Exploring Management

FIFTH EDITION

John R. Schermerhorn, Jr.

Ohio University

Daniel G. Bachrach

University of Alabama

VICE PRESIDENT & DIRECTOR	George Hoffman
EXECUTIVE EDITOR	Lisé Johnson
EXECUTIVE MARKETING MANAGER	Christopher DeJohn
PRODUCT DESIGN MANAGER	Allison Morris
SPONSORING EDITOR	Jennifer Manias
MARKET SOLUTIONS ASSISTANT	Amanda Dallas
SENIOR CONTENT MANAGER	Dorothy Sinclair
SENIOR PRODUCTION EDITOR	Valerie Vargas
DESIGN DIRECTOR	Harry Nolan
SENIOR DESIGNER	Thomas Nery
SENIOR PHOTO EDITOR	Mary Ann Price
COVER PHOTO	© Alfonso Cacciola/iStockphoto

This book was typeset in 11/14 Kepler Std Regular at Aptara®, Inc. and printed and bound by Courier/Kendallville. The cover was printed by Courier/Kendallville.

This book is printed on acid free paper. ∞

Founded in 1807, John Wiley & Sons, Inc. has been a valued source of knowledge and understanding for more than 200 years, helping people around the world meet their needs and fulfill their aspirations. Our company is built on a foundation of principles that include responsibility to the communities we serve and where we live and work. In 2008, we launched a Corporate Citizenship Initiative, a global effort to address the environmental, social, economic, and ethical challenges we face in our business. Among the issues we are addressing are carbon impact, paper specifications and procurement, ethical conduct within our business and among our vendors, and community and charitable support. For more information, please visit our website: www.wiley.com/go/citizenship.

Library of Congress Cataloging-in-Publication Data:
Schermerhorn, John R.
   Exploring management / John R. Schermerhorn, Jr., Ohio University, Daniel G. Bachrach,
University of Alabama. — FIFTH EDITION.
      1 online resource.
   Revised edition of the author's Exploring management.
   Includes index.
   Description based on print version record and CIP data provided by publisher; resource not viewed.
ISBN 978-1-119-14029-0 (pdf) — ISBN 978-1-119-14030-6 (epub) — ISBN 978-1-119-11774-2
(pbk. : alk. paper)   1.   Management.   2.   Executive ability.   3.   Industrial management.
I.   Bachrach, Daniel G.   II.   Title.
   HD31
   658—dc23

ISBN 13 978-1-119-11774-2   2015025127

The inside back cover will contain printing identification and country of origin if omitted from this page. In addition, if the ISBN on the back cover differs from the ISBN on this page, the one on the back cover is correct.

Printed in the United States of America.

10 9 8 7 6 5 4 3 2 1

*I once again dedicate this book
to the person who lovingly helps me explore
and appreciate life's wonders:
My wife, Ann.*

J.R.S.

*For Julie, Sammy, Eliana, Jakey, Jessica, Caleb, and Lilah
—I love you!*

D.G.B.

About the Authors

Dr. John R. Schermerhorn Jr. is the Charles G. O'Bleness Emeritus Professor of Management in the College of Business at Ohio University. He earned a PhD degree in organizational behavior from Northwestern University, after receiving an MBA degree (with distinction) in management and international business from New York University and a BS degree in business administration from the State University of New York at Buffalo.

Dr. Schermerhorn's teaching and writing bridges the gap between the theory and practice of management. At Ohio University he was named a *University Professor*, the university's leading campus-wide award for undergraduate teaching. He has also won awards for teaching excellence at Tulane University and the University of Vermont. He received the excellence in leadership award for his service as Chair of the Management Education and Development Division of the Academy of Management.

Dr. Schermerhorn brings a unique global dimension to his scholarship. He holds an honorary doctorate from the University of Pécs in Hungary, awarded for his international scholarly contributions to management research and education. He served as a Visiting Fulbright Professor at the University of Botswana, Visiting Professor of Management at the Chinese University of Hong Kong, on-site Coordinator of the Ohio University MBA and Executive MBA programs in Malaysia, and Kohei Miura Visiting Professor at the Chubu University of Japan. Presently he is a member of the graduate faculty at Bangkok University Thailand and Permanent Lecturer in the PhD program at the University of Pécs in Hungary.

Educators and students alike know Dr. Schermerhorn as co-author of *Management 13e* (Wiley, 2015) and co-author of *Organizational Behavior13e* (Wiley, 2014). His many books are available in Chinese, Dutch, French, Indonesian, Portuguese, Russian, and Spanish language editions. Dr. Schermerhorn has also published numerous articles in publications such as the *Academy of Management Journal, Academy of Management Review, Academy of Management Executive, Organizational Dynamics, Journal of Management Education,* and the *Journal of Management Development.*

Dr. Schermerhorn is a popular guest speaker. His student and faculty workshop topics include high-engagement instructional approaches, management curriculum innovations, and scholarly manuscript development and textbook writing. His latest projects include video-enhanced e-textbook development for flipped classroom environments.

Dr. Daniel G. Bachrach (Dan) is the Robert C. and Rosa P. Morrow Faculty Excellence Fellow and Professor of Management in the Culverhouse College of Commerce at the University of Alabama, where he teaches graduate and undergraduate courses in management. Dr. Bachrach earned a PhD in organizational behavior and human resource management—with a minor emphasis in strategic management—from Indiana University's Kelley School of Business, an MS in industrial/organizational psychology from the University of Wisconsin-Oshkosh, and a BA in psychology from Bates College in Lewiston Me.

A member of the Academy of Management and the Society for Industrial and Organizational Psychology, Dr. Bachrach serves on the editorial boards of the *Journal of Applied Psychology* and *Organizational Behavior and Human Decision Processes*. He is co-editor of the *Handbook of Behavioral Operations Management: Social and Psychological Dynamics in Production and Service Settings* (Oxford University Press, 2014), co-author of *Transformative Selling: Becoming a Resource Manager and a Knowledge Broker* (Axcess Capon, 2014), and senior co-author *of Becoming More Than a Showroom: How to Win Back Showrooming Customers* (Palgrave-Macmillan, 2015) *and 10 Don'ts on Your Digital Devices: The Non-Techie's Survival Guide to Digital Security and Privacy* (Apress, 2014).

Dr. Bachrach also has published extensively in a number of academic journals including *Organization Science, Journal of Applied Psychology, Strategic Management Journal, Organizational Behavior and Human Decision Processes, Personnel Psychology, Journal of Management, Leadership Quarterly, Production and Operations Management, Journal of Operations Management, Journal of Supply Chain Management,* and *the Journal of Personal Selling and Sales Management.*

Dear Colleague

Welcome to *Exploring Management, Fifth Edition*. You'll quickly see that it is a bit different from traditional textbooks, we hope in a positive way. It has all the content you expect, but . . .

- The writing voice is "personal"—students are made part of the conversation and asked to interact with the subject matter while reading.
- The presentation is "chunked"—short content sections that fit how students read are followed by study guides that check their learning and prompt career thinking.
- The content is "live"—pages are full of timely examples, news items, situations, and reflection questions that make management real and launch meaningful discussions.

Exploring Management is a reflection of how much we have learned from our students about what they value, where they hope to go, and how they like to study and learn. It's also a reflection of our desire to bring the real world into the management class, engage students in interesting discussions of important topics, and offer a variety of assignments and projects that promote critical thinking. And if you are using the flipped classroom or plan to try it, this book is tailored from experience to make "doing the flip" easy.

Instructors have had a lot of success using *Exploring Management* to bring high student engagement to their classes. Chances are that you will, too. Take a moment to review the book's design and built-in pedagogy. Browse some pages to check the writing style, visual presentation, reflection features, and study guides.

Does *Exploring Management* offer what you are looking for to build a great management course? Could it help engage your students to the point where they actually read and think about topics before coming to class?

As management educators we bear a lot of responsibility for helping students learn how to better manage their lives and careers, and help organizations make real contributions to society. *Exploring Management, Fifth Edition*, is our attempt to make it easier for you to fulfill this responsibility in your own way, with lots of instructional options, and backed by solid text content. Thanks for considering it.

Sincerely,
John Schermerhorn
Dan Bachrach

Preface

WHAT MAKES *EXPLORING MANAGEMENT* DIFFERENT?

Students tell us over and over again that they learn best when their courses and assignments fit the context of their everyday lives, career aspirations, and personal experiences. We have written *Exploring Management, Fifth Edition,* to meet and engage a new generation of students in their personal spaces. It uses lots of examples, applications, visual highlights, and learning aids to convey the essentials of management. It also asks students thought-provoking questions as they read. Our hope is that this special approach and pedagogy will help management educators find unique and innovative ways to enrich the learning experiences of their students.

Exploring Management offers a flexible, topic-specific presentation.

The first thing you'll notice is that *Exploring Management* presents "chunks" of material to be read and digested in short time periods. This is a direct response to classroom experiences where our students increasingly find typical book chapters cumbersome to handle.

Students never read more than a few pages in *Exploring Management* before hitting a "Study Guide" that allows them to bring closure to what they have just read. This chunked pedagogy motivates students to read and study assigned material before attending class. And, it helps them perform better on tests and assignments.

Topics are easily assignable and sized for a class session. Although presented in the traditional planning, organizing, leading, and controlling framework, chapters can be used in any order based on instructor preferences. Many options are available for courses of different types, lengths, and meeting schedules, including online and distance-learning formats. It all depends on what fits best with course objectives, learning approaches, and instructional preferences.

Exploring Management uses an integrated learning design.

Every chapter opens with a catchy subtitle and clear visual presentation that quickly draws students into the topic. The opening Management Live vignette hits a timely topic relevant to chapter material. Key learning objectives are listed in Your Chapter Takeaways, while What's Inside highlights four interesting and useful chapter features—Ethics Check, Facts to Consider, Hot Topic, and Quick Case.

Each chapter section begins with a visual overview that poses a Takeaway Question followed by a list of Answers to Come. These answers become the subheadings that organize section content. The section ends with a Study Guide. This one-page checkpoint asks students to pause and check learning before moving on to the next section. The Study Guide elements include:

- *Rapid Review*—bullet-list summary of concepts and points
- *Questions for Discussion*—questions to stimulate inquiry and prompt class discussions
- *Be Sure You Can*—checkpoint of major learning outcomes for mastery
- *Career Situation: What Would You Do?*—asks students to apply section topics to a problem-solving situation
- *Terms to Define*—glossary quiz for vocabulary development

Exploring Management makes "flipping" the classroom easy.

Flipped classrooms shift the focus from instructors lecturing and students listening, to instructors guiding and students engaging. The first step in doing the flip is getting students to read and study assigned materials before class. When they come to class prepared, the instructor has many more options for engagement. The chunked presentations and frequent Study Guides in *Exploring Management*, along with its video-enhanced flipped classroom learning package, help greatly in this regard.

Dan Bachrach has prepared an extensive **Flipped Classroom Guide** that includes authors' videos that students can view before class to highlight core content for each section of every chapter. It also provides easy-to-use lesson plans for engaging students in active discussions and interesting assignments based on chapter features. Our goal with Dan's **Flipped Classroom Guide**—packaged with the pedagogy of *Exploring Management* and WileyPLUS Learning Space—is to give instructors a ready-to-go pathway to implement an active, engaged, and flipped classroom.

Success in flipping the classroom requires a good short quiz and testing program to ensure student learning. Dan has nicely integrated *Exploring Management* with the advanced WileyPLUS Learning Space online environment to make this easy. Success in flipping the classroom also requires a solid inventory of discussion activities, projects, and quick-hitting experiences that turn class and online time into engaged learning time.

Dan has also prepared instructor's guides for each feature in every chapter of *Exploring Management* so that they can be easily used for flipped classroom activities and discussions, and for individual and team assignments. Imagine the possibilities for student engagement when using features like these:

- <u>Ethics Check</u>—poses an ethical dilemma and challenges students with *Your Decision?*

   Examples include "Social Media Checks May Cause Discrimination in Hiring," "My Team Leader is a Workaholic," "Life and Death at an Outsourcing Factory," and "Social Loafing May Be Closer Than You Think."

- <u>Facts to Consider</u>—summarizes survey data to stimulate critical inquiry and asks students *What's Your Take?*

   Examples include "The "Ask Gap"—What It Takes for Women to Get Raises," "Policies on Office Romances Vary Widely," "Disposable Workers are Indispensable to Business Profits," and "Ups and Downs for Minority Entrepreneurs."

- <u>Hot Topics</u>—presents timely, even controversial, issues framed for debate and discussion, and asks students *How About It?*

   Examples include "The $50,000 Retail Worker," "Keep Your Career Plan Tight and Focused, or Loosen Up?" "Rewarding Mediocrity Begins at an Early Age" and, "Can Disharmony Build a Better Team?"

- <u>Quick Case</u>—gives students a short, real-life, scenario that puts them in a challenging work situation and asks *What Do You Do?*

   Examples include "New Dads Say it's Time for Paternity Leave," "Removing the Headphones to Show Team Spirit," "16 Hours to J-Burg," and "It's Time to Ask for a Raise."

Exploring Management uses a conversational and interactive writing style.

The authors' voice in *Exploring Management* speaks with students the way you and we do in the classroom—conversationally, interactively, and using lots of questions. Although it may seem unusual to have authors speaking directly to their audience, our goals are to be real people and approach readers in the spirit of what Ellen Langer calls *mindful learning*.[1] She describes this as engaging students from a perspective of active inquiry rather than as consumers of facts and prescriptions. We view it as a way of moving textbook writing in the same direction we are moving college teaching—being less didactic and more interactive, and doing a better job of involving students in a dialog around meaningful topics, questions, examples, and even dilemmas.

[1] Ellen J. Langer, *The Power of Mindful Learning* (Reading, MA: Perseus, 1994).

Exploring Management helps students earn good grades
and build useful career skills.

Exploring Management is written and designed to help students prepare for quizzes and tests, and build essential career and life skills. In addition to chunked reading and Study Guides, the end-of-chapter Test Prep asks students to answer multiple-choice, short response, and integration and application questions as a starting point for testing success. They are next directed to active learning and personal development activities in the end-of-book *Skill-Building Portfolio*. It offers Self-Assessments, Class Exercises, and Team Projects carefully chosen to match chapter content with skills development opportunities. A further selection of *Cases for Critical Thinking* engages students in analysis of timely situations and events involving real people and organizations.

WileyPLUS LEARNING SPACE

WileyPLUS Learning Space is an innovative, research-based, online environment for effective teaching and learning. It's a place where students can learn and prepare for class while identifying their strengths and nurture core skills. WileyPLUS Learning Space transforms course content into an online learning community whose members experience learning activities, work through self-assessment, ask questions and share insights. As they interact with the course content, peers and their instructor, WileyPLUS Learning Space creates a personalized study guide for each student.

When students collaborate with each other, they make deeper connections to the content. When students work together, they also feel part of a community so that they can grow in areas beyond topics in the course. Students using WileyPLUS Learning Space become invested in their learning experience while using time efficiently and developing skills like critical thinking and teamwork.

WileyPLUS Learning Space is class tested and ready-to-go for instructors. It offers a flexible platform for quickly organizing learning activities, managing student collaboration, and customizing courses—including choice of content as well as the amount of interactivity between students. An instructor using *WileyPLUS Learning Space* is able to easily:

- Assign activities and add special materials
- Guide students through what's important by easily assigning specific content
- Set up and monitor group learning
- Assess student engagement
- Gain immediate insights to help inform teaching

Special visual reports in WileyPLUS Learning Space help identify problem areas in student learning and focus instructor attention and resources on what's most important. With the visual reports, an instructor can see exactly where students are struggling and in need of early intervention. Students can see exactly what they don't know to better prepare for exams, and gain insights into how to study and succeed in a course.

STUDENT AND INSTRUCTOR RESOURCES

Exploring Management is rich in special materials that support instructional excellence and student learning. Our colleagues at John Wiley & Sons have worked hard to design supporting materials that support our learning and engagement.

- **Companion Web Site** The Companion Web site for *Exploring Management* at www.wiley.com/college/schermerhorn contains myriad tools and links to aid both teaching and learning, including nearly all the resources described in this section.

- **Instructor's Resource Guide** The Instructor's Resource Guide includes a *Conversion Guide*, *Chapter Outlines*, *Chapter Objectives*, *Lecture Notes*, *Teaching Notes*, and *Suggested Answers* for all quiz, test, and case questions.
- **Test Bank** The Test Bank consists of nearly 80 true/false, multiple-choice, and short-answer questions per chapter. It was specifically designed so that the questions vary in degree of difficulty, from straightforward recall to challenging, to offer instructors the most flexibility when designing their exams. The *Computerized Test Bank* includes a test-generating program that allows instructors to customize their exams.
- **PowerPoint Slides** A set of interactive PowerPoint slides includes lecture notes and talking points. An *Image Gallery*, containing .jpg files for all of the figures in the text, is also provided for instructor convenience.
- **Management Weekly Updates** These timely updates keep you and your students updated and informed on the very latest in business news stories. Each week you will find links to five new articles, video clips, business news stories, and so much more with discussion questions to elaborate on the stories in the classroom. http://wileymanagementupdates.com
- **Darden Business Cases** Through the Wiley Custom Select Web site, you can choose from thousands of cases from Darden Business Publishing to create a book with any combination of cases, Wiley textbook chapters, and original material. Visit http://www.customselect.wiley.com/collection/dardencases for more information.

ACKNOWLEDGMENTS

Exploring Management, *Fifth Edition*, began, grew, and found life and form in its first four editions over many telephone conversations, conference calls, e-mail exchanges, and face-to-face meetings. It has since matured and been refined as a fifth edition through the useful feedback provided by many satisfied faculty and student users and reviewers.

There wouldn't be an *Exploring Management* without the support, commitment, creativity, and dedication of the following members of the Wiley team. Our thanks go to: Lisé Johnson, *Executive Editor*; George Hoffman, *Vice President and Director*; Jennifer Manias, *Development Editor*; Amanda Dallas, *Market Solutions Assistant*; Chris DeJohn, *Executive Marketing Manager*; Valerie Vargas, *Senior Production Editor*; Harry Nolan, *Creative Director*; Tom Nery, *Senior Designer*; Mary Ann Price, *Photo Manager*; and Jackie Henry, our Project Manager at Aptara.

Focus Group Participants

Maria Aria, *Camden County College;* Ellen Benowitz, *Mercer County Community College;* John Brogan, *Monmouth University;* Lawrence J. Danks, *Camden County College;* Matthew DeLuca, *Baruch College;* David Fearon, *Central Connecticut State University;* Stuart Ferguson, *Northwood University;* Eugene Garaventa, *College of Staten Island;* Scott Geiger, *University of South Florida, St. Petersburg;* Larry Grant, *Bucks County Community College;* Fran Green, *Pennsylvania State University, Delaware County;* F. E. Hamilton, *Eckerd College;* Don Jenner, *Borough of Manhattan Community College;* John Podoshen, *Franklin and Marshall College;* Neuman Pollack, *Florida Atlantic University;* David Radosevich, *Montclair State University;* Moira Tolan, *Mount Saint Mary College.*

Virtual Focus Group Participants

George Alexakis, *Nova Southeastern University;* Steven Bradley, *Austin Community College;* Paula Brown, *Northern Illinois University;* Elnora Farmer, *Clayton State University;* Paul Gagnon, *Central Connecticut State University;* Eugene Garaventa, *College of Staten Island;* Larry Garner, *Tarleton State University;* Wayne Grossman, *Hofstra University;* Dee Guillory, *University of South Carolina, Beaufort;* Julie Hays, *University of St. Thomas;* Kathleen Jones, *University of North Dakota;* Marvin Karlins, *University of South Florida;* Al Laich, *University of Northern Virginia;* Vincent Lutheran, *University of North Carolina, Wilmington;* Douglas L. Micklich, *Illinois State University;* David Oliver, *Edison College;* Jennifer Oyler, *University of Central Arkansas;* Kathleen Reddick, *College of Saint Elizabeth;* Terry L. Riddle, *Central Virginia*

Community College; Roy L. Simerly, *East Carolina University;* Frank G. Titlow, *St. Petersburg College;* David Turnipseed, *Indiana University—Purdue University, Fort Wayne;* Michael Wakefield, *Colorado State University, Pueblo;* George A. (Bud) Wynn, *University of Tampa.*

Reviewers

M. David Albritton, *Northern Arizona University;* Mitchell Alegre, *Niagara University;* Allen Amason, *University of Georgia;* Mihran Aroian, *University of Texas, Austin;* Karen R. Bangs, *California State Polytechnic University;* Heidi Barclay, *Metropolitan State University;* Reuel Barksdale, *Columbus State Community College;* Patrick Bell, *Elon University;* Michael Bento, *Owens Community College;* William Berardi, *Bristol Community College;* Robert Blanchard, *Salem State University;* Laquita Blockson, *College of Charleston;* Peter Geoffrey Bowen, *University of Denver;* Victoria Boyd, *Claflin University;* Ralph R. Braithwaite, *University of Hartford;* David Bright, *Wright State University-Dayton;* Kenneth G. Brown, *University of Iowa;* Diana Bullen, *Mesa Community College;* Beverly Bugay, *Tyler Junior College;* Robert Cass, *Virginia Wesleyan College;* Savannah Clay, *Central Piedmont Community College;* Paul Coakley, *Community College of Baltimore County;* Suzanne Crampton, *Grand Valley State University;* Kathryn Dansky, *Pennsylvania State University;* Susan Davis, *Claflin University;* Jeanette Davy, *Wright State University;* Matt DeLuca, *Baruch College;* Karen Edwards, *Chemeketa Community College;* Valerie Evans, *Lincoln Memorial University;* Paul Ewell, *Bridgewater College;* Gary J. Falcone, *LaSalle University;* Elnora Farmer, *Clayton State University;* Gail E. Fraser, *Kean University;* Nancy Fredericks, *San Diego State University;* Tamara Friedrich, *Savannah State University;* Larry Garner, *Tarleton State University;* Cindy Geppert, *Palm Beach State College;* Richard J. Gibson, *Embry-Riddle University;* Dee Guillory, *University of South Carolina, Beaufort;* Linda Hefferin, *Elgin Community College;* Aaron Hines, *SUNY New Paltz;* Merrily Hoffman, *San Jacinto College;* Jeff Houghton, *West Virginia University;* Tammy Hunt, *University of North Carolina Wilmington;* Debra Hunter, *Troy University;* Kimberly Hurnes, *Washtenaw Community College;* Gary S. Insch, *West Virginia University;* Barcley Johnson, *Western Michigan University;* Louis Jourdan, *Clayton State University;* Brian Joy, *Henderson Community College;* Edward Kass, *University of San Francisco;* Renee King, *Eastern Illinois University;* Judith Kizzie, *Howard Community College;* Robert Klein, *Philadelphia University;* John Knutsen, *Everett Community College;* Al Laich, *University of Northern Virginia;* Susan Looney, *Delaware Technical & Community College;* Vincent Lutheran, *University of North Carolina, Wilmington;* Jim Maddox, *Friends University;* John Markert, *Wells College;* Marcia Marriott, *Monroe Community College;* Brenda McAleer, *Colby College;* Randy McCamery, *Tarleton State University;* Gerald McFry, *Coosa Valley Technical College;* Diane Minger, *Cedar Valley College;* Michael Monahan, *Frostburg State University;* Dave Nemi, *Niagara County Community College;* Nanci Newstrom, *Eastern Illinois University;* Lam Nguyen, *Palm Beach State College;* Joelle Nisolle, *West Texas A&M University;* Penny Olivi, *York College of Pennsylvania;* Jennifer Oyler, *University of Central Arkansas;* Barry Palatnik, *Burlington County Community College;* Kathy Pederson, *Hennepin Technical College;* Sally Proffitt, *Tarrant County College;* Nancy Ray-Mitchell, *McLennan Community College;* Catherine J. Ruggieri, *St. John's University;* Joseph C. Santora, *Essex County College;* Charles Seifert, *Siena College;* Sidney Siegel, *Drexel University;* Gerald F. Smith, *University of Northern Iowa;* Wendy Smith, *University of Delaware;* Howard Stanger, *Canisius College;* Peter Stone, *Spartanburg Community College;* Henry A. Summers, *Stephen F. Austin State University;* Daryl J. Taylor, *Pasadena City College;* Ann Theis, *Adrian College;* Jody Tolan, *University of Southern California, Marshall School of Business;* David Turnipseed, *Indiana University—Purdue University, Fort Wayne;* Robert Turrill, *University of Southern California;* Vickie Tusa, *Embry-Riddle University;* Aurelio Valente, *Philadelphia University;* Michael Wakefield, *Colorado State University, Pueblo;* Charles D. White, *James Madison University;* Daniel Wubbena, *Western Iowa Tech Community College;* Alan Wright, *Henderson State University;* Ashley Wright, *Spartanburg Community College.*

Class Test Participants

Verl Anderson, *Dixie State College;* Corinne Asher, *Henry Ford Community College;* Forrest Aven, *University of Houston Downtown;* Richard Bartlett, *Columbus State Community College;* John Bird, *West Virginia State University;* Dr. Sheri Carder, *Florida Gateway College;* Susie Cox,

McNeese State University; Robert Eliason, *James Madison University;* Trent Engbers, *Indiana University;* Shelly Gardner, *Augustana College;* Ann Gilley, *Ferris State University;* Janie Gregg, *The University of West Alabama;* Jay Hochstetler, *Anderson University;* Tacy Holliday, *Montgomery College;* David Hollomon, *Victor Valley College;* Cheryl Hughes, *Indiana University;* David Jalajas, *Long Island University;* Angelina Kiser, *University of the Incarnate Word;* Cindy Murphy, *Southeastern Community College;* Chandran Mylvaganam, *Northwood University;* Greg Petranek, *Eastern Connecticut State University;* Tracy Porter, *Cleveland State University;* Renee Rogers, *Forsyth Technical Community College;* Richard Sharman, *Lone Star College–Montgomery;* Catherine Slade, *Augusta State University;* Susan Steiner, *The University of Tampa;* Donald Stout, *Saint Martin's University;* Alec Zama, *Grand View University;* Nancy Zimmerman, *The Community College of Baltimore County.*

Brief Contents

Contents

Skill-Building Portfolio

Online Module: Management Learning

Please visit www.wiley.com/college/schermerhorn or your WileyPLUS Learning Space course for access to this module.

WHAT ARE THE LESSONS OF THE CLASSICAL MANAGEMENT APPROACHES?

- Taylor's scientific management sought efficiency in job performance.
- Weber's bureaucratic organization is supposed to be efficient and fair.
- Fayol's administrative principles describe managerial duties and practices.

WHAT ARE THE CONTRIBUTIONS OF THE BEHAVIORAL MANAGEMENT APPROACHES?

- Follett viewed organizations as communities of cooperative action.
- The Hawthorne studies focused attention on the human side of organizations.
- Maslow described a hierarchy of human needs with self-actualization at the top.
- McGregor believed managerial assumptions create self-fulfilling prophecies.
- Argyris suggests that workers treated as adults will be more productive.

WHAT ARE THE FOUNDATIONS OF MODERN MANAGEMENT THINKING?

- Managers use quantitative analysis and tools to solve complex problems.
- Organizations are open systems that interact with their environments.
- Contingency thinking holds that there is no one best way to manage.
- Quality management focuses attention on continuous improvement.
- Evidence-based management seeks hard facts about what really works.

Self-Assessment: Managerial Assumptions

Class Exercise: Evidence-Based Management Quiz

Team Project: Management in Popular Culture

Case Study: Zara International—Fast Fashion's Style Maker

Zappos CEO Tony Hsieh is into happiness. He strives "to set up an environment where the personalities, creativities, and individuality of all different employees come out and shine."

Managers and the Management Process

Everyone Becomes a Manager Someday

Management Live
Gaming Skills Can Be Résumé Builders

© Monalyn Gracia/Corbis Corp.

Do managing large guilds and leading raids while playing World of Warcraft belong in your résumé and online recruiting profiles? Heather Newman thinks so. In a "Leisure/Volunteer Activities" section she highlighted how gaming enhanced her skills at organizing teams of volunteers and communicating. That said, she landed a job as director of marketing and communications for a university. One hiring manager says putting gaming experience on a résumé can be a "conversation starter," but another dismisses it as "all make-believe."

YOUR THOUGHTS?

Can Newman's strategy pay off for you? What "hidden" experiences—not just gaming—might you describe as skill-builders on your résumé?

YOUR CHAPTER 1 TAKEAWAYS

1. Understand what it means to be a manager.
2. Know what managers do and what skills they use.
3. Recognize timely and important career issues.

Takeaway 1.1
What Does It Mean to Be a Manager?

ANSWERS TO COME

- Organizations have different types and levels of managers.
- Accountability is a foundation of managerial performance.
- Effective managers help others achieve high performance and satisfaction.
- Managers are coaches, coordinators, and supporters.

IN A BOOK CALLED *THE SHIFT: THE FUTURE OF WORK IS ALREADY HERE*, SCHOLAR Lynda Gratton describes the difficult times in which we live and work. "Technology shrinks the world but consumes all of our time," she says, while "globalization means we can work anywhere, but must compete with people from everywhere; there are more of us, and we're living longer; traditional communities are being yanked apart as people cluster in cities; and there is rising energy demand and fewer traditional resources."[1]

What does all this mean in terms of planning for career entry and advancement? At a minimum, there are few guarantees of long-term employment. Jobs are increasingly earned and re-earned every day through one's performance accomplishments. Careers are being redefined along the lines of "flexibility," "free agency," "skill portfolios," and "entrepreneurship." The fact is: Career success today requires lots of initiative and self-awareness, as well as continuous learning. The question is: Are you ready?

ORGANIZATIONS HAVE DIFFERENT TYPES AND LEVELS OF MANAGERS.

A **manager** is a person who supports and is responsible for the work of others.

You find them everywhere, in small and large businesses, voluntary associations, government agencies, schools, hospitals, and wherever people work together for a common cause. Even though the job titles vary from team leader to department head, project leader, president, administrator, and more, the people in these jobs all share a common responsibility—helping others do their best work. We call them **managers**—persons who directly supervise, support, and help activate work efforts to achieve the performance goals of individuals, teams, or even an organization as a whole. In this sense, I think you'll agree with the chapter subtitle: Everyone becomes a manager someday.

"ONE GREAT PERSON CAN EASILY DO THE BUSINESS PRODUCTIVITY OF THREE GOOD PEOPLE."

HOT TOPIC

The $50,000 Retail Worker

Courtesy The Container Store

Looking for a job in retail? Want to avoid minimum wage employers? Head for The Container Store.® Its front-line, full-time workers are paid about $50,000 per year for starters, with more coming with positive annual performance reviews. Chairman & CEO Kip Tindell says it's central to his business strategy—hire great people, extensively train them and empower them by paying 50–100% more than what other retailers might pay them. He calls it the "One Equals Three" Foundation Principle. "One great person can easily do the business productivity of three good people," he says. And, he believes other retailers should follow The Container Store's lead. "Better pay," he argues, "leads to higher profitability."

HOW ABOUT IT?

Why would CEO Kip Tindell place so much emphasis on hiring and retaining retail workers for his stores? Is the Container Store's wage policy sustainable in the ups and downs of competitive business? If better pay leads to higher productivity, why do so many employers—think fast-food industry—stick with the minimum wage?

First-Line Managers and Team Leaders

Take a good look at Figure 1.1. It describes an organization as a series of layers, each of which represents different levels of work and managerial responsibilities.[2]

A first job in management typically involves serving as a team leader or supervisor in charge of a small work group. Typical job titles for these **first-line managers** include department head, team leader, and unit manager. For example, the leader of an auditing team is considered a first-line manager, as is the head of an academic department in a university.

Even though most people enter the workforce as technical specialists such as auditor, market researcher, or systems analyst, sooner or later they advance to positions of initial managerial responsibility. And they serve as essential building blocks for organizational performance.[3] Consider these words of Justin Fritz as he describes leading a 12-member team to launch a new product at a medical products company: "I've just never worked on anything that so visibly, so dramatically changes the quality of someone's life."[4]

> **First-line managers** are team leaders and supervisors in charge of people who perform non managerial duties.

Middle Managers

Look again at Figure 1.1. This time consider how Justin may advance in his career. At the next level above team leader we find **middle managers**—persons in charge of relatively large departments or divisions consisting of several smaller work units or teams.

Middle managers usually supervise several first-line managers. Examples include clinic directors in hospitals; deans in universities; and division managers, plant managers, and regional sales managers in businesses. Because of their position "in the middle," these managers must be able to work well with people from all parts of the organization—higher, lower, and side-to-side. As Justin moves up the career ladder to middle management, there will be more pressure and new challenges. But there should also be rewards and satisfaction.

> **Middle managers** oversee the work of large departments or divisions.

Top Managers

Some middle managers advance still higher in the organization, earning job titles such as chief executive officer (CEO), chief operating officer (COO), chief financial officer (CFO), chief information officer (CIO), president, and vice president. These **top managers**, or C-suite executives, are part of a senior management team that is responsible for the performance of an organization as a whole or for one of its larger parts. They must be alert to trends and developments in the external environment, recognize potential problems and opportunities, set strategy, craft the internal culture, build a talent pool, and overall lead the organization to success.[5] The best top managers are future-oriented thinkers who make good decisions even in face of uncertainty, risk, and tough competition.

> **Top managers** guide the performance of the organization as a whole or of one of its major parts.

Boards of Directors

It would be great if all top managers were responsible and successful—always making the right decisions and doing things in their organization's best interests. But, the fact is that

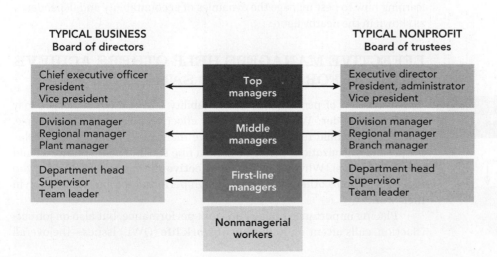

TYPICAL BUSINESS
Board of directors

TYPICAL NONPROFIT
Board of trustees

Chief executive officer / President / Vice president	Top managers	Executive director / President, administrator / Vice president
Division manager / Regional manager / Plant manager	Middle managers	Division manager / Regional manager / Branch manager
Department head / Supervisor / Team leader	First-line managers	Department head / Supervisor / Team leader
	Nonmanagerial workers	

FIGURE 1.1

What Are the Typical Job Titles and Levels of Management in Organizations?

The traditional organization is structured as a pyramid. The top manager, typically a CEO, president, or executive director, reports to a board of directors in a business or to a board of trustees in a nonprofit organization. Middle managers report to top managers, and first-line managers or team leaders report to middle managers.

Ursula Burns Leads Xerox with Confidence and a Strategic Eye

Ramin Talale/Bloomberg/
Getty Images

"Frankness," "sharp humor," "willingness to take risks," "deep industry knowledge," "technical prowess" are all phrases used to describe Ursula Burns, CEO of Xerox Corporation. She started as a mechanical engineering intern and moved up to become the first African American woman to head a *Fortune* 500 firm. Raised by a single mom in public housing, her pride in her achievements comes across loud and clear. "I'm in this job because I believe I earned it through hard work and high performance," says Burns. "Did I get some opportunities early in my career because of my race and gender? Probably . . . I imagine race and gender got the hiring guys' attention. And the rest was really up to me."

some don't live up to expectations. They perform poorly and may even take personal advantage of their positions, perhaps to the point of ethics failures and illegal acts. Who or what keeps CEOs and other senior managers ethical and high performing?

Figure 1.1 shows that even the CEO or president of an organization reports to a higher-level boss. In business corporations, this is a **board of directors**, whose members are elected by stockholders to represent their ownership interests. In nonprofit organizations, such as a hospital or university, top managers report to a *board of trustees*. These board members may be elected by local citizens, appointed by government bodies, or invited to serve by existing members.

In both business and the public sectors, board members are supposed to oversee the affairs of the organization and the performance of its top management. In other words, they are supposed to make sure that the organization is being run right. This is called **governance**, the oversight of top management by an organization's board of directors or board of trustees.[6]

> Members of a **board of directors** are elected by stockholders to represent their ownership interests.

> **Governance** is oversight of top management by a board of directors or board of trustees.

> **Accountability** is the requirement to show performance results to a supervisor.

> An **effective manager** successfully helps others achieve high performance and satisfaction in their work.

> **Quality of work life** is the overall quality of human experiences in the workplace.

ACCOUNTABILITY IS A FOUNDATION OF MANAGERIAL PERFORMANCE.

The term **accountability** describes the requirement of one person to answer to a higher authority for performance achieved in his or her area of work responsibility. This notion of accountability is an important aspect of managerial performance. In the traditional organizational pyramid, accountability flows upward. Team members are accountable to a team leader, the team leader is accountable to a middle manager, the middle manager is accountable to a top manager, and the top manager is accountable to a board of directors.

Let's not forget that accountability in managerial performance is always accompanied by dependency. At the same time that any manager is being held accountable by a higher level for the performance results of her or his area of supervisory responsibility, the manager is dependent on others to do the required work. In fact, we might say that a large part of the study of management is all about learning how to best manage the dynamics of accountability and dependency as shown in the nearby figure.

EFFECTIVE MANAGERS HELP OTHERS ACHIEVE HIGH PERFORMANCE AND SATISFACTION.

This discussion of performance accountability and related challenges may make you wonder: What exactly is an effective manager? Most people, perhaps you, would reply that an effective manager is someone who helps people and organizations perform. That's a fine starting point, but we should go a step further. Why not define an **effective manager** as someone who successfully helps others achieve both high performance and satisfaction in their work?

Placing importance not just on work performance, but also on job satisfaction, calls attention to **quality of work life** (QWL) issues—the overall

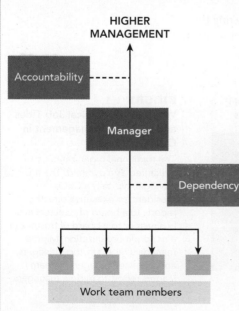

HIGHER
MANAGEMENT

Accountability

Manager

Dependency

Work team members

quality of human experiences in the workplace. Have you experienced a "high QWL" environment? Most people would describe it as a place where they are respected and valued by their employer. They would talk about fair pay, safe work conditions, opportunities to learn and use new skills, room to grow and progress in a career, and protection of individual rights. They would say everyone takes pride in their work and the organization.

Are you willing to work anywhere other than in a high-QWL setting? Would you, as a manager, be pleased with anything less than helping others achieve not just high performance but also job satisfaction? Sadly, the real world doesn't always live up to these expectations. Talk to parents, relatives, and friends who go to work every day. You might be surprised. Too many people still labor in difficult, sometimes even hostile and unhealthy, conditions—ones we would consider low QWL for sure.[7]

MANAGERS ARE COACHES, COORDINATORS, AND SUPPORTERS.

We live and work in a time when the best managers are known more for "helping" and "supporting" than for "directing" and "order giving." The terms "coordinator," "coach," and "team leader" are heard as often as "supervisor" or "boss." The fact is that most organizations need more than managers who simply sit back and tell others what to do.

Figure 1.2 uses the notion of an **upside-down pyramid** to describe a new mindset for managers, one guided by the key words "serve" and "support." All managers—from first-level team leaders to top level executives—should find that this mindset offers a real expression of what it means to act as a coach rather than an order giver.

The **upside-down pyramid** view of organizations puts customers at the top and being served by nonmanagerial workers, who are supported by team leaders and higher-level managers.

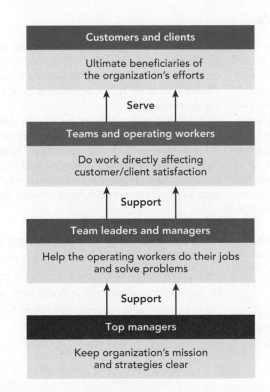

FIGURE 1.2 How Do Mindsets Change When the Organization Is Viewed as an Upside-Down Pyramind?

If we turn the traditional organizational pyramid upside down, we get a valuable look at how managerial work is viewed today. Managers are at the bottom of the upside-down pyramid, and they are expected to support the operating workers above them. Their goal is to help these workers best serve the organization's customers at the top. The appropriate mind-set of this supportive manager is more "coaching" and "helping" than "directing" and "order giving."

Sitting prominent at the top of the upside-down pyramid are nonmanagerial workers. Performing individually and in teams, they interact directly with customers and clients or produce products and services for them. The key word driving their work is "serve." Located just below them are team leaders and managers. Their attention is focused on helping others serve the organization's customers. The key word driving their work is "support."

Top managers and executives are at the bottom of the upside-down pyramid. Their focus is on clarifying mission and crafting strategies that help team leaders and managers take care of their teams and workers. Once again, the key word driving their work is "support." Picture top managers going to work, looking up, and seeing an entire organization balanced on their outstretched hands and depending on them for vital support all day long. Wouldn't you agree this is quite a change of mindset from that of traditional managers who might view themselves standing comfortably on top of the pyramid while those below take care of them?

The upside-down pyramid view leaves no doubt that the organization exists to serve its customers. And, it leaves no doubt that team leaders, managers, and executives are there to help and support the people whose work makes that possible. As the Container Store's CEO Kip Tindell says: "If employees aren't happy, customers aren't happy and then shareholders won't be happy."[8]

Look again at Figure 1.2 and consider the power of the words "serve" and "support." Isn't this a pretty strong endorsement for team leaders and managers at all levels to try flipping the organizational pyramid upside-down?

Working Mother Looks for the Best

Great Employers Put Top Value on People

Masterfile

Working Mother magazine's annual listing of the "100 Best Companies for Working Mothers" has become an important management benchmark—both for employers who want to be among the best and for potential employees who want to work only for the best. The magazine is worth a look for topics ranging from kids to health to personal motivation and more.

Self-described as helping women "integrate their professional lives, their family lives and their inner lives," *Working Mother* mainstreams coverage of work–life balance issues and needs for women. One issue reported on moms who "pushed for more family-friendly benefits and got them." The writer described how Kristina Marsh worked to get lactation support for nursing mothers as a formal benefit at Dow Corning, and how Beth Schiavo started a Working Moms Network in Ernst & Young's Atlanta offices and then got it approved as a corporate program nationwide.

A list of best employers for multicultural women includes Allstate, American Express, Deloitte, Ernst & Young, IBM, and General Mills. *Working Mother* says: "All of our winning companies not only require manager training on diversity issues but also rate manager performance partly on diversity results, such as how many multicultural women advance."

FIND INSPIRATION

Pick up a copy of *Working Mother* magazine or browse the online version. It's a chance to learn more about the complexities of work–life balance, including the challenges faced by women blending motherhood with a career. It's also a place to learn which employers are truly great in respecting quality of work life issues.

STUDYGUIDE

Takeaway 1.1
What Does It Mean to Be a Manager?

Terms to Define

Accountability	First-line managers	Middle managers	Upside-down pyramid
Board of directors	Governance	Quality of work life	
Effective manager	Manager	Top managers	

Rapid Review

- Managers support and facilitate the work efforts of other people in organizations.
- Top managers scan the environment and pursue long-term goals; middle managers coordinate activities among large departments or divisions; first-line managers, like team leaders, supervise and support nonmanagerial workers.
- Everyone in an organization is accountable to a higher-level manager for his or her performance accomplishments; at the highest level, top managers are held accountable by boards of directors or boards of trustees.
- Effective managers help others achieve both high performance and high levels of job satisfaction.
- New directions in managerial work emphasize "coaching" and "supporting," rather than "directing" and "order giving."
- In the upside-down pyramid view of organizations, the role of managers is to support nonmanagerial workers who serve the needs of customers at the top.

Questions for Discussion

1. Other than at work, in what situations do you expect to be a manager during your lifetime?
2. Why should a manager be concerned about the quality of work life in an organization?
3. In what ways does the upside-down pyramid view of organizations offer advantages over the traditional view of the top-down pyramid?

Be Sure You Can

- **explain** how managers contribute to organizations
- **describe** the activities of managers at different levels
- **explain** how accountability operates in organizations
- **describe** an effective manager
- **list** several ways the work of managers is changing from the past
- **explain** the role of managers in the upside-down pyramid

Career Situation: What Would You Do?

When people are promoted to become managers, they often end up supervising friends and colleagues. Put yourself in this situation. As a new manager of a team full of friends, what can and should you do to quickly earn the respect of others and build a smoothly functioning work team?

Takeaway 1.2
What Do Managers Do, and What Skills Do They Use?

ANSWERS TO COME

- Managers plan, organize, lead, and control.
- Managers perform informational, interpersonal, and decisional roles.
- Managers use networking and social capital to pursue action agendas.
- Managers use technical, human, and conceptual skills.
- Managers should learn from experience.

THE MANAGERS WE HAVE BEEN DISCUSSING ARE INDISPENSABLE TO ORGANIZATIONS. Their efforts bring together resources, technology, and human talents to get things done. Some are fairly routine tasks that are repeated day after day. Other tasks are challenging and novel, often appearing as unexpected problems and opportunities. A manager's workday can be intense, hectic, and fast paced, with lots of emphasis on communication and interpersonal relationships.[9] Today, we add the constant demands of smart phones, e-mail and voice-mail in-boxes, instant messages, and social media alerts to any list of managerial preoccupations.[10]

MANAGERS PLAN, ORGANIZE, LEAD, AND CONTROL.

If you are ready to perform as a manager or to get better as one, a good starting point is **Figure 1.3**. It shows the four functions in the **management process**—planning, organizing, leading, and controlling. The belief is that all managers, regardless of title, level, and organizational setting, are responsible for doing each of them well.[11]

The **management process** is planning, organizing, leading, and controlling the use of resources to accomplish performance goals.

Planning

Planning is the process of setting objectives and determining what should be done to accomplish them.

In management, **planning** is the process of setting performance objectives and determining what actions should be taken to accomplish them. When managers plan, they set goals and objectives and select ways to achieve them.

There was a time, for example, when Ernst & Young's top management grew concerned about the firm's retention rates for women.[12] Why? Turnover rates at the time were much higher among women than among men, running some 22% per year and costing the firm about 150% of each person's annual salary to hire and train a replacement. Then Chairman Philip A. Laskawy responded to the situation by setting a planning objective to reduce turnover rates for women.

FIGURE 1.3
What Four Functions Make Up the Management Process?

The management process consists of four functions: planning, organizing, leading, and controlling. Planning sets the direction as performance objectives. Organizing arranges people and tasks to do the work. Leading inspires others to work hard. Controlling measures performance to make sure that plans and objectives are accomplished.

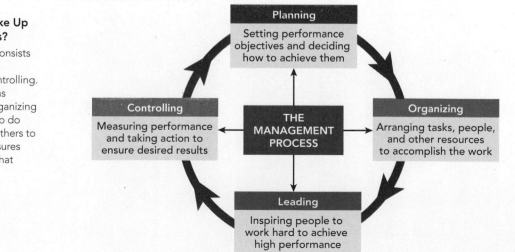

Planning
Setting performance objectives and deciding how to achieve them

Organizing
Arranging tasks, people, and other resources to accomplish the work

THE MANAGEMENT PROCESS

Controlling
Measuring performance and taking action to ensure desired results

Leading
Inspiring people to work hard to achieve high performance

> "'CULTURE FIT' COMES TO MEAN, SUBCONSCIOUSLY, 'PEOPLE LIKE ME,' WHERE 'ME' IS USUALLY A YOUNG MALE FOUNDER."

FACTS TO CONSIDER

Tech Industry No Role Model for Employment Diversity

Monkey Business Images/Shutterstock

Fortune magazine put it this way: "White and Asian men dominate. Everyone else—women, blacks and Hispanics—is severely lacking." Lack of diversity in the technology industry is under fire. One early Facebook employee, Kate Mosse, describes the phenomenon this way: "'Culture fit' comes to mean, subconsciously, 'people like me', where 'me' is usually a young male founder. This is how the diversity data can become so skewed towards white technical men without the companies realizing it." Google is tackling the problem with training in "unconscious bias." Megan Smith, Google X vice president, says: "As a manager you need to be conscious that a whole bunch of people are going to be running at you who might not be as qualified as the person who is not raising their hand." Here are a few recent facts:

- % female in workforce—Apple 30%, Facebook 31%, LinkedIn 39%, Pandora 49%.
- % nonwhite in workforce—Apple 36%, Facebook 26%, LinkedIn 35%, Pandora 15%.
- African Americans hold fewer than 5% of jobs in large technology firms.
- Female engineering graduates in computer and information science are paid 77% of what their male counterparts get.

WHAT'S YOUR TAKE?

What do these tech industry findings mean for you more generally? Is unconscious bias something that you might be facing now or expect to face in the future? What issues and contradictions in employer commitment to diversity have you experienced or heard about? What are the implications for job seekers, job holders, and managers alike?

Organizing

Even the best plans will fail without strong implementation. Success begins with **organizing**, the process of assigning tasks, allocating resources, and coordinating the activities of individuals and groups. When managers organize, they bring people and resources together to put plans into action.

At Ernst & Young, Laskawy organized to meet his planning objective by convening and personally chairing a Diversity Task Force of partners. He also established a new Office of Retention and hired Deborah K. Holmes, now Global Director of Corporate Responsibility, to head it. As retention problems were identified in various parts of the firm, Holmes created special task forces to tackle them and recommend location-specific solutions.

> **Organizing** is the process of assigning tasks, allocating resources, and coordinating work activities.

Leading

The management function of **leading** is the process of arousing people's enthusiasm to work hard and inspiring their efforts to fulfill plans and accomplish objectives. When managers lead, they build commitments to plans and influence others to do their best work in implementing them. This is one of the most talked about managerial responsibilities, and it deserves lots of personal thought. Not every manager is a good leader, but every great manager is one for sure.

Deborah Holmes actively pursued her leadership responsibilities at Ernst & Young. She noticed that, in addition to the intense work at the firm, women often faced more stress because their spouses also worked. She became a champion of improved work–life balance and pursued it relentlessly. She started "call-free holidays," where professionals did not check voice mail or e-mail on weekends and holidays. She also started a "travel sanity" program that limited staffers' travel to four days a week so that they could get home for weekends. And she started a Woman's Access Program to provide mentoring and career development.

> **Leading** is the process of arousing enthusiasm and inspiring efforts to achieve goals.

Controlling

Controlling is the process of measuring work performance, comparing results to objectives, and taking corrective action as needed. As you have surely experienced, things don't always

> **Controlling** is the process of measuring performance and taking action to ensure desired results.

go as planned. When managers control, they stay in contact with people as they work, gather and interpret information on performance results, and use this information to make adjustments.

At Ernst & Young, Laskawy and Holmes regularly measured retention rates for women at the firm and compared them to the rate that existed when their new programs were started. By comparing results with plans and objectives, they were able to track changes in work–life balance and retention rates and pinpoint where they needed to make further adjustments in their programs. Over time, turnover rates for women were, and continue to be, reduced at all levels in the firm.[13]

MANAGERS PERFORM INFORMATIONAL, INTERPERSONAL, AND DECISIONAL ROLES.

INTERPERSONAL ROLES	INFORMATIONAL ROLES	DECISIONAL ROLES
How a manager interacts with other people	How a manager exchanges and processes information	How a manager uses information in decision making
• Figurehead	• Monitor	• Entrepreneur
• Leader	• Disseminator	• Disturbance handler
• Liaison	• Spokesperson	• Resource allocator
		• Negotiator

When you consider the four management functions, don't be unrealistic. The functions aren't always performed one at a time or step by step. Remember that the manager's workday is often intense, fast-paced, and stressful. The reality is that managers must plan, organize, lead, and control continuously while dealing with the numerous events, situations, and problems of the day.

To describe how managers actually get things done, scholar and consultant Henry Mintzberg identified three sets of roles that he believed all good managers enact successfully.[14] A manager's *informational roles* focus on the giving, receiving, and analyzing of information. The *interpersonal roles* reflect interactions with people inside and outside the work unit. The *decisional roles* involve using information to make decisions to solve problems or address opportunities.[15] It is through performing all these roles, so to speak, that managers fulfill their planning, organizing, leading, and controlling responsibilities.

MANAGERS USE NETWORKING AND SOCIAL CAPITAL TO PURSUE ACTION AGENDAS.

SITUATION: An executive is heading to a staff meeting. She encounters a manager from a different department in the hallway. After an exchange of "hellos," she initiates a quick two-minute conversation. She (a) asks two questions and receives helpful information, (b) compliments the other manager for success on a recent project, and, (c) gets the manager's commitment to help on another project.

Can you see the pattern here? In just two short minutes, this general manager accomplished a lot. In fact, she demonstrates excellence with two activities that management consultant and scholar John Kotter considers critical to succeeding with the management process— agenda setting and networking.[16]

Agenda Setting

Agenda setting involves identifying clear action priorities.

Agendas are important in management, and it is through **agenda setting** that managers identify clear action priorities. These agendas may be incomplete and loosely connected in the beginning. But over time, as the manager uses information continually gleaned from many different sources, the agendas become more specific. Kotter says the best managers keep their agendas always in mind so they can quickly recognize and take advantage of opportunities to advance them. What might have happened in the prior example if the manager had simply nodded "hello" to the staff member and continued on to her meeting?

Networking and Social Capital

Networking involves building and maintaining positive relationships with other people.

Much of what managers need to get done is beyond their individual capabilities alone. The support and contributions of other people often make the difference between success and failure. Managers engage in **networking** to build and maintain positive relationships with other people, ideally those whose help might be useful someday in fulfilling their agendas.

Successful managers work hard to network with peers, members of their work teams, higher-level executives, and people at various points elsewhere in the organization. Many are expected to network even more broadly, such as with customers, suppliers, and community representatives.

Think of networking as a pathway to **social capital**—the capacity to attract support and get things done through the help of people you know and relate well with.[17] The executive in the prior vignette needed help from someone who did not report directly to her. She couldn't order the staff person to help her out, but this wasn't a problem. Because of social capital in their network relationship, the person was happy to help when asked.

> **Social capital** is the capacity to attract support and help from others to get things done.

MANAGERS USE TECHNICAL, HUMAN, AND CONCEPTUAL SKILLS.

The discussion of roles, agendas, and networking is but a starting point for inquiry into your personal portfolio of management skills. Another step forward is found in the work of Harvard scholar Robert L. Katz. He classified the essential skills of managers into three categories—technical, human, and conceptual. As shown in **Figure 1.4**, the relative importance of each skill varies by level of managerial responsibility.[18]

Technical Skill

A **technical skill** is the ability to use a special proficiency or expertise to perform particular tasks. Accountants, engineers, market researchers, financial planners, and systems analysts, for example, possess obvious technical skills. Other baseline technical skills for any college graduate today include such things as written and oral communication, computer literacy, and math and numeracy.

> A **technical skill** is the ability to use expertise to perform tasks with proficiency.

In Katz's model, technical skills are very important at career entry levels. So how do you get them? Formal education is an initial source for learning these skills, but continued training and job experiences are important in further developing them. Why not take a moment to inventory your technical skills, the ones you have and the ones you still need to learn for your future career? Katz tells us that the technical skills are especially important at job entry and early career points. Surely, you want to be ready the next time a job interviewer asks the bottom-line question: "What can you really do for us?"

Human Skill

The ability to work well with others is **a human skill**, and it is a foundation for managerial success. How can we excel at networking, for example, without an ability and willingness to relate well with other people? How can we develop social capital without it? A manager with good human skills will have a high degree of self-awareness and a capacity to understand or

> A **human skill** is the ability to work well in cooperation with other people.

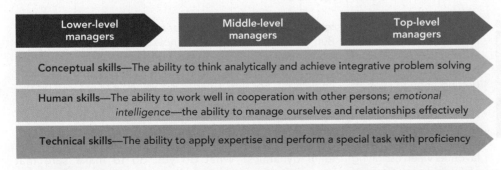

FIGURE 1.4 What Are Three Essential Managerial Skills, and How Does Their Importance Vary Across Levels?

All managers need essential technical, human, and conceptual skills. At lower levels of management, the technical skills are more important than conceptual skills, but at higher levels of management, the conceptual skills become more important than technical skills. Because managerial work is so heavily interpersonal, human skills are equally important across all management levels.

Five Foundations of Emotional Intelligence

1. *Self-awareness*—understanding moods and emotions
2. *Self-regulation*—thinking before acting; controlling disruptive impulses
3. *Motivation*—working hard and persevering
4. *Empathy*—understanding the emotions of others
5. *Social skills*—gaining rapport and building good relationships

empathize with the feelings of others. You would most likely observe this person working with others in a spirit of trust, enthusiasm, and genuine involvement.

A manager with good human skills is also likely to be high in **emotional intelligence** (EI). Considered an important leadership attribute, EI is defined by scholar and consultant Daniel Goleman as the "ability to manage ourselves and our relationships effectively."[19] He believes that emotional intelligence is built on the following five foundations.

Conceptual Skill

Emotional intelligence is the ability to manage ourselves and our relationships effectively.

A **conceptual skill** is the ability to think analytically and solve complex problems.

The ability to think critically and analytically is a **conceptual skill**. It is the capacity to break down problems into smaller parts, see the relations between the parts, and recognize the implications of any one problem for others. Recruiters have described it as "forming your own opinion from a variety of different sources" and "the ability to work with data, to accumulate it, analyze it [and] synthesize it, in order to make balanced assessments and smart decisions."[20] As shown in Figure 1.4, Katz believes conceptual skills are important for all managers, but that they gain in relative importance as we move from lower to higher levels of responsibility. This is because the problems faced at higher levels are often ambiguous and unstructured, accompanied by many complications and interconnections, and full of longer-term consequences for people and organizations.

This conceptual skill set may sound a bit daunting, but it's something you must work hard to develop and that you'll need to show for success in job interviews. When asked a question like—"Talk about how you handled working with a difficult person"—you can bet the job interviewer is trying to judge your capacities for critical thinking.21 In respect to personal development, the question to ask is: "Am I developing the strong critical-thinking and problem-solving capabilities I will need for sustained career success?" The Steps for Further Learning selections at the end of each chapter are good ways to test your conceptual skills in a management context.

MANAGERS SHOULD LEARN FROM EXPERIENCE.

Functions, roles, agendas, networks, skills! How can anyone develop and be consistently good at all these things? How can the capacity to do them all well be developed and maintained for long-term career success?

CHARLES HAS WALKED INTO YOUR CUBICLE AND RANTED ABOUT NOT GETTING ENOUGH SUPPORT FROM YOU AS THE TEAM LEADER.

QUICK CASE

Team Leader Faces Disruptive Team Member

Radius Images/Getty Images

For the third time in a month Charles walks into your cubicle and begins to rant about not getting enough support from you as the team leader. Before you can say anything, he accuses you of playing favorites when assigning projects and failing to show respect for his seniority and expertise. After giving you an angry look, he turns around and stomps off. You've ignored his temper tantrums in the past. Charles is a top software engineer and brings a lot of technical expertise to the team. And, the last time he soon returned to apologize and offer a fist-bump of reconciliation. But, other team members are now complaining to you about his disruptive influence on the work culture. They've been on the receiving end of similar outbursts that make the workday unpleasant. For sure, Charles is a valuable talent, but his disruptive behavior is a call to action.

WHAT DO YOU DO?

How do you handle Charles? How do you handle the team dynamics? What do you do to make sure that everyone, Charles included, achieves high performance and experiences high QWL? Which management functions are being tested here? What essential managerial skills will you need to succeed in this and similar situations?

TABLE 1.1 Six "Must-Have" Managerial Skills

Teamwork: Able to work effectively as team member and leader; strong on team contributions, leadership, conflict management, negotiation, and consensus building

Self-Management: Able to evaluate self, modify behavior, and meet obligations; strong on ethical reasoning, personal flexibility, tolerance for ambiguity, and performance responsibility

Leadership: Able to influence and support others to perform complex and ambiguous tasks; strong on diversity awareness, project management, and strategic action

Critical Thinking: Able to gather and analyze information for problem solving; strong on information analysis and interpretation, creativity and innovation, judgment, and decision making

Professionalism: Able to sustain a positive impression and instill confidence in others; strong on personal presence, initiative, and career management

Communication: Able to express self well in communication with others; strong on writing, oral presentation, giving and receiving feedback, and technology utilization

The challenge for all of us is to be good at **lifelong learning**—the process of continuously learning from our daily experiences and opportunities. Is this a challenge you are confident in meeting? Do you have what the world's largest executive recruiting firm, Korn/Ferry International, calls **learning agility**? Claiming that Korn/Ferry research shows this the top predictor of executive success, CEO Gary Burnison defines it as "willingness to grow, to learn, to have insatiable curiosity."[22]

Why not use **Table 1.1**, Six "Must-Have" Managerial Skills, as a preliminary checklist for assessing your managerial learning and career readiness? How do you stack up? Don't forget the importance of realistic self assessment and willingness to improve over time. Everyone has strengths and weaknesses, and we shouldn't be afraid to recognize ours. But, the challenges of career and life success also require us to be proactive in making positive changes and adapting to new situations.

While we are talking about self reflection, another question is worth asking. Given all the hard work and challenges that it involves, why would anyone want to be a manager or team leader? Beyond the often-higher salaries, there is one very compelling answer—pride of accomplishment! As pointed out by management scholar Henry Mintzberg, being a manager is an important and socially responsible job.[23]

> **Lifelong learning** is continuous learning from daily experiences.

> **Learning agility** is the willingness to grow, to learn, to have insatiable curiosity.

No job is more vital to our society than that of the manager. It is the manager who determines whether our social institutions serve us well or whether they squander our talents and resources. It is time to strip away the folklore about managerial work, and time to study it realistically so that we can begin the difficult task of making significant improvement in its performance.

SELF-MANAGEMENT HELPS US AVOID VIEWING OURSELVES MORE FAVORABLY THAN IS JUSTIFIED.

EXPLORE YOURSELF

Self-Management

When it comes to doing well as a student and in a career, a lot rests on how well you know yourself and what you do with this knowledge. Self-management involves acting with a strong sense of self-awareness, something that helps us build on strengths, overcome weaknesses, and avoid viewing ourselves more favorably than is justified. This capacity is an important career skill. It can be easy to talk about self-management but much harder to master it. Why not use the many self-assessments in this book to get in better touch with this and other important career skills?

> Get to know yourself better by taking the self-assessment on Personal Career Readiness and completing other activities in the *Exploring Management* **Skill-Building Portfolio**.

STUDYGUIDE

Takeaway 1.2
What Do Managers Do, and What Skills Do They Use?

Terms to Define

Agenda setting	Human skill	Management process	Social capital
Conceptual skill	Leading	Networking	Technical skill
Controlling	Learning agility	Organizing	
Emotional intelligence	Lifelong learning	Planning	

Rapid Review

- The daily work of managers is often intense and stressful, involving long hours and continuous performance pressures.
- In the management process, planning sets the direction, organizing assembles the human and material resources, leading provides the enthusiasm and direction, and controlling ensures results.
- Managers perform interpersonal, informational, and decision-making roles while pursuing high-priority agendas and engaging in successful networking.
- Managers rely on a combination of technical skills (ability to use special expertise), human skills (ability to work well with others), and conceptual skills (ability to analyze and solve complex problems).
- Everyday experience is an important source of continuous lifelong learning for managers.

Questions for Discussion

1. Is Mintzberg's view of the intense and demanding nature of managerial work realistic, and if so, why would you want to do it?
2. If Katz's model of how different levels of management use essential skills is accurate, what are its career implications for you?
3. Why is emotional intelligence an important component of one's human skills?

Learning Checks: Can You...?

- **describe** the intensity and pace of a typical workday for a manager
- **give** examples of each of the four management functions
- **list** the three managerial roles identified by Mintzberg
- **explain** how managers use agendas and networks in their work
- **give** examples of a manager's technical, human, and conceptual skills
- **explain** how these skills vary in importance across management levels
- **explain** the importance of experience as a source of managerial learning

Career Situation: What Would You Do?

It's time now to take a first interview for your "dream" job. The interviewer is sitting across the table from you. She smiles, looks you in the eye, and says: "You have a very nice academic record, and we're impressed with your extracurricular activities. Now tell me exactly, what can you do for us that will add value to our organization right from day one?" How do you respond in a way that clearly shows you are "job ready" with strong technical, human, and conceptual skills?

Takeaway 1.3
What Are Some Important Career Issues?

ANSWERS TO COME

- Globalization and job migration have changed the world of work.
- Failures of ethics and corporate governance are troublesome.
- Diversity and discrimination are continuing social priorities.
- Talent is a must-have in a free-agent and on-demand economy.
- Self-management skills are essential for career success.

YOU MIGHT ALREADY HAVE NOTICED THAT THIS TEXT MAY DIFFER FROM OTHERS you've read. I'm going to ask you a lot of questions and expose you to different viewpoints and possibilities. This process of active inquiry begins with the recognition that we live and work in a time of great changes, ones that are not only socially troublesome and personally challenging, but also likely to increase, not decrease, in number, intensity, and complexity in the future.

Are you ready for the challenges ahead? Are you informed about the issues and concerns that complicate our new workplace? Are you willing to admit that this is no time for complacency?

GLOBALIZATION AND JOB MIGRATION HAVE CHANGED THE WORLD OF WORK.

We buy foreign cars like Toyota, Nissan, and Mercedes-Benz that are assembled in America. We buy appliances from the Chinese firm Haier and Eight O'Clock Coffee from India's Tata Group. Top managers at Starbucks, IBM, Sony, Ford, and other global corporations have little need for the words "overseas" or "international" in everyday business vocabulary. They operate as global businesses that serve customers and suppliers wherever in the world they may be located, and that hire talent from around the world wherever it may be available at the lowest costs. Hewlett-Packard operates in 170 countries, and most of its more than 330,000 employees work outside the United States.[24] Although it is headquartered in Palo Alto, California, is HP truly an American company?

There are many faces of **globalization**, the worldwide interdependence of resource flows, product markets, and business competition that characterize our economy.[25] Government leaders now worry about the competitiveness of nations, just as corporate leaders worry about business competitiveness.[26] At a time when more Americans find that their customer service call is answered in Ghana, their CT scan read by a radiologist in India, and their tax return prepared by an accountant in the Philippines, the fact is that globalization offers both opportunities and challenges.

Businesses engage the global economy to sell goods and services to customers around the world. They save money by manufacturing and getting jobs done in countries with lower costs of labor. They also buy the things they need wherever they can be found at the lowest price. This is **global sourcing**—hiring workers and contracting for supplies in other countries.

One controversial side effect to global sourcing is **job migration**, the shifting of jobs from one country to another. The U.S. economy has been a net loser to job migration. Countries such as China, India, and the Philippines have been net gainers. And such countries aren't just sources of unskilled labor anymore. They are now able to offer highly trained workers—engineers, scientists, accountants, health professionals—for portions of the cost of an equivalent U.S. worker.

Politicians and policy makers regularly debate how best to deal with the high costs of job migration, as local workers lose their jobs and their communities lose economic vitality. One side looks for new government policies to stop job migration by protecting the jobs of U.S.

Globalization is the worldwide interdependence of resource flows, product markets, and business competition.

Global sourcing involves contracting for work to be performed in other countries.

Job migration occurs when global outsourcing shifts jobs from one country to another.

Reshoring moves jobs back from foreign to domestic locations.

workers. The other side calls for patience, believing that the global economy will readjust in the long run and create new jobs for U.S. workers. Recent data suggest, in fact, that this is starting to happen as rising global labor and transportation costs make manufacturing at home more attractive. Ford and General Electric are among the firms that have started a practice called **reshoring**. It moves foreign production and jobs back to the United States.[27] Which side are you on—more regulation to save domestic jobs, or letting markets take care of themselves?

FAILURES OF ETHICS AND CORPORATE GOVERNANCE ARE TROUBLESOME.

When Bernard Madoff was sentenced to 150 years in jail for crimes committed with a multi-billion-dollar fraudulent Ponzi scheme, the message was crystal clear.[28] There is no excuse for senior executives in any organization to act illegally. We don't have to tolerate management systems that enrich the few while damaging the many. But not everyone gets the message. We still read and hear about cases where greed overwhelms morality, with negative effects on people, institutions, and society. How would you recover if an employer bankruptcy or major business fraud affected you?

Ethics sets moral standards of what is "good" and "right" behavior in organizations and in our personal lives.

At the end of the day, we depend on individual people, working at all levels of organizations, to act ethically. **Ethics** is a code of moral principles that sets standards of conduct for what is "good" and "right" as opposed to "bad" or "wrong."

Corporate governance is oversight of a company's management by a board of directors.

And, we shouldn't let all the scandals make us cynical about ethical behavior in organizations. Even though ethics failures get most of the publicity, there is still a lot of good happening in the world of work. Look around. You'll find stronger **corporate governance**, described earlier as the active oversight of management decisions, corporate strategy, and financial reporting by a company's board of directors.[29] You'll also find that many people and organizations exemplify an ethical reawakening, one that places high value on personal integrity and moral leadership.

In a book entitled *The Transparent Leader*, Herb Baum argues that integrity is a major key to ethics in leadership. As CEO of Dial Corporation, he walked the talk—no reserved parking place, open door, honest communication, careful listening, and hiring good people. Believing that most CEOs are overpaid, he once gave his annual bonus to the firm's lowest-paid workers.[30]

. . . DISCRIMINATION BASED ON SOCIAL MEDIA INVESTIGATIONS CAN BE UNCONSCIOUS RATHER THAN INTENTIONAL, WITH THE EMPLOYER SHOWING THE BIAS WITHOUT REALIZING IT.

ETHICS CHECK

Social Media Cues May Cause Discrimination in Hiring

Loic Venance/AFP/Getty Images, Inc.

Research suggests that a job candidate's social media postings can contribute to discrimination in hiring. Professor Alessandro Acquisti and colleagues at Carnegie Mellon University distributed 4,000 résumés to job posting sites and associated them with Facebook profiles giving subtle cues—such as background photos and quotes—about the candidates' religion (Muslim or Christian) and sexuality (gay or straight). Religious cues were significant, with Muslims less likely to be called for follow-up interviews than Christians. Sexuality cues made no difference in call-back rates.

Discrimination based on social media investigations can be unconscious rather than intentional, with the employer showing the bias without realizing it. In addition to religion and sexuality, other social media cues that increase the risk of discriminatory behavior are photos of women showing pregnancies or children, and applicants with names often associated with ethnic, racial, or religious communities.

YOUR DECISION?

Is it ethical for employers to use social media to "peek" at the personal lives of prospective candidates? Should there be laws preventing them from doing so? What about individual responsibility? The public visibility of social media postings is well publicized. Isn't it the job seeker's responsibility to avoid and screen out potentially discriminatory information?

Why not make ethics a personal priority? Your management course and this book are good opportunities to build confidence in dealing with ethics challenges. Take time to read and consider the situations presented in the Ethics Check featured in each chapter.

DIVERSITY AND DISCRIMINATION ARE CONTINUING SOCIAL PRIORITIES.

The term **workforce diversity** describes the composition of a workforce in terms of differences among people on gender, age, race, ethnicity, religion, sexual orientation, and physical ability.[31] The diversity trends of changing demographics are well recognized. The U.S. Census Bureau predicts that by 2060 no one racial or ethnic group will be in the majority. Whites will be less than half the population, outnumbered by African Americans, Hispanics, Native Americans, and Asians. Hispanics, the fastest-growing community, will constitute almost one-third of the population by 2060. The U.S. population is also aging. By 2030, more than 20% of the population will be 65 or older. The proportion of the population that is working age will decline to 56.9% by 2060.[32]

Even with the diversity in our society, diversity issues in employment remain as open challenges. When researchers sent out résumés with white-sounding first names like Brett, they received 50% more responses from potential employers than when identical résumés were sent with black-sounding first names, like Kareem.[33] How can this result be explained? U.S. laws prohibit the use of demographic characteristics when employers make decisions on hiring, promotion, and firing. But laws are one thing; actions are another. Some may experience a subtle form of discrimination known as the **glass ceiling effect**. It occurs when an invisible barrier, or "ceiling," prevents members of diverse populations from advancing to high levels of responsibility in organizations.[34]

Do you ever wonder why women and minorities hold few top jobs in large companies? There is little doubt that they still face special work and career challenges.[35]

Although progress is being made—for example, more corporate board seats going to women—diversity bias still exists in too many of our work settings.[36] This bias begins with **prejudice**, the holding of negative, irrational attitudes regarding people who are different from us.

Prejudice becomes active **discrimination** when people in organizations treat minority members unfairly and deny them full membership benefits. Discrimination was evident in the résumés study described earlier. And prejudice also becomes discrimination when a male or female manager refuses to promote a working mother in the belief that "she has too many parenting responsibilities to do a good job at this level."

TALENT IS A MUST-HAVE IN A FREE-AGENT AND ON-DEMAND ECONOMY.

No matter how you look at it, the future poses a complex setting for career success. And current trends indicate job hunters face a challenging **free-agent and on-demand economy**. Like professional athletes, many of us are changing jobs more often while others are working on flexible contracts that connect them temporarily with a shifting mix of employers over time.[37] British scholar and consultant Charles Handy uses the analogy of the **shamrock organization**, shown here, to describe the implications as more workers shift to contract and on-demand work rather than full-time employment.[38]

The first leaf in Handy's shamrock organization is a core group of *permanent, full-time employees* with critical skills, who follow standard career paths. The second leaf consists of workers hired as *freelancers and independent contractors*. They provide organizations with specialized skills and talents for specific projects and then change employers when projects are completed. An increasing number of jobs in the on-demand economy—think Uber—fall into this category. Some call this a time of "giganomics," where even well-trained professionals make their livings moving from one "gig" to the next, instead of holding a traditional full-time job.[39] The third leaf is a group of *temporary part-timers*. Their hours of work increase or decrease as the needs of the business rise or fall. They often work without benefits and are the first to lose their jobs when an employer runs into economic difficulties.

Workforce diversity describes differences among workers in gender, race, age, ethnicity, religion, sexual orientation, and able-bodiedness.

The **glass ceiling effect** is an invisible barrier limiting career advancement of women and minorities.

Prejudice is the display of negative, irrational attitudes toward women or minorities.

Discrimination actively denies women and minorities the full benefits of organizational membership.

In a **free-agent and on-demand economy**, people change jobs more often and many work on-demand as independent contractors with a shifting mix of employers.

A **shamrock organization** operates with a core group of full-time long-term workers supported by others who work with on-demand contracts or as part timers.

The Shamrock Organization

Full-time core workers

Independent contractors

Part-time temporaries

Intellectual capital is the collective brainpower or shared knowledge of a workforce.

The **intellectual capital equation** is: Intellectual Capital = Competency × Commitment.

Knowledge workers use their minds and intellects as critical assets to employers.

Self-management is the ability to understand oneself, exercise initiative, accept responsibility, and learn from experience.

Your **personal brand** is your reputation in the eyes of others and your talents as evidenced by unique and timely skills and capabilities of real value to a potential employer.

As you might guess, today's college graduates must be prepared to succeed in the second and third leaves of Handy's shamrock organization, not just the first. And to achieve success, they need talent in the form of a portfolio of skills that is always up-to-date and attractive to potential employers. And when it comes to talent—yours—it's important to think seriously about **intellectual capital**—what you can offer an employer in terms of brainpower, skills, and capabilities.

A good guide for personal talent development is this **intellectual capital equation**:[40] Intellectual Capital = Competency × Commitment. Competency in this equation represents your talents or job-relevant capabilities; commitment represents your willingness to work hard in applying them to important tasks. Obviously, both are essential. One without the other is not enough to meet anyone's career needs or any organization's performance requirements.

SELF-MANAGEMENT SKILLS ARE ESSENTIAL FOR CAREER SUCCESS.

When it comes to talent and human potential, are well into an *information age* dominated by **knowledge workers**. These are persons whose minds, not just physical capabilities, are critical assets.[41] And things are not standing still. Futurist Daniel Pink says that we are quickly moving into a *conceptual age* in which the most valued intellectual capital will be found in people who are both "high concept"—creative and good with ideas, and "high touch"—joyful and good with relationships.[42]

There is no doubt that the free-agent economy places a premium on your capacity for **self-management**, being able to realistically assess and actively manage your personal development. It means showing emotional intelligence, exercising initiative, accepting responsibility for accomplishments and failures, and continually seeking new learning opportunities and experiences. As a career skill, this ability to self-manage helps us build on strengths, minimize weaknesses, and avoid viewing ourselves both more favorably or more negatively than is justified.

The fact is that what happens from this point forward in your career is largely up to you. There is no better time than the present to start taking charge of what can be called your **personal brand**. This is your reputation in the eyes of others and your talents as evidenced by unique and timely package of skills of real value to a potential employer. Management consultant Tom Peters advises that your brand should be "remarkable, measurable, distinguished, and distinctive" relative to the competition—others who want the same career opportunities that you do.[43] It is also helpful to think of your personal brand as "what I want to be known for."[44]

Have you thought about what employers want? Are you clear and confident about the brand called "You"? Does your intellectual capital portfolio include critical new workplace skills?

Self-Management and *Slumdog Millionaire*

Watner Bros/Photofest

What's your take on this rags-to-riches story of an orphan growing up in Mumbai, India, and finding his way to a TV game show offering him the chance to be a "slumdog millionaire"? When the disgruntled game-show host has the police chief rough up the main character Jamal (Dev Patel) the night before the big show, he asks: "What the hell can a slum boy possibly know?" Facing the chief and the prospect of more mistreatment, Jamal looks him in the eye and says in return: "The answers." And, he didn't fall prey to the quiz master's repeated attempts to deceive and pressure him into not believing his own best answers. It's a classic case of competency with self-management—the capacity to act confidently, with discipline and a strong sense of self-awareness.

STUDYGUIDE

Takeaway 1.3
What Are Some Important Career Issues?

Terms to Define

Corporate governance	Global sourcing	Knowledge workers	Shamrock organization
Discrimination	Globalization	Personal Brand	Workforce diversity
Ethics	Intellectual capital	Prejudice	
Free-agent and on-demand economy	Intellectual capital equation	Reshoring	
Glass ceiling effect	Job migration	Self-management	

Rapid Review

- Globalization has brought increased use of global outsourcing by businesses and concern for the adverse effects of job migration.
- Society increasingly expects organizations and their members to perform with high ethical standards and in socially responsible ways.
- Organizations operate with diverse workforces, and each member should be respected for her or his talents and capabilities.
- Work in the new economy is increasingly knowledge based, relying on people with valuable intellectual capital to drive high performance.
- Careers in the new economy are becoming more flexible, requiring personal initiative to build and maintain skill portfolios that are always up-to-date and valued by employers.

Questions for Discussion

1. How are current concerns about ethics in business, globalization, and changing careers addressed in your courses and curriculum?
2. Is it possible for members of minority groups to avoid being hurt by prejudice, discrimination, and the glass ceiling effect in their careers?
3. In what ways can the capacity for self-management help you to prosper in a free-agent economy?

Learning Checks: Can you. . . ?

- **describe** how corporate governance influences ethics in organizations
- **explain** how globalization and job migration are changing the economy
- **differentiate** prejudice, discrimination, and the glass ceiling effect
- **state** the intellectual capital equation
- **discuss** career opportunities in the shamrock organization
- **explain** the importance of self-management to career success

Career Situation: What Would You Do?

One result of globalization is that many people now work domestically for foreign employers that have set up businesses in their local communities. How about you? Does it make any difference if you receive a job offer in your home state from a foreign employer or a domestic employer? What are the "pluses and minuses" of working at home for a foreign employer? Could the pluses outweigh the minuses for you?

TESTPREP 1

Answers to Test Prep 1 questions can be found at the back of the book.

Multiple-Choice Questions

1. If a sales department supervisor is held accountable by a middle manager for the department's performance, on whom is the department supervisor dependent in making this performance possible?
   (a) Board of directors (b) Top management
   (c) Customers or clients (d) Department salespersons

2. The management function of _____ is being activated when a bookstore manager measures daily sales in the magazine section and compares them with daily sales targets.
   (a) planning (b) agenda setting
   (c) controlling (d) delegating

3. The process of building and maintaining good working relationships with others who may someday help a manager implement his or her work agendas is called _____.
   (a) governance (b) networking
   (c) emotional intelligence (d) entrepreneurship

4. According to Robert Katz, _____ skills are more likely to be emphasized by top managers than by first-line managers.
   (a) human (b) conceptual
   (c) informational (d) technical

5. An effective manager is someone who helps others to achieve high levels of both _____ and _____.
   (a) pay; satisfaction
   (b) performance; satisfaction
   (c) performance; pay
   (d) pay; quality of work life

6. _____ is the active oversight by boards of directors of top management decisions in such areas as corporate strategy and financial reporting.
   (a) Value chain analysis (b) Productivity
   (c) Outsourcing (d) Corporate governance

7. When a manager denies promotion to a qualified worker simply because of personally disliking her because she is Hispanic, this is an example of _____.
   (a) discrimination (b) accountability
   (c) self-management (d) a free-agent economy

8. A company buys cloth in one country, has designs made in another country, has the garments sewn in another country, and sells the finished product in yet other countries. This firm is actively engaging in the practice of _____.
   (a) job migration
   (b) performance effectiveness
   (c) value creation
   (d) global sourcing

9. The intellectual capital equation states: Intellectual Capital × _____ = Commitment.
   (a) Diversity (b) Confidence
   (c) Competency (d) Communication

10. If the direction in managerial work today is away from command and control, what is it toward?
    (a) Coaching and facilitating
    (b) Telling and selling
    (c) Pushing and pulling
    (d) Carrot and stick

11. The manager's role in the "upside-down pyramid" view of organizations is best described as providing _____ so that operating workers can directly serve _____.
    (a) direction; top management
    (b) leadership; organizational goals
    (c) support; customers
    (d) agendas; networking

12. When a team leader clarifies desired work targets and deadlines for a work team, he or she is fulfilling the management function of _____.
    (a) planning (b) delegating
    (c) controlling (d) supervising

13. The research of Mintzberg and others concludes that most managers _____.
    (a) work at a leisurely pace.
    (b) have blocks of private time for planning.
    (c) always live with the pressures of performance responsibility.
    (d) have the advantages of short workweeks.

14. Emotional intelligence helps us to manage ourselves and our relationships effectively. Someone who is high in emotional intelligence will have the capacity to _____, an ability to think before acting and to control potentially disruptive emotions and actions.
    (a) set agendas (b) show motivation
    (c) self-regulate (d) act as a leader

15. Which of the following is a responsibility that is most associated with the work of a CEO, or chief executive officer, of a large company?
    (a) Aligning the company with changes in the external environment
    (b) Reviewing annual pay raises for all employees
    (c) Monitoring short-term performance of lower-level task forces and committees
    (d) Conducting hiring interviews for new college graduates

Short-Response Questions

16. What is the difference between prejudice and workplace discrimination?

17. How is the emergence of a free-agent economy changing career and work opportunities?

18. In what ways will the job of a top manager typically differ from that of a first-line manager?

19. How does planning differ from controlling in the management process?

Integration and Application Question

20. Suppose you have been hired as the new supervisor of an audit team for a national accounting firm. With four years of auditing experience, you feel technically well prepared. However, it is your first formal appointment as a manager. The team has 12 members of diverse demographic and cultural backgrounds and varying work experience. The workload is intense, and there is a lot of performance pressure.

    Questions: To be considered *effective* as a manager, what goals will you set for yourself in the new job? What skills will be important to you, and why, as you seek success as the audit team supervisor?

Steps for
Further Learning

BUILD MARKETABLE SKILLS • **DO** A CASE ANALYSIS • **GET** AND STAY INFORMED

BUILD MARKETABLE SKILLS.

EARN BIG CAREER PAYOFFS!

Don't miss these opportunities in the SKILL-BUILDING PORTFOLIO

SELF-ASSESSMENT 1:
Personal Career Readiness

Rate your personal characteristics . . . start making a solid career development plan.

CLASS EXERCISE 1:
My Best Manager

Compare viewpoints on great managers . . . think about how you can become one.

TEAM PROJECT 1:
The Multigenerational Workforce

Get inside the millennial generation . . . learn to appreciate individual differences at work.

Many learning resources are found at the end of the book and online within **WileyPLUS Learning Space.**

Practice Critical Thinking—Complete the
CHAPTER 1 CASE

Trader Joe's—Managing Less to Gain More

Trader Joe's stands for unique quality items, happy employees, and loyal customers. How did "TJ's" grow from startup to billions in sales and attract an obsessive and diverse cult following of foodies? Much has to do with its unique organizational culture, which affects everything from how the company meticulously plans its store locations, to how it manages its employees, to purchasing and branding strategies. A walk down any aisle shows how management fundamentals helped make Trader Joe's more than just the "average Joe" of food retailers.

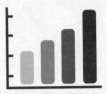

DO A CASE ANALYSIS.

STRENGTHEN YOUR CRITICAL THINKING!

MANAGER'S LIBRARY SELECTION
Read for Insights and Wisdom
Delivering Happiness: A Path to Profits, Passion, and Purpose by Tony Hsieh

"What are you going to be when you grow up?" According to this book by Tony Hsieh, co-founder and CEO of Zappos, "being" something is more of a mindset than an occupation. He thinks the question is answered by simply asking yourself, "What makes you happy?"

Hsieh thinks rules in business are just like rules about hobbies and friends—do what makes you happy with people you like. As Zappos' CEO, Hsieh cultivates a culture in which customers and employees are treated as friends. He considers this the Zappos brand and its secret to success. He emphasizes customer service and employee training and says adults work best when they playfully share discoveries together, much as children do. Fun events sponsored during work hours enable social ties to be cultivated.

GET AND STAY INFORMED.

MAKE YOURSELF VALUABLE!

Zappos welcomes customer calls and online chats as opportunities to create friendly bonds. They aren't timed, no script is used, and agents are guided by personal judgment. Zappos' mission is to "Deliver WOW," and loyal customers receive surprise upgrades to overnight shipping. Employees control career progression by choosing which company-designed courses to take and when to complete them. They receive incremental title and pay boosts rather than infrequent employer-driven reviews. This creates a pipeline of wide-ranging talent.

Finding purpose in work comes with finding happiness; staying connected with others in common purpose beyond self-serving needs feels more like play than work. Hsieh reflects on his childhood worm farm and college pizza business as examples where work and friendship merged meaningfully. He stays busy having fun rather than growing up to be "something."

REFLECT AND REACT Is Hsieh onto something here? Can the workplace really become a fun place? How do you think the rules of work compare or contrast to the rules of play? How are friends and coworkers similar or different? What are your pathways to happiness?

"So if hearing that the CEO of Apple is gay can help someone struggling to come to terms with who he or she is, or bring comfort to anyone who feels alone, or inspire people to insist on their equality, then it's worth the trade-off with my own privacy."

Tim Cook, CEO Apple, Inc.

Ethics and Social Responsibility

2

Character Doesn't Stay Home When We Go to Work

Management Live

Curbing Work Hours to Improve Performance

Spectral-Design/Shutterstock

Does it surprise you that software coders produce higher quality work in 40-hour versus 60-hour weeks? Someone who works long hours gives the impression of being "dependable" and "committed." But at what price? An occupational psychologist says: "We need to see duty of care as part of the role of manager . . . sensible hours needs to be championed by middle managers as well as senior leaders." Not taking care of your health, missing children's life and school events, and inattention to spouse or partner are warning signs. Living with always-on technology doesn't help.

YOUR THOUGHTS?

What social responsibility do employers have to make sure that employees don't work so many hours that they lose productivity and damage their health and personal lives?

WHAT'S INSIDE

ETHICS CHECK
Interns sue employers for back pay

FACTS TO CONSIDER
Manager behavior key to an ethical workplace

HOT TOPIC
App-enabled on-demand workers are not robots

QUICK CASE
Teacher calls about daughter cheating on test

YOUR CHAPTER 2 TAKEAWAYS

1. Understand how ethics and ethical behavior play out in the workplace.

2. Know how to maintain high standards of ethical conduct.

3. Identify when organizations are and are not acting in socially responsible ways.

Takeaway 2.1
How Do Ethics and Ethical Behavior Play Out in the Workplace?

ANSWERS TO COME

- Ethical behavior is values driven.
- Views differ on what constitutes moral behavior.
- What is considered ethical can vary across cultures.
- Ethical dilemmas are tests of personal ethics and values.
- People have tendencies to rationalize unethical behaviors.

DOES LEARNING ABOUT BAD BUSINESS BEHAVIOR SHOCK AND DISMAY YOU? Sensational news headlines are all too frequent. And the underlying stories aren't just ones of incompetence or poor judgment; they include tales of personal failures and greed.[1] It's understandable why so many people feel cynical, pessimistic, and even helpless regarding the state of executive leadership in our society.[2]

Would you say that it is time to get serious about the morality of behavior in and by organizations? Can we agree that in your career, and for any manager, the goal should always be to achieve performance objectives through ethical and socially responsible actions? As you think about these questions, consider this advice from Desmond Tutu, archbishop of Capetown, South Africa, and winner of the Nobel Peace Prize.[3]

> You are powerful people. You can make this world a better place where business decisions and methods take account of right and wrong as well as profitability. . . . You must take a stand on important issues: the environment and ecology, affirmative action, sexual harassment, racism and sexism, the arms race, poverty, the obligations of the affluent West to its less-well-off sisters and brothers elsewhere.

ETHICAL BEHAVIOR IS VALUES DRIVEN.

It is tempting to say that any behavior that is legal can also be considered ethical. But this is too easy; the "letter of the law" does not always translate into what others would consider to be ethical actions.[4] U.S. laws once allowed slavery, permitted only men to vote, and allowed young children to work full-time jobs. Today we consider such actions unethical.

Ethics is defined as the code of moral principles that sets standards of good or bad, or right or wrong, in our conduct.[5] Personal ethics are guides for behavior, helping people make moral choices among alternative courses of action. Most typically, we use the term **ethical behavior** to describe what we accept as "good" and "right" as opposed to "bad" or "wrong."

But, it's one thing to look back and make ethical judgments; it is a bit harder to make them in real time. Is it truly ethical for an employee to take longer than necessary to do a job . . . to make personal telephone calls on company time . . . to call in sick and go on vacation instead? Although these acts are not strictly illegal, many people would consider one or more of them to be unethical. How about you? How often and in what ways have you committed or observed acts that could be considered unethical in your school or workplace?[6]

Consider this situation. About 10% of an MBA class at Duke University was once caught cheating on a take-home final exam.[7] The "cheaters" were also big on music downloads, file sharing, open-source software, text messaging, and electronic collaboration. Some say what happened relates to "postmodern learning," where students are taught to collaborate, work in teams, and use the latest communication technologies. For others, there is no doubt—it was an individual exam, and those students cheated.

Ethical issues and problems arise when people do something that violates their—or someone else's—**values**—underlying beliefs and judgments regarding what is right or

---

Ethics sets standards of good or bad, or right or wrong, in our conduct.

Ethical behavior is "right" or "good" in the context of a governing moral code.

Values are broad beliefs about what is appropriate behavior.

FACTS TO CONSIDER

Behavior of Managers Is Key to an Ethical Workplace

Masterfile

Managers make a big difference in ethical behavior at work, according to a survey conducted for Deloitte & Touche USA. The most common unethical acts by managers and supervisors include verbal, sexual, and racial harassment; misuse of company property; and giving preferential treatment. Some other findings include:

- 91% of workers are more likely to behave ethically when they have work–life balance; but, 30% say they suffer from poor work–life balance.

- Top reasons for unethical behavior are lack of personal integrity (80%) and lack of job satisfaction (60%).
- Most workers consider it unacceptable to steal from an employer, cheat on expense reports, take credit for another's accomplishments, or lie on time sheets.
- Most workers consider it acceptable to ask a work colleague for a personal favor, take sick days when not ill, or use company technology for personal affairs.

WHAT'S YOUR TAKE?

Are there any surprises in these data? Is this emphasis on manager and direct supervisor behavior justified as the key to an ethical workplace? Would you make any changes to what the workers in this survey report as acceptable and unacceptable work behaviors?

---

desirable and that influence individual attitudes and behaviors. The psychologist Milton Rokeach distinguishes between "terminal" and "instrumental" values.[8] **Terminal values** focus on desired ends or what someone wants to achieve, such as the goal of career advancement. Examples of terminal values considered important by managers include self-respect, wealth, and happiness. **Instrumental values** focus on the means one is willing to use to accomplish desired ends, such as honesty in relationships. Instrumental values held important by managers include ambition, courage, imagination, and self-discipline.

Although terminal and instrumental values tend to be quite enduring for any one individual, they can vary considerably from one person to the next. This might help to explain why different people respond quite differently to the same situation. Although they might share the terminal value of career success, they might disagree on how to balance the instrumental values of honesty and ambition in accomplishing it.

Terminal values are preferences about desired end states.

Instrumental values are preferences regarding the means to desired ends.

VIEWS DIFFER ON WHAT CONSTITUTES MORAL BEHAVIOR.

Figure 2.1 summarizes four different philosophical views of ethical behavior—utilitarian, individualism, justice, and moral rights. Each represents an alternative approach to moral reasoning and may conclude differently about whether or not a given behavior is ethical.[9]

Individualism view

Does a decision or behavior promote one's long-term self-interests?

Moral rights view

Does a decision or behavior maintain the fundamental rights of all human beings?

Utilitarian view

Does a decision or behavior do the greatest good for the most people?

Justice view

Does a decision or behavior show fairness and impartiality?

FIGURE 2.1

How Do Alternative Moral Reasoning Approaches View Ethical Behavior?

People often differ in the approaches they take toward moral reasoning, and they may use different approaches at different times and situations. Four ways to reason through the ethics of a course of action are utilitarianism, individualism, moral rights, and justice. Each approach can justify an action as ethical, but the reasoning will differ from that of the other views.

Utilitarian View

In the **utilitarian view**, ethical behavior delivers the greatest good to the most people.

A business owner decides to cut 30% of a small firm's workforce in order to keep the business profitable and save the remaining jobs, rather than lose them all to failure. This decision is considered ethical in the **utilitarian view** because it delivers the greatest good to the greatest number of people.

Founded in the work of 19th-century philosopher John Stuart Mill, the results-oriented utilitarian view tries to assess the moral implications of our actions in terms of their consequences. Business executives, for example, might use profits, efficiency, and other performance criteria to judge when and if a decision is best for the most people. But, we also have to be careful. Utilitarian thinking relies on assessment of future outcomes that can be difficult to predict and hard to measure accurately. What is the economic value of a human life, for example, when deciding how rigid safety regulations need to be on an offshore drilling rig or in an underground coal mine? Is it even appropriate to try to put an economic value on the potential loss of human life?

Individualism View

In the **individualism view**, ethical behavior advances long-term self-interests.

The **individualism view** focuses the ethics analysis on long-term advancement of self-interests. The notion is that people become self-regulating and ethics are maintained as they strive for individual advantage over time. Suppose that you are considering cheating on your next test. With further thought, you realize for any short-term gain might lead to a long-term loss if you are caught and expelled from school. Thus, defense of your self-interest causes you to reject the original inclination to cheat on the exam.

Not everyone, as you might expect, believes we can rely on individualism to ensure that decisions result in ethical behavior. People vary in their capacity for self-regulation, especially when faced with difficult choices and situations that put honesty and integrity to stiff tests. And, a common complaint about individualism in business is that decisions are too often driven by a *pecuniary ethic* fueled by greed and resulting in misbehavior.[10]

Justice View

In the **justice view**, ethical behavior treats people impartially and fairly.

A behavior is ethical under the **justice view** of moral reasoning when people are treated impartially and fairly, and according to legal rules and standards. This view judges the ethics of any decision on the basis of how equitable it is in terms of workplace justice—procedural, distributive, interactional, and commutative.[11]

"HELLO, THIS IS ANN'S FOURTH-GRADE TEACHER.
I'D LIKE TO SET UP A CONFERENCE. SHE'S BEEN CAUGHT CHEATING ON A TEST."

QUICK CASE

Teacher Calls About Daughter Cheating on Test

Ermolaev Alexander/Shutterstock

"Hello, this is Ann's fourth-grade teacher. I'd like to set up a conference. She's been caught cheating on a test." This isn't the telephone message you'd been expecting when answering voice mail from your daughter's school. Just the other day Ann had been telling you how much she enjoyed the class and working in a small group on projects. "It's so much fun working with others," she said. After calling the teacher back you've learned that during a standardized test, one of the students from that group asked for and received an answer from Ann. The teacher hasn't said anything to the students yet, but wants to talk to the parents. You wonder: How does all the emphasis on teamwork, sharing, and collaboration reconcile with a classmate's request for help on a test? The teacher conference is scheduled for tomorrow. Ann will be waiting when you get home from work.

WHAT DO YOU DO?

Can Ann's behavior be justified on ethics grounds? What do you say, ask, and do with her? How can you turn this situation into a learning experience that will help her know right from wrong? How do you handle her emotions . . . and likely questions? What is the line here between ethical and unethical behavior in a culture of teamwork? What do you say, ask, and do with the teacher?

Procedural justice involves the fair administration of policies and rules. For example, does a sexual harassment charge levied against a senior executive receive the same full hearing as one made against a first-level supervisor? **Distributive justice** involves the allocation of outcomes without respect to individual characteristics, such as those based on ethnicity, race, gender, or age. For example, does a woman with the same qualifications and experience as a man receive the same consideration for hiring or promotion?

Interactional justice focuses on treating everyone with dignity and respect. For example, does a bank loan officer take the time to fully explain to an applicant why he or she was turned down for a loan?[12] **Commutative justice** focuses on the fairness of exchanges or transactions. An exchange is considered fair if all parties enter into it freely, have access to relevant and available information, and obtain some type of benefit from the transaction.[13]

> **Procedural justice** focuses on the fair application of policies and rules.
>
> **Distributive justice** focuses on treating people the same regardless of personal characteristics.
>
> **Interactional justice** is the degree to which others are treated with dignity and respect.
>
> **Commutative justice** focuses on the fairness of exchanges or transactions.

Moral Rights View

The **moral rights view** considers behavior to be ethical when it respects and protects the fundamental rights of people. Based on the teachings of John Locke and Thomas Jefferson, this view believes all people have rights to life, liberty, and fair treatment under the law. In organizations, this translates into protecting the rights of employees to privacy, due process, free speech, free consent, health and safety, and freedom of conscience.

> In the **moral rights view**, ethical behavior respects and protects fundamental rights.

This view of ethical reasoning protects individual rights, but it doesn't guarantee that the outcomes will be beneficial to the broader society. What happens, for example, when someone's right to free speech conveys messages hurtful to others? Compounding this problem is the fact that various nations have different laws and cultural expectations. As we grapple with the complexities of global society, human rights are often debated. Even though the United Nations stands by the Universal Declaration of Human Rights passed by the General Assembly in 1948, business executives, representatives of activist groups, and leaders of governments still argue and disagree over rights issues in various circumstances.[14]

> **Excerpts from the Universal Declaration of Human Rights, United Nations**
>
> - **ARTICLE 1**—All human beings are born free and equal in dignity and right.
> - **ARTICLE 18**—Everyone has the right to freedom of thought, conscience, and religion.
> - **ARTICLE 19**—Everyone has the right to freedom of opinion and expression.
> - **ARTICLE 23**—Everyone has the right to work, to free choice of employment, to just and favorable conditions of work.
> - **ARTICLE 26**—Everyone has the right to education.

WHAT IS CONSIDERED ETHICAL CAN VARY ACROSS CULTURES.

SITUATION: A 12-year-old boy is working in a garment factory in Bangladesh. He is the sole income earner for his family. He often works 12-hour days and was once burned quite badly by a hot iron. One day he is told he can't work. His employer was given an ultimatum by the firm's major American customer—"no child workers if you want to keep our contracts." The boy says: "I don't understand. I could do my job very well. My family needs the money."

"Should this child be allowed to work?" This question is but one example among the many ethics challenges faced in international business. Robert Haas, former Levi Strauss CEO, once said that an ethical problem "becomes even more difficult when you overlay the complexities of different cultures and values systems that exist throughout the world."[15] It would probably be hard to find a corporate leader or businessperson engaged in international business who would disagree. Put yourself in their positions. How would you deal with an issue such as child labor in a factory owned by one of your major suppliers?

Those who believe that behavior in foreign settings should be guided by the classic rule of "when in Rome, do as the Romans do" reflect an ethical position of **cultural relativism**.[16] This is the belief that there is no one right way to behave and that ethical behavior is always determined by its cultural context. An American international business executive guided by rules of cultural relativism, for example, would argue that the use of child labor is okay in another country as long as it is consistent with local laws and customs.

> **Cultural relativism** suggests there is no one right way to behave; cultural context determines ethical behavior.

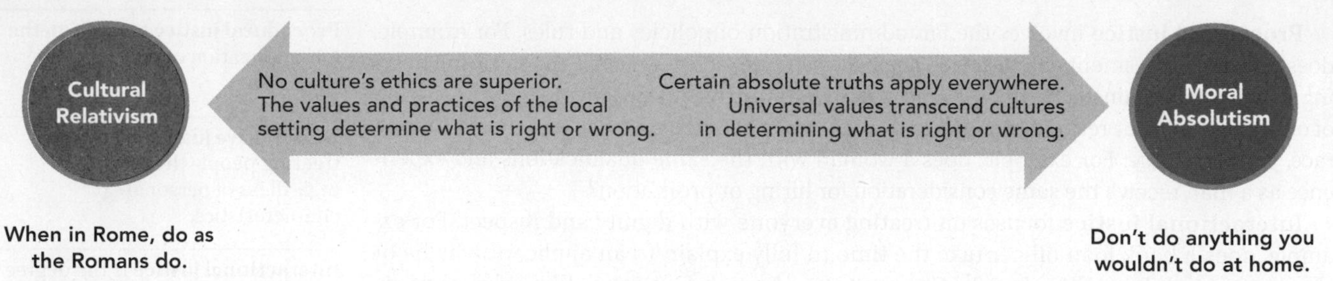

When in Rome, do as
the Romans do.

Don't do anything you
wouldn't do at home.

FIGURE 2.2 How Do Cultural Relativism and Moral Absolutism Influence International Business Ethics?
The international business world is one of the most challenging settings in respect to ethical decision making. This figure identifies two diametrically opposed extremes. Cultural relativism justifies a decision if it conforms to local values, laws, and practices. Moral absolutism justifies a decision only if it conforms to the ways of the home country.
(*Source:* Developed from Thomas Donaldson, "Values in Tension: Ethics Away from Home," *Harvard Business Review*, vol. 74 (September/October 1996), pp. 48–62.)

Moral absolutism suggests ethical standards apply universally across all cultures.

Figure 2.2 contrasts cultural relativism with the alternative of **moral absolutism**. This is a universalist ethical position suggesting that if a behavior or practice is not okay in one's home environment, it is not acceptable practice anywhere else. In other words, ethical standards are absolute and should apply universally across cultures and national boundaries. The American executive in the former example would not do business in a setting where child labor was used because it is unacceptable at home. Critics of the universal approach claim it is a form of **ethical imperialism**, or the attempt to externally impose one's ethical standards on others.

Ethical imperialism is an attempt to impose one's ethical standards on other cultures.

Business ethicist Thomas Donaldson finds fault with both cultural relativism and moral absolutism. He argues instead that fundamental human rights and ethical standards can be preserved while values and traditions of a local culture are respected.[17] The core values or "hypernorms" that must travel across cultural and national boundaries focus on human dignity, basic rights, and good citizenship. But once these core values have been met, Donaldson believes that international business behaviors can be tailored to local cultures. In the case of child labor, the American executive might ensure that any children employed in a factory under contract to his or her business work in safe conditions and are provided regular schooling during scheduled work hours.[18]

ETHICAL DILEMMAS ARE TESTS OF PERSONAL ETHICS AND VALUES.

It's all well and good to discuss cases about ethical behavior in theory and in the safety of the college classroom. The tough personal test, however, occurs when we encounter a real-life situation that challenges our ethical beliefs and standards. Often ambiguous and unexpected, these ethical challenges are inevitable. Think ahead to your next job search. Suppose you have accepted a job offer only to get a better one from another employer two weeks later. Should you come up with an excuse to back out of the first job so that you can accept the second one instead?

An **ethical dilemma** is a situation that, although offering potential benefit or gain, is also unethical.

An **ethical dilemma** is a situation requiring a decision about a course of action that, although offering potential benefits, may be considered unethical. As a further complication, there may be no clear consensus on what is "right" and "wrong." In these circumstances, one's personal values are often the best indicators that something isn't right. An engineering manager speaking from experience sums it up this way: "I define an unethical situation as one in which I have to do something I don't feel good about."[19]

Take a look at **Table 2.1**—Common Examples of Unethical Behavior at Work.[20] Have you been exposed to anything like this? Are you ready to deal with these situations and any ethical dilemmas that they may create?

Managers report that many of their ethical dilemmas arise out of conflicts with superiors, customers, and subordinates.[21] The most frequent issues involve dishonesty in advertising and in communications with top management, clients, and government agencies. Other ethics problems involve dealing with special gifts, entertainment expenses, and kickbacks.

TABLE 2.1 Common Examples of Unethical Behavior at Work

Discrimination: Denying people a promotion or job because of their race, religion, gender, age, or another reason that is not job relevant

Sexual harassment: Making a co-worker feel uncomfortable because of inappropriate comments or actions regarding sexuality or by requesting sexual favors in return for favorable job treatment

Conflicts of interest: Taking bribes, kickbacks, or extraordinary gifts in return for making decisions favorable to another person

Customer privacy: Giving someone privileged information regarding the activities of a customer

Organizational resources: Using a business e-mail account to communicate personal opinions or to make requests from community organizations

Isn't it interesting that managers single out their bosses as frequent causes of ethical dilemmas? They complain about bosses who engage in various forms of harassment, misuse organizational resources, and give preferential treatment to certain persons.[22] They report feeling pressured at times to support incorrect viewpoints, sign false documents, overlook the boss's wrongdoings, and do business with the boss's friends. A surprising two-thirds of chief financial officers in one survey, for example, said that they had been asked by their bosses to falsify financial records. Among them, 45% said they refused the directive; 12% said they complied.[23]

Unrealistically high performance goals often top the lists of bad boss practices.[24] When individuals feel extreme performance pressures, they sometimes act incorrectly and engage in questionable practices in attempting to meet these expectations. As scholar Archie Carroll says: "... otherwise decent people start cutting corners on accuracy or quality, or start covering up incidents, lying or deceiving customers."[25] Carroll also says: "Good management means that one has to be sensitive to how pressure to perform might be perceived by those who want to please the boss."[26]

PEOPLE HAVE TENDENCIES TO RATIONALIZE UNETHICAL BEHAVIORS.

What happens after someone commits an unethical act? Most of us generally view ourselves as "good" people. When we do something that is or might be "wrong," it leaves us doubtful, uncomfortable, and anxious. A common response is to rationalize the questionable behavior to make it seem acceptable in our minds. Although rationalizations might give us a false sense of justification, they come at a high cost.[27]

"It's not really illegal." Wrong—this implies that the behavior is acceptable even in ambiguous situations. When dealing with shady or borderline situations, you may not be able to precisely determine right from wrong. In such cases, it is important to stop and reconsider things. When in doubt about the ethics of a decision, the best advice is: Don't do it.

"It's in everyone's best interests." Wrong—this suggests that just because someone might benefit from the behavior, it is okay. To overcome this "ends justify the means" rationalization, we need to look beyond short-run results and carefully assess longer-term implications.

"No one will ever know about it." Wrong—this implies that something is wrong only if it is discovered. Lack of accountability, unrealistic pressures to perform, and a boss who prefers "not to know" can all reinforce this tendency. But such thinking is risky and hard to accept. Nothing stays secret very long in today's world of great transparency.

"The organization will stand behind me." Wrong—this is misperceived loyalty. If anything, you can expect the organization and its managers to sacrifice you when their self-interests are threatened. If you are caught doing something wrong, do you really want to count on the organization going to bat for you? And when you read about people who have done wrong and then tried to excuse it by saying, "I only did what I was ordered to do," how sympathetic are you?

STUDYGUIDE

Takeaway 2.1
How Do Ethics and Ethical Behavior Play Out in the Workplace?

Terms to Define

Commutative justice	Ethical imperialism	Justice view	Utilitarian view
Cultural relativism	Ethics	Moral absolutism	Values
Distributive justice	Individualism view	Moral rights view	
Ethical behavior	Instrumental values	Procedural justice	
Ethical dilemmas	Interactional justice	Terminal values	

Rapid Review

- Ethical behavior is that which is accepted as "good" or "right" as opposed to "bad" or "wrong."
- The utilitarian, individualism, moral rights, and justice views offer different approaches to moral reasoning; each takes a different perspective of when and how a behavior becomes ethical.
- Cultural relativism argues that no culture is ethically superior to any other; moral absolutism believes there are clear rights and wrongs that apply universally, no matter where in the world one might be.
- An ethical dilemma occurs when one must decide whether to pursue a course of action that, although offering the potential for personal or organizational gain, may be unethical.
- Ethical dilemmas faced by managers often involve conflicts with superiors, customers, and subordinates over requests that involve some form of dishonesty.
- Common rationalizations for unethical behavior include believing the behavior is not illegal, is in everyone's best interests, will never be noticed, or will be supported by the organization.

Questions for Discussion

1. For a manager, is any one of the moral reasoning approaches better than the others?
2. Will a belief in cultural relativism create inevitable ethics problems for international business executives?
3. Are ethical dilemmas always problems, or can they be opportunities?

Be Sure You Can

- **differentiate** between legal behavior and ethical behavior
- **differentiate** between terminal and instrumental values, and give examples of each
- **list** and explain four approaches to moral reasoning
- **illustrate** distributive, procedural, interactive, and commutative justice in organizations
- **explain** the positions of cultural relativism and moral absolutism in international business ethics
- **illustrate** the types of ethical dilemmas common in the workplace
- **explain** how bad management can cause ethical dilemmas
- **list** four common rationalizations for unethical behavior

Career Situation: What Would You Do?

Today's classroom could be a mirror image of tomorrow's workplace. You have just seen one of your classmates snap a cell-phone photo of the essay question on an exam. The instructor has missed this, and you're not sure if anyone else observed what just happened. You know that the instructor is giving an exam to another section of the course starting next class period. Do you let this pass, perhaps telling yourself that it isn't all that important? If so, how do you justify this choice? If you can't let it pass, what action would you take and why?

Takeaway 2.2
How Can We Maintain High Standards of Ethical Conduct?

ANSWERS TO COME

- Personal character and moral development influence ethical decision making.
- Managers as positive role models can inspire ethical conduct.
- Training in ethical decision making can improve ethical conduct.
- Protection of whistleblowers can encourage ethical conduct.
- Formal codes of ethics set standards for ethical conduct.

LOOK AROUND AND YOU'LL SEE MANY PEOPLE AND ORGANIZATIONS OPERATING in ethical and socially responsible ways. Some are quite well known—companies like Patagonia, Stonyfield Farm, and Whole Foods Market are examples. Others are less visible, but still performing every day with high ethical standards. Surely there are examples of small businesses right in your local community that show how "profits with principles" can be achieved. As you think about organizations that do these good things, don't forget that the underlying reasons rest with the people who run them—individuals like you and me.

PERSONAL CHARACTER AND MORAL DEVELOPMENT INFLUENCE ETHICAL DECISION MAKING.

Something called "character" is a major influence on our personal ethics. It comes from family influences, religious beliefs, personal standards, personal values, and even past experiences. And as the chapter subtitle reminds us: Character shouldn't stay home when we go to work. But, it isn't always easy to stand up for what we believe when we are exposed to extreme performance pressures, when we get contradictory or just plain bad advice, or when our career or personal well being is threatened. "Do this or lose your job!" is a terribly intimidating message.

Does it surprise you that 56% of U.S. workers in one survey reported feeling pressured to act unethically in their jobs . . . or, that 48% of them self-reported as having committed questionable acts.[28] It is easier to deal with tough problems and situations when we already have solid **ethical frameworks** in place. These are well-thought-out personal rules and strategies for ethical decision making that give high priority to virtues like honesty, fairness, integrity, and self-respect. Ethical frameworks help us to act consistently and confidently even under the most difficult conditions.

The many personal influences on ethical frameworks come together in the three levels of moral development described by Lawrence Kohlberg and shown in **Figure 2.3**.[29] Kohlberg

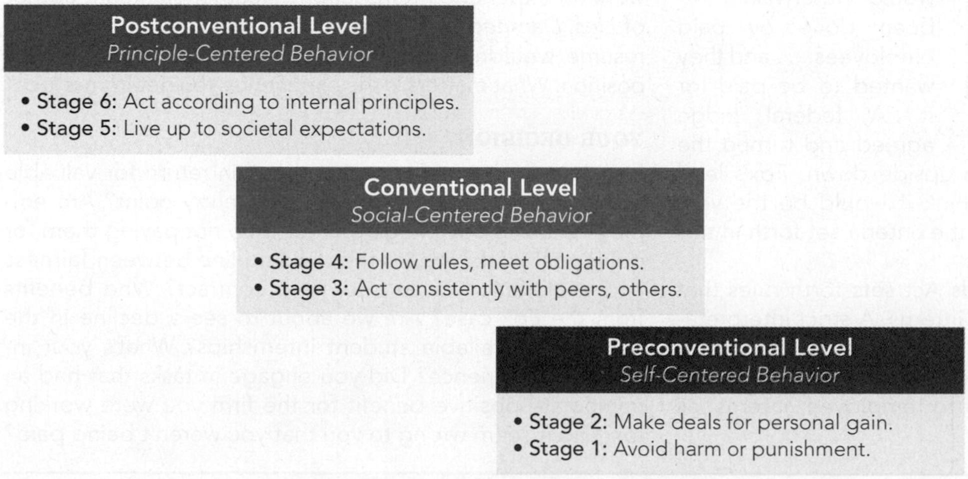

Ethical frameworks are well-thought-out personal rules and strategies for ethical decision making.

Postconventional Level
Principle-Centered Behavior
- **Stage 6:** Act according to internal principles.
- **Stage 5:** Live up to societal expectations.

Conventional Level
Social-Centered Behavior
- **Stage 4:** Follow rules, meet obligations.
- **Stage 3:** Act consistently with peers, others.

Preconventional Level
Self-Centered Behavior
- **Stage 2:** Make deals for personal gain.
- **Stage 1:** Avoid harm or punishment.

FIGURE 2.3
What Are the Stages in Kohlberg's Three Levels of Moral Development?
At the preconventional level of moral development, the individual focuses on self-interests, avoiding harm and making deals for gain. At the conventional level, attention becomes more social centered, and the individual tries to be consistent and meet obligations to peers. At the postconventional level of moral development, principle-centered behavior results in the individual living up to societal expectations and personal principles.

believes that we move step-by-step through the levels as we grow in maturity and education. Not everyone, in fact perhaps only a few of us, will reach the top.

In Kohlberg's *preconventional stage* of moral development, the individual is self-centered and the ethics framework is weak. Moral thinking is largely limited to issues of punishment, obedience, and personal interest. Decisions made in the preconventional stage are likely to be directed toward personal gain and based on obedience to rules.

In the *conventional stage*, by contrast, attention broadens to include more social concerns. Decisions made in this stage are likely to be based on following social norms, meeting the expectations of others, and living up to agreed-upon obligations.

In the *postconventional or principled stage* of moral development, the individual is driven by core principles and beliefs. A strong ethics framework is evident. The individual is willing to break with norms and conventions, even laws, to act consistently with personal principles. An example is the student who passes on an opportunity to cheat on a take-home examination because he or she believes it is wrong, even though the consequence will be a lower grade. Another example is someone who refuses to use pirated computer software, preferring to purchase it and show respect for intellectual property rights.

Chooses to behave unethically

Fails to consider ethics

Immoral manager

Amoral manager

Makes ethical behavior a personal goal

Moral manager

MANAGERS AS POSITIVE ROLE MODELS CAN INSPIRE ETHICAL CONDUCT.

Managers at all levels in all organizations have a lot of power to shape policies and set a moral tone. Some of this power works through the attention given to policies that set high ethics standards—and to their enforcement. Another and significantly large part of this power works through the personal examples managers set as ethics role models. In order to have a positive impact, a manager must walk the ethics talk. An example is to set realistic and achievable performance goals rather than impossible ones.[30] A *Fortune* survey reported that 34% of its respondents felt a company president can help to create an ethical climate by setting reasonable goals "so that subordinates are not pressured into unethical actions."[31]

"A JOB LISTED ON A RESUME WOULDN'T IMPRESS ME JUST BECAUSE IT WAS A PAID POSITION. WHAT MATTERS IS THE EXPERIENCE YOU GET FROM A JOB."

ETHICS CHECK

Interns Are Suing Their Employers for Back Pay

Alex Brandon/AP Photo

Two interns sued Fox Searchlight Pictures claiming their jobs would otherwise have been done by paid employees . . . and they wanted to be paid for it. A federal judge agreed and turned the notion of the unpaid internship upside down. Fox's lead attorney Juno Turner says: "I think it would be the very rare internship that would meet the criteria set forth in this decision."

The U.S. Fair Labor Standards Act sets forth rules that must be followed to hire unpaid interns. A strict interpretation seems to push employers in the direction of offering only paid internships. An exception is the public sector where nonprofits are allowed to employee interns as volunteers.

There's no doubt that internships are a well-established source of valuable experience for students and a job entry point for many. What difference does pay make in this work-for-experience transaction? Heather Huhman, author of *Lies, Damned Lies & Internships*, says: "A job listed on a resume wouldn't impress me just because it was a paid position. What matters is the experience you get from a job."

YOUR DECISION?

Is it right for interns to demand pay in return for valuable work experience and a possible job entry point? Are employers taking advantage of interns by not paying them for doing real work? What's the dividing line between fairness and exploitation in an internship contract? Who benefits from the Fox case? Are we about to see a decline in the number of available student internships? What's your internship experience? Did you engage in tasks that had an immediate positive benefit for the firm you were working for? Did it seem wrong to you that you weren't being paid?

Management scholar Archie Carroll makes distinctions among amoral, immoral, and moral managers.[32] The **immoral manager** chooses to behave unethically. This manager seeks only personal gain and intentionally disregards the ethics of an action. The **amoral manager** also disregards the ethics of a decision, but does so unintentionally. This manager simply fails to consider the ethical consequences of his or her actions. In contrast to both prior types, the **moral manager** has a strong ethics framework and values ethical behavior as a personal goal. This manager always makes decisions in full consideration of ethical issues. In Kohlberg's terms, he or she operates at the postconventional or principled stage of moral development.[33]

Although it may seem surprising, Carroll suggests that most of us act amorally as managers and in our work roles. Although well intentioned, we remain mostly uninformed or undisciplined in considering the ethical aspects of our behavior. Should we just accept this as some natural human tendency? Or is Carroll's observation better considered a personal call to action—a challenge to seek the moral high ground at work and in our personal lives?

> An **immoral manager** chooses to behave unethically.

> An **amoral manager** fails to consider the ethics of her or his behavior.

> A **moral manager** makes ethical behavior a personal goal.

TRAINING IN ETHICAL DECISION MAKING CAN IMPROVE ETHICAL CONDUCT.

It would be nice if everyone had access through their employers to **ethics training** that helps them understand and best deal with ethical aspects of decision making. Although not all will have this opportunity, more and more are getting it, including college students. Most business schools, for example, now offer required and elective courses on ethics or integrate ethics throughout a curriculum.[34]

> **Ethics training** seeks to help people understand the ethical aspects of decision making and to incorporate high ethical standards into their daily behavior.

Time pressures creates one of the biggest differences between facing an ethical dilemma in a college class discussion—where things are safe and easy, and in real life—where real consequences exist. Many times we must, or believe we must, move fast. Instead, ethics training recommends that we pause and double-check important decisions before taking action in uncomfortable circumstances.

Tips to Remember offers a useful seven- step checklist for dealing with ethical dilemmas.[35] Would you agree that the most important of the steps in the decision checklist is Step 6? This is what some call the test of the **spotlight questions**. You might think of it as highlighting the risk of public disclosure for your actions. Asking and answering the spotlight questions is an easy and powerful way to test whether a decision is consistent with your ethical standards.[36] Have you ever been in a situation where these questions would have helped you resolve an ethically challenging situation?

> **TIPS TO REMEMBER**
> ### Checklist for Dealing with Ethical Dilemmas
> **Step 1.** Recognize the ethical dilemma.
> **Step 2.** Get the facts.
> **Step 3.** Identify your options.
> **Step 4.** Test each option by asking: Is it legal? Is it right? Is it beneficial?
> **Step 5.** Decide which option to follow.
> **Step 6.** Double check your decision by asking three spotlight questions.
> - *"How would I feel if my family found out about my decision?"*
> - *"How would I feel if my decision was reported in the local newspaper or posted on the Internet?"*
> - *"What would the person I know who has the strongest character and best ethical judgment say about my decision?"*
> **Step 7.** Take action.

> **Spotlight questions** highlight the risks from public disclosure of one's actions.

PROTECTION OF WHISTLEBLOWERS CAN ENCOURAGE ETHICAL CONDUCT.

SITUATION: Agnes Connolly pressed her employer to report two toxic chemical accidents. . . . Dave Jones reported that his company was using unqualified suppliers in constructing a nuclear power plant. . . . Margaret Newsham revealed that her firm allowed workers to do personal business while on government contracts. . . . Herman Cohen charged that the ASPCA in New York was mistreating animals. . . . Barry Adams complained that his hospital followed unsafe practices.

Whistleblowers expose misconduct of organizations and their members.

Each of these people is a **whistleblower**, someone who exposed organizational misdeeds to preserve ethical standards and protect against wasteful, harmful, or illegal acts.[37] They were also all fired from their jobs.

Whistleblowers take significant career risks when they expose wrongdoing in organizations. Although there are federal and state laws that offer whistleblowers some defense against "retaliatory discharge," the protection is still inadequate overall. Laws vary from state to state, and the federal laws mainly protect government workers. And even with legal protection, the very nature of organizations as power structures creates potential barriers that discourage the practice. A strict chain of command can make it hard to bypass the boss if he or she is the one doing something wrong. Strong work-group identities can discourage whistleblowing and encourage loyalty and self-censorship. And, working with unclear goals and rules can sometimes make it hard to distinguish right from wrong.[38]

FORMAL CODES OF ETHICS SET STANDARDS FOR ETHICAL CONDUCT.

A **code of ethics** is a formal statement of values and ethical standards.

Many, if not most, organizations now operate with a **code of ethics** that formally states the values and ethical principles members are expected to display. Ethics codes may be specific on how to behave in situations susceptible to ethical dilemmas—such as how sales representatives and purchasing agents should handle giving and receiving gifts. They might also specify consequences for unethical acts such as taking bribes and kickbacks. Some employers require new hires to sign and agree to their ethics code as a condition of employment. Don't be surprised if you are asked to do this someday.

Ethics codes are common in the complicated world of international business. Firms use them to make sure partners and suppliers act in ethical ways and avoid misbehaviors that could hurt the reputation of the global company. The use of child labor and forcing workers into unfair or unsafe work conditions, for example, are common complaints that make the news about global supply chains for our popular products. At Gap Inc., global manufacturing is governed by a formal Code of Vendor Conduct that includes statements such as these[39]:

- **Discrimination**—"Factories shall employ workers on the basis of their ability to do the job, not on the basis of their personal characteristics or beliefs."
- **Forced labor**—"Factories shall not use any prison, indentured or forced labor."
- **Working conditions**—"Factories must treat all workers with respect and dignity and provide them with a safe and healthy environment."
- **Freedom of association**—"Factories must not interfere with workers who wish to lawfully and peacefully associate, organize or bargain collectively."

Don't forget that you have to be careful in expecting too much of ethics codes in any setting, not just international ones. They set forth nice standards, but they can't guarantee good conduct.[40] That, we might say, depends once again on employing people with the right moral character and putting them in a work environment where they are led by strong and positive ethics role models.

When Students Share Assignments, Is It Cheating . . . Or Collaborating?

© Christopher Futcher/iStockphoto

When a Harvard professor finished reading take-home final examinations in a government class, the conclusion was: Too many answers said close to the same things. When the faculty member reported the incident to the university administration, Harvard had a "cheating" scandal on its hands. Or did it? From the perspective of some students, "collaborating" is a better choice of words. That's the view of a generation that grew up using the Internet and all sorts of collaborative media, and for whom online courses or class activities are a way of life. So, was it cheating? Or, are the professors out of date? Do test-taking rules need better clarification? Are too many students taking advantage of new situations and technologies?

STUDYGUIDE

Takeaway 2.2
How Can We Maintain High Standards of Ethical Conduct?

Terms to Define

Amoral manager	Ethical frameworks	Immoral manager	Spotlight questions
Code of ethics	Ethics training	Moral manager	Whistleblowers

Rapid Review

- Ethical behavior is influenced by an individual's character and represented by core values and beliefs.
- Kohlberg describes three levels of moral development—preconventional, conventional, and postconventional—with each of us moving step-by-step through the levels as we grow ethically over time.
- Ethics training can help people better understand how to make decisions when dealing with ethical dilemmas at work.
- Whistleblowers who expose the unethical acts of others have incomplete protection from the law and can face organizational penalties.
- All managers are responsible for acting as ethical role models for others.
- Immoral managers choose to behave unethically; amoral managers fail to consider ethics; moral managers make ethics a personal goal.
- Formal codes of conduct spell out the basic ethical expectations of employers regarding the behavior of employees and other contractors.

Questions for Discussion

1. Is it right for organizations to require ethics training of employees?
2. Should whistleblowers have complete protection under the law?
3. Should all managers be evaluated on how well they serve as ethical role models?

Be Sure You Can

- **explain** how ethical behavior is influenced by personal factors
- **list** and explain Kohlberg's three levels of moral development
- **explain** the term "whistleblower"
- **list** three organizational barriers to whistleblowing
- **compare** and contrast ethics training, ethics role models, and codes of conduct for their influence on ethics in the workplace
- **state** the spotlight questions for double-checking the ethics of a decision
- **describe** differences between the inclinations of amoral, immoral, and moral managers when facing difficult decisions

Career Situation: What Would You Do?

One of your first assignments as a summer intern for a corporate employer is to design an ethics training program for the firm's new hires. Your boss says that the program should familiarize newcomers with the corporate code of ethics. But, it should go beyond this to provide them with a foundation for handling ethical dilemmas in a confident and moral way. What will your lesson plan for the training program look like?

Takeaway 2.3
What Should We Know About the Social Responsibilities of Organizations?

ANSWERS TO COME

- Social responsibility is an organization's obligation to best serve society.
- Perspectives differ on the importance of corporate social responsibility.
- Shared value integrates corporate social responsibility into business strategy.
- Social businesses and social entrepreneurs are driven by social responsibility.
- Social responsibility audits measure the social performance of organizations.
- Sustainability is an important social responsibility goal.

Stakeholders are people and institutions most directly affected by an organization's performance.

THE ORGANIZATIONS, GROUPS, AND PERSONS WITH WHOM AN ORGANIZATION interacts and conducts business are known as its **stakeholders** because they have a direct "stake" or interest in its performance. They are affected in one way or another by what the organization does and how it performs. As **Figure 2.4** shows, the stakeholders include customers, suppliers, competitors, regulators, investors/owners, and employees, as well as future generations.

Importantly, an organization's stakeholders can have different interests. Customers typically want value prices and quality products; owners want profits as returns on their investments; suppliers want long-term business relationships; communities want good corporate citizenship and support for public services; employees want good wages, benefits, security, and satisfaction in their work.

SOCIAL RESPONSIBILITY IS AN ORGANIZATION'S OBLIGATION TO BEST SERVE SOCIETY.

Corporate social responsibility is the obligation of an organization to serve its own interests and those of its stakeholders.

The way organizations behave in relationship with their many stakeholders is a good indicator of their underlying ethical characters. When we talk about the "good" and the "bad" in business and societal relationships, **corporate social responsibility** is at issue. Often called CSR, it is defined as an obligation of the organization to act in ways that serve both its own interests and the interests of its stakeholders, representing society at large.

The **triple bottom line** of organizational performance includes financial, social, and environmental criteria.

Even though corporate "irresponsibility" seems to get most of the media's attention, we can't forget that a lot of responsible behavior is taking place as well. Increasingly this has become part of what is called the **triple bottom line**—how well an organization performs when measured not only on financial criteria but also on social and environmental ones.

FIGURE 2.4

Who Are the Stakeholders of Organizations?

Stakeholders are the individuals, groups, and other organizations that have a direct interest in how well an organization performs. A basic list of stakeholders for any organization would begin with the employees and contractors who work for the organization, customers and clients who consume the goods and services, suppliers of needed resources, owners who invest capital, regulators in the form of government agencies, and special-interest groups such as community members and activists.

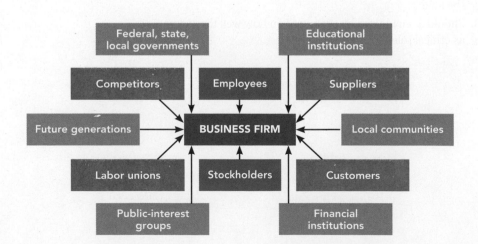

Some call this triple bottom line the **3 Ps of organizational performance**—profit, people, and planet.[41] The triple bottom line in business decision making is checked by asking these questions: Profit—Is the decision economically sound? People—Is the decision socially responsible? Planet—Is the decision environmentally sound?

Showing CSR and valuing the triple bottom line are most likely the ways you'd like your future employers to behave. "Students nowadays want to work for companies that help enhance the quality of life in their surrounding community," says an observer.[42] In one survey, 70% of students reported that "a company's reputation and ethics" was "very important" when deciding whether or not to accept a job offer; in another survey, 79% of 13- to 25-year-olds said they "want to work for a company that cares about how it affects or contributes to society."[43]

> The **3 Ps of organizational performance** are profit, people, and planet.

PERSPECTIVES DIFFER ON THE IMPORTANCE OF CORPORATE SOCIAL RESPONSIBILITY.

It may seem that corporate social responsibility, or CSR, is one of those concepts and goals that most everyone agrees on. There are, however, two contrasting views that stimulate debate in academic and public-policy circles. The classical view takes a stand against making corporate social responsibility a business priority, whereas the socioeconomic view advocates for it.[44]

Classical View of CSR

The **classical view of CSR** holds that management's only responsibility in running a business is to maximize profits and shareholder value. This narrow stakeholder perspective puts the focus on the single bottom line of financial performance. The respected economist and Nobel laureate Milton Friedman says: "Few trends could so thoroughly undermine the very foundations of our free society as the acceptance by corporate officials of social responsibility other than to make as much money for their stockholders as possible."[45]

> The **classical view of CSR** is that business should focus on the pursuit of profits.

Arguments against corporate social responsibility include fears that its pursuit will reduce business profits, raise business costs, dilute business purpose, and give business too much social power. Yet events such as the huge BP oil spill in the Gulf of Mexico seem to argue otherwise. The public was outraged about the oil spill. Demands were quickly made for stronger government oversight and control over corporate practices such as deep-water oil drilling that might put our natural world at risk.

Socioeconomic View of CSR

The **socioeconomic view of CSR** believes that because businesses have vast resources with the potential for great social impact, business executives have ethical obligations to ensure that their firms act in socially responsible ways. This broad stakeholder perspective puts the focus on the triple bottom line of not just profits but also social and environmental performance. It is supported by Paul Samuelson, another distinguished economist and Nobel laureate, who says: "A large corporation these days not only may engage in social responsibility, it had damn well better try to do so."[46]

> The **socioeconomic view of CSR** is that businesses should focus on contributions to society, not just making profits.

Those in favor of corporate social responsibility argue that it will boost long-run profits, improve public images, and help businesses avoid more government regulation. Researchers are describing the worst-case scenario of CSR as no adverse impact on the financial bottom line.[47] The best-case scenario is a **virtuous circle**, where corporate social responsibility leads to improved financial performance that leads to more socially responsible actions in the future.[48]

> A **virtuous circle** exists when corporate social responsibility leads to improved financial performance that leads to more social responsibility.

SHARED VALUE INTEGRATES CORPORATE SOCIAL RESPONSIBILITY INTO BUSINESS STRATEGY.

What's your position on these alternative views of corporate social responsibility? More and more today you will find people arguing that businesses have an obligation to "give back" to society. This means doing more than offering useful products and services and providing jobs. It means that businesses should balance the pursuit of profit with genuine contributions to the public good.

Shared value approaches business decisions with understanding that economic gains and social progress are interconnected.

This thinking is consistent with the notion of **shared value** advocated by Mark Kramer and Michael Porter.[49] They say: "The purpose of a corporation must be redefined as creating shared value, not just profit per se."[50] Their point is that executives can and should make business decisions with full understanding that economic gains and social progress are fundamentally interconnected. In other words, businesses can make profits while striving to do good and overcome social ills such as pollution, poverty, illiteracy, and disease.

Instead of viewing CSR from a win-lose perspective that pits the interests of shareholders and owners against other stakeholders, the notion of shared value offers a win-win perspective. Business decisions are made so that economic value is created by pursuing social value, and business advantage is gained by aligning practices and strategies with social contributions. For example[51]: Procter & Gamble—saves costs by making waste reduction is a top priority. Nestlé—ensures supplies of high-quality products by supporting local sourcing and rural businesses near its factories. IBM—found a new market to help cities use IBM technologies to solve problems with traffic flows, public health, schools, housing, and crime.

SOCIAL BUSINESSES AND SOCIAL ENTREPRENEURS ARE DRIVEN BY SOCIAL RESPONSIBILITY.

A **social business** is one in which the underlying business model directly addresses a social problem.

Muhammad Yunus won a Nobel prize for his pioneering work in Bangladesh creating the Grameen Bank.[52] At one level it was a business innovation—bringing microcredit lending into mainstream financing. But at another level it is a **social business** with a business model that directly addresses a social problem—using microcredit lending to help fight poverty. And in the expanding domain of social businesses and social entrepreneurship, Yunus's ideas and examples have set inspirational benchmarks.

Social businesses are profit driven. But, instead of the profits being returned to investors or owners, they are used to pay off initial start-up costs and then reinvested to expand the social business to serve more clients and customers. These businesses are developed by **social entrepreneurs**, people who take business risk with the goal of finding novel ways to solve pressing social problems at home and abroad.[53] Social entrepreneurs are like business entrepreneurs with one big difference: They are driven by a social mission, not financial gain.[54] They pursue original thinking and innovations to help solve social problems and make lives better for people who are disadvantaged.

Social entrepreneurs take business risks to find novel ways to solve pressing social problems.

You'll be hearing and reading a lot more about social businesses and social entrepreneurs. They are already being called the new "fourth sector" of our economy—joining private for-profit businesses, public government organizations, and nonprofits.[55] As the late management guru Peter Drucker once said: "Every single social and global issue of our day is a business opportunity in disguise."[56] Housing and job training for the homeless . . . bringing technology to poor families . . . improving literacy among disadvantaged youth . . . bringing expanded health-care to impoverished communities . . . and more. What wonderful possibilities. Could social business and social entrepreneurship be part of your future some day?

Gary Hirshberg Goes for Triple Bottom Line at Stonyfield Farm

President, CEO, and co-founder of Stonyfield Farm Gary Hirshberg has made a career out of organic yogurt. He's also a firm believer that "business is the most powerful force in the world." Considered a social entrepreneur, Hirshberg has always been at the forefront of movements for environmental and social transformation. At Stonyfield Farm he has crafted a clear mission: "Offer a pure and healthy product that tastes good and earn a profit without harming the environment." Indeed, Hirshberg says, "we factor the planet into all of our decisions. . . . It's a simple strategy but a powerful one." According to Hirshberg, "Going green is not just the right thing to do, but a great way to build a successful business."

Jodi Hilton/The New York Times /Redux Pictures

SOCIAL RESPONSIBILITY AUDITS MEASURE THE SOCIAL PERFORMANCE OF ORGANIZATIONS.

The social performance of business firms varies along a continuum that ranges from compliance—acting to avoid adverse consequences, to conviction—acting to create positive impact.[57, 59] If we are to get serious about social responsibility and aspire for more positive impact, we need to get rigorous about measuring corporate social performance and holding business leaders accountable for the results. A **social responsibility audit** can be used at regular intervals to report on and systematically assess an organization's performance in various areas of corporate social responsibility. As shown in the small figure, an audit of corporate social performance might cover the organization's performance on four criteria for evaluating socially responsible practices: economic, legal, ethical, and discretionary.[58, 60]

> A **social responsibility audit** measures and reports on an organization's performance in various areas of corporate social responsibility.

An organization is meeting its *economic responsibility* when it earns a profit through the provision of goods and services desired by customers. Although it might seem unusual to focus on financial performance as a component of CSR, a firm's economic performance provides the foundation on which all the other types of responsibility rest. If a firm is not financially viable, it will not be able to take care of its owners or employees or en-

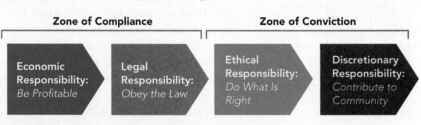

gage in any of the other aspects of CSR. *Legal responsibility* is fulfilled when an organization operates within the law and according to the requirements of various external regulations. An organization meets its *ethical responsibility* when its actions voluntarily conform not only to legal expectations but also to the broader values and moral expectations of society.

The highest level of social performance comes through the satisfaction of *discretionary responsibility*. At this level, the organization moves beyond basic economic, legal, and ethical expectations to provide leadership in advancing the well-being of individuals, communities, and society as a whole. Perhaps you would consider the Starbucks College Achievement Plan as a commitment to discretionary social responsibility. This plan offers employees subsidized online college studies in partnership with Arizona State University. Juniors and seniors get full tuition reimbursement for each year of study completed; freshmen and sophomores get partial scholarship and financial aid support.[59]

SUSTAINABILITY IS AN IMPORTANT SOCIAL RESPONSIBILITY GOAL.

Think about the issues of our day—things like resource scarcity, climate change, carbon footprints, and alternative energy. Think about popular terms and slogans—ones like renew, recycle, conserve, and preserve. They all reflect the importance of **sustainability** as a goal, one that values the rights of both present and future generations as stakeholders of the world's natural resources.

> **Sustainability** is a goal that addresses the rights of present and future generations as stakeholders of the world's natural resources.

"With a global population at 6.5 billion," Gavin Neath, vice president for Unilever, says, "we are already consuming resources at a rate far in excess of nature's capacity to replenish them. Water is becoming scarce and global warming and climate change are accelerating."[60] Little wonder that 93% of CEOs in a recent survey admit that the future success of their firms depends in part on how well they meet sustainability challenges.[61] And as United Nations General Secretary Ban Ki-moon says, "It [sustainability] means thinking differently about how and where we invest, thinking differently about creating markets of the future, and creating opportunities for growth."[62]

Sustainable Business and Sustainable Development

The term **sustainable business** refers to firms that operate in ways that both meet the needs of customers and protect or advance the well-being of our natural environment.[63] Think of it this way. A sustainable business operates in harmony with nature rather than by exploiting nature. Its actions produce minimum negative impact on the environment and help preserve it for future generations. The hallmarks of sustainable business practices include less waste, less toxic materials, more resource efficiency, more energy efficiency, and more renewable energy.

> **Sustainable business** is where firms operate in ways that both meet the needs of customers and protect or advance the well-being of our natural environment.

Sustainable development is making use of natural resources to meet today's needs while also preserving and protecting the environment for use by future generations.

Environmental capital or **natural capital** is the storehouse of natural resources—atmosphere, land, water, and minerals—that we use to sustain life and produce goods and services for society.

ISO 14001 is a global quality standard that certifies organizations that set environmental objectives and targets, account for the environmental impact of their activities, and continuously improve environmental performance.

If sustainability is a business goal, just what is **sustainable development**? The World Business Council for Sustainable Development defines it as "forms of progress that meet the needs of the present without compromising the ability of future generations to meet their needs."[64] At issue here is **environmental capital** or **natural capital**—the storehouse of natural resources that exist in the atmosphere, land, water, and minerals that we use to sustain life and produce goods and services for society.[65] The importance of environmental capital is reflected in **ISO 14001**, a global quality standard that requires certified organizations to set environmental objectives and targets; account for the environmental impact of their activities, products, or services; and continuously improve environmental performance.[66]

The conversation about sustainable development stands at the interface between how people live and organizations operate, and the capacity of the natural environment to support them. We want prosperity, convenience, comfort, and luxury in our everyday lives. But we are also more aware that attention must be given to the "costs" of these aspirations and how those costs can be borne in a way that doesn't impair the future. At PepsiCo, for example, CEO Indra Nooyi has said that her firm's "real profit" should be assessed as: Revenue less Cost of Goods Sold less Costs to Society. "All corporations operate with a license from society," says Nooyi. "It's critically important that we take that responsibility very, very seriously; we have to make sure that what corporations do doesn't add costs to society."[67]

Human Sustainability

Scholar Jeffrey Pfeffer offers a strong case in favor of giving management attention not only to issues of ecological and environmental sustainability—traditional green management themes—but also to social and human sustainability. He says: "Just as there is concern for protecting natural resources, there could be a similar level of concern for protecting human resources. . . . Being a socially responsible business ought to encompass the effect of management practices on employee physical and psychological well-being."[68] You might think of Pfeffer's point this way: While valuing the "planet" as well as "profits," don't forget that "people" are also part of the 3 Ps of organizational performance.

FEDERAL COURTS ARE NOW HEARING LAWSUITS FILED BY ON-DEMAND WORKERS SEEKING MORE EMPLOYMENT RIGHTS. ONE PLAINTIFF SAYS: "WE ARE NOT ROBOTS; WE ARE NOT A REMOTE CONTROL; WE ARE INDIVIDUALS."

HOT TOPIC

App-Enabled On-Demand Workers Are Not Robots

Andrew Caballero-Reynolds/AFP/ Getty Images

Here's the sharing economy business model. Set up a smart device app that matches people needing rides with freelance drivers willing to provide them—think Uber or Lyft. Take a fee for the matchup, monitor and post driver quality and customer satisfaction scores, and keep the technology up to date. Nice!

This ride sharing example is just one of many avenues of on-demand work fast appearing on the employment scene. But what's it like to be one of the app-enabled workers? The opportunity for income with job flexibility is attractive to many—work when you want, as long as want, as often as you want. But, what rights do "on-demand workers" have? If a ride sharing company sets pay schedules, requires certain attire and behaviors, and can fire at will, are the drivers true "employees" or not?

Current U.S. labor laws offer two classifications of workers—traditional and independent contractors. The traditional workers are official employees and have legal protections in respect to minimum wage, anti-discrimination, union membership, and more. Independent contractors lack these protections, and it's mainly a net gain for employers who don't have to deal with legal obligations and offer costly benefits. Federal courts are now hearing lawsuits filed by on-demand workers seeking more employment rights. One plaintiff says: "We are not robots; we are not a remote control; we are individuals."

HOW ABOUT IT?

Uber's head of policy and strategy, David Plouffe, says, "We obviously are comfortable with our business model." Are you? What are the social responsibilities of organizations that hire on-demand workers? Is it enough to offer income opportunity with work flexibility, or should more be on the table as part of the employer-employee contract? Are the sharing economy and the app-enabled workforce good for human sustainability?

STUDYGUIDE

Takeaway 2.3
What Should We Know About the Social Responsibilities of Organizations?

Terms to Define

3 Ps of organizational performance	ISO 14001	Socioeconomic view of CSR	Triple bottom line
Classical view of CSR	Shared value	Stakeholders	Virtuous circle
Corporate social responsibility	Social business	Sustainability	
	Social entrepreneurs	Sustainable business	
Environmental capital or natural capital	Social responsibility audit	Sustainable development	

Rapid Review

- Corporate social responsibility is an obligation of the organization to act in ways that serve both its own interests and the interests of its stakeholders.

- In assessing organizational performance today, the concept of the triple bottom line evaluates how well organizations are doing on economic, social, and environmental performance criteria.

- Criteria for evaluating corporate social performance include how well the corporation meets economic, legal, ethical, and discretionary responsibilities.

- The argument against corporate social responsibility says that businesses should focus on making profits; the argument for corporate social responsibility says that businesses should use their resources to serve broader social concerns.

- The concept of sustainable development refers to making use of environmental resources to support societal needs today while also preserving and protecting the environment for use by future generations.

- Social businesses and social entrepreneurs pursue business models that help to directly address important social problems.

Questions for Discussion

1. Choose an organization in your community. What questions would you ask to complete an audit of its social responsibility practices?

2. Is the logic of the virtuous circle a convincing argument in favor of corporate social responsibility?

3. Should government play a stronger role in making sure organizations commit to sustainable development?

Be Sure You Can

- **explain** the concept of social responsibility
- **summarize** arguments for and against corporate social responsibility
- **illustrate** how the virtuous circle of corporate social responsibility might work
- **explain** the notion of social business

Career Situation: What Would You Do?

It's debate time, and you've been given the task of defending corporate social responsibility. Make a list of all possible arguments for making CSR an important goal for any organization. For each item on the list, find a good current example that confirms its importance based on real events. In what order of priority will you present your arguments in the debate? Next, what arguments "against" CSR will you be prepared to defend against?

TEST PREP **2**

Answers to TestPrep questions can be found at the back of the book.

Multiple-Choice Questions

1. A business owner makes a decision to reduce a plant's workforce by 10% to cut costs and be able to save jobs for the other 90% of employees. This decision could be justified as ethical by using the _____ approach to moral reasoning.
   (a) utilitarian   (b) individualism   (c) justice   (d) moral rights

2. If a manager fails to enforce a late-to-work policy for all workers—that is, by allowing some favored employees to arrive late without penalties—this would be considered a violation of _____.

   (a) human rights   (b) personal values
   (c) distributive justice   (d) cultural relativism

3. According to research on ethics in the workplace, _____ is/are often a major and frequent source of pressures that create ethical dilemmas for people in their jobs.
   (a) Declining morals in society   (b) Long work hours
   (c) Low pay   (d) Requests or demands from bosses

4. Someone who exposes the ethical misdeeds of others in an organization is usually called a/an _____.
   (a) whistleblower   (b) ethics advocate
   (c) ombudsman   (d) stakeholder

5. Two employees are talking about ethics in their workplaces. Jay says that ethics training and codes of ethical conduct are worthless; Maura says they are the only ways to ensure ethical behavior by all employees. Who is right, and why?
   (a) Jay—no one really cares about ethics at work.
   (b) Maura—only the organization can influence ethical behavior.
   (c) Neither Jay nor Maura—training and codes can encourage but never guarantee ethical behavior.
   (d) Neither Jay nor Maura—only the threat of legal punishment will make people act ethically.

6. Which ethical position has been criticized as a source of "ethical imperialism"?
   (a) Individualism (b) Absolutism (c) Utilitarianism (d) Relativism

7. If a manager takes a lot of time explaining to a subordinate why he did not get a promotion and sincerely listens to his concerns, this is an example of an attempt to act ethically according to _____ justice.
   (a) utilitarian (b) commutative (c) interactional (d) universal

8. At what Kohlberg calls the _____ level of moral development, an individual can be expected to act consistent with peers, meet obligations, and follow rules of social conduct.
   (a) postconventional   (b) conventional
   (c) preconventional   (d) nonconventional

9. In respect to the link between bad management and ethical behavior, research shows that _____.
   (a) managers who set unrealistic goals can cause unethical behavior
   (b) most whistleblowers just want more pay
   (c) only top managers really serve as ethics role models
   (d) a good code of ethics makes up for any management deficiencies

10. A person's desires for a comfortable life and family security represent _____ values, whereas his or her desires to be honest and hard working represent _____ values.

    (a) terminal; instrumental   (b) instrumental; terminal
    (c) universal; individual   (d) individual; universal

11. A proponent of the classical view of corporate social responsibility would most likely agree with which of these statements?
    (a) Social responsibility improves the public image of business.
    (b) The primary responsibility of business is to maximize profits.
    (c) By acting responsibly, businesses avoid government regulation.
    (d) Businesses should do good while they are doing business.

12. The triple bottom line of organizational performance would include measures of financial, social, and _____ performance.
    (a) philanthropic   (b) environmental   (c) legal   (d) economic

13. An amoral manager _____.
    (a) always acts in consideration of ethical issues
    (b) chooses to behave unethically
    (c) makes ethics a personal goal
    (d) acts unethically but does so unintentionally

14. In a social responsibility audit of a business firm, positive behaviors meeting which of the following criteria would measure the highest level of commitment to socially responsible practices?
    (a) Legal—obeying the law
    (b) Economic—earning a profit
    (c) Discretionary—contributing to community
    (d) Ethical—doing what is right

15. What organizational stakeholder would most likely get top priority attention if a corporate board is having a serious discussion regarding how the firm could fulfill its obligations in respect to sustainable development?
    (a) Owners or investors   (b) Customers
    (c) Suppliers   (d) Future generations

Short-Response Questions

16. How does distributive justice differ from procedural justice?

17. What are the three spotlight questions that people can use for double-checking the ethics of a decision?

18. If someone commits an unethical act, how can he or she rationalize it to make it seem right?

19. What is the virtuous circle of corporate social responsibility?

Integration and Application Questions

20. A small outdoor clothing company in the United States has just received an attractive proposal from a business in Tanzania to manufacture the work gloves that it sells. Accepting the offer from the Tanzanian firm would allow for substantial cost savings compared to the current supplier. However, the clothing company's manager has recently read reports that some businesses in Tanzania are forcing people to work in unsafe conditions in order to keep their costs down. The manager is now seeking your help in clarifying the ethical aspects of this opportunity.

    Question: How would you describe to this manager his or her alternatives in terms of cultural relativism and moral absolutism? What would you identify as the major issues and concerns in terms of the cultural relativism position versus the absolutist position? Finally, what action would you recommend in this situation, and why?

Steps for Further Learning

BUILD MARKETABLE SKILLS • **DO** A CASE ANALYSIS • **GET** AND STAY INFORMED

BUILD MARKETABLE SKILLS.

EARN BIG CAREER PAYOFFS!

Don't miss these opportunities in the SKILL-BUILDING PORTFOLIO

SELF-ASSESSMENT 2:
Terminal Values

Values count and values differ . . . what do you hold as important?

CLASS EXERCISE 2:
Confronting Ethical Dilemmas

No one can predict when a dilemma will hit . . . now is a good time to test your ethics.

TEAM PROJECT 2:
Organizational Commitment to Sustainability

Sustainability is easy to talk about . . . it can be hard to measure how well organizations really do.

Many learning resources are found at the end of the book and online within **WileyPLUS Learning Space.**

Practice Critical Thinking—Complete the CHAPTER 2 CASE

CASE SNAPSHOT: Patagonia: Leading a Green Revolution

Patagonia has stayed green and profitable even when the economy is down and consumers are tight for cash. How has the firm achieved economic success while being socially responsible? A look to the firm's founder, Yvon Chouinard, provides lots of insight. Patagonia succeeds by staying true to his vision of having a successful outdoor clothing company that is steadfastly committed to environmental sustainability. "They've become the Rolls-Royce of their product category," says one industry analyst. "When people were stepping back, and the industry became copycat, Chouinard didn't sell out, lower prices, and dilute the brand. Sometimes, the less you do, the more provocative and true of a leader you are."

DO A CASE ANALYSIS.

STRENGTHEN YOUR CRITICAL THINKING!

MANAGER'S LIBRARY SELECTION
Read for Insights and Wisdom
Conscious Capitalism: Liberating the Heroic Spirit of Business by John Mackey and Raj Sisodia

Business and capitalism have received lots of criticism in the aftermath of the global financial crisis. Does that mean they are fundamentally bad for society? John Mackey and Raj Sisodia argue just the opposite in this book. Business and capitalism are fundamentally good, they say, while adding that it's the job of business leaders to make sure things turn out that way.

GET AND STAY INFORMED.

MAKE YOURSELF VALUABLE!

Mackey and Sisodia's book has been called "chicken soup for the Davos soul" by *The Wall Street Journal*—a reference to the annual global economic forum in Davos, Switzerland, where economic ideas are presented and debated. The concept behind the acclaim is "conscious capitalism." Think of it as capitalism pursued by leaders who understand that business can create lots of value for society, act ethically, and help people and communities gain prosperity.

The key to conscious capitalism is considering the needs of all stakeholders and realizing that the purpose of the business goes beyond making profit for the owners. As Mackey, CEO founder of Whole Foods Market, and Sisodia, Bentley College marketing professor, say: "When any profession becomes primarily about making money, it starts to lose its true identity and its interests start to diverge from what is good for society." But on the bright side, they point out that capitalism becomes "heroic" when businesses do the right things that have positive societal impact on people, planet, and environment. In order to get there, business leaders must be "primarily motivated by service to the purposes of the business and its stakeholders, and not by the pursuit of power and personal enrichment."

REFLECT AND REACT Is "conscious capitalism" something that can be achieved on a broad scale across a society. Or, is it something that is mainly evidenced by a few special companies and organizations that have enlightened founders with lots of power to do things their own ways?

"Estamos bien en el réfugio–los 33." For 69 days shift leader Luis Urzúa kept the men trapped in the Chilean mine organized and hopeful. On the 70th day, he was the last man safely out.

Managers as Decision Makers

3

There Is No Substitute for a Good Decision

Management Live

Making the "Right" Job Choices

John Lund/Getty Images

It's a great offer ... or is it? Whether talking about your first job or a later step in career progression, this is one of the most important decisions you'll ever make. Too bad it's often wrong. A survey by Development Dimensions found only 51% of new hires confirming they made the right decisions. Many said they missed important information during the recruitment process—things like travel requirements, actual hours of work, work team dynamics, organizational finances, and job turnover rates. Unmet and unrealistic expectations lead to later job disengagement, causing many new hires to later want out.

YOUR THOUGHTS?

Recruiters should provide full information to job candidates, including the potential downsides of a job and employer. But, many still go for the traditional "tell and sell" approach. How can you get realistic job previews and then use this information well to make your job choice decisions?

WHAT'S INSIDE

ETHICS CHECK
Left to die on Mt. Everest

FACTS TO CONSIDER
The "Ask Gap"—what it takes for women to get raises

HOT TOPIC
Bye-bye telecommuting?

QUICK CASE
Time for a pay boost

YOUR CHAPTER 3 TAKEAWAYS

1. Recognize how managers use information to solve problems.
2. Identify five steps in the decision-making process.
3. Understand current issues in managerial decision making.

Takeaway 3.1
How Do Managers Use Information to Solve Problems?

ANSWERS TO COME

- Managers use technological, informational, and analytical competencies to solve problems.
- Managers deal with problems posing threats and offering opportunities.
- Managers can be problem avoiders, problem solvers, or problem seekers.
- Managers make programmed and nonprogrammed decisions.
- Managers use both systematic and intuitive thinking.
- Managers use different cognitive styles to process information for decision making.
- Managers make decisions under conditions of certainty, risk, and uncertainty.

WHEN THE SAN JOSÉ COPPER AND GOLD MINE COLLAPSED IN CHILE, 32 MINERS, along with their shift leader, Luis Urzúa, were trapped inside.[1] "The most difficult moment was when the air cleared and we saw the rock," said Urzúa, "I had thought maybe it was going to be a day or two days, but not when I saw the rock. . . ." In fact, the miners were trapped 2,300 feet below the surface for 69 days. Their plight caught the attention of the entire world. After the rescue shaft was completed, Urzúa was the last man out. "The job was hard," he said, "they were days of great pain and sorrow." But the decisions Urzúa made as shift leader—organizing the miners into work shifts, keeping them busy, studying mine diagrams, making escape plans, raising morale—all contributed to the successful rescue. After embracing Urzúa when he arrived at the surface, Chile's President Sebastian Pinera said, "He was a shift boss who made us proud."

Most managers will never have to face such an extreme crisis, but decision making and problem solving are parts of every manager's job. Not all decisions are going to be easy ones, and some will have to be made under tough conditions. And, not all decisions will turn out right. But as demonstrated by Luis Urzúa, the goal is to do the best you can under the circumstances.

MANAGERS USE TECHNOLOGICAL, INFORMATIONAL, AND ANALYTICAL COMPETENCIES TO SOLVE PROBLEMS.

All those case studies, experiential exercises, class discussions, and even essay exam questions are intended to engage students in the complexities of managerial decision making, the potential problems and pitfalls, and even the pressures of crisis situations. From the classroom forward, however, it's all up to you. Only you can determine whether you step ahead and make the best of very difficult problems or collapse under pressure.

Problem solving is the process of identifying a discrepancy between an actual and a desired state of affairs and then taking action to resolve it. The context for managerial problem solving is depicted in **Figure 3.1**. It shows why managers fit the definition of **knowledge workers**, persons whose value to organizations rests with their intellectual and analytical talents, not physical capabilities.[2]

All managers continually solve problems as they gather, give, receive, and process information from many sources. In fact, your career and personal success increasingly requires three "must-have" competencies. **Technological competency** is the ability to understand new technologies and use them to their best advantage. In many ways this involves moving skills we already use in everyday personal affairs—social media, smart devices, and more— into work-related applications. **Information competency** is the ability to locate, retrieve, organize, and display information of potential value to decision making and problem solving.

Problem solving involves identifying and taking action to resolve problems.

Knowledge workers add value to organizations through their intellectual capabilities.

Technological competency is the ability to understand new technologies and to use them to their best advantage.

Information competency is the ability to gather and use information to solve problems.

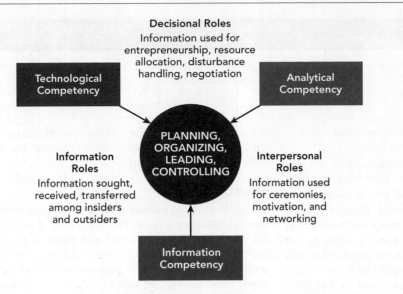

FIGURE 3.1

In What Ways Do Managers Serve as Information Nerve Centers in Organizations?

Managers sit at the center of complex networks of information flows; they serve as information-processing hubs or nerve centers. Each of the management functions—planning, organizing, leading, and controlling—requires the gathering, use, and transfer of information in these networks. Managers must have the information competencies needed to perform well in these roles.

This does not just mean, for example, getting information from hearsay or off the Internet; it means locating credible and valuable information. **Analytical competency** is the ability to evaluate and analyze information to find meaningful patterns, make decisions, and solve real problems.[3] This involves being able to digest and sort through information, even very large amounts of data, and then use it well to make good decisions that solve real problems How about it—are you ready?

> **Analytical competency** is the ability to evaluate and analyze information to make decisions and solve real problems.

MANAGERS DEAL WITH PROBLEMS POSING THREATS AND OFFERING OPPORTUNITIES.

The most obvious problem-solving situation is a **performance threat** that appears as an actual or potential performance deficiency. Simply put: Something is wrong or is likely to be wrong in the near future. But let's not forget that problem solving often deals with a **performance opportunity**. This is a situation that offers the possibility of a better future if the right steps are taken now. Suppose a regional manager notices that sales at one retail store are unusually high. If she just says "Great" and goes on about her business, that's an opportunity missed. A really sharp manager says: "Wait a minute, something is happening here that I could learn from and possibly transfer to other stores. I had better find out what's going on." That's an opportunity gained.

> A **performance threat** is a situation where something is wrong or likely to be wrong.

> A **performance opportunity** is a situation that offers the possibility of a better future if the right steps are taken.

MANAGERS CAN BE PROBLEM AVOIDERS, PROBLEM SOLVERS, OR PROBLEM SEEKERS.

What do you do when you receive a lower grade than expected on an exam or assignment? Do you get the grade, perhaps complain a bit to yourself or friends, and then forget it? Or do you get the grade, recognize that a problem exists, and try to learn from it so that you can do better in the future? Managers are just like you and me. They approach problem solving in different ways and realize different consequences.

Some managers are *problem avoiders*. They ignore information that would otherwise signal the presence of a performance threat or opportunity. They are not active in gathering information and prefer not to make decisions or deal with problems. Other managers are *problem solvers*. They make decisions and try to solve problems, but only when required. They are reactive, gathering information and responding to problems when they occur, but not before. These managers may deal reasonably well with performance threats, but they are likely to miss many performance opportunities.

Still other managers—the really good ones—are *problem seekers*. They are always looking for problems to solve or opportunities to explore. True problem seekers are proactive as information gatherers, and they are forward thinking. They anticipate threats and opportunities, and they are eager to take action to gain the advantage in dealing with them.

QUICK CASE

Time for a Pay Boost

Jetta Productions Blend Images/Newscom

Situation: You want a raise.

Problem: How do you get your boss to agree that you deserve one?

Insight: Researchers tell us that when negotiating a raise it's better to *not* use a round number as a target—such as "about $65,000," and better to use a precise number—such as "$63,750." The round number suggests a person has only a general idea of the market for their skills, whereas the precise number gives the impression that they've done the research and know their facts.

WHAT DO YOU DO?

Describe what you will say and do to get your boss to agree that you deserve a raise. Prepare a narrative that presents the exact words, justifications, and dollar target you would use to ask for a raise in your current job. Alternatively, assume you have been working in your chosen career field for five years, have developed lots of expertise and earned high performance reports, and now want a raise.

MANAGERS MAKE PROGRAMMED AND NONPROGRAMMED DECISIONS.

> A **decision** is a choice among possible alternative courses of action.

So far in this discussion, we have used the word "decision" rather casually. From this point forward let's agree that a **decision** is a choice among possible alternative courses of action. Let's also agree that decisions can be made in different ways and that some ways work better than others in various circumstances.

> A **programmed decision** applies a pre-existing solution to a routine problem.

Routine and repetitive management problems can be solved by **programmed decisions** that apply preplanned solutions based on past experience. These types of decisions work well for structured problems that are familiar and have clear-cut information needs. In human resource management, for example, decisions always have to be made on things such as vacation and holiday schedules. Forward-looking managers can use the lessons of past experience to plan ahead to make these decisions in programmed, not spontaneous, ways.

> A **nonprogrammed decision** crafts a unique solution to a new and unstructured problem.

New or unusual problems full of ambiguities and information deficiencies require **nonprogrammed decisions**. These decisions craft novel solutions to meet the unique demands of unstructured problems. Consider the situation faced by Sony Pictures CEO Michael Lynton when his firm's computer systems were hacked just prior to the release of a comedy, *The Interview*. No programmed solution could handle this problem—thousands of employee social security numbers were lost, prerelease movies were stolen, computer systems were disabled, and threats were made of further harm if the movie was released. Lynton and his team did what they believed best, first cancelling the release and then reversing course to open in a limited number of theatres as well as in pay-for-view. Their nonprogrammed decisions, made in difficult and dynamic circumstances, were hotly debated. Only time would tell if they were the right ones.

MANAGERS USE BOTH SYSTEMATIC AND INTUITIVE THINKING.

> **Systematic thinking** approaches problems in a rational and analytical fashion.

A person approaching problems using **systematic thinking** addresses them in a rational, step-by-step, and analytical fashion. You might recognize this when someone you are working with tries to break a complex problem into smaller components that can be addressed one by one. We might expect systematic managers to make a plan before taking action and to search for information and proceed with problem solving in a fact-based and step-by-step fashion.

> **Intuitive thinking** approaches problems in a flexible and spontaneous fashion.

Someone using **intuitive thinking** is more flexible and spontaneous than the systematic thinker, and they may be quite creative.[4] You might observe this pattern in someone who always seems to come up with an imaginative response to a problem, often based on a quick and broad evaluation of the situation. Intuitive managers tend to deal with many aspects of a problem at once, jump quickly from one issue to another, and act on hunches based on experience or on spontaneous ideas.

A systematic thinker approaches problems in a step-by-step and linear fashion

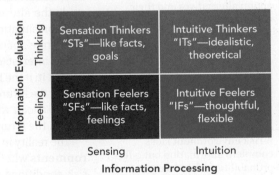

An intuitive thinker approaches problems in flexible and spontaneous fashion

Amazon.com's Jeff Bezos says that when it's not possible for the firm's top managers to make systematic fact-based decisions, "you have to rely on experienced executives who've honed their instincts" and are able to make good judgments.[5] In other words, there's a place for both systematic and intuitive decision making in management.

MANAGERS USE DIFFERENT COGNITIVE STYLES TO PROCESS INFORMATION FOR DECISION MAKING.

SITUATION: US Airways Flight 1549 took off from LaGuardia airport on January 15, 2009. All was normal until the plane hit a flock of birds and both engines failed. It was going to crash. Pilot Chesley Sullenberger quickly realized he couldn't get to an airport and decided to land in the Hudson River—a highly risky move. But he had both a clear head and a clear sense of what he had been trained to do. The landing was successful, and no lives were lost.

Called a "hero" for his efforts, Sullenberger described his thinking this way. "I needed to touch down with the wings exactly level. I needed to touch down with the nose slightly up. I needed to touch down at . . . a descent rate that was survivable. And I needed to touch down just above our minimum flying speed but not below it. And I needed to make all these things happen simultaneously."[6]

This example raises the issue of **cognitive styles**, or the way individuals deal with information while making decisions. Contrasting tendencies toward information gathering (sensation vs. intuition) and information evaluation (feeling vs. thinking) result in these four master cognitive styles.[7]

Cognitive style is the way an individual deals with information while making decisions.

- *Sensation thinker*—STs tend to emphasize the impersonal rather than the personal and take a realistic approach to problem solving. They like hard "facts," clear goals, certainty, and situations of high control.
- *Intuitive thinkers*—ITs are comfortable with abstraction and unstructured situations. They tend to be idealistic, prone to intellectual and theoretical positions; they are logical and impersonal but also avoid details.
- *Intuitive feelers*—IFs prefer broad and global issues. They are insightful and tend to avoid details, being comfortable with intangibles; they value flexibility and human relationships.
- *Sensation feelers*—SFs tend to emphasize both analysis and human relations. They tend to be realistic and prefer facts; they are open communicators and sensitive to feelings and values.

		Sensing	Intuition
Information Evaluation	Thinking	Sensation Thinkers "STs"—like facts, goals	Intuitive Thinkers "ITs"—idealistic, theoretical
	Feeling	Sensation Feelers "SFs"—like facts, feelings	Intuitive Feelers "IFs"—thoughtful, flexible

Information Processing

Pilot Sullenberger would most likely score high in both sensation and thinking, and that is probably an ideal type for his job. But people vary widely in cognitive styles, and they don't always fit well with specific problem situations. The descriptions just listed show that we may approach problems and make decisions in ways quite different from one another. This is why it's so important to understand our cognitive styles and those of others. The more diverse the cognitive styles in our work teams, families, and organizations, the more difficulty we might expect as they try to make decisions.

MANAGERS MAKE DECISIONS UNDER CONDITIONS OF CERTAINTY, RISK, AND UNCERTAINTY.

It's not just personal styles that differ in problem solving. The environment counts, too. **Figure 3.2** shows three different conditions or problem environments in which managers make decisions—certainty, risk, and uncertainty.

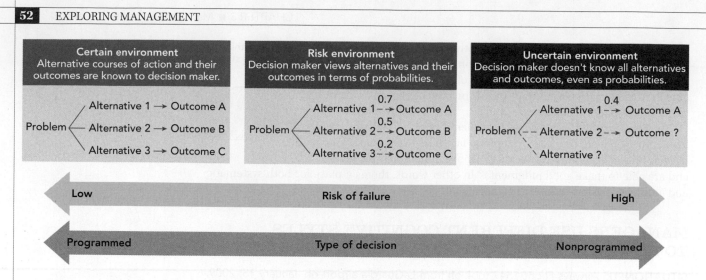

FIGURE 3.2 What Are the Differences Between Certain, Risk, and Uncertain Decision-Making Environments?
Managers rarely face a problem where they can know all the facts, identify all alternatives and their consequences, and chart a clear course of action. Such *certainty* is more often than not replaced by problem environments involving risk and uncertainty. *Risk* is where alternatives are known but their consequences can be described in terms of probabilities. *Uncertainty* is where all alternatives are not known, and their consequences are highly speculative.

A **certain environment** offers complete information on possible action alternatives and their consequences.

A **risk environment** lacks complete information but offers probabilities of the likely outcomes for possible action alternatives.

An **uncertain environment** lacks so much information that it is difficult to assign probabilities to the likely outcomes of alternatives.

As you might expect, the levels of risk and uncertainty in problem environments tend to increase the higher one moves in management ranks. You might think about this each time you hear about Apple, Samsung, Microsoft, or some other tech firm launching a new product or advertising campaign. Are the top executives making these decisions *certain* that the results will be successful? Or are they taking *risks* in market situations that are *uncertain* as to whether the new product or ad will be positively received by customers?

It would be nice if we could all make decisions and solve problems in the predictability of a **certain environment**. This is an ideal decision situation where factual information exists on the alternative courses of action and their consequences. A decision maker only needs to study the alternatives and choose the best solution. But it isn't easy to find examples of decision situations with such certain conditions. One possibility is a decision to take out a "fixed-rate" loan—say for college studies or a new car. You can make the decision knowing future interest costs and repayment timetables. But this situation changes significantly, doesn't it, if the lender offers a "variable-rate" loan? In this case the interest rate you pay will vary in the future according to what happens with market interest rates. How willing are you to take a loan while not knowing if interest rates will go down (to your gain) or up (to your loss) in the future?

The reality in our personal lives and in management is that we most often face **risk environments** where information and facts are incomplete, and the future is hard to predict. In risk conditions such as the variable-rate loan scenario, alternative courses of action and their consequences can be analyzed only as *probabilities* (e.g., 4 chances out of 10). One way of dealing with risk is by gathering as much information as possible, perhaps in different ways. In the case of a new product, such as a new soft drink flavor or even a college textbook like this one, it is unlikely that marketing executives would make go-ahead decisions without lots of data gathering and analysis. This often involves getting reports from multiple focus groups that test the new product in its sample stages.

An **uncertain environment** exists when facts are few and information is so poor that managers have a hard time even assigning probabilities to things. This is the most difficult decision condition and more common than you may think.[8] Decisions made in uncertain conditions depend greatly on intuition, judgment, informed guessing, and hunches—all of which leave considerable room for error. And, the borderline between risk and uncertainty isn't always clear. When the Japanese built a nuclear power plant at Fukushima—on the seacoast and in an earthquake zone—were decision makers just taking a calculated risk, or were they acting in the face of absolute uncertainty? How did they factor into their decisions the likelihood of a massive tsunami damaging the reactors and leading to population evacuation and radiological contamination—a situation that eventually occurred?

STUDYGUIDE

Takeaway 3.1
How Do Managers Use Information to Solve Problems?

Terms to Define

Analytical competency	Information competency	Performance opportunity	Risk environment
Certain environment	Intuitive thinking	Performance threat	Systematic thinking
Cognitive styles	Knowledge workers	Problem solving	Technological competency
Decision	Nonprogrammed decision	Programmed decision	Uncertain environment

Rapid Review

- A problem can occur as a threat or an opportunity; it involves an existing or potential discrepancy between an actual and a desired state of affairs.
- Managers can deal with structured and routine problems using programmed decisions; novel and unique problems require special solutions developed by nonprogrammed decisions.
- Managers deal with problems in different ways, with some being problem avoiders, others being reactive problem solvers, and still others being proactive problem seekers.
- Managers using systematic thinking approach problems in a rational step-by-step fashion; managers using intuitive thinking approach them in a more flexible and spontaneous way.
- Managers display different cognitive styles when dealing with information for decision making—sensation thinkers, intuitive thinkers, intuitive feelers, and sensation feelers.
- The problems that managers face occur in environments of certainty, risk, or uncertainty.

Questions for Discussion

1. Can a manager be justified for acting as a problem avoider in certain situations?
2. Would an organization be better off with mostly systematic or mostly intuitive thinkers?
3. Is it possible to develop programmed decisions for use in conditions of risk and uncertainty?

Be Sure You Can

- **explain** the importance of information competency for successful problem solving
- **differentiate** programmed and nonprogrammed decisions
- **describe** different ways managers approach and deal with problems
- **discuss** the differences between systematic and intuitive thinking
- **identify** differences between the four cognitive styles used in decision making
- **explain** the challenges of decision making under conditions of certainty, risk, and uncertainty environments

Career Situation: What Would You Do?

Even though some problems in organizations seem to "pop up" unexpectedly, many of them can be anticipated. Examples are an employee who calls in sick at the last minute, a customer who is unhappy with a product or service and wants a refund, and even a boss who asks you to do something that isn't job relevant. How might you anticipate handling such situations as a decision maker?

Takeaway 3.2
What Are Five Steps in the Decision-Making Process?

ANSWERS TO COME

■ Step 1—Identify and define the problem.
■ Step 2—Generate and evaluate alternative courses of action.
■ Step 3—Decide on a preferred course of action.
■ Step 4—Take action to implement the decision.
■ Step 5—Evaluate results.
■ Ethical reasoning is important at all steps in decision making.

The **decision-making process** begins with identification of a problem and ends with evaluation of implemented solutions.

THE FIVE STEPS IN THE **DECISION-MAKING PROCESS** are shown in **Figure 3.3**—Identify and define the problem, generate and evaluate alternative solutions, decide on a preferred course of action, implement the decision, and then evaluate results. The figure also shows a commitment to ethical decision making. An ethics double-check should be done at each step along the way.[9] Let's look at this process with an example of how competition, changing times, and the forces of globalization can take their toll on organizations, the people who work for them, and the communities in which they operate. How would you feel as one of the affected employees, as the town mayor, or as an executive having to make tough decisions in this situation?

The Ajax Case

On December 31, the Ajax Company decided to close down its Murphysboro plant. Market conditions and a recessionary economy were forcing layoffs, and the company hadn't been able to find a buyer for the business. Of the 172 employees, some had been with the company as long as 18 years, others as little as 6 months. Ajax needed to terminate all of them. Under company policy, they would be given severance pay equal to one week's pay per year of service.

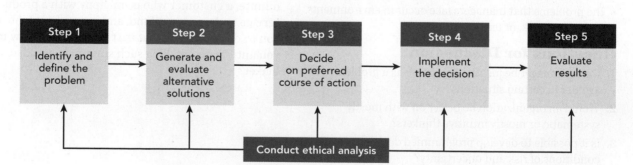

FIGURE 3.3 What Are Five Steps in the Decision-Making Process?
Decision making can be viewed as a series of steps—(1) find and define the problem, (2) generate and evaluate solutions, (3) choose a preferred alternative, (4) implement the decision, and (5) evaluate the results. It is important to conduct ethical analysis at all steps in the decision-making process—from initial problem identification all the way to the evaluation of results. When the ethics of a decision are questioned, it's time to stop and rethink the entire process. This helps the decision maker to be confident that all underlying moral problems have been identified and dealt with in the best possible ways.

STEP 1—IDENTIFY AND DEFINE THE PROBLEM.

The first step in decision making is to identify and define the problem. This is a stage of information gathering, information processing, and deliberation. It is where goals are clarified to specify exactly what a decision should accomplish. However, three mistakes are common in the rush to set goals and get rid of a problem.

Mistake 1—defining the problem too broadly or too narrowly. To take a classic example, instead of stating the problem as "Build a better mousetrap," we define it as "Get rid of the mice." Ideally, problems are defined in ways that give them the best possible range of problem-solving options.

Mistake 2—focusing on symptoms instead of causes. Symptoms are indicators that problems may exist; they aren't the problems themselves. Of course, it's important to be good at spotting problem symptoms such as a drop in a team member's performance. But instead of treating symptoms, say by clarifying targets and encouraging higher performance, this team leader needs to identify and address the problem's root causes—in this case, lack of training in a complex new computer system.

Mistake 3—choosing the wrong problem to deal with. This can happen when we are rushed and time is short or when there are many things happening at once. Instead of just doing something—anything—when something goes wrong, it's important to do the right things. This means setting wise priorities and dealing with the most important problems first.

Back to the Ajax Case

Closing the plant will result in a loss of jobs for a substantial number of people from the small community of Murphysboro. The unemployment created will negatively affect these individuals, their families, and the community as a whole. The loss of the Ajax tax base will further hurt the community. Ajax management, therefore, defines the problem as how to minimize the adverse impact of the plant closing on the employees, their families, and the community.

STEP 2—GENERATE AND EVALUATE ALTERNATIVE COURSES OF ACTION.

After the problem is defined, the next step in decision making is to gather relevant facts and information. Managers must be clear here on exactly what they know and what they need to know. They should identify alternative courses of action as well as their anticipated consequences on key stakeholders. In the case of plant closings and layoffs by General Motors, for example, a union negotiator once said: "While GM's continuing decline in market share isn't the fault of workers or our communities, it is these groups that will suffer."[10]

It's helpful to use some form of **cost-benefit analysis** to evaluate alternative courses of action. This compares what an alternative will cost with its expected benefits. At a minimum, benefits should exceed costs. In addition, an alternative should be timely, acceptable to as many stakeholders as possible, and ethically sound. And most often, the better the pool of alternatives and the better the analysis and the more likely it is that a good decision will result.

Cost-benefit analysis involves comparing the costs and benefits of each potential course of action.

Back to the Ajax Case

Ajax will definitely close the plant; keeping it open is no longer an option. These alternatives are considered—close the plant on schedule and be done with it; delay the plant closing and try again to sell it to another firm; offer to sell the plant to the employees and/or local interests; close the plant and offer employees transfers to other Ajax plant locations; close the plant, offer transfers, and help the employees find new jobs in and around Murphysboro.

STEP 3—DECIDE ON A PREFERRED COURSE OF ACTION.

The **classical decision model** describes decision making with complete information.

An **optimizing decision** chooses the alternative providing the absolute best solution to a problem.

The **behavioral decision model** describes decision making with limited information and bounded rationality.

A **satisficing decision** chooses the first satisfactory alternative that presents itself.

Management theory recognizes two quite different ways that alternatives get explored and decisions get made—the classical and behavioral models shown in **Figure 3.4**. The **classical decision model** views the manager as acting rationally and in a fully informed manner. The problem is clearly defined, all possible action alternatives are known, and their consequences are clear. As a result, he or she makes an **optimizing decision** that gives the absolute best solution to the problem.

Although the classical decision model sounds ideal, most of the time it's too good to be true. To begin, it's rare to face problems in environments of complete certainty. And to further complicate things, there are limits to human information-processing capabilities. Something called *cognitive limitations* makes it is hard for us to be fully informed and make perfectly rational decisions in all situations.

The **behavioral decision model** accepts the presence of cognitive limitations and recognizes risk and uncertainty in most decision environments. Its premise is that people act only in terms of their perceptions, which are frequently imperfect. Armed with only partial knowledge about the available action alternatives and their consequences, decision makers are likely to choose the first alternative that appears satisfactory. Herbert Simon, who won a Nobel prize for his work, calls these **satisficing decisions**.[11] What do you think? Does this seem accurate in describing how we make a lot of decisions?

Back to the Ajax Case

Ajax executives decide to close the plant, offer employees transfers to company plants in another state, and offer to help displaced employees find new jobs in and around Murphysboro.

STEP 4—TAKE ACTION TO IMPLEMENT THE DECISION.

Once a preferred course of action is chosen, action must be taken to fully implement it. Otherwise nothing new can or will happen to solve the problem. This means that managers

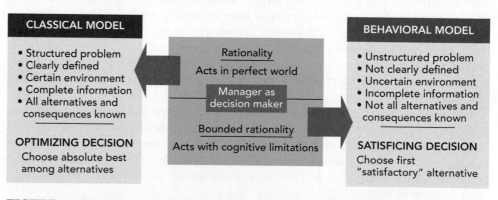

FIGURE 3.4 How Does the Classical Model of Managerial Decision Making Differ from the Behavioral Model?

The classical model views decision makers as having complete information and making optimum decisions that are the absolute best choices to resolve problems. The behavioral model views decision makers as having limited information-processing capabilities. They act with incomplete information and make satisficing decisions, choosing the first satisfactory alternative that comes to their attention.

HOT TOPIC

Bye-bye Telecommuting?

© Mango Productions/Corbis

Situation All eyes were on Marissa Mayer when she left a successful stint at Google to become Yahoo!'s CEO. But not everyone liked what they heard when she told employees there would be no more working from home. "Bye-bye telecommuting" was the message. Mayer's stated goal was to bring face-to-face collaboration back to the Yahoo! culture—and increase innovation in the process.

Critics of Mayer's decision claim it flies in the face of evidence that says not only do most employees want the option of telecommuting—as high as 80% in some reports—but they're both hardworking and more satisfied when they can spend time working from home. "Telecommuting. . . has allowed me to have a career as well as be a mother," said a posting by "digital mom" on Babble.com, an online Web site for parents.

Those who support Mayer's decision point to other employers—including Bank of America, Google, and Twitter—that are either cutting back on or discouraging work-at-home choices. When asked, "How many people telecommute at Google?" the firm's chief financial officer replied: "As few as possible."

HOW ABOUT IT?

What is your position on telecommuting? Does experience tell you that it works or that it doesn't? Is it something that you are looking for in an employer? Does Mayer's decision show courage in the face of a popular but not necessarily performance-friendly practice? Or, was it a premature rush to blame work-at-home practices for what she perceived as Yahoo!'s failures of collaboration and innovation?

---

need more than the determination and creativity to arrive at decisions. They must be able and willing to take action. And, they must have the people skills needed to rally the actions of others on their teams and in their organizations. More often than you might realize, it is lack of support from others that sabotages the implementation of many perfectly good decisions.

Managers commit the **lack-of-participation error** when they fail to include in the decision-making process those persons whose support is necessary for implementation. Managers who use participation wisely avoid this error and get the right people involved from the beginning. This not only brings their inputs and insights to bear on the problem and strengthens decision making, it also builds their commitments to follow through with the actions needed to make sure things turn out as intended.

Lack-of-participation error is failure to include the right people in the decision-making process.

Back to the Ajax Case

Ajax management ran an ad in the local and regional newspapers for several days. It announced to potential employers an "Ajax skill bank" composed of "qualified, dedicated, and well-motivated employees with a variety of skills and experiences." The ad urged interested employers to contact Ajax for further information.

STEP 5—EVALUATE RESULTS.

A decision isn't much good if it doesn't achieve the desired outcomes or causes undesired side effects. This is why the decision-making process is not complete until results are evaluated. This is a form of management control where data are gathered so that results can be measured against goals. If things aren't going well, corrective actions can be taken and earlier steps in the decision-making process can be revisited. If things are going better than expected, it's possible to learn why and save these lessons for use in the future.

ETHICS CHECK

Left to Die on Mt. Everest

STR/AFP/Getty Images

Some 40 climbers are winding their way to the top of Mt. Everest. About 1,000 feet below the summit sits a British mountain climber in trouble, collapsed in a shallow snow cave. Most of those on the way up just look while continuing their climbs. Sherpas from one passing team pause to give him oxygen before moving on. Within hours, David Sharp, 34, is dead of oxygen deficiency on the mountain.

A climber who passed by says: "At 28,000 feet it's hard to stay alive yourself . . . he was in very poor condition . . . it was a very hard decision . . . he wasn't a member of our team."

Someone who made the summit in the past says: "If you're going to go to Everest . . . I think you have to accept responsibility that you may end up doing something that's not ethically nice . . . you have to realize that you're in a different world."

After hearing about this case, the late Sir Edmund Hillary, who reached the top in 1953, said: "Human life is far more important than just getting to the top of a mountain."

YOUR DECISION?

Who's right and who's wrong here? And, by the way, in our personal affairs, daily lives, and careers, we are all, in our own ways, climbing Mt. Everest. What are the ethics of our climbs? How often do we notice others in trouble, struggling along the way? And, like the mountain climbers heading to the summit of Everest, how often do we pass them by to continue our own journeys? Can you identify examples—from business, school, career, sports, and so on—that pose similar ethical dilemmas?

Back to the Ajax Case

How effective was Ajax's decision? Well, we don't know for sure. After Ajax ran the skill-bank advertisement for 15 days, the plant's industrial relations manager said: "I've been very pleased with the results." However, we really need a lot more information for a true evaluation. How many employees got new jobs locally? How many transferred to other Ajax plants? How did the local economy perform in the following months? Probably you can add evaluation questions of your own to this list.

ETHICAL REASONING IS IMPORTANT AT ALL STEPS IN DECISION MAKING.

If you look back to Figure 3.3, you'll see that each step in the decision-making process is linked with ethical reasoning.[12] Careful attention to ethical analysis helps identify any underlying moral problems as the decision maker moves from one step to another. You can think of this as an ongoing "ethics double-check," one that can be accomplished by asking and answering tough ethics questions.

A good first step in checking the ethics of a decision is to evaluate it on these four criteria described in the work of ethicist Gerald Cavanagh and his associates.[13] *Utility*—Does the decision satisfy all constituents or stakeholders? *Rights*—Does the decision respect the rights and duties of everyone? *Justice*—Is the decision consistent with the canons of justice? *Caring*—Is the decision consistent with my responsibilities to care?

A strong second step is to test the ethics of a decision by opening it up to public disclosure and the prospect of shame.[14] The so-called **spotlight questions** listed here are especially powerful.

Spotlight questions highlight the risks of public disclosure of one's actions.

1. "How would I feel if my family found out about this decision?"
2. "How would I feel if this decision was published in the local newspaper or posted on the Internet?"
3. "What would the person I know who has the strongest character and best ethical judgment say about my decision?"

STUDYGUIDE

Takeaway 3.2
What Are Five Steps in the Decision-Making Process?

Terms to Define

Behavioral decision model	Cost-benefit analysis	Lack-of-participation error	Satisficing decision
Classical decision model	Decision-making process	Optimizing decision	Spotlight questions

Rapid Review

- The steps in the decision-making process are (1) identify and define the problem, (2) generate and evaluate alternatives, (3) decide on the preferred course of action, (4) implement the decision, (5) evaluate the results, and conduct ethics double-check in all steps.
- A cost-benefit analysis compares the expected costs of a decision alternative with its expected results.
- In the classical model, an optimizing decision chooses the absolute best solution from a known set of alternatives.
- In the behavioral model, cognitive limitations lead to satisficing decisions that choose the first satisfactory alternative to come to attention.
- The ethics of a decision can be checked on the criteria of utility, rights, justice, and caring, as well as by asking the spotlight questions.

Questions for Discussion

1. Do the steps in the decision-making process have to be followed in order?
2. Do you see any problems or pitfalls for managers using the behavioral decision model?
3. Is use of the spotlight questions sufficient to ensure an ethical decision?

Be Sure You Can

- **list** the steps in the decision-making process
- **apply** these steps to a sample decision-making situation
- **explain** cost-benefit analysis
- **compare** and contrast the classical and behavioral decision models
- **illustrate** optimizing and satisficing in your personal decision-making experiences
- **list** and explain the criteria for evaluating the ethics of a decision
- **list** three questions for double-checking the ethics of a decision

Career Situation: What Would You Do?

You are under a lot of pressure as a team leader because of social loafing and poor performance by one of your team members. You have come up with a reason to remove her from the team. But, you feel very uneasy. After doing the ethics analysis, the decision you are about to make fails all three of the recommended spotlight questions. What do you do now?

Takeaway 3.3
What Are Current Issues in Managerial Decision Making?

ANSWERS TO COME

- Creativity can be unlocked for better decision making.
- Group decision making has both advantages and disadvantages.
- Judgmental heuristics and other biases may cause decision-making errors.
- Managers must prepare for crisis decision making.

ONCE YOU ACCEPT THE FACT THAT EACH OF US IS LIKELY TO MAKE IMPERFECT decisions at least some of the time, it makes sense to probe even further into the hows and whys of decision making in organizations. One popular issue is creativity and how to unlock its power in decision making. Other current issues relate to the handling of group versus individual decisions, judgmental heuristics and decision biases, and decision making under crisis conditions.

CREATIVITY CAN BE UNLOCKED FOR BETTER DECISION MAKING.

SITUATION: Elevator riders in a new high-rise building are complaining about long waiting times.

Building engineer's advice—upgrade the entire system at substantial cost. Why? He assumed that any solutions to a slow elevator problem had to be mechanical ones.

Creativity consultant's advice—place floor-to-ceiling mirrors by the elevators. Why? People, she suspected, would not notice waiting times because they were distracted by their and others' reflections.

Outcome—the mirrors were installed and the complaints ceased. The creativity consultant was right.[15]

> **Creativity** is the generation of a novel idea or unique approach that solves a problem or crafts an opportunity.

> **Big-C creativity** occurs when extraordinary things are done by exceptional people.

> **Little-C creativity** occurs when average people come up with unique ways to deal with daily events and situations.

We can define **creativity** as the generation of a novel idea or unique approach to solving performance problems or exploiting performance opportunities.[16] And don't forget—the potential for creativity is one of our greatest personal assets, even though this capability may be too often unrecognized by us and by others.

Big-C Creativity

One reason we often underestimate our creativity skills is too much focus on what researchers call **Big-C creativity**—when extraordinary things are done by exceptional people.[17] Think Big-C creativity when you use or see someone using an iPhone—Steve Jobs's creativity, or browse Facebook—Mark Zuckerberg's creativity, or chat on WhatsApp—Brian Acton's and Jan Koum's creativity.

Little-C Creativity

Now switch gears. Even though not always aware of it, most of us also show a lot of **Little-C creativity**—when average people come up with unique ways to deal with daily events and situations. Think Little-C creativity, for example, the next time you solve relationship problems at home, build something for the kids, or even find ways to pack too many things into too small a suitcase.

Just imagine what can be accomplished with all the creative potential—Big-C and Little-C—that exists in an organization. How do you turn that potential into creative decisions? Is creativity something that is built into some of us and not

Personal Creativity Drivers

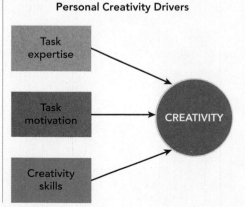

built into others? Or, is creativity something that one can work to develop along with other personal skills and competencies?

Personal Creativity Drivers

Here are some insights from the nearby three-component model of personal creativity drivers.[18] Creative decisions are more likely to occur when the person or team has a lot of task expertise. This is because creativity often extends in new directions something we are already good at or know something about. Creative decisions are more likely when people are highly task motivated. When people work exceptionally hard to resolve a problem, they often end up accomplishing something new and different. Creative decisions are also more likely when people have strong creativity skill sets. Just what are we talking about here? Most researchers tend to agree that most of us can develop creativity skill sets like the following: hold ground in face of criticism, stay resourceful when things get difficult, think "outside the box," transfer learning from one setting to others, and step back to question assumptions.[19]

> ### Team Decisions Have Advantages and Disadvantages
>
> Potential Advantages of Making Decisions as a Team
>
> *More information available*—members offer information, expertise, and viewpoints for problem solving.
>
> *More alternatives considered*—members generate and consider more alternative courses of action.
>
> *Increased understanding*—members gain understanding and are more likely to accept decisions.
>
> *Greater commitment*—members gain commitment to work hard and support decisions.
>
> Potential Disadvantages of Making Decisions as a Team
>
> *Social pressures to conform*—some members may "go along" because they feel intimidated.
>
> *Domination by a few*—a small coalition of members may dominate discussion and decision making.
>
> *Time delays*—it takes time for many people to make decisions together.

GROUP DECISION MAKING HAS BOTH ADVANTAGES AND DISADVANTAGES.

Whether to make decisions alone or with the help of others shouldn't be an either/or choice. Effective managers and team leaders typically switch back and forth between individual and group decision making, trying to use the best methods for the problems at hand. After all, group or team decision approaches have both advantages and disadvantages, as shown in the nearby box.[20]

In respect to advantages, group decisions can be good because they bring greater amounts of information, knowledge, and expertise to bear on a problem. They often expand the number and even the creativity of action alternatives examined. Participation also helps group members gain a better understanding of any decisions reached. This increases the likelihood that they will both accept decisions made and work hard to help implement them.

In respect to disadvantages, we all know that it is sometimes difficult and time consuming for people to make group decisions. The more people involved, the longer it can take to reach a group decision, and the more likely it is that problems will arise. There may be social pressure to conform that leads to premature consensus and agreement in group situations. Some individuals may feel intimidated or compelled to go along with the apparent wishes of others who have authority or who act in aggressive and uncompromising ways. Minority domination might cause some members to feel forced or railroaded into a decision advocated by one vocal individual or a small coalition. And, lots of decisions suffer when they get made quickly or at the last minute just because a group is running out of meeting time.

Video Games May Be Good for Decision Making

Believe it or not, and contrary to public opinion, researchers are starting to talk about gaming being good for our brains. Consider these data—Starcraft players show faster thought and movements; players of action video games were 25% faster than nonplayers in decision making; game players can track six things at once, while nonplayers track four; surgeons who play games at least three hours a week make fewer surgical errors. Of course there's a lot of downside risk, too. Players of violent video games seem to have more aggressive thoughts and are less caring toward others. Perhaps your gaming, well considered, can be a decision-making asset—boosting creativity and multitasking skills.

Jerzyworks/Masterfile

FACTS TO CONSIDER

The "Ask Gap"—What It Takes for Women to Get Raises

PeopleImages/iStock/Getty Images

Women in the tech industry earn an average of $6,538 less per year than men. Women with children suffer a "mom penalty" of minus $11,247 per year. But when Microsoft CEO Satya Nadella was asked for career advice at a conference on women in computing, he said: "It's not really about asking for the raise but knowing and having faith that the system will actually give you the right raises as you go along." Facing flak and outrage once his comments hit the news, Nadella issued a retraction: "I answered that question completely wrong. . . . If you think you deserve a raise, you should just ask." Nevertheless, facts show that women ask for raises less frequently than men.

- 44% of women in a Condé Nast *Glamour* survey believed they would be getting higher pay if they were a man.

- 39% of women and 54% of men in the survey said they asked for more pay when negotiating for a new job. Of the women who asked for more pay, 75% got it.

- 27% of women in a Citi/LinkedIn survey said they asked for more pay last year. Of them, 84% said they were successful.

WHAT'S YOUR TAKE?

Why don't more women ask for raises and promotions? What are the implications for women and men when top executives, managers, and team leaders say "just trust the system and everything will work out for you." Have you ever asked for more pay and career advancement? What were your experiences? And if you've never asked, will you in the future? If so, are you prepared to put forth your best case?

JUDGMENTAL HEURISTICS AND OTHER BIASES MAY CAUSE DECISION-MAKING ERRORS.

Why do well-intentioned people sometimes make bad decisions? One reason is because we often use simplifying strategies when making decisions with limited information, time, and even energy. These strategies, known as heuristics, can cause decision-making errors.[21]

The **availability heuristic** uses readily available information to assess a current situation.

The **availability heuristic** occurs when people use information "readily available" from memory as a basis for assessing a current event or situation. You may decide, for example, not to buy running shoes from a company if your last pair didn't last long. The potential bias is that the readily available information may be wrong or irrelevant. Even though your present running shoes are worn out, you may have purchased the wrong model for your needs or used them in the wrong conditions.

The **representativeness heuristic** assesses the likelihood of an occurrence based on a stereotyped set of similar events.

The **representativeness heuristic** occurs when people assess the likelihood of something happening based on its similarity to a stereotyped set of past occurrences. An example is deciding to hire someone for a job vacancy simply because he or she graduated from the same school attended by your last and most successful new hire. Using the representative stereotype may mask the truly important factors relevant to the decision—the real abilities and career expectations of the new job candidate; the school attended may be beside the point.

The **anchoring and adjustment heuristic** adjusts a previously existing value or starting point to make a decision.

The **anchoring and adjustment heuristic** involves making decisions based on adjustments to a previously existing value or starting point. For example, a manager may set a new salary level for a current employee by simply raising the prior year's salary by a percentage increment. The problem is that this increment is anchored in the existing salary level, one that may be much lower than the employee's true market value. Rather than being pleased with the raise, the employee may be unhappy and start looking elsewhere for another, higher-paying job.

MANAGERS ARE DECISION MAKERS AND IMPLEMENTORS . . . THE BEST ARE ALSO SELF REGULATORS.

EXPLORE YOURSELF

Self-confidence

Managers are decision makers. And if they are to make consistently good decisions, they must be skilled at gathering and processing information.

Managers are implementers. Once decisions are made, managers are expected to rally people and resources to put them into action. This is how problems get solved and opportunities get explored in organizations.

The best managers and team leaders are also self regulators. They understand potential decision biases and traps, and they are able to avoid these pitfalls through self and situational awareness, and disciplined action.

In order for all this to happen, managers must have the **self-confidence** to turn decisions into action accomplishments. They must believe in their decisions and the informa-

tion foundations for them. A good understanding of the many topics in this chapter can improve your decision-making skills. A better understanding of your personal style in gathering and processing information can also go a long way toward building your self-confidence as a decision maker.

> Get to know yourself better by taking the self-assessment on **Maximizer or Satisficer Self Check** and completing other activities in the *Exploring Management* **Skill-Building Portfolio**.

In addition to heuristic biases, **framing error** is another potential decision trap. Framing occurs when managers evaluate and resolve a problem in the context in which they perceive it—either positive or negative. You might consider this as the "glass is half empty versus the glass is half full" dilemma. Suppose marketing data show that a new product has a 40% market share. What does this really mean? A negative frame says there's a problem because the product is missing 60% of the market. "What are we doing wrong?" is the likely follow-up question. But if the marketing team used a positive frame and considered the 40% share as a success story, the conversation might well be: "How can we do even better?" By the way, we are constantly exposed to framing in the world of politics; the word used to describe it is "spin."

Another of our tendencies is to try to find ways to justify a decision after making it. In the case of unethical acts, for example, we try to rationalize with statements such as "No one will ever find out" or "The boss will protect me." Such thinking causes a decision-making trap known as **confirmation error**. This means that we notice, accept, and even seek out only information that confirms or is consistent with a decision we have already made. Other and perhaps critical information is downplayed or denied. This is a form of selective perception. The error is that we neglect other points of view or disconfirming information that might lead us to a different decision.

Yet another decision-making trap is **escalating commitment**. This is a tendency to increase effort and perhaps apply more resources to pursue a course of action that signals indicate is not working.[22] It is an inability or unwillingness to call it quits even when the facts suggest that this is the best decision under the circumstances. Ego and the desire to avoid being associated with a mistake can play a big role in escalation.

How about it? Are you disciplined enough to minimize the risk of escalating commitments to previously chosen, but erroneous, courses of action? Fortunately, researchers have provided the following ideas on how to avoid the escalation trap.[23]

- Set advance limits on your involvement in and commitment to a particular course of action; stick with these limits.
- Make your own decisions; don't follow the lead of others because they are also prone to escalation.
- Carefully determine just why you are continuing a course of action; if there are insufficient reasons to continue, don't.
- Remind yourself of the costs of a course of action; consider saving these costs as a reason to discontinue.

Framing error evaluates and resolves a problem within the context in which it is perceived.

Confirmation error is when we attend only to information that confirms a decision already made.

Escalating commitment is the continuation of a course of action even though it is not working.

MANAGERS MUST PREPARE FOR CRISIS DECISION MAKING.

A **crisis** is an unexpected problem that can lead to disaster if not resolved quickly and appropriately.

Think back to the chapter-opening example of shift leader Luis Urzúa and the Chilean mine disaster that opened this chapter. One of the most challenging of all decision situations is the **crisis**. This is an unexpected problem that can lead to disaster if not resolved quickly and appropriately.

Although not all crises are as sensational and life-threatening as the mine disaster, they still require special handling, and they still generate lots of mistakes. Indeed, the ability to deal successfully with crises could well be the ultimate test of any manager's decision-making capabilities.

Managers sometimes react to crises by doing exactly the wrong things. Instead of opening up and reaching out, they end up isolating themselves and trying to solve the problem alone or in a small, closed group.[24] This denies them access to crucial information at the very time that they need it the most. It not only sets them up for poor decisions, but may create even more problems.

Many organizations are developing formal crisis management programs. They train managers in rules of crisis decision making like those shown in Tips to Remember. They also assign people ahead of time to crisis management teams, and they develop crisis management plans to deal with various contingencies.

> ## TIPS TO REMEMBER
> ### Six Rules for Crisis Management
>
> 1. *Figure out what is going on*—Dig in to thoroughly understand what's happening and the conditions under which the crisis must be resolved.
> 2. *Remember that speed matters*—Attack the crisis as quickly as possible, trying to catch it before it gets overwhelmingly large.
> 3. *Remember that slow counts, too*—Know when to back off and wait for a better opportunity to make progress with the crisis.
> 4. *Respect the danger of the unfamiliar*—Understand the danger of entering all-new territory where you and others have never been before.
> 5. *Value the skeptic*—Don't look for and get too comfortable with early agreement; appreciate skeptics and let them help you see things differently in sorting out what to do.
> 6. *Be ready to "fight fire with fire"*—When things are going wrong and no one seems to care, you may have to fuel the crisis to get their attention.

Fire and police departments, the Red Cross, and community groups plan ahead and train to best handle civil and natural disasters; airline crews train for flight emergencies. In the same way, managers and work teams can plan ahead and train to best deal with organizational crises.[25] This only makes sense, doesn't it?

STUDYGUIDE

Takeaway 3.3

What Are Some Current Issues in Managerial Decision Making?

Terms to Define

Anchoring and
  adjustment heuristic

Availability heuristic

Big-C creativity

Confirmation error

Creativity

Crisis

Escalating commitment

Framing error

Little-C creativity

Representativeness
  heuristic

Rapid Review

- Creativity in decision making can be enhanced by the personal creativity drivers of individual creativity skills, task expertise, and motivation.
- Group decisions offer the potential advantages of more information, greater understanding, and expanded commitments; a major disadvantage is that they are often time consuming.
- Judgmental heuristics such as availability, anchoring and adjustment, and representativeness can bias decisions by oversimplifying the situation.
- Framing errors influence decisions by placing them in either a negative or a positive situational context; confirmation error focuses attention only on information that supports a decision.
- Escalating commitment occurs when one sticks with a course of action even though evidence indicates that it is not working.
- A crisis problem occurs unexpectedly and can lead to disaster if managers fail to handle it quickly and properly.

Questions for Discussion

1. How can you avoid being hurt by the anchoring and adjustment heuristic in your annual pay raises?
2. What are some real-world examples of how escalating commitment is affecting decision making in business, government, or people's personal affairs?
3. Is it really possible to turn a crisis into an opportunity, and, if so, how?

Be Sure You Can

- **identify** personal factors that can be developed or used to drive greater creativity in decision making
- **list** potential advantages and disadvantages of group decision making
- **explain** the availability, representativeness, and anchoring and adjustment heuristics
- **illustrate** framing error and continuation error in decision making
- **explain** and give an example of escalating commitment
- **describe** what managers can do to prepare for crisis decisions

Career Situation: What Would You Do?

You have finally caught the attention of senior management. Top executives asked you to chair a task force to develop ideas that can breathe new life into an existing product line. First, you need to select the members of the task force. What criteria will you use to choose members who are most likely to bring high levels of creativity to this team?

TEST PREP 3

Answers to Test Prep questions can be found at the back of the book.

Multiple-Choice Questions

1. A manager who is reactive and works hard to address problems after they occur is described as a _____.
   (a) problem seeker
   (b) problem solver
   (c) rational thinker
   (d) strategic opportunist

2. A problem is a discrepancy between a/an _____ situation and a desired situation.
   (a) unexpected
   (b) risk
   (c) actual
   (d) uncertain

3. If a manager approaches problems in a rational and analytical way, trying to solve them in step-by-step fashion, he or she is well described as a/an _____.
   (a) systematic thinker
   (b) intuitive thinker
   (c) problem seeker
   (d) behavioral decision maker

4. The first step in the decision-making process is to _____.
   (a) generate a list of alternatives
   (b) assess the costs and benefits of each alternative
   (c) identify and define the problem
   (d) perform the ethics double-check

5. When the members of a special task force are asked to develop a proposal for hitting very aggressive targets for the international sales of a new product, this problem most likely requires a _____ decision.
   (a) routine
   (b) programmed
   (c) crisis
   (d) nonprogrammed

6. Costs, benefits, timeliness, and _____ are among the recommended criteria for evaluating alternative courses of action in the decision-making process.
   (a) ethical soundness
   (b) past history
   (c) availability
   (d) simplicity

7. The _____ decision model views managers as making optimizing decisions, whereas the _____ decision model views them as making satisficing decisions.
   (a) behavioral; judgmental heuristics
   (b) classical; behavioral
   (c) judgmental heuristics; ethical
   (d) crisis; routine

8. One reason why certainty is the most favorable environment for problem solving is because the problems can be addressed by using _____ decisions.
   (a) satisficing
   (b) optimizing
   (c) programmed
   (d) intuitive

9. A common mistake made by managers facing crisis situations is _____.
   (a) trying to get too much information before responding
   (b) relying too much on group decision making
   (c) isolating themselves to make crisis decisions alone
   (d) forgetting to use their crisis management plan

10. In which decision environment does a manager deal with probabilities regarding possible courses of action and their consequences?
    (a) Risk
    (b) Certainty
    (c) Uncertainty
    (d) Optimal

11. A manager who decides against hiring a new employee who just graduated from Downstate University because the last person hired from there turned out to be a low performer is falling prey to _____ error.
    (a) availability
    (b) adjustment
    (c) anchoring
    (d) representativeness

12. Which decision-making error is most associated with the old adage: "If at first you don't succeed, try, try again"?
    (a) Satisficing
    (b) Escalating commitment
    (c) Confirmation
    (d) Too late to fail

13. You go to your boss and ask for a pay raise. She says: "Well, let's take a look first at what you are making now." The risk you face in this situation is that your boss's decision will be biased because of _____.
    (a) a framing error
    (b) escalating commitment
    (c) anchoring and adjustment
    (d) strategic opportunism

14. Personal creativity drivers include creativity skills, task expertise, and _____.
    (a) strategic opportunism
    (b) management support
    (c) organizational culture
    (d) task motivation

15. The last step in the decision-making process is to _____.
    (a) choose a preferred alternative
    (b) evaluate results
    (c) find and define the problem
    (d) generate alternatives

Short-Response Questions

16. How does an optimizing decision differ from a satisficing decision?

17. What is the difference between a risk environment and an uncertain environment in decision making?

18. How can you tell from people's behavior if they tend to be systematic or intuitive in problem solving?

19. What is escalating commitment, and how can it be avoided?

Integration and Application Question

20. With the goals of both expanding your résumé and gaining valuable experience, you have joined a new mentoring program between your university and a local high school. One of the first activities is for you and your teammates to offer "learning modules" to a class of sophomores. You have volunteered to give a presentation and engage them in some learning activities on the topic: "Individual versus group decision making: Is one better than the other?"

    Question: What will you say and do, and why?

Steps for Further Learning

BUILD MARKETABLE SKILLS • **DO** A CASE ANALYSIS • **GET** AND STAY INFORMED

BUILD MARKETABLE SKILLS.

EARN BIG CAREER PAYOFFS!

Don't miss these opportunities in the SKILL-BUILDING PORTFOLIO

SELF-ASSESSMENT 3:
Maximizer or Satisficer Quick Check

Check your decision-making tendencies . . . turn decision making into a personal skill.

CLASS EXERCISE 3:
Lost at Sea

Sometimes group decisions are best . . . how do you make a good group decision?

TEAM PROJECT 3:
Crisis Management Realities

Crisis handling is always a hot topic . . . turn the experiences of others into learning for yourself.

Many learning resources are found at the end of the book and online within **WileyPLUS Learning Space.**

Practice Critical Thinking—Complete the CHAPTER 3 CASE

CASE SNAPSHOT: Amazon.com—Keeping the Fire Hot

Not only is Amazon.com the e-commerce company to beat, it also keeps changing as it grows. No one is ever sure what will come next under the guidance of founder and CEO Jeff Bezos. Seeming not to worry about current earnings per share, Bezos keeps investing to make his company stronger and harder to catch. Its millions of square feet of distribution fulfillment space keep growing domestically and around the globe. The firm's products and services are continuously upgraded and expanded. What drives Bezos's decisions, and will his investments pay off in the years to come?

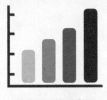

DO A CASE ANALYSIS.

STRENGTHEN YOUR CRITICAL THINKING!

MANAGER'S LIBRARY SELECTION
Read for Insights and Wisdom
The Shallows: What the Internet Is Doing to Our Brains (2010, W. W. Norton & Company) by Nicolas Carr

Although the Internet has enlightened us in various ways, it may also be lightening our thinking by replacing deep thought and reflection with shallow-minded pursuits. In this book, author Nicholas Carr discusses how human minds have changed along with communication technologies ranging from the spoken word to the written tablet, and the printing press to the Internet. He cites research shows that brains are "rewired" when using the Web as the "hypermedia" of links and audiovisual stimuli overwhelm its cognitive capacity. Studies show that brains cope with information overload by changing their neural networks of operation. "Linear" thought—deep thinking and slow reflection using long-term memory—is replaced by "non-linear" thought—temporary thinking and rapid scanning using short-term memory. Further, book readers are found to outperform "hypertext" readers in comprehension, memory, and learning.

GET AND STAY INFORMED.

MAKE YOURSELF VALUABLE!

Internet brains are distracted by abundant stimuli and grow their short-term memory circuits by converting and replacing long-term memory circuits. Because permanent memory requires time and calm for ideas to pass into the unconscious mind, Carr describes the Internet as a "technology of forgetfulness" and a "Web of distraction." He warns that critical mental skills are lost with too much reliance on the Internet. He thinks Internet users should be purpose-driven, focus on fewer tasks simultaneously, and spend time away from the Web to read, ponder, and discuss ideas verbally.

Carr concedes that new skills are developed by Net use, such as "power browsing" through titles, content pages, and abstracts to quickly obtain ideas. He admits that Internet "hunting and gathering" is efficient for locating additional and varied facts. He also speculates that Web use may someday advance brains to multitask effectively. But Carr worries that those tasks may be less complex as humans' brains evolve to accommodate the shallow thinking demands of the Internet.

REFLECT AND REACT Does your use of the Internet make you more, or less, smart? Do you agree with Carr's view that the Internet is a web of distraction? How can Internet distractions be managed?

"Considering the future of our children and young people . . .we have no choice but to go ahead with the village-wide evacuation." Mayor Noro Kanno of Kawamata-cho town, after a 9.0 earthquake and monster tsunami wrecked nuclear power facilities in Fukushima, Japan.

Plans and Planning Techniques

4

Get There Faster with Objectives

Management Live

Picking a Major Based on Projected Future Salaries

Kristian Husar/iStock/Getty Images

The choice of major, or majors, is one of the most important plans a college student ever makes. It may not be the absolute key to career and life success, but it certainly sets the stage for a college experience that should build talents for long-term accomplishments. Lots of students take out large loans to pay for their studies, but data show that different majors command different starting salaries. How many students plan well to turn their choice of major into real career opportunities, including having enough earning power to quickly pay off their loans?

YOUR THOUGHTS?

Will your major and career choice allow you to meet your family obligations? Will the ratio of your earnings to debt be something you can manage? Will your major selection make you competitive in your career? How do you answer these questions, and what are the implications of your answers?

WHAT'S INSIDE

ETHICS CHECK
E-waste graveyards offer easy way out

FACTS TO CONSIDER
Policies on office romances vary widely

HOT TOPIC
Keep your career plan tight and focused, or loosen up?

QUICK CASE
New dads say it's time for paternity leave

YOUR CHAPTER 4 TAKEAWAYS

1. Understand how and why managers use the planning process.
2. Identify the types of plans used by managers.
3. Describe useful planning tools and techniques.

Takeaway 4.1
How and Why Do Managers Use the Planning Process?

ANSWERS TO COME

- Planning is one of the four functions of management.
- Planning sets objectives and identifies how to achieve them.
- Planning improves focus and flexibility.
- Planning improves action orientation.
- Planning improves coordination and control.
- Planning improves time management.

IT CAN BE EASY TO GET SO ENGROSSED IN THE PRESENT THAT WE FORGET ABOUT the future. Yet a mad rush to the future can sometimes go off track without solid reference points in the past. The trick is to blend past experiences and lessons with future aspirations and goals and to be willing to adjust as new circumstances arise. The management function of **planning** helps us do just that. It is a process of setting goals and objectives and determining how to best accomplish them. Said a bit differently, planning involves looking ahead, identifying exactly what you want to accomplish, and deciding how best to go about it.

> **Planning** is the process of setting performance objectives and determining how to accomplish them.

PLANNING IS ONE OF THE FOUR FUNCTIONS OF MANAGEMENT.

Among the four management functions shown in **Figure 4.1**, planning comes first. When done well, it sets the stage for the others: organizing—allocating and arranging resources to accomplish tasks; leading—guiding the efforts of human resources to ensure high levels of task accomplishment; and controlling—monitoring task accomplishments and taking necessary corrective action.

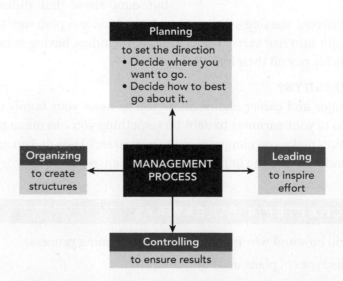

FIGURE 4.1 Why Does Planning Play a Central Role in the Management Process?
Planning is the first of the four management functions. It is the process of setting objectives—deciding where you want to go—and then identifying how to accomplish them—determining how to get there. When planning is done well, it provides a strong foundation for success with the other management functions.

In today's demanding organizational and career environments, effective planning is essential to staying one step ahead of the competition. An Eaton Corporation annual report, for example, once stated: "Planning at Eaton means taking the hard decisions before events force them upon you, and anticipating the future needs of the market before the demand asserts itself."[1]

You really should take these words to heart. But instead of a company, think about your personal situation. What hard decisions do you need to make? Where are the job markets going? Where do you want to be in your career and personal life in the next 5 or 10 years?

PLANNING SETS OBJECTIVES AND IDENTIFIES HOW TO ACHIEVE THEM.

From experience alone, you are probably familiar with planning and all that it involves. But it also helps to understand **Table 4.1**—How to Implement the Planning Process—and its action implications. Skill in handling each step in the planning process can deliver many career and personal benefits.

Step 1 in planning is to define your **objectives** and to identify the specific results or desired goals you hope to achieve. This step is important enough to stop and reflect a moment. Whether you call them goals or objectives, they are targets. They point us toward the future and provide a frame of reference for evaluating progress. With them, as the module subtitle suggests, you should get where you want to go, and get there faster.

Step 2 in planning is to compare where you are at present with the objectives. This establishes a baseline for performance; the present becomes a standard against which future progress can be gauged.

Step 3 in planning is to formulate premises about future conditions. It is where one looks ahead, trying to figure out what may happen and with what potential consequences.

Step 4 in planning is to make an actual **plan**. This is a list of actions that must be taken to accomplish the objectives.

Step 5 in planning is to implement the plan and evaluate results. This is where action takes place and measurement happens. Results are compared with objectives, and if needed, plans are modified to improve things in the future.

Have you thought about how well you plan, and how you might do it better? Managers should be asking the same question. They rarely get to plan while working alone in quiet rooms free from distractions. Because of the fast pace and complications of the typical workday, managerial planning is ongoing. It takes place even as one deals with a constant flow of problems in a sometimes hectic and demanding work setting.[2] Yet it's all worth it: Planning offers many benefits to people and organizations.[3]

Objectives are specific results that one wishes to achieve.

A **plan** is a statement of intended means for accomplishing objectives.

TABLE 4.1 How to Implement the Planning Process

Step 1. Define your objectives Know where you want to go; be specific enough to know you have arrived when you get there and how far off you are along the way.

Step 2. Determine where you stand vis-à-vis objectives Know where you presently stand in reaching the objectives; identify strengths that work in your favor and weaknesses that can hold you back.

Step 3. Develop premises regarding future conditions Generate alternative scenarios for what may happen; identify for each scenario things that may help or hinder progress toward your objectives.

Step 4. Make a plan Choose the action alternative most likely to accomplish your objectives; describe what must be done to implement this course of action.

Step 5. Implement the plan and evaluate results Take action; measure progress toward objectives as implementation proceeds; take corrective actions and revise the plan as needed.

Good Planning Makes Us and Our Organizations . . .

- **ACTION ORIENTED**—Planning gives us a results-driven sense of direction
- **PRIORITY ORIENTED**—Planning highlights the most important things for our attention
- **ADVANTAGE ORIENTED**—Planning makes sure that resources are used to best advantage
- **CHANGE ORIENTED**—Planning helps us anticipate and deal with problems and opportunities

PLANNING IMPROVES FOCUS AND FLEXIBILITY.

Planning can help sharpen focus and increase flexibility, both of which improve performance. An organization with focus knows what it does best and what it needs to do. Individuals with focus know where they want to go in a career or personal situation, and they keep that focus even when difficulties arise. An organization with flexibility is willing and able to change and adapt to shifting circumstances. An individual with flexibility adjusts career and life plans to fit new and developing opportunities.

PLANNING IMPROVES ACTION ORIENTATION.

The **complacency trap** is being lulled into inaction by current successes or failures.

Planning focuses attention on priorities and helps us avoid the **complacency trap** of being passively carried along by the flow of events. It's easy to be lulled into inaction by successes or failures of the moment. Instead of being caught in the present, however, planning keeps us alert and actively moving toward the future.

Management consultant Stephen R. Covey points out that planning gives us not just an action orientation, but also one guided by a clear set of priorities.[4] He says the most successful executives "zero in on what they do that adds value to an organization." They know what is important and what can wait, and they work first on the things that really count. They are results oriented, quick to avoid the complacency trap, and don't waste time by working on too many things at once.

Would a friend or relative describe you as focused on priorities, or as always jumping from one thing to another? Could you achieve more by getting your priorities straight and working hard on things that really count?

HOT TOPIC

Keep Your Career Plan Tight and Focused, or Loosen Up?

bikeriderlondon/Shutterstock

Executive A. "Career planning is more art than science. . . . Nonetheless, some form of plan can greatly enhance the evaluation of various opportunities and enable you to make better career decisions. A career plan allows you to identify how to use your basic strengths to maximum advantage, set major career objectives, and establish immediate milestones to measure personal development and advancement."

Executive B. "A career . . . is a series of accidental changes of job and shifts of scenery on which you look back later, weaving through the story retroactively some thread of logic that was not visible at the time. If you try to carefully to plan your life, the danger is that you will succeed—succeed in narrowing your options and closing off avenues of adventure that cannot now be imagined."

Those in favor of tight career planning are likely to say: "You need a plan to give yourself a sense of direction". . . "Having a career objective is highly motivating" . . . "Without a plan you'll wander and not accomplish much of anything."

Those against tight career planning are likely to say: "How can you know today what the future might offer?" . . . "If you are too tightly focused, you won't spot unique opportunities" . . . "We grow and change over time—our career plans should, too."

HOW ABOUT IT?

Is executive A's advice on target—careers should be carefully planned and then implemented step-by-step to achieve a long-term goal? Is executive B's view worth considering—careers are best built with flexibility and spontaneity to take advantage of opportunities that pop up along the way? How do these perspectives fit with what we know about job markets and career directions today? Which position do you favor? Or, would you rather blend a bit of both to carve a pathway to career success?

PLANNING IMPROVES COORDINATION AND CONTROL.

Organizations consist of many people and subsystems doing many different things at the same time. But even as they pursue the various tasks, their accomplishments must add together meaningfully if the organization is to succeed.

Good planning facilitates coordination by linking people and subsystems in a **hierarchy of objectives**. This is a means–ends chain in which lower-level objectives (the means) lead to the accomplishment of higher-level objectives (the ends). Think, for example, about the challenge of coordinating all people and systems in an organization around a total quality commitment. Strategic quality goals set at the top should be meaningful across all organization levels and for all work units and their members. Good planning helps accomplish this coordination by creating a hierarchy of objectives such as the one shown in **Figure 4.2**.

Good planning also sets the stage for controlling in the management process. The link begins when planning objectives and standards are set. It's hard to exercise control if you don't have objectives. Without control, even the best of plans may fail because of a lack of follow-through. With both good planning and good controlling, it's a lot easier to recognize when things aren't going well and make the necessary adjustments.

> In a **hierarchy of objectives**, lower-level objectives help to accomplish higher-level ones.

PLANNING IMPROVES TIME MANAGEMENT.

When Daniel Vasella was CEO of Novartis AG and its 98,000 employees spread across 140 countries, he was calendar bound—"locked in by meetings, travel and other constraints." To stay on track, he would list priorities of things to do. As CEO of ING US Wealth Management, Kathleen Murphy was also calendar bound, with conferences and travel booked a year ahead. She scheduled meetings at half-hour intervals, worked 12-hour days, and spent 60% of her time traveling. She also made good use of her time on planes, where, she says, "no one can reach me by phone and I can get reading and thinking done."[5]

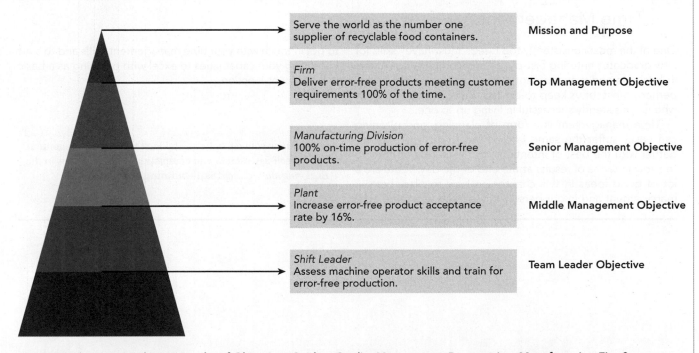

FIGURE 4.2 How Might a Hierarchy of Objectives Guide a Quality Management Program in a Manufacturing Firm?

A hierarchy of objectives identifies a means–ends chain through which lower-level objectives become the pathways for accomplishing higher-level ones. In the case of total quality management, the top-level objective (delivering error-free products that meet customer needs 100% of the time) moves step-by-step down the hierarchy until the point where a shift supervisor supports TQM with the objective of making sure that machine operators are trained well enough to do error-free work.

How to Better Manage Your Time

- Set priorities for what really needs to get done.
- Work on the most important things first.
- Leave details for later, or delegate them to others.
- Say "No!" to requests that divert attention from your priorities.
- Take charge of your schedule; don't let others control what you do and when.
- Stick with your choices; not everything deserves immediate attention.

These are common executive stories—tight schedules, little time alone, lots of meetings and phone calls, and not much room for spontaneity. And the keys to success in such classic management scenarios rest, in part at least, on another benefit of good planning—time management. It is an important management skill and competency, and a lot of time management comes down to discipline and priorities. Lewis Platt, former chairman of Hewlett-Packard, once said: "Basically, the whole day is a series of choices."[6] These choices have to be made in ways that allocate your time to the most important priorities.

Surely you have experienced difficulties in balancing time-consuming commitments and requests. Indeed, it is all too easy to lose track of time and fall prey to what consultants identify as "time wasters." Of course, you have to be careful in defining "waste." It isn't a waste of time to occasionally relax, take a breather from work, and find humor and pleasure in social interactions. Such breaks help us gather and replenish energies to do well in our work. But it is a waste to let other people or nonessential activities dominate your time.[7]

Although to-do lists can help, they aren't much good unless the lists contain the high-priority things. We need to distinguish between things that we must do (top priority), should do (high priority), might do (low priority), and really don't need to do (no priority). We also need to guard against the **planning fallacy**—underestimating the time required to complete a task. Research suggested the typical error can be as high as 40%. It also indicates that breaking a large task into smaller ones and mentally going through a task before starting the work makes for more realistic time estimates.[8]

The **planning fallacy** is underestimating the time required to complete a task.

TO-DO LISTS PUT TOGETHER WITH BEST INTENTIONS OFTEN FAIL TO DELIVER RESULTS AT THE END OF THE DAY.

EXPLORE YOURSELF

Time Management

One of the most consistently top rated "must-have" skills for new graduates entering fast-paced and complicated careers in business and management is **time management**. Many, perhaps most, of us keep to-do lists. But it's the rare person who is consistently successful in living up to one.

Time management is a form of planning, and planning can easily suffer the same fate as the to-do lists—put together with the best of intentions, but with little or nothing to show in terms of results at the end of the day. There are a lot of good ideas in this chapter on how to plan, both in management and in our personal lives. Now is a good time to get in touch with your time management skills and to start improving your capabilities to excel with planning as a basic management function.

Get to know yourself better by taking the **Time Management Profile** self-assessment and completing other activities in the *Exploring Management* **Skill-Building Portfolio**.

STUDYGUIDE

Takeaway 4.1
How and Why Do Managers Use the Planning Process?

Terms to Define

Complacency trap	Objectives	Planning
Hierarchy of objectives	Plan	Planning fallacy

Rapid Review

- Planning is the process of setting performance objectives and determining how to accomplish them.
- A plan is a set of intended actions for accomplishing important objectives.
- The steps in the planning process are (1) define your objectives, (2) determine where you stand vis-à-vis objectives, (3) develop premises regarding future conditions, (4) make a plan to best accomplish objectives, (5) implement the plan, and evaluate results.
- The benefits of planning include better focus and action orientation, better coordination and control, and better time management.
- Planning improves time management by setting priorities and avoiding time wasters.

Questions for Discussion

1. Should all employees plan, or just managers?
2. Which step in the planning process do you think is the hardest to accomplish?
3. How could better planning help in your personal career development?

Be Sure You Can

- **explain** the importance of planning as the first of four management functions
- **list** the steps in the formal planning process
- **explain** the important link between planning and controlling as management functions
- **illustrate** the benefits of planning for a business or an organization familiar to you
- **illustrate** the benefits of planning for your personal career development
- **list** at least three things you can do now to improve your time management

Career Situation: What Would You Do?

Someone you really care about wants you to take a step forward in time management. She asks you to make a list of all the things you plan to do tomorrow and identify which ones are (A) *most important*—top priority, (B) *important*—not top priority, and (C) *least important*—low priority. Next, she says to double-check your Bs—asking if any should be As or Cs, and your As—to see if any should be Bs or Cs? So do it, and see how things turn out. Can an exercise like this help you take charge of your time and get the really important things done first?

Takeaway 4.2
What Types of Plans Do Managers Use?

ANSWERS TO COME

- Managers use short-range and long-range plans.
- Managers use strategic and operational plans.
- Organizational policies and procedures are plans.
- Budgets are plans that commit resources to activities.

MANAGERS FACE DIFFERENT PLANNING CHALLENGES IN THE FLOW AND PACE OF activities in organizations. In some cases, the planning environment is stable and predictable. In others, it is more dynamic and uncertain. To meet these different needs, managers rely on a variety of plans.

MANAGERS USE SHORT-RANGE AND LONG-RANGE PLANS.

We live and work in a fast-paced world where planning horizons are becoming compressed. We now talk about planning in Internet time, where businesses are continually changing and updating plans. Even most top managers would likely agree that *long*-range planning is becoming shorter and shorter. A reasonable rule of thumb in this context is that **short-range plans** cover a year or less, whereas **long-range plans** look ahead three or more years into the future.[9]

Quite frankly, the advent of Internet time and shorter planning horizons might be an advantage for many of us. Management researcher Elliot Jaques found that very few people have the capacity to think long term.[10] As shown in the figure, he believes that most of us work comfortably with only three-month time spans; some can think about a year into the future; only about one person in several million can handle a 20-year time frame.

Do Jaques's conclusions match your experience? And if we accept his findings, what are their implications for managers and career development? Although a team leader's planning challenges may rest mainly in the weekly or monthly range, a chief executive needs to have a vision extending at least some years into the future. Career progress to higher management levels still requires the conceptual skills to work well with longer-range time frames.[11]

Short-range plans usually cover a year or less.

Long-range plans usually cover three years or more.

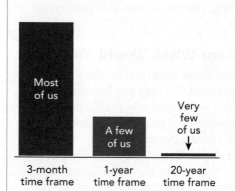

| 3-month time frame | 1-year time frame | 20-year time frame |

MANAGERS USE STRATEGIC AND OPERATIONAL PLANS.

When planning for the organization as a whole or a major component, the focus is on **strategic plans**. These longer-term plans set broad and comprehensive directions for an organization. Well-crafted strategic plans create a framework for allocating resources for best long-term performance impact. They take a **vision** that clarifies the purpose of the organization and what it hopes to be in the future and set out the ways to turn that vision into reality.

When a sports team enters a game, it typically does so with a "strategy." Most often this strategy is set by the head coach in conjunction with assistants. The goal is clear: Win the game! But as the game unfolds, a variety of situations arise that require adjustments and responses to solve problems or exploit opportunities. They call for "tactics" that deal with the situation at hand while advancing the overall strategy for winning against the competition. These tactics are often decided on by assistant coaches, perhaps in consultation with the head coach.

The same logic holds true for organizations. **Operational plans**, also called **tactical plans**, are developed to implement strategic plans. They are shorter-term and step-by-step means for putting the strategies into action. In the sports context, you might think of tactical plans as involving the use of "special teams" plans or as "special plays" designed to meet a particular threat or opportunity. In business, tactical plans often take the form of **functional plans**

A **strategic plan** identifies long-term directions for the organization.

A **vision** clarifies the purpose of the organization and expresses what it hopes to be in the future.

An **operational plan** or **tactical plan** sets out ways to implement a strategic plan.

A **functional plan** identifies how different parts of an enterprise will contribute to accomplishing strategic plans.

QUICK CASE

New Dads Say It's Time for Paternity Leave

KidStock/Getty Images

As the Human Resources Director for a medium-sized business with 800 employees, you've been asked by the CEO to draft a paternity leave policy. New moms get up to 8 weeks off with pay and have the option of taking another 4 weeks off without pay. New dads would like official time off but worry about negative consequences for their careers and job security. At present they are informally allowed to take up to a week off, and many do. It's your task to not only develop the new policy on paternity leave, but also make sure it is accepted by all stakeholders.

WHAT DO YOU DO?

How will you go about getting good information to make this paternity leave policy? Who will you include in the process? How will you make sure the new policy is a good for both the organization and its employees? What will you do to make sure new dads take advantage of the new policy and aren't afraid to use it because of job and career concerns?

---

that indicate how different parts of the enterprise will contribute to the overall strategy. Such functional plans might include things like:

- *Financial plans* deal with money required to support various operations.
- *Facilities plans* deal with facilities development and work layouts.
- *Marketing plans* deal with the requirements of selling and distributing goods or services.
- *Human resource plans* deal with the recruitment, selection, and placement of people into various jobs.
- *Production plans* deal with the methods and technology needed by people in their work.

ORGANIZATIONAL POLICIES AND PROCEDURES ARE PLANS.

In addition to strategic and operational plans, organizations also need plans that provide members with day-to-day guidance on such things as attendance, hiring practices, ethical behavior, privacy, trade secrets, and more. This is often provided in the form of organizational policies and procedures.

A **policy** communicates broad guidelines for making decisions and taking action in specific circumstances. Common human resource policies address such matters as employee hiring, termination, performance appraisals, pay increases, promotions, discipline, and civility. Consider the issue of sexual harassment. How should individual behavior be guided? A sample sexual harassment policy states: "Sexual harassment is specifically prohibited by this organization. Any employee found to have violated the policy against sexual harassment will be subject to immediate and appropriate disciplinary action including but not limited to possible suspension or termination."

> A **policy** is a standing plan that communicates broad guidelines for decisions and action.

Procedures, or *rules*, describe exactly what actions to take in specific situations. They are often found in employee handbooks or manuals as SOPs (standard operating procedures). Whereas a policy sets broad guidelines, procedures define specific actions to be taken. A sexual harassment policy, for example, should be backed up with procedures that spell out how to file a sexual harassment complaint, as well as the steps through which any complaint will be handled.[12]

> A **procedure** or rule precisely describes actions to take in specific situations.

BUDGETS ARE PLANS THAT COMMIT RESOURCES TO ACTIVITIES.

A **budget** is a plan that commits resources to activities, programs, or projects. It is a powerful tool that allocates scarce resources among multiple and often competing uses. Managers

> A **budget** is a plan that commits resources to projects or activities.

FACTS TO CONSIDER

Policies on Office Romances Vary Widely

Allison Michael Orenstein/Getty Images

A former CEO of Boeing was asked to resign by the firm's board after his relationship with a female executive became public. But, employer policies on office relationships vary.

• 80% prohibit relationships between supervisors and subordinates.

• 24% prohibit relationships among persons in the same department.

• 13% prohibit relationships among persons who have the same supervisor.

• 5% have no restrictions on office romances.

• New trend—"love contracts," where employees pledge that their romantic relationships in the office won't interfere with their work.

WHAT'S YOUR TAKE?

Do you know anyone who has been involved in an office relationship? What are your thoughts? Is this an area that employers should be regulating, or should office romance be left to the best judgments of those involved?

---

typically negotiate with their bosses to obtain budgets that support the needs of their work units or teams. They are also expected to achieve performance objectives while keeping within their budgets.

Managers deal with and use various types of budgets. *Financial budgets* project cash flows and expenditures. *Operating budgets* plot anticipated sales or revenues against expenses. *Nonmonetary budgets* allocate resources such as labor, equipment, and space. A *fixed budget* allocates a fixed amount of resources for a specific purpose, such as $50,000 for equipment purchases in a year. A *flexible budget* allows resources to vary in proportion with various levels of activity, such as monies to hire temporary workers when workloads exceed certain levels.

All budgets play important roles in organizations by linking planned activities with the resources needed to accomplish them. But budgets can also get out of control. Sometimes, perhaps much too often, they creep higher and higher without getting enough critical scrutiny. If in doubt, just tune in to the latest debates over local and national government budgets.

A **zero-based budget** allocates resources as if each budget was brand new.

One of the most common budgeting problems is that resource allocations are rolled over from one time period to the next without any real performance review. A **zero-based budget** deals with this problem by approaching each budget period as if it were brand new. No guarantee exists for renewing any past funding. Instead, all proposals compete with a fresh start for available resources. This helps eliminate waste by making sure scarce resources are not spent on unproductive, outdated, or low-priority activities.

Apple Plans for a Rebirth of "Made in USA"

Paul Sakuma/AP

There was a time early in Apple's life when all Mac computers were made at U.S. factories. Then the strategy shifted to outsourcing with foreign suppliers and assembly plants. But problems with worker safety and employments conditions in some of its contractors' plants created uncomfortable publicity. Political pressures to bring jobs home added more fuel to the outsourcing fires. Now Apple CEO Tim Cook—considered the genius behind the firm's global supply chains—is planning to shift at least some of that foreign production of Macs back to American soil. It won't be easy, and the plan is not a guaranteed success, say analysts. Labor costs, worker skills, and even Federal Trade Commission rules on importing parts and qualifying for "Made in USA" labeling all add risk to the move.

STUDYGUIDE

Takeaway 4.2
What Types of Plans Do Managers Use?

Terms to Define

Budget	Operational (tactical) plan	Procedure	Vision
Functional plan		Short-range plan	Zero-based budget
Long-range plan	Policy	Strategic plan	

Rapid Review

- Short-range plans tend to cover a year or less, whereas long-range plans extend out to three years or more.
- Strategic plans set critical long-range directions; operational plans are designed to support and help implement strategic plans.
- Policies, such as a sexual harassment policy, are plans that set guidelines for the behavior of organizational members.
- Procedures are plans that describe actions to take in specific situations, such as how to report a sexual harassment complaint.
- Budgets are plans that allocate resources to activities or projects.
- A zero-based budget allocates resources as if each new budget period is brand new; no "rollover" resource allocations are allowed without new justifications.

Questions for Discussion

1. Is there any need for long-range plans in today's fast-moving environment?
2. What types of policies do you believe are essential for any organization?
3. Are there any possible disadvantages to zero-based budgeting?

Be Sure You Can

- **differentiate** short-range and long-range plans
- **differentiate** strategic and operational plans
- **explain** how strategic and operational plans complement one another
- **differentiate** policies and procedures, and give examples of each
- **explain** the benefits of a zero-based budget

Career Situation: What Would You Do?

One of the persons under your supervision has contacted you about a "possible" sexual harassment complaint against a co-worker. But, she says that the organization's procedures are not clear. You also decide they're not clear and take the matter to your boss. He tells you to draft a set of procedures that can be taken to top management for approval. What procedures will you recommend so that future sexual harassment complaints can be dealt with in a fair manner?

Takeaway 4.3
What Are Some Useful Planning Tools and Techniques?

ANSWERS TO COME

- Forecasting tries to predict the future.
- Contingency planning creates backup plans for when things go wrong.
- Scenario planning crafts plans for alternative future conditions.
- Benchmarking identifies best practices used by others.
- Goal setting aligns plans and activities.
- Goals can have downsides and must be well managed.
- Participatory planning builds implementation capacities.

It's easy to recognize and talk about key concerns of the day—food security, income inequality, climate change, water shortages, social strife and conflict, pandemics, cyber security, and more. Why, then, do we seem to have such a hard time in our personal lives, in organizations, and in governments getting on top of the issues and making constructive plans to deal with them? The risks of computer viruses and hacking, for example, are well known. So, how is it that a major corporation such as Sony Pictures would have its computer systems shut down and its film files and employee data stolen by hackers? All the information and signals were available to Sony's decision makers, but where was the planning?

FORECASTING TRIES TO PREDICT THE FUTURE.

Forecasting attempts to predict the future.

Forecasting is the process of predicting what will happen in the future. Periodicals such as *Bloomberg Business, Fortune*, and *The Economist* regularly report forecasts of industry conditions, interest rates, unemployment trends, and national economies, among other issues.[13] Some rely on qualitative forecasting, which uses expert opinions to predict the future. Others involve quantitative forecasting, which uses mathematical models and statistical analysis of historical data and surveys.

Most plans involve forecasts of some sort. But, any forecast should be used with caution. Forecasts are planning aids, not planning substitutes. It is said that a music agent once told Elvis Presley: "You ought to go back to driving a truck because you ain't going nowhere." That's the problem with forecasts. They always rely on human judgment, and that judgment can be wrong.

CONTINGENCY PLANNING CREATES BACKUP PLANS FOR WHEN THINGS GO WRONG.

Of course things often go wrong. It is highly unlikely that any plan will ever be perfect. But picture this scene. A golfer is striding down the golf course with an iron in each hand. The one in her right hand is "the plan"; the one in her left is the "backup plan." Which club she uses will depend on how the ball lies on the fairway. One of any professional golfer's greatest strengths is being able to adjust to the situation by putting the right club to work in the circumstances at hand.

Planning in our work and personal affairs is often like that of the golfer. By definition, planning involves thinking ahead. But the more uncertain the environment, the more likely one's original assumptions, forecasts, and intentions are to prove inadequate or wrong. And when they do, the best managers and organizations have alternative plans ready to go.

Contingency planning identifies alternative courses of action that can be implemented to meet the needs of changing circumstances. A really good contingency plan will contain "trigger points" for activating preselected alternatives. This is really an indispensable planning tool. But, it's surprising how many organizations lack good contingency plans to deal with unexpected events.

Poor contingency planning was very much in the news when debates raged over how BP managed the disastrous *Deepwater Horizon* oil spill in the Gulf of Mexico. Everyone from the public at large to U.S. lawmakers to oil industry experts criticized BP not only for failing to contain the spill quickly, but also for failing to anticipate and have contingency plans in place to handle such a crisis.

A BP spokesperson initially said—"You have here an unprecedented event . . . the unthinkable has become thinkable and the whole industry will be asking questions of itself."

An oil industry expert responded—"There should be a technology that is preexisting and ready to deploy at the drop of a hat . . . it shouldn't have to be designed and fabricated now, from scratch."

Former BP CEO Tony Hayward finally admitted—"There are some capabilities that we could have available to deploy instantly, rather than creating as we go."[14]

The lesson in the BP example is hard-earned but very clear. Contingency planning can't prevent crises from occurring. But when things do go wrong, there's nothing better to have in place than good contingency plans.

SCENARIO PLANNING CRAFTS PLANS FOR ALTERNATIVE FUTURE CONDITIONS.

A long-term version of contingency planning, called **scenario planning**, identifies several alternative future scenarios. Managers then make plans to deal with each, so they will be better prepared for whatever occurs.[15] In this sense, scenario planning forces them to really think far ahead.

This approach was developed years ago at Royal Dutch/Shell, when top managers asked themselves a perplexing question: "What will Shell do after its oil supplies run out?" Although recognizing that scenario planning can never be inclusive of all future possibilities, a Shell executive once said that it helps "condition the organization to think" and better prepare for "future shocks."[16]

Shell uses scenario planning to tackle such issues as climate change, sustainable development, fossil-fuel alternatives, human rights, and biodiversity. Most typically it involves descriptions of "worst cases" and "best cases." In respect to oil supplies, for example, a worst-case scenario might be that global conflict and devastating effects on the natural environment occur as nations jockey with one another to secure increasingly scarce supplies of oil and other natural resources. A best-case scenario might be that governments work together to find pathways that take care of everyone's resource needs while supporting the sustainability of global resources.

BENCHMARKING IDENTIFIES BEST PRACTICES USED BY OTHERS.

All too often managers become too comfortable with the ways things are going. They fall into the complacency trap discussed earlier, letting habits and overconfidence trick them into believing the past is a good indicator of the future. Planning helps us deal with such tendencies by challenging the status quo and reminding us not to always accept things as they are. One way to do this is through **benchmarking**, a planning technique that makes use of external comparisons to better evaluate current performance.[17]

Contingency planning identifies alternative courses of action to take when things go wrong.

Scenario planning identifies alternative future scenarios and makes plans to deal with each.

Benchmarking uses external comparisons to gain insights for planning.

ETHICS CHECK

E-Waste Graveyards Offer Easy Way Out

budgetstockphoto/iStockphoto

"Give me a plan," says the boss. "We need to get rid of our electronic waste."

This isn't an uncommon problem. Have you ever considered where your old cell phone or computer monitor ends up when discarded in favor of a new one? Rapid changes in technology, effective advertising, and planned or built-in product obsolescence—designing a product with a limited useful life so that it becomes obsolete—have fueled what may be called an "e-waste monster."

Lots of e-waste ends up in less-developed countries in Asia and Africa. The waste arrives by sea container or barge and goes into huge dumps. Local laborers, perhaps including children, disassemble the waste products under unsafe conditions and using methods like open-air incineration and acid baths. Their goal is to salvage valuable metals such as platinum, silver, and gold and base metals like copper, iron, and aluminum.

Exporting to e-waste graveyards overseas may be less expensive than dealing with the waste at home, but what are the adverse environmental and health effects? What is the harm to people and planet? It isn't a stretch to say that the workers often inhale toxic fumes; nearby streams can be polluted with runoff waste; and even the streets and living areas of the workers become cluttered with electronic debris. Monitors or TVs with cathode-ray tubes contain up to four pounds of toxic lead. Disposed of improperly, it can cause harm to health and environment. Hazardous substances such as lead, cadmium, mercury, and chromium are part of many electronics. When released, they can pollute groundwater and cause neurological damage in children.

It can be expensive to properly dispose of electronic waste. Regulatory controls or laws on its export tend to be light. Going offshore with e-waste may be cheap and easy. But, is it the correct thing to do?

YOUR DECISION?

As countries become profitable hosts for e-waste, their governments may look the other way when it comes to environmental and human costs. Some even argue that e-waste business helps with a country's development. Whose responsibility is it to deal with the adverse consequences of e-waste disposal? Is it just a local matter? Do the originating country and consumer have obligations as well? If a manager gives the directive to "ship the waste overseas" is this acceptable business practice?

Best practices are methods that lead to superior performance.

Managers use benchmarking to discover what other people and organizations are doing well and plan how to incorporate these ideas into their own operations. They search for **best practices** inside and outside the organization and among competitors and noncompetitors alike. These are things that others are doing and that help them to achieve superior performance. As a planning tool, benchmarking is basically a way of learning from the successes of others. There's little doubt that sports stars benchmark one another; scientists and scholars do it; executives and managers do it. Could you be doing it, too?

Many top firms make good use of best practices benchmarks. Xerox, for example, has benchmarked L. L. Bean's warehousing and distribution methods, Ford's plant layouts, and American Express's billing and collections. In building its "world car," the Fiesta, Ford benchmarked BMW's 3 series. James D. Farley, Ford's global marketing head says: "The ubiquity of the 3 series engenders trust in every part of the world, and its design always has a strong point of view."[18] And in the fast-moving apparel industry, the Spanish retailer Zara has become a benchmark for both worried competitors and others outside the industry.[19] Zara is praised for excellence in affordable "fast-fashion." The firm's design and manufacturing systems allow it to get new fashions from design to stores in 2 weeks, whereas competitors may take months. Zara produces only in small batches that sell out and create impressions of scarcity. Shoppers at Zara know they have to buy now because an item will not be replaced, whereas at competitors, shoppers often wait for sales and inventory clearance bargains.

GOAL SETTING ALIGNS PLANS AND ACTIVITIES.

In the dynamic and highly competitive technology industry, CEO T. J. Rodgers of Cypress Semiconductor Corp. supports a planning system where employees work with clear and quantified work goals that they help set. He believes the system helps people find problems before they interfere with performance. Says Rodgers: "Managers monitor the goals, look for problems, and expect people who fall behind to ask for help before they lose control of or damage a major project."[20]

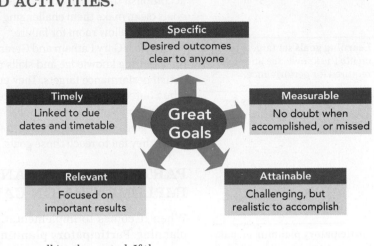

Although Rodgers makes us aware of the importance of goal setting in management, he may make it look too easy. Just how goals are set can make a big difference in whether they work well or poorly to point people in the right directions and make sure plans are well implemented. If they are to have the desired effects, goals and objectives have to be good ones; they should push us to achieve substantial, not trivial, things. Jack Welch, former CEO of GE, believed in **stretch goals**—performance targets that we have to work extra hard and really stretch to reach.[21] Would you agree that stretch goals as shown here can add real strength to the planning process, for organizations and for individuals?

Stretch goals are performance targets that we have to work extra hard and stretch to reach.

Even when individual goals are well set as part of a plan, managers must still make sure that the goals and plan for one person or work unit help accomplish the goals of the organization as a whole. It's always important to align goals from one level to the next so that the right things happen at the right times throughout an organization. Goals set anywhere in the organization should ideally help advance its overall mission or purpose. Strategic goals set by top management should cascade down the organization to become goals and objectives for lower levels. Ideally, goals link together across levels in a consistent "means–end" fashion as suggested earlier in Figure 4.2. When a hierarchy of goals and objectives is well defined through good planning, this helps improve coordination among the multiple tasks, components, and levels of work in organizations.

GOALS CAN HAVE DOWNSIDES AND MUST BE WELL MANAGED.

SCANDAL: The Ohio state auditor charged that teachers and principals in the Columbus school district were pressured to change student test scores and attendance rosters in order to improve the district's performance scorecard on goals that affected state funding.[22]

SCANDAL: An internal audit of the U.S. Veterans Affairs system charged that managers covered up long appointment waiting times and used bogus lists in order meet tight scheduling goals and receive personal bonuses. More than 120,000 veterans failed to get care, and at least 23 died awaiting treatment.[23]

It isn't enough to set goals for you and for others; the goals and the quest for their accomplishment must also be well managed. Just look at the scandals reported above. They show that goals that can have a "dark" as well as positive side.[24] Stretch goals are one thing, but when the "stretch" becomes unrealistic, bad things can happen. The unrealistic goals tied to performance rewards in the prior scandals contributed to ethics and performance failures. Teachers and principals—not the students—became the cheaters in the Ohio school district. At the VA, auditors said, "Pressures were placed on schedulers to utilize unofficial lists or engage in inappropriate practices in order to make waiting times appear more favorable."[25]

Goals that are set unrealistically high can have negative consequences that include excessive stress for the goal seeker, poor performance results, and possible unethical or illegal behavior. This is especially the case when people are expected to meet high goals over and over again, and when those striving to meet high goals don't have the support needed to accomplish them.[26] Good management of goal setting helps to avoid such problems—keep goals clear, make them challenging but attainable, allow participation, set and discuss goals frequently, allow room for failure.[27]

Scholars Gary Latham and Gerard Seijts also distinguish between **learning goals** focused on acquiring knowledge and skills necessary for performance, and **outcome goals** that set actual performance targets. They point out that undesirable effects of goal setting are likely when outcome goals are emphasized at the expense of learning goals prerequisite to them. Latham and Seijts say: "It is foolish and even immoral for organizations to assign employees stretch goals without equipping them with the resources to succeed—and still punish them when they fail to reach those goals."[28]

> **Learning goals** set targets to create the knowledge and skills required for performance.

> **Outcome goals** set targets for actual performance results.

PARTICIPATORY PLANNING BUILDS IMPLEMENTATION CAPACITIES.

When it comes to implementation, participation can be a very important word in planning. **Participatory planning**, as shown in **Figure 4.3**, includes in all steps of the process those people whose ideas and inputs can benefit the plans and whose support is needed for implementation. And, it unlocks the advantages of group decision making.

> **Participatory planning** includes the persons who will be affected by plans and/or who will be asked to implement them.

Participatory planning can increase the creativity and information available, it can increase understanding and acceptance of plans, and it can build stronger commitments to a plan's success. When 7-Eleven executives planned for new upscale products and services, such as selling fancy meals-to-go, they learned this lesson the hard way. Although their ideas sounded good at the top, franchise owners and managers disagreed. Their resistance taught the executives the value of taking time to involve lower levels in planning new directions for the stores.[29]

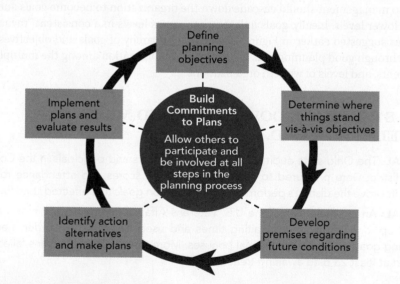

FIGURE 4.3 How Do Participation and Involvement Help Build Commitments to Plans?

Any plan needs the efforts and support of many people to make it work. It is easier and more likely to get this commitment when the people responsible for implementation have had the opportunity to participate in developing the plans in the first place. When managers use participatory planning and allow others to become involved in the planning process, it leads to better plans, a deeper understanding of the plans, and a strengthened commitment to fully implementing the plans.

STUDYGUIDE

Takeaway 4.3
What Are Some Useful Planning Tools and Techniques?

Terms to Define

Benchmarking	Forecasting	Participatory planning	Stretch goals
Best practices	Learning goals	Scenario planning	
Contingency planning	Outcome goals		

Rapid Review

- Forecasting, which attempts to predict what might happen in the future, is a planning aid but not a planning substitute.
- Contingency planning identifies alternative courses of action to implement if and when circumstances change and an existing plan fails.
- Scenario planning analyzes the implications of alternative versions of the future.
- Benchmarking utilizes external comparisons to identify best practices that could become planning targets.
- Participation and involvement open the planning process to valuable inputs from people whose efforts are essential to the effective implementation of plans.

Questions for Discussion

1. If forecasting is going to be imperfect, why bother with it?
2. Shouldn't all planning provide for contingency plans?
3. Are stretch goals a good fit for today's generation of college students when they enter the workplace?

Be Sure You Can

- **differentiate** among forecasting, contingency planning, scenario planning, and benchmarking
- **explain** the importance of contingency planning
- **describe** the benefits of participatory planning as a special case of group decision making

Career Situation: What Would You Do?

As CEO you've decided to hire a consulting firm to help write a strategic plan for your organization. The plan is important, but you are worried about getting "buy-in" from all members, not just those at the top. What guidelines will you give the consultants so that they come up with a solid strategic plan that has strong commitments to its implementation by all members of your organization?

TEST PREP 4

Answers to Test Prep questions can be found at the back of the book.

Multiple-Choice Questions

1. Planning is best described as the process of _____ and _____.
   - (a) developing premises about the future; evaluating them
   - (b) measuring results; taking corrective action
   - (c) measuring past performance; targeting future performance
   - (d) setting objectives; deciding how to accomplish them

2. The benefits of planning often include _____.
   - (a) improved focus
   - (b) less need for controlling
   - (c) more accurate forecasts
   - (d) guaranteed success

3. The first step in the planning process is to _____.
   - (a) decide how to get where you want to go
   - (b) define your objectives
   - (c) identify possible future conditions or scenarios
   - (d) act quickly to take advantage of opportunities

4. As a first step to help implement her firm's strategic plans, the CEO of a business firm would want marketing, manufacturing, and finance executives to develop clear and appropriate _____.
   - (a) procedures
   - (b) operational plans
   - (c) zero-based budgets
   - (d) forecasts

5. _____ planning identifies alternative courses of action that can be quickly taken if problems occur with the original plan.
   - (a) Benchmark
   - (b) Participatory
   - (c) Staff
   - (d) Contingency

6. Having a clear sexual harassment policy won't help an organization much unless it is accompanied by clear _____ that let all members know for sure how it will be implemented.
   - (a) contingencies
   - (b) benchmarks
   - (c) procedures
   - (d) budgets

7. When a manager is asked to justify a new budget proposal on the basis of projected activities rather than as an incremental adjustment to the prior year's budget, this is an example of _____.
   - (a) zero-based budgeting
   - (b) strategic planning
   - (c) operational planning
   - (d) contingency planning

8. One of the expected benefits of participatory planning is _____.
   - (a) faster planning
   - (b) less need for forecasting
   - (c) greater attention to contingencies
   - (d) more commitment to implementation

9. When managers use benchmarking in the planning process, they usually try to _____.
   - (a) set up flexible budgets
   - (b) identify best practices used by others
   - (c) find the most accurate forecasts that are available
   - (d) use expert staff planners to set objectives

10. In a hierarchy of objectives, plans at lower levels are supposed to act as _____ for accomplishing higher-level plans.
    - (a) means
    - (b) ends
    - (c) scenarios
    - (d) benchmarks

11. If a team leader wants to tap the advantages of participatory planning, what type of decision-making method should he or she use?
    - (a) Authority
    - (b) Quantitative
    - (c) Group
    - (d) Zero-based

12. From a time management perspective, which manager is likely to be in best control of his or her time? One who _____.
    - (a) tries to never say "no" to requests from others
    - (b) works on the most important things first
    - (c) immediately responds to instant messages
    - (d) always has "an open office door"

13. A marketing plan in a business firm would most likely deal with _____.
    - (a) production methods and technologies
    - (b) money and capital investments
    - (c) facilities and workforce recruiting
    - (d) sales and product distribution

14. The best planning goals or objectives would have which of the following characteristics?
    - (a) Easy enough so that no one fails to reach them
    - (b) Realistic and possible to achieve, while still challenging
    - (c) Open ended, with no clear end point identified
    - (d) No set timetable or due dates

15. The planning process isn't complete until _____.
    - (a) future conditions have been identified
    - (b) stretch goals have been set
    - (c) plans are implemented and results evaluated
    - (d) budgets commit resources to plans

Short-Response Questions

16. List the five steps in the planning process, and give examples of each.

17. How does planning facilitate controlling?

18. What is the difference between contingency planning and scenario planning?

19. Why is participation good for the planning process?

Integration and Application Question

20. My friends Curt and Rich own a local bookstore. They are very interested in making plans for improving the store and better dealing with competition from the other bookstores that serve college students in our town. I once heard Curt saying to Rich: "We should be benchmarking what some of the successful coffee shops, restaurants, and novelty stores are doing." Rich replied: "I don't see why; we should only be interested in bookstores. Why don't we study the local competition and even look at what the best bookstores are doing in the big cities?"

    Questions: Who is right, Curt or Rich? If you were hired as a planning consultant to them, what would you suggest as the best way to utilize benchmarking as a planning technique to improve their bookstore? And, how would you use the planning process to help Curt and Rich come to a point of agreement on the best way forward for their bookstore?

Steps for Further Learning

BUILD MARKETABLE SKILLS • **DO** A CASE ANALYSIS • **GET** AND STAY INFORMED

BUILD MARKETABLE SKILLS.

EARN BIG CAREER PAYOFFS!

Don't miss these opportunities in the SKILL-BUILDING PORTFOLIO

SELF-ASSESSMENT 4:
Time Management Profile
Time does count, but who really counts time? . . . check your time management skills.

CLASS EXERCISE 4:
The Future Workplace
Good jobs are hard to find . . . look ahead and prepare for tomorrow's opportunities.

TEAM PROJECT 4:
Personal Career Planning
Your career planning should have started yesterday . . . it's not too late to build a plan for success.

Many learning resources are found at the end of the book and online within **WileyPLUS Learning Space.**

Practice Critical Thinking—Complete the CHAPTER 4 CASE

CASE SNAPSHOT: Nordstrom—"High Touch" with "High Tech"

A trip to the local department store isn't always a turn on. But a trip to Nordstrom's . . . well, that's usually a trip worth taking. How has Nordstrom managed to stay fashionable and profitable in an economy of recession-weary consumers? How does it keep up with, or ahead of, changing fashion trends and intense competition among retailers? The fourth generation of family members running this business has brought time-honored retail practices into a new era. But in many ways, it's just the basics with an added dash of technology that makes the difference. Nordstrom provides a quality customer experience via personalized service, a compelling merchandise offering, a pleasant shopping environment, and tight inventory management. Acute attention to detail and well-laid plans have allowed the company to navigate difficult times better than many rivals.

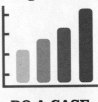

DO A CASE ANALYSIS.

STRENGTHEN YOUR CRITICAL THINKING!

MANAGER'S LIBRARY SELECTION
Read for Insights and Wisdom
***Analytics at Work: Smarter Decisions, Better Results* (2010, Harvard Business Press) by Thomas Davenport, Jeanne Harris, and Robert Morison**

Authors Thomas Davenport, Jeanne Harris, and Robert Morison argue that organizations can improve their strategies by making better use of available information to guide decisions. A key point is that organizations have access to vast amounts of data but often fail to leverage it for competitive gain. Analytical approaches to decision making can yield smarter choices with improved results. And, all aspects of organizations are ripe for analytic improvement. Customer relationships can be enhanced by segmenting types, understanding preferences, predicting desires, and identifying loyal or departing patrons. Supply chains can be streamlined by optimizing inventory levels, delivery routes, and production schedules. Human resources can be improved by hiring those likely to stay and predicting those prone to depart.

GET AND STAY INFORMED.

MAKE YOURSELF VALUABLE!

Analytics are great tools, and we need to get better at using them. The authors say organizations are more intelligent when managers use facts, and not feelings, to guide decisions. Face the facts—those gut feelings could be misleading you.

REFLECT AND REACT How might a business that you are familiar with use data and analytics to plan improvements in customer relationship management? For example, how might it determine which products are most popular, most profitable, or trending toward less popular? How might it optimize inventory levels or hire better workers? And by the way, do you also agree that better analytics can help improve personal planning?

"Self-awareness is crucial . . . but when it comes to understanding how others see us, many of us are in the dark . . . leads to bad decisions and spoiled relationships."

Zhan min-Imaginechina/AP

Controls and Control Systems

What Gets Measured Happens

Management Live
Mastering Self-Control for Life Success

Flickr RF/Getty

The lesson begins with the marshmallow test. Picture this. Several 4- to 6-year-old children are at a table, each with two marshmallows in front of them. A researcher tells them they can eat one now or get both if they hold off eating for 5 minutes. What would you do? About one third of the kids delayed gratification long enough to get two marshmallows instead of one. Forty years later these "high self-control" students were found to have entered college with higher SATs, graduated with higher averages, and earned more money than their "quick gratification" counterparts.

HOW ABOUT IT?

How would you do on the marshmallow test? To what extent is self-control a personal strength . . . or a weakness? What can you do to make it a real personal asset going forward in life?

WHAT'S INSIDE

ETHICS CHECK
Boss wants staff to lose a few pounds

FACTS TO CONSIDER
Everyday distractions can be goal killers

HOT TOPIC
Should parents pay for children's grades?

QUICK CASE
Flexible work hour policy starting to be abused

YOUR CHAPTER 5 TAKEAWAYS

1. Understand how and why managers use the control process.

2. Identify types of controls used by managers.

3. Describe useful control tools and techniques.

Takeaway 5.1
How and Why Do Managers Use the Control Process?

ANSWERS TO COME

- Controlling is one of the four functions of management.
- Step 1—Control begins with objectives and standards.
- Step 2—Control measures actual performance.
- Step 3—Control compares results with objectives and standards.
- Step 4—Control takes corrective action as needed.

"KEEPING IN TOUCH" . . . "STAYING INFORMED" . . . "BEING IN CONTROL." These are important responsibilities for every manager. Yet "control" is a word like "power." If you aren't careful when and how the word is used, it leaves a negative connotation. But control plays a positive and necessary role in the management process. To have things "under control" is good; for things to be "out of control" is generally bad.[1] So, what happened at these well-known companies?[2]

> *Toyota*—Recalled more than 6 million vehicles to fix throttle problems. Toyota North America's president and COO Jim Lentz said: "I am truly sorry for the concern our recalls have caused, and want you to know we're doing everything we can—as fast as we can—to make things right. . . . We'll continue to do everything we can to meet—and exceed—your expectations and justify your continued trust in Toyota."

> *Lululemon*—Recalled black yoga pants and offered full refunds after customers discovered that they were see-through when worn. The cost to the firm was damaged reputation plus some $60 million in lost revenues. Lululemon's CEO Christine Day, since replaced, said: "The only way to test for the problem is to put the pants on and bend over."

CONTROLLING IS ONE OF THE FOUR FUNCTIONS OF MANAGEMENT.

Controlling is the process of measuring performance and taking action to ensure desired results.

Managers understand **controlling** as a process of measuring performance and taking action to ensure desired results. Its purpose is straightforward—to make sure that plans are achieved and that actual performance meets or surpasses objectives. As with any aspect of decision making, the foundation of control is information. Henry Schacht, former CEO of Cummins Engine Company, once discussed control in terms of what he called "friendly facts." "Facts that reinforce what you are doing are nice," he said, "because they help in terms of psychic reward. Facts that raise alarms are equally friendly, because they give you clues about how to respond, how to change, where to spend the resources."[3]

Just how does control fit in with the other management functions? Planning sets the directions. Organizing arranges people and resources for work. Leading inspires people toward their best efforts. And as shown in Figure 5.1, controlling sees to it that the right things happen, in the right way, and at the right time. If things go wrong, control helps get things back on track.

After-action review is a structured review of lessons learned and results accomplished through a completed project, task force assignment, or special operation.

Effective control offers the great opportunity of learning from experience. Consider, for example, the program of **after-action review** pioneered by the U.S. Army and now used in many other organization settings. It is a structured review of lessons learned and results accomplished through a completed project, task force assignment, or special operation. Participants answer questions such as: "What was the intent?" "What actually happened?" "What did we learn?"[4] The after-action review encourages everyone involved to take responsibility for his or her performance efforts and accomplishments.

Even though improving performance through learning is one of the great opportunities offered by the control process, the potential benefits are realized only when learning is translated into corrective actions. For example, after IBM executives learned that male attitudes were creating barriers to the success of female managers, they made male senior executives report annually on the progress of women managers in their divisions. This action substantially increased the percentage of women in IBM's senior management ranks.[5]

STEP 1—CONTROL BEGINS WITH OBJECTIVES AND STANDARDS.

The control process consists of the four steps shown in **Figure 5.2**. The process begins with setting performance objectives and standards for measuring them. It can't start any other way. This is the planning part: setting the performance objectives against which results can eventually be compared. Measurement standards are important, too. It isn't always easy to set them, but they are essential.

We often hear about earnings per share, sales growth, market shares, service or delivery time, and error rates as standards for measuring business performance. How about other types of organizations? When the Cleveland Symphony Orchestra wrestled with performance standards, the members weren't willing to rely on vague generalities like "we played well," "the audience seemed happy," and "not too many mistakes were made." Rather, they decided to track standing ovations, invitations to perform in other countries, and how often other orchestras copied their performance styles.[6]

Things like earnings per share for a business and standing ovations for a symphony are examples of **output standards**. They measure actual outcomes or work results. When Allstate Corporation launched a new diversity initiative, it created a "diversity index" to quantify performance on diversity issues. The standards included how well employees met the goals of bias-free customer service and how well managers met the firm's diversity expectations.[7] GE created measurement standards to track ethics compliance in its global workforce. Each business unit was required to report quarterly on how many of its members attended ethics training sessions and what percentage signed the firm's "Spirit and Letter" ethics guide.[8]

The control process also uses **input standards** to measure work efforts. These are helpful in situations where outputs are difficult or expensive to measure. Examples of input standards for a college professor might be having an orderly course syllabus, showing up at all class sessions, and returning exams and assignments in a timely fashion. Of course, as this example might suggest, measuring inputs doesn't mean that outputs, such as high-quality teaching and learning, are necessarily achieved. Other examples of input standards in the workplace include conformance with rules and procedures, efficiency in the use of resources, and work attendance or punctuality.

STEP 2—CONTROL MEASURES ACTUAL PERFORMANCE.

The second step in the control process is to measure actual performance. Accurate and timely measurement is essential to spot differences between what is really taking place and what was originally planned. Unless we are willing to measure, very little control is possible. But willingness to measure has its rewards. As the well-quoted adage states: What gets measured tends to happen.

FIGURE 5.1 Why Is Controlling So Important in the Management Process?

Controlling is one of the four management functions. It is the process of measuring performance—finding out how well you are doing, and taking action to ensure desired results—making sure results meet expectations. When controlling is done well, it sets a strong foundation for performance. Remember: What gets measured happens.

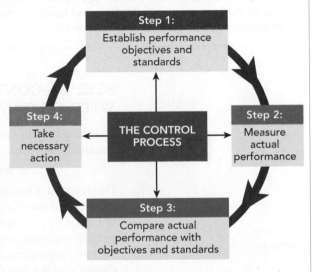

FIGURE 5.2 What Are the Four Steps in the Control Process?

The control process is straightforward: (1) set performance objectives and standards, (2) measure actual performance, (3) compare actual performance with objectives and standards, (4) take corrective action as needed. Although essential to management, these steps apply equally well to personal careers. Without career objectives, how do you know where you really want to go? How can you allocate time and other resources to take best advantage of opportunities? Without measurement, how can you assess how well you are doing and make adjustments to do better in the future?

An **output standard** measures performance results in terms of quantity, quality, cost, or time.

An **input standard** measures work efforts that go into a performance task.

FACTS TO CONSIDER

Distractions can be Goal Killers

Hiya Images/Corbis Corp.

Most of us work with good intentions. But when distractions hit, focus gets lost, plans fall by the wayside, and progress suffers. Whether it's chatting with co-workers, following social media, or tackling electronic in-boxes, interruptions are more plentiful than we might admit.

- Office workers get distracted as often as once every 3 minutes, and it takes an average of 23 minutes to refocus after a major interruption.
- Handling up to 100 electronic messages can kill up to half a workday.
- Facilitators of disruptions include open-plan office spaces, use of multiple electronic devices, and constant checking of social media and messaging windows.

Lacy Roberson, eBay's director of learning and organization development, calls the situation "an epidemic" and says it's hard for people to get their work done with all the interruptions and the stress they cause. The fight against disruptions causes some workers to start extra early or stay late to get their jobs done. Employers are starting to fight back and try to protect "real work" time.

"No devices" is a rule at some eBay meetings. Intel is experimenting with allowing workers blocks of "think time" where they don't answer messages or attend meetings. Abbot Laboratories is retraining workers to use the telephone rather than e-mail for many internal office communications.

WHAT'S YOUR TAKE?

How prone are you to letting distractions consume your time? Does this problem apply to your personal affairs and relationships, not just work? It's interesting that some employers are trying to step in and set policies that might minimize the negative impact of distractions, particularly electronic ones. Where's the self-control? Aren't there things we can all do to protect our time and keep our work and goals on track?

STEP 3—CONTROL COMPARES RESULTS WITH OBJECTIVES AND STANDARDS.

The third step in the control process is to compare actual results with objectives and standards. You might remember its implications by this **control equation**:

$$\text{Need for Action} = \text{Desired Performance} - \text{Actual Performance.}$$

When actual is less than desired, a performance threat or deficiency exists. When actual is more than desired, a performance opportunity exists. One important point to remember—the value of the control equation depends on having goals that clearly identify desired performance and measurements that clearly define actual performance.

Some organizations use *engineering comparisons* to identify desired performance. An example is UPS. The firm carefully measures the routes and routines of its drivers to establish the times expected for each delivery. When a delivery manifest is scanned as completed, the driver's time is registered in an electronic performance log closely monitored by supervisors. Some make use of *historical comparisons*. These use past experience as a basis for evaluating current performance. And, *relative comparisons* are also common. They benchmark performance against that being achieved by other people, work teams, or organizations.

STEP 4—CONTROL TAKES CORRECTIVE ACTION AS NEEDED.

The final step in the control process occurs when action is taken to address gaps between desired and actual performance. You might hear the term **management by exception** used in this regard. It is the practice of giving attention to high-priority situations that show the greatest need for action.

Management by exception focuses attention on differences between actual and desired performance.

Management by exception basically adds discipline to our use of the control equation by focusing attention not just on needs for action but also on the highest-priority needs for action. In this way it can save valuable time, energy, and other resources that might be spent addressing things of little or no importance while those of great importance get missed or delayed.

STUDYGUIDE

Takeaway 5.1
How and Why Do Managers Use the Control Process?

Terms to Define

After-action review	Controlling	Management by exception
Control equation	Input standards	Output standards

Rapid Review

- Controlling is the process of measuring performance and taking corrective action as needed.
- The control process begins when performance objectives and standards are set; both input standards for work efforts and output standards for work results can be used.
- The second step in control is to measure actual performance in the control process.
- The third step compares results with objectives and standards to determine the need for corrective action.
- The final step in the control process involves taking action to resolve problems and improve things in the future.
- The control equation states: Need for action = Desired performance − Actual performance.
- Management by exception focuses attention on the greatest need for action.

Questions for Discussion

1. What performance standards should guide a hospital emergency room or fire department?
2. Can one control performance equally well with input standards and output standards?
3. What are the possible downsides to management by exception?

Be Sure You Can

- **explain** the role of controlling in the management process
- **list** the steps in the control process
- **explain** how planning and controlling should work together in management
- **differentiate** output standards and input standards
- **state** the control equation
- **explain** management by exception

Career Situation: What Would You Do?

A work colleague comes to you and confides that she feels "adrift in her career" and "just can't get enthused about what she's doing anymore." Your take is that this might be a problem of self-management and personal control. How will you explain to her that using the steps in the management control process might help in better understanding and correcting her situation?

Takeaway 5.2
What Types of Controls Are Used by Managers?

ANSWERS TO COME

- Managers use feedforward, concurrent, and feedback controls.
- Managers use both internal and external controls.
- Managing by objectives helps integrate planning and controlling.

MANAGERS USE FEEDFORWARD, CONCURRENT, AND FEEDBACK CONTROLS.

It's helpful to view organizations and work teams as open systems that interact with their environments in a dynamic input-throughput-output cycle. **Figure 5.3** shows how each of these phases link with three types of managerial controls—feedforward, concurrent, and feedback.[9]

Feedforward control ensures clear directions and needed resources before the work begins.

Feedforward controls, also called *preliminary controls*, take place before work begins. Their goal is to prevent problems before they occur. This is a forward-thinking and proactive approach to control, one that we should all try to follow whenever we can. At fast food restaurants, for example, preliminary control of food ingredients plays an important role in quality programs. Suppliers—say of hamburger buns—produce them to exact specifications, covering everything from texture to uniformity of color.[10]

Concurrent control focuses on what happens during the work process.

Concurrent controls focus on what happens during the work process; they take place while people are doing their jobs. The goal is to solve problems as they occur. Sometimes called *steering controls*, they make sure that things are always going according to plan. The ever-present shift leaders at fast-food restaurants are a good example of how this happens through direct supervision. They constantly observe what is taking place, even while helping out with the work. They are trained to correct things on the spot. The question continually asked is: "What can we do to improve things right now?"

Feedback control takes place after completing an action.

Feedback controls, or *post-action controls*, take place after a job or project is completed. Think about your experiences as a student. Most course evaluation systems ask, "Was this a good learning experience?" only when the class is almost over. Think also about your experiences as a restaurant customer. Very often we're asked "Was everything all right?" when it's already time to pay the bill. And think of the electronic devices you buy. Probably the last question a cell phone maker asks before your device is shipped from the factory floor is, "Does it work?" Although such questions are asked in good faith, results for customers can be mixed.

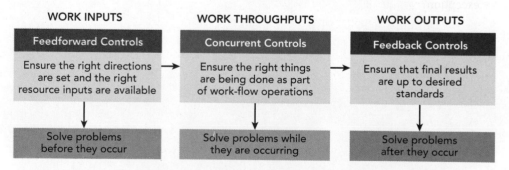

FIGURE 5.3 What Are the Differences Between Feedforward, Concurrent, and Feedback Controls?

Organizations are input-throughput-output systems, and each point in the cycle offers its own opportunities for control over performance. Feedforward controls try to solve problems before they occur, by making sure the production systems have high-quality inputs. Concurrent controls try to solve problems as they occur, by monitoring and correcting problems during the work process. Feedback controls try to correct problems after they have occurred and inform the system so that similar mistakes can be avoided in the future.

IF THEIR BEHAVIOR SPREADS TO OTHERS, IT WON'T BE LONG
BEFORE THE BOSS DISCONTINUES THE PROGRAM. . . .

QUICK CASE

Flexible Work Hour Policy Starting to Be Abused

Hero Images/Getty Images

Just over 2 years ago, your employer started a flexible working hours program. It allows workers (there are only 11 of you) to vary starting and ending times on a daily basis depending on your personal circumstances and preferences. The only requirements are that everyone be present from 9:30 AM to 3 PM (with time off for lunch) and that a full 8-hour workday be completed. The program has been a big hit, and staff morale quickly rose and stayed high . . . until now, when attitudes are starting to falter. The issue relates to two staff members who have started to abuse the policy. They are arrive well after 9:30 AM some days, they are often out the door right at 3 PM or a bit earlier, and they aren't shouldering a fair share of the workload. If their behavior spreads to others, it won't be long before the boss discontinues the program, although for now she seems unaware of what is happening.

WHAT DO YOU DO?

You don't want to lose the program. Is this an issue for the employees to discuss as a full team? Should you approach the two "abusers" on your own? Should you go to the boss with the information? In short, there are a range of things you can do, including nothing. So, what's it going to be?

Feedback controls may prevent you from receiving a defective cell phone; they don't help you much after taking a poorly organized college course or eating an unsatisfactory meal.

MANAGERS USE BOTH INTERNAL AND EXTERNAL CONTROLS.

We all exercise self-control in our daily lives; we do so in respect to managing our money, our relationships, our work–life balance, and more.[11] Managers and team leaders can take advantage of this human capacity by unlocking and setting up conditions that support **internal control**, or **self-control**, in the workplace. Management theorists have long recognized that people are ready and willing to exercise self-control in their work.[12] This potential is increased on a team, for example, when members have a clear sense of the team task and purpose, know their own and each other's goals, have task-relevant abilities, and are supported with the resources needed to do their jobs well.

> **Internal control**, or **self-control**, occurs as people exercise self-discipline in fulfilling job expectations.

In addition to encouraging and supporting internal control, managers and team leaders also use various forms of **external control** to structure situations so that things happen as planned.[13] The alternatives include bureaucratic or administrative control, clan control, and market control.

> **External control** occurs through direct supervision or administrative systems.

The logic of **bureaucratic control** is that authority, policies, procedures, job descriptions, budgets, and day-to-day supervision help make sure that people behave in ways consistent with organizational interests. For example, organizations typically have policies and procedures regarding sexual harassment. They are designed to make sure people behave toward one another respectfully and without sexual pressures or improprieties.

> **Bureaucratic control** influences behavior through authority, policies, procedures, job descriptions, budgets, and day-to-day supervision.

Whereas bureaucratic control emphasizes hierarchy and authority, **clan control** influences behavior through social norms and peer expectations. This is the power of collective identity. Persons who share values and identify strongly with each other tend to behave in ways that are consistent with one another's expectations. Just look around the typical college classroom and campus. You'll see clan control reflected in dress, language, and behavior as students tend to act in a way that is consistent with the expectations of those peers and groups they identify with. The same holds true in organizations where close-knit employees display common behavior patterns.

> **Clan control** influences behavior through social norms and peer expectations.

Market control is essentially the influence of competition on the behavior of organizations and their members. Business firms adjust products, pricing, promotions, and other practices in response to customer feedback and competitor moves. Think about the growing emphasis on "green" products and practices. When a firm such as Walmart starts to get good publicity from its expressed commitment to eventually power all its stores with renewable energy, the

> **Market control** is essentially the influence of market competition on the behavior of organizations and their members.

ETHICS CHECK

Boss Wants Staff to Lose a Few Pounds

Lucy Young/eyevine/Redux

Here's the deal. The CEO, a fitness addict, has decided that it's her responsibility to help everyone on staff to adopt a healthier lifestyle. She just sent an email to all with the following statements: "I have just subscribed to a health and wellness service for the entire company. A personal trainer will be on premises every Wednesday from 7:00 AM until 1:00 PM. The trainer will offer classes on nutrition and fitness, and will conduct sessions on Pilates and meditation. I've arranged for a large meeting room to be converted to a wellness facility. My expectation is that everyone will take advantage of this opportunity. In order to justify the expense, the trainer will hold individual conferences that set measurable wellness targets for

each of us. Progress in meeting these targets will be assessed at 3-month intervals. Individuals meeting or exceeding their targets each period will earn one additional personal leave day. Individuals who do not meet targets AND who have poor attendance records at the available activities will lose one personal leave day. I really hope this program works to the benefit of everyone. Remember: I'm part of the program, so my progress is on the line just as well as yours."

YOUR DECISION?

Is this CEO onto something that others should follow—making organization-supported wellness activities available and mandatory during work hours? Or, is the CEO going a step too far? Is wellness a personal issue that should not be part of workplace expectations? Can an employer's attempts to control staff wellness be justified ethically? Is this CEO operating within acceptable boundaries of management control?

---

effect is felt by its competitors.[14] They have to adjust practices to avoid giving up this public relations advantage to Walmart. In this sense, the time-worn phrase "Keeping up with the competition" is really another way of expressing the dynamics of market controls in action.

MANAGING BY OBJECTIVES HELPS INTEGRATE PLANNING AND CONTROLLING.

Managing by objectives is a
process of joint objective setting
between a superior and a
subordinate.

Managing by objectives is a technique that helps integrate planning and controlling within work teams. Often called MBO, it is a structured process of regular communication in which a team leader and a team member jointly set performance objectives and review accomplished results.[15] As **Figure 5.4** shows, the process creates an agreement between the two parties regarding performance objectives for a given time period, plans and resources for accomplishing them, standards for measuring results, and timetables for reviewing accomplishments.

When a team leader and team member are working together in a managing by objectives approach, it is helpful to consider two types of objectives that might be discussed.

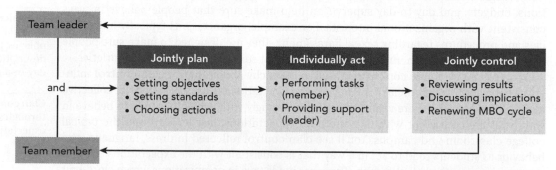

FIGURE 5.4 How Does Managing by Objectives Help to Integrate Planning and Controlling?
Managing by objectives is a structured process of communication between a supervisor and a subordinate, or team leader and team members. Planning is accomplished when both parties communicate to identify the subordinate's performance objectives. This is a form of participatory planning, and the goal is agreement. Informed by the objectives, the supervisor provides support for the subordinate as work progresses. Controlling is accomplished when the two parties meet at scheduled times to jointly discuss progress and results and make new plans setting future performance objectives.

Finding Quality at Whole Foods Markets
Employees Control the Tone for High Performance

Rebecca Cook/NewsCom

Whole Foods Market is a sweetheart of the supermarket industry. And the Austin, Texas, company's management philosophies leave no room for complacency. It competes in a $560 billion industry with profit margins described by one business writer as "slimmer than angel-hair pasta." The high-end retail grocer has survived a squeamish economy and cutbacks in discretionary consumer spending. You may wonder how. A good place to start is its culture of "open books, open doors, and open people."

Included in *Fortune* magazine's annual list of the "100 Best Companies to Work For" every year since the list began, Whole Foods is a benchmark for continuous improvement. The company's employees embrace its mission to promote a healthy lifestyle.

Co-CEO Walter Robb emphasizes that "employees are everything." One of the company's core values is team member happiness and excellence. Robb says, "That is something we believe in our hearts and something that guides our actions every day as a company. . . . If we're taking care of one another, the customers are going to feel that." The company's culture is one of inclusiveness so that employees feel that not only are they being taken care of, they have responsibilities to take care of one another.

FIND INSPIRATION

Whole Foods Market caps the salaries of top executives at 19 times the average worker pay every year. "It helps us keep faith with one another," says Robb, who emphasizes the importance of "all living by the same rules." He also criticizes traditional CEO salaries that can run to 400 times that of average worker pay. Although some companies struggle to find ways to improve performance, Whole Foods Market trusts its employees to deliver. Control for whole foods comes from inside the culture. Shouldn't this be the case in all organizations?

Improvement objectives focus on improving performance in a specific way. An example is "to reduce quality rejects in our apparel supply chain by 10%." **Personal development objectives** focus on expanding job knowledge or skills. An example is "to learn the latest version of our firm's customer relationship management software."

Whether we are talking about improvement or personal objectives, it's important to remember that the best objectives are specified as clearly as possible and associated with timetables. Ideally, this involves agreement on a *measurable end product*—for example, "to reduce building electricity costs by 15% by the end of the fiscal year." But achieving this level of measurement specificity can be hard to do in some cases. An alternative is to state performance objectives as *verifiable work activities*. For example, a team leader who wants to improve communications with team members (hard to measure) may commit to holding weekly team meetings (easy to measure). The justification is that the weekly meetings should be good for team communications.

You might already be wondering if managing by objectives can become too complicated a process.[16] The answer is "yes." Critics note that problems arise when objectives are linked too closely with pay, focused too much on easy accomplishments, involve excessive paperwork, and end up being dictated by supervisors.

It's also true that there are many advantages to making objectives a clear part of the ongoing conversation between managers and those reporting to them.[17] This keeps workers focused on the most important tasks and priorities. And, it keeps supervisors focused on the best ways to help them meet agreed-upon objectives. Because managing by objectives requires lots of communication, furthermore, it helps build good interpersonal relationships. By increasing participation in goal setting, it also builds trust and encourages self-management.[18]

Improvement objectives document intentions to improve performance in a specific way.

Personal development objectives document intentions to accomplish personal growth, such as expanded job knowledge or skills.

TIPS TO REMEMBER

How to Write a Good Performance Objective

- *Clarify the target*—be specific; clearly describe the key result to be accomplished.
- *Make it measurable*—state how the key result will be measured and documented.
- *Define the timetable*—identify a date by which the key result will be accomplished.
- *Avoid the impossible*—be realistic; don't promise what cannot be accomplished.
- *Add challenge*—be optimistic; build in "stretch" to make the accomplishment significant.
- *Don't overcomplicate*—stick to the essentials; write to fit a Post-it note reminder.

STUDYGUIDE

Takeaway 5.2
What Types of Controls Are Used by Managers?

Terms to Define

Bureaucratic control

Clan control

Concurrent control

External control

Feedback control

Feedforward control

Improvement objectives

Internal control

Managing by objectives

Market control

Personal development objectives

Self-control

Rapid Review

- Feedforward controls try to make sure things are set up right before work begins; concurrent controls make sure that things are being done correctly; feedback controls assess results after an action is completed.
- Internal control is self-control that occurs as people take personal responsibility for their work.
- External control is accomplished by use of bureaucratic, clan, and market control systems.
- Management by objectives is a process through which team leaders work with team members to "jointly" set performance objectives and "jointly" review performance results.

Questions for Discussion

1. How does bureaucratic control differ from clan control?
2. What is Douglas McGregor's main point regarding internal control?
3. Can MBO work when there are problems in the relationship between a team leader and a team member?

Be Sure You Can

- **illustrate** the use of feedforward, concurrent, and feedback controls
- **explain** the nature of internal control or self-control
- **differentiate** among bureaucratic, clan, and market controls
- **list** the steps in the MBO process as it might operate between a team leader and a team member

Career Situation: What Would You Do?

You have a highly talented work team whose past performance has been outstanding. Recently, though, team members are starting to act like the workday is mainly a social occasion. Getting the work done seems less important than having a good time, and performance is on the decline. How can you use external controls in a positive way to restore team performance to high levels?

Takeaway 5.3
What Are Some Useful Control Tools and Techniques?

ANSWERS TO COME

- Quality control is a foundation of management.
- Gantt charts and CPM/PERT improve project management and control.
- Inventory controls help save costs.
- Breakeven analysis shows where revenues will equal costs.
- Financial ratios measure key areas of financial performance.
- Balanced scorecards keep the focus on strategic control.

MOST ORGANIZATIONS USE A VARIETY OF COMPREHENSIVE AND SYSTEM-WIDE controls. As to the basics, you should be familiar with quality control, purchasing and inventory controls, and breakeven analysis, as well as the use of key financial controls and balanced scorecards.

QUALITY CONTROL IS A FOUNDATION OF MANAGEMENT.

If managing for high performance is a theme of the day, "quality control" is one of its most important watchwords. The term **total quality management (TQM)** describes efforts to make quality an everyday performance objective and strive to do things right the first time.[19] A core element in TQM is the quest for **continuous improvement**, always looking for new ways to improve on current performance.[20] The underlying notion is that you can never be satisfied—that something always can and should be done better.[21]

Measurement is the cornerstone of quality control in any setting. If you want quality, you have to tally defects, analyze and trace them to the sources, make corrections, and keep records of what happens afterwards.[22] **Control charts**, for example, are quality tools often used in manufacturing. They graphically display measures so that trends and exceptions to quality standards can be spotted. In the figure, for example, an upper control limit and a lower control limit specify the allowable tolerances for measurements of a machine part. As long as part measurements fall within these limits, things are "in control." But as soon as measurements start to fall outside the limits, it is clear that something is going wrong that is affecting quality. The process can then be investigated, or even shut down, to identify the source of the errors and correct them.

Total quality management (TQM) commits to quality objectives, continuous improvement, and doing things right the first time.

Continuous improvement involves always searching for new ways to improve work quality and performance.

Control charts are graphical ways of displaying trends so that exceptions to quality standards can be identified.

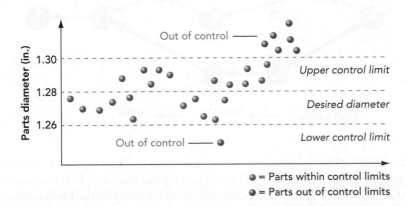

The use of statistics adds power to sampling as a basis for decision making and quality management. Many manufacturers now use a **Six Sigma** program, meaning that statistically the firm's quality performance will tolerate no more than 3.4 defects per million units

Six Sigma is a quality standard of 3.4 defects or less per million products or service deliveries.

of goods produced or services completed. This translates to a perfection rate of 99.9997%. As tough as it sounds, Six Sigma is a common quality standard for many, if not most, major competitors in our demanding global marketplace.

GANTT CHARTS AND CPM/PERT IMPROVE PROJECT MANAGEMENT AND CONTROL.

It might be something personal such as planning an anniversary party for one's parents, preparing for a renovation to your home, or watching the completion of a new student activities building on a campus. What these examples and others like them share in common is that they are relatively complicated tasks. Multiple components must be completed in a certain sequence, within budget, and by a specified date. In management we call them **projects**.

Project management is responsibility for the overall planning, supervision, and control of projects. Basically, a project manager's job is to ensure that a project is well planned and then completed according to plan—on time, within budget, and consistent with objectives. In practice, this is often assisted by two control techniques known as Gantt charts and CPM/PERT.

A **Gantt chart** like the one shown here graphically displays the scheduling of tasks that go into completing a project. Developed by Henry Gantt, an industrial engineer, this tool has become a mainstay of project management. One of the biggest problems with projects, for example, is that delays in early activities create problems for later ones. The Gantt chart's visual overview shows what needs to be done when, and allows for progress checks to be taken at different time intervals. This helps with activity sequencing to make sure that things get accomplished in time for later work to build on them.

A more advanced use of the Gantt chart is found in something called **CPM/PERT**, which combines the critical path method and the program evaluation and review technique. Project planning based on CPM/PERT uses network charts that break a project into a series of small sub-activities with clear beginning and end points. These points become "nodes" in the charts and the arrows between nodes show in what order things must be done. The full CPM/PERT diagram shows all the interrelationships that must be coordinated for the entire project to be successfully completed.

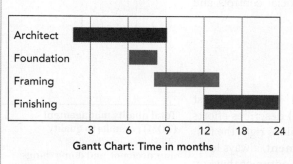

Gantt Chart: Time in months

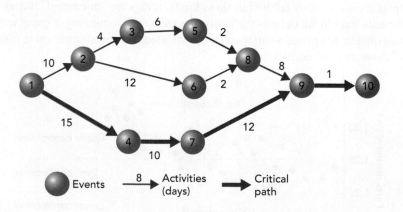

Events → 8 → Activities (days) → Critical path

Use of CPM/PERT techniques helps project managers track activities to make sure they happen in the right sequence and on time. If you look at the CPM/PERT network shown here, you should notice that the time required for each activity can be easily computed and tracked. The pathway from start to conclusion that involves the longest completion times is called the **critical path**. It represents the quickest time in which the entire project can be finished, assuming everything goes according to schedule and plans. In the example, the critical path is 38 days.

Projects are one-time activities with many component tasks that must be completed in proper order and according to budget.

Project management makes sure that activities required to complete a project are planned well and accomplished on time.

A **Gantt chart** graphically displays the scheduling of tasks required to complete a project.

CPM/PERT is a combination of the critical path method and the program evaluation and review technique.

The **critical path** is the pathway from project start to conclusion that involves the longest completion times.

INVENTORY CONTROLS HELP SAVE COSTS.

Cost control ranks right up there with quality control as an important performance concern. And a very good place to start is with inventory. The goal of **inventory control** is to make sure that any inventory is only big enough to meet one's immediate performance needs.

The **economic order quantity** form of inventory control, shown in the figure, automatically orders a fixed number of items every time an inventory level falls to a predetermined point. The order sizes are mathematically calculated to minimize costs of inventory. A good example is your local supermarket. It routinely makes hundreds of daily orders on an economic order quantity basis.

Another and very popular approach to inventory control is **just-in-time scheduling (JIT)**. First made popular by the Japanese, these systems reduce costs and improve workflow by scheduling materials to arrive at a workstation or facility just in time for use. Because JIT reduces the carrying costs of inventories, it is an important business productivity tool. But, the tsunami and nuclear disaster in Japan also showed some of the risks of JIT. Many global companies faced product delays when just-in-time shipments were disrupted as Japanese firms in their supply chains were closed or their operations scaled back because of the disaster.[23]

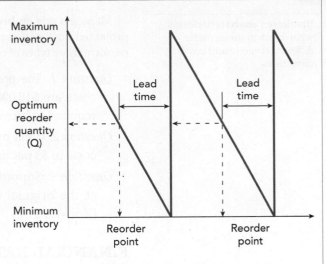

Inventory control ensures that inventory is only big enough to meet immediate needs.

The **economic order quantity** method places new orders when inventory levels fall to predetermined points.

Just-in-time scheduling (JIT) routes materials to workstations just in time for use.

The **breakeven point** occurs where revenues just equal costs.

BREAKEVEN ANALYSIS SHOWS WHERE REVENUES WILL EQUAL COSTS.

When business executives are deliberating new products or projects, a frequent control question is: "What is the **breakeven point**?" Figure 5.5 shows that breakeven occurs at the point where revenues just equal costs. You can also think of it as the point where losses end and profit begins. A breakeven point is computed using this formula.

$$\text{Breakeven Point} = \text{Fixed Costs} \div (\text{Price} - \text{Variable Costs})$$

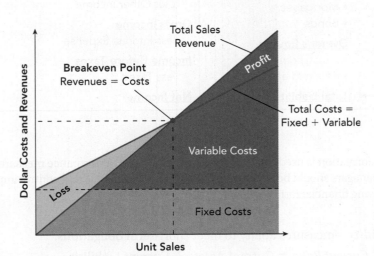

FIGURE 5.5 How Do Managers Use Breakeven Analysis to Make Informed What-If Decisions?

A common question asked by managers when considering a new product or service investment is: "What is the breakeven point?" A breakeven point is computed using this formula: Breakeven Point × Fixed Costs ÷ (Price − Variable Costs). As shown in this figure, breakeven occurs at the point where revenues just equal costs. You can also think of it as the point where losses end and profit begins. This approach helps managers perform what-if calculations under different projected cost and revenue conditions.

Breakeven analysis performs what-if calculations under different revenue and cost conditions.

Managers rely on **breakeven analysis** to perform what-if calculations under different projected cost and revenue conditions. Take the following tests. Business executives perform these types of cost control analyses every day.

Question 1. The proposed target price for a new product is $8 per unit, fixed costs are $10,000, and variable costs are $4 per unit. What sales volume is required to break even? (*Answer:* Breakeven at 2,500 units.)

Question 2. What happens if you are good at cost control and can keep variable costs to $3 per unit? (*Answer:* Breakeven at 2,000 units.)

Question 3. Suppose you can only produce 1,000 units in the beginning and at the original costs. At what price must you sell them to break even? (*Answer:* $14.)

FINANCIAL RATIOS MEASURE KEY AREAS OF FINANCIAL PERFORMANCE.

The pressure is always on for organizations to use their financial resources well to achieve high performance. And, the analysis of an organization's financial performance is an important aspect of managerial control.

A **balance sheet** shows assets and liabilities at one point in time.

An **income statement** shows profits or losses at one point in time.

The foundation for analysis using financial controls rests with a firm's balance sheet and income statement. The **balance sheet** shows assets and liabilities at a point in time. It will be displayed in an Assets = Liabilities format. The **income statement** shows profits or losses at a point in time. It will be displayed in a Sales − Expenses = Net Income format.

Balance Sheet

Assets	Liabilities
Current Assets	**Current Liabilities**
• Cash	• Accounts payable
• Receivables	• Accrued expenses
• Inventories	• Taxes payable
Fixed Assets	**Long-term Liabilities**
• Land	• Mortgages
• Buildings	• Bonds
Less Depreciation	**Owner's Equity**
	• Outstanding stock
	• Retained earnings
Total Assets =	**Total Liabilities**

Income Statement

Gross Sales
less Returns

Net Sales
less Expenses and Cost of Goods Sold

Operating Profits
plus Other Income

Gross Income
less Interest Expense

Income Before Taxes
less Taxes

Net Income

The information is used to create a variety of financial performance measures. At a minimum, managers should be able to understand the performance and control implications of the following financial ratios.

Liquidity—measures ability to meet short-term obligations.
- *Current Ratio* = Current Assets ÷ Current Liabilities
- *Quick Ratio* = (Current Assets − Inventory) ÷ Current Liabilities
- ↑ Higher is better: You want more assets and fewer liabilities.

Leverage—measures use of debt.
- *Debt Ratio* = Total Debts ÷ Total Assets
- ↓ Lower is better: You want fewer debts and more assets.

Asset Management—measures asset and inventory efficiency.

- *Asset Turnover* = Sales ÷ Total Assets
- *Inventory Turnover* = Sales ÷ Average Inventory
- ↑ Higher is better: You want more sales and fewer assets or lower inventory.

Profitability—measures profit generation.

- *Net Margin* = Net Income ÷ Sales
- *Return on Assets* (ROA) = Net Income ÷ Total Assets
- *Return on Equity* (ROE) = Net Income ÷ Owner's Equity
- ↑ Higher is better: You want as much net income or profit as possible for sales, assets, and equity.

Financial ratios can be used for historical comparisons within the firm and for external benchmarking relative to industry performance. They can also be used to set company-level financial targets or goals to be shared with employees and tracked to indicate success or failure. At Civco Medical Instruments, for example, financial results are distributed monthly to all employees. They always know exactly how well the firm is doing. This helps them focus on what they can do differently and better to help improve the firm's bottom line.[24]

BALANCED SCORECARDS KEEP THE FOCUS ON STRATEGIC CONTROL.

If "what gets measured happens," then managers should take advantage of "scorecards" to record and track performance results. When an instructor takes class attendance and assigns grades based on it, students tend to come to class. When an employer tracks the number of customers each employee serves per day, employees tend to serve more customers. Do the same principles hold for organizations?

Strategic management consultants Robert S. Kaplan and David P. Norton think so. They advocate using what is called the **balanced scorecard** in respect to management control.[25] It gives top managers, as they say, "a fast but comprehensive view of the business." The basic principle is that to do well and to win, you have to keep score. And like sports teams, organizations perform better when all members know the score.

> A **balanced scorecard** measures performance on financial, customer service, internal process, and innovation and learning goals.

Developing a balanced scorecard for any organization begins with a clarification of the organization's mission and vision—what it wants to be and how it wants to be perceived by its key stakeholders. Next, the following questions are asked and answered to develop balanced scorecard goals and performance measures.

WE NEED THE COURAGE TO ADMIT WHEN THINGS ARE GOING WRONG.

EXPLORE YOURSELF

Resiliency

The control process is one of the ways through which managers help organizations best use their resources and systems. In many ways our daily lives are similar quests for productivity, and the control process counts there, too. But how well we do depends a lot on our capacity for **resiliency**—the ability to call on inner strength and keep moving forward even when things are tough.

Resilient people are willing to self assess. They face up to challenges rather than hide or back away from them. And, they have the courage and confidence to admit when

things are going wrong, to change ways that aren't working well, and to keep moving forward even in the face of adversity.

> Get to know yourself better by taking the self-assessment on **Internal/External Control** and completing other activities in the *Exploring Management* **Skill-Building Portfolio**.

HOT TOPIC

Should Parents Pay for Children's Grades?

© Tetra Images/Alamy

Managing is a lot like parenting, and allocating rewards isn't easy in either situation. So, what's the balanced scorecard for family life?

Start with the kids' schooling. How often have you heard someone say: "We pay for A's"? Perhaps you've said it yourself, or plan to. But is this the correct thing to do? Can paying for grades improve parental control over children's study habits?

Those in favor of paying for grades are likely to say: "It gets the kid's attention". . . "It motivates them to study more" . . . "It gets them ready for work where pay and performance go together." *Those against the practice are likely to say:* "Once they get paid for A's, they'll be studying for financial gain, not real learning" . . . "It hurts those who work hard but still can't get the high grades" . . . "If there's more than one child in the family, it's unfair if they don't all get rewards."

HOW ABOUT IT?

As a parent, will you pay for grades or not? How can you justify your position? There are a number of issues here that any manager, leader, or parent needs to understand—pay for performance, equity in rewards, valuing effort versus valuing achievement. By the way, what can parenting teach us about managing people at work?

- *Financial Performance*—"How well do our actions directly contribute to improved financial performance?" To improve financially, how should we appear to our shareholders? Sample goals: survive, succeed, and prosper. Sample measures: cash flow, sales growth and operating income, increased market share, and return on equity.

- *Customer Satisfaction*—"How well do we serve our customers and clients?" To achieve our vision, how should we appear to our customers? Sample goals: new products, responsive supply. Sample measures: percentage sales from new products, percentage on-time deliveries.

- *Internal Process Improvement*—"How well do our activities and processes directly increase value provided to our customers and clients?" To satisfy our customers and shareholders, at what internal business processes should we excel? Sample goals: manufacturing productivity, design excellence, new product introduction. Sample measures: cycle times, engineering efficiency, new product time.

- *Innovation and Learning*—"How well are we learning, changing, and improving things over time?" To achieve our vision, how will we sustain our ability to change and improve? Sample goals: technology leadership, time to market. Sample measures: time to develop new technologies, new product introduction time versus competition.

When balanced scorecard measures are taken, recorded, shared, and critically reviewed, Kaplan and Norton expect organizations to perform better. Use of a balanced scorecard helps keep important goals and their status in the limelight. As we've said before: What gets measured happens.

Think about the possibilities here. Couldn't the balanced scorecard approach work in an elementary school, a hospital, a community library, a mayor's office, a fast-food restaurant? It doesn't have to be just a big business tool. Couldn't balanced scorecards be created to help individuals like you and us keep our priorities clear and assess our performance progress? And if balanced scorecards make sense, why is it that more organizations and individuals don't use them?

STUDYGUIDE

Takeaway 5.3
What Are Some Useful Control Tools and Techniques?

Terms to Define

Balance sheet	Control chart	Income statement	Six Sigma
Balanced scorecard	Critical path	Inventory control	Total quality management (TQM)
Breakeven analysis	CPM/PERT	Just-in-time scheduling (JIT)	
Breakeven point	Economic order quantity	Project	
Continuous improvement	Gantt chart	Project management	

Rapid Review

- Total quality management tries to meet customers' needs and do things right on time, the first time, and all the time.
- Organizations use control charts and statistical techniques such as the Six Sigma system to measure the quality of work samples for quality control purposes.
- Economic order quantities and just-in-time deliveries are common approaches to inventory cost control.
- The breakeven equation is: Breakeven Point = Fixed Costs ÷ (Price − Variable Costs).
- Breakeven analysis identifies the points where revenues will equal costs under different pricing and cost conditions.
- Financial control of business performance is facilitated by use of financial ratios, such as those dealing with liquidity, leverage, assets, and profitability.
- The balanced scorecard measures overall organizational performance in respect to four areas: financial, customers, internal processes, and innovation.

Questions for Discussion

1. Can a firm such as Walmart ever go too far in controlling its inventory costs?
2. Is the concept of total quality management out of date?
3. Does the "balanced scorecard" as described in this chapter measure the right things?

Be Sure You Can

- **explain** the role of continuous improvement in TQM
- **explain** how Gantt charts and CPM/PERT help organizations with project management
- **explain** two common approaches to inventory cost control
- **state** the equation to calculate a breakeven point and its use in explaining breakeven analysis
- **state** the common financial ratios used in organizational control
- **identify** the balanced scorecard components and control questions

Career Situation: What Would You Do?

You've had 3 years of solid work experience after earning your undergraduate degree. A lot of your friends are talking about going to graduate school, and they're pushing you to take time out to earn an MBA degree. There are potential costs and benefits if you go for the MBA. How can breakeven analysis help you make the decision to: (1) go or not go, (2) go full time or part time, and (3) even where to go?

TEST PREP **5**

Answers to Test Prep questions can be found at the back of the book.

Multiple-Choice Questions

1. After objectives and standards are set, what step comes next in the control process?
   (a) Measure results.
   (b) Take corrective action.
   (c) Compare results with objectives.
   (d) Modify standards to fit circumstances.

2. When a soccer coach tells her players at the end of a losing game, "You did well in staying with our game plan," she is using a/an _____ as a measure of performance.
   (a) input standard
   (b) output standard
   (c) historical comparison
   (d) relative comparison

3. When an automobile manufacturer is careful to purchase only the highest-quality components for use in production, this is an example of an attempt to ensure high performance through _____ control.
   (a) concurrent   (b) statistical
   (c) inventory   (d) feedforward

4. Management by exception means _____.
   (a) managing only when necessary
   (b) focusing attention where the need for action is greatest
   (c) the same thing as concurrent control
   (d) the same thing as just-in-time delivery

5. A total quality management program is most likely to be associated with _____.
   (a) EOQ
   (b) continuous improvement
   (c) return on equity
   (d) breakeven analysis

6. The _____ chart graphically displays the scheduling of tasks required to complete the project.
   (a) exception   (b) Taylor
   (c) Gantt   (d) after-action

7. When MBO is done right, who does the review of a team member's performance accomplishments?
   (a) The team member
   (b) The team leader
   (c) Both the team member and team leader
   (d) The team leader, the team member, and a lawyer

8. A good performance objective is written in such a way that it _____.
   (a) has a flexible timetable
   (b) is general and not too specific
   (c) is impossible to accomplish
   (d) can be easily measured

9. A team leader is not living up to the concept of MBO if he or she _____.
   (a) sets performance objectives for individual team members
   (b) stays in touch and tries to support team members in their work
   (c) jointly reviews performance results with each team member
   (d) keeps a written record of performance objectives for team members

10. If an organization's top management establishes a target of increasing new hires of minority and female candidates by 15% in the next 6 months, this is an example of a/an _____ standard for control purposes.
    (a) input   (b) output
    (c) clan   (d) market

11. When a supervisor works alongside an employee and corrects him or her immediately when a mistake is made, this is an example of _____ control.
    (a) feedforward   (b) external
    (c) concurrent   (d) preliminary

12. When one team member advises another team member that "your behavior is crossing the line in terms of our expectations for workplace civility," she is exercising a form of _____ control over the other person's inappropriate behaviors.
    (a) clan   (b) market
    (c) internal   (d) preliminary

13. In CPM/PERT, "CPM" stands for _____.
    (a) critical path method
    (b) control planning management
    (c) control plan map
    (d) current planning matrix

14. In a CPM/PERT analysis, the focus is on _____ and the event _____ that link them together with the finished project.
    (a) costs; budgets
    (b) activities; sequences
    (c) timetables; budgets
    (d) goals; costs

15. Among the financial ratios often used for control purposes, Current Assets/Current Liabilities is known as the _____.
    (a) debt ratio
    (b) net margin
    (c) current ratio
    (d) inventory turnover ratio

Short-Response Questions

16. What type of control is being exercised in the U.S. Army's after-action review?

17. How could clan control be used in a TQM program?

18. How can a just-in-time system reduce inventory costs?

19. What four questions could be used to set up a balanced scorecard for a small business?

Integration and Application Question

20. Put yourself in the position of a management consultant who specializes in MBO. The local Small Business Enterprise Association has asked you to be the speaker for its luncheon next week. The president of the association says that the group would like to learn more about the topic "How to Use Management by Objectives for Better Planning and Control."

    Questions: Your speech will last 15 to 20 minutes. What is the outline for your speech? How will you explain the potential benefits of MBO to this group of small business owners?

Steps for Further Learning

BUILD MARKETABLE SKILLS • **DO** A CASE ANALYSIS • **GET** AND STAY INFORMED

BUILD MARKETABLE SKILLS.

EARN BIG CAREER PAYOFFS!

Don't miss these opportunities in the SKILL-BUILDING PORTFOLIO

SELF-ASSESSMENT 5:
Internal/External Control

Is what happens up to you, or not?...Learn about your control tendencies.

CLASS EXERCISE 5:
Stakeholder Maps

Organizations can have lives of their own...gain insight into stakeholder perspectives.

TEAM PROJECT 5:
After Meeting Project Review

It's rare that things go perfectly right...a good review process can make things go better the next time.

Many learning resources are found at the end of the book and online within **WileyPLUS Learning Space.**

Practice Critical Thinking—Complete the CHAPTER 5 CASE

CASE SNAPSHOT: Chipotle—Control Keeps Everything Fresh

If controlling is the process of measuring performance and taking action to ensure desired results, your next meal from Chipotle should be a good one. Since its humble beginnings in Denver, Colorado, Chipotle has implemented the control process with fervor, catapulting the company to where it is today. Nothing is left to chance, and everything counts. Input standards make sure that meal ingredients are up to the firm's high expectations. After all, putting good ingredients in makes it more likely that good burritos will come out. Output standards measure performance results in terms of quantity, quality, cost, or time. For Chipotle this means reviewing sales-to-cost ratios and same-store sales figures, speeding checkout times during peak lunch hour, and tracking its stock performance. All those burritos come from a high-performance culture that thrives on control.

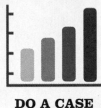

DO A CASE ANALYSIS.

STRENGTHEN YOUR CRITICAL THINKING!

MANAGER'S LIBRARY SELECTION
Read for Insights and Wisdom
Lean In: Women, Work and the Will to Lead (2013, Knopf)
by *Sheryl Sandberg*

First-time author Sheryl Sandberg got lots of attention with this book. Chief Operating Officer of Facebook, Sandberg says women have to take charge of their careers and stop making bad decisions. She believes they do too much "leaning back"—such as taking a back or corner seat at a meeting table, and do too much "leaning out"—such as not accepting new responsibilities because motherhood is planned sometime in the future. Instead, Sandberg's advises women to "lean in" and "don't leave before you leave." Think of this as women taking control of their own destinies.

GET AND STAY INFORMED.

MAKE YOURSELF VALUABLE!

Sandberg admits that stereotypes, corporate cultures, and traditional structures can hold women back. And she calls for better policies on things like maternity and paternity leave. She also warns about "benevolent sexism," where men act sympathetic but still treat women differently. But, her book is really about empowering women to take control and make better career decisions. Sandberg wants women to believe in their dreams and in themselves . . . and to achieve their full potential.

REFLECT AND REACT Is Sandberg on to something here, or is she being too critical? Have you witnessed or experienced the "leaning back" or "leaning out" types of behaviors? Can this call for women to take charge of their careers really lead to positive change? Is it broadly applicable? Or, is Sandberg talking from the largely unrealistic position of a super-successful and wealthy businesswoman—someone who "has it all," so to speak?

"There is a fundamental disconnect between the providers of education and the consumers of education . . . this whole online debate or what's happening now is actually starting to clarify things. At Khan Academy we're 100% focused on the learning side. . . ."

Salman Khan, founder of the Khan Academy

$$e^{it} = \cos x + i \sin$$

$$e^{i\pi} = \cos \pi - i \sin$$

$$e^{i\pi} = -1$$

Sal Khan

Strategy and Strategic Management

6

Insight and Hard Work Deliver Results

Management Live

Diversity in Leadership Linked to Financial Performance

Compassionate Eye Foundation/Martin Barraud/Getty Images

A McKinsey study of 366 companies found that financial performance was higher as the percentage of women and minorities in top management teams increased. Gender diversity delivered a 15% performance benefit, and the advantage for ethnic diversity was 35%. One of the study's authors stated, however: "Very few U.S. companies yet have a systematic approach to diversity that is able to consistently achieve a diverse global talent pool."

YOUR THOUGHTS?

If the diversity advantage is real, why aren't more U.S. companies making it part of their performance strategies? If the diversity advantage applies in large organizations, does it hold true in smaller ones? How about your teams—work and personal? Are they getting the most out of the diversity advantage?

WHAT'S INSIDE

ETHICS CHECK
Life and death at an outsourcing factory

FACTS TO CONSIDER
Disposable workers are indispensable to business profits

HOT TOPIC
Can the sharing economy create good jobs?

QUICK CASE
Kickstarting a friend's business idea

YOUR CHAPTER 6 TAKEAWAYS

1. Identify the types of strategies used by organizations.
2. Understand how managers formulate and implement strategies.

Takeaway 6.1
What Types of Strategies Are Used by Organizations?

ANSWERS TO COME

- Strategy is a comprehensive plan for achieving competitive advantage.
- Organizations use corporate, business, and functional strategies.
- Growth strategies focus on expansion.
- Restructuring and divestiture strategies focus on consolidation.
- Global strategies focus on international business opportunities.
- Cooperation strategies focus on alliances and partnerships.
- E-business strategies use the Web and apps for business success.

DON'T TAKE THE OPENING PHOTO OF SAL KHAN TOO LIGHTLY. HIS INNOVATIVE ONLINE Khan Academy has the goal of "changing education for the better by providing a free world-class education for anyone anywhere." Its success helped spur the development of MOOCs—massive open online courses—as "disrupters" of the traditional university model of face-to-face delivery of pay-per-credit courses.[1] Some MOOCs are free, they're being launched in increasing numbers from top universities, and start-ups such as Coursera and Udacity are marketing them on a global scale.

Fast Company magazine once said: "If you want to make a difference as a leader, you've got to make time for strategy."[2] And, higher education today ranks high among industries facing strategic challenges. But leaders in any industry should remember past lessons. There was a time when Henry Ford could say: "The customer can have any color he wants as long as it's black." Those days are gone for the automakers, and they're gone for universities, public institutions, and businesses as well. A senior IBM executive described this shift in strategic landscape as the "difference between a bus which follows a set route, and a taxi which goes where customers tell it to go."[3]

There are lots of strategy and strategic management lessons and insights in this chapter. As you read, remember that everything applies equally well to you and your career. What's your personal strategy? Are you acting like the bus following the set route, the taxi following opportunities, or some combination of both?

STRATEGY IS A COMPREHENSIVE PLAN FOR ACHIEVING COMPETITIVE ADVANTAGE.

A strategy is a comprehensive action plan for allocating resources to accomplish long-term goals. And importantly, strategy focuses attention on the competitive environment. Whether we are talking about a government, a large or small business, a nonprofit, or a personal career, a strategy represents a "best guess" about what to do in order to be successful in the face of rivalry and changing conditions.

A good strategy provides a plan for allocating and using resources with a consistent sense of **mission**—a clear and ideally lofty sense of purpose or why you exist, and **strategic intent**—a clear and lofty sense of where you are going in the future. At the nonprofit Khan Academy, discussed earlier, the mission is to provide "a free world-class education for anyone anywhere." The strategic intent may be stated as "to inspire the world to learn."[4] While mission and strategic intent provide the targets, strategy provides the plan for reaching them. In the case of the Khan Academy, this strategy involves using technology to empower learners to study for free at their own pace and timetable. This partnership of mission and strategic intent—the ends, and strategy—the means, keeps everyone headed in the same direction, avoids having things veer off track, and gets the best value from resource utilization.[5]

A strategy is a comprehensive plan for allocating resources to achieve long-term organization goals.

Mission is a clear and lofty sense of why you exist.

Strategic intent is a clear and lofty sense of where you are going.

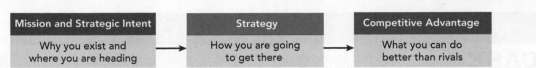

Mission and Strategic Intent	Strategy	Competitive Advantage
Why you exist and where you are heading	How you are going to get there	What you can do better than rivals

Ultimately, a good strategy helps an organization achieve **competitive advantage**—being able to outperform rivals. Think about Apple and its iPad. It was first to market with an innovative product linking design, technology, and customer appeal. And, it was all backed by a super-efficient supply chain. As one industry analyst said, "Apple moved the goal posts before most of their competitors even took the field."[6] The very best strategies provide something more—**sustainable competitive advantage**. This doesn't mean that the competitive advantage lasts forever, but it does mean that it's hard for competitors to imitate for some period of time.

Part of what makes strategy so challenging today is that a fast-changing environment is shrinking the period of time that competitive advantage can be maintained. How long does it take one of Apple's competitor's to come out with a new smart phone? How long did it take for Uber-like ride sharing services to pop up around the globe? Will one smart watch rule them all? And, how about the Khan Academy? Its competitive advantage comes from an ever-expanding online selection of high-quality exercises and video lessons, all supported by a community of expert "virtual coaches."[7] Nice. But is this competitive advantage sustainable? That's the question the Khan Academy leadership team grapples with every day.

> A **competitive advantage** is an ability to outperform rivals.

> A **sustainable competitive advantage** is achieved in ways that are difficult to imitate.

ORGANIZATIONS USE CORPORATE, BUSINESS, AND FUNCTIONAL STRATEGIES.

You can identify strategies at three levels in most organizations. At the top level, **corporate strategy** provides direction and guides resource allocation for the organization as a whole. The *strategic question* at the corporate strategy level is: In what industries and markets should we compete? In large, complex organizations, such as PepsiCo, IBM, and General Electric, decisions on corporate strategy identify how the firm intends to compete across multiple industries, businesses, and markets.

> A **corporate strategy** sets long-term direction for the total enterprise.

Business strategy focuses on the strategic intent for a single business unit or product line. The *strategic question* at the business strategy level is: How are we going to compete for customers within this industry and in this market? Typical business strategy decisions include choices about product and service mix, facilities locations, new technologies, and the like. For smaller, single-business enterprises, business strategy is the corporate strategy.

> A **business strategy** identifies how a division or strategic business unit will compete in its product or service domain.

Functional strategy guides activities to implement higher-level business and corporate strategies. This level of strategy unfolds within a specific functional area such as marketing, manufacturing, finance, and human resources. The *strategic question* for functional strategies is: How can we best utilize resources within the function to support implementation of the business strategy? Answers to this question involve a wide variety of practices and initiatives to improve things such as operating efficiency, product quality, customer service, or innovativeness.

> A **functional strategy** guides activities within one specific area of operations.

GROWTH STRATEGIES FOCUS ON EXPANSION.

We often read and hear about organizations trying to get bigger. They are pursuing **growth strategies** to increase the size and scope of current operations. Many executives view growth as necessary for long-run profitability. But you should probably question this assumption and probe deeper right from the start. Is growth always the best path? And if the strategic choice is to grow, how should it be accomplished?

> A **growth strategy** involves expansion of the organization's current operations.

A strategy of growth through **concentration** seeks expansion within an existing business area, one in which the firm has experience and presumably expertise. You don't see Chipotle trying to grow by buying bookstores or gasoline stations; it keeps opening more restaurants. You don't see Walmart trying to grow by buying a high-end department store chain or a cell-phone company; it keeps opening more Walmart stores. These are classic growth by concentration strategies.

> Growth through **concentration** means expansion within an existing business area.

QUICK CASE

Kickstarting a Friend's Business Idea

Radharc Images/Alamy

Situation: You've worked hard, made a fair amount of money, and have a nice stock portfolio. You're also known among your friends as "the guy with the money." As with lottery winners, you've become a bit of a target—some want handouts, some loans, and others just do their share of freeloading. But now one of your friends has come with a business proposal. She's just back from a trip to Southeast Asia and is raving about all the neat fabrics available in local markets in places like Cambodia, Thailand, and Vietnam. She's also a great fan of the TV show *Project Runway*. So, she wants to import fabrics, buy some sewing machines and materials, rent a small storefront, and set up a shop called The Design Place. The basic idea is that a customer can come in, find fabrics, use workspace, and then design and sew their own fashions. She thinks the idea will be a winner, but has come to you for advice and—she hopes—some startup financing.

WHAT DO YOU DO?

What questions will you ask and what will you say to give your friend a good strategic analysis of her business idea? Without knowing any more than you do now, what do you believe is the real strategic potential of The Design Place? Are there other examples of do-it-yourself stores within other product spaces that could serve as guides for your evaluation and help develop her business proposal?

Growth through diversification means expansion by entering related or new business areas.

Growth can also take place through **diversification**, where expansion occurs by entering new business areas. As you might expect, diversification involves risk because the firm may be moving outside existing areas of competency. One way to moderate the risk is to pursue *related diversification*, expanding into similar or complementary new business areas. PepsiCo did this when it purchased Tropicana. Although Tropicana's fruit juices were new to Pepsi, the business is related to its expertise in the beverages industry.

Some firms pursue *unrelated diversification* by seeking growth in entirely new business areas. Did you know that Exxon once owned Izod? Does that make sense? Can you see the risk here and understand why growth through unrelated diversification might cause problems? Research is quite clear that business performance may decline for firms that get into too much unrelated diversification.[8]

Growth through vertical integration occurs by acquiring suppliers or distributors.

Diversification can also take the form of **vertical integration**. This is where a business acquires its suppliers (*backward vertical integration*) or its distributors (*forward vertical integration*). Backward vertical integration is evident at Apple Computer. The firm has bought chip manufacturers to give it more privacy and sophistication in developing microprocessors for its products. In beverages, both Coca-Cola and PepsiCo have pursued forward vertical integration by purchasing some of their major bottlers.

RESTRUCTURING AND DIVESTITURE STRATEGIES FOCUS ON CONSOLIDATION.

A retrenchment strategy changes operations to correct weaknesses.

When organizations run into performance difficulties, perhaps because of too much growth and diversification, these problems have to be solved. A **retrenchment strategy** seeks to correct weaknesses by making radical changes to current ways of operating.

Liquidation occurs when a business closes and sells its assets to pay creditors.

The most extreme form of retrenchment is **liquidation**, where a business closes down and sells its assets to pay creditors. A less extreme and more common form of retrenchment is **restructuring**. This involves making major changes to cut costs and buy time to try new strategies to improve future success.

Restructuring reduces the scale or mix of operations.

Chapter 11 bankruptcy protects an insolvent firm from creditors during a period of reorganization to restore profitability.

When a firm is in desperate financial condition and unable to pay its bills, a situation faced by Chrysler and General Motors during the financial crisis, restructuring by **Chapter 11 bankruptcy** is an option under U.S. law. This protects the firm from creditors while management reorganizes things in an attempt to restore solvency. The goal is to emerge from bankruptcy as a stronger and profitable business, something achieved by both GM and Chrysler.

Downsizing is a restructuring approach that cuts the size of operations and reduces the workforce.[9] When you learn of organizations downsizing by across-the-board cuts, however, you might be a bit skeptical. Research shows that downsizing is most successful when cutbacks are done selectively and focused on key performance objectives.[10]

> **Downsizing** decreases the size of operations.

Finally, restructuring by **divestiture** involves selling parts of the organization to refocus on core competencies, cut costs, and improve operating efficiency. This type of retrenchment often occurs when organizations have become too diversified. eBay once spent $3.1 billion to buy Skype. But, when the expected synergies between Skype and eBay's online auction business never developed, Skype was sold to private investors.[11] They, in turn, sold it to Microsoft, which is still working to integrate Skype into its business model.

> **Divestiture** involves selling off parts of the organization to refocus attention on core business areas.

GLOBAL STRATEGIES FOCUS ON INTERNATIONAL BUSINESS OPPORTUNITIES.

The world's diverse populations and economies offer a variety of growth opportunities for businesses. Many large U.S. firms—including Yum Brands, IBM, and Colgate-Palmolive—now get the majority of their revenues internationally. But, the growth opportunities of international business pose challenges that firms strategically address in different ways.[12]

Firms pursuing a **globalization strategy** tend to view the world as one large market. They try to advertise and sell standard products for use everywhere. For example, Gillette sells and advertises its latest razors around the world; you get the same product in Italy or South Africa as in America. Firms pursuing a **multidomestic strategy**, by contrast, customize products and advertising to fit local cultures and needs. Bristol Myers, Procter & Gamble, and Unilever all vary their products to match consumer preferences in different countries and cultures.[13]

> A **globalization strategy** uses standardized products and advertising worldwide.

> A **multidomestic strategy** customizes products and advertising to fit local markets.

Firms using the **transnational strategy** try to tap business resources and customer markets worldwide. A transnational firm tries to operate without a strong national identity, hoping instead to blend seamlessly with the global economy. "Ford," for example, strives to become a global brand, not just an American one. It draws on design, manufacturing, and distribution expertise all over the world to build car platforms. These are then modified within regions to build cars that meet local tastes.

> A **transnational strategy** integrates global operations without having a strong national identity.

THE WORK IS MEANINGLESS, NO CONVERSATION IS ALLOWED ON THE PRODUCTION LINES, AND BATHROOM BREAKS ARE LIMITED.

ETHICS CHECK

Life and Death at an Outsourcing Factory

Jason Lee/Reuters/Newscom

Foxconn, the trade name for Hon Hai Precision Industry, is a major outsourcing firm. Its plants in China make products for Apple, Dell, and Hewlett-Packard, among others. One large complex employs more than 300,000 people.

The firm has been the target of complaints over worker safety, overtime, and underage hiring practices. A clash between workers and security forces focused on rules perceived as too strict for China's newest generation of workers. At a factory in Shenzen, China, safety netting was draped around dormitories after a rash of employee suicides.

Foxconn employees have complained that the work is meaningless, no conversation is allowed on the production lines, and bathroom breaks are limited. One says: "I do the same thing every day. I have no future."

A Foxconn supervisor points out that the firm provides counseling services, and that most workers are young and away from their homes for the first time. "Without their families," says the supervisor, "they're left without direction. We try to provide them with direction and help." Recent changes at the company include more focus on working conditions, higher wages, less overtime, and even more automation of simple jobs.

YOUR DECISION?

What ethical responsibilities do global firms have when outsourcing in foreign plants? Whose responsibility is it to make sure workers are well treated? Should price-conscious consumers support bad practices by buying products from firms whose outsourcing partners treat workers poorly?

COOPERATION STRATEGIES FOCUS ON ALLIANCES AND PARTNERSHIPS.

In a **strategic alliance**, organizations join together in partnership to pursue an area of mutual interest.

The trend today is toward more cooperation among organizations, often in **strategic alliances**, where two or more organizations join together in partnership to pursue an area of mutual interest. A common form involves *outsourcing alliances*, contracting to purchase specialized services from another organization. An example is the organization that outsources its IT function in the belief that these services are better provided by a firm with special expertise in this area. Cooperation also takes the form of *supplier alliances*—which guarantee a smooth and timely flow of quality supplies among alliance partners, and *distribution alliances*—where firms join together to accomplish product or services sales and distribution.

Co-opetition is the strategy of working with rivals on projects of mutual benefit.

Some cooperation strategies even involve strategic alliances with competitors. Known as **co-opetition**, it has been called a "revolution mindset" that business competitors can be co-operating partners.[14] United and Lufthansa are international competitors, but they cooperate in the Star Alliance network that allows customers to book both airlines' flights and share frequent flyer programs. Likewise, luxury car competitors Daimler and BMW cooperate to co-develop new motors and components for hybrid cars.[15]

E-BUSINESS STRATEGIES USE THE WEB AND APPS FOR BUSINESS SUCCESS.

An **e-business strategy** strategically uses the Web and mobile apps to gain competitive advantage.

A common question asked of business executives is: "What is your **e-business strategy**?" This refers to the strategic use of the Web and mobile apps to gain competitive advantage. Table 6.1—Sample Web-Based Business Models—lists some examples.[16]

B2C business strategies link businesses with customers.

B2C business strategies are business-to-customer. They use the Web and apps to link businesses directly with customers. Whenever you buy a music download from Apple's iTunes Store, order a book from Amazon.com, or shop Patagonia.com for the latest outdoor gear, you are the "C" in a B2C strategy.

B2B business strategies link businesses together within supply chains.

B2B business strategies are business-to-business. They link businesses with members of their supply chains. For example, Dell Computer sets up special Web site services that allow major corporate customers to manage their accounts online. Walmart ties suppliers into its information systems so they can electronically manage inventories for their own products.

C2B business strategies link customers to businesses that can supply what they need.

C2B business strategies use the Web and apps to link customers with businesses that might provide a needed product or service. In contrast to B2C, the C2B strategy puts the initiative for the transaction in the hands of the potential customer. A timely

TABLE 6.1 Sample Web-Based Business Models

Advertising model: Provide free information or services and then generate revenues from paid advertising to viewers (e.g., Yahoo!, Google)

Brokerage model: Bring buyers and sellers together for online business transactions and take a percentage from the sales (e.g., eBay, Priceline)

Community model: Provide a meeting point sold by subscription or supported by advertising (e.g., eHarmony, Facebook)

Freemium model: Offer a free service and encourage users to buy extras (e.g., Skype, Zynga)

Infomediary model: Provide a free service while collecting information on users and selling it to other businesses (e.g., Epinions, Yelp)

Merchant model: Sell products direct to customers through e-tailing (e.g., Amazon, Apple iTunes Store)

Referral model: Provide free listings and get referral fees from online merchants after directing customers to them (e.g., Shopzilla, PriceGrabber)

Subscription model: Sell access to high-value content through a subscription Web site (e.g., Netflix, Wall Street Journal Interactive)

example in our free-agent and on-demand economy is Elance, which links customers needing a special project completed—say a Web animation or a document translation task—with businesses and independent contractors who are willing to bid on and complete the project.

C2C business strategies are customer-to-customer. They use the Web and apps to link customers to one another, with the host site collecting a fee for setting up the opportunity. You can find C2C in online marketplaces such as eBay and Etsy, where customers sell, buy, and trade items with one another.

The power of our daily Web "connections" and "communities" has also moved us into **P2P business strategies**. These peer-to-peer connections are part of the sharing economy where the Web and apps link persons needing services with those willing to provide them. Examples are Uber—matching riders with drivers, TaskRabbit—matching small jobs with "taskers" willing to do them, and Airbnb—matching travelers with host residences.

There's a lot of buzz today about **social media strategy**. Think of this as an organization using social media such as Facebook or Twitter to better engage with customers, clients, and external audiences. How often do you hear or read "Find us on Facebook"? That's what Procter & Gamble says. Its Facebook page on Pampers sells the product, hosts a discussion forum for users, and encourages viewers to enter free Pampers sweepstakes.

There's also a lot of buzz about **crowdsourcing** as a special type of social media strategy. It uses the Web to engage customers and potential customers to make suggestions and express opinions on products and their designs. An example is Threadless.com. The firm's online visitors submit designs for T-shirts. The designs are voted on by other viewers—the "crowd"—and top-rated ones get selected for production and sale to customers.[17]

> **C2C business strategies** link customers together to make business transactions.

> **P2P business strategies** link persons needing services with those willing to provide them.

> A **social media strategy** uses social media to better engage with an organization's customers, clients, and external audiences in general.

> A **crowdsourcing** strategy uses the Web to allow customers to provide opinions and suggestions on products and their designs.

"IT IS A GREAT DEAL FOR THE OWNERS, BUT A BAD ONE FOR WORKERS."

HOT TOPIC

Can the Sharing Economy Create Good Jobs?

Press-Telegram, StephenCarr/© AP/Wide World Photos

The advice is increasingly frequent in everyday conversations. Need a ride? Check your Uber app instead of calling a taxi. Need a small job done in your home or small business? Go online with TaskRabbit and book a "tasker" ready to jump on it. Need someone to watch your dog while you take a long weekend in the city? Let Dogvacay match you with a nearby dog sitter. And surely there's more to come in this sharing economy with its boundless opportunities for Web and app-driven business innovation.

A PricewaterhouseCoopers survey found 7% of U.S. workers already active on shared economy platforms, and the number is growing rapidly. They range from those supplementing full-time jobs with extra income, to those who can't find traditional full-time employment, to those wanting to work but needing flexibility in schedules.

Clients seem delighted for the most part. But, is this sharing economy good for workers?

While the income is good, most of those driving the cars, doing the tasks, and walking the pets work without benefits and legal protections traditional workers enjoy. One columnist argues: "It is a great deal for the owners, but a bad one for workers." Critics say that the sharing economy contributes to income disparity between those holding really good jobs with attractive futures and those doing as-available jobs for low pay and few long term growth prospects.

HOW ABOUT IT?

The sharing economy is here, but what are its implications for large and small employers, for career seekers, and for society at large? Is this a hot spot for innovation and eventual job creation, or is another sign that income inequalities are here to stay? How can the sharing economy be turned into a real strategic opportunity that benefits employers and workers alike? What are the career strategy implications of all this for you?

STUDYGUIDE

Takeaway 6.1
What Types of Strategies Are Used by Organizations?

Terms to Define

B2B business strategy	Co-opetition	Globalization strategy	Social media strategy
B2C business strategy	Corporate strategy	Growth strategy	Strategic alliance
Business strategy	Crowdsourcing	Liquidation	Strategic intent
C2B business strategy	Diversification	Mission	Strategy
C2C business strategy	Divestiture	Multidomestic strategy	Sustainable competitive advantage
Chapter 11 bankruptcy	Downsizing	P2P business strategies	
Competitive advantage	E-business strategy	Restructuring	Transnational strategy
Concentration	Functional strategy	Retrenchment strategy	Vertical integration

Rapid Review

- A strategy is a comprehensive plan that sets long-term direction for an organization and guides resource allocations to achieve competitive advantage, operating in ways that outperform the competition.
- Corporate strategy sets the direction for an entire organization; business strategy sets the direction for a large business unit or product division; functional strategy sets the direction within business functions.
- Growth strategies seek to expand existing business areas through concentration or add new ones by related or unrelated diversification.
- Retrenchment strategies try to streamline or consolidate organizations for better performance through restructuring and divestiture.
- Global strategies pursue international business opportunities.
- Cooperative strategies make business use of alliances and partnerships.
- E-business strategies use the Internet to pursue competitive advantage.

Questions for Discussion

1. With things changing so fast today, is it really possible for a business to achieve "sustainable" competitive advantage?
2. Why is growth such a popular business strategy?
3. Is it good news or bad news for investors when a business announces that it is restructuring?

Be Sure You Can

- **differentiate** strategy, strategic intent, and competitive advantage
- **differentiate** corporate, business, and functional levels of strategy
- **list** and explain major types of growth and diversification strategies
- **list** and explain restructuring and divestiture strategies
- **explain** alternative global strategies
- **differentiate** B2B and B2C as e-business strategies

Career Situation: What Would You Do?

A neighborhood business association has members from the local coffee bistro, bookstore, drugstore, hardware store, and bicycle shop. The owners of these businesses are interested in how they might "cooperate" for better success. Be a business consultant to the association. What would you propose as possible strategic alliances and cooperation strategies so that these businesses can work together for mutual gain?

Takeaway 6.2
How Do Managers Formulate and Implement Strategies?

ANSWERS TO COME

- The strategic management process formulates and implements strategies.
- SWOT analysis identifies strengths, weaknesses, opportunities, and threats.
- Porter's five forces model analyzes industry attractiveness.
- Porter's competitive strategies model identifies business or product strategies.
- Portfolio planning examines strategies across multiple businesses or products.
- Strategic leadership ensures strategy implementation and control.

THE LATE, GREAT MANAGEMENT GURU PETER DRUCKER ONCE SAID: "THE FUTURE will not just happen if one wishes hard enough. It requires decision—now. It imposes risk—now. It requires action—now. It demands allocation of resources, and above all, of human resources—now. It requires work—now."[18] Drucker's point fits squarely with the chapter subtitle: Insight and hard work deliver results. It's now time to talk more about the hard work of strategic management.

THE STRATEGIC MANAGEMENT PROCESS FORMULATES AND IMPLEMENTS STRATEGIES.

Figure 6.1 shows **strategic management** as the process of formulating and implementing strategies to accomplish long-term goals and sustain competitive advantage. **Strategy formulation** is the process of crafting strategy to fit mission and strategic intent, objectives, and environmental conditions.[19] It sets forth a strategic plan to deliver future competitive advantage. **Strategy implementation** is the process of putting strategies into action. It activates the entire organization to put strategies to work.

Can you see that success is only possible when strategies are both well formulated and well implemented? Success—in business or in personal life—doesn't just happen. It is

Strategic management is the process of formulating and implementing strategies.

Strategy formulation is the process of creating strategies to deliver competitive advantage.

Strategy implementation is the process of putting strategies into action.

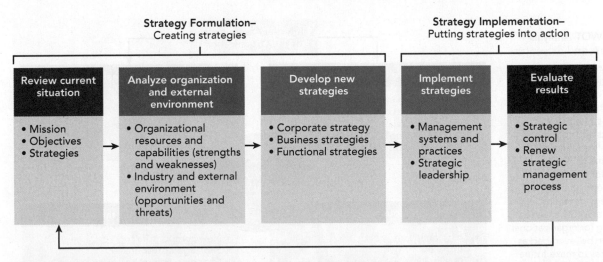

Strategy Formulation—Creating strategies

Strategy Implementation—Putting strategies into action

Review current situation	Analyze organization and external environment	Develop new strategies	Implement strategies	Evaluate results
• Mission • Objectives • Strategies	• Organizational resources and capabilities (strengths and weaknesses) • Industry and external environment (opportunities and threats)	• Corporate strategy • Business strategies • Functional strategies	• Management systems and practices • Strategic leadership	• Strategic control • Renew strategic management process

FIGURE 6.1 What Are the Steps in the Strategic Management Process?
The strategic management process involves responsibilities for both formulating and implementing organizational strategies. The process begins with review of existing mission, objectives, and strategies to set a baseline for further action. Next, organizational strengths and weaknesses as well as environmental opportunities and threats are analyzed. Strategies are then crafted at corporate, business, and functional levels. Finally, the strategies are put into action. This requires strategic leadership and control to ensure that all organizational resources and systems fully support strategy implementation.

TIPS TO REMEMBER
Key Operating Objectives of Organizations

- Profits—operating with revenues greater than costs
- Cost efficiency—operating with low costs; finding ways to lower costs
- Market share—having a solid and sustainable pool of customers
- Product quality—producing goods and services that satisfy customers
- Talented workforce—attracting and retaining high-quality employees
- Innovation—using new ideas to improve operations and products
- Social responsibility—earning the respect of multiple stakeholders
- Sustainability—developing sustainable processes, products, and supply chains

created when good strategies are implemented to full advantage.

Strategic success in business achieves operating objectives like those shown in the box. Strategic success in our personal lives achieves objectives like family prosperity and career advancement. But in both cases, strategic success requires more than reliance on solid one-time front-end analysis. In times of fast change, strategies and their implementations have to be flexible and adaptive. Strategic management has to continuously adjust to new conditions.

SWOT ANALYSIS IDENTIFIES STRENGTHS, WEAKNESSES, OPPORTUNITIES, AND THREATS.

A **SWOT analysis** examines organizational strengths and weaknesses, as well as environmental opportunities and threats.

A **core competency** is a special strength that gives an organization a competitive advantage.

A **SWOT analysis** involves a detailed examination of organizational strengths and weaknesses as well as environmental opportunities and threats. As **Figure 6.2** shows, the results of this examination can be portrayed in a straightforward and very useful planning matrix.

When looking at the organization's *strengths*, one goal is to identify **core competencies**. These are special strengths that the organization has or does exceptionally well in comparison with its competitors. When an organization's core competencies are unique and costly for others to imitate—say, for example, Amazon's "1-Click" order technology and efficient logistics—they become potential sources of competitive advantage.[20] Organizational *weaknesses* are the flip side of the picture. They must also be understood to gain a realistic sense of the organization's capabilities.

The same analytical discipline holds when examining conditions in the environment. It's not only the *opportunities* that count—such as new markets, a strong economy, weak competitors, and emerging technologies. The *threats* count, too—perhaps the emergence of new competitors, resource scarcities, changing customer tastes, and new government regulations.

By the way, don't forget the career planning implications of this discussion. If you were to analyze your strategic readiness for career entry or advancement right now, what would your personal SWOT look like?

FIGURE 6.2
What Does a SWOT Analysis Try to Discover?

The SWOT analysis is a way of identifying organizational strengths and weaknesses as well as environmental opportunities and threats. It forces strategists to discover key facts and conditions with potential consequences for strategic performance. It also organizes this information in a structured manner that is useful for making strategy decisions. Managers using a SWOT analysis should be looking for organizational strengths that can be leveraged as core competencies to make future gains, as well as environmental opportunities that can be exploited.

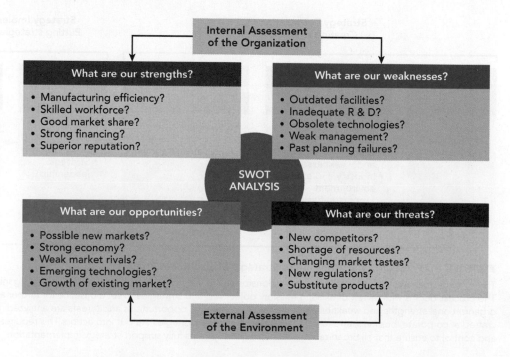

PORTER'S FIVE FORCES MODEL ANALYZES INDUSTRY ATTRACTIVENESS.

Harvard scholar and consultant Michael Porter says, "A company without a strategy is willing to try anything."[21] With a good strategy in place, by contrast, Porter believes an organization can best focus its resources on mission and objectives. He goes on to suggest that the first step in crafting a good strategy is to understand the nature of competition within an industry. This requires solid analysis, something that benefits from the strategy based on these "five forces":

Force 1: *Competitors*—intensity of rivalry among firms in the industry

Force 2: *New entrants*—threats of new competitors entering the market

Force 3: *Suppliers*—bargaining power of suppliers

Force 4: *Customers*—bargaining power of buyers

Force 5: *Substitutes*—threats of substitute products or services[22]

Porter's five forces model of industry attractiveness is shown in **Figure 6.3**. An unattractive industry will have intense competitive rivalries, substantial threats in the form of possible new entrants and substitute products, and powerful suppliers and buyers who dominate any bargaining with the firm. As you might expect, this is a very challenging environment for strategy formulation. A very attractive industry will have little existing competition, few threats from new entrants or substitutes, and low bargaining power among suppliers and buyers. These are much more favorable conditions for strategy formulation.

PORTER'S COMPETITIVE STRATEGIES MODEL IDENTIFIES BUSINESS OR PRODUCT STRATEGIES.

Once industry forces are understood, attention shifts to how a business or its products can be strategically positioned relative to competitors. Porter believes that competitive strategies can be built around differentiation, cost leadership, and focus.

A **differentiation strategy** seeks competitive advantage through uniqueness. This means developing goods and services that are clearly different from the competition. The strategic objective is to attract customers who stay loyal to the firm's products and lose interest in those of its competitors.

Success with a differentiation strategy depends on customer perceptions of product quality and uniqueness. This requires organizational strengths in marketing, research and development, and creativity. An example is Polo Ralph Lauren, retailer of upscale classic fashions and accessories. In Ralph Lauren's words, "Polo redefined how American style and quality is perceived. Polo has always been about selling quality products by creating worlds and inviting our customers to be part of our dream."[23] If you've seen any Polo ads in magazines or on television, you'll know that the company aggressively markets this perception.

> A **differentiation strategy** offers products that are unique and different from those of the competition.

FIGURE 6.3 What Is Porter's Five Forces Model of Industry Attractiveness?

Strategic management is very challenging in an *unattractive industry* that has intense competitive rivalries, substantial threats in the form of possible new entrants and substitute products, and powerful suppliers and buyers who dominate any bargaining with the firm. Strategy management is less of a problem in an *attractive industry* that has little existing competition, few threats from new entrants or substitutes, and low bargaining power among suppliers and buyers.

A **cost leadership strategy** seeks to operate with lower costs than competitors.

A **focused differentiation strategy** offers a unique product to a special market segment.

A **focused cost leadership strategy** seeks the lowest costs of operations within a special market segment.

A **cost leadership strategy** seeks competitive advantage by operating with lower costs than competitors. This allows organizations to make profits while selling products or services at low prices their competitors can't profitably match. The objective is to continuously improve operating efficiencies in purchasing, production, distribution, and other organizational systems.

Success with the cost leadership strategy requires tight cost and managerial controls, as well as products or services that are easy to create and distribute. This is what might be called the "Walmart" strategy—do everything you can to keep costs so low that you can offer customers lower prices than competitors and still make a reasonable profit.

Porter describes two forms of the focus strategy, both of which try to serve the needs of a narrow market segment better than anyone else. The **focused differentiation strategy** offers a unique product to customers in a special market segment. For example, NetJets offers air travel by fractional ownership of private jets to wealthy customers. The **focused cost leadership strategy** tries to be the low-cost provider for a special market segment. Low-fare airlines, for example, offer heavily discounted fares and "no frills" service for customers who want to travel point-to-point for the lowest prices.

Can you apply these four competitive strategies to an actual situation—say, alternative sodas in the soft-drink industry? Porter would begin by asking and answering two questions for each soda: What is the market scope—broad or narrow? What is the potential source of competitive advantage—low price or product uniqueness? **Figure 6.4** shows how answers to these questions might strategically position some soft drinks with which you might be familiar.

The makers of Coke and Pepsi follow a differentiation strategy. They spend millions on advertising to convince consumers that their products are of high quality and uniquely desirable. Bubba Cola, a Save-A-Lot Brand, and Go2 Cola, a Safeway Brand, sell as cheaper alternatives. To make a profit at the lower selling price, these stores must follow a cost leadership strategy.

What about a can of A & W Root Beer or a can of Mountain Dew? In Porter's model, they represent a strategy of focused differentiation—products with unique tastes for customers wanting quality brands. This is quite different from the strategy behind Giant Store's Quist or Stop & Shop's Sun Pop. These are classic cases of focused cost leadership—a product with a unique taste for customers who want a low price.

PORTFOLIO PLANNING EXAMINES STRATEGIES ACROSS MULTIPLE BUSINESSES OR PRODUCTS.

As you might expect, strategic management gets quite complicated for companies that operate multiple businesses selling many different products and services. A good example is the global conglomerate General Electric. The firm owns a portfolio of diverse businesses ranging from jet engines, to medical systems, to power systems, and even more. The CEO of

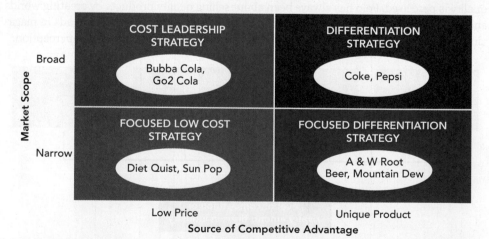

FIGURE 6.4 What Are the Strategic Options in Porter's Competitive Strategies Model?
Porter's competitive strategies model asks two basic questions to identify alternative business and product strategies. First, what is the market scope—broad or narrow? Second, what is the expected source of competitive advantage—lower price or product uniqueness? The four possible combinations of answers result in differentiation, cost leadership, focused differentiation, and focused cost leadership strategies. The figure uses examples from the soft-drink industry to show how these strategies can be used for different products.

GE faces a difficult strategic question all the time: How to allocate the firm's resources across this mix, or portfolio, of businesses? Portfolio-planning questions like this are better made systematically than haphazardly.[24]

A very basic but still insightful portfolio planning approach developed by the Boston Consulting Group is summarized in **Figure 6.5**. Known as the **BCG Matrix**, this strategic management framework analyzes business and product strategies based on market growth rate and market share.[25]

Stars in the BCG Matrix have high market shares in high-growth markets. They produce large profits through substantial penetration of expanding markets. The preferred strategy for stars is growth. The BCG Matrix recommends making further resource investments in them. Stars are not only high performers in the present, they also offer future potential to do the same or even better.

Cash cows have high market shares in low-growth markets. They produce large profits and a strong cash flow, but with little upside potential. Because the markets offer little growth opportunity, the preferred strategy for cash cows is stability or modest growth. Like real dairy cows, the BCG Matrix advises firms to "milk" these businesses to generate cash for investing in other more promising areas.

Question marks have low market shares in high-growth markets. Although they may not generate much profit at the moment, the upside potential is there because of the growing markets. Question marks make for difficult strategic decision making. The BCG Matrix recommends targeting only the most promising question marks for growth, while retrenching those that are less promising.

Dogs have low market shares in low-growth markets. They produce little if any profit, and they have low potential for future improvement. The preferred strategy for dogs is straightforward: retrenchment by divestiture.

The **BCG Matrix** analyzes business opportunities according to market growth rate and market share.

STRATEGIC LEADERSHIP ENSURES STRATEGY IMPLEMENTATION AND CONTROL.

In order to successfully put strategies into action, the entire organization and all its resources and systems must be mobilized to support them. This involves the complete management process from planning and organizing through leading and controlling. No matter how well or elegantly planned, a strategy has to be well executed to achieve success. It requires supporting structures, a good allocation of tasks and workflow designs, and the right people to staff all aspects of operations. The strategy also needs to be enthusiastically supported by leaders at all levels who are capable of motivating everyone, building individual performance commitments, and utilizing teams and teamwork to their best advantage.

The premium today is on **strategic leadership**—the capability to inspire people to successfully implement organizational strategies.[26] In order to excel at strategic leadership, you must have the ability to make strategic choices. But, you must also be alert and confident in recognizing when strategies aren't working and need to be changed. Ultimately, you

Strategic leadership inspires people to implement organizational strategies.

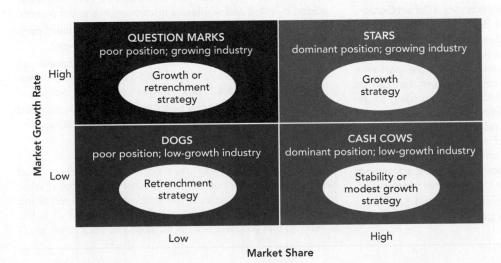

	QUESTION MARKS poor position; growing industry	STARS dominant position; growing industry
High	Growth or retrenchment strategy	Growth strategy
	DOGS poor position; low-growth industry	CASH COWS dominant position; low-growth industry
Low	Retrenchment strategy	Stability or modest growth strategy
	Low	High

Market Growth Rate (vertical axis) — Market Share (horizontal axis)

FIGURE 6.5

Why Is the BCG Matrix Useful in Strategic Planning?

The BCG Matrix is useful in situations where managers must make strategic decisions that allocate scarce organizational resources among multiple and competing uses. This is a typical situation for organizations that have a range of businesses or products. The BCG Matrix sorts businesses or products into four strategic types (dogs, stars, question marks, and cash cows), based on market shares held and market growth rates. Specific master strategies are recommended for each strategic type.

must be able to rally the entire organization around the twin tasks of strategy implementation and positive change. Michael Porter describes the strategic leadership role this way:[27]

- *A strategic leader has to be the guardian of trade-offs.* It is the leader's job to make sure that the organization's resources are allocated in ways consistent with the strategy. This requires the discipline to sort through many competing ideas and alternatives to stay on course and not get sidetracked.

- *A strategic leader needs to create a sense of urgency.* The leader must not allow the organization and its members to grow slow and complacent. Even when doing well, the leader keeps the focus on getting better and being alert to conditions that require adjustments to the strategy.

- *A strategic leader must make sure that everyone understands the strategy.* Unless strategies are understood, the daily tasks and contributions of people lose context and purpose. Everyone might work very hard, but unless efforts are aligned with strategy, the impact is dispersed and fails to advance common goals.

- *A strategic leader must be a teacher.* It is the leader's job to teach the strategy and make it a "cause," says Porter. In order for strategy to work, it must become an ever-present commitment throughout the organization. This means that a strategic leader must be a great communicator. Everyone must understand the strategy and how it makes the organization different from others.

To Porter's list we must add the following: *A strategic leader must be the champion of control.* One of the lessons business firms learn from economic crisis is that a strategic leader has to maintain **strategic control**. This means that the CEO and other top managers stay closely in touch with the strategy, know whether it is generating performance success or failure, and recognize when the strategy needs to be tweaked or changed.[28]

> **Strategic control** makes sure strategies are well implemented and that poor strategies are scrapped or changed.

A posting on Patagonia's Web site once said: "During the past thirty years, we've made many mistakes but we've never lost our way for very long."[29] Not only is the firm being honest, it is also communicating an important point about the strategic management process: Mistakes will be made, and strategic leaders both correct and learn from them.

FACTS TO CONSIDER

Disposable Workers Are Indispensable to Business Profits

Stuart Rayner/iStockphoto

We're now in the era of the disposable worker, says Northwestern University economist Robert Gordon. And the facts certainly support his claim. Businesses seem enamored with the idea of hiring fewer full timers and hiring more part-time or temporary workers that can be added and let go according to demand. Professor Susan J. Lambert of the University of Chicago blames some of the switch to disposable workers on labor union decline. Others simply point out the cost advantages to employers who only have to pay for workers as needed.

- A McKinsey survey of 2,000 employers found 58% planning to hire more workers on a part-time, temporary, and contract basis.

- The U.S. Bureau of Labor Statistics reports that 1 million full-time jobs have been cut and 500,000 part-time ones added by retail and wholesale employers in the last 6 years.

- Almost 3 of every 10 retail/wholesale jobs are filled part-time. Among part-timers, 30.6% want full-time work.

- Compensation for part-timers in retail/wholesale averaged $10.92 per hour ($8.90 wages and $2.02 benefits) versus $17.18 for full-timers ($12.25 wages and $4.93 benefits).

- A survey of retailers in New York City found half of jobs filled by part-timers. Only 1 in 10 of them had set work schedules.

WHAT'S YOUR TAKE?

Is this switch to employing more disposable workers a good long-term strategy for businesses and other organizations? What are the possible downsides to the employer and the remaining full-time employees? How might this trend affect you? Is this something that you have already factored into your career plan?

STUDYGUIDE

Takeaway 6.2
How Do Managers Formulate and Implement Strategies?

Terms to Define

BCG Matrix	Focused cost leadership strategy	Strategic control	Strategy implementation
Core competencies		Strategic leadership	
Cost leadership strategy	Focused differentiation strategy	Strategic management	SWOT analysis
Differentiation strategy		Strategy formulation	

Rapid Review

- Strategic management is the process of formulating and implementing strategies to achieve a sustainable competitive environment.
- A SWOT analysis sets a foundation for strategy formulation by systematically assessing organizational strengths and weaknesses as well as environmental opportunities and threats.
- Porter's five forces model analyzes industry attractiveness in terms of competitors, threat of new entrants, substitute products, and the bargaining powers of suppliers and buyers.
- Porter's competitive strategies describes business and product strategies based on differentiation (distinguishing one's products from the competition), cost leadership (minimizing costs relative to the competition), and focus (concentrating on a special market segment).
- The BCG Matrix is a portfolio-planning approach that describes strategies for businesses classified as stars, cash cows, question marks, or dogs.
- Strategic leadership is the responsibility for activating people, organizational resources, and management systems to continually pursue and fully accomplish strategy implementation.

Questions for Discussion

1. Can an organization have a good strategy but a poor sense of mission?
2. Would a monopoly receive a perfect score for industry attractiveness in Porter's five forces model?
3. Does the BCG Matrix oversimplify a complex strategic management problem?

Be Sure You Can

- **describe** the strategic management process
- **explain** Porter's five forces model
- **explain** Porter's competitive strategies model
- **describe** the purpose and use of the BCG Matrix
- **explain** the responsibilities of strategic leadership

Career Situation: What Would You Do?

For some years now, you've owned a small specialty bookshop in a college town. You sell some textbooks but mainly cater to a broader customer base. Your store always stocks the latest fiction, nonfiction, and children's books. Recent numbers show a steep decline in sales, including of books that would normally be considered best sellers. You suspect this is because of the growing popularity of e-books and e-readers such as the Amazon Kindle and Barnes & Noble Nook. Some of your friends say it's time to close up because your market is dying. Is it hopeless, or is there a business strategy that might yet save the store?

TEST PREP 6

Answers to Test Prep questions can be found at the back of the book.

Multiple-Choice Questions

1. Which is the best question to ask to start the strategic management process?
   (a) "What is our mission?"
   (b) "How well are we currently doing?"
   (c) "How can we get where we want to be?"
   (d) "Why aren't we doing better?"

2. The ability of a business firm to consistently outperform its rivals is called _____.
   (a) vertical integration
   (b) competitive advantage
   (c) strategic intent
   (d) core competency

3. General Electric is a complex conglomerate that owns many firms operating in very different industries. The strategies pursued for each individual firm within the GE umbrella would best be called _____ level strategies.
   (a) corporate   (b) business
   (c) functional   (d) transnational

4. An organization that is downsizing by cutting staff to reduce costs can be described as pursuing a _____ strategy.
   (a) liquidation   (b) divestiture
   (c) retrenchment   (d) stability

5. When you buy music downloads online, the firm selling them to you is engaging in which type of e-business strategy?
   (a) B2C   (b) B2B
   (c) infomediary   (d) crowdsourcing

6. The alliances that link firms in supply chain management relationships are examples of how businesses can use _____ strategies.
   (a) B2C   (b) growth
   (c) cooperation   (d) concentration

7. Among the global strategies that international businesses might pursue, the _____ strategy most directly tries to customize products to fit local needs and cultures in different countries.
   (a) concentration   (b) globalization
   (c) transnational   (d) multidomestic

8. If Google's top management were to announce that the firm was going to buy Federal Express, this would be a strategy of growth by _____.
   (a) diversification
   (b) concentration
   (c) horizontal integration
   (d) vertical integration

9. _____ are special strengths that an organization has or does exceptionally well and that help it outperform competitors.
   (a) Core competencies
   (b) Strategies
   (c) Alliances
   (d) Operating objectives

10. A _____ in the BCG Matrix would have a high market share in a low-growth market.
    (a) dog   (b) cash cow
    (c) question mark   (d) star

11. In Porter's five forces model, which of the following conditions is most favorable from the standpoint of industry attractiveness?
    (a) Many competitive rivals
    (b) Many substitute products
    (c) Low bargaining power of suppliers
    (d) Few barriers to entry

12. The two questions Porter asks to identify the correct competitive strategy for a business or product line are: 1—What is the market scope? 2—What is the _____?
    (a) market share
    (b) source of competitive advantage
    (c) core competency
    (d) industry attractiveness

13. When Coke and Pepsi spend millions on ads trying to convince customers that their products are unique, they are pursuing what Porter calls a _____ strategy.
    (a) transnational
    (b) concentration
    (c) diversification
    (d) differentiation

14. A firm that wants to compete with rivals by selling a very low-priced product in a broad market would need to successfully implement a _____ strategy.
    (a) retrenchment   (b) differentiation
    (c) cost leadership   (d) diversification

15. In addition to focusing on strategy implementation and strategic control, the responsibility for strategic leadership of an organization involves success with _____.
    (a) motivating a disposable workforce
    (b) the process of continuous change
    (c) Chapter 11 bankruptcy
    (d) growth by liquidation

Short-Response Questions

16. What is the difference between corporate strategy and functional strategy?

17. Why is a cost leadership strategy so important when one wants to sell products at lower prices than competitors?

18. What strategy should be pursued for a "question mark" in the BCG Matrix, and why?

19. What is strategic leadership?

Integration and Application Question

20. Kim Harris owns and operates a small retail store that sells the outdoor clothing of an American manufacturer to a predominantly college-student market. A large national-chain department store has come to town and started selling similar but lower-priced clothing manufactured in China, Thailand, and Bangladesh. Kim is losing business to this store. She has asked your instructor to have a student team analyze the situation and propose some strategic alternatives to best deal with this threat. You are on the team.

    Questions: How can a SWOT analysis be helpful in addressing Kim's strategic management problem? How could Porter's competitive strategies model be helpful as well?

Steps for
Further Learning

BUILD MARKETABLE SKILLS • **DO** A CASE ANALYSIS • **GET** AND STAY INFORMED

BUILD MARKETABLE SKILLS.

EARN BIG CAREER PAYOFFS!

Don't miss these opportunities in the SKILL-BUILDING PORTFOLIO

SELF-ASSESSMENT 6:
Facts and Inferences

Not all situations are clear-cut ... get better at separating facts from inferences.

CLASS EXERCISE 6:
Strategic Scenarios

It's risky to make decisions on past experience ... practice getting a sense of the future.

TEAM PROJECT 6:
Contrasting Strategies

There's often more than one way to a goal ... but some strategies are still better than others

Many learning resources are found at the end of the book and online within **WileyPLUS Learning Space.**

Practice Critical Thinking—Complete the CHAPTER 6 CASE

CASE SNAPSHOT: Dunkin' Donuts—Growth Feeds a Sweet Tooth

Long before Starbucks was even a glimmer in anyone's entrepreneurial mind, Dunkin' Donuts was as a well-known chain of coffee shops in the Northeast. It began in Boston in 1950, grew nicely, and today has positioned itself as a global player. This java giant is expanding both its food and coffee menus to ride the wave of fresh trends appealing to a new generation of more health-conscious customers. Dunkin's reputation for quality gives it an advantage in earning the trust of customers. In a highly competitive industry, change has to constantly be on the menu. Will great strategic management keep customers "Runnin' on Dunkin'"?

DO A CASE ANALYSIS.

STRENGTHEN YOUR CRITICAL THINKING!

MANAGER'S LIBRARY SELECTION
Read for Insights and Wisdom
Rebooting Work: Transform How You Work in the Age of Entrepreneurship (2013, John Wiley & Sons) by Maynard Webb

It's time to get your career strategy up to date. Strategy and strategic management isn't just for organizations, it also applies to personal affairs and goals. Career strategy is right up there in importance. Things are changing so fast today that the career strategies that helped past generations to succeed might not work as well for present ones.

GET AND STAY INFORMED.

MAKE YOURSELF VALUABLE!

Maynard Webb's book is a practical guide to navigating the new era of what many call the "entrepreneurial workplace." A silicon valley angel investor, philanthropist, entrepreneur, and company builder, he describes a decline in face-to-face mentoring between senior managers and their juniors. Reasons include technology replacing in-person communication and the shorter and more temporary tenure of employment contracts. Flatter organizations that operate with fewer middle managers also offer fewer mentoring opportunities.

Even though Webb claims that "the mentor-protégé model has gone the way of the mainframe computer," mentoring is still high on his list of career priorities, but as a strategy driven by the power of self-management. It's important, he says, to take control of your own destiny and abandon the dated notion that an employer will take care of your professional development.

Webb's message is that mentors are out there, but we have to find and access them on our own. Good developmental job opportunities exist, but we have to seek out the new roles and responsibilities for ourselves. Webb recommends we "seek mentors and aspire to be a mentor" and "focus on being voted on the team each day." With proper self management it's possible to stay inspired, empowered, and successful in the entrepreneurial workplace.

REFLECT AND REACT Does this notion of the entrepreneurial workplace seem to describe the career settings ahead for you? How about the mentoring strategy? If you don't have a mentor and your employer isn't being helpful, how can you get yourself one? Can mentoring work as well in online as face-to-face relationships?

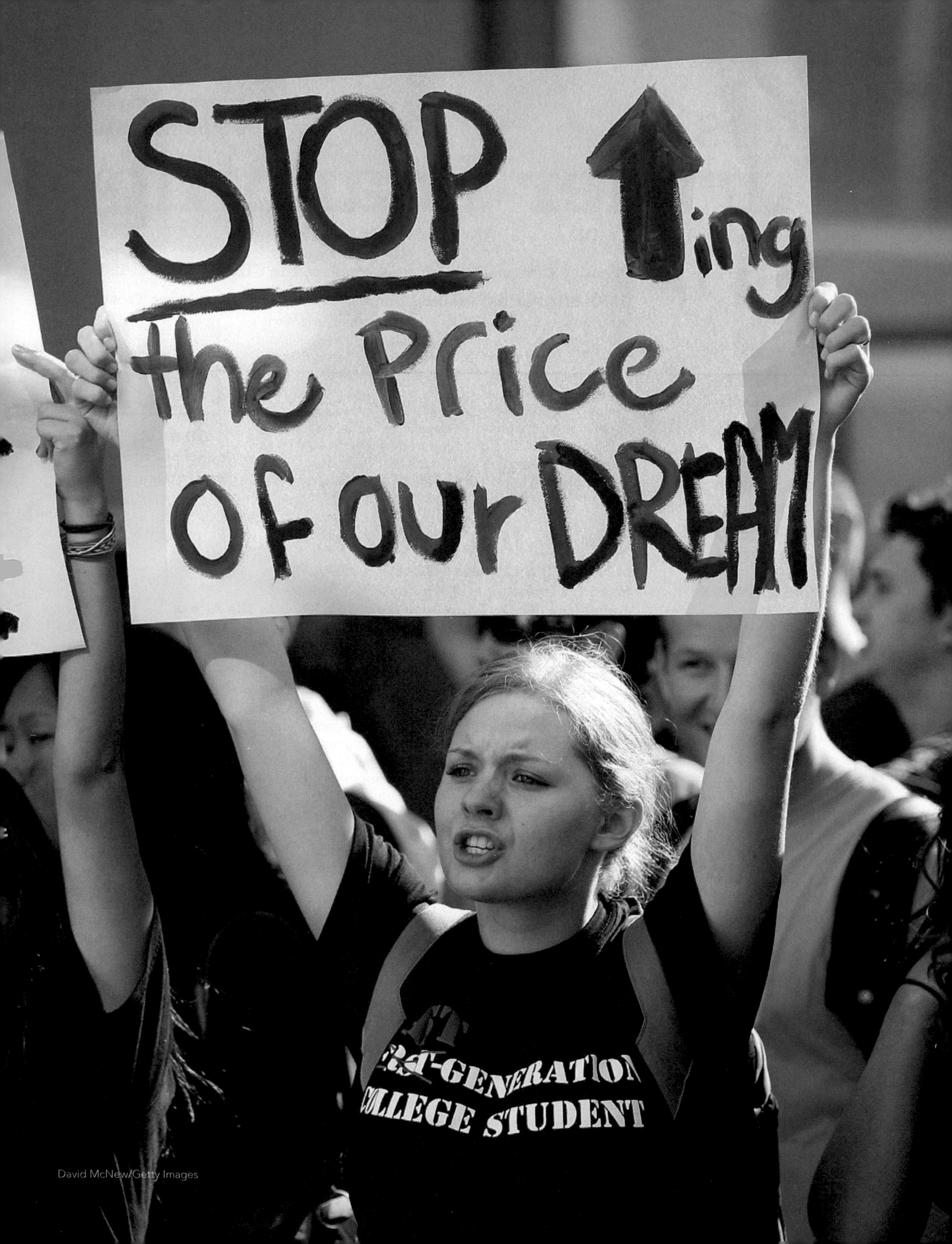

David McNew/Getty Images

Organization Structure and Design

It's All About Working Together

Management Live

Skills Gap found in College Students

Mediaphotos/Istockphoto/Getty Images

The data are sobering. Complex reasoning skills—lacking in 4 of 10 graduating college students. Read a data plot, construct a clear argument, evaluate evidence in an argument, identify a logical fallacy—many graduates can't do them. Critical thinking and written communication—14% of graduating seniors fail a standardized test and 25% score with only "basic" skills. A survey of business owners reports that 9 of 10 believe college graduates are "poorly prepared" for work.

HOW ABOUT IT?

Richard Arum, author of *Academically Adrift*, says: "Colleges are increasing their attention to the social aspects on campus to keep students happy; there is not enough rigorous academic instruction." Is this the case on your campus and with you? Are our colleges and universities well organized to serve students' long-term needs?

YOUR CHAPTER 7 TAKEAWAYS

1. Understand organizing as a managerial responsibility.
2. Identify common types of organization structures.
3. Recognize current trends in organizational design.

Takeaway 7.1
What Is Organizing as a Managerial Responsibility?

ANSWERS TO COME

- Organizing is one of the management functions.
- Organization charts describe formal structures of organizations.
- Organizations also have informal structures.
- Informal structures have good points and bad points.

IT IS MUCH EASIER TO TALK ABOUT high-performing organizations than to actually create them. There is no one best way to do things; no one organizational form meets the needs of all circumstances. And what works well at one moment in time can quickly become outdated, even dysfunctional, in another. This is why you often read and hear about organizations making changes and reorganizing in an attempt to improve their performance. But beware. Whenever job assignments and reporting relationships change, whenever the organization grows or shrinks, whenever old ways of doing things are reconfigured, people naturally struggle to understand the new ways of working.[1] And perhaps even more important, they will worry about the implications for their jobs and careers.

ORGANIZING IS ONE OF THE MANAGEMENT FUNCTIONS.

Most of us like to be organized—at home, at work, when playing games. We tend to get uncomfortable and anxious when things are disorganized. It shouldn't surprise you, therefore, that people in organizations need answers to such questions as: "Where do I fit in?" "How does my work relate to that of others?" and "Who runs things?"[2] Employees need these answers when they first join an organization, when they take new jobs, and whenever things are substantially changed. The risk of disengagement rises when they don't get good answers. And disengagement fosters absenteeism, turnover, dissatisfaction, and lower performance.[3]

This is where and why **organizing** plays a key role as one of the four functions of management shown in **Figure 7.1**. Think of it as the process of arranging people and resources so that they can work together to accomplish goals. Once goals are set in the planning phase of management, organizing puts people and resources in place to carry them out.[4] Organizing clarifies jobs and working relationships. It identifies who is to do what and who is in charge

> **Organizing** arranges people and resources to work toward a common goal.

FIGURE 7.1

What Is the Importance of Organizing in the Management Process?

Organizing is one of the four management functions. It is the process of arranging people and resources to create structures so that they work well together in accomplishing goals. Key organizing decisions made by managers include those that divide up the work to be done, staff jobs with talented people, position resources for best utilization, and coordinate activities.

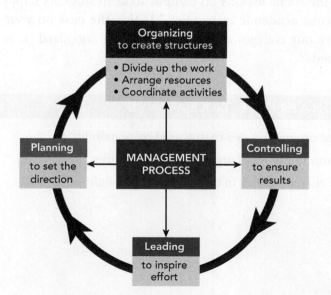

of whom. And it sets the stage so that different people and different parts of the organization are coordinated and work well with one another. All this, of course, can be accomplished in different ways. The manager's challenge is to choose the best organizational form—or structure—to fit the people, the strategy, and other situational demands.

ORGANIZATION CHARTS DESCRIBE FORMAL STRUCTURES OF ORGANIZATIONS.

When managers organize things, they arrange people and jobs into meaningful working relationships. They spell out who is to do what, who is in charge of whom, and how different people and work units are supposed to cooperate. This creates what we call the **organization structure**, a formal arrangement of people, tasks, positions, and reporting relationships.

You probably know the concept of structure best in terms of an **organization chart**. This is a diagram of positions—job titles, and reporting relationships—the hierarchy of authority, within a team or organization.[5] This chart describes a **division of labor** that is designed to support organizational performance by assigning important tasks to individuals and groups.

You can learn from an organization chart, but only in respect to the **formal structure**. This is the "official" structure or the way things are supposed to operate.[6] Think of it as a "best guess" for how to align positions, people, and responsibilities to get work done. But as with most guesses, things don't always work as intended. Circumstances change, tasks change, people change, and more. And every time they do, the formal structure moves a bit further away from the current situation it is supposed to fit. This is why managers often find themselves tinkering with the formal structure in attempting to get the alignment right.

ORGANIZATIONS ALSO HAVE INFORMAL STRUCTURES.

SITUATION: A worker in his office cubicle overhears a conversation taking place in the next cubicle. Words such as "project being terminated" and "job cuts will be necessary" are used. At lunch he shares this with friends. Word quickly spreads around the building that the employer is going to announce layoffs.

What's happening in this situation falls outside the formal structure of the organization. It takes place in the "shadows" and won't appear on any organization chart. An important fact of organizational life is that behind every formal structure also lies an **informal structure**—a network of unofficial relationships between organizational members. Like any

Organization structure is a formal arrangement of tasks, reporting relationships, and communication linkages.

An **organization chart** describes the arrangement of work positions within a team or organization.

The **division of labor** assigns important tasks to individuals and groups.

Formal structure is the official structure of the organization.

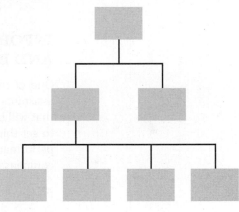

The **informal structure** or **shadow organization** is the network of unofficial relationships among an organization's members.

Holacracy Wants to Change Organization Charts and Say "Goodbye" to CEO Power

© Minerva Studio/iStockphoto

Welcome to a fashion-forward Holacracy. Trademarked by HolacracyOne, it is described as a "new 'operating system'" that "replaces today's top-down predict-and-control paradigm with a new way of achieving control by distributing power." Employees—as "partners"—hold power distributed to them by the Holacracy Constitution. Managers are gone. Partners agree to things like creating and acting on projects to fulfil roles, tracking progress, helping one another, and spotting tensions indicating things could be better. When Zappos adopted Holacracy, CEO Tony Hsieh justified the shift this way: "There's the org chart on paper, and then the one that is exactly how the company operates for real, and then there's the org chart that it would like to have in order to operate more efficiently. . . . [With Holacracy] the idea is to process tensions so that the three org charts are pretty close together."

Informal Structures and the Shadow Organization

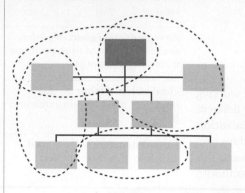

shadow, the shape of the informal structure emerges and changes over time. You may have to work hard to understand its full complexities.

If you could draw the informal structure for your organization—and this would be an interesting exercise—you would find relationships cutting across levels and moving from side to side. Some would be work related, reflecting how people have found the best ways to get their jobs done. Many others would be personal, reflecting who meets for coffee, stops in for office chats, meets together in exercise groups, and spends time together as friends, not just co-workers.[7]

It used to be that most informal structures were based on face-to-face relationships. Now, technology is the driving force behind many of them. Messaging and social media links people together within organizations as well as outside of them. As organizations try to tap technology to create things like knowledge-sharing networks and crowdsourcing support for problem solving, the relationships they empower make boundaries between "informal" and "formal" structures increasingly hard to define.

INFORMAL STRUCTURES HAVE GOOD POINTS AND BAD POINTS.

One of the first things you probably learned in college was that knowing department assistants is a very good way to get into classes that are "closed" or find out about new courses that will be offered. This is just one of any number of ways people use informal structures to get things done. And this can be a very positive influence on the organization and its performance. Simply put, informal structures often fill gaps in the formal structure and help compensate for its inadequacies.

Good Points About Informal Structures

The relationships available in the informal structure can connect people to get things done, learn new jobs, and solve problems. People assist each other within the informal structure because they know and trust one another, not because the structure requires it. As you already know from personal experience, it can be really helpful to tap into the wisdom of friends or even an anonymous social media crowd when needing advice on a particular problem. And, informal relationships also provide a lot of social and emotional support. They give people access to friendships, support groups, conversations, and advice that can help make the normal workday pleasant and a bad workday less troublesome. Informal structures can be especially helpful during periods of change, when out-of-date formal structures just don't deal well with new situations. Because it takes time to change or modify formal structures, the informal structure helps fill the void while things are in transition.

It's increasingly common to use **social network analysis** to identify active informal structures. This analysis asks people to name others they ask for help most often, whom they communicate with regularly, and who energizes and de-energizes them.[8] The results are depicted in a network map that shows how a lot of work really gets done. This information becomes a roadmap for redesigning the formal structure for better performance and identifying key candidates for leadership and mentoring roles.[9]

Social network analysis identifies the informal structures and their embedded social relationships that are active in an organization.

Downsides of Informal Structures

Things sometimes happen within informal structures that work against the best interests of the organization as a whole. Shadow structures can be susceptible to rumor, carry inaccurate information, breed resistance to change, and even distract members from their work. And if you happen to end up as an "outsider" rather than an "insider" in the informal networks, you may feel less a part of things.

Crises or difficult situations sometimes accentuate the bad points of informal structures. The Society for Human Resource Management reported a 23% increase in workplace eavesdropping and a 54% increase in "gossip and rumors about downsizings and layoffs" during the last economic crisis. Cafeterias were hotspots for gossip, and one HR director says she even noticed people trying to hang out in hallways and sit as close as possible to executives in cafeterias in attempts to overhear conversations.[10]

STUDYGUIDE

Takeaway 7.1
What Is Organizing as a Managerial Responsibility?

Terms to Define

Division of labor	Informal structure	Organization structure	Shadow organization
Formal structure	Organization chart	Organizing	Social network analysis

Rapid Review

- Organizing is the process of arranging people and resources to work toward a common goal.
- Structure is the system of tasks, reporting relationships, and communication that links people and positions within an organization.
- Organization charts describe the formal structure and how an organization should ideally work.
- The informal structure of an organization consists of the unofficial relationships that develop among its members.
- Informal structures create helpful relationships for social support and task assistance, but they can be susceptible to rumors.

Questions for Discussion

1. Why is organizing such an important management function?
2. If organization charts are imperfect, why bother with them?
3. Could an organization consistently perform well without the help of its informal structure?

Be Sure You Can

- **explain** what you can learn from an organization chart
- **differentiate** formal and informal structures
- **discuss** potential good and bad points about informal structures

Career Situation: What Would You Do?

As the new manager of a branch bank location, you will be supervising 22 employees, most of whom have worked together for a number of years. How will you identify the informal structure of the branch? How will you try to use this structure to help establish yourself as an effective manager in the new situation?

Takeaway 7.2
What Are the Most Common Organization Structures?

ANSWERS TO COME

■ Functional structures group together people using similar skills.

■ Divisional structures group together people by products, customers, or locations.

■ Matrix structures combine the functional and divisional structures.

■ Team structures make extensive use of permanent and temporary teams.

■ Network structures make extensive use of strategic alliances and outsourcing.

A TRADITIONAL PRINCIPLE OF ORGANIZING IS THAT HIGH PERFORMANCE DEPENDS on having a well defined and coordinated division of labor. The process of arranging people by tasks and work groups is called **departmentalization**.[11] The traditional forms are the functional, divisional, and matrix structures. Increasingly popular today are team and network structures. These are examples of **horizontal structures** designed to tap the power of technology, teams, collaboration, and networks. As you read about each type of structure, don't forget that organizations rarely use only one. Most often they will have a mixture, with various parts and levels of the organization using different structures to meet their unique needs.

FUNCTIONAL STRUCTURES GROUP TOGETHER PEOPLE USING SIMILAR SKILLS.

Take a look at **Figure 7.2**. What organizing logic do you see? These are **functional structures** where people having similar skills and performing similar tasks are grouped together into

Departmentalization is the process of grouping together people and jobs into work units.

Horizontal structures are designed to tap the power of technology, teams, collaboration, and networks.

A **functional structure** groups together people with similar skills who perform similar tasks.

FIGURE 7.2
What Does a Typical Functional Organization Structure Look Like?

Functional structures are common in organizations of all types and sizes. In a typical business you might have vice presidents or senior managers heading the traditional functions of accounting, human resources, finance, manufacturing, marketing, and sales. In a bank, they may head such functions as loans, investments, and trusts. In a hospital, managers or administrators are usually in charge of functions such as nursing, clinics, and patient services.

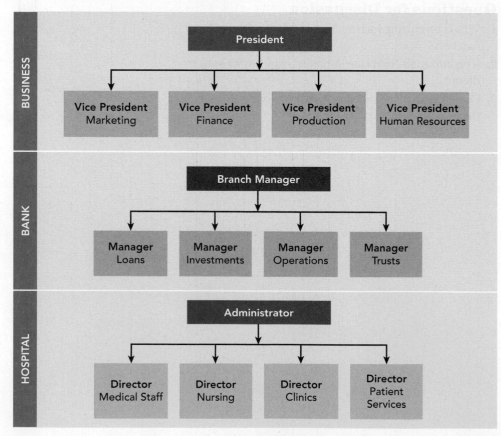

formal work units. The assumption is that if the functions are well chosen and each acts properly, the organization should operate successfully. In business, for example, typical functions include marketing, finance, accounting, production, management information systems, and human resources. But functional structures are not limited to businesses. The figure also shows how other organizations such as banks and hospitals may use them.

> ### Potential Advantages of Functional Structures
>
> - Economies of scale make efficient use of human resources.
> - Functional experts are good at solving technical problems.
> - Training within functions promotes skill development.
> - Career paths are available within each function.

Functional structures work well for small organizations that produce only one or a few products or services. They also tend to work best for organizations, or parts of organizations, that have relatively stable environments where the problems are predictable and demands for change are limited. And they offer benefits to individuals. Within a given function—say, marketing—people share technical expertise, interests, and responsibilities. They can also advance in responsibilities and pursue career paths within the function.

Although functional structures have a clear logic, there are some potential downsides as well. When an organization is divided into functions, it can be hard to pinpoint responsibilities for things such as cost containment, product or service quality, and innovation. And with everyone focused on meeting functional goals, the sense of working for the good of the organization as a whole may get lost. People may also find that they get trapped in functional career niches that are hard to break out of to gain career-broadening experiences in other areas.

Another concern about functional structures is something called the **functional chimneys** or **functional silos problem**. Shown in the small figure, this problem occurs as a lack of communication, coordination, and problem solving across functions. Instead of cooperating with one another, members of functional units sometimes end up either competing or selfishly focusing on functional goals rather than broader organizational objectives.

> The **functional chimneys** or **functional silos problem** is a lack of communication and coordination across functions.

Former Yahoo CEO Carol Bartz described a functional silo problem this way: "The home page people didn't want to drive traffic to the finance page because they wanted to keep them on the home page."[12] Such problems of poor cooperation and even just plain lack of helpfulness across functions can be very persistent. When Paul Michaels took over as CEO of Mars, Inc., he found, "The top team was siloed and replete with unspoken agendas. Members did not see the benefit of working together as a team; they were only concerned about success in their own region." Michaels tried to break the functional thinking by realigning people and mindsets around teams and teamwork.[13]

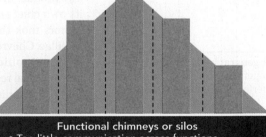

Functional chimneys or silos
- Too little communication across functions
- Too many problems referred upward for solution

DIVISIONAL STRUCTURES GROUP TOGETHER PEOPLE BY PRODUCTS, CUSTOMERS, OR LOCATIONS.

A second organizational alternative is the **divisional structure** shown on the next page in **Figure 7.3**. It groups together people who work on the same product, serve similar customers, and/or are located in the same area or geographical region.[14]

> A **divisional structure** groups together people working on the same product, in the same area, or with similar customers.

The intent of the division structure is to overcome the disadvantages of a functional structure, such as the functional chimneys problem. Toyota, for example, shifted to divisions in its North American operations. Engineering, manufacturing, and sales were brought together under a common boss, instead of each function reporting to its own top executive. One analyst said the problem was that "every silo reported back to someone different" and "they need someone in charge of the whole choir."[15]

Product structures group together jobs and activities devoted to a single product or service. They identify a common point of managerial responsibility for costs, profits, problems, and successes in a defined market area. An expected benefit is that the product division will be able to respond quickly and effectively to changing market demands and customer tastes. When Fiat took over Chrysler, CEO Sergio Marchionne said he wanted a new structure to "speed decision making and improve communication flow." He reorganized

> A **product structure** groups together people and jobs working on a single product or service.

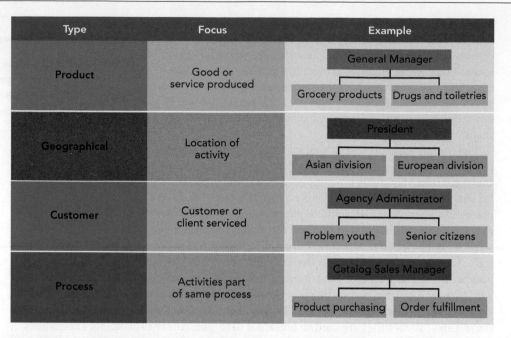

Type	Focus	Example
Product	Good or service produced	**General Manager** — Grocery products / Drugs and toiletries
Geographical	Location of activity	**President** — Asian division / European division
Customer	Customer or client serviced	**Agency Administrator** — Problem youth / Senior citizens
Process	Activities part of same process	**Catalog Sales Manager** — Product purchasing / Order fulfillment

FIGURE 7.3 **What Are Some Ways Organizations Use Divisional Structures?**
In products structures, divisions are based on the product or service provided, such as consumer products and industrial products. In geographic structures, divisions are based on geography or territories, such as an Asia–Pacific division and a North American division. In customer structures, divisions are based on customers or clients served, such as graduate students and undergraduate students in a university.

into product divisions for the firm's three brands—Chrysler, Jeep, and Dodge. Each was given its own chief executive and assigned responsibility for its own profits and losses.[16] General Motors took the same approach and reorganized around four product divisions—Buick, Cadillac, Chevrolet, and GMC.[17]

> A **geographical structure** brings together people and jobs performed in the same location.

Geographical structures group together jobs and activities in the same areas or geographical regions. Companies use geographical divisions when they need to focus attention on the unique product tastes or operating requirements of particular regions. As UPS operations expanded worldwide, for example, the company announced a change from a product to a geographical organizational structure. The company created two geographical divisions—the Americas and Europe/Asia—with each area responsible for its own logistics, sales, and other business functions.

Potential Advantages of Divisional Structures

- Expertise is focused on special products, customers, or regions.
- Better coordination exists across functions within divisions.
- There is better accountability for product or service delivery.
- It is easier to grow or shrink in size as conditions change.

> A **customer structure** groups together people and jobs that serve the same customers or clients.

Customer structures group together jobs and activities that serve the same customers or clients. The major appeal of customer divisions is the ability to best serve the special needs of the different customer groups. This is a common structure for complex businesses in the consumer products industries. 3M Corporation, for example, structures itself to focus on such diverse markets as consumer and office, specialty materials, industrial, health care, electronics and communications, transportation, graphics, and safety. Customer structures are also useful in service companies and social agencies. Banks, for example, use them to give separate attention to consumer and commercial customers for loans; government agencies use them to focus on different client populations.

Divisional structures are supposed to avoid some of the major problems of functional structures, including functional chimneys. But, as with any structural alternative, they also have potential disadvantages. They can be costly when economies of scale are lost through the duplication of resources and efforts across divisions. They can also create unhealthy rivalries where divisions end up competing with one another for scarce resources, prestige, or special top management attention.

MATRIX STRUCTURES COMBINE THE FUNCTIONAL AND DIVISIONAL STRUCTURES.

The **matrix structure**, often called the *matrix organization*, combines the functional and divisional structures to try to gain the advantages of each. This is accomplished by setting up permanent teams that operate across functions to support specific products, projects, or programs.[18] Workers in a typical matrix structure, like **Figure 7.4**, belong to at least two formal groups at the same time—a functional group and a product, program, or project team. They also report to two bosses—one within the function and the other within the team.

The use of permanent **cross-functional teams** in matrix structures creates several potential advantages. These are teams whose members come together from different functional departments to work on a common task. Everyone, regardless of his or her departmental affiliation, is required to work closely with others and focus on team goals—no functional chimney thinking is allowed. Expertise and information is shared to solve problems at the team level and make sure that things are accomplished in the best ways possible.

Still, matrix structures aren't perfect; they can't overcome all the disadvantages of their functional and divisional parents. The two-boss system of the matrix can lead to power struggles if functional supervisors and team leaders make confusing or conflicting demands on team members. Matrix structures can be costly because they require a whole new set of managers to lead the cross-functional teams.[19] As you might guess, team meetings in the matrix can be time consuming.

The matrix structure has gained a strong foothold in the workplace. Applications are found in such diverse settings as manufacturing (e.g., aerospace, electronics, pharmaceuticals), service industries (e.g., banking, brokerage, retailing), professional fields (e.g., accounting, advertising, law), and the nonprofit sector (e.g., government agencies, hospitals, universities).

> A **matrix structure** combines functional and divisional approaches to emphasize project or program teams.

> A **cross-functional team** brings together members from different functional departments.

Potential Advantages of Matrix Structures

- Performance accountability rests with program, product, or project managers.
- Better communication exists across functions.
- Teams solve problems at their levels.
- Top managers spend more time on strategy.

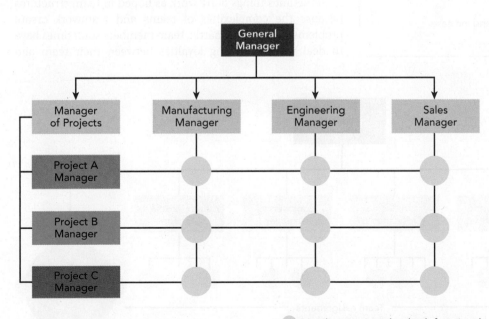

Members assigned to both functional departments and cross-functional teams

FIGURE 7.4 How Does a Matrix Structure Combine Functional and Divisional Structures?
A matrix structure is designed to combine the best of the functional and divisional forms. In a typical matrix, the normal functions create a traditional vertical structure, with heads of marketing and manufacturing, and so on. Then a new horizontal structure is added to create cross-functional integration. This is done using teams that are staffed by members from the functions.

Biotech Entrepreneurs Ride the Cutting Edge of Virtual Networks

samsonovs/Shutterstock

It used to be that it took a corporate giant to create a new drug—big investments, big staff, big and formal organization. But we live in a new connected economy where technology makes new things possible. Leonide Saad and Ilyas Washington, co-founders of the biotech firm Akeus Pharmaceuticals, want to cure childhood blindness. But if you want to see their operation you'll be surprised at what you find: zero full-time employees, zero fixed office and lab space, and zero salaries. Akeus works in virtual space; everything moves fast at minimum cost. Saad and Washington hire consultants, outsource to labs, and hold meetings in temporary meeting spaces like a nearby Au Bon Pain. Saad says: "The cost savings and flexibility advantages are enormous."

TEAM STRUCTURES MAKE EXTENSIVE USE OF PERMANENT AND TEMPORARY TEAMS.

A **team structure** uses permanent and temporary cross-functional teams to improve lateral relations.

Many organizations adopt **team structures** that extensively use permanent and temporary teams to solve problems, complete special projects, and accomplish day-to-day tasks.[20] As **Figure 7.5** shows, these are horizontal structures in which teams are often formed across functions and staffed with members whose talents match team tasks.[21] The goals are to reduce the functional chimneys problem, tap the full benefits of group decision making, and gain as much creativity and speed in problem solving as possible. Consultant and scholar Gary Hamel says that one of the forces driving managers to build team structures is the growing presence of "younger workers" who are "impatient with old hierarchies and value systems."[22] Could this description apply to you? Might it suggest the type of organization structure you would be most comfortable working in?

Sometimes things don't work as hoped in team structures because the complexities of teams and teamwork create problems. As with the matrix, team members sometimes have to deal with conflicting loyalties between their team and

Potential Advantages of Team Structures

- Team assignments improve communication, cooperation, and decision making.
- Team members get to know each other as persons, not just job titles.
- Team memberships boost morale and increase enthusiasm and task involvement.

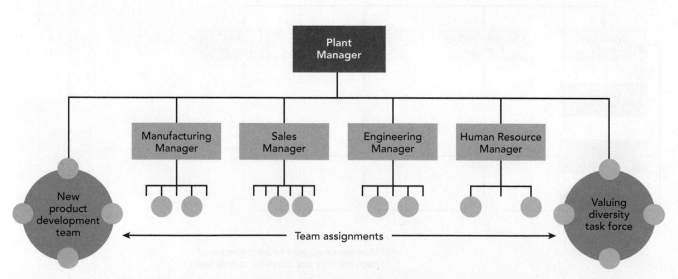

FIGURE 7.5 How Do Team Structures Capture the Benefits of Cross-Functional Teams?

Team structures make extensive use of teams to improve organizations through better communication and problem solving across functions. Some teams are temporary, such as a project team that convenes to create a new product and then disbands when finished. Other teams are more permanent. They bring together members from different functions to work together on standing issues and common problems, such as quality control, diversity management, labor–management relations, or health care benefits.

functional assignments. Teamwork always takes time. And as in any team situation, the quality of results often depends on how well the team is managed and how well team members gel as a group. This is why you'll most likely find that organizations with team structures invest heavily in team building and team training, as well as special office space designs to encourage teamwork and support informal structures.

NETWORK STRUCTURES MAKE EXTENSIVE USE OF STRATEGIC ALLIANCES AND OUTSOURCING.

Another development in organizational structures uses a network of strategic alliances and outsourcing to dramatically reduce the need for full-time staff. Shown in **Figure 7.6**, a **network structure** links a central core of full-time employees with outside suppliers and service contractors. Because the central core is small and the surrounding networks can be expanded or shrunk as needed, the potential advantages are lower costs, more speed, and greater flexibility in dealing with changing environments.[23]

A **network structure** uses IT to link with networks of outside suppliers and service contractors.

The example in Figure 7.6 shows a network structure for a company that sells lawn and deck furniture over the Internet and by mail order. The firm employs only a few full-time "core" employees. Other business requirements are met through a network of alliances and outsourcing relationships. A consultant creates product designs, and suppliers produce them at low-cost sites around the world. A supply chain management firm gets products shipped to and distributed from an outsourced warehouse. A quarterly catalog is mailed as part of a strategic alliance with two other firms that sell different home furnishings. Accounting services are outsourced. Even the company's IT services that support customers and network relationships are maintained by an outside contractor.

This notion of the network structure may sound a bit radical, but it isn't. It is an increasingly common arrangement that raises lots of entrepreneurial opportunities—the growing

> ### Potential Advantages of Network Structures
>
> - Lower costs due to fewer full-time employees.
> - Better access to expertise through specialized alliance partners and contractors.
> - Easy to grow or shrink with market conditions.

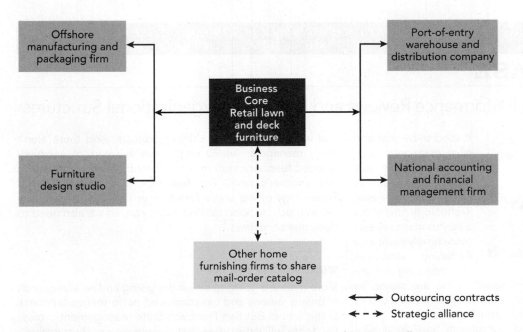

FIGURE 7.6 How Do Network Structures Take Advantage of Strategic Alliances and Outsourcing?

Organizations using network structures replace some full-time positions and functions with services provided by alliance partners and outsourcing contractors. In these structures, "core" employees perform essential operations at the center of a "network" that links them with a shifting mix of outside partners and contractors. The example in this figure shows that a small group of people can run an online and mail-order business in this manner. Network activities are made easy and cost efficient by using the latest information technologies.

popularity of network organization concepts could make it easier for you to start your own business someday. But even if network structures are highly streamlined, efficient, and adaptable, don't they sometimes have problems? The answer is "Yes."

Problems with network structures include the management complications of having to deal with a vast and sometimes shifting network of contracts and alliances. They also include the uncertainties associated with reliance on outside contractors for key supplies and services. When one part of the network breaks down or fails to deliver, the entire system may suffer the consequences. Also, too much reliance on outsourcing might have hidden costs, including poor product and service quality. What was behind a Delta Air announcement that it was shutting down its call-center operations in India? They did it because so many customers complained about communication difficulties with service providers.[24]

A **virtual organization** uses information technologies to operate as a shifting network of alliances.

As things continue to evolve, a network variation called the **virtual organization** is appearing. It uses information technologies that allow the organization to function as a constantly shifting network of alliances.[25] The goal is to create virtual networks that eliminate structural boundaries that would traditionally separate a firm from its suppliers and customers, and separate its internal departments and divisions from one another. These virtual relationships can be called into action on demand. When the work is done, they are disbanded or left idle until the next time they are needed.

Traditional boundaries fade as virtual alliances shift in and out over time.

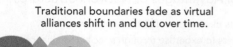

If you really think about it, each of us is probably already a part of virtual organizations. Do you see similarities, for example, with the Facebook, Twitter, or LinkedIn communities? Isn't the virtual organization concept similar to how we manage our online relationships— signing on, signing off, getting things done as needed with different people and groups, and all taking place instantaneously, temporarily, and without the need for face-to-face contacts?

ALL 90 EMPLOYEES ARE PART OF A CROWDSOURCED FEEDBACK SYSTEM THAT ALLOWS THEM TO COMMENT ON ONE ANOTHER'S WORK.

QUICK CASE

Crowdsourcing Performance Reviews and Flattening Organizational Structures

sindlera/Shutterstock

It used to be that one of a manager's most important tasks was conducting annual performance reviews. Technology now offers a way to make reviews more timely while also flattening structures and reducing administrative costs. "Bye-bye, manager!" some are saying as more performance reviews move online and crowdsourcing becomes the feedback mechanism of choice.

Management scholars and consultants have long suggested the value of 360° reviews that include feedback from peers and others working with or for the person being assessed. New technology makes it easy to do all this, and more, online and in real time—think anyone, anytime, any project.

Online reviews are in at the San Francisco–based social media outfit Hearsay Social, Inc. The firm runs on teamwork and involves constantly shifting projects. And there aren't many managers. All 90 employees are part of a crowdsourced feedback system that allows them to comment on one another's work. The feedback is anonymous. Chief Technology officer Steve Garrity says: "We are decentralizing as much decision making as we can, so we also need to decentralize reviews."

WHAT WOULD YOU DO?

More of us are going to be on the giving and receiving ends of online reviews and crowdsourced performance feedback in the future. But San Francisco State management professor John Sullivan worries that people may end up evaluating others whose jobs they don't know enough about. Online peer reviews are easy and cost effective, but are they good replacements for the formal sit-down with a team leader or manager? When does technology flatten a structure too far?

STUDYGUIDE

Takeaway 7.2
What Are the Most Common Types of Organization Structures?

Terms to Define

Cross-functional team	Functional chimneys or functional silos problem	Geographic structure	Product structure
Customer structure		Horizontal structures	Team structure
Departmentalization	Functional structure	Matrix structure	Virtual organization
Divisional structure		Network structure	

Rapid Review

- Functional structures group people using similar skills to perform similar activities.
- Divisional structures group people who work on a similar product, work in the same geographical region, or serve the same customers.
- A matrix structure uses permanent cross-functional teams to try to gain the advantages of both the functional and divisional approaches.
- Team structures make extensive use of permanent and temporary teams, often cross-functional ones, to improve communication, cooperation, and problem solving.
- Network structures maintain a staff of core full-time employees and use contract services and strategic alliances to accomplish many business needs.

Questions for Discussion

1. Why use functional structures if they are prone to functional chimneys problems?
2. Could a matrix structure improve performance for an organization familiar to you?
3. How can the disadvantages of group decision making hurt team structures?

Be Sure You Can

- **compare** the functional, divisional, and matrix structures
- **draw** charts to show how each structure might be used in a business
- **list** advantages and disadvantages of each structure
- **explain** the functional chimneys problem
- **describe** how cross-functional and project teams operate in team structures
- **illustrate** how an organization familiar to you might operate as a network structure
- **list** advantages and disadvantages of the network approach to organizing

Career Situation: What Would You Do?

The typical university business school is organized on a functional basis, with departments such as accounting, finance, information systems, management, and marketing all reporting to a dean. Practice your consulting skills. How would you redesign things to increase communication and collaboration across departments, as well as improve curriculum integration across all areas of study?

Takeaway 7.3
What Are the Trends in Organizational Design?

ANSWERS TO COME

- Organizations are becoming flatter and using fewer levels of management.
- Organizations are increasing decentralization.
- Organizations are increasing delegation and empowerment.
- Organizations are becoming more horizontal and adaptive.
- Organizations are using more alternative work schedules.

JUST AS ORGANIZATIONS VARY IN SIZE AND TYPE, SO, TOO, DO THE VARIETY OF problems and opportunities they face.[26] This is why they use different ways of organizing—from the functional, divisional, and matrix structures to the team and network approaches reviewed in the last section. Now it's time to probe further. There is still more to the story of how managers try to align structures with the unique situations their organizations face.

This process of alignment is called **organizational design**. It deals with the choices managers make to configure their organizations to best meet the problems and opportunities posed by their environments.[27] And because every organization faces unique challenges, there is no "one size fits all" best design. Organizational design is a problem-solving activity where managers strive to get the best configuration to meet situational demands.

> **Organizational design** is the process of configuring organizations to meet environmental challenges.

ORGANIZATIONS ARE BECOMING FLATTER AND USING FEWER LEVELS OF MANAGEMENT.

When organizations grow in size, they tend to get taller by adding more and more levels of management. This raises costs. It also increases the distance between top management and lower levels, making it harder for the levels to communicate with one another. Even with the benefits of new technologies, this increases the risks of slow and poorly informed decisions.

Taller organizations are generally viewed as less efficient, less flexible, and less customer sensitive.[28] You shouldn't be surprised that the trend is toward flatter structures. But, one of the issues behind the chapter opening photo is that many universities seem to be doing just the opposite—adding administrative positions and nonacademic units. A Purdue professor says, "I have no idea what these people do." A University of Arkansas professor says, "Administrative bloat is clearly contributing to the overall cost of higher education."[29]

One of the things affected when organizations do get flatter is **span of control**—the number of persons directly reporting to a manager. When span of control is narrow, as shown nearby, a manager supervises only a few people. Taller organizations have many levels of management and narrow spans of control. A manager with a wide span of control supervises many people. Flatter organizations with fewer levels of management have wider spans of control.

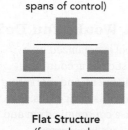

Tall Structure
(more levels; narrower spans of control)

Flat Structure
(fewer levels; wider spans of control)

> **Span of control** is the number of persons directly reporting to a manager.

ORGANIZATIONS ARE INCREASING DECENTRALIZATION.

While we are talking about levels of management, the next question becomes: Should top management make the decisions and the lower levels just carry them out? The answer is "No," at least not for all decisions. When top management keeps the power to make most decisions, the setup is called **centralization**. When top management allows lower levels to make decisions on matters where they are best prepared or informed, the setup is called **decentralization**.

> With **centralization**, top management keeps the power to make most decisions.

> With **decentralization**, top management allows lower levels to help make many decisions.

> "IT DOESN'T MATTER WHAT INDUSTRY YOU'RE IN. PEOPLE HAVE BLIND SPOTS ABOUT WHERE THEY ARE WEAK."

FACTS TO CONSIDER

Bosses May Be Overestimating Their Delegating Skills

Karen Moskowitz/Getty Images

A survey by Development Dimensions International, Inc., finds that managers may be overestimating their managing skills. Skills rated as needing most development were delegating, gaining commitment, and coaching. But not everyone is prepared to admit their weaknesses. "It doesn't matter what industry you're in. People have blind spots about where they are weak," says DDI vice president Scott Erker, whose survey of 1,100 first-year managers found the following.

- 72% never question their ability to lead others.
- 58% claim planning and organizing skills as strengths.
- 53% say they are strong in decision making.
- 50% say they are strong in communication.
- 32% claim proficiency in delegating.

YOUR THOUGHTS?

Would you, like managers in this survey, probably overestimate your strengths in management skills? What might explain such tendencies toward overconfidence? And among the skills needing work, why would delegating be the one about which even very confident managers still feel some inadequacy?

If you had to choose right now, wouldn't you go for decentralization? Well, you wouldn't be wrong, given the trends.[30] But you wouldn't be exactly right, either. Do you really want lower levels making major decisions and changing things whenever they see fit?

The reality is that there is no need for a trade-off; an organization can have both. One of the unique opportunities of today's high-tech world is that top management can decentralize and still maintain centralized control. Computer technology and information systems allow top managers to easily stay informed about day-to-day performance results throughout an organization. This makes it easier for them to operate in more decentralized ways.[31]

ORGANIZATIONS ARE INCREASING DELEGATION AND EMPOWERMENT.

Decentralization brings with it another trend that is good for organizations and their members: increased delegation and empowerment. **Delegation** is the process of entrusting work to others by giving them the right to make decisions and take action. Think of it as setting the foundation for decentralization by following these three steps. (1) *Assign responsibility*—explain tasks and expectations to others. (2) *Grant authority*—allow others to act as needed to complete tasks. (3) *Create accountability*—require others to report back on the completed tasks.

Every manager really needs to know how and when to delegate. Even if you are already good at it, there are probably ways to get even better. On those days when you complain, "I just can't get everything done," the real problem may be that you are trying to do everything yourself. Delegation involves deciding what work to do yourself and what you should allow others to accomplish. It sounds easy, but there is skill in doing delegation right.[32]

A classical management principle states that authority should equal responsibility when a supervisor delegates work to a subordinate. In other words, managers shouldn't delegate a task without giving the subordinate sufficient authority to perform it. Can you think of a time when you were asked to get something done but didn't have the authority to do it? This was probably frustrating, and it may have even caused you to lose respect for the manager.

Some managers mistakenly go even one step further: They fail to delegate at all. Whether because managers are unwilling or unable to trust others or are too inflexible in how they want things done, the failure to delegate is more common than you might think. And it creates problems. A failure to delegate not only makes it hard for people to do their jobs, but it also overloads the manager with work that really should be done by others.

Delegation is the process of entrusting work to others.

Three Steps in Delegation

Step 1: Assign Responsibility
Explain key tasks and performance expectations to others

Step 2: Grant Authority
Allow others to take necessary actions

Step 3: Create Accountability
Require others to report back on progress and completed tasks

ETHICS CHECK

Empowered into Exhaustion

Tom Gril/Getty Images

Dear Stress Doctor:

My boss has this great idea of cutting some supervisor positions and reassigning the work to those of us who remain. She says this is all part of a new management approach to operate with a flatter structure and more empowerment.

For me this means a lot more work. I can't get everything cleaned up on my desk most days, and I end up taking a lot of paperwork home.

As my organization "restructures" we get exhausted and our families get shortchanged, even angry. I feel guilty now taking time to watch my daughter play soccer on a weekday evening and Saturday morning. Sure, there's some decent pay involved, but that doesn't make up for the heavy price I'm paying in terms of lost family time.

But you know what? My boss doesn't get it.

I never hear her ask: "Henry, are you working too much; don't you think it's time to get back on a reasonable schedule?" No! What I often hear instead is "Look at Andy; he handles our new management model really well. He's real go-getter. I don't think he's been out of here one night this week before 8 PM."

Am I missing something in regard to this "empowerment"?

Sincerely,
Overworked in Cincinnati

YOUR DECISION?

Is it ethical to restructure, cut management levels, and expect the remaining managers to do more work? Or is it simply the case that managers used to the "old" ways of doing things need extra training and care while learning how to handle empowerment? And what about this person's boss—is she on track with her management skills? Aren't managers supposed to help people understand their jobs, set priorities, and fulfill them, while still maintaining a reasonable work–life balance?

> **Empowerment** gives people freedom to do their jobs as they think best.

Let's remember that the trend is toward more, not less, delegation. And let's not forget that when delegation is done well, it leads to **empowerment**. This is the process of giving people the freedom to contribute ideas, make decisions, show initiative, and do their jobs in the best possible ways. Empowerment unlocks the full power of talent, experience, and intellect that people bring to their jobs. It is the engine that powers decentralization. And when it becomes part of the organizational culture, it helps everyone act faster and be more flexible when dealing with today's dynamic environments.

ORGANIZATIONS ARE BECOMING MORE HORIZONTAL AND ADAPTIVE.

> A **bureaucracy** emphasizes formal authority, rules, order, fairness, and efficiency.

You have heard about and, ideally, studied the concept of **bureaucracy**. We typically view it as a vertical, tight, and rigid form of organization. Its distinguishing features are clear-cut division of labor, strict hierarchy of authority, formal rules and procedures, and promotion based on competency. According to Max Weber, bureaucracies should be orderly, fair, and highly efficient.[33] Yet chances are that your experience suggests an organization bogged down with "red tape," acting slowly and impersonally, and overcome to the point of inadequacy by never-ending rules and procedures.

Where, you might ask, are the decentralization, delegation, and empowerment that we have just been talking about? Well, researchers have looked into the question and arrived at some interesting answers. When Tom Burns and George Stalker investigated 20 manufacturing firms in England, they found that two quite different organizational forms could be successful.[34] The key was the "fit" between the form and challenges in the external environment.

> Fair
> Impersonal
> Career managers
> Clear division of labor
> Promotion based on merit
> Formal hierarchy of authority
> Written rules and standard procedures

A more bureaucratic form of organization, which Burns and Stalker called the **mechanistic design**, thrived in stable environments. It was good at doing routine things in predictable situations. But in rapidly changing and uncertain situations, a much less bureaucratic

> **Mechanistic designs** are bureaucratic, using a centralized and vertical structure.

form, called the **organic design**, performed best. It was adaptable and better suited to handle change and less-predictable situations.

Figure 7.7 portrays these two approaches as opposite extremes on a continuum of organizational design alternatives. You can see that organizations with mechanistic designs typically operate as "tight" structures of the traditional vertical and bureaucratic form.[35] They are good for production efficiency and work well for, say, your local fast-food restaurant. But how about Microsoft or Facebook—does bureaucracy serve it well?

Businessweek once claimed that Microsoft suffers from "bureaucratic red tape" and endless meetings that bog employees down and limit their abilities to be creative and on top of market demands.[36] The *Wall Street Journal* suggested it should be broken into smaller pieces to free the firm from "bureaucracy that's stifling entrepreneurial spirits."[37] In other words, over time and with increasing size, Microsoft may have become too mechanistic for its own good.

Organizations, perhaps Microsoft, can benefit from an organic organizational design that is more horizontal and less vertical than its mechanistic counterpart. Organic designs are good for creativity and innovation. They emphasize empowerment and teamwork, with a lot of work getting done through informal structures and interpersonal networks.[38] The result is an adaptive and flexible organization whose employees are empowered to be spontaneous in using their talents to deal with changing circumstances.[39]

> **Organic designs** are adaptive, using a decentralized and horizontal structure.

ORGANIZATIONS ARE USING MORE ALTERNATIVE WORK SCHEDULES.

There's yet another organizing trend that's quite likely to become very important to you someday, if it isn't already—the use of alternative work schedules. The fact is that just because it was normal to work 40 hours each week in the past doesn't make this the only or best way to schedule work time.[40] Here are some possibilities.

A **compressed workweek** allows a worker to complete a full-time job in less than the standard 5 days of 8-hour shifts.[41] The most common form is the "4–40," that is, accomplishing 40 hours of work in four 10-hour days. It's well used at USAA, a diversified financial services company that ranks among the 100 best companies to work for in America. A large part of the firm's San Antonio workforce is on a 4-day schedule, with some working Monday through Thursday and others working Tuesday through Friday.[42] Although compressed workweeks can cause scheduling problems, possible customer complaints, and even union objections, the benefits are there as well. USAA reports improved morale, lower overtime costs, less absenteeism, and decreased use of sick leave.

> A **compressed workweek** allows a worker to complete a full-time job in less than five days.

The term **flexible working hours**, also called *flextime*, describes any work schedule that gives employees some choice in daily work hours. A typical flextime schedule offers choices

> **Flexible working hours** give employees some choice in daily work hours.

MECHANISTIC DESIGNS
Bureaucratic organizations

ORGANIC DESIGNS
Adaptive organizations

Mechanistic		Organic
Predictability	Goal	Adaptability
Centralized	Authority	Decentralized
Many	Rules and procedures	Few
Narrow	Spans of control	Wide
Specialized	Tasks	Shared
Few	Teams and task forces	Many
Formal and impersonal	Coordination	Informal and personal

FIGURE 7.7

What Are the Major Differences Between Mechanistic and Organic Organizations Designs?

Some indicators of a more organic design are decentralization, few rules and procedures, wider spans of control, sharing of tasks, use of teams and task forces, and informal or personal approaches to coordination. This organic design is most associated with success in dynamic and changing environments. The more mechanistic design has mainly bureaucratic features and is more likely to have difficulty in changing environments but to be successful in more stable ones.

of starting and ending times, while still putting in a full workday. Some may start earlier and leave earlier, while others do the opposite. The flexibility provides opportunities to attend to personal affairs such as parenting, elder care, medical appointments, and home emergencies. All top 100 companies in *Working Mother* magazine's list of best employers for working moms offer flexible scheduling. They find it reduces stress and unwanted job turnover.[43]

Telecommuting, such as work-from-home or remote work, uses technology to allow workers to do their jobs from outside the office.

More and more workers now do some form of **telecommuting**, often called **work-from-home** or **remote work**.[44] They spend at least a portion of scheduled work time outside of the office and linked through technology with co-workers, customers, and bosses.[45] From the employer side it makes for savings in office space and real estate. It's a good recruiting tool—reports indicate that up to 80% of employees desire it. Evidence also suggests most telecommuters are hard working and satisfied.[46] Positives on the employee side include freedom to be your own boss and having more free time.

Even though the evidence largely supports telecommuting or work-at-home practices, there are potential downsides. Some telecommuters say they end up working too much and actually have less time to themselves and for family.[47] And, some employers worry about adverse impact on teamwork and collaboration. Yahoo! CEO Marissa Mayer received lots of criticism when she decided to ban working from home. Rightly or wrongly, she believed that doing so would help revitalize face-to-face collaboration and increase innovation at the firm.[48]

A **co-working center** is a place where telecommuters share office space outside the home.

A recent development in telecommuting is the **co-working center**, essentially a place where telecommuters go to share an office environment outside the home. A marketing telecommuter says: "We have two kids, so the ability to work from home—it just got worse and worse. I found myself saying, 'If daddy could just have two hours. . . .'" Now he has started his own co-working center to cater to his needs and those of others. One of those using his center says: "What you're paying for is not the desk, it's access to networking creativity and community."[49]

Job sharing splits one job between two people.

Yet another flexible scheduling option is **job sharing**, where two or more persons split one full-time job. This often involves each person working one-half day, but it can also be done via weekly or monthly sharing arrangements. Both the employees and the organizations benefit when talented people who cannot work full days or weeks are kept in or brought back into the workforce.

WORKERS SPEND 40% TO 60% OF THEIR INTERACTION TIME TALKING WITH THEIR IMMEDIATE NEIGHBORS.

HOT TOPIC

Playing Musical Chairs to Increase Collaboration

Monkey Business Images/Shutterstock

Goodbye, private office . . . goodbye, permanent work space . . . and, "Hello, stranger!" The childhood game of musical chairs is very likely coming to your workplace!

One of the latest trends in office design is to move employees into new workspaces every few months, as a way to increase communication and collaboration. The moves end up putting employees from different departments and work functions into contact with one another. Seating assignments may be planned based on tasks or employees' personalities, or even done randomly. But regardless of the method used, the goal is the same: break down functional silos and habits that limit communication across internal boundaries, and put people side-by-side to talk, learn, and be creative together.

Research indicates that workers spend roughly 40% to 60% of their interaction time every workday talking with their immediate neighbors. They have only a 5% to 10% chance of interacting with someone even just a few steps further away. The CEO of Sociometric Solutions, a consulting firm that works on such issues, says, "If I change the organizational chart and you stay in the same seat, it doesn't have much of an effect. If I keep the organization chart the same but change where you sit, it is going to massively change everything."

HOW ABOUT IT?

Is musical chairs in the office going a step too far? What's your reaction to this approach? Would you enjoy changing desks every month or so, or hate it, and why? Can this idea be used in larger organizations, or is the usefulness of the approach really likely to be limited to smaller firms and startups employing a lot of new college graduates? Overall, is this a useful way to break down "functional silos," or is it just a passing fad that will soon lose its appeal? What do you think?

STUDYGUIDE

Takeaway 7.3
What Are the Trends in Organizational Design?

Terms to Define

Bureaucracy	Decentralization	Job sharing	Remote work
Centralization	Delegation	Mechanistic designs	Span of control
Compressed workweek	Empowerment	Organic designs	Telecommuting
Co-working center	Flexible working hours	Organizational design	Work-from-home

Rapid Review

- Organizations are becoming flatter—having fewer management levels, combining decentralization with centralization, and using more delegation and empowerment.
- Mechanistic organizational designs are vertical and bureaucratic; they perform best in stable environments with mostly routine and predictable tasks.
- Organic organizational designs are horizontal and adaptive; they perform best in change environments requiring adaptation and flexibility.
- Organizations are using alternative work schedules such as the compressed workweek, flexible working hours, and job sharing.

Questions for Discussion

1. Is "empowerment" just a buzzword, or is it something that can really make a difference in organizations today?
2. Knowing your personality, will you fit in better with an organization that has a mechanistic or an organic design?
3. How can alternative work schedules work to the benefit of both organizations and their members?

Be Sure You Can

- **illustrate** the link between tall or flat organizations and spans of control
- **explain** how decentralization and centralization can work together
- **list** the three steps in delegation
- **differentiate** mechanistic and organic organizational designs
- **differentiate** compressed workweek, flexible working hours, and job sharing
- **list** advantages and disadvantages of telecommuting

Career Situation: What Would You Do?

As the owner of a small computer repair and services business, you would like to allow employees more flexibility in their work schedules. But, you also need consistency of coverage to handle drop-in customers as well as at-home service calls. There are also times when customers need "emergency" help outside normal 8 AM to 5 PM office hours. A meeting with the employees is scheduled for next week. How can you work with them to develop a staffing plan that includes flexible work options that meet their needs as well as yours?

TESTPREP 7

Answers to Test Prep questions can be found at the back of the book.

Multiple-Choice Questions

1. The main purpose of organizing as a management function is to _____.
   (a) make sure that results match plans
   (b) arrange people and resources to accomplish work
   (c) create enthusiasm for the needed work
   (d) link strategies with operational plans

2. An organization chart is most useful for _____.
   (a) mapping informal structures
   (b) eliminating functional chimneys
   (c) showing designated supervisory relationships
   (d) describing the shadow organization

3. Rumors and resistance to change are potential disadvantages often associated with _____.
   (a) virtual organizations   (b) informal structures
   (c) functional chimneys   (d) cross-functional teams

4. When an organization chart shows that vice presidents of marketing, finance, manufacturing, and purchasing all report to the president, top management is using a _____ structure.
   (a) functional   (b) matrix
   (c) network   (d) product

5. The "two-boss" system of reporting relationships is both a potential source of problems and one of the key aspects of _____ structures.
   (a) functional   (b) matrix
   (c) network   (d) product

6. A manufacturing business with a functional structure has recently acquired two other businesses with very different product lines. The president of the combined company might consider using a _____ structure to allow a better focus on the unique needs of each product area.
   (a) virtual   (b) team
   (c) divisional   (d) network

7. An organization using a _____ structure should expect that more problems will be solved at lower levels and that top managers will have more time free to engage in strategic thinking.
   (a) virtual   (b) matrix
   (c) functional   (d) product

8. The functional chimneys problem occurs when people in different functions _____.
   (a) fail to communicate with one another
   (b) try to help each other work with customers
   (c) spend too much time coordinating decisions
   (d) focus on products rather than functions

9. An organization that employs just a few "core" or essential full-time employees and outsources a lot of the remaining work shows signs of using a _____ structure.
   (a) functional   (b) divisional
   (c) network   (d) team

10. A "tall" organization will likely have _____ spans of control than a "flat" organization with the same number of members.
    (a) wider   (b) narrower
    (c) more ambiguous   (d) less centralized

11. If a student in one of your course groups volunteers to gather information for a case analysis and the other members tell him to go ahead and choose the information sources he believes are most important, the group is giving this student _____ to fulfill the agreed-upon task.
    (a) responsibility
    (b) accountability
    (c) authority
    (d) values

12. The bureaucratic organization described by Max Weber is similar to the _____ organization described by Burns and Stalker.
    (a) adaptive
    (b) mechanistic
    (c) organic
    (d) horizontal

13. Which organization design would likely be a good fit for a dynamic and changing external environment?
    (a) Vertical   (b) Centralized
    (c) Organic   (d) Mechanistic

14. Workers following a compressed workweek schedule often work 40 hours in _____ days.
    (a) 3 ½   (b) 4
    (c) 5   (d) a flexible schedule of

15. Which alternative work schedule is identified by *Working Mother* magazine as being used by all companies on its list of "100 Best Employers for Working Moms"?
    (a) Telecommuting
    (b) Job sharing
    (c) Flexible hours
    (d) Part-time

Short-Response Questions

16. Why should an organization chart be trusted "only so far"?

17. In what ways can informal structures be good for organizations?

18. How does a matrix structure combine functional and divisional forms?

19. Why is an organic design likely to be quicker and more flexible in adapting to changes than a mechanistic design?

Integration and Application Question

20. Imagine you are a consultant to your university or college president. The assignment is: Make this organization more efficient without sacrificing its educational goals. Although the president doesn't realize it, you are a specialist in network structures. You are going to suggest building a network organization, and your ideas are going to be radical and provocative.

    Questions: What would be the core of the network—is it the faculty members, who teach the various courses, or is it the administration, which provides the infrastructure that students and faculty use in the learning experience? What might be out-sourced—grounds and facilities maintenance, food services, security, recreation programs, even registration? What types of alliances might prove beneficial—student recruiting, faculty, even facilities?

Steps for
Further Learning

BUILD MARKETABLE SKILLS • **DO** A CASE ANALYSIS • **GET** AND STAY INFORMED

BUILD MARKETABLE SKILLS.

EARN BIG CAREER PAYOFFS!

Don't miss these opportunities in the SKILL-BUILDING PORTFOLIO

SELF-ASSESSMENT 7:
Empowering Others

It can be hard to let go . . . check your willingness to loosen the strings.

CLASS EXERCISE 7:
Organizational Metaphors

Organizations as brains? . . . metaphors can be a key to greater understanding.

TEAM PROJECT 7:
Network "U"

Times are changing at the nation's universities . . . is it reasonable that students could help design better ones?

Many learning resources are found at the end of the book and online within **WileyPLUS Learning Space.**

Practice Critical Thinking—Complete the CHAPTER 7 CASE

CASE SNAPSHOT: Nike—Spreading Out to Stay Together

Nike is indisputably a giant in the athletics industry. The Portland, Oregon, company has reached the top by knowing how to stay small, focusing on core competencies—and outsourcing other tasks and functions. Nike is known worldwide for its products, none of which it actually makes. But if you don't make anything, what do you actually do? If you outsource everything, what's left?

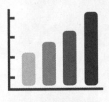

DO A CASE ANALYSIS.

STRENGTHEN YOUR CRITICAL THINKING!

MANAGER'S LIBRARY SELECTION
Read for Insights and Wisdom
The Truth About Middle Managers: Heroes, Villains, and the Reinvention of Middle Management (2008, Harvard Business School Publishing Corporation) by Paul Osterman

In this book Paul Osterman describes the changing landscape for managers nestled between levels of top management and hourly workers. Restructuring trends—fewer levels of management between top management and hourly workers and fewer employees overall—require middle managers to assume broader duties and work longer hours. They have less autonomy because top managers are closer in the hierarchy, and less control as information technology allows monitoring and feedback, anytime, anywhere.

GET AND STAY INFORMED.

MAKE YOURSELF VALUABLE!

Osterman notes that middle managers have increased job insecurity because of restructuring. Job tenure, or length of time spent with one employer, is decreasing, and middle managers are more likely to job hop. Stress has increased due to new realities, and they are less loyal to employers. They see top management as greedy, self-serving, and distant and are frustrated by executive hires outside the organization. Many lose ambition because flat hierarchies mean fewer paths to the top.

Despite the challenges, Osterman believes middle managers are highly committed to their work. They enjoy their jobs as craft and thrive on skill execution. Restructuring has pushed high-level duties on many, and they welcome new strategic roles. They make key decisions involving resource allocations and negotiations with varied interests. They spend more time in informal interaction and unplanned activities and experience more variety and complexity in assignments.

REFLECT AND REACT Organizations now have fewer management levels and employees, so how would you describe middle management jobs and skills? Middle managers view work not only as a means to an end—money or promotion, but an end in itself—craftwork and fulfillment. Why is this? And by the way, what is the future likely to hold for middle managers as more organizations take on team, network, and virtual characteristics?

"We're very clear not everyone fits in this quirky company. We put potential hires through seven to eight interviews. Sometimes people look at us like we're crazy and run away. When employees don't understand the team atmosphere, we let them go. . . ."

Kip Tindell, CEO of Container Store

Organizational Cultures, Innovation, and Change

Adaptability and Values Set the Tone

Management Live

"Go Along to Get Along" Culture Is a Danger Signal

Westend61/Getty Images

"**D**on't tell the boss" . . . "Don't bring it up." These are warning signs of what experts call "a tendency for people in large, hierarchical organizations to tell bosses what they want to hear." GM's new CEO Mary Barra had to change what she claimed was a culture of the "GM nod"—agree but take no action, and the "GM salute"—directing responsibility to others and covering up rather than confronting problems. The *Wall Street Journal* calls this malaise a "go along to get along" culture.

HOW ABOUT IT?

Have you been in settings where something similar to the GM nod and GM salute was standard behavior? Where do shared expectations like this come from? And, perhaps more importantly, what can a leader do to avoid the downsides of "go along to get along"?

YOUR CHAPTER 8 TAKEAWAYS

1. Understand the nature of organizational culture.
2. Recognize how organizations support and achieve innovation.
3. Describe how managers lead the process of organizational change.

Takeaway 8.1
What Is the Nature of Organizational Culture?

ANSWERS TO COME

- Organizational culture is the personality of the organization.
- Organizational culture shapes behavior and influences performance.
- Not all organizational cultures are alike.
- The observable culture is what you see and hear as an employee or customer.
- The core culture is found in the underlying values of the organization.
- Value-based management supports a strong organizational culture.

YOU PROBABLY HEAR THE WORD "CULTURE" A LOT THESE DAYS. IN TODAY'S GLOBAL economy, how can we fail to appreciate the cultural differences between people or nations? However, there's another type of culture that can be just as important: the cultures of organizations. Just as nations, ethnic groups, and families have cultures, organizations do, too. These cultures help distinguish organizations from one another and give members a sense of collective identity. The Container Store example in the opening photo suggests that the "fit" between the individual and an organization's culture is very important. A good fit should be good for both parties. And, how to find the right fit is a real career issue for you to consider.

ORGANIZATIONAL CULTURE IS THE PERSONALITY OF THE ORGANIZATION.

Organizational culture is a system of shared beliefs and values guiding behavior.

Think of the stores that you shop in, the restaurants that you patronize, the places where you work and enjoy leisure activities. What is the "atmosphere" like, and does it draw you in or hurry you out? Do you notice how major retailers such as Anthropologie, J. Crew, and Williams-Sonoma have store climates that seem to fit their brands and customer identities?[1] Such aspects of the internal environments of organizations are important in management. They represent the **organizational culture** as a system of shared beliefs and values that develops within an organization and guides the behavior of its members.[2]

Healthy Living Sets the Tone at Clif Bar

Chicago Tribune/Getty Images IncImages Inc

Have you had your Clif Bar today? Lots of people have, thanks to a long bike ride during which Gary Erickson decided he just couldn't eat another of the available energy bars. He went back to experiment in his mother's kitchen and produced the first Clif Bar 2 years later.

Despite its growth from small startup to a large operation, Clif's still runs with a commit-ment to what it calls the "5 aspirations"—"sustaining our planet . . . community . . . people . . . business . . . brands." This includes creating a high-quality work life for employees. Picture the "Clifies" working this way.

- Every employee an owner.
- Paid sabbatical leaves of 6 to 8 weeks after 7 years.
- Flexible schedule to get every other Friday free.
- Pay for 2.5 hours of workout time each week.
- Bring your pet to work and wear casual clothes.
- Get $6,500 toward a hybrid or biodiesel automobile.

FIND INSPIRATION

Clif's core values are evident not only in the firm's healthy organic foods and philanthropy, but also in the quality of working life offered to employees. The culture is unique. Why can't more of us find jobs in places like this?

Whenever someone speaks of "the way we do things here," he or she is talking about the organization's culture. Sometimes called the *corporate culture*, it communicates the personality of the organization. And, it can have a strong impact on an organization's performance and the quality of work experiences of its members. For example, check out Zappos.com. Its CEO, Tony Hsieh, has built a fun, creative, and customer-centered organizational culture. He says that "the original idea was to add a little fun," and things moved to the point where the notion of an unhappy Zappos customer is almost unthinkable: "They may only call once in their life," says Hsieh, "but that is our chance to wow them. If we get the culture right most of the other stuff, like brand and the customer service, will just happen."[3, 4]

ORGANIZATIONAL CULTURE SHAPES BEHAVIOR AND INFLUENCES PERFORMANCE.

Although culture isn't the only determinant of what happens in organizations, it's an important one. Organizational culture helps to set values, shape attitudes, reinforce beliefs, direct behavior, and establish performance expectations and the motivation to fulfill them.[5] In **strong culture** organizations, the culture is clear, well defined, and widely shared by members. Does this sound good to you? It can be. But you also have to be careful. A strong culture can have downsides as well as upsides.

> **Strong cultures** are clear, well defined, and widely shared among organization members.

When the strong culture is positive, it supports high performance by forging a good fit between the nature of the business and the talents of the employees. It discourages dysfunctional behaviors and encourages helpful ones while keeping a clear performance vision front and center for all to rally around. But when the strong culture is negative—look back to the "go along to get along" cultures highlighted in the chapter-opening Management Live feature—it becomes a performance inhibitor. Everyday behaviors reinforced and shared in the culture work to the disadvantage of the organization.[6]

Strong and positive cultures don't happen by chance. They are created by leaders who set the tone, and they are reinforced through **socialization** practices.[7] This is the process through which new members learn the culture and values of the team or organization, as well as the behaviors and attitudes that are shared among its members.[8] Each new Disney employee, for example, attends a carefully planned onboarding program called "traditions." It introduces the Disney culture by educating them on the company mission, history, language, lore, traditions, and expectations. This commitment to employees bound together in a strong culture began with the founder, Walt Disney. He once said: "You can dream, create, design and build the most wonderful place in the world, but it requires people to make the dream a reality."[9]

> **Socialization** is the process through which new members learn the culture of a team or organization.

NOT ALL ORGANIZATIONAL CULTURES ARE ALIKE.

It takes a keen eye to be able to identify and understand an organization's culture. But such understanding can be a real asset to employees and job hunters alike. Who wants to end up in a situation with a bad person–culture fit? Management scholars offer ideas for reading organizational cultures by asking questions like these:[10]

• How tight or loose is the structure? • Do most decisions reflect change or the status quo? What outcomes or results are most highly valued? • How widespread are empowerment and worker involvement? • What is the competitive style, internal and external? • What value is placed on people, as customers and employees? • Is teamwork a way of life in this organization?

A useful way to describe organizational cultures is shown in the small figure. Based on a model called the competing values framework, it identifies four different culture types.[11] *Hierarchical cultures* emphasize authority, tradition, and clear roles. *Rational cultures* emphasize process, efficiency, and slow change. *Entrepreneurial cultures* emphasize change, growth, creativity, and competition. *Team cultures* emphasize teamwork, collaboration, and trust.

Alternative Organizational Cultures	
Team Culture	**Hierarchial Culture**
• Authority shared, distributed • Teams and teamwork rule • Collaboration, trust valued • Emphasis on mutual support	• Authority runs the system • Traditions, roles clear • Rules, hierarchy valued • Emphasis on predictability
Entrepreneurial Culture	**Rational Culture**
• Authority goes with ideas • Flexibility and creativity rule • Change and growth valued • Emphasis on entrepreneurship	• Authority serves the goals • Efficiency, productivity rule • Planning, process valued • Emphasis on modest change

How do these organizational culture options sound to you? According to a study by LeadershipIQ, employees are likely to give entrepreneurial cultures the highest marks for engagement and motivation, and as good places to work.[12] Think about the organizations that are important to you—employer, voluntary, school, and sports teams. Just where in this competing values model do their cultures fall? And importantly, how good is the "fit" between that culture and you?

THE OBSERVABLE CULTURE IS WHAT YOU SEE AND HEAR AS AN EMPLOYEE OR CUSTOMER.

Figure 8.1 shows how you might think of organizational culture as an iceberg. What lies below the surface and is harder to see is the "core culture." What stands out above the surface and is visible to the eye is the "observable culture."[13] Both are important to understand, and both influence behavior in organizations.

The **observable culture** is what you see in people's behaviors and hear in their conversations. It is reflected in how people dress at work, arrange their offices, speak to and behave toward one another, and talk about and treat their customers. You'll notice it not only as an employee but also as a customer or client. Test this out the next time you go into a store, restaurant, or service establishment. How do people look, act, and behave? How do they treat one another? How do they treat customers? What's in their conversations? Are they enjoying themselves? When you answer these questions, you are starting to describe the observable culture of the organization.

The observable culture is also found in the stories, heroes, rituals, and symbols that are part of daily organizational life. In the university, it includes the pageantry of graduation and honors ceremonies; in sports teams, it's the pregame rally, sideline pep talk, and all the "thumping and bumping" that takes place after a good play. In workplaces it can be spontaneous celebrations of a work accomplishment or personal milestone such as a co-worker's birthday or wedding. And in organizations like Apple, Hewlett-Packard, Zappos, Google, and Amazon, it's in the stories told about the founders and the firm's history.

> The **observable culture** is what you see and hear when walking around an organization.

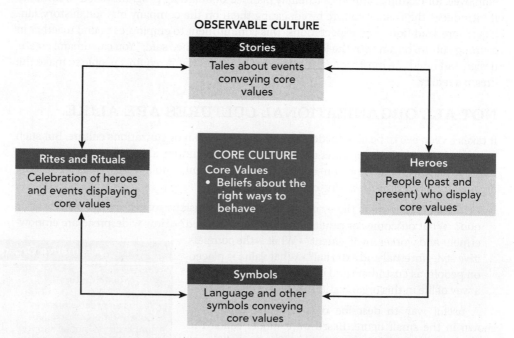

FIGURE 8.1 What Are the Main Components of Organizational Culture?

With a bit of effort, one can easily identify the organizational culture. The most visible part is the observable culture. It is shown in the stories, rituals, heroes, and symbols that are part of the everyday life of the organization. The deeper, below-the-surface part is the core culture. It consists of the values that influence the beliefs, attitudes, and work practices among organizational members.

HOT TOPIC

Saying "OK" to Chest Bumps at the Office

© Media Bakery13/Shutterstock

Bring a bit of ritual to the office culture and increase performance. At least that's the wisdom being followed by some forward-thinking organizations. When was the last time you shared a chest bump with a co-worker? In many workplaces people are afraid to even try, given the concerns about sexual harassment and unwanted physical contact. But at others, the organization culture welcomes such practices.

Rituals are in at Salo LLC, a Minneapolis human resource management company. A ringing gong signals a deal that has been closed. You might even see a couple of employees doing a chest bump to celebrate a success. What's it all about? Answer: harnessing the power of organizational culture as a performance booster.

Researchers note that many of us follow rituals before doing things—like the major league baseball player who tightens and re-retightens his batting gloves before each pitch. Some consider rituals confidence boosters. When rituals move into the office, they are linked with increased employee involvement and a higher sense of connection among team members. Of course, newcomers may have to be treated with extra care. At Salo, for example, new marketing manager Maureen Sullivan was surprised to see the chest bumping. But she learned to accept it, saying: "Alrighty, that's what we do here. We just really get into it."

HOW ABOUT IT?

Is this taking organizational culture a step too far? Would you be comfortable in an office environment where chest bumps were part of the daily ritual? Suppose it was a "shoulder bump"—would that help? Do you find such activities a source of celebration, camaraderie, and engagement? Or, are they a real turnoff? As a team leader, would you try to make rituals part of the team culture?

The presence or absence of these observable things, and the ways they are practiced, can say a lot about an organization's culture. They represent, communicate, and carry the culture over time, keeping it visible and clear in all members' eyes. New members learn the organization's culture through them, and all members keep the culture alive by sharing and joining in them.

THE CORE CULTURE IS FOUND IN THE UNDERLYING VALUES OF THE ORGANIZATION.

In the iceberg metaphor of organizational culture, what lies below the surface is called the **core culture**, consisting of the **core values** or underlying assumptions and beliefs that shape and guide people's behaviors. Positive examples include things like performance excellence, innovation, social responsibility, integrity, worker involvement, customer service, and teamwork.[14]

It's common to find values statements on corporate Web sites, in mission statements, and in executive speeches. Here are some examples: Whole Foods—"Creating ongoing win-win partnerships with our suppliers" . . . UnderArmour—"Innovation, Inspiration, Reliability and Integrity" . . . Tesla—"the best electric car and electric power trains in the world" . . . Honest Tea—"We strive to live up to our name in the way we conduct our business."[15] Nice, we might say. But, don't be fooled by values statements alone when trying to understand an organization's core culture. It's easy to write a set of values, post them on the Web, and talk about them. It's a lot harder to live up to them.

If an organization's stated values are to have positive effects, everyone in the organization from top to bottom must know the values and live up to them in day-to-day actions. It's in this sense that managers have a special responsibility to "walk the values talk" and make the expressed values real. After all, how might you react if you found out senior executives in your organization talked up values such as honesty and ethical behavior, but were also known to spend company funds on lavish private parties and vacations?

The **core culture** is found in the underlying values of the organization.

Core values are beliefs and values shared by organization members.

FACTS TO CONSIDER

Family Values Put Pressure on Organization Cultures

Ariel Skelley\Ariel Skelley/Getty Images

The pressure is on organizations to pay more attention to family values and the work–life balance issues faced by their employees. Talk to friends and relatives to check facts such as these.

- 78% of American couples are dual-wage earners.
- 63% believe they don't have enough time for their spouses or partners.
- 74% believe they don't have enough time for their children.
- 35% are spending time caring for elderly relatives.
- 80+% across generations rate flexible work as important.
- 60+% across generations want to work remotely at least part of the time.

YOUR THOUGHTS?

What organizational culture issues are raised by family values today? What should employers do to best respond to them? Can employers make respect for family values and work–life balance a recruiting and retention tool?

VALUE-BASED MANAGEMENT SUPPORTS A STRONG ORGANIZATIONAL CULTURE.

SITUATION: After making a big investment in a new deodorant, founder Tom Chappell of Tom's of Maine learned that customers were very dissatisfied with it. He quickly decided to reimburse customers and pull the product from the market, even though it would cost the company more than $400,000. Tom had founded the company on values of fairness and honesty in all matters. Rather than trying to save costs, he did what he believed was the right thing.[16]

Value-based management actively develops, communicates, and enacts shared values.

When managers practice the core values, model them for others, and communicate and reinforce them in all that they do, this is called **value-based management**. That's what Tom Chappell displayed in this situation. His decision to reimburse customers and pull the product lived up to the company's values and set a positive example for others in the firm to follow in the future. And it set an enduring precedent. When employees faced difficult situations and dilemmas in the future, they could check their behavior by asking this important values question: What would Tom do?

Workplace spirituality involves practices that create meaning and shared community among organizational members.

The notion of **workplace spirituality** is sometimes discussed along with value-based management. Although the first tendency might be to associate the term "spirituality" with religion, it is used in management to describe practices that try to enrich people's lives by bringing meaning to their work and helping them engage one another with a sense of shared community.[17]

A culture of workplace spirituality will have strong ethical foundations, recognize the value of individuals and respect their diversity, and focus efforts on meaningful jobs that offer real value to society. Anyone working in a culture of workplace spirituality should derive pleasure from knowing that what is being accomplished is personally meaningful, created through community, and valued by others. Anyone who leads a culture of workplace spirituality values people by emphasizing meaningful purpose, trust and respect, honesty and openness, personal growth and development, worker-friendly practices, and ethics and social responsibility.

STUDYGUIDE

Takeaway 8.1
What Is the Nature of Organizational Culture?

Terms to Define

Core culture	Observable culture	Socialization	Value-based management
Core values	Organizational culture	Strong cultures	Workplace spirituality

Rapid Review

- Organizational culture is a climate of shared values and beliefs that guides the behavior of members; it creates the character and personality of the organization and sets its performance tone.
- The observable culture is found in the everyday rites, rituals, stories, heroes, and symbols of the organization.
- The core culture consists of the core values and fundamental beliefs on which the organization is based.
- Value-based management communicates, models, and reinforces core values throughout the organization.
- Symbolic leadership uses words, symbols, and actions to communicate the organizational culture.

Questions for Discussion

1. Can an organization achieve success with a good organizational design but a weak organizational culture?
2. When you are in your local bank or any other retail establishment as a customer, what do you see and hear around you that identifies its observable culture?
3. What core values would you choose if you were creating a new organization and wanted to establish a strong performance-oriented culture?

Be Sure You Can

- **explain** organizational culture as the personality of an organization
- **describe** how strong cultures influence organizations
- **define** and explain the process of socialization
- **distinguish** between the observable and the core cultures
- **explain** value-based management
- **explain** symbolic leadership

Career Situation: What Would You Do?

You have two really nice job offers and will soon have to choose between them. They are both in the same industry, but you wonder which employer would be the "best fit" for you. Make a list of the key aspects of the cultures of these organizations that you would investigate to help make your job choice. Why are these aspects of organizational culture important to you?

Takeaway 8.2
How Do Organizations Support and Achieve Innovation?

ANSWERS TO COME

- Organizations pursue process, product, and business model innovations.
- Green innovations advance the goals of sustainability.
- Social innovations seek solutions to important societal problems.
- Commercializing innovation turns new ideas into salable products.
- Disruptive innovation uses new technologies to displace existing practices.
- Innovative organizations share many common characteristics.

THE iPAD, KINDLE, POST-IT NOTES, SUPER-SOAKER WATER GUN, ATMs, streaming movie rentals, overnight package deliveries, and more. Name your favorites! These examples are all brought to us through **innovation**, the process of developing new ideas and putting them into practice.[18] The late management consultant Peter Drucker called innovation "an effort to create purposeful, focused change in an enterprise's economic or social potential."[19] Today's organizations and entrepreneurs thrive on cultures of innovation.

> **Innovation** is the process of developing new ideas and putting them into practice.

ORGANIZATIONS PURSUE PROCESS, PRODUCT, AND BUSINESS MODEL INNOVATIONS.

Innovation takes different forms. **Process innovations** create better ways of doing things. **Product innovations** create new or improved goods and services. **Business model innovations** create new ways of making money.[20] Consider these examples.

> **Process innovations** result in better ways of doing things.

> **Product innovations** result in new or improved goods or services.

> **Business model innovations** result in ways for firms to make money.

- *Process innovation*—Southwest Airlines streamlines operations to fit its low-cost business strategy; IKEA sells furniture and fixtures in assemble-yourself kits; Amazon.com's "one-click" makes online shopping easy; Nike lets customers design their own sneakers.
- *Product innovation*—Apple introduced the iPod, iPhone, and iPad and made the "app" a must-have for smart phones and tablets; Amazon brought us the Kindle e-book reader; Facebook and Twitter made social media a part of everyday life; Uber made ride-sharing an easy taxi alternative.
- *Business model innovation*—Netflix turned movie rental into a subscription business; eBay profits by connecting users of its online marketplace; Zynga made paying for "extras" profitable with free online games; Salesforce.com introduced cloud-based software not as a product but as a service.

GREEN INNOVATIONS ADVANCE THE GOALS OF SUSTAINABILITY.

> **Green innovation** or **sustainable innovation** reduces the carbon footprint of an organization or its products.

Today we can add **green innovation,** or **sustainable innovation**, to the list of innovation types. These innovations advance sustainability by creating ways to reduce the carbon footprint of an organization or its products. Look for them in areas like energy use, water use, packaging, waste management, and transportation practices, as well as in new product development. The possibilities abound. Replacing air travel with videoconferencing not only reduces travel costs for the organization, it also reduces carbon emissions otherwise put out by air travel. Getting energy from biogas or solar energy may cut electricity costs for a business, but it also reduces air pollution. Recycling used garments and reweaving the fibers into new clothing can save on both energy costs and carbon emissions.[21]

SOCIAL INNOVATIONS SEEK SOLUTIONS TO IMPORTANT SOCIETAL PROBLEMS.

Although the tendency is to view innovation in an economic business context, it's important to remember that it applies equally well to societal issues such as poverty, famine, literacy, and disease. **Social innovation** is business innovation driven by a social conscience. It is spearheaded by **social entrepreneurs** who pursue creative ways to solve pressing social problems.[22] Peter Drucker was an early and vocal champion of this notion. "Every single social and global issue of our day," he said, "is a business opportunity in disguise."[23] His message is still right on for today. Dipak C. Jain, respected scholar and dean, says that business schools "should be producing leaders of real substance who put their knowledge to work in ways that make the world a better place."[24]

Social innovation is business innovation driven by a social conscience.

Social entrepreneurs pursue innovative ways to solve pressing social problems.

COMMERCIALIZING INNOVATION TURNS NEW IDEAS INTO SALABLE PRODUCTS.

Whatever the goal—new product, improved process, unique business model, better sustainability, or social problem solving, the innovation process begins with *invention*—the act of discovery—and ends with *application*—the act of use.[25] The business process of **commercializing innovation** turns new ideas—the inventions—into actual products, services, or processes—the applications—that generate profits.[26] 3M Corporation, for example, owes its success to the imagination of employees such as Art Fry. He's the person whose creativity turned an adhesive that "wasn't sticky enough" into the blockbuster product known worldwide today as Post-it Notes.

Commercializing innovation is the process of turning new ideas into applications that generate profits.

It's tempting to believe that commercializing an innovation such as the Post-it Note is easy. You might even consider it a "no-brainer." But it isn't necessarily so. Art Fry and his colleagues had to actively "sell" the Post-it idea to 3M's marketing group and senior management. It took quite some time before they got the financial support needed to turn their invention into a salable product.

Figure 8.2 shows how new product ideas such as Post-it might move through the typical steps of commercializing innovation. One of the newer developments to pass through this process is called **reverse innovation** or *trickle-up innovation*. The concept got its start in the world of global business when firms stopped viewing innovation as something only done "at home" and then transferred to "foreign or emerging markets."[27]

Reverse innovation recognizes the potential for valuable innovations to be launched from lower organizational levels and diverse locations, including emerging markets.

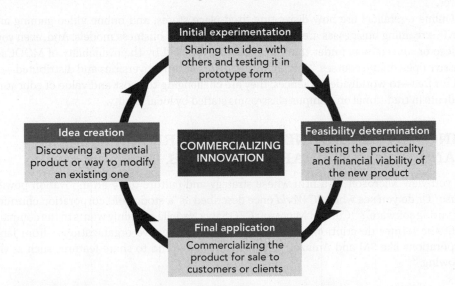

FIGURE 8.2 How Do Organizations Commercialize Innovation?

In business it is the process of commercializing innovation that turns new ideas into actual products, services, or processes that can increase profits through greater sales or reduced costs. This requires management encouragement and support for idea creation (invention and the act of discovery), experimentation and feasibility determination, and final application (actually putting the tested idea into use).

Social Entrepreneur Empowers Small Farmers to Fight Rural Poverty

Khalik Senosi/AP

Chronic hunger is the leading cause of death among African children. So, what can be done? Sympathy wasn't enough for Andrew Youn. He's a social entrepreneur whose efforts have made a world of difference for many African families. Using $7,000 of his own money, he set up an innovative program called the One Acre Fund. It provides small loans to poor families in Burundi, Kenya, and Rwanda, enabling them to work their land with high-quality seed, fertilizer, equipment, and training. The goal is to help farmers "grow their way out of poverty" by finding ways to increase crop yields and avoid the devastating effects of Kenya's 3-month "hunger season." Farmer repayments to the fund have reached $10 million annually. The One Acre Fund won the SC Johnson Award for Socially Responsible Entrepreneurship and has expanded into Rwanda. Says Youn: "The mothers are absolutely inspiring. The things they do out of necessity are heroic."

Reverse innovation takes products and services developed in emerging markets and finds ways to use them elsewhere. Management scholar C. K. Prahalad goes so far as to call cost-conscious emerging markets "laboratories for radical innovation."[28] GE is a big believer. The firm developed handheld and portable electrocardiogram and ultrasound machines to sell in India for a fraction of the price of larger units. Their success prompted GE to move them through reverse innovation into the United States, where portability and lower prices made them popular with emergency services.

DISRUPTIVE INNOVATION USES NEW TECHNOLOGIES TO DISPLACE EXISTING PRACTICES.

Disruptive innovation creates products or services that become so widely used that they largely replace prior practices and competitors.

At times the innovation process is so successful that **disruptive innovation** occurs. Harvard Scholar Clay Christensen defines it as the creation of an innovative product or service that starts out small scale and then moves "up market" to where it is so widely used it displaces prior practices and competitors.[29] Historical examples include cellular phones that disrupted traditional landlines and discount retailers that disrupted traditional full-line department stores.

Online e-retailers are now disrupting fixed-place stores, and online video gaming and movie streaming businesses are disrupting "buy and own" business models. And, even your college or university is under the disruptive threat posed by the availability of MOOCs—massive open online courses.[30] Taught by professors at top universities and distributed—often for free—to worldwide audiences, they are challenging the cost and value of educating students in traditional on-campus classrooms staffed by local faculty.

INNOVATIVE ORGANIZATIONS SHARE MANY COMMON CHARACTERISTICS.

Do you view Microsoft as a firm whose strategy and culture drive an innovation powerhouse? Or do you see what *PC World* once described as "a stodgy old corporation churning out boring software"?[31] Current Microsoft CEO Satya Nadella certainly wants to the company to fit the former description, not the latter. Truly innovative organizations—from large corporations like 3M and Amazon to small start-ups—tend to share features such as the following.[32]

HIGHLY INNOVATIVE ORGANIZATIONS				
Strategy includes innovation	Culture values innovation	Structures support innovation	Staffing builds talent for innovation	Leadership drives innovation

In highly innovative organizations the *corporate strategy and culture embrace innovation*. The strategies of the organization target innovation; the culture of the organization values an innovation spirit. If you go to the Web site for the design firm IDEO, you'll find this description: "Our values are part mad scientist (curious, experimental), bear-tamer (gutsy, agile), *reiki* master (hands-on, empathetic), and midnight tax accountant (optimistic, savvy). These qualities are reflected in the smallest details to the biggest endeavors, composing the medium in which great ideas are born and flourish."[33] There's little doubt that core values at IDEO encourage innovation and allow new ideas to continually flourish.

In highly innovative organizations, *organization structures support innovation*. Bureaucracy is the enemy of innovation. Innovative organizations take advantage of organic designs and team structures that empower people and eliminate cumbersome bureaucratic ways. *Businessweek* says: "Instead of assembly line, think swarming beehive. Teams of people from different disciplines gather to focus on a problem. They brainstorm, tinker and toy with different approaches."[34] The term **skunkworks** is often used to describe special work units set free from the formal organizational structure and given separate locations, special resources, and their own managers, all with the purpose of achieving innovation.

In highly innovative organizations, *staffing builds talent for innovation*. Step 1 in meeting this goal is to make creativity important when hiring and moving people into positions of responsibility. Step 2 is allowing their creative talents to fully operate by inspiring and empowering them by the practices just discussed—strategy, culture, and structure, as well as the right leadership.

In highly innovative organizations, *leadership drives innovation*. Sometimes leadership support for innovation is policy driven. Google, for example, gives engineers freedom to spend 20% of their time on projects of their own choosing. Other times this support is style driven. Innovation leaders not only encourage new ideas, they also tolerate criticism and differences of opinion. They know that success doesn't always come in a straight line and admit that mistakes are often part of the innovation process. When talking about the firm's innovative electronic reader, the Kindle, Amazon's CEO Jeff Bezos said: "Our willingness to be misunderstood, our long-term orientation and our willingness to repeatedly fail are the three parts of our culture that make doing this kind of thing possible."[35]

> **Skunkworks** are special creative units set free from the normal structure for the purpose of innovation.

Innovation in Work Scheduling Helps Employers Beat the "Mommy Drain"

Mango Productions/Corbis Corp

It's well known that attracting and retaining talented workers should be one of the top priorities for any organization. But what happens with new moms? How do you get them onboard when you want to hire them? How do you keep them onboard when you already have them? The "Mommy drain"— loss of mothers from the workforce—is real. And now we're also starting to talk about a "Daddy drain." Could this be one of those areas where the top innovators win the employee talent prizes?

STUDYGUIDE

Takeaway 8.2
How Do Organizations Support and Achieve Innovation?

Terms to Define

Business model innovation	Disruptive innovation	Product innovations	Social innovation
Commercializing innovation	Green innovation	Reverse innovation	Sustainable innovation
	Innovation	Skunkworks	
	Process innovations	Social entrepreneurs	

Rapid Review

- Innovation is a process that turns creative ideas into products or processes that benefit organizations and their customers.
- Organizations pursue process, product, and business model innovations.
- Organizations pursue green innovations that support sustainability.
- Organizations pursue social business innovations to tackle important societal problems.
- The process of commercializing innovation turns new ideas into useful applications.
- Highly innovative organizations tend to have supportive cultures, strategies, structures, staffing, and top management.

Questions for Discussion

1. Are there any potential downsides to making organizational commitments to green innovation?
2. What are the biggest trouble points in a large organization that might prevent a great idea from becoming a commercialized innovation?
3. What difference does a leader make in terms of how innovative an organization becomes?

Be Sure You Can

- **discuss** differences among process, product, and business model innovations
- **explain** green innovation and social business innovation
- **list** five steps in the process of commercializing innovation
- **list** and explain four characteristics of innovative organizations

Career Situation: What Would You Do?

Take a look around your present organization, be it a school or workplace. What three ideas can you come up with right away for possible innovations? How would your ideas, if implemented, benefit both the organization and society at large? What are the potential obstacles to getting your ideas implemented? What steps could you take as an "innovation champion" to turn your ideas into real practices?

Takeaway 8.3
How Do Managers Lead the Processes of Organizational Change?

ANSWERS TO COME

- Organizations and teams need change leaders.
- Organizational change can be transformational or incremental.
- Three phases of planned change are unfreezing, changing, and refreezing.
- Times of complexity require improvising in the change process.
- Managers use force-coercion, rational persuasion, and shared power change strategies.
- Change leaders identify and deal positively with resistance to change.

WHAT IF THE EXISTING STRUCTURE OR CULTURE OF AN ORGANIZATION IS FLAWED, doesn't drive high performance, and in general causes problems? Just "change things," you might say. The fact is that we use the word "change" so much that the tendency may be to think changing things is easy, almost a matter of routine. But that's not always the case.[36] Former British Airways CEO Sir Rod Eddington once said, for example, that "altering an airline's culture is like trying to perform an engine change in flight."[37]

ORGANIZATIONS AND TEAMS NEED CHANGE LEADERS.

Just look at the business news. You'll always find firms that are struggling, and it's not always because they don't have the right ideas—it's because they aren't adapting well to new circumstances. In other words, they have difficulty creating organizational change. There are times when managers at all levels in organizations have to succeed as **change leaders** and take initiative to change the existing pattern of behavior of another person or social system.[38]

A **change leader** tries to change the behavior of another person or social system.

Change leaders are supposed to make things happen even when inertia has made systems and people reluctant to embrace new ways of doing things. They are supposed to be alert to cultures, situations, and people needing change; open to good ideas and opportunities; and ready and able to support the implementation of new ideas in actual practice. But, the reality described in the small figure shows a big difference between true change leaders and status quo managers. All too often people in organizations have major tendencies toward the status quo—accepting things as they are and not wanting to change. And it's the status quo that creates lots of difficulties when managers and team leaders push organizations and teams to innovate and adapt to changing times.

Change leaders	Status quo managers
• Confident of ability	• Threatened by change
• Willing to take risks	• Bothered by uncertainty
• Seize opportunity	• Prefer predictability
• Expect and embrace surprise	• Support the status quo
• Make things happen	• Wait for things to happen

ORGANIZATIONAL CHANGE CAN BE TRANSFORMATIONAL OR INCREMENTAL.

Changes led from top levels are likely to be large-scale, strategic, and *frame breaking*. They are repositioning changes targeting big issues that affect the organization as a whole. We call this **transformational change**. It is supposed to result in a major and comprehensive redirection of the organization—a new vision, new strategy, new culture, new structure, and even new people.[39]

Transformational change results in a major and comprehensive redirection of the organization.

As you might expect, transformational change is intense, stressful, and hard to achieve. Lots of large-scale change efforts actually fail, and the main reason for failure is bad implementation.[40] One of the most common implementation mistakes is management failure to build commitments so that everyone accepts and works hard to accomplish change goals.[41] Instead of setting the stage for change and getting key people on board before the process begins, they just "order and hope." Popular advice to would-be leaders of large-scale changes includes the following guidelines:[42]

- Establish a sense of urgency for change.
- Form a powerful coalition to lead the change.
- Create and communicate a change vision.
- Empower others to move change forward.
- Celebrate short-term wins, and recognize those who help.
- Build on success; align people and systems with new ways.
- Stay with it; keep the message consistent; champion the vision.

Incremental change bends and adjusts existing ways to improve performance.

There is another more modest and *frame-bending* side to organizational change. It deals with ongoing adjustments in structures, systems, technologies, products, and staffing. This is **incremental change** that tweaks and nudges people, systems, and practices to better align them with emerging problems and opportunities. The intent here isn't to break and remake the system, but to move it forward through continuous improvements.

Leadership of incremental change focuses on building upon existing ways of doing things with the goal of doing them better in the future. Common incremental changes involve new products, processes, technologies, work systems, and human resource approaches.

Don't get the idea, by the way, that incremental change is inferior to transformational change. You are likely to find that organizations are most successful over time when they successfully put transformational and incremental change together, as shown in the organizational change pyramid.[43] Think of it this way. Incremental changes keep things tuned up—like the engine on a car, in between transformations—when the old car is replaced with a new one.

Organizational Change Pyramid

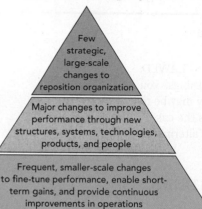

Few strategic, large-scale changes to reposition organization

Major changes to improve performance through new structures, systems, technologies, products, and people

Frequent, smaller-scale changes to fine-tune performance, enable short-term gains, and provide continuous improvements in operations

THREE PHASES OF PLANNED CHANGE ARE UNFREEZING, CHANGING, AND REFREEZING.

Managers seeking to lead change in organizations can benefit from a simple but helpful model developed by the psychologist Kurt Lewin. Shown in **Figure 8.3**, it describes how change situations can be analyzed and addressed in three phases: *unfreezing*—preparing

FIGURE 8.3

What Are the Change Leader Responsibilities in Lewin's Three Phases of Planned Change?

Kurt Lewin identified three phases of the planned change process. The first is unfreezing, where people open up and become receptive to the possibility of change. The second is changing, where real change happens. Third is refreezing, where changes become part of everyday routines. Lewin believed that change agents often neglect unfreezing, thus setting the stage for change failures. They may also neglect refreezing, with the result that any achieved change has only temporary effects.

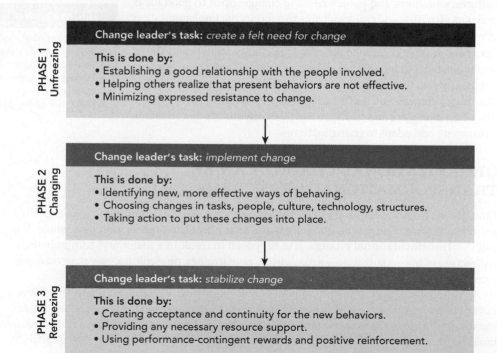

PHASE 1 Unfreezing

Change leader's task: *create a felt need for change*

This is done by:
- Establishing a good relationship with the people involved.
- Helping others realize that present behaviors are not effective.
- Minimizing expressed resistance to change.

PHASE 2 Changing

Change leader's task: *implement change*

This is done by:
- Identifying new, more effective ways of behaving.
- Choosing changes in tasks, people, culture, technology, structures.
- Taking action to put these changes into place.

PHASE 3 Refreezing

Change leader's task: *stabilize change*

This is done by:
- Creating acceptance and continuity for the new behaviors.
- Providing any necessary resource support.
- Using performance-contingent rewards and positive reinforcement.

a system for change; *changing*—making actual changes in the system; and *refreezing*—stabilizing the system after change.[44]

Unfreezing is the stage in which managers help others to develop, experience, and feel a real need for change. The goal here is to get people to view change as a way of solving a problem or taking advantage of an opportunity. Some might call this the "burning bridge" phase, arguing that to get people to jump off a bridge, you might just have to set it on fire. Managers can simulate the burning bridge by engaging people with facts and information that communicate the need for change—environmental pressures, declining performance, and examples of alternative approaches. And as you have probably experienced, conflict can help people to break old habits and recognize new ways of thinking about or doing things.

The **changing** phase is where actual change takes place. Ideally these changes are planned in ways that give them the best opportunities for success, having maximum appeal and posing minimum difficulties for those being asked to make them. Although this phase should follow unfreezing in Lewin's model, he believes it is often started too early. When change takes place before people and systems are ready for it, the likelihood of resistance and change failure is much greater. In this sense Lewin might liken the change process to building a house: You need to put a good foundation in place before you begin the framing.

The final stage in the planned change process is **refreezing**. Here, the focus is on stabilizing the change to make it as long lasting as needed. Linking change with rewards, positive reinforcement, and resource support all help with refreezing. Of course, in today's dynamic environments there may not be a lot of time for refreezing before things are ready to change again. You may well find that refreezing in Lewin's sense probably gives way quite often to another phase of evaluating and reassessing. In other words, we begin preparing for or undertaking more change even while trying to take full advantage of the present one.

Unfreezing is the phase during which a situation is prepared for change.

Changing is the phase where a planned change actually takes place.

Refreezing is the phase at which change is stabilized.

TIMES OF COMPLEXITY REQUIRE IMPROVISING IN THE CHANGE PROCESS.

Lewin's three-phase model gives the impression that change is a linear, step-by-step process having clear beginning and end points. But the complexity facing organizations today introduces an important reality: change is most often dynamic and ongoing, and its outcomes may be uncertain and transitory. Change leaders often deal with the change phases simultaneously, and new changes may begin before refreezing ever takes place with an old one. This

AN ARCHITECT PROPOSES A DESIGN THAT DOES AWAY WITH PRIVATE OFFICES AND SHIFTS SALES REPRESENTATIVES TO "HOTDESKING."

QUICK CASE

Proposal for Open Office Design and Hotdesking

Stephane Lagoutte/Challenges-REA/Redux

You are just starting to work with an architect on designs for a new office space for your fast-growing tech startup. She proposes a design that does away with private offices, includes two or three personal cubicles with flexible dividers, and provides lots of flexible open spaces for casual and arranged meetings. She also proposes a shift to "hotdesking" for the sales representatives because they spend a lot of time away from the office. This means that they will not have permanent space and will instead "sign up" to use temporary cubicle desks when they come into the office.

You really like the design concept because it supports collaboration and teamwork while also saving space and facilities costs as the firm grows. But you're worried about possible resistance because everyone is used to having private office space. So, you sit down to write a list of "pros" and "cons" for the architect's proposal. You also make some notes on how to engage the staff with these ideas in order to head off any problems.

WHAT DO YOU DO?

What's on your pros and cons list? What are your notes, and what are their implications for how you will approach this change situation? What's your strategy? What kind of change leadership approach do you think will be most likely to work with this group?

Improvisational change makes continual adjustments as changes are being implemented.

complexity creates a need for **improvisational change**, where change is viewed as an ongoing process and adjustments are continually made as changes are being implemented.[45]

Consider the case of bringing new technology into an organization or work unit. A technology that is attractive in concept may appear complicated to the new users. The full extent of its benefits or inadequacies may not become known until it is tried. To succeed in such situations, a change leader should be continually gathering feedback on how the change is going and then improvising to adjust the new technology to best meet users' needs. And while this change is underway, another newer or related technology may emerge that places further demands on change leadership.

MANAGERS USE FORCE-COERCION, RATIONAL PERSUASION, AND SHARED POWER CHANGE STRATEGIES.

How does a manager or team leader actually move people and systems toward change? The answer in **Figure 8.4** shows three common change strategies—force-coercion, rational persuasion, and shared power. Each should be understood and most likely used by all change leaders.[46]

A **force-coercion strategy**
pursues change through formal authority and/or the use of rewards or punishments.

A **force-coercion strategy** uses the power bases of legitimacy, rewards, and punishments as the primary inducements to change.[47] It comes in two forms. In a *direct forcing* strategy, the change agent takes direct and unilateral action to command that change take place. This involves the exercise of formal authority or legitimate power, offering special rewards, and/or threatening punishment. In *political maneuvering*, the change agent works indirectly to gain special advantage over other persons to force the change. This involves bargaining, obtaining control of important resources, forming alliances, or granting favors.

Most people will probably respond to force-coercion with temporary compliance. They'll act in a limited way and only out of fear of punishment or hope for a reward. But the new behavior continues only so long as the possibilities for rewards and punishments exist. This is why force-coercion may be most useful as an unfreezing strategy. It can help to break people from old habits and try new ones that eventually prove valuable enough to be self-sustaining.

A **rational persuasion strategy**
pursues change through empirical data and rational argument.

The **rational persuasion strategy** seeks to bring about change through persuasion backed by special knowledge, information, facts, and rational argument. The likely outcome is compliance with reasonable commitment. This is actually the strategy that you learn and practice so much in school when writing reports and making formal presentations on group projects. You'll do a lot of rational persuasion in the real world as well. But as you probably realize, success with this change strategy depends on having very good facts and information—the rational part, and then being able to communicate them well—the persuasion part.

The rational persuasion strategy works best when the change agent has credibility as an expert. This credibility can come from possessing special information or having a reputation as an expert. It can also be gained from bringing in external consultants or experts, showing case examples or benchmarks, and conducting demonstration projects. Ford, for example, has sent

FIGURE 8.4

What Happens When a Change Leader Uses Different Types of Change Strategies?

Force-coercion strategies use authority, offers of rewards, and threats of punishment to push change forward. The likely outcome is, at best, temporary compliance. Rational persuasion strategies use information, facts, and logic to present a persuasive case in support of change. The likely outcomes are compliance with reasonable commitment. Shared power strategies allow others to participate in the change process, from initial planning through implementation. The likely outcomes are more internalization and greater commitment to change.

Change Strategy	Power Bases	Managerial Behavior	Likely Outcomes
Force–Coercion Using position power to create change by decree and formal authority	Legitimacy Rewards Punishments	*Direct forcing* and unilateral action *Political maneuvering* and indirect action	Faster, but low commitment and only temporary compliance
Rational Persuasion Creating change through rational persuasion and empirical argument	Expertise	*Informational efforts* using credible knowledge, demonstrated facts, and logical argument	
Shared Power Developing support for change through personal values and commitments	Reference	*Participative efforts* to share power and involve others in planning and implementing change	Slower, but high commitment and longer term internalization

ETHICS CHECK

Hidden Agendas in Organizational Change

Image Source/Alamy

Sharing power is a popular choice when implementing a change strategy. It means allowing others to have a decision-making role and to be involved throughout the change process. This approach can generate a lot of good ideas and helps establish all-important "buy-in" to support the proposed change. But, suppose the ideas offered and the ensuing conversations move in a direction that top management thinks is wrong? What happens then?

Some managers are afraid of losing influence while sharing power during organizational change. So, they resort to hidden agendas. They handpick key members to be on their change teams. They also ask them to take prominent roles in discussions and support only the "right" ideas. The goal is to make sure that change heads in the predetermined "preferred" direction while still giving everyone involved a sense of being included and empowered. It's a very political way of appearing to share power—enjoying the image-related benefits of inclusiveness, but still getting your way.

YOUR DECISION?

Although this situation happens frequently in organizations, does that make it right? What are the ethical issues involved? When is such an approach more or less likely to be ethical? As a manager, would you handpick the leaders of a change effort in order to get your way—even if that meant that alternative points of view were likely to be excluded from the process? What if your boss selected you to represent your department on a task force just because you agreed with his or her favored approach? If you knew that most of your co-workers disagreed, would you do what your boss wanted you to do, or would you try to represent the wishes of the majority of your co-workers? What are the potential risks associated with your choice?

---

managers to Disney World to learn about customer loyalty, hoping to stimulate them to lead customer service initiatives of their own. A Ford vice president says, "Disney's track record is one of the best in the country as far as dealing with customers."[48] In this sense the power of rational persuasion is straightforward: If it works for Disney, why can't it work for Ford?

A **shared power strategy** engages people in a collaborative process of identifying values, assumptions, and goals from which support for change will naturally emerge. Although slow, the process is likely to yield high commitment. Sometimes called a *normative re-educative strategy*, this approach relies on empowerment and participation. The change leader engages others as a team to develop the consensus needed to support change. This requires being comfortable and confident in allowing others to influence decisions that affect the planned change and its implementation. And because it entails a high level of involvement, this strategy is often quite time consuming. But shared power can deliver major benefits in terms of longer-lasting and internalized change.

> A **shared power strategy** pursues change by participation in assessing change needs, values, and goals.

The great strength of the shared power strategy lies with unlocking the creativity and experience of people within the system. Still, many managers hesitate to use it for fear of losing control or of having to compromise on important organizational goals. Harvard scholar Teresa M. Amabile points out, however, that managers and change leaders can share power regarding choice of means and processes, even if they can't debate the goals. "People will be more creative," she says, "if you give them freedom to decide how to climb particular mountains. You needn't let them choose which mountains to climb."[49]

CHANGE LEADERS IDENTIFY AND DEAL POSITIVELY WITH RESISTANCE TO CHANGE.

You may have heard the adage that "change can be your best friend." At this point, however, we should probably add: "but only if you deal with resistance in the right ways."

When people resist change, they are most often defending something important to them and that now appears threatened. It is tempting to view such resistance as something that must be overcome or defeated. But this mindset can easily cause problems. Perhaps a better

TABLE 8.1 Why People May Resist Change

Fear of the unknown—not understanding what is happening or what comes next

Disrupted habits—feeling upset to see the end of the old ways of doing things

Loss of confidence—feeling incapable of performing well under the new ways of doing things

Loss of control—feeling that things are being done "to" you rather than "by" or "with" you

Poor timing—feeling overwhelmed by the situation or feeling that things are moving too fast

Work overload—not having the physical or psychic energy to commit to the change

Loss of face—feeling inadequate or humiliated because it appears that the old ways weren't good ways

Lack of purpose—not seeing a reason for the change and/or not understanding its benefits

way is to view resistance as feedback, as a source of information about how people view the change and its impact on them. A change leader can learn a lot by listening to resistance and then using it to develop ideas for improving the change and the change process.[50]

The list in **Table 8.1**—Why People May Resist Change—probably contains some familiar items. Surely you've seen some or all of these types of change resistance in your own experience. And honestly now, haven't you also been a resister at times? When you were, how did the change leader or manager respond? How do you think they should have responded?

Researchers have found that once resistance appears in organizations, managers try to deal with it in various ways, and some of their choices are better than others.[51] *Education and communication* use discussions, presentations, and demonstrations to educate people about a change before it happens. *Participation and involvement* allows others to contribute ideas and help design and implement the change. *Facilitation and support* provide encouragement and training, channels for communicating problems and complaints, and ways of helping to overcome performance pressures. *Negotiation and agreement* offer incentives to those who are actively resisting or ready to resist, trying to make trade-offs in exchange for cooperation.

Two others are considerably more risky and prone to negative side effects. Change leaders who use *manipulation and cooptation* try to covertly influence resisters by providing information selectively and structuring events in favor of the desired change. Those using *explicit and implicit coercion* try to force resisters to accept change by threatening them with a variety of undesirable consequences if they don't go along as asked. Would you agree that most people don't like to be on the receiving end of these strategies?

TOLERANCE FOR AMBIGUITY IS A GOOD PREDICTOR OF HOW YOU DEAL WITH CHANGE.

EXPLORE YOURSELF

Tolerance for Ambiguity

The next time you are driving somewhere and following a familiar route only to find a "detour" sign ahead, test your **tolerance for ambiguity**. Is the detour no big deal and you go forward without any further thought? Or is it a bit of a deal, perhaps causing anxiety or anger and demonstrating your tendencies to resist change in your normal routines?

Your tolerance for ambiguity is a good predictor of how you like to work and deal with change. Some of us embrace change, whereas others resist it. But remember, people today are being asked to be ever more creative and innovative in their work; organizations are, too.

At work we are expected to support change initiatives launched from the top; we are also expected to be change leaders in our own teams and work units. This is a good time to check your readiness to meet the challenges of change in organizations and in personal affairs.

Get to know yourself better by taking the self-assessment on **Tolerance for Ambiguity** and completing other activities in the *Exploring Management* **Skill-Building Portfolio.**

STUDYGUIDE

Takeaway 8.3
How Do Managers Lead the Processes of Organizational Change?

Terms to Define

Change leader	Incremental change	Rational persuasion	Shared power strategy
Changing	Improvisational	strategy	Transformational change
Force-coercion strategy	change	Refreezing	Unfreezing

Rapid Review

- Transformational change makes radical changes in organizational directions; incremental change makes continuing adjustments to existing ways and practices.
- Change leaders are change agents who take responsibility for helping to change the behavior of people and organizational systems.
- Lewin's three phases of planned change are unfreezing (preparing a system for change), changing (making a change), and refreezing (stabilizing the system with a new change in place).
- Successful change agents understand the force-coercion, rational persuasion, and shared power change strategies, and the likely outcomes of each.
- People resist change for a variety of reasons, including fear of the unknown and force of habit; this resistance can be a source of feedback that can help improve the change process.
- Change agents deal with resistance to change in a variety of ways, including education, participation, facilitation, negotiation, manipulation, and coercion.

Questions for Discussion

1. When is it better to pursue incremental rather than transformational change?
2. Can the refreezing phase of planned change ever be completed in today's dynamic environment?
3. Should managers avoid the force-coercion change strategy altogether?

Be Sure You Can

- **differentiate** transformational and incremental change
- **discuss** a change leader's responsibilities for each phase of Lewin's change process
- **explain** the force-coercion, rational persuasion, and shared power change strategies
- **list** reasons why people resist change
- **identify** strategies for dealing with resistance to change

Career Situation: What Would You Do?

Times are tough at your organization, and, as the director of human resources, you have a problem. The company's senior executives have decided that 10% of the payroll has to be cut immediately. Instead of laying off people, you would like to have everyone cut back their work hours by 10%. This would cut the payroll but let everyone keep their jobs. You've heard this idea isn't popular with all the workers. Some are already grumbling that it's a "bad idea" and the company is just looking for excuses "to cut wages." How can you best handle this situation as a change leader?

TESTPREP 8

Answers to Test Prep questions can be found at the back of the book.

Multiple-Choice Questions

1. Stories told about an organization's past accomplishments and heroes such as company founders are all part of what is called the _____ culture.
   - (a) observable
   - (b) underground
   - (c) functional
   - (d) core

2. Planned and spontaneous ceremonies and celebrations of work achievements illustrate how the use of _____ helps build strong corporate cultures.
   - (a) rewards
   - (b) structures
   - (c) rites and rituals
   - (d) core values

3. An organization with a strong culture is most likely to have a _____.
   - (a) tight, bureaucratic structure
   - (b) loose, flexible design
   - (c) small staff size
   - (d) clearly communicated mission

4. Honesty, social responsibility, and customer service are examples of _____ that can become foundations for an organization's core culture.
   - (a) rites and rituals
   - (b) values
   - (c) subsystems
   - (d) ideas

5. Product innovations create new goods or services for customers, whereas _____ innovations create new ways of doing things in the organization.
   - (a) content
   - (b) process
   - (c) quality
   - (d) task

6. The Kindle e-reader by Amazon and the iPad by Apple are examples of _____ innovations.
   - (a) business model
   - (b) social
   - (c) product
   - (d) process

7. Movie downloads by subscription (Netflix) and advertising revenues from Internet searches (Google) are examples of _____ innovations.
   - (a) business model
   - (b) social
   - (c) product
   - (d) process

8. Green innovation is most associated with the concept of _____.
   - (a) observable culture
   - (b) core culture
   - (c) sustainability
   - (d) skunkworks

9. The innovation process isn't really successful in an organization until a new idea is _____.
   - (a) tested as a prototype
   - (b) proven to be financially feasible
   - (c) put into practice
   - (d) discovered or invented

10. The basic purpose of a starting a skunkworks is to _____.
    - (a) add more bureaucratic structure to the innovation process
    - (b) provide special space for people to work together and achieve innovation
    - (c) make sure that any innovation occurs according to preset plans
    - (d) give people free time in their jobs to be personally creative

11. _____ change results in a major change of direction for an organization, whereas _____ change makes small adjustments to current ways of doing things.
    - (a) Frame breaking; radical
    - (b) Frame bending; incremental
    - (c) Transformational; frame breaking
    - (d) Transformational; incremental

12. A manager using a force-coercion strategy is most likely relying on the power of _____ to bring about planned change.
    - (a) expertise
    - (b) reference
    - (c) legitimacy
    - (d) information

13. The most participative of the planned change strategies is _____.
    - (a) negotiation and agreement
    - (b) rational persuasion
    - (c) shared power
    - (d) education and communication

14. The responses most likely to be associated with use of a force-coercion change strategy are best described as _____.
    - (a) internalized commitment
    - (b) temporary compliance
    - (c) passive cooptation
    - (d) active resistance

15. When a change leader tries to deal with resistance by trying to covertly influence others, offering only selective information and/or structuring events in favor of the desired change, this is an example of _____.
    - (a) rational persuasion
    - (b) manipulation and cooptation
    - (c) negotiation
    - (d) facilitation

Short-Response Questions

16. What core values might be found in high-performance organizational cultures?

17. What are the differences among process, product, and business model innovations?

18. How do a manager's responsibilities for change leadership vary among Lewin's three phases of planned change?

19. What are the possible differences in outcomes for managers using force-coercion and shared power change strategies?

Integration and Application Question

20. One of the common experiences of new college graduates in their first jobs is that they often "spot things that need to be changed." They are full of new ideas, and they are ready and quick to challenge existing ways of doing things. They are enthusiastic and well intentioned. But more often than most probably expect, their new bosses turn out to be skeptical, not too interested, or even irritated; co-workers who have been in place for some time may feel and act the same.

    Questions: What is the new employee to do? One option is to just forget it and take an "I'll just do my job" approach. Let's reject that. So then, how can you be an effective change leader in your next new job? How can you use change strategies and deal with resistance from your boss and co-workers in a manner that builds your reputation as someone with good ideas for positive change?

Steps for
Further Learning

CHAPTER 8

BUILD MARKETABLE SKILLS • **DO** A CASE ANALYSIS • **GET** AND STAY INFORMED

BUILD MARKETABLE SKILLS.

EARN BIG CAREER PAYOFFS!

Don't miss these opportunities in the SKILL-BUILDING PORTFOLIO

SELF-ASSESSMENT 8:
Tolerance for Ambiguity

Measure your reactions to ambiguity ... make it a friend, not a foe.

CLASS EXERCISE 8:
Force-Field Analysis

Change situations are complex ... mapping the forces can clarify the pathways.

TEAM PROJECT 8:
Organizational Culture Walk

Organizational cultures are all around us ... we can learn a lot as informed observers.

Many learning resources are found at the end of the book and online within **WileyPLUS Learning Space.**

Practice Critical Thinking—Complete the CHAPTER 8 CASE

CASE SNAPSHOT: Gamification—Games Join the Corporate Culture

Would you be surprised if you approached a co-worker only to realize that he was playing a video game, and the boss didn't care? It is more and more common to see people playing games at work and being praised—not criticized—for doing it. Companies are increasingly using video games or "gamification" as a way to enhance productivity and increase creativity and satisfaction in the workplace.

DO A CASE ANALYSIS.

STRENGTHEN YOUR CRITICAL THINKING!

MANAGER'S LIBRARY SELECTION
Read for Insights and Wisdom
Change by Design: How Design Thinking Transforms Organizations and Inspires Innovation (2009, HarperCollins), by Tim Brown

Some people like strong coffee and a quiet space to dream up new ideas, whereas other people prefer crowded social settings and hands-on activities to get their creative juices flowing. Either approach helps, because creative thinking breaks the routine and moves out of the box. Maybe the key to innovation is just to avoid an ordinary mindset and try not to think straight!

GET AND STAY INFORMED.

MAKE YOURSELF VALUABLE!

In this book Tim Brown, CEO of the design firm Ideo, claims that "design thinking" requires belief that people are all innovators, not just artists, engineers, and marketers. He believes that human-centered ideas, not technology-centered ones, capture sustainable gains. New ideas should consider and alter human experiences—those of customers, employees, or business partners—and avoid use of existing resources to improve functionality for incremental but predictable gains. Services are particularly ripe for design thinking. Brown encourages ideas with emotional benefits, saying a shift to an "experience economy" means consumers are actively seeking emotive experiences in products and services and avoiding basic feature improvements.

The anecdotes in this book come from Brown's career as a design consultant. He advocates building prototypes early in the design phase—ones that are rough and cheap. The goal is not to have working models, but to generate tangible results from abstract thought and realize their strengths and weaknesses. Prototyping "slows down the process to speed it up."

REFLECT AND REACT What products or services in your everyday living give you an emotional experience rather than pure functional utility? What are the implications for you as a customer? Now, choose one or two products and services that lack this emotional connection. Design ways to turn their pure functional value into something bigger and more encompassing, ideally an emotional connection. And by the way, do you agree with Brown's point that slowing down to speed up enables creative thinking?

A Pew Research study reports that 50% of working fathers and 56% of working mothers have "very" or "somewhat difficult" times balancing work and family . . . 50% of working fathers and 23% of working mothers feel they "spend too little time with kids."

Human Resource Management

9

Nurturing Turns Potential into Performance

Management Live
Lessons for a Succesful Interview

Blend Images/Alamy

Today's graduates are facing both improved job prospects and more specific interview questions. So what are employers looking for? Director of global university programs Jennifer Boden's list at Amazon includes the ability to influence others, strong bias for action and teamwork, and customer obsession. A typical question for job candidates is: "Tell us about times you've owned a project from start to finish." Candidates err by focusing on where they've been instead of what they've done, and by not explaining how they delivered results. Boden says: "People should make sure their résumés highlight what impact they've had."

HOW ABOUT IT?

Choose what is or could be your target employer. Exactly what can you say—right now—when asked to describe a project you've owned start to finish. What are you doing—right now—to build career readiness skills plus experiences that persuasively communicate them to recruiters?

WHAT'S INSIDE

ETHICS CHECK
Personality test? Drug test? Social media test?

FACTS TO CONSIDER
Human resource executives worry about performance measurement

HOT TOPIC
Underemployment affects almost one fifth of U.S. workers

QUICK CASE
Athletic director's dilemma

YOUR CHAPTER 9 TAKEAWAYS

1. Understand the purpose and legal context of human resource management.

2. Identify essential human resource management practices.

3. Recognize current issues in human resource management.

Takeaway 9.1
What Are the Purpose and Legal Context of Human Resource Management?

ANSWERS TO COME

■ Human resource management attracts, develops, and maintains a talented workforce.

■ Strategic human resource management aligns human capital with organizational strategies.

■ Laws protect against employment discrimination.

■ Laws can't guarantee that employment discrimination will never happen.

> The key to managing people in ways that lead to profit, productivity, innovation, and real organizational learning ultimately lies in how you think about your organization and its people. . . . When you look at your people, do you see costs to be reduced? . . . Or, when you look at your people do you see intelligent, motivated, trustworthy individuals—the most critical and valuable strategic assets your organization can have?

THESE COMMENTS ARE FROM JEFFREY PFEFFER'S BOOK, *THE HUMAN EQUATION: Building Profits by Putting People First*.[1] What is your experience? Do you find employers treating people as costs or as assets? And what difference does this seem to make? Pfeffer and his colleague, John F. Veiga, believe it makes a performance difference, a potentially big one. They conclude: "There is a substantial and rapidly expanding body of evidence . . . that speaks to the strong connection between how firms manage their people and the economic results achieved."[2] Simply put, organizations perform better when they treat their members better.[3] And when it comes to talent and how people are treated at work, we are in the territory of human resource management.

HUMAN RESOURCE MANAGEMENT ATTRACTS, DEVELOPS, AND MAINTAINS A TALENTED WORKFORCE.

Human resource management (HRM) is the process of attracting, developing, and maintaining a high-quality workforce.

A marketing manager at IDEO, the Palo Alto–based design firm, once said: "If you hire the right people . . . if you've got the right fit . . . then everything will take care of itself."[4] It really isn't quite that simple, but getting the right people on board is certainly a great starting point for success. The process of **human resource management (HRM)** is supposed to do just that—attract, develop, and maintain a talented and engaged workforce. These core HRM tasks or responsibilities can be described this way:

1. *Attracting a quality workforce*—focus on employee recruitment and selection

2. *Developing a quality workforce*—focus on employee orientation, training and development, and performance management

3. *Maintaining a quality workforce*—focus career development, work–life balance, compensation and benefits, retention and turnover, and labor–management relations

There are many career opportunities in human resource management. HRM departments are must-haves in most organizations. And HRM specialists of many types are increasingly important in an employment environment complicated by legal issues, talent shortages, economic turmoil, new corporate strategies, changing social values, and more. Such complexity has led to the growth of HRM firms that provide expert services in recruiting, compensation, training, outplacement, HR data mining, and the like. The Society for Human Resource Management, or SHRM, is a professional organization dedicated to keeping

The Office Sensationalized Dysfunction in Human Resource Management

Want a laugh? Watch some old episodes of *The Office*. Want to learn what you shouldn't do as a manager? Watch some more. Although many of the politically incorrect situations may make you cringe, the show's diverse and outrageous characters also challenge us to think about how we could improve our workplaces. Almost every episode focuses attention on critical issues in human resource management. If you're willing to look behind the laughs, good answers to basic questions can be found. What behavior violates employment law? Should employees attend diversity training sessions? How can we do a better job of handling rivalries between colleagues? When does trying to be funny cross the line into being unprofessional?

© AF archive/Alamy

its membership up to date in all aspects of HRM from fundamental practices to current events and issues.

STRATEGIC HUMAN RESOURCE MANAGEMENT ALIGNS HUMAN CAPITAL WITH ORGANIZATIONAL STRATEGIES.

The purpose of human resource management is to ensure that organizations always have the right people in the right places doing the right jobs to advance performance success. It focuses management attention on **human capital**, the talents people bring to organizations in the forms of abilities, knowledge, experience, ideas, energies, and commitments. Job titles like Chief People Officer and Chief Talent Officer are becoming more common in the executive teams or C-suites of organizations. Such job titles and their presence in the top management ranks indicate that an organization is strategically committed to people and talent development.

It's the job of **strategic human resource management** to align human capital—people and their talents—with organizational strategies and objectives. And in many ways it's the people part of this challenge that counts the most.[5] They are the implementers whose talents, we hope, put strategies into action. We often focus on strategy as the key to business success, says Lord Livingston, the UK trade minister, "but it's actually one part strategy and nine parts execution." And according to Andy Mattes, CEO of Diebold: "A mediocre strategy well executed will yield far better results that a perfect idea poorly done."[6]

The concept of "fit" is critical in activating talent through strategic human resource management. At the organization and team levels there must be a good fit between people and the specific jobs to be accomplished, and between people and the overall culture of the organization. **Person–job fit** is the extent to which an individual's knowledge, skills, experiences, and personal characteristics are consistent with job requirements. **Person–culture fit** is the extent to which an individual's values, interests, and behavior are consistent with the culture of the organization. The importance of a good fit is highlighted to the extreme at Zappos.com. Believe it or not, if a new employee is unhappy with the firm after going through initial training, Zappos pays them to quit. At last check the "bye-bye bounty" was $4,000, and some 2% to 3% of new hires were taking it each year.[7]

Strategic HRM puts into place **employee value propositions** that create and sustain good person–job and person–culture fits. Called EVPs, these are packages of opportunities and rewards, such as pay, benefits, meaningful work, and advancement possibilities that make diverse and talented people want to belong to and work hard for the organization. Organizations with compelling EVPs have the edge over others in hiring and retaining talented people in scarce labor markets. Starbuck's, for example, teamed up with Arizona State University to offer online degree programs for employees who work at least 20 hours per week. In return for paying part of the tuition bills, Starbuck's expects to attract and retain talented workers while lowering its hiring and training costs.[8]

LAWS PROTECT AGAINST EMPLOYMENT DISCRIMINATION.

"Why didn't I get invited for a job interview? Is it because my first name is Omar?" "Why didn't I get that promotion? Is it because I'm so visibly pregnant?" If valuing people is at the

Human capital is the talent people offer organizations in the form of abilities, knowledge, experience, ideas, energies, and commitments.

Strategic human resource management aligns human capital with organizational strategies and objectives.

Person–job fit is the extent to which an individual's knowledge, skills, experiences and personal characteristics are consistent with job requirements.

Person–culture fit is the extent to which an individual's values, interests, and behavior are consistent with the culture of the organization.

Employee value propositions are packages of opportunities and rewards that make diverse and talented people want to belong to and work hard for the organization.

Job discrimination occurs when someone is denied a job or job assignment for non-job-relevant reasons.

Equal employment opportunity (EEO) is the right to employment and advancement without regard to race, sex, religion, color, or national origin.

Affirmative action is an effort to give preference in employment to women and minority group members.

heart of human resource management, **job discrimination** is the enemy. It occurs when an organization denies someone employment or a job assignment or an advancement opportunity for reasons that are not performance relevant.[9] **Figure 9.1** provides an overview of legal protections for U.S. workers.

An important cornerstone of U.S. laws designed to protect workers from job discrimination is Title VII of the Civil Rights Act of 1964, amended by the Equal Employment Opportunity Act of 1972 and the Civil Rights Act (EEOA) of 1991. These acts provide for **equal employment opportunity (EEO)**, giving everyone the right to employment without regard to sex, race, color, national origin, or religion. It is illegal under Title VII to use any of these as criteria when making decisions about hiring, promoting, compensating, terminating, or otherwise changing someone's terms of employment.

The intent of Title VII and equal employment opportunity is to ensure everyone the right to gain and keep employment based only on their ability and job performance. The Equal Employment Opportunity Commission (EEOC) enforces the legislation through its federal power to file civil lawsuits against organizations that do not provide timely resolution of any discrimination charges lodged against them. These laws generally apply to all public and private organizations that employ 15 or more people.

Title VII also requires organizations to show **affirmative action** in their efforts to ensure equal employment opportunity for members of *protected groups*, those historically underrepresented in the workforce. Employers are expected to analyze existing workforce demographics, compare them with those in the relevant labor markets, and set goals for correcting any underrepresentation that might exist. These goals are supported by *affirmative action plans* that are designed to ensure that an organization's workforce represents women and minorities in proportion to their labor market availability.[10]

You are likely to hear discussion over the pros and cons of affirmative action. Critics tend to focus on the use of group membership, female or minority status, as a criterion in employment decisions.[11] The issues raised include claims of *reverse discrimination* toward members of majority populations. White males, for example, may claim that preferential treatment given to minorities in a particular situation interferes with their individual rights.

FIGURE 9.1
Sample of U.S. Laws Against Employment Discrimination.
The U.S. legal environment contains many protections against employment discrimination. Title VII of the Civil Rights Act of 1964 and its amendments are the cornerstones. Employment discrimination issues still occur and legal protections are continually evolving in a changing society.

Equal Pay Act of 1963	Requires equal pay for men and women performing equal work in an organization.
Title VII of the Civil Rights Act of 1964 (as amended)	Prohibits discrimination in employment based on race, color, religion, sex, or national origin.
Age Discrimination in Employment Act of 1967	Prohibits discrimination against persons over 40; restricts mandatory retirement.
Occupational Health and Safety Act of 1970	Establishes mandatory health and safety standards in workplaces.
Pregnancy Discrimination Act of 1978	Prohibits employment discrimination against pregnant workers.
Americans with Disabilities Act of 1990	Prohibits discrimination against a qualified individual on the basis of disability.
Civil Rights Act of 1991	Reaffirms Title VII of the 1964 Civil Rights Act; reinstates burden of proof by employer, and allows for punitive and compensatory damages.
Family and Medical Leave Act of 1993	Allows employees up to 12 weeks of unpaid leave with job guarantees for childbirth, adoption, or family illness.

As a general rule, the legal protections of EEO do not restrict an employer's right to establish **bona fide occupational qualifications**. These are criteria for employment that an organization can clearly justify as relating to a person's capacity to perform a job. However, EEO bars the use of employment qualifications based on race and color under any circumstances; those based on sex, religion, and age are very difficult to support.[12]

> **Bona fide occupational qualifications** are employment criteria justified by capacity to perform a job.

LAWS CAN'T GUARANTEE THAT EMPLOYMENT DISCRIMINATION WILL NEVER HAPPEN.

QUESTION: "I was interviewing for a sales job and the manager asked me what child care arrangements I had made. . . . Was his question legal?"

ANSWER BY LABOR ATTORNEY: This is "a perfect example of what not to ask a job applicant" and "could be considered direct evidence of gender bias against women based on negative stereotypes."[13]

A look back to Figure 9.1 offers a reminder that legal protection against employment discrimination is quite extensive. But, the example just given shows that we must still be realistic. Laws help fight discrimination but can't guarantee that it won't happen. Consider issues like the following.

Pay discrimination that compensates men and women differently for doing the same work is against the law. So when Lilly Ledbetter was about to retire from Goodyear and realized that male co-workers were being paid more, she sued. She initially lost the case because the Supreme Court said she had waited too long to file the claim. But she was smiling when the Lilly Ledbetter Fair Pay Act became the very first bill signed by President Barack Obama. It expanded workers' rights to sue employers on equal pay issues. When he signed the Lilly Ledbetter Fair Pay Act, the President said: "Making our economy work means making sure it works for everybody."[14]

> **Pay discrimination** occurs when men and women are paid differently for doing equal work.

How about **pregnancy discrimination**? It's also against the law, but pregnancy bias complaints filed with the U.S. Equal Employment Opportunity Commission are still common. A spokesperson for the National Partnership of Women & Families said that problems of pregnancy discrimination are "escalating" and require "national attention."[15] And, research paints a bleak picture as well. One study had actors play roles of being visibly pregnant and nonpregnant while applying for jobs as corporate attorneys and college professors. Results showed that interviewers were more negative toward the "pregnant" females, even making comments such as "She'll try to get out of doing work" and "She would be too moody."[16]

> **Pregnancy discrimination** penalizes a woman in a job or as a job applicant for being pregnant.

Age discrimination is against the law. But the EEOC reports an increased number of age bias complaints. Federal age discrimination laws protect employees aged 40 and up, and the proportion of workers in this age group is increasing with the "graying" of the American workforce. The possibility of age discrimination exists whenever an older worker is laid off or loses his or her job. But as one attorney points out: "There's always the fine line between discrimination and a legitimate business decision."[17] About 20% of age discrimination suits result in some financial settlement in favor of the person filing the claim. However, this doesn't always include getting the job back.

> **Age discrimination** penalizes an employee in a job or as a job applicant for being over the age of 40.

Issues surrounding **employee privacy**—the right to privacy both on and off the job, are sensitive and debatable.[18] Technology makes it easy for employers to monitor telephone calls, e-mails, social media usage, and Internet searches. These employer practices can become invasive and cross legal and ethical lines. The best advice is to assume you have no privacy at work and act accordingly. But what about right to privacy *outside* of work?

> **Employee privacy** is the right to privacy both on and off the job.

While vacationing in Europe, a Florida teacher posted to her "private setting" Facebook pages photos that showed her drinking alcoholic beverages. After it came to the attention of school administrators, she was asked to resign. She did, but later filed a lawsuit stating her resignation was forced.[19] The number of such social media lawsuits is growing. Just how they are resolved should help clear up what is and is not against the law in the respect to employee privacy.

STUDYGUIDE

Takeaway 9.1
What Are the Purpose and Legal Context of Human Resource Management?

Terms to Define

Affirmative action

Age discrimination

Bona fide occupational qualifications

Employee privacy

Employee value propositions

Equal employment opportunity (EEO)

Human capital

Human resource management (HRM)

Job discrimination

Pay discrimination

Person–job fit

Person–culture fit

Pregnancy discrimination

Strategic human resource management

Rapid Review

- The human resource management process involves attracting, developing, and maintaining a quality workforce.
- Job discrimination occurs when someone is denied an employment opportunity for reasons that are not job relevant.
- Equal employment opportunity legislation guarantees people the right to employment and advancement without discrimination.
- Current legal issues in the work environment deal with workplace privacy, pay, pregnancy, and age, among other matters.

Questions for Discussion

1. How might the forces of globalization affect human resource management in the future?
2. Are current laws protecting American workers against discrimination in employment sufficient, or do we need additional ones?
3. What employee-rights issues and concerns would you add to those discussed here?

Be Sure You Can

- **explain** the purpose of human resource management
- **differentiate** job discrimination, equal employment opportunity, and affirmative action
- **identify** major U.S. laws protecting against employment discrimination
- **explain** the issues of workplace privacy that today's college graduates should be prepared to face

Career Situation: What Would You Do?

If you were appointed to a student committee asked to investigate gender equity in sports on your campus, what would you propose the committee look at? Based on your understanding of campus affairs, what changes would you suggest in athletic funding and administration to improve gender equity?

Takeaway 9.2
What Are the Essentials of Human Resource Management?

ANSWERS TO COME

- Psychological contracts set the exchange of value between individuals and organizations.
- Recruitment attracts qualified job applicants.
- Selection makes decisions to hire qualified job applicants.
- Onboarding introduces new hires to the organization.
- Training develops employee skills and capabilities.
- Performance reviews assess work accomplishments.
- Career development provides for retention and career paths.

HUMAN RESOURCE MANAGEMENT IS ALL ABOUT MATCHING TALENTED PEOPLE WITH THE NEEDS OF TEAMS AND ORGANIZATIONS. Doing this well requires knowing what types of people and skill sets are needed. It also requires having the right value propositions in place to attract these people and turn them into enthusiastic and high-performing employees. Basic tasks like recruitment, selection, onboarding, training, and performance management are the foundations of successful HRM.

PSYCHOLOGICAL CONTRACTS SET THE EXCHANGE OF VALUE BETWEEN INDIVIDUALS AND ORGANIZATIONS.

In the last section we defined the *employee value proposition* as a package of opportunities and rewards that make diverse and talented people want to belong to and work hard for the organization. It comes to life as a **psychological contract** in which the organization and the individual exchange value with one another.[20] As shown in **Figure 9.2**, the value offered by the individual—what the employer gets—includes things like effort, loyalty, commitment, creativity, and skills. The value offered by the employer—what the employee gets—includes things like pay, benefits, meaningful work, flexible schedules, and personal development opportunities.

The process of building and maintaining psychological contracts begins with initial recruitment of new hires and extends over their careers. Perceived fairness is critical. Any sense of imbalance in the exchange of value is likely to cause problems. From the individual's side, a perceived lack of inducements from the employer may cause dissatisfaction, loss of motivation, and poor performance. From the employer's side, a perceived lack of

> **The psychological contract** is the exchange of value between the individual and the organization in the employment relationship.

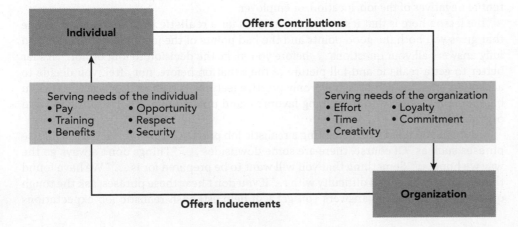

FIGURE 9.2
The Psychological Contract Links Individuals and Organizations.
The psychological contract summarizes an exchange of values. The individual offers things like effort, loyalty, commitment, creativity, and skills. The employer offers things like pay, benefits, meaningful work, and development opportunities.

contributions from the individual may cause a loss of confidence in and commitment to the employee as well as reduced rewards for work delivered.

RECRUITMENT ATTRACTS QUALIFIED JOB APPLICANTS.

Recruitment is a set of activities designed to attract a qualified pool of job applicants.

Employers engage in **recruitment** to attract a qualified pool of applicants to the organization. The word "qualified" is especially important here. Recruiting should bring employment opportunities to the attention of people whose skills, abilities, and interests meet job requirements. The process involves advertising the job, collecting a pool of applicants, and screening them in terms of potential employability. Technology and social media are moving this process in ways that are important to understand—for both employers and job candidates alike.

Online Recruiting

Recruiters now rely heavily on the Web to disseminate job openings and search for qualified applicants, and to cultivate relationships with potential job seekers. Job seekers follow sites like Monster.com and CareerBuilder.com, and social media sites are becoming go-to-for-sure options.[21] Among professionals, LinkedIn is still a top choice. It's especially useful for "opportunistic" recruiting where potential—not necessarily active—candidates can keep credentials visible to employers who may be browsing résumés looking for desireable skill sets.

Initial job interviews are often conducted by telephone or video conferencing. These make-or-break moments shouldn't be taken lightly. After being asked to describe past accomplishments, one job candidate said, "I was taken aback by how specific the interviewer was getting."[22] Are you ready? Check out Tips to Remember for ideas on how to succeed in telephone and online interviews.[23]

TIPS TO REMEMBER
Steps to Success in Telephone and Video Interviews

- *Prepare ahead of time*—Study the organization; carefully list your strengths and capabilities; have materials ready for note taking.
- *Interview in private*—Make sure you are in a quiet place, with privacy and free of interruptions; turn off phone and computer alerts.
- *Dress professionally*—Don't be casual, even if at home; dressing right increases confidence and sets a professional tone.
- *Practice your "voice" and "screen presence"*—Your impression will be made quickly; you must sound and look right to succeed.
- *Have a list of questions ready*—Don't be caught unprepared; be sure to interject your best questions during the interview.
- *Ask what happens next*—Find out how to follow up; ask what other information you can provide; clarify the time frame for a decision.
- *Follow up*—Don't forget to send a thank-you email that reiterates your interest in the job.

Realistic Recruiting

Did you know that almost 50% of new hires end up not being sure they made the right choice when accepting a job offer?[24] The big reason is that they come out of the interview process with unrealistic expectations. It's easy to not ask the hard questions as the candidate if you are over-eager for the job. And, it's easy to be misled by an interviewer who adopts a traditional "tell-and-sell" approach, perhaps trying to hide or gloss over the potential negatives of the job, location, or employer.

Realistic job previews provide job candidates with all pertinent information about a job and organization.

The lesson here is that it's important to press for a **realistic job preview**. This is one that gives you both the good points and the bad points of the job and organization and fully answers all your questions . . . before you make the decision to join or not.[25] It's far better to get a realistic and full picture of the situation before, not after, you decide to accept an offer. Instead of "selling" only positive features, a realistic job preview tries to be open and balanced in describing favorable and unfavorable aspects of the job and organization.

How can you tell if you are getting a realistic job preview? The interviewer might use phrases such as "Of course, there are some downsides . . ." "Things don't always go the way we hope . . ." "Something that you will want to be prepared for is . . ." "We have found that some new hires had difficulty with . . ." If you don't hear these phrases, ask the tough questions yourself. The answers you get will help establish realistic job expectations and better prepare you for the inevitable ups and downs of a new job. Recruiters also benefit when new hires have higher levels of early job satisfaction and less inclination to quit prematurely.

SELECTION MAKES DECISIONS TO HIRE QUALIFIED JOB APPLICANTS.

Once a good set of job candidates is identified, the next step is **selection,** choosing to hire applicants with the greatest performance potential. This is really an exercise in prediction—trying to anticipate whether the candidate will perform well once on the job. The typical sequence involves in-depth interviewing, some form of testing, and perhaps a real-time assessment of how well the candidate works on actual or simulated job tasks. Background checks increasingly include Web searches and reviews of personal postings on social media sites.

It's quite common for job candidates to be asked to take employment tests. Some test job-specific knowledge and skills; others focus more on intelligence, aptitudes, personality, and even ethics. Regardless of the intent, any employment test should be both reliable and valid. **Reliability** means consistency. A reliable test returns a consistent score for an individual each time they take it. **Validity** means predictability. Scores on a valid test are good predictors of future job performance, with a high score associated with high job performance and vice versa.

One of the popular developments in employment testing is the use of **assessment centers**. They allow recruiters to evaluate a person's job potential by observing his or her performance in experiential activities designed to simulate daily work.

A related approach is **work sampling**, which asks candidates to work on actual job tasks while observers grade their performance. Google uses a form of this called "Code Jams." These are essentially contests that the firm runs to find the most brilliant software coders. Winners get financial prizes and job offers. Code Jams are held worldwide, and a company spokesperson says: "Wherever the best talent is, Google wants them."[26]

Something called a **job audition** is becoming more popular as a selection device. Think of it as a "trial hire" where job candidates are given short-term employment contracts—say four to six weeks—to demonstrate their performance capabilities. When the contract is up the employer decides whether or not to offer a full-time job. This gives the candidate a chance to actually show what they can do, while giving the employer a chance to reduce the risk of making a hiring mistake.

Selection is choosing whom to hire from a pool of qualified job applicants.

Reliability means that a test gives consistent results over repeated measures.

Validity means that scores on a test are good predictors of future job performance.

An **assessment center** evaluates job candidates in simulated work situations.

Work sampling evaluates job candidates as they perform actual work tasks.

A **job audition** is a trial hire where the job candidate is given a short-term employment contract to demonstrate performance capabilities.

SINCE WHEN IS SOMEONE'S FACEBOOK PROFILE MEANT TO BE AN ONLINE RÉSUMÉ?

ETHICS CHECK

Personality Test? Drug Test? Social Media Test?

Jin Lee/Bloomberg/Getty Images

It used to be that preparing for a job interview meant being ready to answer questions about your education, work experience, interests, and activities. Now there's another question to prepare for: What's your social media user name and password?

Many interviewers don't want just a quick glance at the public profile; they want access to the private profile. It's time to get worried when the recruiter says, "Please friend me." Although a social media profile can be a treasure chest of information for recruiters and employers, it is less clear whether it is ethical to tap this resource to measure candidates' characters and make employment decisions. Since when is a Facebook profile meant to be an online résumé?

YOUR DECISION?

What are the ethical issues of recruiters asking for access to personal social media pages? Should it be held against applicants if they refuse? Is it okay for managers to search online sites to check up on employees and job applicants? Should what someone does in school or outside of work cost them a good job? Where do the lines of responsibility fall?

ONBOARDING INTRODUCES NEW HIRES TO THE ORGANIZATION.

Socialization influences the expectations, behavior, and attitudes of new members of groups and organizations.

Onboarding is a program of activities that introduce a new hire to the policies, practices, expectations, and culture of the organization and its teams.

Orientation sessions for new hires **communicate key information, set expectations, and answer questions.**

Once hired, a new member of any organization has to "learn the ropes" and become familiar with "the way things are done." **Socialization** is the process of influencing the expectations, behavior, and attitudes of new members to a group or organization. The process comes to life in employment through **onboarding**—a program of activities that introduces a new hire to the policies, practices, expectations, and culture of the organization and its teams. A common first step is some form of **orientation** where HR and other staff members meet with new hires in formal sessions to communicate key information, share expectations, and answer questions.

For years, Disney has been considered a master at socialization and onboarding. During orientation sessions at its Disney World Resort in Buena Vista, Florida, new employees learn the corporate culture. They also learn that the company places a premium on personality and expects all employees—from entertainers to ticket sellers to groundskeepers—"to make the customer happy." A Disney HRM specialist says: "We want people who are enthusiastic, who have pride in their work, who can take charge of a situation without supervision."[27]

TRAINING DEVELOPS EMPLOYEE SKILLS AND CAPABILITIES.

Coaching assigns an experienced person to provide performance advice to a new hire.

Mentoring assigns early-career employees as long term protégés of more senior ones.

We all need training. But it's especially critical today because new knowledge and technologies quickly make existing skills obsolete. A great employer won't let this happen. Instead of trying to avoid or cut training to save costs, it willingly spends on training as an investment in human resources.[28] You really should ask about training opportunities in any job interview. And if the recruiter struggles for answers or evades the questions, you're getting a pretty good indication that the organization isn't likely to pass the "great employer" test.

One training approach you might inquire about is **coaching**. This is where an experienced person is assigned to provide ongoing advice to the new hire. You should also ask about **mentoring**. This is where a new or early-career employee becomes a protégé of a

---

FACTS TO CONSIDER

Human Resource Executives Worry about Performance Measurement

enis izgi/iStockphoto

A survey of human resource executives published in the *Wall Street Journal* reveals they aren't pleased with the way managers in their organizations do performance reviews. Some are so concerned that they suggest dropping reviews altogether. Among survey findings:

- 30% of the HR executives believed that employees trust their employer's performance measurement system.
- 40% rated their performance review systems as B, and only 3% rated them as A.

- Many were concerned that managers aren't willing to face employees and give constructive feedback.
- Many also complained that employees don't have a clear enough understanding of what rates as good and bad performance.

WHAT'S YOUR TAKE?

Performance measurement is often a hot topic these days as things like "merit pay" and "performance accountability" are discussed in many job settings. Based on your experience, what should be done about it? Is it really possible to have a performance measurement system that is respected by all? Can a performance review be accomplished in ways that are good for employers and workers alike?

respected senior one. Mentors are supposed to take a long term interest in the junior person, and provide guidance and advice on skills development and career advancement. Some employers even offer **reverse mentoring.** This gives younger employees a chance to mentor seniors—for example, on how to better use social media in their work. A human resource management consultant says: "It's exactly the kind of thing that's needed today because Gen Ys really want to be involved."[29]

> In **reverse mentoring**, younger and newly hired employees mentor their seniors.

PERFORMANCE REVIEWS ASSESS WORK ACCOMPLISHMENTS.

Once a person is hired and on the job, various techniques of **performance review** or **performance appraisal** are used to formally assess and give feedback on their work accomplishments.[30] These reviews can serve two purposes. First, they measure and document accomplishments for the record. Second, they set the stage for development activities that can improve performance in the future.[31] To be credible in both respects, performance reviews must satisfy the criteria of reliability—consistency, and validity—predictability, discussed earlier.[32]

> **Performance review** or **performance appraisal** is the process of formally assessing performance and providing feedback to a jobholder.

The **graphic rating scale** is one of the most basic performance review methods. Think of it as a checklist or scorecard for rating an employee on criteria such as work quality, attendance, and punctuality. Although simple and quick, graphic rating scales have questionable reliability across raters and poor validity as predictors of future performance. They should probably be used only along with additional assessment tools.

> A **graphic rating scale** uses a checklist of traits or characteristics to evaluate performance.

The **behaviorally anchored rating scale (BARS)** describes actual behaviors that illustrate various levels of performance achievement. The example in **Figure 9.3** shows a BARS for a customer service representative. Note that "Extremely poor" performance is described with the behavioral anchor "treats a customer rudely and with disrespect." Because BARS assessments are linked with specific descriptions of work behavior, they are more reliable and valid than the graphic rating scale.

> A **behaviorally anchored rating scale (BARS)** uses specific descriptions of actual behaviors to rate various levels of performance.

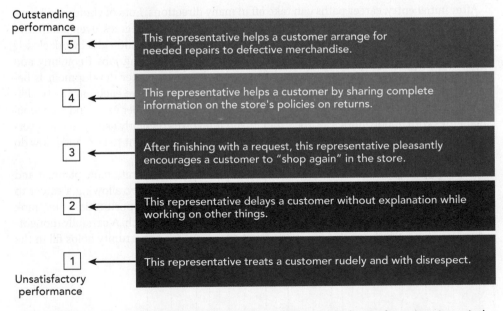

Outstanding performance

5 — This representative helps a customer arrange for needed repairs to defective merchandise.

4 — This representative helps a customer by sharing complete information on the store's policies on returns.

3 — After finishing with a request, this representative pleasantly encourages a customer to "shop again" in the store.

2 — This representative delays a customer without explanation while working on other things.

1 — This representative treats a customer rudely and with disrespect.

Unsatisfactory performance

FIGURE 9.3 Sample of a Behaviorally Anchored Rating Scale for Performance Appraisal. A behaviorally anchored rating scale, or BARS, uses actual descriptions of positive and negative job behaviors to anchor performance ratings. In this example, helping a customer arrange repairs for defective merchandise would earn the salesperson a rating of "5—Outstanding." By contrast, rude or disrespectful behavior toward customers by a salesperson would earn a rating of "1—Unsatisfactory." This specificity makes the BARS more reliable and valid than simple graphic rating scales.

The **critical-incident technique** keeps a log of someone's effective and ineffective job behaviors.

360° feedback includes superiors, subordinates, peers, and even customers in the appraisal process.

A **multiperson comparison** rates and ranks one person's performance against that of others.

The **critical-incident technique** keeps an actual log of a person's effective and ineffective job behavior. A critical-incident log for a customer service representative might include this *positive example*: "Took extraordinary care of a customer who had purchased a defective item from a company store in another city." Or, it might include this *negative example*: "Acted rudely in dismissing the complaint of a customer who felt that we mistakenly advertised a sale item."

Not all performance reviews are completed by one's immediate boss or team leader. In **360° feedback**, superiors, subordinates, peers, and even internal and external customers are asked to review a jobholder's performance.[33] The process typically starts with a self-appraisal that is then compared with reviews from the 360° cohort. New technologies allow 360° feedback to be gathered online in real time. An example is Work.com, which allows users to post feedback questions in 140 characters or less. Someone might ask, for example, "What did you think of my presentation?" or "How could I have run that meeting better?" Software compiles the anonymous responses and sends 360° feedback to the person posting the query.[34]

A common problem faced by those doing performance reviews is the tendency to rate everyone about the same. This can be avoided by using **multiperson comparisons** that rate and rank people relative to one another. Comparisons can be done by *rank-ordering* people from top to bottom with no ties allowed. They can be done as *paired comparisons* that evaluate each person against every other and then create a summary ranking based on the number of superior scores. They can also be done by *forced distributions* that place each person into a frequency distribution with fixed performance classifications, such as top 10%, next 40%, next 40%, and bottom 10%.

CAREER DEVELOPMENT PROVIDES FOR RETENTION AND CAREER PATHS.

Career development is the process of managing how a person grows and progresses in a career.

It seems a no-brainer that employers are foolish to neglect efforts to retain the best employees for as long as possible. Yet many fail the test. Sometimes it's a problem with compensation and benefits. But often it's an issue of **career development**—the process of managing how a person grows and progresses from one point in a career to the next.

After initial entry, career paths can take off in many directions. Lots of choices will have to be made about promotions, transfers, training, mentors, higher degrees, even alternative employment and eventual retirement. Ideally, the employer and the individual work closely together in making these choices. With more people now changing jobs frequently and working as independent contractors and freelancers, however, career development is becoming more and more a personal responsibility. This means that we each have to be diligent in **career planning**, the process of systematically matching career goals and individual capabilities with opportunities for their fulfillment. It involves regularly asking and answering such questions as "Who am I?" "What can I do?" "Where do I want to go?" and "How do I get there?"

Career planning is the process of matching career goals and individual capabilities with opportunities for their fulfillment.

Some suggest that we should view a career as something to be rationally planned and pursued in a careful step-by-step fashion. Others argue for flexibility, allowing a career to unfold along different pathways as we respond to unexpected opportunities. But think about it. A well-managed career will probably include elements of each. A carefully thought-out career plan helps point you in a clear direction; an eye for opportunity helps fill in the details as you proceed along the way. Are you ready?

STUDYGUIDE

Takeaway 9.2
What Are the Essentials of Human Resource Management

Terms to Define

Assessment center	Graphic rating scale	Performance review	Socialization
Behaviorally anchored rating scale (BARS)	Job audition	Psychological contract	360° feedback
	Mentoring	Realistic job previews	Validity
Career development	Multiperson comparison	Recruitment	Work sampling
Career planning	Onboarding	Reliability	
Coaching	Orientation	Reverse mentoring	
Critical-incident technique	Performance appraisal	Selection	

Rapid Review

- Recruitment is the process of attracting qualified job candidates to fill vacant positions; realistic job previews try to provide candidates with accurate information on the job and organization.
- Assessment centers and work sampling that mimic real job situations are increasingly common selection techniques.
- Orientation is the process of formally introducing new employees to their jobs and socializing them to the culture and performance expectations.
- Training keeps workers' skills up to date and job relevant; important training approaches include coaching and mentoring.
- Performance appraisal methods include graphic rating scales, behaviorally anchored rating scales, the critical-incidents technique, 360° feedback, and multiperson comparisons.
- Employee retention programs try to keep skilled workers in jobs and on career paths satisfying to them and beneficial to the employer.

Questions for Discussion

1. Is it realistic to expect that you can get a realistic job preview during the interview process?
2. If a new employer doesn't formally assign someone to be your coach or mentor, what should you do?
3. What are some of the possible downsides to receiving 360° feedback?

Be Sure You Can

- **list** steps in the recruitment process
- **explain** realistic job previews
- **illustrate** reliability and validity in employment testing
- **illustrate** how an assessment center might work
- **explain** the importance of socialization and orientation
- **describe** coaching and mentoring as training approaches
- **discuss** strengths and weaknesses of alternative performance appraisal methods

Career Situation: What Would You Do?

After taking a new job as head of retail merchandising at a department store, you are disappointed to find that the salesclerks are evaluated on a graphic rating scale. It uses a simple list of traits to gauge their performance. You want to propose an alternative and better approach that will make performance reviews really valuable. Your boss says: "Give me a plan." Exactly what will you suggest in your proposal, and how will you present it to the salesclerks as well as the boss?

Takeaway 9.3
What are Current Issues in Human Resource Management?

ANSWERS TO COME

- Today's lifestyles increase demands for flexibility and work–life balance.
- Organizations are using more independent contractors and contingency workers.
- Compensation plans influence recruitment and retention.
- Fringe benefits are an important part of compensation.
- Labor relations and collective bargaining are closely governed by law.

"HIRING GOOD PEOPLE IS TOUGH," STARTS AN ARTICLE IN THE *HARVARD BUSINESS REVIEW*. The sentence finishes with "keeping them can be even tougher."[35] The point is that it isn't enough to hire and train workers to meet an organization's immediate needs. They must also be successfully nurtured, supported, and retained. When the Society for Human Resource Management surveyed employers, it learned that popular tools for maintaining a quality workforce included flexible work schedules and personal time off, as well as competitive salaries and good benefits—especially health insurance.[36]

TODAY'S LIFESTYLES INCREASE DEMANDS FOR FLEXIBILITY AND WORK–LIFE BALANCE.

E-MAIL FROM WORKING DAD TO TEAM MEMBERS—"Folks, can I propose a slight change? I decided to work from home this morning so I could take my toddler to day care and help my wife with our newborn. . . . May I suggest a conference call? Dial-in information below."[37]

Work–life balance involves balancing career demands with personal and family needs.

Fast-paced and complicated lifestyles raise concerns about **work–life balance**. You have or will soon encounter it as the balance—or lack of balance—between the demands of careers and personal and family needs.[38] Not surprisingly, the "family-friendliness" of an employer is now frequently used as a screening criterion by job candidates. It is also used in "best employer" rankings by magazines such as *Business Week*, *Working Mother*, and *Fortune*.

Work–life balance improves when we have flexibility in scheduling work hours, work locations, and even such things as vacation days and personal time off. This helps manage both personal needs and work responsibilities. The results can be good for both the individual—greater job satisfaction, and the employer—less intention to leave.[39] About four out of five employees say they would like the work-at-home or telecommuting option and consider it a "significant job perk."[40] But, employers also worry that too much flexibility disrupts schedules and causes a loss of important face-to-face work time.[41] Marisa Mayer, Yahoo!'s CEO, for example, decided to disallow telecommuting because working from home detracted from Yahoo!'s collaborative culture and ability to innovate. However, this decision was highly criticized.[42]

Employers have many options for increasing job flexibility and work–life balance. Some directly help workers handle family matters by providing such things as on-site day care and elder care. Some have moved into innovative programs like work sabbaticals—Schwab offers 4 weeks after 5 years' employment; unlimited vacation days, unlimited vacation—Netflix lets workers take as many vacation days as they want; purchased vacation time—Xerox allows workers to buy vacation days using payroll deductions; and on-call medical care—Microsoft sends doctors to employees' homes to keep them out of emergency rooms.[43]

ORGANIZATIONS ARE USING MORE INDEPENDENT CONTRACTORS AND CONTINGENCY WORKERS.

Employer–employee compacts are changing, and the shift is away from permanent long-term employment to temporary and contract employment.[44] Don't be surprised if you are

HOT TOPIC

Underemployment Affects Almost One Fifth of U.S. Workers

© Beau Lark/Corbis

The Gallup organization tracks the percent of the U.S. workforce that is underemployed, meaning either part-time or unemployed people who want full-time work. A recent count showed 18.6% of people over 18 falling into this category.

The underemployment figure for recent college graduates is even higher—44%!

- Adults aged 18 to 29 are almost twice as likely (31%) to be underemployed as 30-to-49-year-olds (17%) and 50-to-65-year-olds (17%).
- Underemployed Americans report spending 36% less than their employed counterparts on average, costing the U.S. economy hundreds of millions of dollars.
- Underemployed individuals in the South (42%) and East (40%) are more optimistic about finding full-time employment than those in the West (38%) and Midwest (36%).

HOW ABOUT IT?

Check these facts against the latest data available. Are things getting better or worse for job seekers? What are the implications of underemployment for organizations and the people they recruit? What are the implications for the economy as a whole? Is there anything an organization can do to keep the underemployed high performing, motivated, and loyal? Is a high level of underemployment likely to affect the wages of fully employed workers?

---

asked some day to work as an **independent contractor**. This means you work "on demand" as a "freelancer" taking a "gig" for an agreed-upon period or for an agreed-upon task. Drive for Uber, you're on demand; build Web pages for a fee, you're a freelancer. You may be paid well, but there's no job security. Don't be surprised either if you are offered a job but with less than full-time hours. Most new jobs being created in—what is often called the *permatemp economy* or *on-demand economy* are filled by such **contingency workers**. They supplement the full-time workforce by working as-needed part-time schedules, often on a long-term basis.[45]

Employers like the permatemp economy because independent contractors and contingency workers are easy to hire and fire to control costs and manage cyclical work loads.[46] *Businessweek* sums up the employer's advantage this way: "easy to lay off, no severance; no company funded retirement plan; pay own health insurance; get zero sick days and no vacation."[47] Workers find things can be a lot less rosy. They may be paid less than full-timers, experience stress due to their temporary and intermittent job status, and lack access to fringe benefits such as health insurance, pension plans, and paid vacations.

Independent contractors are hired on temporary contracts and are not part of the organization's permanent workforce.

Contingency workers work as needed and part-time, often on a longer-term basis.

COMPENSATION PLANS INFLUENCE RECRUITMENT AND RETENTION.

Pay! It may be that no other work issue receives as much attention. And, the trend in compensation today is largely toward "pay-for-performance."[48] **Merit pay** systems link pay to some assessment of actual performance. A high merit raise sends a positive signal to high performers, whereas a low one sends a negative signal to poor performers. The notion is that this encourages both to work hard in the future.

Although the pay-for-performance logic makes sense, they are only as good as the methods used to measure performance. And this can be a problem. A survey reported by the *Wall Street Journal* found that only 23% of employees believed they understood their companies' systems.[49] Typical questions are: Who assesses performance? Suppose the employee doesn't agree with the assessment? Is the system fair and equitable to everyone involved? Is there enough money available to make the merit increases meaningful for those who receive them?

Merit pay awards pay increases in proportion to performance contributions.

Although some employers struggle with merit pay plans, others use them well and even creatively. If you are one of the high-performing employees that Applebee's managers want to retain, you might be on the receiving end of "Applebucks"—small cash awards that are given to reward performance and raise loyalty to the firm.[50] This is an example of **bonus pay**—one-time or lump-sum payments to employees based on the accomplishment of specific performance targets or some other extraordinary contribution. Wouldn't you like to someday receive a letter like one sent to two top executives by Amazon.com's chairman Jeff Bezos? "In recognition and appreciation of your contributions," his letter read, "Amazon.com will pay you a special bonus in the amount of $1,000,000."[51]

In contrast to giving outright bonuses, **profit sharing** distributes to employees a proportion of net profits earned by the organization in a performance period. **Gain sharing** extends the profit-sharing concept by allowing groups of employees to share in any savings or "gains" realized when their efforts result in measurable cost reductions or productivity increases.[52]

Yet another merit pay approach is to grant employees **stock options** linked to their performance.[53] Stock options give them the right to buy shares of stock at a future date at a fixed price. Employees holding options gain financially when the stock price rises above the original option price; they lose when it moves lower. Some companies "restrict" the stock options so that they come due only after designated periods of employment. This practice is meant to tie high performers to the employer and is often called the "golden handcuff."

Bonus pay plans provide one-time payments based on performance accomplishments.

Profit sharing distributes to employees a proportion of net profits earned by the organization.

Gain sharing allows employees to share in cost savings or productivity gains realized by their efforts.

Stock options give the right to purchase shares at a fixed price in the future.

FRINGE BENEFITS ARE AN IMPORTANT PART OF COMPENSATION.

Benefits! They rank right up there with pay as a way of helping to attract and retain workers. How many times does a graduating college student hear, "Be sure to get a job with benefits!"?[54] An employee's **fringe benefits** include nonmonetary forms of compensation such as health insurance and retirement plans. And, they can be a hot button in conversations about work today.

Some benefits are required by law, such as contributions to Social Security, unemployment insurance, and workers' compensation insurance. Others are available at the employer's discretion. The best employers offer health care insurance and retirement plans, as well as additional benefits that help attract and retain highly qualified employees. **Family-friendly benefits** help with work–life balance—things like child care, elder care, flexible schedules, personal days, and parental leave. Also popular are **flexible benefits** that give employees budgets and allow them to choose a set of benefits that best meet their needs. There are also **employee assistance programs** that help with troublesome personal problems, such as dealing with stress, counseling on alcohol and substance abuse, domestic violence and sexual abuse, and family and marital difficulties.

As nice as these benefits sound, the majority of U.S. workers still don't have access to them. Although the Family and Medical Leave Act requires employers to offer unpaid leaves

Fringe benefits are nonmonetary forms of compensation such as health insurance and retirement plans.

Family-friendly benefits help employees achieve better work–life balance.

Flexible benefits programs allow choice to personalize benefits within a set dollar allowance.

Employee assistance programs help employees cope with personal stresses and problems.

The Truth About Why Great Employees Quit

No one wants to lose a great employee. But when they do, many employers are caught by surprise. They think everything is fine and have no idea that their best employees might be thinking about leaving. When 18,000 professionals were asked in a LinkedIn survey what caused them to think about changing employers, their top thoughts were to get better compensation and benefits, better work–life balance, and career advancement. But when 7,530 actual job switchers were surveyed, they reported that the decision to leave was most often driven by career advancement, followed by opportunities to work for organizations with better leadership. Getting more pay came in third.

© diego_cervo/iStockphoto

for medical and family problems, for example, President Obama told a Summit on Working Families: "There is only one country in the world that does not offer paid maternity leave, and that is us."[55] And when it comes to the "working sick" problem, some 40 million Americans lack paid sick leave benefits.[56]

The fact is that benefit costs, especially medical insurance and retirement, can add as much as 20% or more to a typical worker's compensation package. This is why you find employers opting out of discretionary benefits programs and shifting ever more retirement planning and health insurance costs to their employees. And, many are hiring contingency workers to minimize benefit costs or avoid them altogether.

LABOR RELATIONS AND COLLECTIVE BARGAINING ARE CLOSELY GOVERNED BY LAW.

Labor unions are organizations to which workers belong and that deal with employers on the workers' behalf. They act as a collective "voice" for their members, one that wouldn't be available to them as individuals. Historically, this voice of the unions has played an important role in American society. And even though unions are often associated with wage and benefit concerns, workers also join unions because of things like

> **A labor union** is an organization that deals with employers on the workers' collective behalf.

THE TEAM CAPTAIN HAS JUST PRESENTED YOU WITH A PETITION SIGNED BY 70% OF THE PLAYERS THAT REQUESTS PERMISSION TO START THE PROCESS LEADING TO UNIONIZATION.

QUICK CASE

Athletic Director's Dilemma

You are the athletic director at a large private university with a highly comprehensive, highly competitive intercollegiate athletics program. Most years the football team is ranked in the top 25 and is in the hunt for an NCAA Division I

Sean De Burca/Corbis

bowl game. The team captain has just presented you with a petition signed by 70% of the players that requests permission to start the process leading to unionization. The players aren't asking to be paid, but they believe it is in their best interests to have union protection when it comes to their physical well-being, academic progress, and financial affairs.

Because you are at a private university, the players are within their rights and can speak with unions such as the National College Players Association about representing them. The next step in the process will be for the players to distribute formal "union cards" for signatures. If at least 30% sign the cards, they could ask the National Labor Relations Board to endorse their request to unionize. This is a complete surprise to you. In fact, you are so surprised that you're not sure what to do next.

WHAT DO YOU DO?

Before reaching for the telephone to call the football coach and university president, you decide to make notes on "goals, critical issues, possible outcomes, and next steps." What's on your list and why? How will you handle the implications of this request for the entire football team, other teams and their coaches, and the university as a whole?

poor relationships with supervisors, favoritism or lack of respect by supervisors, little or no influence with employers, and failure of employers to provide a mechanism for grievance and dispute resolution.[57]

The overall percentage of workers in the United States who belong to unions has been on the decline. Figures show that 11.3% of workers now belong to unions versus 20.3% in 1983, the year records first became available. But, the percentage of public-sector workers who belong to unions—teachers, police, firefighters, and local government employees—is on the increase. It now stands at 35.7% of workers versus 6.6% in the private sector.[58] Just what explains the downward trend in private-sector union membership? And, why do you think union membership is increasing in the public sector?

Unions negotiate legal contracts affecting many aspects of the employment relationship for their members. These **labor contracts** typically specify the rights and obligations of employees and management with respect to wages, work hours, work rules, seniority, hiring, grievances, and other conditions of work.

The front line in labor–management relationship is **collective bargaining**, the process that brings management and union representatives together in negotiating, administering, and interpreting labor contracts. During a collective bargaining session, these parties exchange a variety of demands, proposals, and counterproposals. Several rounds of bargaining may take place before a contract is reached or a dispute resolved. Sometimes the process breaks down, and one or both parties walk away. The impasse can be short or lengthy, in some cases leading to labor actions that can last months and even years before agreements are reached.

One of the areas where unions and employers can find themselves on different sides of the bargaining issue relates to so-called **two-tier wage systems**. These are systems that pay new hires less than more senior workers already doing the same jobs. Agreeing to a two-tier system in collective bargaining isn't likely to be the preference of union negotiators. At a Goodyear factory in Alabama where a two-tiered system is in place, one of the high-seniority workers says: "If I was doing the same job, working just as hard and earning what they make, I'd be resentful."[59] Management offers a counterargument: the two-tier agreement helps keep the firm profitable and retain jobs in America that would otherwise be lost to foreign outsourcing.[60]

When labor–management relations take on the adversarial character shown in **Figure 9.4**, the conflict can be prolonged and costly for both sides. That's not good for anyone, and there is quite a bit of pressure these days for more cooperative union–management relationships. Wouldn't it be nice if unions and management would work together in partnership, trying to address the concerns of both parties in ways that best meet the great challenges and competitive pressures of a global economy?

A **labor contract** is a formal agreement between a union and an employer about the terms of work for union members.

Collective bargaining is the process of negotiating, administering, and interpreting a labor contract.

Two-tier wage systems pay new hires less than workers already doing the same jobs with more seniority.

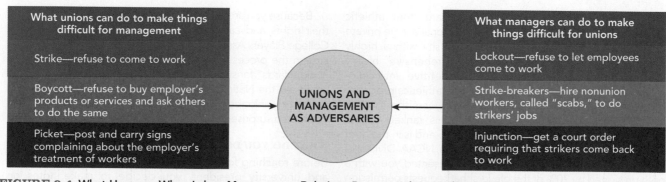

FIGURE 9.4 **What Happens When Labor–Management Relations Become Adversarial?**
When union and management representatives meet in collective bargaining, it would be nice if things were always cooperative. Unfortunately, they sometimes turn adversarial, and each side has weapons at its disposal to make things hard for the other. Unions can resort to strikes, boycotts, and picketing. Management can use lockouts, strike-breakers, and court injunctions to force strikers back to work. Although each side can find justifications in defense of using such tactics, they can also come with high price tags in terms of lost worker earnings and company profits.

STUDYGUIDE

Takeaway 9.3
What Are Current Issues in Human Resource Management?

Terms to Define

Bonus pay	Flexible benefits	Independent contractors	Stock options
Collective bargaining	Family-friendly benefits	Labor contract	Two-tier wage systems
Contingency workers		Labor union	Work–life balance
Employee assistance programs	Fringe benefits	Merit pay	
	Gain sharing	Profit sharing	

Rapid Review

- Complex job demands and family responsibilities have made work–life balance programs increasingly important in human resource management.
- Compensation and benefits packages must be attractive so that an organization stays competitive in labor markets.
- Labor unions are organizations to which workers belong and that deal with employers on the employees' behalf.
- Collective bargaining is the process of negotiating, administering, and interpreting a labor contract.
- Labor relations and collective bargaining are closely governed by law and can be cooperative or adversarial in nature.

Questions for Discussion

1. Are we giving too much attention these days to issues of work–life balance?
2. Can a good argument be made that merit pay just doesn't work?
3. Given economic trends, is it likely that unions will gain in future popularity?

Be Sure You Can

- **define** work–life balance and discuss its significance for the human resource management process
- **explain** why compensation and benefits are important in human resource management
- **differentiate** bonuses and profit sharing as forms of performance-based pay
- **define** the terms "labor union," "labor contract," and "collective bargaining"
- **compare** the adversarial and cooperative approaches to labor–management relations

Career Situations: What Would You Do?

You have become aware of a drive to organize the faculty of your institution and have them represented by a union. The student leaders on campus are holding a forum to gather opinions on the pros and cons of a unionized faculty. Because you represent a student organization in your college, you are asked to participate in the forum. What will you say, and why?

TEST PREP **9**

Answers to Test Prep questions can be found at the back of the book.

Multiple-Choice Questions

1. Human resource management is the process of _____, developing, and maintaining a high-quality workforce.
   (a) attracting
   (b) compensating
   (c) appraising
   (d) selecting

2. A _____ is a criterion that organizations can legally justify for use in screening job candidates.
   (a) job description
   (b) bona fide occupational qualification
   (c) realistic job preview
   (d) BARS

3. _____ programs are designed to ensure equal employment opportunities for groups historically underrepresented in the workforce.
   (a) Realistic recruiting
   (b) Mentoring
   (c) Affirmative action
   (d) Coaching

4. Which of the following questions can an interviewer legally ask a job candidate during a telephone interview?
   (a) Are you pregnant or planning to soon start a family?
   (b) What skills do you have that would help you do this job really well?
   (c) Will you be able to work at least 10 years before hitting the retirement age?
   (d) Do you get financial support from a spouse or companion who is also a wage earner?

5. An employment test that yields different results over time when taken by the same person lacks _____.
   (a) validity
   (b) reliability
   (c) realism
   (d) behavioral anchors

6. Which phrase is most consistent with a recruiter offering a job candidate a realistic job preview?
   (a) "There are just no downsides to this job."
   (b) "No organization is as good as this one."
   (c) "I can't think of any negatives."
   (d) "Here's something you might not like about the job."

7. Socialization of newcomers occurs during the _____ step of the staffing process.
   (a) orientation
   (b) recruiting
   (c) selection
   (d) advertising

8. The assessment center approach to employee selection uses _____ to evaluate a candidate's job skills.
   (a) intelligence tests
   (b) simulations and experiential exercises
   (c) 360° feedback
   (d) formal one-on-one interviews

9. The selection technique known as _____ asks a job candidate to actually perform on the job for a period of time while being observed by a recruiter.
   (a) mentoring
   (b) work sampling
   (c) job coaching
   (d) critical incident testing

10. The _____ purpose of performance review is being addressed when a manager describes training options that might help an employee improve future performance.
    (a) development
    (b) evaluation
    (c) judgmental
    (d) legal

11. When a team leader must rate 10% of team members as "superior," 80% as "good," and 10% as "unacceptable," this is an example of the _____ approach to performance appraisal.
    (a) graphic
    (b) critical-incident
    (c) behaviorally anchored rating scale
    (d) forced distribution

12. What is one of the reasons why employers are hiring more part-time or contingency workers?
    (a) It's hard to get people to work full-time anymore.
    (b) Part-timers are known to work much harder than full-timers.
    (c) Full-time employees don't have up-to-date job skills.
    (d) It's easy to hire part-timers when you need them and let them go when you don't.

13. Whereas bonus plans pay employees for special accomplishments, gain-sharing plans reward them for _____.
    (a) helping to recruit new workers
    (b) regular attendance
    (c) positive work attitudes
    (d) cost reductions that have been achieved

14. An employee with family problems that are starting to interfere with work would be pleased to learn that his employer had a(n) _____ plan.
    (a) employee assistance
    (b) flexible benefits
    (c) comparable worth
    (d) stock options

15. When representatives of management and a labor union meet and negotiate the terms of a new labor contract, this process is known as _____.
    (a) boycotting
    (b) collective bargaining
    (c) 360° feedback
    (d) profit sharing

Short-Response Questions

16. Why is onboarding important in the HRM process?

17. How does mentoring work as an on-the-job training approach?

18. When is an employment test or a performance appraisal method reliable?

19. How do the graphic rating scale and the BARS differ as performance appraisal methods?

Integration and Application Question

20. Sy Smith is not doing well in his job. The problems began to appear shortly after Sy's job changed from a manual to a computer-based operation. He has tried hard but is just not doing well in learning how to use the computer to meet performance expectations. He is 45 years old and has been with the company for 18 years. Sy has been a great worker in the past and is both popular and influential among his peers. Along with his performance problems, you have also noticed that Sy is starting to sometimes "badmouth" the firm.

   Questions: As Sy's manager, what options would you consider in terms of dealing with the issue of his retention in the job and in the company? What could you do by way of career development for Sy, and why?

Steps for Further Learning

CHAPTER 9

BUILD MARKETABLE SKILLS • **DO** A CASE ANALYSIS • **GET** AND STAY INFORMED

BUILD MARKETABLE SKILLS.

EARN BIG CAREER PAYOFFS!

Don't miss these opportunities in the SKILL-BUILDING PORTFOLIO

SELF-ASSESSMENT 9:
Performance Review Assumptions

Test your judgment when assessing others . . . make the best of performance management.

CLASS EXERCISE 9:
Upward Appraisal

Sometimes feedback has to flow up . . . with practice, you can get better at it.

TEAM PROJECT 9:
Future of Labor Unions

Union membership is on the decline . . . does this mean all is well in the workplace?

Many learning resources are found at the end of the book and online within **WileyPLUS Learning Space.**

Practice Critical Thinking—Complete the CHAPTER 9 CASE

CASE SNAPSHOT: TWO-TIER WAGES—Same Job, Different Pay

When domestic auto manufacturers were hit hard by recession and foreign competition, they struggled to control costs and maintain profitability. One response was a two-tier wage system that pays new workers significantly less than existing ones doing the same job. What is the future for such two-tier wage systems?

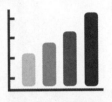

DO A CASE ANALYSIS.

STRENGTHEN YOUR CRITICAL THINKING!

MANAGER'S LIBRARY SELECTION
Read for Insights and Wisdom
Profit at the Bottom of the Ladder: Creating Value by Investing in Your Workforce **(Harvard Business Press Books, 2010) by Jody Heymann.**

It is said that employees are responsible for 90% of a company's profitability. Yet many firms invest only in their most highly skilled, best-educated workers, while cutting wages and benefits for workers at the bottom of the ladder as a quick way to improve profits. Researcher Jody Heymann, Dean of UCLA's Fielding School of Public Health, challenges this approach by providing evidence that investing in front-line employees has a powerful impact on corporate profit-ability.[61] Her book draws on thousands of interviews with organizations around the world. Findings show how organizations have profited by improving the working conditions of their least-skilled employees. Examples of practices that improve productivity are higher pay, flexible working opportunities, increased training, and career development.

GET AND STAY INFORMED.

MAKE YOURSELF VALUABLE!

REFLECT AND REACT "Underemployment . . . minimum wage workers . . . income inequality"—these are all topics and buzzwords of our day. In a perfect world where everyone worked for an employer that valued them and invested in their human capital, you'd think these words wouldn't even be on our vocabulary lists. But the fact is that they are and that all employers are not "the best." What's it all mean to workers today and to those seeking jobs and careers in the future? How will you deal with the challenge of finding an employer that values you?

"I have a dream," said Martin Luther King, Jr., and his voice traveled from the steps of the Lincoln Memorial in Washington, D.C., on August 28, 1963, across generations. Like other visionary leaders, he communicated shared dreams and inspired others to pursue lofty goals.

Leadership

10

A Leader Lives in Each of Us

Management Live

Building Charisma through "Leadership Speech"

Hill Street Studios/Getty Images

Who really listens when you speak? Who seems ready to accept and act on what you are proposing? That's the test of "leadership speech"—saying things in ways that cause others to respond positively. We're talking about people who have charismatic leadership skills that turn listeners into followers. Some skills are verbal—breaking things down into easy lists, using metaphors, telling stories, asking rhetorical questions, taking a moral stand, and setting high goals. Others are nonverbal—using voice modulations, gestures, and facial expressions to accent what you are saying.

HOW ABOUT IT?

Instead of putting charismatic leadership on an unreachable pedestal, perhaps learning specific techniques of "leadership speech" is a pathway to success. Is there opportunity here for you to turn everyday conversations into influential acts of leadership?

WHAT'S INSIDE

ETHICS CHECK
A step over the line into community service

FACTS TO CONSIDER
Followers report shortcomings of leaders

HOT TOPIC
Making "No" part of the follower's vocabulary

QUICK CASE
Playing favorites as a team leader

YOUR CHAPTER 10 TAKEAWAYS

1. Understand the foundations for effective leadership.
2. Identify insights of the contingency leadership theories.
3. Discuss current issues and directions in leadership development.

Takeaway 10.1
What Are the Foundations for Effective Leadership?

ANSWERS TO COME

- Leadership is one of the four functions of management.
- Leaders use power to achieve influence.
- Leaders bring vision to teams and organizations.
- Leaders display different traits in the quest for effectiveness.
- Leaders display different styles in the quest for effectiveness.

Leadership is the process of inspiring others to work hard to accomplish important tasks.

A GLANCE AT THE SHELVES IN YOUR LOCAL BOOKSTORE WILL QUICKLY CONFIRM that **leadership**, the process of inspiring others to work hard to accomplish important tasks, is one of the most popular management topics.[1] Consultant and author Tom Peters says that the leader is "rarely—possibly never—the best performer."[2] They don't have to be; leaders thrive through and by the successes of others. But not all managers live up to these expectations. Warren Bennis, a respected scholar and consultant, claims that too many U.S. corporations are "over-managed and under-led." Grace Hopper, the first female admiral in the U.S. Navy, advised that "you manage things; you lead people."[3] The bottom line is that leaders become great by bringing out the best in people.

LEADERSHIP IS ONE OF THE FOUR FUNCTIONS OF MANAGEMENT.

Leadership is one of the four functions that make up the management process shown in **Figure 10.1**. *Planning* sets the direction and objectives; *organizing* brings together the resources to turn plans into action; *leading* builds the commitment and enthusiasm that allow people to apply their talents to help accomplish plans; and *controlling* makes sure things turn out right.

Of course, managers sometimes face daunting challenges in their quest to succeed as leaders. The time frames for getting things accomplished are becoming shorter. Second chances are sometimes few and far between. The problems to be resolved through leadership

FIGURE 10.1

Why Is Leading So Important in the Management Process?

Leading is one of the four management functions. It is the process of inspiring others to work hard to accomplish important tasks. Managers who are effective leaders act in ways that create high levels of enthusiasm among people to use their talents fully to accomplish tasks and pursue important plans and goals.

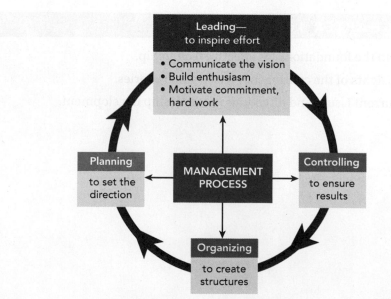

are often complex, ambiguous, and multidimensional. And, leaders are expected to stay focused on long-term goals even while dealing with problems and pressures in the short term.[4]

Anyone aspiring to career success in leadership must rise to these challenges and more. They must become good at using interpersonal skills like power and influence, communication, motivation, teamwork, conflict, and negotiation. Where do you stand on leadership skills and capabilities? If, as the chapter subtitle states, "A leader lives in each of us," what leader resides in you?

LEADERS USE POWER TO ACHIEVE INFLUENCE.

Are you surprised that our discussion of leadership starts with power? Harvard professor Rosabeth Moss Kanter once called it "America's last great dirty word."[5] She worries that too many managers are uncomfortable with the concept and don't realize it is indispensable to leadership.

Power is the ability to get someone else to do something you want done, to make things happen the way you want them to. Isn't that a large part of management, being able to influence other people? And given so, where and how do managers get power? Most often we talk about managers and leaders relying on two sources of power that you might remember by this *managerial power equation*:[6]

> **Power** is the ability to get someone else to do something you want done.

$$\text{Managerial Power} = \text{Position Power} \times \text{Personal Power.}$$

The first source of power comes from the position, being the "manager" or the "leader." This power includes rewards, coercion, and legitimacy. The second source comes from the person, who you are and what your presence means in a situation. This power includes expertise, reference, and relationships. Of course, some of us do far better than others at mobilizing and using the different types of power.[7]

Position Power

If you look at the small figure, you'll see that **reward power** is the capability to offer something of value as a means of achieving influence. To use reward power, a manager says, in effect: "If you do what I ask, I'll give you a reward." Common rewards are things like pay raises, bonuses, promotions, special assignments, and compliments. As you might expect, reward power can work well as long as people want the reward and the manager or leader makes it continuously available. But take the value of the reward or the reward itself away, and that power is quickly lost.

> **Reward power** achieves influence by offering something of value.

> **Coercive power** achieves influence by punishment.

Coercive power is the capability to punish or withhold positive outcomes as a way of influencing others. To mobilize coercive power, a manager is really saying: "If you don't do what I want, I'll punish you." Managers have access to lots of possible punishments including reprimands, pay penalties, bad job assignments, and even termination. But how do you feel when on the receiving end of such threats? If you're like us, you'll most likely resent both the threat and the person making it. You might act as requested or at least go through the motions, but you're unlikely to continue doing so once the threat no longer exists.

> Power of the POSITION:
> *Based on things managers can offer to others*
>
> Rewards: "If you do what I ask, I'll give you a reward."
>
> Coercion: "If you don't do what I ask, I'll punish you."
>
> Legitimacy: "Because I am the boss, you *must* do as I ask."

Legitimate power is the capacity to influence through formal authority. It is the right of the manager to exercise control over persons in subordinate positions. To use legitimate power, a manager is basically saying: "I am the boss; therefore, you are supposed to do as I ask." When an instructor assigns homework, exams, and group projects, don't you most often do what is requested? Why? You do it because the requests seem legitimate to the course. But if the instructor moves outside course boundaries, perhaps asking you to attend a sports event, the legitimacy is lost and your compliance is less likely.

> **Legitimate power** achieves influence by formal authority.

Personal Power

Position power alone isn't enough for any manager or team leader. How much personal power you can mobilize through expertise, reference, and relationships often makes the difference between leadership success and failure.

> **Power of the PERSON:**
> *Based* on how ma*nagers are viewed by others*
>
> **Expertise**—as a source of special knowledge and information
>
> **Reference**—as a person with whom others like to identify
>
> **Relationship power**—as a trustworthy person others are connected with

Expert power achieves influence by special knowledge.

Reference power achieves influence by personal identification.

Relationship power achieves influence through connections and social capital.

Expert power is the ability to influence the behavior of others because of special knowledge and skills. When a manager uses expert power, the implied message is: "You should do what I want because of my special expertise or information." A leader's expertise may come from technical understanding or access to information relevant to the issue at hand. It can be acquired through formal education and evidenced by degrees and credentials. It is also acquired on the job, through experience, and by gaining a reputation as a high performer that really understands the work. Building expertise is one of the biggest early career challenges.

Think of the high-visibility athletes and personalities advertising consumer products. What's really going on here? The intent is to attract customers through identification with the athletes and personalities. The same holds true in leadership. **Reference power** is the ability to influence the behavior of others because they admire and want to identify positively with you. When a manager uses referent power, the implied message is: "You should do what I want in order to maintain a positive self-defined relationship with me."

If referent power is so valuable, how do you get it? The answer is: "It's a lot easier to get people to do what you want when they like you than when they dislike you." Isn't this good advice for how to approach your job and the people with whom you work every day? Reference power largely comes from admiration and respect, things we gain by being pleasant and engaging when interacting and working with others.

Relationship power comes from the ability to get things done through connections and social capital, or who you know. When a manager uses relationship power the implied message is: "We know one another and often help each other out. Now, I'd like you to do this for me."

Think of the power that you can develop by nurturing good relationships with persons in and around your workplace and in your friendship groups. A person high in relationship power is embedded in an extensive array of social networks. And importantly, he or she is well regarded in these networks. Relationship power comes not just from having connections, but from being viewed as a trustworthy contact who believes in reciprocity—willingness to help one another.

LEADERS BRING VISION TO TEAMS AND ORGANIZATIONS

"Great leaders," it is said, "get extraordinary things done in organizations by inspiring and motivating others toward a common purpose."[8] In other words, they use their power

Leadership Turns Vision into Inspiration

Lorraine Monroe Led the Frederick Douglass Academy to Excellence

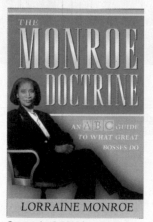

Dr. Lorraine Monroe began her career in the New York City Schools as a teacher. She went on to found the Frederick Douglass Academy, a public school in Harlem named after an escaped slave, prominent abolitionist, and civil rights leader. She believes leadership must be vision driven and follower centered. Leaders must always start at the "heart of the matter," she says, and "the job of a good leader is to articulate a vision that others are inspired to follow." Everyone should know that they are valued and that their advice is welcome.

While serving as a consultant on public leadership, she stated: "We can reform society only if every place we live—every school, workplace, church, and family—becomes a site of reform." Her many leadership ideas are summarized in what is called the "Monroe Doctrine." It begins with this advice: "The job of the leader is to uplift her people—not just as members of and contributors to the organization, but as individuals of infinite worth in their own right."

FIND INSPIRATION

Is visionary leadership something that works only at the very top of organizations? Should the leader of a work team also have a vision? Follower-centered leadership is high on Lorraine Monroe's list of priorities. And she's made a fine career by putting its principles to work. What is there in the Monroe Doctrine that can help you succeed as a leader? Do you have what it takes to truly value people who look up to you for leadership?

exceptionally well. And frequently today, successful leadership is associated with **vision**—a future that one hopes to create or achieve in order to improve on the present state of affairs. According to the late John Wooden, a standout men's basketball coach at UCLA for 27 years: "Effective leadership means having a lot of people working toward a common goal. And when you have that with no one caring who gets the credit, you're going to accomplish a lot."[9]

The term **visionary leadership** describes a leader who brings to the situation a clear and compelling sense of the future, as well as an understanding of the actions needed to get there successfully.[10] But simply having the vision of a desirable future is not enough. Truly great leaders are extraordinarily good at turning their visions into accomplishments. This means being good at communicating the vision and getting people motivated and inspired to pursue the vision in their daily work. You can think of it this way. Visionary leadership brings meaning to people's work; it makes what they do seem worthy and valuable.

A **vision** is a clear sense of the future.

Visionary leadership brings to the situation a clear sense of the future and an understanding of how to get there.

LEADERS DISPLAY DIFFERENT TRAITS IN THE QUEST FOR EFFECTIVENESS.

For centuries, people have recognized that some persons use power well and perform successfully as leaders, whereas others do not. You've certainly seen this yourself. How can such differences in leadership effectiveness be explained?

An early direction in leadership research tried to answer this question by identifying traits and personal characteristics shared by well-regarded leaders.[11] Not surprisingly, results showed that physical characteristics such as height, weight, and physique make no difference. But a study of more than 3,400 managers found that followers rather consistently admired leaders who were honest, competent, forward-looking, inspiring, and credible.[12] Another comprehensive review is summarized in **Table 10.1**—Traits Often Shared by Effective Leaders.[13] You might use this list as a quick check of your leadership potential.

LEADERS DISPLAY DIFFERENT STYLES IN THE QUEST FOR EFFECTIVENESS.

In addition to leadership traits, researchers have also studied how successful and unsuccessful leaders behave when working with followers. Most of this research focused on two sets of behaviors: task-oriented behaviors and people-oriented behaviors. A leader high in concern for task plans and defines work goals, assigns task responsibilities, sets clear work standards, urges task completion, and monitors performance results. A leader high in concern for people acts warm and supportive toward followers, maintains good relations with them, respects their feelings, shows sensitivity to their needs, and displays trust in them.

Leaders who show different combinations of task and people behaviors are often described as having unique leadership styles, such as you have probably observed in your own experiences. A popular summary of classic **leadership styles** used by managers is shown in **Figure 10.2**.[14]

Someone who emphasizes task over people is often described as an **autocratic leader**. This manager focuses on authority and obedience, delegates little, doesn't share information, and acts in a unilateral command-and-control fashion. Have you ever worked for someone fitting this description? How would you score his or her leadership effectiveness?

Leadership style is the recurring pattern of behaviors exhibited by a leader.

An **autocratic leader** acts in unilateral command-and-control fashion.

TABLE 10.1 Traits Often Shared by Effective Leaders

Drive—Successful leaders have high energy, display initiative, and are tenacious.

Self-confidence—Successful leaders trust themselves and have confidence in their abilities.

Creativity—Successful leaders are creative and original in their thinking.

Cognitive ability—Successful leaders have the intelligence to integrate and interpret information.

Business knowledge—Successful leaders know their industry and its technical foundations.

Motivation—Successful leaders enjoy influencing others to achieve shared goals.

Flexibility—Successful leaders adapt to fit the needs of followers and the demands of situations.

Honesty and integrity—Successful leaders are trustworthy; they are honest, predictable, and dependable.

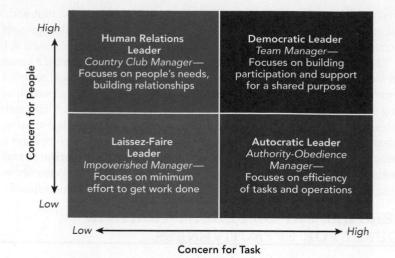

FIGURE 10.2 What Are the Classic Leadership Styles?

It is common to describe leaders in terms of how their day-to-day styles show concern for people and concern for task. In this figure the leader low in concern for both people and task is described as "laissez-faire" and is very ineffective. The leader high in concern for task but low in concern for people is "autocratic" and focused on performance. The leader high in concern for people and low in concern for task has a "human relations" style that focuses mainly on people and relationships. The "democratic" leader is high in concern for both people and task. This person is often highly successful as a true team manager who is able to engage people to accomplish common goals.

A **human relations leader** emphasizes people over tasks.

A leader who emphasizes people over task is often referred to as a **human relations leader**. This leader is interpersonally engaging, cares about others, is sensitive to feelings and emotions, and tends to act in ways that emphasize harmony and good working relationships.

Interestingly, researchers at first believed that the human relations style was the most effective for a leader. However, after pressing further, the conclusion emerged that the most effective leaders were strong in concerns for both people and task.[15] Called a **democratic leader**, a manager with this high-high style shares decisions with followers, encourages participation, and supports the teamwork needed for high levels of task accomplishment.

A **democratic leader** encourages participation with an emphasis on task and people.

One result of this research on leader behaviors was the emergence of training programs designed to help people become better leaders by learning how to be good at both task-oriented and people-oriented behaviors. How about you? Where do you fit on this leadership diagram? What leadership training would be best for you? Let's hope you're not starting out as an a **laissez-faire leader**, low on both task and people concerns.

A **laissez-faire leader** is disengaged, showing low task and people concerns.

LEADERS WITH INTEGRITY ARE HONEST, CREDIBLE, HUMBLE, AND CONSISTENT.

EXPLORE YOURSELF

Integrity

Leaders with **integrity** are honest, credible, humble, and consistent in all that they do. They walk the talk by living up to high ethical standards and personal values in all their actions. Great leadership—from the team level to the organization as a whole—operates on a foundation of integrity. The very concept of moral leadership is centered on integrity. And, a servant leader represents integrity in action. Why is it, then, that in the news and in everyday experiences we so often end up wondering where leadership integrity has gone?

Get to know yourself better by taking the self-assessment on **Least Preferred Co-Worker Scale** and completing other activities in the *Exploring Management* **Skill-Building Portfolio**.

STUDYGUIDE

Takeaway 10.1
What Are the Foundations for Effective Leadership?

Terms to Define

Autocratic leader	Human relations leader	Legitimate power	Reward power
Coercive power	Laissez-faire leader	Power	Vision
Democratic leader	Leadership	Referent power	Visionary leadership
Expert power	Leadership style	Relationship power	

Rapid Review

- Leadership, as one of the management functions, is the process of inspiring others to work hard to accomplish important tasks.
- Leaders use power from two primary sources: position power—which includes rewards, coercion, and legitimacy, and personal power—which includes expertise and reference.
- The ability to communicate a vision or clear sense of the future is considered essential to effective leadership.
- Personal characteristics associated with leadership success include honesty, competency, drive, integrity, and self-confidence.
- Research on leader behaviors focused attention on concerns for task and concerns for people, with the leader high on both and using a democratic style considered most effective.

Questions for Discussion

1. When, if ever, is a leader justified in using coercive power?
2. How can a young college graduate gain personal power when moving into a new job as team leader?
3. Why might a leader with a human relations style have difficulty getting things done in an organization?

Be Sure You Can

- **illustrate** how managers use position and personal power
- **define** vision and give an example of visionary leadership
- **list** five traits of successful leaders
- **describe** alternative leadership styles based on concern for task and concern for people

Career Situation: What Would You Do?

Some might say it's bad luck. Others will say it's life and you'd better get used to it. You've just gotten a new boss, and within the first week it was clear that she is as autocratic as can be. The previous boss led in a very democratic way, and so does the next-higher-level manager with whom you have a good working relationship. So, do you just sit tight and live with it? Or, are there things you and your co-workers can do to remedy this situation without causing harm to anyone, including the new boss?

Takeaway 10.2
What Can We Learn from the Contingency Leadership Theories?

ANSWERS TO COME

- Fiedler's contingency model matches leadership styles with situational differences.
- The Hersey-Blanchard situational model matches leadership styles with the maturity of followers.
- House's path-goal theory matches leadership styles with task and follower characteristics.
- Leader–member exchange theory describes how leaders treat in-group and out-group followers.
- The Vroom-Jago model describes how leaders use alternative decision-making methods.

EVEN AS YOU CONSIDER YOUR LEADERSHIP STYLE AND TENDENCIES, YOU SHOULD know that researchers eventually concluded that no one style always works best. Not even the democratic, or "high-high," leader is successful all the time. This finding led scholars to explore a **contingency leadership perspective**, one that recognizes that what is successful as a leadership style varies according to the nature of the situation and people involved.

> The **contingency leadership perspective** suggests that what is successful as a leadership style varies according to the situation and the people involved.

FIEDLER'S CONTINGENCY MODEL MATCHES LEADERSHIP STYLES WITH SITUATIONAL DIFFERENCES.

One of the first contingency models of leadership was put forth by Fred Fiedler. He proposed that leadership success depends on achieving a proper match between your leadership style and situational demands.[16] He also believed that each of us has a predominant leadership style that is strongly rooted in our personalities. This is important because it suggests that a person's leadership style, yours or mine, is going to be enduring and hard to change.

Fiedler uses an instrument called the *least-preferred co-worker scale (LPC)* to classify our leadership styles as either task motivated or relationship motivated. The LPC scale is available in the end-of-book *Skill-Building Portfolio*. Why not complete it now and see how Fiedler would describe your style?

Leadership situations are analyzed in Fiedler's model according to three contingency variables—leader–member relations, task structure, and position power. These variables can exist in eight different combinations, with each representing a different leadership challenge. The most favorable situation provides high control for the leader. It has good leader–member relations, high task structure, and strong position power. The least favorable situation puts the leader in a low-control setting. Leader–member relations are poor, task structure is low, and position power is weak.

Fiedler's research revealed an interesting pattern when he studied the effectiveness of different styles in different leadership situations. As shown in Figure 10.3, a task-motivated leader is most successful in either very favorable (high-control) or very unfavorable (low-control) situations. In contrast, a relationship-motivated leader is more successful in situations of moderate control.

Don't let the apparent complexity of the figure fool you. Fiedler's logic is quite straightforward and, if on track, has some interesting career implications. It suggests that you must know yourself well enough to recognize your predominant leadership style. You should seek out or create leadership situations for which this style is a good match. And, you should avoid situations for which your style is a bad match.

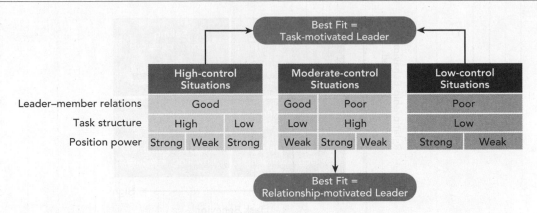

FIGURE 10.3 What Are the Best Matches of Leadership Style and Situation According to Fiedler's Contingency Model?
Fiedler believes that leadership success requires the right style–situation match. He classifies leadership styles as either task motivated or relationship motivated and views them as strongly rooted in our individual personalities. He describes situations according to the leader's position power, quality of leader–member relations, and amount of task structure. In situations that are most favorable and unfavorable for leaders, his research shows the task-motivated style as the best fit. In more intermediate situations, the relationship-motivated style provides the best fit.

Let's do some quick examples. First, assume that you are the leader of a team of bank tellers. The tellers seem highly supportive of you, and their job is clearly defined. You have the authority to evaluate their performance and to make pay and promotion recommendations. This is a high-control situation consisting of good leader–member relations, high task structure, and high position power. By checking Figure 10.3, you can see that a task-motivated leader is recommended.

Now suppose you are chairperson of a committee asked to improve labor–management relations in a manufacturing plant. Although the goal is clear, no one knows exactly how to accomplish it—task structure is low. Further, not everyone believes that a committee is even the right way to approach the situation—poor leader–member relations are likely. Finally, committee members are free to quit any time they want—you have little position power. Figure 10.3 shows that in this low-control situation, a task-motivated leader should be most effective.

Finally, assume that you are the new head of a fashion section in a large department store. Because you won the job over one of the popular salesclerks you now supervise, leader–member relations are poor. Task structure is high because the clerk's job is well defined. Your position power is low because clerks work under a seniority system, with a fixed wage schedule. Figure 10.3 shows that this moderate-control situation requires a relationship-motivated leader.

THE HERSEY-BLANCHARD SITUATIONAL MODEL MATCHES LEADERSHIP STYLES WITH THE MATURITY OF FOLLOWERS.

In contrast to Fiedler's notion that leadership style is hard to change, the Hersey-Blanchard situational leadership model suggests that successful leaders do adjust their styles. They do so contingently and based on the maturity of followers, as indicated by their readiness to perform in a given situation.[17] "Readiness," in this sense, is based on how able and willing or confident followers are to perform required tasks. As shown in **Figure 10.4**, the possible combinations of task and relationship behaviors result in four leadership styles.

- *Delegating*—allowing the group to take responsibility for task decisions; a low-task, low-relationship style
- *Participating*—emphasizing shared ideas and participative decisions on task directions; a low-task, high-relationship style

FIGURE 10.4

What Are the Leadership Implications of the Hersey-Blanchard Situational Leadership Model?

The Hersey-Blanchard situational leadership model suggests that successful leaders adjust their styles based on the maturity of followers or how willing and able they are to perform in a given situation. The four style–follower matches are delegating style for able and willing followers, participating style for able but unwilling followers, selling style for unable but willing followers, and telling style for unable and unwilling followers.

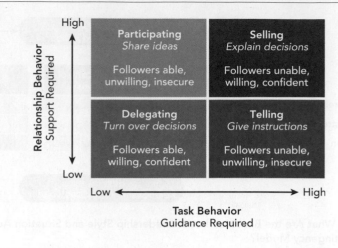

- *Selling*—explaining task directions in a supportive and persuasive way; a high-task, high-relationship style
- *Telling*—giving specific task directions and closely supervising work; a high-task, low-relationship style

The delegating style works best in high-readiness situations with able and willing or confident followers. The telling style works best at the other extreme of low readiness, where followers are unable and unwilling or insecure. The participating style is recommended for low-to-moderate readiness (followers are able but unwilling or insecure); the selling style works best for moderate-to-high readiness (followers are unable but willing or confident).

Hersey and Blanchard further believe that leadership styles should be adjusted as followers change over time. The model also implies that if the correct styles are used in lower-readiness situations, followers will "mature" and grow in ability, willingness, and confidence. This allows the leader to become less directive as followers mature. Although this situational leadership model is intuitively appealing, limited research has been accomplished on it to date.[18]

HOUSE'S PATH-GOAL THEORY MATCHES LEADERSHIP STYLES WITH TASK AND FOLLOWER CHARACTERISTICS.

Another contingency leadership approach is the path-goal theory advanced by Robert House.[19] This theory suggests that leaders are effective when they help followers move along paths through which they can achieve both work goals and personal goals. The best leaders create positive path-goal linkages, raising motivation by removing barriers and rewarding progress.

Like Fiedler's approach, House's path-goal theory seeks the right fit between leadership and situation. But unlike Fiedler, House believes that a leader can move back and forth among the four leadership styles: directive, supportive, achievement-oriented, and participative.

When choosing among the different styles, House suggests that the leader's job is to "add value" to a situation. This means acting in ways that contribute things that are missing and not doing things that can otherwise take care of themselves. If you are the leader of a team whose members are expert and competent at their tasks, for example, why would you need to be directive? Members have the know-how to provide their own direction. More likely, the value you can add to this situation would be found in a participative leadership style that helps unlock the expertise of team members and apply it fully to the tasks at hand.

Path-goal theory provides a variety of research-based guidance of this sort to help leaders contingently match their styles with situational characteristics.[20] When job assignments are unclear, *directive leadership* helps to clarify task objectives and expected rewards. When worker self-confidence is low, *supportive leadership* can increase confidence by emphasizing individual abilities and offering needed assistance. When task

Four Leadership Styles in House's Path-Goal Theory

1. *Directive leader*—lets others know what is expected; gives directions, maintains standards
2. *Supportive leader*—makes work more pleasant; treats others as equals, acts friendly, shows concern
3. *Achievement-oriented leader*—sets challenging goals; expects high performance, shows confidence
4. *Participative leader*—involves others in decision making; asks for and uses suggestions

challenge is insufficient in a job, *achievement-oriented leadership* helps to set goals and raise performance aspirations. When performance incentives are poor, *participative leadership* might clarify individual needs and identify appropriate rewards.

This contingency thinking has contributed to the recognition of what are called **substitutes for leadership**.[21] These are aspects of the work setting and the people involved that can reduce the need for a leader's personal involvement. In effect, they make leadership from the "outside" unnecessary because leadership is already provided from within the situation.

Possible substitutes for leadership include subordinate characteristics such as ability, experience, and independence; task characteristics such as how routine it is and the availability of feedback; and organizational characteristics such as clarity of plans and formalization of rules and procedures. When these substitutes are present, managers are advised to avoid duplicating them. Instead, they should concentrate on doing other and more important things.

> **Substitutes for leadership** are factors in the work setting that direct work efforts without the involvement of a leader.

LEADER–MEMBER EXCHANGE THEORY DESCRIBES HOW LEADERS TREAT IN-GROUP AND OUT-GROUP FOLLOWERS.

One of the things you may have noticed in your work and study groups is the tendency of leaders to develop "special" relationships with some team members. This notion is central to leader–member exchange theory, or LMX theory, as it is often called.[22] The theory is highlighted in the nearby figure and recognizes that in most, or at least many, leadership situations, not everyone is treated the same. People fall into "in-groups" and "out-groups," and the group you are in can have quite a significant influence on your experience with the leader.

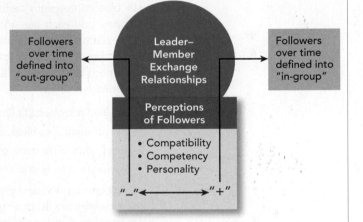

The premise underlying leader–member exchange theory is that as a leader and follower interact over time, their exchanges end up defining the follower's role.[23] Those in a leader's in-group are often considered the best performers. They enjoy special and trusted high-exchange relationships with the leader that can translate into special assignments, privileges, and access to information. Those in the out-group are often excluded from these benefits due to low-exchange relationships with the leader.

For the follower in a high-LMX relationship, being part of the leader's inner circle or in-group can be a real positive. It's often motivating and satisfying to be on the inside of things in terms of getting rewards and favorable treatments. Being in the out-group because of a low-LMX relationship, however, can be a real negative, bringing fewer rewards and less-favorable treatment. As to the leader, it is nice to be able to call on and depend on the loyal support of those in the in-group. But the leader may also be missing out on opportunities that might come from working more closely with out-group members.

Research on leader–member exchange theory places most value on its usefulness in describing leader–member interactions. The notions of high-LMX and low-LMX relationships seem to make sense and correspond to working realities experienced by many people. Look around, and you're likely to see examples of this in classroom situations between instructors and certain students, and in work situations between bosses and certain subordinates. In such settings, research finds that members of in-groups get more positive performance evaluations, report higher levels of satisfaction, and are less prone to turnover than are members of out-groups.[24]

THE VROOM-JAGO MODEL DESCRIBES HOW LEADERS USE ALTERNATIVE DECISION-MAKING METHODS.

Yet another contingency leadership theory focuses on how managers lead through their use of decision-making methods. The Vroom-Jago leader-participation model views a manager as having three decision options, and in true contingency fashion, no one option is always superior to the others.[25]

An **authority decision** is made by the leader and then communicated to the group.

A **consultative decision** is made by a leader after receiving information, advice, or opinions from group members.

A **group decision** is made by group members themselves.

1. **Authority decision**—The manager makes an individual decision about how to solve the problem and then communicates the decision to the group.

2. **Consultative decision**—The manager makes the decision after sharing the problem with and getting suggestions from individual group members or the group as a whole.

3. **Group decision**—The manager convenes the group, shares the problem, and then either facilitates a group decision or delegates the decision to the group.

Leadership success results when the manager's choice of decision-making method best matches the nature of the problem to be solved.[26] The rules for making the choice involve three criteria: (1) *decision quality*—based on who has the information needed for problem solving; (2) *decision acceptance*—based on the importance of follower acceptance of the decision to its eventual implementation; and (3) *decision time*—based on the time available to make and implement the decision. These rules are shown in **Figure 10.5**.

In true contingency fashion, each of the decision methods is appropriate in certain situations, and each has advantages and disadvantages.[27] Authority decisions work best when leaders have the expertise needed to solve the problem, they are confident and capable of acting alone, others are likely to accept and implement the decision they make, and little time is available for discussion. By contrast, consultative and group decisions are recommended when:

• The leader lacks sufficient expertise and information to solve this problem alone.

• The problem is unclear, and help is needed to clarify the situation.

• Acceptance of the decision and commitment by others are necessary for implementation.

• Adequate time is available to allow for true participation.

Using consultative and group decisions offers important leadership benefits.[28] Participation helps improve decision quality by bringing more information to bear on the problem. It helps improve decision acceptance as others gain understanding and become committed to the process. It also contributes to leadership development by allowing others to gain experience in the problem-solving process. However, a potential cost of participation is lost efficiency. Participation often adds to the time required for decision making, and leaders don't always have extra time available. When problems must be resolved immediately, the authority decision may be the only option.[29]

FIGURE 10.5

What Are the Leadership Implications of the Vroom-Jago Leader-Participation Model?

The leader-participation model suggests that leaders are effective when they use the appropriate decision method to solve a problem situation. Three criteria govern the choice among possible authority, consultative, and team or group decisions: (1) *decision quality*—based on who has the information needed for problem solving; (2) *decision acceptance*—based on the importance of follower acceptance of the decision to its eventual implementation; and (3) *decision time*—based on the time available to make and implement the decision.

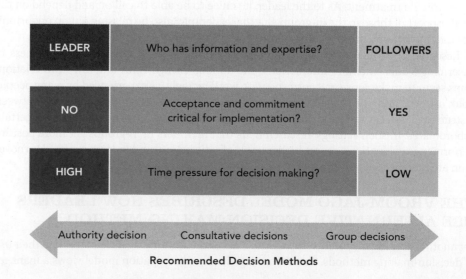

STUDYGUIDE

Takeaway 10.2
What Can We Learn from the Contingency Leadership Theories?

Terms to Define

Authority decision

Consultative decision

Contingency leadership perspective

Group decision

Substitutes for leadership

Rapid Review

- Fiedler's contingency model describes how situational differences in task structure, position power, and leader–member relations may influence the success of task-motivated and relationship-motivated leaders.

- The Hersey-Blanchard situational model recommends using task-oriented and people-oriented behaviors, depending on the "maturity" levels of followers.

- House's path-goal theory describes how leaders add value to situations by using supportive, directive, achievement-oriented, and/or participative styles as needed.

- Leader–member exchange theory recognizes that leaders respond differently to followers in their in-groups and out-groups.

- The Vroom-Jago leader-participation theory advises leaders to choose decision-making methods—authority, consultative, group—that best fit the problems to be solved.

Questions for Discussion

1. What are the potential career development lessons of Fiedler's contingency leadership model?

2. What are the implications of follower maturity for leaders trying to follow the Hersey-Blanchard situational leadership model?

3. Is it wrong for a team leader to allow the formation of in-groups and out-groups in his or her relationships with team members?

Be Sure You Can

- **explain** Fiedler's contingency model for matching leadership style and situation

- **identify** the three variables used to assess situational favorableness in Fiedler's model

- **identify** the four leadership styles in the Hersey-Blanchard situational leadership model

- **explain** the importance of follower "maturity" in the Hersey-Blanchard model

- **describe** the best use of directive, supportive, achievement-oriented, and participative leadership styles in House's path-goal theory

- **explain** how leader–member exchange theory deals with in-groups and out-groups among a leader's followers

Career Situation: What Would You Do?

You've just been hired as a visual effects artist by a top movie studio. Members of the team you are joining have already been working together for about 2 months. There's obviously an in-group when it comes to team leader and team member relationships. This job is important to you, and the movie is going to be great résumé material. But, you're worried about the leadership dynamics and your role as a newcomer to the team. What can you do to quickly become a valued team member?

Takeaway 10.3
What Are Current Issues and Directions in Leadership Development?

ANSWERS TO COME

- Transformational leadership inspires enthusiasm and great performance.
- Emotionally intelligent leadership handles emotions and relationships well.
- Interactive leadership emphasizes communication, listening, and participation.
- Moral leadership builds trust through personal integrity.
- Servant leadership is follower centered and empowering.

YOU SHOULD NOW BE THINKING SERIOUSLY ABOUT YOUR LEADERSHIP QUALITIES, tendencies, styles, and effectiveness. You should also be thinking about your personal development as a leader. If you really look at what people say about leaders in their workplaces, you should be admitting that most of us have considerable room to grow in this regard.[30]

TRANSFORMATIONAL LEADERSHIP INSPIRES ENTHUSIASM AND GREAT PERFORMANCE.

It is popular to talk about "superleaders," persons whose visions and strong personalities have an extraordinary impact on others.[31] Martin Luther King, in his famous "I have a dream" speech delivered in August 1963 on the Washington Mall, serves as a good example. Some call people like King **charismatic leaders** because of their ability to inspire others in exceptional ways. We used to think charisma was limited to only a few lucky persons. Today, it is considered one of several personal qualities—including honesty, credibility, and competence—that can be developed with foresight and practice.

Leadership scholars James MacGregor Burns and Bernard Bass have pursued this theme. They begin by describing the traditional leadership approaches we have discussed so far as **transactional leadership**.[32] You might picture the transactional leader engaging followers in a somewhat mechanical fashion, "transacting" with them by using power, employing behaviors and styles that seem to be the best choices at the moment for getting things done.

What is missing in the transactional approach, say Burns and Bass, is attention to things typically linked with superleaders—enthusiasm and inspiration, for example. These are among the charismatic qualities that they associate with something called **transformational leadership**.[33]

Transformational leaders use their personalities to inspire followers and get them so highly excited about their jobs and organizational goals that they strive for truly extraordinary performance accomplishments. Indeed, the easiest way to spot a truly transformational leader is through his or her followers. They are likely to be enthusiastic about the leader and loyal and devoted to his or her ideas and to work exceptionally hard together to support them.

The goal of achieving excellence in transformational leadership is a stiff personal development challenge. It is not enough to possess leadership traits, know the leadership behaviors, and understand leadership contingencies. One must also be prepared to lead in an inspirational way and with a compelling personality. Transformational leaders raise the confidence, aspirations, and performance of followers through special qualities like these.[34]

- *Vision*—has ideas and a clear sense of direction; communicates them to others; develops excitement about accomplishing shared "dreams"
- *Charisma*—uses the power of personal reference and emotion to arouse others' enthusiasm, faith, loyalty, pride, and trust in themselves

A **charismatic leader** develops special leader–follower relationships and inspires followers in extraordinary ways.

Transactional leadership directs the efforts of others through tasks, rewards, and structures.

Transformational leadership is inspirational and arouses extraordinary effort and performance.

FACTS TO CONSIDER

Followers Report Shortcomings of Leaders

Anderson Ross/Blend/Getty Images

Harris Interactive periodically conducts surveys of workers' attitudes toward their jobs and employers. The results for a query about how workers view "leaders" and "top managers" reveal lots of shortcomings. It makes you wonder—how do these same leaders see themselves?

- 39% believe leaders most often act in the best interest of organization.

- 37% believe their top managers display integrity and morality.
- 33% perceive their managers as "strong leaders."
- 25% of women and 16% of men believe their organizations pick the best people for leadership
- 22% see leaders as ready to admit mistakes.

YOUR THOUGHTS?

How do the leaders you have experienced stack up—strong or weak, moral or immoral? How do you believe these leaders view themselves? Is their self-awareness of leadership effectiveness high or low? What makes the most difference in the ways leaders are viewed in the eyes of followers?

- *Symbolism*—identifies "heroes" and holds spontaneous and planned ceremonies to celebrate excellence and high achievement
- *Empowerment*—helps others grow and develop by removing performance obstacles, sharing responsibilities, and delegating truly challenging work
- *Intellectual stimulation*—gains the involvement of others by creating awareness of problems and stirring their imaginations
- *Integrity*—is honest and credible; acts consistently and out of personal conviction; follows through on commitments

EMOTIONALLY INTELLIGENT LEADERSHIP HANDLES EMOTIONS AND RELATIONSHIPS WELL.

The role of personality in transformational leadership raises another area of inquiry in leadership development—**emotional intelligence**. Popularized by the work of Daniel Goleman, emotional intelligence, or EI for short, is an ability to understand emotions in yourself and others and use this understanding to handle one's social relationships effectively.[35] "Great leaders move us," say Goleman and his colleagues. "Great leadership works through emotions."[36]

Emotional intelligence is an important influence on leadership success, especially in more senior management positions. In Goleman's words: "The higher the rank of the person considered to be a star performer, the more emotional intelligence capabilities showed up as the reason for his or her effectiveness."[37] This is a pretty strong endorsement for making EI one of your leadership assets.[38] In fact, you'll increasingly hear the term **EQ**, or **emotional intelligence quotient**, used in this regard as more employers start to actually measure it as a part of their recruitment screening.

Consider the four primary emotional intelligence competencies shown in the small figure. *Self-awareness* is the ability to understand our own moods and emotions and to understand their impact on our work and on others. *Social awareness* is the ability to empathize, to understand the emotions of others, and to use this understanding to better deal with them. *Self-management,* or self-regulation, is the ability to

Emotional intelligence (EI) is the ability to manage our emotions in leadership and social relationships.

Emotional intelligence quotient (EQ) is a measure of a person's ability to manage emotions in leadership and social relationships.

Self-awareness | Social awareness | Emotional intelligence competencies | Self-management | Relationship management

think before acting and to be in control of otherwise disruptive impulses. *Relationship management* is the ability to establish rapport with others in ways that build good relationships and influence their emotions in positive ways.

INTERACTIVE LEADERSHIP EMPHASIZES COMMUNICATION, LISTENING, AND PARTICIPATION.

When Sara Levinson was president of NFL Properties Inc., she once asked the all-male members of her management team: "Is my leadership style different from a man's?"[39] Would you be surprised to learn that they answered "Yes," telling her that just by asking the question she was providing evidence of the difference? They described her as a leader who emphasized communication, always gathering ideas and opinions from others. And when Levinson probed further by asking, "Is this a distinctly 'female' trait?" they again said yes, it was.

Are there gender differences in leadership? Before you jump in with your own answer, consider three things. First, research largely supports the **gender similarities hypothesis** that males and females are very similar to one another in terms of psychological properties.[40] Second, research leaves no doubt that both women and men can be effective leaders.[41] Third, research shows that men and women are sometimes perceived as using different leadership styles, perhaps arriving at success from different angles.[42]

Some studies report that male leaders are viewed as directive and assertive, using position power to get things done in traditional command-and-control ways.[43] Other studies report female leaders are viewed as more participative than men. They are also rated by peers, subordinates, and supervisors as strong on motivating others, emotional intelligence, persuading, fostering communication, listening to others, mentoring, and supporting high-quality work.[44] Yet another study found that women were rated more highly than men in all but one area of leadership—visioning.[45] A possible explanation is that women aren't considered as visionaries because they are perceived as acting less directive as leaders.

The pattern of behaviors associated with female leaders has been called **interactive leadership**.[46] Interactive leaders are democratic, participative, and inclusive, often approaching problems and decisions through teamwork.[47] They focus on building consensus and good interpersonal relations through emotional intelligence, communication, and involvement. They tend to get things done with personal power, seeking influence over others through support and interpersonal relationships.

Rosabeth Moss Kanter says that in many ways, "Women get high ratings on exactly those skills required to succeed in the Global Information Age, where teamwork and partnering

> The **gender similarities hypothesis** holds that males and females have similar psychological makeups.

> **Interactive leadership** is strong on communicating, participation, and dealing with problems by teamwork.

THE LAST PERSON YOU RECOMMENDED FOR PROMOTION WAS A GOOD FRIEND AND A MEMBER OF YOUR BIWEEKLY POKER NIGHT CLUB.

QUICK CASE

Playing Favorites as a Team Leader

Jirsak/iStockphoto/Getty Images

One of your colleagues just returned from a leadership training session at which the instructor presented the LMX, or leader–member exchange, theory. Listening to her talk about the training caused you to think about your own leader behaviors, and you came to a somewhat startling conclusion: You may be playing "favorites." In fact, the last person you recommended for promotion was a good friend and a member of your biweekly poker night club. Of course he was competent and is doing a good job in the new position. But as you think more about it, there were two others on the team who may well have been equally good choices. Did you give them a fair chance when preparing your promotion recommendation, or did you shortchange them in favor of your friend?

WHAT DO YOU DO?

It's a new day for the team, and basically the start of the rest of your leadership career. What can you do as a team leader to make sure that tendencies toward favoritism don't disadvantage some members? What kinds of signals can you use to determine whether you are playing favorites?

are so important."[48] Her observations are backed up by data showing that firms with more female directors and executives outperform others.[49] But let's be careful. One of the risks here is placing individual men and women into boxes in which they don't necessarily belong.[50] It may be better to focus instead on the notion of interactive leadership. The likelihood is that this style is a very good fit with the needs of today's organizations and workers.[51] And, isn't there every reason to believe that both men and women can do interactive leadership equally well?

MORAL LEADERSHIP BUILDS TRUST THROUGH PERSONAL INTEGRITY.

As discussed many times in this book, society expects organizations to be run with **moral leadership**. This is leadership by ethical standards that clearly meet the test of being "good" and "correct."[52] We should expect anyone in a leadership position to practice high ethical standards of behavior and help others to also behave ethically in their work. But the facts don't always support this aspiration.

Are you surprised by the Harris poll reported in Facts to Consider? Why are so few people willing to describe their top managers as acting with "integrity and morality"?[53] Based on that result, it may not surprise you that a *Businessweek* survey found that just 13% of top executives at large U.S. firms rated "having strong ethical values" as a top leadership characteristic.[54]

In contrast to the findings just described, is there any doubt that society today is demanding more ethical leadership? We want business, government, and nonprofit leaders to act ethically and maintain ethical organizational cultures. We want them to help and require others to behave ethically in their work.[55] Such themes should be clear throughout this book. Ideally, too, you will agree that long-term success in your work and life can be built only on a foundation of solid ethical behavior.[56]

But how and where do we start when facing up to the challenge of building personal capacities for ethical leadership? A good answer is to focus on **integrity**.[57] You must start with honest, credible, and consistent behavior that puts your values into action. Words like "principled," "fair," and "authentic" should come immediately to mind.

When a leader has integrity, he or she earns the trust of followers. And when followers believe that their leaders are trustworthy, they are more willing to try to live up to the

> **Moral leadership** has integrity and appears to others as "good" or "right" by ethical standards.

> **Integrity** in leadership is honesty, credibility, and consistency in putting values into action.

> THE ASSISTANT MANAGER FOLLOWED "OFFICER SCOTT'S" INSTRUCTIONS TO THE POINT WHERE THE 18-YEAR-OLD EMPLOYEE IS NAKED AND DOING JUMPING JACKS.

HOT TOPIC

Making "No" Part of the Follower's Vocabulary

michaeljung/iStockphoto/Getty Images

McDonald's Restaurant— A telephone caller claiming to be a police officer and to have "corporate" on the line, directs the assistant store manager to take a female employee into the back room and question her while he is on the line. The interrogation lasted 3 hours. The assistant manager followed "Officer Scott's" instructions to the point where the 18-year-old employee is naked and doing jumping jacks. The hoax was discovered only when the assistant manager called her boss to check out the story. The caller was later arrested and found to have tried similar tricks at more than 70 McDonald's restaurants.

Managers and leaders are supposed to make decisions, and the rest of us are supposed to follow. Isn't that the conventional wisdom? But perhaps the word "no" deserves more attention as part of a follower's vocabulary.

HOW ABOUT IT?

If obedience isn't always the right choice, how do we know when it's time to disobey? Should we give students more training on both spotting bad directives and learning how to say "No"? Do management courses have enough to say about tendencies to obey, how to double-check decisions to make sure our obedience is justified, and even about the price of disobedience? Is it possible to educate and train students to be "principled" followers—ones who don't always follow orders and sometimes question them?

leader's expectations. Southwest Airlines CEO Gary Kelly says: "Being a leader is about character . . . being straightforward and honest, having integrity, and treating people right." And there's a payoff. One of his co-workers says this about Kelly's leadership impact: "People are willing to run through walls for him."[58]

A word of caution: Dean Nitin Nohria of the Harvard Business School says, "The world isn't neatly divided into good people and bad people."[59] One of the risks we face in living up to the expectations of moral leadership is **moral overconfidence**. This occurs as an overly positive view of one's integrity and strength of character.[60] It may cause a leader to act unethically without recognizing it or while justifying it by inappropriate rationalizations. "I'm a good person, so I can't be wrong on this," a leader might say with moral overconfidence.

Moral overconfidence is an overly positive view of one's integrity and strength of character.

SERVANT LEADERSHIP IS FOLLOWER CENTERED AND EMPOWERING.

A classic observation about great leaders is that they view leadership as a responsibility, not a rank.[61] This is consistent with the notion of **servant leadership**. It means serving others and helping them use their talents to the fullest so that the organization benefits society.[62]

Servant leadership means serving others and helping them use their talents to help organizations benefit society.

You might think of servant leadership by asking this question: Who is most important in leadership, the leader or the followers? For those who believe in servant leadership, there is no doubt about the correct answer: the followers. Servant leadership is "other centered" and not "self-centered." It shifts the leader's focus away from the self and toward others, and creates **empowerment** by giving people job freedom and opportunities to influence what happens in the organization.[63]

Empowerment gives people job freedom and power to influence affairs in the organization.

Max DePree, former CEO of Herman Miller and a noted leadership author, praises leaders who "permit others to share ownership of problems—to take possession of the situation."[64] Lorraine Monroe of the School Leadership Academy says: "The real leader is a servant of the people she leads . . . a really great boss is not afraid to hire smart people. You want people who are smart about things you are not smart about."[65] Robert Greenleaf, credited with coining the term "servant leadership," says: "Institutions function better when the idea, the dream, is to the fore, and the person, the leader, is seen as servant to the dream."[66]

Think about these ideas and then take a good look in the mirror. Is the leader in you capable of being a servant?

ETHICS CHECK

A Step over the Line into Community Service

Ravi Tahilraman/iStockphoto

What if your company's CEO is active in a local community group? It sounds great, and she gets a lot of press for philanthropy and leadership in the local Red Cross, homeless shelter, food bank, and more. The company's reputation for social responsibility also gains from her outreach efforts. But, first thing this morning she appeared in your office and asked you to spend a good part of the workweek helping organize a fundraising event for one of her local charities. Caught off guard, you've given her a weak "okay."

Now that you've had time to think a bit more about it, you're not sure you should comply. After all, you've already got a lot of top-priority work on your desk, there's no direct connection between the charity and the firm's business, and the charity isn't one that you personally support.

Helping your boss with this request will obviously be good for her. You'll also probably benefit from increased goodwill in your relationship with her. However, the organization could actually end up being worse off as your regular work slips behind schedule, affecting not only you but client activities that depend on you. Sure, you're getting paid to do what she asks—but who benefits?

YOUR DECISION?

Is it ethical to help your manager in the situation just described? Are you doing a disservice to the organization's other stakeholders if you go along with this request? Is it acceptable for a manager or team leader or top executive to ask others to help them with tasks and activities that are not directly tied to work?

STUDYGUIDE

Takeaway 10.3
What Are Current Issues and Directions in Leadership Development?

Terms to Define

Charismatic leader

Emotional intelligence (EI)

Emotional intelligence quotient (EQ)

Empowerment

Gender similarities hypothesis

Integrity

Interactive leadership

Moral leadership

Moral overconfidence

Servant leadership

Transactional leadership

Transformational leadership

Rapid Review

- Transformational leaders use charisma and emotion to inspire others toward extraordinary efforts to achieve performance excellence.
- Emotional intelligence, the ability to manage our emotions and relationships effectively, is an important leadership capability.
- The interactive leadership style, sometimes associated with women, emphasizes communication, involvement, and interpersonal respect.
- Moral or ethical leadership is built from a foundation of personal integrity, creating a basis for trust and respect between leaders and followers.
- A servant leader is follower centered, not self-centered, and empowers others to unlock their personal talents in the quest for goals and accomplishments that help society.

Questions for Discussion

1. Should all managers be expected to excel at transformational leadership?
2. Do women lead differently than men?
3. Is servant leadership inevitably moral leadership?

Be Sure You Can

- **differentiate** transformational and transactional leadership
- **list** the personal qualities of transformational leaders
- **explain** how emotional intelligence contributes to leadership success
- **discuss** research findings on interactive leadership
- **explain** the role of integrity as a foundation for moral leadership
- **explain** the concept of servant leadership

Career Situation: What Would You Do?

Okay, so it's important to be "interactive" in leadership. By personality, though, you tend to be a bit withdrawn. If you could do things by yourself, that's the way you would behave. Yet here you are taking over as a team leader as the first upward career step in your present place of employment. How can you bend your personality to take advantage of interactive leadership and best master the challenges of your new role?

TEST PREP **10**

Answers to Test Prep questions can be found at the back of the book.

Multiple-Choice Questions

1. When managers use offers of rewards and threats of punishments to try to get others to do what they want them to do, they are using which type of power?
   (a) Formal authority   (b) Position
   (c) Referent   (d) Personal

2. When a manager says, "Because I am the boss, you must do what I ask," what power base is being put into play?
   (a) Reward   (b) Legitimate
   (c) Moral   (d) Referent

3. The personal traits that are now considered important for managerial success include _____.
   (a) self-confidence   (b) gender
   (c) age   (d) personality

4. In the research on leader behaviors, which style of leadership describes the preferred "high-high" combination?
   (a) Transformational
   (b) Transactional
   (c) Laissez-faire
   (d) Democratic

5. In Fiedler's contingency model, both highly favorable and highly unfavorable leadership situations are best dealt with by a _____-motivated leadership style.
   (a) task   (b) vision
   (c) ethics   (d) relationship

6. Which leadership theorist argues that one's leadership style is strongly anchored in personality and therefore very difficult to change?
   (a) Daniel Goleman   (b) Peter Drucker
   (c) Fred Fiedler   (d) Robert House

7. Vision, charisma, integrity, and symbolism are all attributes typically associated with _____ leaders.
   (a) people-oriented   (b) democratic
   (c) transformational   (d) transactional

8. In terms of leadership behaviors, someone who focuses on doing a very good job of planning work tasks, setting performance standards, and monitoring results would be described as _____.
   (a) task oriented
   (b) servant oriented
   (c) achievement oriented
   (d) transformational

9. In the discussion of gender and leadership, it was pointed out that some perceive women as having tendencies toward _____, a style that seems a good fit with developments in the new workplace.
   (a) interactive leadership
   (b) use of position power
   (c) command-and-control
   (d) transactional leadership

10. In House's path-goal theory, a leader who sets challenging goals for others would be described as using the _____ leadership style.
    (a) autocratic   (b) achievement-oriented
    (c) transformational   (d) directive

11. Someone who communicates a clear sense of the future and the actions needed to get there is considered a _____ leader.
    (a) task-oriented
    (b) people-oriented
    (c) transactional
    (d) visionary

12. Managerial Power = _____ Power $\times$ _____ Power.
    (a) Reward; Punishment
    (b) Reward; Expert
    (c) Legitimate; Position
    (d) Position; Personal

13. The interactive leadership style is characterized by _____.
    (a) inclusion and information sharing
    (b) use of rewards and punishments
    (c) command-and-control behavior
    (d) emphasis on position power

14. A leader whose actions indicate an attitude of "do as you want and don't bother me" would be described as having a(n) _____ leadership style.
    (a) autocratic
    (b) country club
    (c) democratic
    (d) laissez-faire

15. The critical contingency variable in the Hersey-Blanchard situational model of leadership is _____.
    (a) follower maturity
    (b) LPC
    (c) task structure
    (d) emotional intelligence

Short-Response Questions

16. Why are both position power and personal power essential in management?

17. Use Fiedler's terms to list the characteristics of situations that would be extremely favorable and extremely unfavorable to a leader.

18. Describe the situations in which House's path-goal theory would expect (a) a participative leadership style and (b) a directive leadership style to work best.

19. How do you sum up in two or three sentences the notion of servant leadership?

Integration and Application Question

20. When Marcel Henry took over as leader of a new product development team, he was both excited and apprehensive. "I wonder," he said to himself on the first day in his new assignment, "if I can meet the challenges of leadership." Later that day, Marcel shares this concern with you during a coffee break.

    Question: How would you describe to Marcel the personal implications of current thinking on transformational and moral leadership and how they might be applied to his handling of this team setting?

Steps for
Further Learning

BUILD MARKETABLE SKILLS • **DO** A CASE ANALYSIS • **GET** AND STAY INFORMED

BUILD MARKETABLE SKILLS.

EARN BIG CAREER PAYOFFS!

Don't miss these opportunities in the SKILL-BUILDING PORTFOLIO

SELF-ASSESSMENT 10:
Least-Preferred
Co-worker Scale

Assess your leadership personality . . . learn more about leadership success.

CLASS EXERCISE 10:
Leading by Participation

There are different ways to make decisions . . . great leaders choose the right ones.

TEAM PROJECT 10:
Leadership Believe-
It-or-Not

Not everyone knows how to lead . . . sometimes the mistakes are almost unbelievable.

Many learning resources are found at the end of the book and online within **WileyPLUS Learning Space.**

Practice Critical Thinking—Complete the
CHAPTER 10 CASE
CASE SNAPSHOT: Zappos—They Do It with Humor

When Zappos CEO Tony Hsieh was the featured guest on *The Colbert Report*, host Stephen Colbert grilled him about the company's success and customer loyalty. Hsieh replied that it's Zappos's goal to deliver "*WOW*" in every shoe or clothing box. The company is consistently ranked highly as one of *Fortune's* "Best Companies to Work For." As Hsieh devotes more time to community service, can the Zappos culture survive growth and a possible leadership transition? Will Zappos continue to succeed while being the home of fashion-forward cultural practices?

DO A CASE ANALYSIS.

STRENGTHEN YOUR CRITICAL THINKING!

MANAGER'S LIBRARY SELECTION
Read for Insights and Wisdom
Power: Why Some People Have It and Others Don't
(2010, HarperCollins) by Jeffrey Pfeffer

Do yourself some good and schedule a power trip—your career depends on it! That's the advice offered in this book by Stanford scholar Jeffrey Pfeiffer. His research shows the most critical factor for success is having power in the form of authority and control over work environments, resources, and decisions. Power correlates positively with career success, job performance, salary, and even one's life span.

Pfeffer's career advice is to use political savvy to gain stature, control resources, and make decisions that build power, status, and influence. All this requires will and skill. Personal qualities of ambition, energy, and focus are needed. Ambition keeps attention focused on achieving influence over others, especially those higher up. Energy fuels hard work and effort. It is contagious and signals commitment to others. Focus limits activities and skills to areas that will lead to more power, status, and influence.

GET AND STAY INFORMED.

MAKE YOURSELF VALUABLE!

REFLECT AND REACT How are members selected and dismissed, and how are tasks assigned in your organizations? How are resources selected and used? How are decisions made and by whom? Are those in power perceived positively or negatively, as intelligent or weak? Do you agree that "gaining power" should be on your "to do" list as an organizational and team member?

You don't have to look in a mirror to gain more self-awareness. What does your smart phone, tablet, or computer screen say about your personality?

Individual Behavior

There's Beauty in Individual Differences

Management Live

The Death of Work–Life Balance

YekoPhotoStudio/iStockphoto/Getty Images

The problem is: When does work end and leisure time begin? We used to "go" to work and then come "home" where we relaxed with family and pursued personal affairs. Now we work "on the go" anytime, from anywhere, and often at someone else's beck and call. "Check your e-mail at Thanksgiving?" asks one commentator who laments the "death of work–life balance." Do others expect you to be always online, or do you have a compulsion to be online, or both? What does work–life balance really mean? How far is an employer willing to go to put some "balance" into our lives?

HOW ABOUT IT?

Do you pass or fail the Thanksgiving e-mail test? Instead of just talking work–life balance, Patagonia lets employees work flexible hours with day care available on site. Exercise time is encouraged at no cost to the employee. Are these the types of things that we need to avoid the death of work–life balance?

YOUR CHAPTER 11 TAKEAWAYS

1. Understand how perceptions influence individual behavior.

2. Understand how personalities influence individual behavior.

3. Understand how attitudes, emotions, and moods influence individual behavior.

Takeaway 11.1
How Do Perceptions Influence Individual Behavior?

ANSWERS TO COME

- Perception filters information received from our environment.
- Perceptual distortions can hide individual differences.
- Perception can cause attribution errors.
- Impression management influences how others perceive us.

KAREN NUSSBAUM LEFT HER JOB AS A SECRETARY AT HARVARD UNIVERSITY AND FOUNDED 9 TO 5, a nonprofit devoted to improving women's salaries and promotion opportunities in the workplace. She describes "the incident that put her over the edge" this way: "One day I was sitting at my desk at lunchtime, when most of the professors were out. A student walked into the office and looked me dead in the eye and said, 'Isn't anyone here?'" Nussbaum started 9 to 5 with a commitment to "remake the system so that it does not produce these individuals."[1]

PERCEPTION FILTERS INFORMATION RECEIVED FROM OUR ENVIRONMENT.

Perception is the process through which people receive and interpret information from the environment.

When people communicate with one another, everything passes through two silent but influential shields: the "perceptions" of both sender and the receiver. **Perception** is the process through which people receive and interpret information from the environment. It is the way we form impressions about ourselves, other people, and daily life experiences.

As suggested in **Figure 11.1**, you might think of perception as a bubble that surrounds us and significantly influences the way we receive, interpret, and process information received from our environments.[2] And because our individual idiosyncrasies, backgrounds, values, and experiences influence our perceptions, this means that people can and do view the same things quite differently. These differences in perceptions influence how we communicate and behave in relationship to one another.

PERCEPTUAL DISTORTIONS CAN HIDE INDIVIDUAL DIFFERENCES.

We live and work in an activity-rich world that constantly bombards us with information. To deal with this complexity, we find ways to simplify and organize our perceptions.

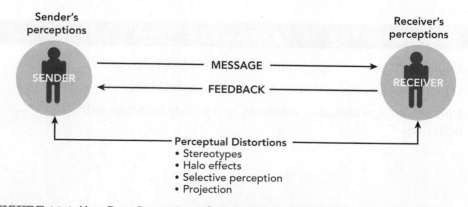

FIGURE 11.1 How Does Perception Influence Communication?
Perception is the process of receiving and interpreting information from our environment. It acts as a screen or filter through which we interpret messages in the communication process. Perceptions influence how we behave in response to information received. And, because people often perceive the same things quite differently, perception is an important issue in respect to individual behavior.

One of the most common perceptual simplifications is the **stereotype**. This occurs when you identify someone with a group or category, and then use the attributes associated with the group or category to describe the individual. Although this makes things easier by reducing the need to deal with unique individual characteristics, it is a distorting simplification. By relying on the stereotype, we end up missing the real individual.

Consider how gender stereotyping might cause managers to misconstrue work behavior. Only a small portion, about 17%, of managers sent on international assignments are women. Do you wonder why? It's not lack of desire; there are as many women as men wanting those jobs. A Catalyst study of women in global business blames gender stereotypes that place women at a disadvantage to men for these jobs. The perception seems to be that women lack the abilities or willingness for working abroad.[3]

A **halo effect** occurs when we use one characteristic of a person or situation to form an overall impression. You probably do this quite often, as do I. When meeting someone new, for example, receiving a positive smile might create a halo effect that results in a positive impression. By contrast, the halo effect of an unfamiliar hairstyle or manner of dressing may create a negative impression.

Halo effects cause the same problems as stereotypes. They obscure individual differences. The person who smiles might have a very negative work attitude; the person with the unique hairstyle might be a top performer. Halo effects are especially significant in performance evaluations where one factor, such as a person's punctuality or lack of it, may become the halo that inaccurately determines the overall performance rating.

Selective perception is the tendency to focus attention on aspects of a situation or a person that reinforce or appear consistent with existing beliefs, needs, or actions.[4] In short, we perceive what fits and screen out the rest. This often happens in organizations when people from different departments or functions—such as marketing or information systems—tend to see things only from their own point of view.

Like the other perceptual distortions, selective perception can bias our views of situations and individuals. One of the great benefits of teamwork and consultative decision making is the pooling of ideas and perceptions of many people, thus making it harder for selective perception to create problems.

Projection occurs when we assign our personal attributes to other individuals. Some call this the "similar-to-me" error. An example is to assume that other persons share our needs, desires, and values. Suppose you enjoy a lot of responsibility and challenge in your work as a team leader. You might try to increase responsibilities and challenges for team members, wanting them to experience the same satisfactions as you. But this involves projection. Instead of designing jobs to best fit their needs, you have designed their jobs to

Common Perceptual Distortions

- *Stereotypes*—put people into categories and then use attributes of the category to describe the individual. Example: He's close to retirement; too old to learn the new technology.
- *Halo effects*—use one characteristic of a person or situation to form an overall impression. Example: She's always at work early; she's a great performer.
- *Selective perception*—focuses attention on things consistent with existing beliefs, needs, and actions. Example: Sales are down; I knew the new product design was flawed.
- *Projection*—assumes others are just like us and assigns our attributes to them. Example: I'll schedule planning meetings for 7:30 AM; it feels good to get an early start.

A **stereotype** assigns attributes commonly associated with a group to an individual.

A **halo effect** uses one attribute to develop an overall impression of a person or situation.

Selective perception focuses attention on things consistent with existing beliefs, needs, or actions.

Projection assigns personal attributes to other individuals.

Bias Against Black Leaders Found on the Football Field

Are black leaders at a disadvantage when leadership success is evaluated? The answer is "yes" according to research reported in the *Academy of Management Journal*. Scholars Andrew M. Carton and Ashleigh Shelby Rosette studied how the performance of football quarterbacks was reported in the news. They found that successful performances by black quarterbacks were attributed less often to competence—such as "making decisions under pressure"—and more often to factors that made up for incompetence—such as having "the speed to get away." The researchers expressed concern that black leaders may suffer from poor career advancement because of biased evaluations.

Sportschrome/NewsCom

fit yours. An individual team member may be quite satisfied and productive doing his or her current job, one that seems routine to you. We can control projection errors through self-awareness and a willingness to communicate and empathize with other persons—that is, to try to see things through their eyes.

PERCEPTION CAN CAUSE ATTRIBUTION ERRORS.

Attribution is the process of creating explanations for events.

One of the ways in which perception exerts its influence on behavior is through **attribution**. This is the process of developing explanations for events and their perceived causes. It is natural for people to try to explain what they observe and the things that happen to them. Suppose you perceive that someone else in a job or student group isn't performing up to expectations. How do you explain this? And, depending on the explanation, what do you do to try to correct things?

When considering so-called poor performance by someone else, we are likely to commit something called **fundamental attribution error**. This is a tendency to blame other people when things go wrong, whether or not this is really true. If I perceive that a student is doing poorly in my course, for example, this error pops up as a tendency to criticize the student's lack of ability or unwillingness to study hard enough. But that perception may not be accurate, as you may well agree. Perhaps there's something about the course design, its delivery, or my actions as an instructor that is contributing to the problem—a deficiency in the learning environment, not the individual.

The **fundamental attribution error** overestimates internal factors and underestimates external factors as influences on someone's behavior.

Self-serving bias underestimates internal factors and overestimates external factors as influences on someone's behavior.

Suppose you are having a performance problem—at school, at work, wherever. How do you explain it? Again, the likelihood of attribution error is high; this time it is called **self-serving bias**. It's the tendency for people to blame personal failures or problems on external causes rather than accept personal responsibility. This is the "It's not my fault!" error. The flip side is to claim personal responsibility for any successes—"It was me; I did it!"

Fundamental Attribution Error *"It's their fault."* ← They are performing poorly | I am performing poorly → Self-Serving Bias *"It's not my fault."*

The significance of these attribution errors can be quite substantial. When we perceive things incorrectly, we are likely to take the wrong actions and miss solving a lot of problems in the process. Think about self-serving bias the next time you hear someone blaming your

---

ABOUT 15%, CALLED "HIGH MEDIA MULTITASKERS," PERFORMED BETTER WHEN MIXING THINGS LIKE MUSIC AND E-MAIL WITH THEIR WORK.

HOT TOPIC

Perception Alert! Some Teens Do Best While Multitasking

Eugenio Marongiu/iStockphoto/Getty Images

"She's multitasking again. I'll have to get her refocused." How often has a parent, teacher, or supervisor said something to this effect? It's a common belief that multitasking—called polychronicity by psychologists—is bad, but overgeneralizing can be a perceptual mistake.

An award-winning research project by two high school students in Portland, Oregon, suggests this isn't always the case. In a study of 400 teens, Sara Caulfield and Alexandra Ulmer found that the performance of most suffered

when they were multitasking, consistent with the stereotype. But about 15% performed better when mixing things like music and e-mail with their work. Called "high media multitaskers," they performed contrary to the stereotype. When it comes to multitasking and performance, Caulfield and Ulmer suggest the lesson may be that one size doesn't fit all.

HOW ABOUT IT?

Are you a multitasker when it comes to things like schoolwork and teamwork? How does it influence your performance? Does this research sound on-target or not? How can a team leader support "high media multitaskers" who perform well while discouraging multitasking by those who don't?

instructor for a poor course grade. And think about the fundamental attribution error the next time you jump on a group member who didn't perform according to your standards. Our perceptions aren't always wrong, but they should always be double-checked and tested for accuracy. There are no safe assumptions when it comes to the power of attributions.

IMPRESSION MANAGEMENT INFLUENCES HOW OTHERS PERCEIVE US.

Richard Branson, CEO of the Virgin Group, may be one of the richest and most famous executives in the world. One of his early business accomplishments was the successful start-up of Virgin Airlines, which became a new competitive force in the airline industry. The former head of British Airways, Lord King, once said: "If Richard Branson had worn a shirt and tie instead of a goatee and jumper, I would not have underestimated him."[5] This is an example of how much our impressions count—both positive and negative. Knowing this, scholars now emphasize the importance of **impression management**, the systematic attempt to influence how others perceive us.[6]

> **Impression management** tries to create desired perceptions in the eyes of others.

You might notice that we often do bits and pieces of impression management as a matter of routine in everyday life. This is especially evident when we enter new situations—perhaps a college classroom or new work team; in what we post on Facebook or Twitter; and as we prepare to meet people for the first time, such as going out with a new friend for a social occasion or heading off to a job interview. In these and other situations we tend to dress, talk, act, and surround ourselves with things that help convey a desirable self-image to other persons.

Impression management that is well done can help us advance in jobs and careers, form relationships with people we admire, and even create pathways to desired social memberships. Some basic tactics are worth remembering: knowing when to dress up and when to dress down to convey positive appeal in certain situations, using words to flatter other people in ways that generate positive feelings toward you, making eye contact and smiling when engaged in conversations to create a personal bond, and displaying a high level of energy that indicates work commitment and initiative.[7]

AMBITION SHOWS UP IN PERSONALITY AS COMPETITIVENESS AND A DESIRE TO BE THE BEST.

EXPLORE YOURSELF

Ambition

People are different; our styles vary in the way we work, the way we relate to others, and even in how we view ourselves. One of the differences you might observe when interacting with other people is in **ambition**, or the desire to succeed and reach for high goals.

Ambition is one of those traits that can certainly have a big impact on individual behavior. It is evident in how we act and what we try to achieve at work, at home, and in leisure pursuits. It comes out in personality as competitiveness and desire to be the best at something.

At it's best, ambition is a personal differentiator to be admired. But beware of its downsides. Overly ambitious people may exaggerate their accomplishments to themselves and others. They also may try to do too much and end up highly stressed and even accomplishing less than

they otherwise could. And, ambitious people who lack integrity can get trapped into corruption and misbehavior. They sacrifice right from wrong in the quest for success.

It's important to keep ambition on your side. The more we understand ambition in our lives, the more successful we're likely to be in accomplishing our goals and helping others do the same.

Get to know yourself better by taking the **Stress Test** self-assessment and completing other activities in the *Exploring Management* **Skill-Building Portfolio**.

STUDYGUIDE

Takeaway 11.1
How Do Perceptions Influence Individual Behavior?

Terms to Define

Attribution

Fundamental attribution error

Halo effect

Impression management

Perception

Projection

Selective perception

Self-serving bias

Stereotype

Rapid Review

- Perception acts as a filter through which all communication passes as it travels from one person to the next.
- Different people may perceive the same things differently.
- Stereotypes, projections, halo effects, and selective perception can distort perceptions and reduce communication effectiveness.
- Fundamental attribution error occurs when we blame others for their performance problems, without considering possible external causes.
- Self-serving bias occurs when, in judging our own performance, we take personal credit for successes and blame failures on external factors.
- Through impression management, we influence the way that others perceive us.

Questions for Discussion

1. How do advertising firms use stereotypes to influence consumer behavior?
2. Are there times when a self-serving bias is actually helpful?
3. Does the notion of impression management contradict the idea of personal integrity?

Be Sure You Can

- **describe** how perception influences behavior
- **explain** how stereotypes, halo effects, selective perceptions, and projection might operate in the workplace
- **explain** the concepts of attribution error and self-serving bias
- **illustrate** how someone might use impression management during a job interview

Career Situation: What Would You Do?

While standing in line at the office coffee machine, you overhear the person in front of you saying this to his friend: "I'm really tired of having to deal with the old-timers here. It's time for them to call it quits. There's no way they can keep up the pace and handle all the new technology we're getting these days." You can listen and forget, or you can listen and act. Take the action route. What would you do or say here, and why?

Takeaway 11.2
How Do Personalities Influence Individual Behavior?

ANSWERS TO COME

- The Big Five personality traits describe important individual differences.
- The Myers-Briggs Type Indicator is a popular approach to personality assessment.
- Personalities vary on personal conception traits.
- People with Type A personalities tend to stress themselves.
- Stress has consequences for performance and health.

THINK OF HOW MANY TIMES YOU'VE COMPLAINED ABOUT SOMEONE'S "BAD personality" or told a friend how much you like someone else because they had such a "nice personality." Well, the same holds true at work. Perhaps you have been part of or the subject of conversations like these: "I can't give him that job. He's a bad fit; with a personality like that, there's no way he can work with customers." Or "Put Erika on the project; her personality is perfect for the intensity that we expect from the team."

The term **personality** describes the combination or overall profile of enduring characteristics that make each of us unique. And as the prior examples suggest, this uniqueness can have consequences for how we behave and how that behavior is regarded by others.

Personality is the profile of characteristics making a person unique from others.

THE BIG FIVE PERSONALITY TRAITS DESCRIBE IMPORTANT INDIVIDUAL DIFFERENCES.

We all know that variations among personalities are both real and consequential in our relationships with everyone from family to friends to co-workers. Scholars have identified a significant list known as the Big Five: extraversion, agreeableness, conscientiousness, emotional stability, and openness to experience.[8]

Take a look at the descriptions in Tips to Remember—How to Identify the Big Five Personality Traits. You can probably spot variations in the Big Five pretty easily in people with whom you work, study, and socialize, as well as in yourself. And while you're at it, why not use the tips as a quick check of your personality? Ask: What are the implications for my personal and work relationships?

A considerable body of research links the Big Five personality traits with work

> **TIPS TO REMEMBER**
> How to Identify the Big Five Personality Traits
>
> **Extraversion**—An extravert is talkative, comfortable, and confident in interpersonal relationships; an introvert is more private, withdrawn, and reserved.
>
> **Agreeableness**—An agreeable person is trusting, courteous, and helpful, getting along well with others; a disagreeable person is self-serving, skeptical, and tough, creating discomfort for others.
>
> **Conscientiousness**—A conscientious person is dependable, organized, and focused on getting things done; a person who lacks conscientiousness is careless, impulsive, and not achievement oriented.
>
> **Emotional stability**—A person who is emotionally stable is secure, calm, steady, and self-confident; a person lacking emotional stability is excitable, anxious, nervous, and tense.
>
> **Openness to experience**—A person open to experience is broad-minded, imaginative, and open to new ideas; a person who lacks openness is narrow-minded, has few interests, and resists change.

and career outcomes. The expectation is that people with more extraverted, agreeable, conscientious, emotionally stable, and open personalities will have more positive relationships and experiences in organizations.[9] Conscientious persons tend to be highly motivated and high-performing in their work, whereas emotionally stable persons tend to handle change situations well. It's also likely that Big Five traits are implicit criteria used by managers when making judgments about people at work, handing out job assignments, building teams, and more. Psychologists even use the Big Five to steer people in the direction of career choices that may provide the best personality–job fits. Extraversion, for example, is a good predictor of success in management and sales positions.

THE MYERS-BRIGGS TYPE INDICATOR IS A POPULAR APPROACH TO PERSONALITY ASSESSMENT.

Something known as the Myers-Briggs Type Indicator is a popular approach to personality assessment. It uses a sophisticated questionnaire to examine how people act or feel in various situations. Called the MBTI for short, it was developed by Katherine Briggs and her daughter Isabel Briggs Myers from foundations set forth in the work of psychologist Carl Jung.[10]

Jung's model of personality differences included three main distinctions. First are personality differences in ways people relate with others—extraversion (being outgoing and sociable) or introversion (being shy and quiet). Second is how people vary in the way they gather information—by sensation (emphasizing details, facts, and routine) or by intuition (looking for the "big picture" and being willing to deal with various possibilities). Third, are differences in evaluating information—by thinking (using reason and analysis) or by feeling (responding to the feelings and desires of others).

Briggs and Briggs Myers adopted Jung's personality model but added a fourth dimension to it. It describes how people vary in the ways they relate to the outside world—judging (seeking order and control) or perceiving (acting with flexibility and spontaneity). What is now called the Myers-Briggs Type Indicator includes all four of the following personality dimensions:[11]

- *Extraversion versus introversion (E or I)*—whether a person tends toward being outgoing and sociable or shy and quiet.
- *Sensing versus intuitive (S or N)*—whether a person tends to focus on details or on the big picture in dealing with problems.
- *Thinking versus feeling (T or F)*—whether a person tends to rely on logic or emotions in dealing with problems.
- *Judging versus perceiving (J or P)*—whether a person prefers order and control or acts with flexibility and spontaneity.

Sample Myers-Briggs Personality Types

ESTJ (extraverted, sensing, thinking, judging)—practical, decisive, logical, and quick to dig in; common among managers.

ENTJ (extraverted, intuitive, thinking, judging)—analytical, strategic, forceful, quick to take charge; common for leaders.

ISFJ (introverted, sensing, feeling, judging)—conscientious, considerate, and helpful; common among team players.

INTJ (introverted, intuitive, thinking, judging)—insightful, free thinking, determined; common for visionaries.

The MBTI instrument can be easily found and completed online. A person's scores allow them to be categorized into one of 16 possible personality types, such as the sample personalities shown in the small box. This neat and understandable classification has made the MBTI very popular in management training and development, although it receives mixed reviews from researchers.[12] Employers and consultants tend to like it because once a person is "typed" on the Myers-Briggs, for example as an ESTJ or ISFJ, they can be trained to both understand their own styles and to learn how to better work with people having different styles.

PERSONALITIES VARY ON PERSONAL CONCEPTION TRAITS.

YES OR NO? There are certain subjects in college that I'll never do well in.

YES OR NO? I study every day because it is important.

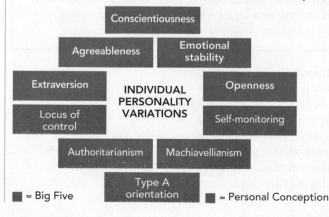

= Big Five   = Personal Conception

Questions like those just posed are sources of personality insight. They and others like them are often used in personality screening by potential employers, colleges and graduate schools, and even relationship partners.

Think about it. What personality do you project when interacting with others socially and at work? Look at the figure. How do you stack up on the Big Five? And, how do you stack up on additional personal conception traits like locus of control, authoritarianism, Machiavellianism, self-monitoring, and Type A orientation.[13]

Look back at the above questions. They really test the extent to which you believe your future is controlled by others and outside events ("Yes" to the first question) or by yourself ("Yes" to the second question).[14] Scholars call this a difference in **locus of control**. Their point is that some people believe they control their destinies, whereas others believe what happens is beyond their control.[15] "Internals" are more self-confident and accept responsibility for their own actions. "Externals" are prone to blaming others and outside forces when bad things happen. Interestingly, research suggests that internals tend to be more satisfied and less alienated from their work.

> **Locus of control** is the extent to which one believes what happens is within one's control.

Authoritarianism is the degree to which a person defers to authority and accepts status differences.[16] Someone with an authoritarian personality might act rigid and control-oriented as a leader. Yet, this same person is often subservient as a follower. People with an authoritarian personality tend to obey orders. Of course, this can create problems when their supervisors ask them to do unethical or even illegal things.

> **Authoritarianism** is the degree to which a person defers to authority and accepts status differences.

In his 16th-century book *The Prince*, Niccolo Machiavelli gained lasting fame for his advice on how to use power to achieve personal goals.[17] Today we use the term **Machiavellianism** to describe someone who acts manipulatively and emotionally detached when using power. We usually view a "high-Mach" personality as exploitative and unconcerned about others, seemingly guided only by a belief that the end justifies the means. Those with "low-Mach" personalities, by contrast, allow others to exert power over them.

> **Machiavellianism** is the degree to which someone uses power manipulatively.

Finally, **self-monitoring** reflects the degree to which someone is able to adjust and modify behavior in new situations.[18] Persons high in self-monitoring tend to be learners, comfortable with feedback, and both willing and able to change. Because they are flexible, however, others may perceive them as constantly shifting gears and hard to read. A person low in self-monitoring is predictable and tends to act consistently. But this consistency may not fit the unique needs of differing circumstances.

> **Self-monitoring** is the degree to which someone is able to adjust behavior in response to external factors.

PEOPLE WITH TYPE A PERSONALITIES TEND TO STRESS THEMSELVES.

Stress is a state of tension experienced by individuals facing extraordinary demands, constraints, or opportunities.[19] As you consider stress in your life and in your work, you might think about how your personality deals with it. Researchers describe the **Type A personality**, also shown among the personality traits in the last figure, as someone who is oriented toward high achievement, impatience, and perfectionism. Because of this, Type A's are likely to bring stress on themselves even in circumstances that others find relatively stress-free.[20]

> **Stress** is a state of tension experienced by individuals facing extraordinary demands, constraints, or opportunities.

> A **Type A personality** is oriented toward extreme achievement, impatience, and perfectionism.

The work environment has enough potential *stressors*, or sources of stress, without this added burden of a stress-prone Type A personality. Some 87% of American workers in one

---

COME TO THE OFFICE A BIT EARLY, SAY 7:30 AM, HE'S ALREADY THERE. DO A BIT EXTRA AND LEAVE AT 6 PM, HE'S STILL HARD AT WORK.

ETHICS CHECK

My Team Leader Is a Workaholic

Hero Images/Getty Images

Dear Management Coach: I'm stuck. My new team leader is an absolute workaholic. I mean he's great in terms of personality, support, task direction— all things a great team leader is supposed to be. But the killer is that he just works all the time; I don't know if he ever sleeps. Come to the office a bit early, say 7:30 AM, he's already there. Do a bit extra and leave at 6 PM, he's still hard at work. What I'm worried about is the hidden expectation in his behavior: "If I can do it, you can, too!" I'm ready to work hard and put in extra hours as needed. However, I have a personal life and lots of other responsibilities. I need this job and I like the work. I'm getting stressed out over what is going to come up when performance reviews are due in about 2 months. Should I confront him with my concerns?

YOUR DECISION?

As the coach, what do you recommend? And how do you read the ethics issues? When a team leader works day and night, is this putting pressure on team members to do the same? Should a team leader who behaves this way "come clean" and tell everyone upfront that they shouldn't let it influence their behavior? When team members see a leader or teammate behaving this way, should they bring the issue up to clarify expectations and make sure that the behavior pattern isn't a signal of personal problems that need attention?

survey said they experienced stress at work, whereas 34% of workers in another survey said that their jobs were so stressful that they were thinking of quitting.[21] The stress they were talking about comes from long hours of work, unreasonable workloads, low pay, difficult bosses or co-workers, and not working in a desired career field.[22]

As if work stress isn't enough for Type A's to deal with, there's the added kicker of always-on technology and complicated personal lives. Things such as family events (e.g., the birth of a new child), economics (e.g., a sudden loss of extra income), and personal issues (e.g., a preoccupation with a bad relationship) are sources of potential emotional strain for most people, but especially for Type A's. Such personal stressors can spill over to negatively affect our behavior at work. Of course, the reverse also holds true—work stressors can spill over to affect our personal lives.

STRESS HAS CONSEQUENCES FOR PERFORMANCE AND HEALTH.

It's tempting to view stress all in the negative. But remember the analogy of a violin.[23] When a violin string is too loose, the sound produced by even the most skilled player is weak and raspy. When the string is too tight, the sound gets shrill and the string might even snap. But when the tension on the string is just right, it creates a beautiful sound.

Constructive stress is a positive influence on effort, creativity, and diligence in work.

Constructive stress is energizing and performance enhancing.[24] You've probably felt it as a student. Don't you sometimes do better work "when the pressure is on," as we like to say? Moderate but not overwhelming stress can help us by encouraging effort, stimulating creativity, and enhancing diligence. But just like tuning a violin string, achieving the right balance of stress for each person and situation is difficult.

Destructive stress is a negative influence on one's performance.

Intense or Long-term Stress → **Exhaustion and Burnout** • Lack of energy • Emotional distress • Bad attitude • Poor self-esteem → **Possible Effects** • Lower performance • Lower satisfaction • Workplace rage • Personal problems • Poor health

Destructive stress is or seems so intense or long-lasting that it overloads and breaks down a person's physical and mental systems. One of its workplace outcomes is **job burnout**. This is a sense of physical and mental exhaustion that drains our energies both personally and professionally. Too much stress can also cause **flameout**, where someone communicates extreme agitation in interpersonal relationships or electronic messages. Think of it as the e-mail message that you wish you'd thought twice about before hitting the "send" button.

Job burnout is physical and mental exhaustion from work stress.

A flameout occurs when we communicate extreme agitation in interpersonal relationships or electronic messages.

Yet another possible outcome of excessive stress is **workplace rage** in the form of overly aggressive—even violent—behavior toward co-workers, bosses, or customers.[25] An extreme example called "bossnapping" made the news when French workers at a Caterpillar plant held their manager hostage for 24 hours in protest of layoffs. A local sociologist said: "Kidnapping your boss is not legal. But it's a way workers have found to make their voices heard."[26]

Workplace rage is aggressive behavior toward co-workers or the work setting.

Medical research also indicates that too much stress can be bad for health. It reduces resistance to disease and increases the likelihood of hypertension, ulcers, substance abuse, overeating, and depression.[27] But, the good news is that it can be managed.

The best stress management strategy is to prevent it from reaching excessive levels in the first place. If we know we have a Type A personality and can identify our stressors, we can often take action to avoid or minimize their negative consequences. And as managers, we can take steps to help others who are showing stress symptoms. Things like temporary changes in work schedules, reduced performance expectations, long deadlines, and even reminders to take time off can all help.

Personal wellness is the pursuit of a personal health-promotion program.

Ultimately, there is really no substitute for **personal wellness** in the form of a personal health-promotion program.[28] It begins by taking personal responsibility for your physical and mental health. It means getting rest, getting plenty of exercise, and eating a balanced diet. It means dealing with addictions to cigarettes, alcohol, or drugs. And it means committing to a healthy lifestyle, one that helps you deal with stress and the demands of life and work.

STUDYGUIDE

Takeaway 11.2
How Do Personalities Influence Individual Behavior?

Terms to Define

Agreeableness	Emotional stability	Machiavellianism	Stress
Authoritarianism	Extraversion	Openness to experience	Type A personality
Conscientiousness	Flameout	Personal wellness	Workplace rage
Constructive stress	Job burnout	Personality	
Destructive stress	Locus of control	Self-monitoring	

Rapid Review

- The Big Five personality factors are extraversion, agreeableness, conscientiousness, emotional stability, and openness.
- The Myers-Briggs Type Indicator (MBTI) identifies personality types based on extraversion–introversion, sensing–intuitive, thinking–feeling, and judging–perceiving.
- Additional personality dimensions of work significance are locus of control, authoritarianism, Machiavellianism, self-monitoring, and Type A orientation.
- Stress is a state of tension that accompanies extraordinary demands, constraints, or opportunities.
- For some people, having a Type A personality creates stress as a result of continual feelings of impatience and pressure.
- Stress can be destructive or constructive; a moderate level of stress can have a positive impact on performance.

Questions for Discussion

1. Which personality trait would you add to the Big Five to make it the Big "Six"?
2. What are the advantages and disadvantages of having people of different MBTI types working on the same team?
3. Can you be an effective manager and not have a Type A personality?

Be Sure You Can

- **list** the Big Five personality traits and give work-related examples of each
- **list** five more personality traits and give work-related examples for each
- **list** and explain the four dimensions used to create personality types in the MBTI
- **identify** common stressors in work and personal life
- **describe** the Type A personality
- **differentiate** constructive and destructive stress
- **explain** personal wellness as a stress management strategy

Career Situation: What Would You Do?

You've noticed that one of your co-workers is always rushing, always uptight, and constantly criticizing herself while on the job. She never takes time for coffee with the rest of the team. Even at lunch it's hard to get her to sit and just talk for awhile. Your guess is that she's a Type A and fighting stress from some source or sources other than the nature of the job itself. How can you help her out?

Takeaway 11.3
How Do Attitudes, Emotions, and Moods Influence Individual Behavior?

ANSWERS TO COME

■ Attitudes predispose people to act in certain ways.

■ Job satisfaction is a positive attitude toward one's job and work experiences.

■ Job satisfaction influences work behaviors.

■ Job satisfaction has a complex relationship with job performance.

■ Emotions and moods are states of mind that influence behavior.

AT ONE TIME, CHALLIS M. LOWE WAS ONE OF ONLY TWO AFRICAN-AMERICAN women among the five highest-paid executives in more than 400 U.S. corporations.[29] She attained this success after a 25-year career that included several changes of employers and lots of stressors—working-mother guilt, a failed marriage, gender bias on the job, and an MBA degree earned part-time. "I've never let being scared stop me from doing something," she said. "Just because you haven't done it before doesn't mean you shouldn't try." Would you agree that Lowe has what we often call a "can-do" attitude?

ATTITUDES PREDISPOSE PEOPLE TO ACT IN CERTAIN WAYS.

> An **attitude** is a predisposition to act in a certain way.

An **attitude** is a predisposition to act in a certain way toward people and environmental factors.[30] Challis Lowe seemed disposed to take risks and embrace challenges. This positive attitude influenced her behavior when dealing with the inevitable problems, choices, and opportunities of work and career.

The three components shown in the small figure help us understand attitudes. First is the *cognitive component* of the attitude. It reflects a belief or value. You might believe, for example, that your management course is very interesting. Second is the *affective* or *emotional component*, which reflects a specific feeling. For example, you might feel very good about being a management major. Third is the *behavioral component*, which reflects an intention to behave consistent with the belief and feeling. Using the same example again, you might say to yourself: "I am going to work hard and try to get A's in all my management courses."

Have you noticed that attitudes don't always predict behavior? Despite pledging to work hard as a student, you might not. Despite wanting a more challenging job, you might keep the current one. In such cases we fail to live up to our own expectations. Usually it's not a good feeling.

Three Components of Attitudes

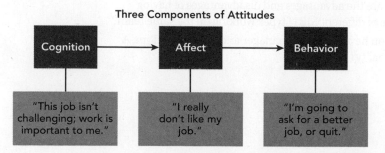

> **Cognitive dissonance** is discomfort felt when attitude and behavior are inconsistent.

The psychological concept of **cognitive dissonance** describes the discomfort we feel in situations where our attitude is inconsistent with our behavior.[31] Most of us manage this dissonance by modifying our attitude to better fit the behavior ("Oh well, work isn't really that important, anyway"), changing future behavior to fit the attitude (not putting extra time in at work; focusing more attention on leisure and personal hobbies), or rationalizing in ways that make the attitude and behavior seem compatible ("I'm in no hurry; there will be a lot of opportunities for better jobs in the future").

JOB SATISFACTION IS A POSITIVE ATTITUDE TOWARD ONE'S JOB AND WORK EXPERIENCES.

People hold attitudes about many things in the workplace—bosses, each other, tasks, organizational policies, performance goals, paychecks, and more. A comprehensive or catch-all work attitude is **job satisfaction**, the degree to which an individual feels positive or negative about various aspects of his or her job and work experiences.[32]

> **Job satisfaction** is the degree to which an individual feels positive about a job and work experience.

If you watch or read the news, you'll regularly find reports on job satisfaction. You'll also find lots of job satisfaction studies in the academic literature. Interestingly, the majority of people tend to report being at least somewhat satisfied with their jobs. But the trend is down.[33]

The least satisfying things about people's jobs often relate to feeling underpaid, not having good career advancement opportunities, and being trapped in the current job. And in respect to things that create job satisfaction, a global study finds that pay is less important than things like opportunities to do interesting work, recognition for performance, work–life balance, chances for advancement, and job security.[34]

> ### Aspects of Job Satisfaction
>
> - *Job tasks*—responsibility, interest, challenge.
> - *Quality of supervision*—task help, social support.
> - *Co-workers*—harmony, respect, friendliness.
> - *Opportunities*—promotion, learning, growth.
> - *Pay*—actual and comparative.
> - *Work conditions*—comfort, safety, support.
> - *Security*—job and employment.

JOB SATISFACTION INFLUENCES WORK BEHAVIORS.

Researchers tell us that there is a strong relationship between job satisfaction and the **withdrawal behaviors** of *absenteeism*—not showing up for work—and *turnover*—quitting one's job. In respect to absenteeism, workers who are more satisfied with their jobs are absent less often than those who are dissatisfied. In respect to turnover, satisfied workers are more likely to stay and dissatisfied workers are more likely to quit their jobs. The consequences of absenteeism and excessive turnover can be expensive for employers. In fact, one study found that changing retention rates—up or down—results in similar changes to corporate earnings.[35]

> **Withdrawal behaviors** include absenteeism (not showing up for work) and turnover (quitting one's job).

Researchers also identify a relationship between job satisfaction and **organizational citizenship behaviors**.[36] They show up as a willingness to "go beyond the call of duty" or "go the extra mile."[37] A person who is a good organizational citizen does things that, although not required, help advance the performance of the organization. You might observe this as a service worker who takes especially good care of a customer, a team member who always takes on extra tasks, or a friend who is working extra hours without pay just to make sure things are done right for his employer.

> **Organizational citizenship behaviors** are things people do to go the extra mile in their work.

The flip side of positive organizational citizenship is antisocial and counterproductive behavior that disrupts work processes, relationships, teamwork, satisfaction, and performance.[38] **Incivility** is antisocial behavior that shows up as individual or group displays of disrespectful acts, social exclusion, and use of language that is hurtful to others. **Bullying** is antisocial behavior, again individual or group, that is intentionally aggressive, intimidating, demeaning, and/or abusive toward the recipients. Both incivility and bullying behaviors are clearly different from what might be considered just one-time "bad" behaviors.[39]

> **Incivility** is antisocial behavior in the forms of disrespectful acts, social exclusion, and use of hurtful language.

> **Bullying** is antisocial behavior that is intentionally aggressive, intimidating, demeaning, and/ or abusive.

Job satisfaction is also tied with **employee engagement**, a strong sense of belonging or connection with one's job and employer. It shows up both in *high involvement*—being willing to help others and always trying to do something extra to improve performance, and in *high commitment*—feeling and speaking positively about the organization. A survey of American workers by the Gallup Organization suggests that more engaged workforces generate higher profits for employers.[40] Things that counted most toward employee engagement in this research were believing one has the opportunity to do the best every day, believing one's opinions are valued, believing fellow workers are committed to quality, and believing there is a direct connection between one's work and the company's mission.

> **Employee engagement** is a strong sense of belonging and connection with one's work and employer.

FACTS TO CONSIDER

Paying a High Price for Incivility at Work

ProStockStudio/Shutterstock.com

Look for losses in the bottom line when rudeness rules the workplace. Most managers say they are against incivility and try to stop it whenever they can. But it's also the case that managers don't have a good handle on the real costs incurred when employees are rude and disrespectful toward one another. When researchers asked 800 workers from different industries about how they responded when exposed to incivility at work, results showed:

- 80% lost work time due to worry
- 78% were less committed to the organization
- 63% performed less well
- 48% decreased work effort
- 47% cut back time spent at work
- 25% took frustration out on customers

YOUR THOUGHTS?

Have you been on the receiving end of incivility? Is incivility taking a toll on the teams and organizations in your life? Is improved civility a hidden pathway to higher performance in our workplaces? How can such improvements be achieved? Are you, for one, ready to put your best foot forward?

JOB SATISFACTION HAS A COMPLEX RELATIONSHIP WITH JOB PERFORMANCE.

We know that job satisfaction influences withdrawal, citizenship, and engagement. But, does it influence performance? The data are, as you might expect, somewhat complicated.[41] Consider a sign that once hung in a tavern near a Ford plant in Michigan: "I spend 40 hours a week here, am I supposed to work too?" Three different arguments on the satisfaction and performance relationship are shown in the small figure. Can you make a case for each argument based on your personal experiences?

There is probably a modest link between job satisfaction and performance.[42] But emphasize the word "modest." We can't conclude that making people happy is a surefire way to improve their job performance. The reality is that some people will like their jobs, be very satisfied, and still not perform very well. That's part of the complexity of individual behavior.

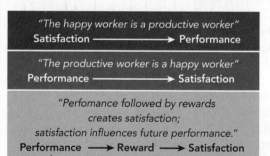

"The happy worker is a productive worker"
Satisfaction ⟶ Performance

"The productive worker is a happy worker"
Performance ⟶ Satisfaction

"Performance followed by rewards creates satisfaction; satisfaction influences future performance."
Performance ⟶ Reward ⟶ Satisfaction

It's also true that high-performing workers are likely to feel satisfied. But again, some people may work with high performance without experiencing high job satisfaction. Has this ever happened for you?

Finally, job satisfaction and job performance do influence each other. But the relationship depends a lot on rewards. High performance followed by rewards that are valued and perceived as fair is likely to create job satisfaction. This satisfaction, in turn, can be expected to increase motivation to work hard to achieve high performance in the future. The catch to this relationship, however, is difficulty making sure rewards are valued and perceived as fair by the recipient.

EMOTIONS AND MOODS ARE STATES OF MIND THAT INFLUENCE BEHAVIOR.

SITUATION: The Boeing 787 Dreamliner is falling further behind on its promised delivery schedule. Boeing's head of Asia-Pacific sales, John Wojick, is in a meeting with his boss. After a "heated" discussion over delivery dates and customer promises, Wojick storms out. He says: "Quite frankly we were failing at meeting our commitment to customers. Some of us may have been able to handle our emotions a little better than others." Wojick is described by others as having "an understated manner" and an underlying "fiery temper."[43]

Looking at this incident we might say that Wojick was emotional about the fact that his customers weren't being well served. His temper flared and anger got the better of him during the meeting. Whether that was good or bad for his customers . . . for him . . . and for his boss, is an open question. But for a time at least, he and the boss both probably ended up in bad moods because of their stressful confrontation.

Emotions

An **emotion** is a strong positive or negative feeling directed toward someone or something. For example, you might feel positive emotion or elation when an instructor congratulates you on a fine class presentation; you might feel negative emotion or anger when an instructor criticizes you in front of the class. In both cases the object of your emotion is the instructor, but in each case the impact of the instructor's behavior on your feelings is quite different. And your behavior in response to the aroused emotions is likely to differ as well—perhaps breaking into a wide smile with the compliment or making a nasty side comment in response to criticism.

Emotional intelligence is an important human skill for managers and an important leadership capability. Daniel Goleman defines "EI" as an ability to understand emotions in ourselves and in others and to use this understanding to manage relationships effectively.[44] His point in highlighting the importance of emotional intelligence is that we perform better in work and social situations when we are good at recognizing and dealing with emotions in ourselves and others. In other words, EI allows us to avoid having our emotions "get the better of us." But what is an "emotion"? And, how does it influence our behavior—positively and negatively?

Moods

Whereas emotions tend to be short-term and clearly targeted, **moods** are generalized positive and negative states of mind that may persist for some time. Everyone seems to have occasional moods, and we each know the full range of

> **Understanding Emotions**
>
> "I was really mad when Prof. Nitpicker criticized my presentation."
> - Linked with a specific cause
> - Tends to be brief or episodic
> - Specific effect on attitude, behavior
> - Might turn into a mood

Emotions are strong feelings directed toward someone or something.

Emotional intelligence, or **EI**, is an ability to understand emotions and manage relationships effectively.

Moods are generalized positive and negative states of mind.

> **Understanding Moods**
>
> "I just feel lousy today and don't have any energy. I've been down all week."
> - Hard to identify cause
> - Tends to linger, be long-lasting
> - General effect on attitude, behavior
> - Can be "negative" or "positive"

15% OF AMERICAN WORKERS DON'T TAKE ALL THEIR VACATION DAYS . . . SOME EUROPEANS CONSIDER THIS SOMETHING JUST SHORT OF CRAZY.

QUICK CASE

Come On, Take Your Vacation Already

PBNJ Productions/Getty Images

Once again Julie is leaving vacation days on the table. Out of the 3 weeks available to her this year she used just 6 days! She's always talking about things she'd like to do in her free time, people she'd like to spend more time with, and places she would like to visit. But it's all talk. She just works. You just heard on the radio that 15% of American workers don't take all their vacation days, and that some Europeans consider this something just short of crazy. The reporter said that some sacrifice vacations to create positive impressions in the quest for promotions. Others consider it a badge of honor—"I haven't taken vacation in 2 years!" Still others just seem addicted to their work.

WHAT DO YOU DO

What's a team leader to do when people don't take vacation? Is it a personal choice and none of the team leader's business? Or, is it something to worry about in terms of stress, burnout, and potential lost productivity? Julie reports to you. Is this a "turn a blind eye" situation for you, or is it one that merits active intervention as team leader? Just what will you do and why?

possibilities they represent. How often do you wake up in the morning and feel excited, refreshed, and just happy? Or, wake up feeling low, depressed, and generally unhappy? How do these different moods affect your behavior with friends and family, and at work or school?

When it comes to moods in the workplace, a *Businessweek* article claims that it pays to be likable.[45] Harsh is out and caring is in. Some CEOs are even hiring executive coaches to help them manage emotions and moods so as to come across as more personable and friendly in relationships with others.

There's a bit of impression management to consider here. If a CEO—or team leader or manager—goes to a meeting in a good mood and gets described as "cheerful," "charming," "humorous," "friendly," and "candid," she or he may be viewed as on the upswing. But if a person is in a bad mood and comes away perceived as "prickly," "impatient," "remote," "tough," "acrimonious," or even "ruthless," she or he may be seen as on the downhill slope.

> **Mood contagion** is the spillover of one's positive or negative moods onto others.

Researchers are very interested in **mood contagion**, the spillover effects of one's mood onto others.[46] It turns out that positive emotions of leaders can be "contagious," causing followers to display more positive moods and also be both more attracted to the leaders and willing to rate the leaders more highly. As you might expect, such contagion can also spread negative moods. And, unfortunately, we tend to be self-centered when thinking about our moods. But, it's important to recognize their possible contagion effects on the moods of co-workers and teammates, as well as family and friends.[47]

Little Things Are Big Things at Life Is Good

You Can Decide You're Going to Be Happy Today

Erick Jacobs/The New York Times/Redux Pictures

Imagine! Yes, you can! Go for it! Life is good.

Thoughts like these can help turn your dreams into reality. They also built a multimillion-dollar company that really is named Life Is Good. It began with two brothers—Bert and John Jacobs—making T-shirts adorned with smiling faces and happy slogans for street sales. Picture an empty card table and the two brothers realizing they have come up with a viable business idea.

Bert—Chief Executive Optimist—and John—Chief Creative Optimist—built a company devoted to humor and humility. John says: "It's important that we're saying 'Life is good,' not 'Life is great' or 'Life is perfect'; there's

a big difference. . . . . Don't determine that you're going to be happy when you get the new car or the big promotion or meet that special person. You can decide that you're going to be happy today." That's the message of the Life Is Good brand: "The little things in life are the big things."

Life Is Good didn't start with business degrees or experience. But Bert and John had good instincts, creativity, and a positive view on life. They stuck to their values while learning about business as their firm grew. They still live the brand while enjoying leisure pursuits and supporting philanthropic enterprises.

FIND INSPIRATION

Just how far can positive thinking carry these two entrepreneurs? How about the rest of us? Is there more to be gained by looking for positives than negatives in our everyday experiences and relationships with others? Who's in charge of the "good" factor in your life?

STUDYGUIDE

Takeaway 11.3
How Do Attitudes, Emotions, and Moods Influence Individual Behavior?

Terms to Define

Attitude	Emotional intelligence	Mood	Withdrawal behaviors
Bullying	Employee engagement	Mood contagion	
Cognitive dissonance	Incivility	Organizational citizenship behaviors	
Emotion	Job satisfaction		

Rapid Review

- An attitude is a predisposition to respond in a certain way to people and things.
- Cognitive dissonance occurs when a person's attitude and behavior are inconsistent.
- Job satisfaction is an important work attitude, reflecting a person's evaluation of the job, co-workers, and other aspects of the work setting.
- Job satisfaction influences withdrawal behaviors of absenteeism and turnover, and organizational citizenship behaviors.
- Job satisfaction has a complex and reciprocal relationship with job performance.
- Emotions are strong feelings that are directed at someone or something; they influence behavior, often with intensity and for short periods of time.
- Moods are generalized positive or negative states of mind that can be persistent influences on one's behavior.

Questions for Discussion

1. Is cognitive dissonance a good or bad influence on us?
2. How can a manager deal with someone who has high job satisfaction but is a low performer?
3. What are the lessons of mood contagion for how a new team leader should behave?

Be Sure You Can

- **identify** the three components of an attitude
- **explain** cognitive dissonance
- **describe** possible measures of job satisfaction
- **explain** the consequences of job satisfaction for absenteeism and turnover
- **explain** the link between job satisfaction, organizational citizenship, and employee engagement
- **list** and describe three alternative explanations in the job satisfaction–performance relationship
- **explain** how emotions and moods influence work behavior

Career Situation: What Would You Do?

Your team leader has just told you that some of your teammates have complained that you have been in a really bad mood lately and it is rubbing off on the others. They like you and point out that this isn't characteristic of you at all. They don't know what to do about it. Can they do anything to help? Is there anything your team leader might do? What is your responsibility here, and how can you best handle the situation?

TEST PREP 11

Answers to Test Prep questions can be found at the back of the book.

Multiple-Choice Questions

1. Among the Big Five personality traits, _____ indicates someone who tends to be responsible, dependable, and careful in respect to tasks.
   (a) authoritarian
   (b) agreeable
   (c) conscientious
   (d) emotionally stable

2. A person with a/an _____ personality would most likely act unemotional and manipulative when trying to influence others to achieve personal goals.
   (a) extroverted
   (b) sensation-thinking
   (c) self-monitoring
   (d) Machiavellian

3. When a person tends to believe that he or she has little influence over things that happen in life, this indicates a/an _____ personality.
   (a) low emotional stability
   (b) external locus of control
   (c) high self-monitoring
   (d) intuitive-thinker

4. How is a person with an authoritarian personality expected to act?
   (a) Strong tendency to obey orders
   (b) Challenges the authority of others
   (c) Tries to play down status differences
   (d) Always flexible in personal behavior

5. A new team leader who designs jobs for persons on her work team mainly "because I would prefer to work the new way rather than the old" is committing a perceptual error known as _____.
   (a) the halo effect
   (b) stereotyping
   (c) impression management
   (d) projection

6. If a manager allows one characteristic of a person—say, a pleasant personality—to bias performance ratings of that individual overall, the manager is falling prey to a perceptual distortion known as _____.
   (a) the halo effect
   (b) impression management
   (c) stereotyping
   (d) projection

7. Use of special dress, manners, gestures, and vocabulary words when meeting a prospective employer in a job interview are all examples of how people use _____ in daily life.
   (a) the halo effect
   (b) impression management
   (c) introversion
   (d) mood contagion

8. _____ is a form of attribution error that involves blaming the environment for problems that we may have caused ourselves.
   (a) Self-serving bias
   (b) Fundamental attribution error
   (c) Projection
   (d) Self-monitoring

9. _____ is a form of attribution error that involves blaming others for problems that they may not have caused for themselves.
   (a) Self-serving bias
   (b) Fundamental attribution error
   (c) Projection
   (d) Self-monitoring

10. The _____ component of an attitude is what indicates a person's belief about something, whereas the _____ component indicates a specific positive or negative feeling about it.
    (a) cognitive; affective
    (b) emotional; affective
    (c) cognitive; attributional
    (d) behavioral; attributional

11. The term for the discomfort someone feels when his or her behavior is inconsistent with a previously expressed attitude is _____.
    (a) alienation
    (b) cognitive dissonance
    (c) job dissatisfaction
    (d) job burnout

12. Job satisfaction is known from research to be a strong predictor of _____.
    (a) personality
    (b) job burnout
    (c) conscientiousness
    (d) absenteeism

13. A person who is always willing to volunteer for extra work or to help someone else with his or her work is acting consistent with strong _____.
    (a) job performance
    (b) self-serving bias
    (c) emotional intelligence
    (d) organizational citizenship

14. A/an _____ represents a rather intense but short-lived feeling about a person or a situation, whereas a/an _____ describes a more generalized positive or negative state of mind.
    (a) attitude; emotion
    (b) external locus of control; internal locus of control
    (c) self-serving bias; halo effect
    (d) emotion; mood

15. Which statement about the job satisfaction–job performance relationship is most accurate based on research?
    (a) A happy worker will be a productive worker.
    (b) A productive worker will be a happy worker.
    (c) A productive worker well rewarded for performance will be a happy worker.
    (d) There is no relationship between being happy and being productive in a job.

Short-Response Questions

16. What is the most positive profile of Big Five personality traits in terms of positive impact on work behavior?

17. What is the relationship between personality and stress?

18. How does the halo effect differ from selective perception?

19. If you were going to develop a job satisfaction survey, exactly what would you try to measure?

Integration and Application Question

20. When Scott Tweedy picked up a magazine article on "How to Manage Health Care Workers," he was pleased to find some apparent advice. Scott was concerned about poor performance by several of the respiratory therapists in his clinic. The author of the article said that the "best way to improve performance is to make your workers happy." Well, Scott was happy on reading this and made a pledge to himself to start doing a much better job of "making the therapists happy in the future."

    Questions: Is Scott on the right track? Should he charge ahead as planned, or should he be concerned about this advice? What do we know about the relationship between job satisfaction and performance, and how can this understanding be used by Scott in this situation?

Steps for Further Learning

BUILD MARKETABLE SKILLS • **DO** A CASE ANALYSIS • **GET** AND STAY INFORMED

BUILD MARKETABLE SKILLS.

EARN BIG CAREER PAYOFFS!

Don't miss these opportunities in the SKILL-BUILDING PORTFOLIO

SELF-ASSESSMENT 11:
Stress Test

Stress can take its toll . . . learn how to recognize the symptoms.

CLASS EXERCISE 11:
Job Satisfaction Preferences

Not everyone wants the same things . . . it's important to understand individual differences.

TEAM PROJECT 11:
Difficult Personalities

Sometimes it's hard to get along . . . difficult personalities are a challenge.

Many learning resources are found at the end of the book and online within **WileyPLUS Learning Space.**

Practice Critical Thinking—Complete the CHAPTER 11 CASE

CASE SNAPSHOT: Panera—A Company with Personality

Panera Bread is in the business of satisfying customers. With fresh-baked breads, gourmet soups, and efficient service, the franchise has surpassed all expectations for success. How did a start-up food company grow so fast and stay so successful? To answer this question, you have to study founder Ron Shaich, understand his background and values, and appreciate both his entrepreneurship and his personality.

DO A CASE ANALYSIS.

STRENGTHEN YOUR CRITICAL THINKING!

MANAGER'S LIBRARY SELECTION
Read for Insights and Wisdom
Women Count: *A Guide to Changing the World* (2010, Purdue University Press) by Susan Bulkeley Butler

The bottom line in Susan Bulkeley Butler's book is that action is needed to ensure the progress of more women into leadership roles. She urges women to stop accepting underrepresentation in leadership and, instead, to take action. Butler advises women to start by helping themselves, which may require rebalancing roles in their work, home, and personal life. She believes that women can't master these roles separately and thus suffer from obligation guilt. So, they must redefine the roles with the help of employers. An example is the attorney who relocated so her children's grandparents could assist with child care. The firm assigned her cases she could work on from home, and the flexibility in rebalancing her work, family, and personal roles was essential to her success.

GET AND STAY INFORMED.

MAKE YOURSELF VALUABLE!

Butler cites research that women are good for performance. Companies with the most women either on their board of directors or in top management positions outperform those with the least women measured by return on equity. She asserts that this is because women possess behavioral advantages over men—things like being more compassionate, less ego-driven, listening better, taking fewer risks, and tending to be consensus builders. In response, Butler advises organizations to appoint at least two women to the board, have women report directly to the CEO, and create mentoring programs for female leaders. Policies allowing women to rebalance life roles must also be commonplace.

REFLECT AND REACT If women are good for performance, why don't more women already lead large companies? Do you expect this situation to change substantially during your career? How can work, family, and personal roles of women conflict? What can organizations and their leaders do in support of professional females? What can a woman really do to "balance" multiple role expectations?

When J. K. Rowling finished the first of her Harry Potter books, she was a single mother living on just over $100 a week. "You sort of start thinking anything's possible," she once said, "if you've got enough nerve."

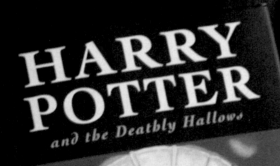

Motivation

12

Respect Unlocks Human Potential

Management Live

Dear CEO—"How About a $10,000 Raise?"

Glowimages/Getty Images

That's the message sent to Wells Fargo bank's CEO John Stumpf by Tyrel Oates, a $15 per hour employee. The e-mail pointed out that Stumpf earned $19 million the past year. Claiming that the issue was "income inequality," Oates said: "My proposal is to take $3 billion, just a small fraction of what Wells Fargo pulls in annually, and raise every employee's annual salary by $10,000 . . . an hourly raise of $4.71 per hour." He encouraged Stumpf to lead by example and show "it is very possible to maintain a profitable company that not only looks out for its consumers and shareholders, but its employees as well."

HOW ABOUT IT?

Where do you stand on the income inequality issue? Does Oates have a legitimate point? Are CEOs overpaid relative to hourly workers? And, by the way, Oates sent a copy of his e-mail to 200,000 Wells Fargo employees. Was he in the wrong to share his message so widely?

WHAT'S INSIDE

ETHICS CHECK
Information goldmine is an equity dilemma

FACTS TO CONSIDER
Europe turns to quotas to increase female board members

HOT TOPIC
Rewarding mediocrity begins at an early age

QUICK CASE
Restaurant chain serves up no-tipping policy

YOUR CHAPTER 12 TAKEAWAYS

1. Describe how human needs influence motivation to work.

2. Identify how thoughts and decisions affect motivation to work.

3. Understand how reinforcement influences motivation to work.

Takeaway 12.1
How Do Human Needs Influence Motivation to Work?

ANSWERS TO COME

- Maslow describes a hierarchy of needs topped by self-actualization.
- Alderfer's ERG theory discusses existence, relatedness, and growth needs.
- McClelland identifies acquired needs for achievement, power, and affiliation.
- Herzberg's two-factor theory focuses on higher-order need satisfaction.
- The core characteristics model integrates motivation and job design.

Did you know that J. K. Rowling's first *Harry Potter* book was rejected by 12 publishers; that the Beatles' "sound" cost them a deal with Decca Records; and, that Walt Disney lost a newspaper job because he supposedly "lacked imagination"?[1] Thank goodness they didn't give up. Their "motivation" to stay engaged, hard working, and confident in their work paid off abundantly—for them and for the millions who have enjoyed the fruits of their labors.

Did you also know that only about 13% of global workers surveyed by Gallup self-report as actively "engaged" while 24% say they are actively "disengaged" on any given workday . . . that 25% of American employers believe their workers have low morale . . . that up to 40% of workers say that they have trouble staying motivated?[2] They sure aren't acting like J. K. Rowling, the Beatles, or Walt Disney. Instead, their behavior raises questions: Why do some of us work enthusiastically, persevere in the face of difficulty, and often exceed the requirements of our jobs? Why do others hold back, quit at the first negative feedback, and do the minimum needed to avoid reprimand or termination? What can be done to ensure that the best possible performance is achieved by every person, at every task, in every job, on every workday?

In management, we use the term **motivation** to describe forces within the individual that account for the level, direction, and persistence of effort expended at work. Simply put, a highly motivated person works hard at a job; an unmotivated person does not. A manager who leads through motivation creates conditions that consistently inspire other people to work hard.

MASLOW DESCRIBES A HIERARCHY OF NEEDS TOPPED BY SELF-ACTUALIZATION.

One of the best starting points in exploring the issue of motivation are theories from psychology that deal with differences in individual **needs**—unfulfilled desires that stimulate people to behave in ways that will satisfy them. And as you might expect, there are different theories about human needs and how they may affect people at work.

Abraham Maslow's theory of human needs is an important foundation in the history of management thought. He described a hierarchy built on a foundation of **lower-order needs** (physiological, safety, and social concerns) and moving up to **higher-order needs** (esteem and self-actualization).[3] Whereas lower-order needs focus on physical well-being and companionship, the higher-order needs reflect psychological development and growth.

A key part of Maslow's thinking relies on two principles. The *deficit principle* states that a satisfied need is not a motivator of behavior. People act in ways that satisfy deprived needs, ones for which a "deficit" exists. We eat because we are hungry; we call a friend when we are lonely; we seek approval from others when we are feeling insecure. The *progression principle* states that people try to satisfy lower-level needs first and then move step by step up the hierarchy. This happens until the level of self-actualization is reached. The more

---

Motivation accounts for the level, direction, and persistence of effort expended at work.

A **need** is an unfulfilled physiological or psychological desire.

Lower-order needs are physiological, safety, and social needs in Maslow's hierarchy.

Higher-order needs are esteem and self-actualization needs in Maslow's hierarchy.

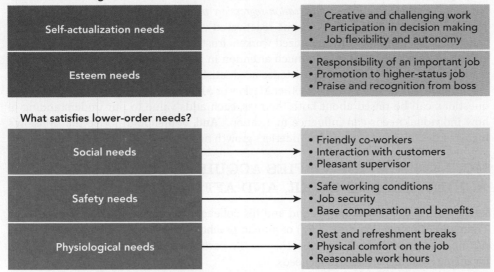

What satisfies higher-order needs?

| Self-actualization needs | → | • Creative and challenging work
• Participation in decision making
• Job flexibility and autonomy |
| Esteem needs | → | • Responsibility of an important job
• Promotion to higher-status job
• Praise and recognition from boss |

What satisfies lower-order needs?

Social needs	→	• Friendly co-workers • Interaction with customers • Pleasant supervisor
Safety needs	→	• Safe working conditions • Job security • Base compensation and benefits
Physiological needs	→	• Rest and refreshment breaks • Physical comfort on the job • Reasonable work hours

FIGURE 12.1 What Are the Opportunities for Need Satisfaction in Maslow's Hierarchy?
For higher-order need satisfaction, people realize self-actualization by doing creative and challenging work and participating in important decisions; they boost self-esteem through promotions and praise and by having responsibility for an important job. For lower-order need satisfaction, people meet social needs through positive relationships with co-workers, supervisors, and customers; they achieve safety needs in healthy working conditions and a secure job with good pay and benefits; and they realize physiological needs by having reasonable work hours and comfortable work spaces.

these needs are satisfied, the stronger they will grow. Maslow believes opportunities for self-fulfillment should continue to motivate a person as long as the other needs remain satisfied.

Maslow's theory is a good starting point for examining human needs and their potential influence on motivation. It seems to make sense, for example, that managers should try to understand the needs of people working with and for them. And isn't it a manager's job to help others find ways of satisfying their needs through work? **Figure 12.1** gives some suggestions along these lines.

ALDERFER'S ERG THEORY DISCUSSES EXISTENCE, RELATEDNESS, AND GROWTH NEEDS.

A well-regarded alternative to Maslow's work is the ERG theory proposed by Clayton Alderfer.[4] His theory collapses Maslow's five needs into three. **Existence needs** are desires for physiological and material well-being. **Relatedness needs** are desires for satisfying interpersonal relationships. **Growth needs** are desires for continued psychological growth and development.

Growth needs are essentially the higher-order needs in Maslow's hierarchy. And they are important. Consider this example.[5] Laine Seator lost her management job and started volunteering during the recession. After putting in 35-hour weeks working for five different organizations, she realized her time helping others was well spent. She gained new skills in grant writing and strategic planning that strengthened her résumé. "In a regular job," she says, "you'd need to be a director or management staff to be able to do these types of things, but on a volunteer basis they welcome the help." And at a United Way in Boise, Idaho, volunteer Rick Overton says: "It's hard to describe how much better it feels to get to the end of the day and, even if you haven't made any money, feel like you did some good for the world." Don't Laine and Rick sound like motivated workers finding lots of higher-order growth need satisfaction through volunteer and nonprofit work?

It's worth noting that ERG theory disagrees with Maslow's deficit and progression principles. Instead, Alderfer suggests that any or all of the needs can influence individual behavior

Existence needs are desires for physiological and material well-being.

Relatedness needs are desires for satisfying interpersonal relationships.

Growth needs are desires for continued psychological growth and development.

at any given time. He also believes that a satisfied need doesn't lose its motivational impact. Instead, Alderfer describes a *frustration-regression principle* through which an already-satisfied lower-level need can become reactivated when a higher-level need cannot be satisfied. Perhaps this is why unionized workers frustrated by assembly-line jobs (lacking growth need satisfaction) give so much attention in labor negotiations to things like job security and wage levels (offering existence need satisfaction).

You shouldn't be quick to reject either Maslow or Alderfer in favor of the other. Although questions can be raised about both theories, each adds value to our understanding of how individual needs can influence motivation.[6] And, you should notice that Maslow's higher-order needs match up with Alderfer's growth needs.

MCCLELLAND IDENTIFIES ACQUIRED NEEDS FOR ACHIEVEMENT, POWER, AND AFFILIATION.

> **Need for achievement** is the desire to do something better, to solve problems, or to master complex tasks.
>
> **Need for power** is the desire to control, influence, or be responsible for other people.
>
> **Need for affiliation** is the desire to establish and maintain good relations with people.

In the late 1940s, David McClelland and his colleagues began experimenting with the Thematic Apperception Test (TAT) of human psychology.[7] The TAT asks people to view pictures and write stories about what they see. Researchers then analyze the stories, looking for themes that display individual needs.

From this research McClelland identified three acquired needs that he considers central to understanding human motivation. The **need for achievement** is the desire to do something better or more efficiently, to solve problems, or to master complex tasks. The **need for power** is the desire to control other people, to influence their behavior, or to be responsible for them. The **need for affiliation** is the desire to have friendly and warm relations with other people.

Work Preferences of High Need Achievers
• Individual responsibilities
• Challenging but achievable goals
• Performance feedback

McClelland encourages managers to learn how to recognize the strength of these needs in themselves and in other people. Because each need can be associated with a distinct set of work preferences, his insights offer helpful ideas for designing jobs and creating work environments that are rich in potential motivation.

Consider someone high in the need for achievement. Do you, for example, like to put your competencies to work, take moderate risks in competitive situations, and often prefer to work alone? Need achievers are like this, and their work

HopeLab Fights Disease with Fun
Video Games Motivates Kids to Take Medicine

Joshua Sudock/MCT/Newscom

Although many teens play video games just for fun, teens with cancer can now play ones that can help them beat the disease. Picture a teenager who has a tough time keeping up with cancer medication schedules. Now imagine him playing the video game called Re-Mission and maneuvering a nanobot called Roxxi through the body of a cancer patient to destroy cancer cells. And, then think about an article in the medical journal *Pediatrics* that says teen patients who play the game at least 1 hour a week do a better job of sticking to their medication schedules.

What's taking place is the brainchild of HopeLab, founded by Pam Omidyar. An immunology researcher and gaming enthusiast, she saw the possible link between games and fighting disease. The nonprofit's mission is combining "rigorous research with innovative solutions to improve the health and quality of life of young people with chronic illness."

One of HopeLabs' recent products is Zamzee, described as a "game-based website." It includes an activity meter where kids earn points for movement and activity. A research study using a control group concluded that "kids using Zamzee increased their moderate-to-vigorous physical activity (MVPA) by an average of 59%—or approximately 45 additional minutes of MVPA per week."

FIND INSPIRATION

Re-Mission is one positive step in the war against childhood cancer. One of HopeLab's current priorities is to use video gaming in the fight against childhood obesity. Think about how creative approaches to motivation might be used to improve lives in other ways as well.

preferences usually follow a pattern. Persons high in need for achievement like work that offers challenging but achievable goals, feedback on performance, and individual responsibility. If you take one or more of these away, they are likely to become frustrated, and their performance may suffer. As a manager, these preferences offer pretty straightforward insights for dealing with a high need achiever. And if you are high in need for achievement, these are things you should be talking about with your manager.

McClelland's theory offers good insights about the other needs as well. People high in the need for affiliation prefer jobs offering companionship, social approval, and satisfying interpersonal relationships. People high in the need for power are motivated to behave in ways that have a clear impact on other people and events; they enjoy being in positions of control.

Importantly, McClelland distinguishes between two forms of the power need.[8] The need for *personal power* is exploitative and involves manipulation purely for the sake of personal gratification. As you might imagine, this type of power need is not respected in management. By contrast, the *need for social power* is the positive face of power. It involves the use of power in a socially responsible way, one that is directed toward group or organizational objectives rather than personal ones. This need for social power is essential to managerial leadership.

> ### Two Types of Power Needs
>
> • *Need for personal power*—seeking power for personal gratification.
> • *Need for social power*—seeking power to help people and groups achieve goals.

One interesting extension of McClelland's research found that successful senior executives often had high needs for social power that, in turn, were higher than their also strong needs for affiliation. Can you explain these results? It may be that managers high in the need for affiliation alone may let their desires for social approval interfere with business decisions. But with a higher need for power, they may be more willing to sometimes act in ways that other persons may disagree with. In other words, they'll do what is best for the organization, even if it makes some people unhappy. Does this make sense?

HERZBERG'S TWO-FACTOR THEORY FOCUSES ON HIGHER-ORDER NEED SATISFACTION.

Frederick Herzberg's work on human needs took a slightly different route. He began with extensive interviews of people at work and then content-analyzed their answers. The result is known as the two-factor theory.[9]

When questioned about what "turned them on," Herzberg found that workers mainly talked about the nature of the job itself—such things as a sense of achievement, feelings of recognition, a sense of responsibility, the opportunity for advancement, and feelings of personal growth. In other words, they told him about what they did. Herzberg called these **satisfier factors**, or *motivator factors*, and described them as part of *job content*. They are consistent with the higher-order needs of Maslow, growth needs of Alderfer, and achievement and power needs of McClelland.

A **satisfier factor** is found in job content, such as a sense of achievement, recognition, responsibility, advancement, or personal growth.

When questioned about what "turned them off," Herzberg found that his respondents talked about quite different things—working conditions, interpersonal relations, organizational policies and administration, technical quality of supervision, and base wage or salary. They were telling him about where they worked, not about what they did. Herzberg called these **hygiene factors** and described them as part of *job context*. They seem most associated with Maslow's lower-order needs, Alderfer's existence and relatedness needs, and McClelland's affiliation need.

A **hygiene factor** is found in the job context, such as working conditions, interpersonal relations, organizational policies, and salary.

Herzberg's two-factor theory is shown in **Figure 12.2**. Hygiene factors influence job dissatisfaction, whereas satisfier factors influence job satisfaction. The distinction is important. Herzberg is saying that you can't increase job satisfaction by improving the hygiene factors. You will only get less dissatisfaction. Although minimizing dissatisfaction is a worthy goal, you can't expect much by way of increased motivation. At least that's his theory.

Scholars have criticized Herzberg's research as method-bound and difficult to replicate. But still, the two-factor theory makes us think about both job content and job context.[10] It's a

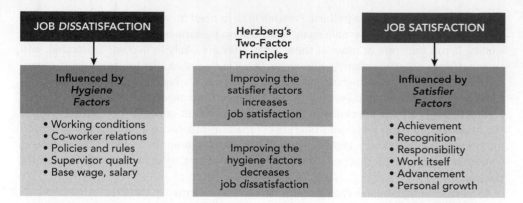

FIGURE 12.2 What Are the Motivational Implications of Job Content and Job Context in Herzberg's Two-Factor Theory?

Scholars criticize this theory because of its research foundations. However, Herzberg makes an interesting and useful distinction between the motivational implications of job content and job context. He believes that you can't increase job satisfaction and motivation by improving hygiene factors in the job context, for example, by increasing wages. This only reduces levels of dissatisfaction. Instead, he argues in favor of improving satisfier factors in the job content, things like responsibility and recognition. In the two-factor theory, such changes are pathways to higher job satisfaction and motivation.

reminder that managers shouldn't expect too much in the way of motivational gains from investments in things like pleasant work spaces and even high base salaries. Instead, it focuses our attention on building jobs to provide opportunities for responsibility, growth, and other sources of higher-order need satisfactions. And to create these high-content jobs, Herzberg suggests allowing people to manage themselves and exercise self-control over their work.

THE CORE CHARACTERISTICS MODEL INTEGRATES MOTIVATION AND JOB DESIGN.

If you really think about it, you should see that for a job to be highly motivational, there has to be a good fit between the needs and talents of the individual and tasks to be performed. And as you might expect, just what constitutes a good fit is going to vary from one individual and situation to the next. **Job design** is the allocation of specific work tasks to individuals and groups.[11] Its goal is a good person–job fit.

Herzberg, known for the two-factor theory just discussed, poses the job design challenge this way: "If you want people to do a good job, give them a good job to do."[12] He goes on to argue that this is best done through **job enrichment**, the practice of designing jobs rich in content that offer opportunities for higher-order need satisfaction. For him, an enriched job allows the individual to perform planning and controlling duties normally done by supervisors. In other words, job enrichment involves a lot of self-management.

Modern management theory values job enrichment and its motivating potential. In true contingency fashion, however, it recognizes that not everyone wants or needs an enriched job. The core characteristics model developed by J. Richard Hackman and his associates helps managers design jobs that best fit the needs of different people.[13]

Figure 12.3 shows that the core characteristics model approaches job design with a focus on five "core" job characteristics: skill variety, task identity, task significance, autonomy, and job feedback. Can you think of specific jobs that might score high and low on these characteristics? Here's a bit more detail on them.

Job design is the allocation of specific work tasks to individuals and groups.

Job enrichment increases job content by adding work planning and evaluating duties normally performed by the supervisor.

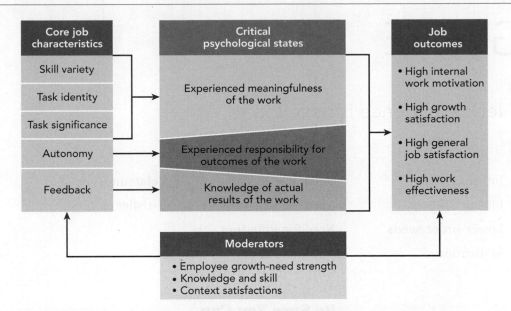

FIGURE 12.3 How Do Core Characteristics Influence Motivation Through Job Design?

This model shows how jobs can be designed according to five core characteristics—skill variety, task identity, task significance, autonomy, and feedback. Jobs that are high in these characteristics provide jobholders with experienced meaningfulness and responsibility as well as knowledge of results. Under the right contingency conditions—high growth need strength and satisfaction with job context—these critical psychological states are motivational and set the stage for positive job outcomes.

1. *Skill variety*—the degree to which a job requires a variety of different activities to carry out the work and involves the use of a number of different skills and talents of the individual

2. *Task identity*—the degree to which the job requires completion of a "whole" and identifiable piece of work, one that involves doing a job from beginning to end with a visible outcome

3. *Task significance*—the degree to which the job has a substantial impact on the lives or work of other people elsewhere in the organization or in the external environment

4. *Autonomy*—the degree to which the job gives the individual freedom, independence, and discretion in scheduling work and in choosing procedures for carrying it out

5. *Feedback from the job itself*—the degree to which work activities required by the job result in the individual obtaining direct and clear information on his or her performance

The higher a job scores on the five core characteristics, the more enriched it is. But as you consider this model, don't forget the contingency logic. It recognizes that not everyone will be a good fit for a highly enriched job. Whether a person does fit well in an enriched job depends on the presence of three "moderators," also shown Figure 12.3. People are expected to respond most favorably to job enrichment when they have strong growth needs, have appropriate job knowledge and skills, and are otherwise satisfied with the job context. When these conditions are weak or absent, the fit between the individual and an enriched job may turn out less favorably than expected.

STUDYGUIDE

Takeaway 12.1
How Do Human Needs Influence Motivation to Work?

Terms to Define

Existence needs	Job design	Need	Relatedness needs
Growth needs	Job enrichment	Need for achievement	Satisfier factors
Higher-order needs	Lower-order needs	Need for affiliation	
Hygiene factors	Motivation	Need for power	

Rapid Review

- Motivation involves the level, direction, and persistence of effort expended at work; a highly motivated person can be expected to work hard.
- Maslow's hierarchy of human needs moves from lower-order physiological, safety, and social needs up to higher-order ego and self-actualization needs.
- Alderfer's ERG theory identifies existence, relatedness, and growth needs.
- McClelland's acquired needs theory identifies the needs for achievement, affiliation, and power, all of which may influence what a person desires from work.
- Herzberg's two-factor theory identifies satisfier factors in job content as influences on job satisfaction; hygiene factors in job context are viewed as influences on job dissatisfaction.
- The core characteristics model of job design focuses on skill variety, task identity, task significance, autonomy, and feedback.

Questions for Discussion

1. Was Maslow right in suggesting we each have tendencies toward self-actualization?
2. Is high need for achievement always good for managers?
3. Why can't job enrichment work for everyone?

Be Sure You Can

- **describe** work practices that can satisfy higher-order needs in Maslow's hierarchy
- **contrast** Maslow's hierarchy with ERG theory
- **explain** needs for achievement, affiliation, and power in McClelland's theory
- **differentiate** the needs for personal and social power
- **describe** work preferences for a person with a high need for achievement
- **describe** differences in hygiene and satisfier factors in Herzberg's theory
- **explain** how a person's growth needs and job skills might affect his or her responses to job enrichment

Career Situation: What Would You Do?

Two student workers are being considered for promotions at a campus recreation center that you manage. One works really well with people and seems to thrive on teamwork and social interaction. The other tackles tough jobs with enthusiasm and always wants to do her best, while preferring to do things alone rather than with others. The center's staff is expanding and you have flexibility to design jobs to best fit each student. What jobs might you create for them, and why?

Takeaway 12.2
How Do Thoughts and Decisions Affect Motivation to Work?

ANSWERS TO COME

- Equity theory explains how social comparisons motivate individual behavior.
- Expectancy theory focuses on the decision to work hard, or not.
- Goal-setting theory shows that the right goals can be motivating.

HAVE YOU EVER RECEIVED AN EXAM OR PROJECT GRADE AND FELT GOOD ABOUT IT, only to get discouraged when you hear about someone who didn't work as hard getting the same or a better grade? Or, have you ever suffered a loss of motivation when the goal set by your boss or instructor seems so high that you don't see any chance at all of succeeding?

My guess is that most of us have had these types of experiences, and perhaps fairly often. They raise the question of exactly what influences decisions to work hard or not in various situations. The equity, expectancy, and goal-setting theories of motivation offer possible answers.

EQUITY THEORY EXPLAINS HOW SOCIAL COMPARISONS MOTIVATE INDIVIDUAL BEHAVIOR.

The equity theory of motivation is best known in management through the work of J. Stacy Adams.[14] Based on the logic of social comparisons, it pictures us continually checking our rewards for work accomplished against those of others. Any perceived inequities in these comparisons are uncomfortable. This makes us motivated to act in ways that restore a sense of equity to the situation. Think of it this way.

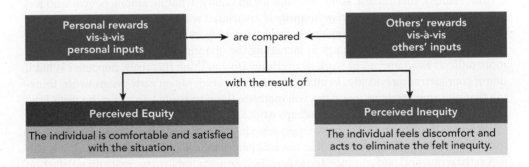

| Personal rewards vis-à-vis personal inputs | are compared | Others' rewards vis-à-vis others' inputs |

with the result of

| Perceived Equity | Perceived Inequity |
| The individual is comfortable and satisfied with the situation. | The individual feels discomfort and acts to eliminate the felt inequity. |

Check these equity dynamics against your own experiences. How have you reacted when your grade seems unfair compared with others? Did you reduce your efforts in the future . . . drop the course . . . rationalize that you really didn't work that hard . . . complain to the instructor and request a higher grade? All of these are ways to reduce the perceived grading inequity. And they are the same types of behaviors that perceived inequity can motivate people to engage in at work. Only instead of grades, the sources of inequity are more likely to be pay raises, job assignments, work schedules, office "perks," and the like. Pay, of course, is the really big one!

Research on equity theory has largely occurred in the laboratory. It is most conclusive with respect to **perceived negative inequity**—feeling uncomfortable at being unfairly treated. People who feel underpaid, for example, may experience disappointment or even a sense of anger. They will be motivated to try to restore perceived equity to the situation. This might be done by reducing work efforts to compensate for the missing rewards—"If that's all I'm going to get, I'm going to do a lot less!"; asking for more rewards or better treatment—"Next stop the boss's office: I should get what I deserve!"; or even by quitting the job—"That's it, I'm out of here!"[15]

Perceived negative inequity is discomfort felt over being harmed by unfair treatment.

ETHICS CHECK

Information Goldmine Is an Equity Dilemma

Image Source/Getty Images

A worker opens the top of the office photocopier and finds a document someone has left behind. It's a list of performance evaluations, pay, and bonuses for 80 co-workers.

She reads the document. Lo and behold, someone she considers a "nonstarter" is getting paid more than others regarded as "super workers." New hires are also being brought in at much higher pay and bonuses than those of existing staff. And to make matters worse, she's in the middle of the list and not near the top, where she would have expected to be. The fact is she makes a lot less money than many others.

Looking at the data, she begins to question why she is spending extra hours working on her laptop evenings and weekends at home, trying to do a really great job for the firm. She wonders to herself: "Should I pass this information around anonymously so that everyone knows what's going on? Or should I quit and find another employer who fully values me for my talents and hard work?"

In the end she decides to quit, saying: "I just couldn't stand the inequity." She also decides not to distribute the information to others in the office because "it would make them depressed, like it made me depressed."

YOUR DECISION?

What would you do in this situation? You're going to be concerned and perhaps upset. Would you hit "print," make about 80 copies, and put them in everyone's mailboxes—or even just leave them stacked in a couple of convenient locations? That would get the information out into the gossip chains pretty quickly. But is this ethical? If you don't send out the information, on the other hand, is it ethical to let other workers go about their days with inaccurate assumptions about the firm's pay practices? By quitting and not sharing the information, did this worker commit an ethics mistake?

Perceived positive inequity is discomfort felt over benefitting from unfair treatment.

Interestingly, there is also some evidence for an equity dynamic among people who feel overpaid. This **perceived positive inequity** is associated with a sense of guilt. It is discomfort felt over benefitting from unfair treatment. The individual is motivated to restore perceived equity by doing such things as increasing the quantity or quality of work, taking on more difficult assignments, or working overtime. Do you think this really happens? What if one of your instructors decides to inflate the grades of students on early assignments, thinking that perceived positive inequities will motivate them to study harder for the rest of the course? Would you work harder or perhaps work less?

Although there are no clear answers available in equity theory, there are some very good insights. The theory is a reminder that rewards perceived as equitable should positively affect satisfaction and performance; those perceived as inequitable may create dissatisfaction and cause performance problems.[16] Probably the best advice is to anticipate potential equity problems from social comparisons whenever rewards of any type are being allocated. It's important to recognize that people may compare themselves not only with co-workers but also with others elsewhere in the organization, including senior executives, and even persons employed by other organizations. And, we should always remember that people behave according to their perceptions. If someone perceives inequity in a work situation, it is likely to affect his or her behavior whether the manager sees things the same way or not.

EXPECTANCY THEORY FOCUSES ON THE DECISION TO WORK HARD, OR NOT.

Expectancy is a person's belief that working hard will result in high task performance.

Victor Vroom offers another approach to understanding motivation. His expectancy theory asks: What determines the willingness of an individual to work hard at tasks important to the organization?[17] Vroom answers this question with an equation: Motivation = Expectancy × Instrumentality × Valence.

The terms in this expectancy equation are defined as follows. **Expectancy** is a person's belief that working hard will result in achieving a desired level of task performance (sometimes called *effort-performance expectancy*). **Instrumentality** is a person's belief that successful performance will lead to rewards and other potential outcomes (sometimes called *performance-outcome expectancy*). **Valence** is the value a person assigns to the possible rewards and other work-related outcomes. Think of them this way.

Instrumentality is a person's belief that various outcomes will occur as a result of task performance.

Valence is the value a person assigns to work-related outcomes.

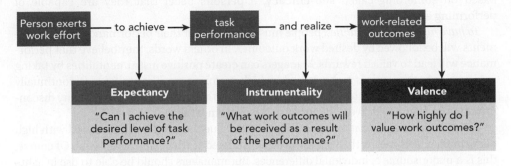

Expectancy	**Instrumentality**	**Valence**
"Can I achieve the desired level of task performance?"	"What work outcomes will be received as a result of the performance?"	"How highly do I value work outcomes?"

The use of multiplication signs in the expectancy equation ($M = E \times I \times V$) has important implications. Mathematically speaking, a zero at any location on the right side of the equation will result in zero motivation. This means that we cannot neglect any of the three factors—expectancy, instrumentality, or valence. For motivation to be high, all three must be positive.

Are you ready to test this theory? Most of us assume that people will work hard to get promoted. But is this necessarily true? Expectancy theory predicts that motivation to work hard for a promotion will be low if any one or more of three conditions apply. If *expectancy is low*, motivation suffers. The person feels that he or she cannot achieve the performance level necessary to get promoted. So why try? If *instrumentality is low*, motivation suffers. The person lacks confidence that high performance will actually result in being promoted. So why try? If *valence is low*, motivation suffers. The person doesn't want a promotion, preferring less responsibility in the present job. So, if it isn't a valued outcome, why work hard to get it?

Figure 12.4 summarizes the management implications of expectancy theory. It is a reminder that different people are likely to come up with different answers to the question: Why should I work hard today? Knowing that their answers will differ, Vroom's point is that each person must be respected as an individual with unique work needs, preferences, and concerns. His theory identifies the following ways to do this while creating work environments that are high in motivating potential.

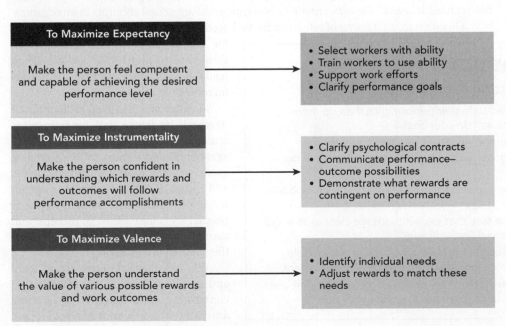

FIGURE 12.4

How Can Managers Use the Insights of the Expectancy Theory of Motivation?

Managers should act in ways that maximize expectancies, instrumentalities, and valences for others. To maximize expectancy, they need to hire capable workers, train and develop them continuously, and communicate goals and confidence in their skills. To maximize instrumentality, managers must clarify and stand by performance-reward linkages. Finally, to maximize valence, they need to understand individual needs and try to tie work outcomes to important sources of need satisfaction.

To have high expectancies, people must believe in their abilities; they must believe that if they try hard to do something, they can perform well at it. Managers can help build these expectancies by selecting workers with the right abilities for the jobs to be done, providing them with the best training and development, and supporting them with resources so that the jobs can be done very well. All these factors stimulate motivation based on something called **self-efficacy**, a person's belief that they are capable of performing a task.

To have high instrumentalities, people must perceive that their performance accomplishments will be followed by desired work outcomes. In others words, they believe that performance will lead to valued rewards. Managers can create positive instrumentalities by taking care to clarify the rewards to be gained by high performance. They must also continually confirm this "promise," so to speak, by actually delivering the expected results. Any disconfirmation or failure to deliver will diminish the instrumentality.

To have high and positive valences, people must value the outcomes associated with high performance. This means that the reward being offered is what they really want. Of course, this is a major source of individual differences. But managers should be able to use insights of the content theories—Maslow, Alderfer, and McClelland, for example—to best match important individual needs with the rewards and outcomes that can be earned through high performance.

> **Self-efficacy** is a person's belief that they are capable of performing a task.

GOAL-SETTING THEORY SHOWS THAT THE RIGHT GOALS CAN BE MOTIVATING.

Steven A. Davis's pathway to success began as a child growing up with a lot of encouragement from his parents. "They never said that because you are an African American you can only go this far or do only this or that," he says, "they just said 'go for it.'" Davis set goals when he graduated from college—to be corporate vice president in 10 years and a president in 20. He made it; Davis rose through a variety of management jobs to become president of Long John Silver's and chairman and CEO of Bob Evans Farms.[18]

Goal Setting Essentials

If asked to comment on this example, scholar Edwin Locke would likely point out that Davis found lots of motivation through the goals he set as a college graduate. The basic premise of Locke's goal-setting theory is that task goals can be a great source of motivation.[19] But, they become motivational only if they are the right goals and if they are set in the right ways.[20]

Goals give direction to people in their work. Goals clarify the performance expectations between leaders and followers, among co-workers, and even across subunits in an organization. Goals establish a frame of reference for task feedback, and they provide a foundation for control and self-management.[21] In these and related ways, Locke believes goal setting is a very practical and powerful motivational tool.

So, what makes a goal motivational? Research by Locke and his associates answer this question by advising managers and team leaders to focus on goal *specificity*—the more specific the better, and on goal *difficulty*—challenging but not impossible. They also point out that people are more likely to accept and commit to accomplishing goals when they participate in setting them.[22]

Although these findings sound ideal and good, we have to be realistic. We can't always choose our own goals. There are many times in work when goals come

---

TIPS TO REMEMBER

How to Make Goal Setting Work for You

- *Set specific goals:* They lead to higher performance than do more generally stated ones, such as "do your best."
- *Set realistic but challenging goals:* When viewed as realistic and attainable, more difficult goals lead to higher performance than do easy goals.
- *Build goal acceptance and commitment:* People work harder for goals they accept and believe in; they resist goals forced on them.
- *Clarify goal priorities:* Make sure that expectations are clear as to which goals should be accomplished first, and why.
- *Provide feedback on goal accomplishment:* Make sure that people know how well they are doing with respect to goal accomplishment.
- *Reward goal accomplishment:* Don't let positive accomplishments pass unnoticed; reward people for doing what they set out to do.

FACTS TO CONSIDER

Europe Turns to Quotas to Increase Female Board Members

Digital Vision/Getty Images

The consulting firm McKinsey & Company reports that women are hired to fill more than 50% of professional jobs in America's large corporations. But then they start leaking from the career pipeline. Diane Segalen, senior executive at a Paris-based executive search company, says: "Some men over 60 think suitable females don't exist because they have never had women as their peers. They think women can't take the pressure involved in serving on a board." In response to this problem, European countries are turning to quotas.

- Norway, Spain, Iceland, and France have adopted mandatory quotas of 40% female board members.
- Legislation is proposed to appoint women to 40% of non-executive board seats throughout the EU.
- A Heidrick & Struggles survey in the United States showed 51% of women directors supporting quotas like those appearing in Europe. Only 25% of men directors voiced similar support.

YOUR THOUGHTS?

Is underrepresentation of women on boards a "pipeline" problem—not enough qualified women available, or a "discrimination" problem—men aren't ready to open the doors to female candidates? And when it comes to correcting the problem, are quotas the way to motivate positive action?

to us from above, and we are expected to help accomplish them. Does this mean that the motivational properties of goal setting are lost? Not necessarily. Even when the goals are set, there may be opportunities to create motivation by allowing people to participate in choosing how to best pursue them. It is also true that a lack of time may make participation hard or impossible. But, Locke's research also suggests that workers will respond positively to externally imposed goals if they trust the supervisors assigning them and they believe the supervisors will adequately support them.

Goal-Setting Downsides

It is important to remember that poorly set and managed goals can have a downside that actually turns the motivation to accomplish them into performance negatives rather than positives.[23] A good example is the scandal over patient waiting times in U.S. Veteran's Affairs hospitals and clinics, where more than 120,000 veterans failed to get care and at least 23 died while awaiting treatment.[24] A VA audit report described the negative effects of working with unrealistic goals—a maximum of 14 days for patient waiting times—this way: "simply not attainable" . . . "an organizational leadership failure." The audit also said that the pressures to meet unattainable goals to achieve pay bonuses motivated some schedulers "to utilize unofficial lists or engage in inappropriate practices in order to make waiting times appear more favorable."[25] Lawmakers at a congressional hearing claimed the VA had an "outlandish bonus culture" and that the fabricated records were motivated by a "quest for monetary gain."[26]

Research offers clear warnings that goal-setting has downsides when managers and leaders set unrealistically high goals, when individuals are expected to meet high goals over and over again, and when people striving to meet high goals aren't given the support they need to accomplish them.[27] Scholars Gary Latham and Gerard Seijts say: "It is foolish and even immoral for organizations to assign employees stretch goals without equipping them with the resources to succeed—and still punish them when they fail to reach those goals. This lack of guidance often leads to stress, burnout, and in some instances, unethical behavior."[28]

STUDYGUIDE

Takeaway 12.2
How Do Thoughts and Decisions Affect Motivation to Work?

Terms to Define

Expectancy	Perceived negative	Perceived positive	Self-efficacy
Instrumentality	inequity	inequity	Valence

Rapid Review

- Adams's equity theory recognizes that social comparisons take place when rewards are distributed in the workplace.
- In equity theory, any sense of perceived inequity is considered a motivating state that causes a person to behave in ways that restore equity to the situation.
- Vroom's expectancy theory states that Motivation = Expectancy × Instrumentality × Valence.
- Managers using expectancy theory are advised to make sure rewards are achievable (maximizing expectancies), predictable (maximizing instrumentalities), and individually valued (maximizing valence).
- Locke's goal-setting theory emphasizes the motivational power of goals that are specific and challenging as well as set through participatory means.

Questions for Discussion

1. Is it against human nature to work harder as a result of perceived positive inequity?
2. Can a person with low expectancy ever be motivated to work hard at a task?
3. Will goal-setting theory work if the goals are fixed and only the means for achieving them are open for discussion?

Be Sure You Can

- **explain** the role of social comparison in Adams's equity theory
- **list** possible ways people with felt negative inequity may behave
- **differentiate** the terms "expectancy," "instrumentality," and "valence"
- **explain** the reason for "×" signs in Vroom's expectancy equation, M = E × I × V
- **explain** Locke's goal-setting theory
- **describe** the link between goal-setting theory and MBO

Career Situation: What Would You Do?

It's apparent that something is wrong with Kate. Her great performance as a Web designer got her promoted to team leader for Web Design Services. But you notice that she now appears anxious, stressed, and generally unhappy in the new assignment. This is quite a contrast from the highly motivated and happy Kate you knew in her old job. What might be wrong here, and what can you, as her supervisor, do to help fix it?

Takeaway 12.3
How Does Reinforcement Influence Motivation to Work?

ANSWERS TO COME

■ Operant conditioning influences behavior by controlling its consequences.

■ Operant conditioning uses four reinforcement strategies.

■ Positive reinforcement connects desirable behavior with pleasant consequences.

■ Punishment connects undesirable behavior with unpleasant consequences.

THE THEORIES DISCUSSED SO FAR FOCUS ON SATISFYING NEEDS, RESOLVING felt inequities, creating positive expectancies, and setting task goals. Instead of looking within the individual to explain motivation in these ways, reinforcement theory takes a different approach. It views human behavior as determined by its environmental consequences.

OPERANT CONDITIONING INFLUENCES BEHAVIOR BY CONTROLLING ITS CONSEQUENCES.

The premises of reinforcement theory rely on what E. L. Thorndike called the **law of effect**: People repeat behavior that results in a pleasant outcome and avoid behavior that results in an unpleasant outcome.[29] Psychologist B. F. Skinner used this notion to popularize the concept of **operant conditioning**. This is the process of influencing behavior by manipulating its consequences.[30]

You may think of operant conditioning as learning by reinforcement. **Figure 12.5** shows how team leaders and managers stimulate it by using four reinforcement strategies.[31]

> The **law of effect** states that behavior followed by pleasant consequences is likely to be repeated; behavior followed by unpleasant consequences is not.

> **Operant conditioning** is the control of behavior by manipulating its consequences.

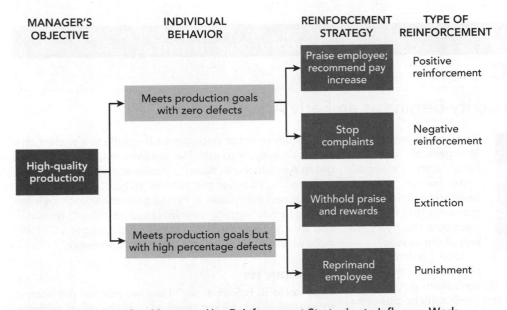

MANAGER'S OBJECTIVE	INDIVIDUAL BEHAVIOR	REINFORCEMENT STRATEGY	TYPE OF REINFORCEMENT
High-quality production	Meets production goals with zero defects	Praise employee; recommend pay increase	Positive reinforcement
		Stop complaints	Negative reinforcement
	Meets production goals but with high percentage defects	Withhold praise and rewards	Extinction
		Reprimand employee	Punishment

FIGURE 12.5 How Can Managers Use Reinforcement Strategies to Influence Work Behavior?

To strengthen quality work a team leader or manager might use positive reinforcement by praising the individual or use negative reinforcement by no longer complaining about poor-quality work. To discourage poor-quality work a supervisor might use extinction—withholding things that are positively reinforcing, or punishment—associating poor-quality work with unpleasant outcomes.

OPERANT CONDITIONING USES FOUR REINFORCEMENT STRATEGIES

If you look again at the case in Figure 12.5, you'll see that the team leader's goal is to improve work quality by an individual performer as part of a total quality management program. This goal can be reached if she can get the individual to display more positive quality behaviors and stop engaging in ones that harm or disregard quality goals. Notice in the four reinforcement strategies that follow that both the positive and negative reinforcement strategies are used to strengthen desirable behaviors. The punishment and extinction strategies are used to weaken or eliminate undesirable behaviors.

> **Positive reinforcement** strengthens a behavior by making a desirable consequence contingent on its occurrence.

> **Negative reinforcement** strengthens a behavior by making the avoidance of an undesirable consequence contingent on its occurrence.

> **Punishment** discourages a behavior by making an unpleasant consequence contingent on its occurrence.

> **Extinction** discourages a behavior by making the removal of a desirable consequence contingent on its occurrence.

Strengthening Desirable Behaviors

Positive reinforcement strengthens or increases the frequency of desirable behavior by making a pleasant consequence contingent on its occurrence. *Example:* A team leader nods to express approval to someone who makes a useful comment during a staff meeting.

Negative reinforcement increases the frequency of or strengthens desirable behavior by making the avoidance of an unpleasant consequence contingent on its occurrence. *Example:* A manager who criticizes a worker every day about tardiness does stops the criticism when the worker comes to work on time.

Eliminating Undesirable Behaviors

Punishment decreases the frequency of or eliminates an undesirable behavior by making an unpleasant consequence contingent on its occurrence. *Example:* A manager issues a written reprimand to an employee whose careless work creates quality problems.

Extinction decreases the frequency of or eliminates an undesirable behavior by making the removal of a pleasant consequence contingent on its occurrence. *Example:* After observing that teammates are providing social approval to a disruptive employee, a team leader counsels them to stop giving this approval.

THE STUDENT COMPLAINED: "I'LL NEVER GET AN A IN THIS COURSE NOW . . . YOU'VE RUINED MY GPA . . . I'LL NEVER GET INTO LAW SCHOOL."

HOT TOPIC

Rewarding Mediocrity Begins at an Early Age

Steve Debenport/Getty Images

Your child plays soccer. She gets to have fun, have some exercise, make friends, and experience coaching and teamwork. But does she deserve a trophy at the end of the season?

One parent complained to the local newspaper that every player on his son's team got a trophy and that "this practice of rewarding mediocrity begins at an early age." Members of the Millennial generation have been called "trophy kids" that grow up getting so much positive reinforcement that they come to believe that "satisfactory" is really "excellent" and that "effort" is the same as "accomplishment."

A faculty member once gave a B– grade to a student on a small quiz early in course. The student complained: "I won't get an A in this course now. . . . You've ruined my grade point average. . . . I'll never get into law school." One week later she dropped the course. A Pac-12 basketball coach criticizes parents for not teaching their kids accountability. "I know parents who go to a school and say, 'Why did he get a C? I was there when he was working hard, doing homework.'"

HOW ABOUT IT?

What would B. F. Skinner say? Have we reached the point in society that young children are given so much positive reinforcement for less than stellar performance that they fail to distinguish between hard work and real performance accomplishment? Are parents, teachers, and team leaders falling into the trap of "satisfactory underperformance," positively rewarding as excellent anything a bit better than poor-average performance?

POSITIVE REINFORCEMENT CONNECTS DESIRABLE BEHAVIOR WITH PLEASANT CONSEQUENCES.

Positive reinforcement deserves special attention among the reinforcement strategies. It should be part of any manager's motivational toolkit. In fact, it should be one of our personal life skills as well—as parents working with children, for example.

> **Guidelines for Positive Reinforcement**
>
> Positive Reinforcement
>
> • Clearly identify desired work behaviors.
> • Maintain a diverse inventory of rewards.
> • Inform everyone what must be done to get rewards.
> • Recognize individual differences when allocating rewards.
> • Follow the laws of immediate and contingent reinforcement.

Shaping

One of the ways to mobilize the power of positive reinforcement is through **shaping**. This is the creation of a new behavior by the positive reinforcement of successive approximations to it.

Sir Richard Branson, well-known founder of Virgin Group, is a believer in shaping through positive reinforcement. "For the people who work for you or with you, you must lavish praise on them at all times," he says. "If a flower is watered, it flourishes. If not, it shrivels up and dies."[32]

David Novak, CEO of Yum! Brands, Inc., is another believer. He claims, "You can never underestimate the power of telling someone he's doing a good job."[33] And Zappos' CEO Tony Hsieh takes all this one step further. If an employee spots someone doing a good thing, they can immediately give them a "Wow" award worth $50.[34]

> **Shaping** is positive reinforcement of successive approximations to the new behavior.

Scheduling Reinforcement

Whether we are talking about verbal praise, a pay raise, or any other forms of positive reinforcement, two laws govern the process. The **law of contingent reinforcement** ties reinforcement directly to behavior. It states: For a reward to have maximum reinforcing value, it must be delivered only if the desired behavior is exhibited. The **law of immediate reinforcement** uses time to advantage. It states: The more immediate the delivery of a reward after the occurrence of a desirable behavior, the greater the reinforcing value of the reward.

> **Law of contingent reinforcement**—deliver the reward only when desired behavior occurs.
>
> **Law of immediate reinforcement**—deliver the reward as soon as possible after the desired behavior occurs.

> "WE DON'T REALLY FEEL THAT FOLKS SHOULD HAVE TO PAY SOMETHING ADDITIONAL FOR US TO APPRECIATE THAT THEY'RE CHOOSING US OVER ANOTHER RESTAURANT."

QUICK CASE

Restaurant Chain Serves Up No-Tipping Policy

© CandyBoxImages/iStockphoto

Most restaurant servers rely on tips to make a decent living from below-minimum-wage jobs. So, how about a "no tip" policy combined with a higher hourly wage?

You've just gotten startup funding for a new campus diner. As part of your planning, you attended business development seminar where the CEO of a fast-growing restaurant chain described her success with a no-tipping policy. On the customer side she said: "We don't really feel that folks should have to pay something additional for us to appreciate that they're choosing us over another restaurant." Customers don't have to worry whether they should add 10%, 15%, or 20% to their bills. On the server side, she added: "One of our beliefs is that you have to appreciate and value serving others and not expect something extra for it." Servers don't have to worry about how much they'll earn; they're already at or above minimum wage.

WHAT DO YOU DO?

Is this CEO on to something that you should copy? Is she getting reinforcement right? What do you see as the motivational pros and cons of a no-tipping policy?

PUNISHMENT CONNECTS UNDESIRABLE BEHAVIOR WITH UNPLEASANT CONSEQUENCES.

Punishment is part of everyday life and is also important to understand as a reinforcement strategy. It tries to eliminate undesirable behavior by making an unpleasant consequence contingent with its occurrence. To punish an employee, for example, a manager may deny a valued reward such as verbal praise or merit pay. Alternatively, she could punish by delivering an unpleasant outcome such as a verbal or written reprimand.

Like positive reinforcement, punishment can be done poorly or it can be done well. All too often, it is done both too frequently and poorly. Shown here is some useful advice on how to best handle punishment when it is necessary.

Whether talking about using punishment or positive reinforcement, some people complain about the underlying reinforcement principles. They believe that any use of operant conditioning techniques ignores the individuality of people, restricts their freedom of choice, and fails to recognize that they can be motivated by things other than rewards delivered by others. Such critics view operant conditioning as inappropriate manipulation and control of human behavior. Advocates agree that reinforcement involves the control of behavior, but argue that control is part of every manager's or parent's job. The ethical issue, they say, isn't whether or not to use reinforcement principles. It is about whether or not we use them well—at work and in everyday living.[35]

How about you? Do you see reinforcement theory as full of useful insights, or as something to be feared? Are you prepared to tap the full potential of positive reinforcement and to do your best when punishment is called for?

Guidelines for Punishment

- Tell the person what is being done wrong.
- Tell the person what is being done right.
- Make sure the punishment matches the behavior.
- Administer the punishment in private.
- Follow the laws of immediate and contingent reinforcement.

EXPLORE YOURSELF

Engagement

There's a lot of attention being given these days to the levels of **engagement** displayed by people at work. Differences in engagement are evident in a variety of ways. Is someone enthusiastic or lethargic, diligent or lazy, willing to do more than expected or at best willing to do only what is expected?

Managers want high engagement by members of their work units and teams, and the ideas in this chapter offer many insights on how to create engagement by using the different theories of motivation as well as reinforcement principles.

Consider your experiences as a customer. When you're disappointed, perhaps with how a banking transaction or how a flight delay is handled, ask: Would a higher level of employee engagement generate better customer service in such situations? And if so, how do we get there?

Take a look around the classroom. What do you see and what would you predict for the career futures of your classmates based on the engagement they now show as students? Who might you want to hire for an important job someday, and who would you pass over?

Get to know yourself better by taking the **Two-Factor Profile** self-assessment and completing other activities in the *Exploring Management* **Skill-Building Portfolio.**

STUDYGUIDE

Takeaway 12.3
How Does Reinforcement Influence Motivation to Work?

Terms to Define

Extinction	Law of effect	Negative reinforcement	Punishment
Law of contingent reinforcement	Law of immediate reinforcement	Operant conditioning	Shaping
		Positive reinforcement	

Rapid Review

- Reinforcement theory views human behavior as determined by its environmental consequences.
- The law of effect states that behavior followed by a pleasant consequence is likely to be repeated; behavior followed by an unpleasant consequence is unlikely to be repeated.
- Managers use strategies of positive reinforcement and negative reinforcement to strengthen desirable behaviors.
- Managers use strategies of punishment and extinction to weaken undesirable work behaviors.
- Positive reinforcement and punishment both work best when applied according to the laws of contingent and immediate reinforcement.

Questions for Discussion

1. Is operant conditioning a manipulative way to influence human behavior?
2. When is punishment justifiable as a reinforcement strategy?
3. Is it possible for a manager, or parent, to only use positive reinforcement?

Be Sure You Can

- **explain** the law of effect and operant conditioning
- **illustrate** how positive reinforcement, negative reinforcement, punishment, and extinction can influence work behavior
- **explain** the reinforcement technique of shaping
- **describe** how managers can use the laws of immediate and contingent reinforcement when allocating rewards
- **list** ways to make punishment effective

Career Situation: What Would You Do?

You can predict with great confidence that when Jason comes to a meeting of your student team, he will spend most of his time cracking jokes, telling stories, and otherwise entertaining other team members. He doesn't do any real work. In fact, his behavior makes it hard for the team to accomplish much in its meetings. But Jason's also a talented guy. How can you put reinforcement theory to work here and turn Jason the mischief maker into a solid team contributor?

TEST PREP **12**

Answers to Test Prep questions can be found at the back of the book.

Multiple-Choice Questions

1. Maslow's progression principle stops working at the level of _____ needs.
   (a) growth
   (b) self-actualization
   (c) achievement
   (d) self-esteem

2. Lower-order needs in Maslow's hierarchy correspond to _____ needs in ERG theory.
   (a) growth
   (b) affiliation
   (c) existence
   (d) achievement

3. A worker high in need for _____ power in McClelland's theory tries to use power for the good of the organization.
   (a) position
   (b) expert
   (c) personal
   (d) social

4. In the _____ theory of motivation, an individual who feels under-rewarded relative to a co-worker might be expected to reduce his or her work efforts in the future.
   (a) ERG
   (b) acquired needs
   (c) two-factor
   (d) equity

5. Which of the following is a correct match?
   (a) McClelland–ERG theory
   (b) Skinner–reinforcement theory
   (c) Vroom–equity theory
   (d) Locke–expectancy theory

6. In Herzberg's two-factor theory, base pay is considered a/an _____ factor.
   (a) hygiene
   (b) satisfier
   (c) equity
   (d) higher-order

7. The expectancy theory of motivation says that Motivation = Expectancy × Instrumentality × _____.
   (a) Rewards   (b) Valence   (c) Equity   (d) Growth

8. When a team member shows strong ego needs in Maslow's hierarchy, the team leader should find ways to _____.
   (a) link this person's compensation with team performance
   (b) provide the individual with praise and recognition for good work
   (c) encourage more social interaction with other team members
   (d) assign challenging individual performance goals

9. When someone has a high and positive "expectancy" in expectancy theory of motivation, this means that the person _____.
   (a) believes he can achieve performance expectations
   (b) highly values the rewards being offered
   (c) sees a performance–reward link
   (d) believes rewards are equitable

10. The law of _____ states that behavior followed by a positive consequence is likely to be repeated, whereas behavior followed by an undesirable consequence is not likely to be repeated.
    (a) reinforcement
    (b) contingency
    (c) goal setting
    (d) effect

11. When a job allows a person to do a complete unit of work, it is high on which core characteristic?
    (a) Task identity
    (b) Task significance
    (c) Task autonomy
    (d) Feedback

12. _____ is a positive reinforcement strategy that rewards successive approximations to a desirable behavior.
    (a) Extinction
    (b) Negative reinforcement
    (c) Shaping
    (d) Merit pay

13. The purpose of negative reinforcement as an operant conditioning technique is to _____.
    (a) punish bad behavior
    (b) discourage bad behavior
    (c) encourage desirable behavior
    (d) cancel the effects of shaping

14. The basic premise of reinforcement theory is that _____.
    (a) behavior is a function of environment
    (b) motivation comes from positive expectancy
    (c) higher-order needs stimulate hard work
    (d) rewards considered unfair are demotivators

15. Both Barry and Marissa are highly motivated students. Knowing this, an instructor can expect them to be _____ in the management course.
    (a) hard working   (b) high performing
    (c) highly satisfied   (d) highly dissatisfied

Short-Response Questions

16. What preferences does a person high in the need for achievement bring to the workplace?

17. How can a team leader use goal-setting theory in working with individual team members?

18. What are three ways a worker might react to perceived negative inequity over a pay raise?

19. How can shaping be used to encourage desirable work behaviors?

Integration and Application Question

20. I once overheard a conversation between two Executive MBA students. One was telling the other: "My firm just contracted with Muzak to have mood music piped into the offices at various times of the workday." The other replied: "That's a waste of money; there should be things to spend money on if the firm is really interested in increasing motivation and performance."

    Question: Is the second student right or wrong, and why?

Steps for
Further Learning

BUILD MARKETABLE SKILLS • **DO** A CASE ANALYSIS • **GET** AND STAY INFORMED

BUILD MARKETABLE SKILLS.

EARN BIG CAREER PAYOFFS!

Don't miss these opportunities in the SKILL-BUILDING PORTFOLIO

SELF-ASSESSMENT 12:
Two-Factor Profile

Motivation is complicated . . . it helps to know the difference between job content and job context.

CLASS EXERCISE 12:
Why We Work

Work means different things to different people . . . practice finding each person's story.

TEAM PROJECT 12:
CEO Pay

CEOs often earn quite a lot, some think too much . . . are CEOs paid what they are worth?

Many learning resources are found at the end of the book and online within **WileyPLUS Learning Space.**

Practice Critical Thinking—Complete the CHAPTER 12 CASE

CASE SNAPSHOT: Salesforce.com: Instant Praise, Instant Criticism

Instead of waiting a year for a performance review, how would you like to know where you stand and always get immediate feedback about how you're doing? The annual performance review can feel like an archaic, inaccurate, time-warped, boss-administered feedback session. Some human resource professionals call it "little more than a dysfunctional pretense." It can be a case of information overload, covering everything from past performance, to goal setting, to pay, to improvement needs. How valuable and motivating is recognition and feedback received 12 months from now? Suppose you could get feedback by asking colleagues, managers, and peers online questions like: "What did you think of my presentation?" or "What can be done better?"

DO A CASE ANALYSIS.

STRENGTHEN YOUR CRITICAL THINKING!

MANAGER'S LIBRARY SELECTION
Read for Insights and Wisdom
Drive: The Surprising Truth about What Motivates Us (2009, Riverhead Books), by Daniel H. Pink

What drives you? In this book, author Daniel Pink argues that more attention should be given to a drive he calls "intrinsic motivation." It includes our desire to do activities because we enjoy and are gratified by them. They give us purpose and satisfy our need to do what we choose and value without others telling us. We do them not because we need to (buy groceries), or have to (avoid errors), but because we want to (enjoy work).

GET AND STAY INFORMED.

MAKE YOURSELF VALUABLE!

Pink urges managers to change reward systems to improve opportunities for intrinsic motivation. He points out that the economy has shifted from algorithmic work—routine, ruled-based work like product assembly, toward heuristic work—knowledge-driven, creative work that requires intuition and self-direction. Reward systems need to shift, too. Extrinsic rewards like pay that drive algorithmic work might appeal to heuristic workers initially. But once a "baseline" level of security is achieved, motivation becomes more linked to things that excite and give them purpose. That's where intrinsic motivation kicks in.

REFLECT AND REACT Make two lists, one of things you do because you have to and the other of things you do because you want to. How do the lists differ in the activities represented? How do they differ in motivational impact on you? Can you spend a whole day doing only what you have to? Do the "have to's" sometimes make it difficult to find motivation and satisfaction from the "want to's"? What does this exercise say about what drives you . . . and about what should drive you?

"The way a team plays as a whole determines its success. You may have the greatest bunch of individual stars in the world, but if they don't play together, the club won't be worth a dime."

Former UCLA basketball coach John Wooden, quoting Hall-of-Famer Babe Ruth

Teams and Teamwork

13

Two Heads Really Can Be Better Than One

Management Live

When Teams Stand Up, Decisions Speed Up

Cultura Creative/Alamy

Did you ever wonder how to move decisions along faster in team meetings? One solution is simple: Take away the seats. At the software firm Atomic Object, seats are out and speed is in—the typical meeting lasts less than 5 minutes. At the team meeting that begins each workday, every one shows up on time, stands up, and is expected to stay on task. Don't plan on playing Angry Birds or chatting. Even tables are frowned upon. A vice president declares: "They make it too easy to lean or rest laptops." Stand-up meetings are popular in the tech industry, where some call them "agile meetings."

WHAT'S INSIDE

ETHICS CHECK
Social loafing may be closer than you think

FACTS TO CONSIDER
Unproductive meetings are major time wasters

HOT TOPIC
Can disharmony build a better team?

QUICK CASE
Removing the headphones to show team spirit

YOUR THOUGHTS?

Might stand up meetings play a role in your workplace? Many people are starting to work at stand-up desks—why not hold meetings the same way? What are the limits? And, are there other ways to speed up meetings and add "agility" to team vocabularies?

YOUR CHAPTER 13 TAKEAWAYS

1. Understand the importance of teams and teamwork.
2. Identify the building blocks of successful teamwork.
3. Understand how managers create and lead high-performance teams.

Takeaway 13.1
Why Is It Important to Understand Teams and Teamwork?

ANSWERS TO COME

- Teams offer synergy and other benefits.
- Teams can suffer from performance problems.
- Organizations are networks of formal teams and informal groups.
- Organizations use committees, task forces, and cross-functional teams.
- Virtual teams use technology to bridge distances.
- Self-managing teams are a form of job enrichment for groups.

WE ARE ALL PART OF TEAMS EVERY DAY, AND IT'S TIME TO RECOGNIZE A BASIC FACT: Teams are hard work, but they are mostly worth it. The beauty of teams is accomplishing something far greater than what's possible for an individual alone. But even though two heads can be better than one, the key word is "can." Have you ever heard someone say, "Too many cooks spoil the broth" or "A camel is an elephant put together by a committee"? There are good reasons why such sayings are well used. So, let's start this discussion realistically.

On one level there seems little to debate. Groups and teams have a lot to offer organizations. But at another level you have to sometimes wonder if the extra effort is really worth it. There's no doubt that teams can sometimes be more pain than gain. There's a lot to learn about them, their roles in organizations, and how we participate in and help lead them for real performance gains.[1]

TEAMS OFFER SYNERGY AND OTHER BENEFITS.

A **team** is a collection of people who regularly interact to pursue common goals.

Teamwork is the process of people actively working together to accomplish common goals.

Synergy is the creation of a whole greater than the sum of its individual parts.

A **team** is a small group of people with complementary skills who work together to accomplish shared goals while holding each other mutually accountable for performance results.[2] Teams are essential to organizations of all types and sizes. Many tasks are well beyond the capabilities of individuals alone.[3] And in this sense, **teamwork**, people actually working together to accomplish a shared goal, is a major performance asset.[4]

The term **synergy** means the creation of a whole that exceeds the sum of its parts. When teams perform well, it's because of synergy that pools many diverse talents and efforts to create extraordinary results. *Check synergy and team success in the NBA.* Scholars find that both good and bad basketball teams win more the longer the players have been together. Why? A "teamwork effect" creates wins because players know one another's moves and playing tendencies. *Check synergy and team success in the hospital operating room.* Scholars notice the same heart surgeons have lower death rates for similar procedures performed in hospitals where the surgeons did more operations. Why? A teamwork effect—the doctors had more time working together with the surgery teams—anesthesiologists, nurses, and other surgical technicians. They say it's not only the surgeon's skills that count; the skills of the team and the time spent working together count, too.[5]

Don't forget—teams are not only good for performance, they're also good for their members.[6] Just as in life overall, being part of a work team or informal group can strongly influence our attitudes and behaviors. The personal relationships can help with job performance—making contacts, sharing ideas, responding to favors, and bypassing roadblocks. And being part of a team often helps satisfy important needs that are unfulfilled in the regular work setting or life overall. Teams provide members with social relationships, security, a sense of belonging, and emotional support.

Why Teams Are Good for Organizations

- More resources for problem solving
- Improved creativity and innovation
- Improved quality of decision making
- Greater commitment to tasks
- Increased motivation of members
- Better control and work discipline
- More individual need satisfaction

TEAMS CAN SUFFER FROM PERFORMANCE PROBLEMS.

We all know that working in teams isn't always easy or productive. Problems not only happen; they are common.[7] Teams often suffer from personality conflicts and work style differences that disrupt relationships and accomplishments. Group members sometimes battle over goals or competing visions. Sometimes they withdraw from active participation because of uncertainty over tasks and relationships. Ambiguous agendas or ill-defined problems can cause teamwork fatigue. Motivation can fall when teams work too long on the wrong things and end up having little to show for it. And, not everyone is always ready to jump in and do a great job on a team. These and other difficulties can easily turn the great potential of teams into frustration and failure.

One of the most troublesome team problems is **social loafing**—the presence of one or more "free-riders" who slack off and allow other team members to do most of the work.[8] For whatever reason, perhaps the absence of spotlight on personal performance, individuals sometimes work less hard, not harder, when they are part of a group.

What can a team leader do when someone is free-riding? The possibilities include a variety of actions to make individual contributions more visible—rewarding individuals for their contributions, making task assignments more interesting, and keeping group size small so that free-riders are more noticeable. This makes the loafers more susceptible to pressures from peers and to critical leader evaluations. And if you've ever considered free-riding as a team member, think again. You may get away with it in the short term, but your reputation will suffer, and sooner or later it will be "payback" time.

> ### How to Handle Social Loafing
>
> - Reward individuals for contributions.
> - Make individuals visible by keeping team size small.
> - Encourage peer pressure to perform.
> - Make task assignments more interesting.

Social loafing is the tendency of some people to avoid responsibility by free-riding in groups.

"I'LL BE ACTIVE IN DISCUSSIONS, BUT I CAN'T BE A LEADER OR VOLUNTEER FOR ANY EXTRA WORK."

ETHICS CHECK

Social Loafing May Be Closer Than You Think

Quiet Noise Creative/Getty Images

Psychology study: A German researcher asks people to pull on a rope as hard as they can. First, individuals pull alone. Second, they pull as part of a group. Results show people pull harder when working alone than when working as part of a team. Such social loafing is the tendency to reduce effort when working in groups.

Faculty office: A student wants to speak with the instructor about his team's performance on the last group project. There were four members, but two did almost all the work. The two loafers largely disappeared, showing up only at the last minute to be part of the formal presentation. His point is that the team was disadvantaged because the two free-riders caused a loss of performance capacity.

Telephone call from the boss: "John, I really need you to serve on this committee. Will you do it? Let me know tomorrow." In thinking about this, I ponder: I'm overloaded, but I don't want to turn down the boss. I'll accept but let the committee members know about my situation. I'll be active in discussions and try to offer viewpoints and perspectives that are helpful. However, I'll let them know up front that I can't be a leader or volunteer for any extra work.

YOUR DECISION?

Whether you call it social loafing, free-riding, or just plain old slacking off, the issue is the same. What right do some people have to sit back in team situations and let other people do all or most of the work? Is this ethical? Does everyone in a group have an ethical obligation to do his or her fair share of the work? Does the fact that John is going to be honest with the other committee members make any difference? Won't he still be a loafer who gets credit with the boss for serving on the committee? Would it be more ethical for him to decline the boss's request?

ORGANIZATIONS ARE NETWORKS OF FORMAL TEAMS AND INFORMAL GROUPS.

A **formal team** is officially recognized and supported by the organization.

A **formal team** is officially designated for a specific organizational purpose. You'll find such teams described by different labels on organization charts—examples are *departments* (e.g., market research department), *work units* (e.g., audit unit), *teams* (e.g., customer service team), or *divisions* (e.g., office products division).

Formal teams are headed by supervisors, managers, department heads, team leaders, and the like. It is common, in fact, to describe organizations as interlocking networks of teams in which managers and leaders play "linking pin" roles.[9] This means that they serve both as head of one work team and as a regular member in the next-higher-level one. It's also important to recognize, as shown here, that managers play more than one role in groups and teams. In addition to serving as the supervisor or team leader, they also act as network facilitators, team members, and coaches.

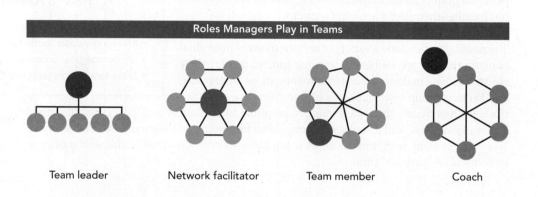

Roles Managers Play in Teams

| Team leader | Network facilitator | Team member | Coach |

An **informal group** is unofficial and emerges from relationships and shared interests among members.

The informal structure of an organization also consists of **informal groups**. They emerge from natural or spontaneous relationships and offer members opportunities for social satisfactions as well as contacts for getting work done. Some are *interest groups*, whose members pursue a common cause, such as a women's career network. Some are *friendship groups* that develop for a wide variety of personal reasons, including shared hobbies and other nonwork interests. Others are *support groups* in which members basically help one another out in work and personal affairs.

WORKERS AROUND THE WORLD SAY MOST MEETINGS ARE "INEFFECTIVE."

FACTS TO CONSIDER

Unproductive Meetings Are Major Time Wasters

© Leontura/iStockphoto

A survey of some 38,000 workers around the world links low productivity with bad meetings, poor communication, and unclear goals.

- 69% of meetings attended are considered ineffective.

- 32% of workers complain about team communication.
- 31% complain about unclear objectives and priorities.

WHAT'S YOUR TAKE?

Do these data match your experiences with team meetings? Given the common complaints about meetings, what can a team leader do to improve them? Think about the recent meetings you have attended. In what ways were the best meetings different from the worst ones? Did your behavior play a significant role in both these cases?

ORGANIZATIONS USE COMMITTEES, TASK FORCES, AND CROSS-FUNCTIONAL TEAMS.

Among the formal teams and groups in organizations, a **committee** brings together people outside their daily job assignments to work in a small team for a specific purpose.[10] A designated head or chairperson typically leads the committee and is held accountable for the task agenda. Organizations, for example, often have committees dealing with issues like diversity, quality, and compensation.[11]

Project teams or **task forces** put people together to work on common problems, but on a temporary rather than a continuing basis. Project teams, for example, might be formed to develop a new product or service, redesign workflows, or provide specialized consulting for a client.[12] A task force might be formed to address employee retention problems or come up with ideas for improving work schedules.[13]

The **cross-functional team** brings together members from different functional units.[14] They are supposed to work together on specific problems or tasks, sharing information and exploring new ideas. They are expected to help knock down the "functional chimneys" or "walls" that otherwise separate departments and people in the organization. Some organizations also use **employee involvement teams**. These groups of workers meet on a regular basis with the goal of using their expertise and experience for continuous improvement. The **quality circle**, for example, is a team that meets regularly to discuss and plan specific ways to improve work quality.[15]

VIRTUAL TEAMS USE TECHNOLOGY TO BRIDGE DISTANCES.

SCENE: U.S.-based IT manager needs to meet with team members in Brazil, the Philippines, and Poland. Rather than pay for everyone to fly to a common location, he checks world time zones, sends an e-mail to schedule, and then joins other team members online at the scheduled time using AppleFaceTime or Skype.

The constant emergence of new technologies is making virtual collaboration both easier and more common. At home it may be Twitter, LinkedIn, or Instagram; at the office it's likely to be a wide variety of online meeting resources. Members of **virtual teams**, also called **distributed teams**, work together and solve problems through computer-mediated rather than face-to-face interactions.[16] They operate like other teams with respect to what gets done. It's the way things get done in virtual teams that is different.

As you probably realize already from working in college study teams, virtual teamwork has many advantages. It allows teamwork by people who may be located at great distances from one another, offering cost and time efficiencies. It makes it easy to widely share lots of information, keep records of team activities, and maintain databases. And, virtual teamwork can help reduce interpersonal problems that might otherwise occur when team members are dealing face-to-face with controversial issues.[17]

Are there any downsides to virtual teams? Yes, for sure, and often they're the same as in other groups.[18] Social loafing can still occur, goals may be unclear, meeting requests may be too frequent. Members of virtual teams can also have difficulties establishing good working relationships. The lack of face-to-face interaction limits the role of emotions and nonverbal cues in the communication and may depersonalize member relations.[19] "Human beings are social animals for whom building relationships matters a great deal," says one scholar. "Strip away the social side of teamwork and, very

---

A **committee** is designated to work on a special task on a continuing basis.

A **project team** or **task force** is convened for a specific purpose and disbands after completing its task.

A **cross-functional team** operates with members who come from different functional units of an organization.

An **employee involvement team** meets on a regular basis to help achieve continuous improvement.

A **quality circle** is a team of employees who meet periodically to discuss ways of improving work quality.

Members of a **virtual team** or **distributed team** work together and solve problems through computer-based interactions.

TIPS TO REMEMBER
Steps to Successful Virtual Teams

- Select team members with positive attitudes and capable of self-starting.
- Select members high in initiative and with proven records of hard work.
- Begin with social messaging that allows members to exchange information about one another to personalize the process.
- Assign clear goals and roles so that members can focus while working alone and also know what others are doing.
- Gather regular feedback from members about how they think the team is doing and how it might do better.
- Provide regular feedback to team members about team accomplishments.
- Make sure the team has the best virtual meeting technology.

quickly, people feel isolated and unsupported."[20] Even with these potential problems, virtual teams proved their performance potential.[21] They're fast becoming a way of organizational life.

SELF-MANAGING TEAMS ARE A FORM OF JOB ENRICHMENT FOR GROUPS.

Members of a **self-managing team** have the authority to make decisions about how they share and complete their work.

In a growing number of organizations, traditional work units of supervisors and subordinates are being replaced with **self-managing teams**. Sometimes called *autonomous work groups*, these are teams whose members have been given collective authority to make many decisions about how they work, ones previously made by higher-level managers.[22] The expected advantages include better performance, decreased costs, and higher morale.

As shown in **Figure 13.1**, the "self-management" responsibilities of self-managing teams include planning and scheduling work, training members in various tasks, distributing tasks, meeting performance goals, ensuring high quality, and solving day-to-day operating problems. In some settings the team's authority may even extend to "hiring" and "firing" its members when necessary. A key feature is multitasking, in which team members help each other develop the skills needed to perform several different jobs. A quick check of a true self-managing team returns "Yes" answers to questions like these: Members collectively accountable for results? Members decide how to distribute tasks and schedule work? Members train and support one another in job skills? Members assess one another's performance?

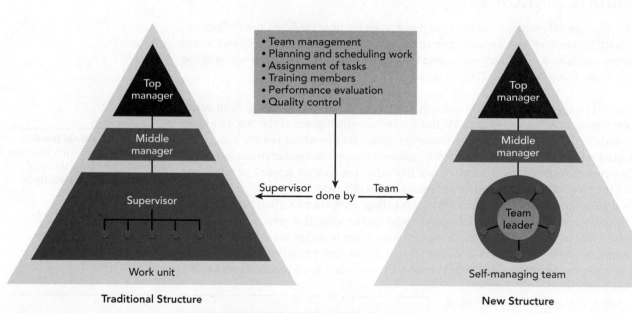

FIGURE 13.1 **What Are the Management Implications of Self-Managing Teams?**
Members of self-managing teams make decisions together on team membership, task plans and job assignments, training and performance evaluations, and quality control. Because they essentially manage themselves in these ways, they no longer need a traditional supervisor or department head. Instead, the team leader performs this role with the support of team members. The team leader and team as a whole report to the next higher level of management and are held accountable for performance results.

STUDYGUIDE

Takeaway 13.1
Why Is It Important to Understand Teams and Teamwork?

Terms to Define

Committee	Formal team	Self-managing team	Team
Cross-functional team	Informal group	Social loafing	Teamwork
Distributed team	Project team	Synergy	Virtual team
Employee involvement team	Quality circle	Task force	

Rapid Review

- A team consists of people with complementary skills working together for shared goals and holding one another accountable for performance.
- Teams benefit organizations by providing for synergy that allows the accomplishment of tasks that are beyond individual capabilities alone.
- Social loafing and other problems can limit the performance of teams.
- Organizations use a variety of formal teams in the form of committees, task forces, project teams, cross-functional teams, and virtual teams.
- Self-managing teams allow team members to perform many tasks previously done by supervisors.

Questions for Discussion

1. Do committees and task forces work better when they are given short deadlines?
2. Are there some things that should be done only by face-to-face teams, not virtual ones?
3. Why do people in teams often tolerate social loafers?

Be Sure You Can

- **define** "team" and "teamwork"
- **describe** the roles managers play in teams
- **explain** synergy and the benefits of teams
- **discuss** social loafing and other potential problems of teams
- **differentiate** formal and informal groups
- **explain** how committees, task forces, and cross-functional teams operate
- **describe** potential problems faced by virtual teams
- **list** the characteristics of self-managing teams

Career Situation: What Would You Do?

It's time for the initial meeting of the task force that you have been assigned to lead. This is a big opportunity for you because it's the first time your boss has given you this level of responsibility. There are seven members of the team, all of whom are your peers and co-workers—no direct reports. The task is to develop a proposal for increased use of flexible work schedules and telecommuting in the organization. What will your agenda be for the first meeting, and what opening statement will you make?

Takeaway 13.2
What Are the Building Blocks of Successful Teamwork?

ANSWERS TO COME

- Teams need the right members to be effective.
- Teams need the right setting and size to be effective.
- Teams need the right processes to be effective.
- Teams move through different stages of development.
- Team performance is influenced by norms.
- Team performance is influenced by cohesiveness.
- Team performance is influenced by task and maintenance activities.
- Team performance is influenced by communication networks.

AFTER TALKING ABOUT THE TYPES OF TEAMS IN ORGANIZATIONS, IT'S TIME TO focus on the teamwork that can make them successful.[23] Look at **Figure 13.2**. It diagrams a team as an open system that, like the organization itself, transforms a variety of inputs into outputs.[24] It also shows that an **effective team** should be accomplishing three output goals—task performance, member satisfaction, and team viability.[25]

The first outcome of an effective team is high *task performance*. When you are on a team, ask: Did we accomplish our tasks and meet expectations? The second outcome of an effective team is *member satisfaction*. Ask: Are we individually and collectively pleased with our participation in the process? The third outcome of an effective team is *viability for future action*. Ask: Can this team be successful again in the future?[26]

> An **effective team** achieves high levels of task performance, membership satisfaction, and future viability.

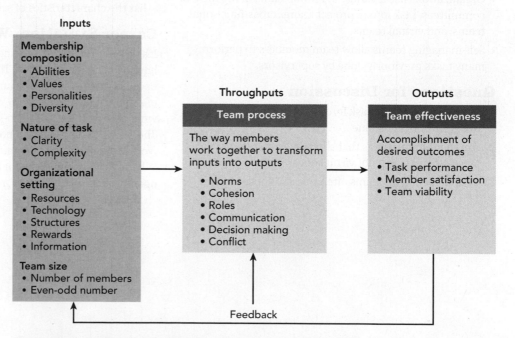

FIGURE 13.2 What Are the Foundations of Team Effectiveness?

An effective team achieves high levels of task performance and member satisfaction and remains viable for the future. The foundations of effectiveness begin with inputs—things such as membership composition, nature of the task, resources and support in the organizational setting, and team size. The foundations of effectiveness further rest with team process—how well the members utilize their talents and other inputs to create the desired outputs. Key process factors on any team include the stages of development, norms and cohesion, task and maintenance activities, communication, and decision making.

You might hear an effective team described as one that has "the right players in the right seats on the same bus, headed in the same direction."[27] The open-systems model in Figure 13.2 shows this thinking. A team's effectiveness is influenced by *inputs*—getting the right players and putting them in the right seats, and by *process*—making sure everyone knows they're on the same bus and headed in the same direction. A team with either input or process deficiencies, or both, is going to underperform. But when the inputs and processes are both right for the tasks at hand, the full benefits of team synergy are likely to be achieved.

TEAMS NEED THE RIGHT MEMBERS TO BE EFFECTIVE.

The foundations for team effectiveness are set when a team is formed. The better the inputs, the more likely are good teamwork and performance success.[28] And when it comes to inputs for team success, the starting point is the selection of members.

Member Talents

Ability counts in team membership. You want talent available to accomplish the tasks at hand. In an ideal world, team members, talents, and interests fit well with the job to be done. If you were in charge of a new team, wouldn't you want to start this way?

The talents needed to accomplish relatively simple tasks are easy to identify. It's harder to identify those needed for more complex tasks. And because complex tasks require more information exchange and intense interaction among team members, they put more pressure on teamwork.

Think complexity the next time you fly. And check out the ground crews. You should notice similarities between them and teams handling pit stops for NASCAR racers. In fact, members of some ramp crews have been through "Pit Crew U," run by Pit Instruction & Training in Mooresville, North Carolina. Real racing crews at this facility have trained ramp workers to work under pressure while meeting the goals of timeliness, safety, and job preparedness. The goal is better teamwork to reduce aircraft delays and poor service.[29]

> **"Must Have" Team Contributions**
>
> - Using talents
> - Encouraging and motivating others
> - Listening to different points of view
> - Sharing information and ideas
> - Resolving conflict
> - Building consensus
> - Fulfilling commitments
> - Avoiding disruptive behavior

Member Diversity

Team diversity also counts in team membership. It represents the mix of skills, experiences, backgrounds, and personalities among team members. The presence or absence of diversity can affect both relationships among members and team performance. And when diversity is present, just how well it is managed can make the difference between a team that struggles between failure or modest success and one that achieves something truly great.

It is easier to manage relationships among members of **homogeneous teams**—those whose members share similar characteristics. But this sense of harmony can come at a price. Researchers warn about risks when team members are too similar in background, training, and experience. Such teams may underperform, especially on complex or creative tasks, even though the members may feel very comfortable with one another.[30]

It is harder to manage relationships among members of more **heterogeneous teams**—those whose members are quite dissimilar to one another.[31] But, the potential complications of membership diversity also come with special performance opportunities. When heterogeneous teams are well managed, the variety of ideas, perspectives, and experiences within them can be helpful for problem solving. Highly creative teams, for example, are often ones that mix experienced people with those who haven't worked together before.[32] The experienced members have the connections, whereas the newcomers add fresh thinking.

What are your experiences with diversity in team membership? Do you get along better in teams whose members are pretty much all alike? Have you encountered problems on teams whose members are quite different from one another?

Team diversity is the mix of skills, experiences, backgrounds, and personalities of team members.

> **Input Foundations for Team Effectiveness**
>
> - *Membership composition*—talent and skills, diversity of experiences, backgrounds, personalities
> - *Nature of task*—clear and defined versus open-ended and complex
> - *Organizational setting*—information, resources, technology, space
> - *Team size*—smaller versus larger, odd/even count

Homogeneous teams have members with similar personal characteristics.

Heterogeneous teams have members with diverse personal characteristics.

TEAMS NEED THE RIGHT SETTING AND SIZE TO BE EFFECTIVE.

As you might expect, the *organizational setting* influences team outputs. A key issue here is how well the organization supports the team in terms of information, material resources, technology, organization structures, available rewards, and even physical space. Teams are much more likely to perform well when they are given the right support than when they lack it.

Team size also makes a difference. The number of potential interactions increases exponentially as teams increase in size. This affects how members communicate, work together, handle disagreements, and reach agreements. So, just how big should a team be? The general answer is five to seven members for creative tasks. The more members, the harder it is to engage in the interactions needed for good problem solving. And, when voting is required, teams should have odd numbers of members to prevent ties.

TEAMS NEED THE RIGHT PROCESSES TO BE EFFECTIVE.

> **Team process** is the way team members work together to accomplish tasks.

Although having the right team inputs—membership composition, task, setting, and size—is important, it's no guarantee of team success. **Team process** counts, too. Think of it as the way the members of any team actually work together as they transform inputs into outputs. This **team effectiveness equation** is well worth remembering:

$$\text{Team Effectiveness} = \text{Quality of Inputs} + (\text{Process Gains} - \text{Process Losses}).$$

The process aspects of any team, also called *group dynamics*, include how members get to know one another, develop expectations and loyalty, communicate, handle conflicts, and make decisions. And, the simple fact is that group dynamics aren't always pretty. Haven't you been on teams where people seemed to spend more time dealing with personality conflicts than with the task? How often have you read or heard about high-talent college sports teams where a lack of the right "chemistry" among players meant subpar team performance?

A positive team process takes full advantage of group inputs to raise team effectiveness. These are process gains in the team effectiveness equation. On the flip side, it's all too common for team problems to create process losses that reduce effectiveness.

"YOU SHOULD TAKE OFF THE HEADPHONES IN THE OFFICE. THAT'S NOT THE WAY WE DO THINGS HERE."

QUICK CASE

Removing the Headphones to Show Team Spirit

Westend61/Getty Images

Sean has just started a new job on your team where everyone works in an open plan office. He's just out of college, acts happy, and is really getting into his new responsibilities. A music lover, he has been wearing headphones during the day while working on the computer at his workstation. But yesterday an older colleague came over and offered him this unsolicited advice. "You should take off the headphones in the office," she said. "It's not the way we do things here. People are starting to say that you aren't a team player."

Now Sean has come to you as his team leader. He wants to know if he's in the wrong or in the right. "And by the way," he says, "I like music and it helps me to work better." There's no company policy against headphones in the office, but the "advice" he's getting suggests he's taken individuality a step too far in this team setting.

WHAT DO YOU DO?

Headphones are as common in some offices as they are on the streets. But, when someone puts the headphones on the message being broadcast, intended or not, may be: Don't disturb! What do you say to Sean, and why? What do you say to the teammates and team as a whole, and why? Is this an opportunity to build new norms with the team, or is it a case of "headphones on, team spirit off"?

Scholar and consultant Daniel Goleman says process failures show a lack of **team IQ** or "the ability of teams to perform well."[33] He points out that "champion" teams excel because their members know how to use their talents in cooperation with others and are able to handle occasional disharmony and interpersonal conflicts. In other words, great teams combine talent with emotional intelligence and positive team processes to create a winning performance combination.

Team IQ is the ability of a team to perform well by using talent and emotional intelligence.

TEAMS MOVE THROUGH DIFFERENT STAGES OF DEVELOPMENT.

Teams tend to change as they age. Things are often very different for a newly formed team than for one whose members have been together for a long time. It turns out that one of the factors determining the success or failure of a team is how well problems and opportunities are handled over different phases of its life cycle. Scholars like to talk about this issue in terms of the five stages of team development listed here.[34]

1. *Forming*—a stage of initial orientation and interpersonal testing
2. *Storming*—a stage of conflict over tasks and working as a team
3. *Norming*—a stage of consolidation around task and operating agendas
4. *Performing*—a stage of teamwork and focused task performance
5. *Adjourning*—a stage of task completion and disengagement

Diversity and Team Development

An effective team meets and masters key process challenges as it moves through each of the prior stages, maximizing process gains and minimizing process losses. Try using the nearby figure to understand how membership diversity can challenge team development.

Here's what we know. Team diversity can expand the talents, ideas, perspectives, and experiences useful in problem solving.[35] But, relationships and processes can get more complicated as diversity grows. It's important to not let process losses overwhelm the opportunity for performance gains. When teams do well at managing diversity, especially through the "critical zone" of storming and norming, the chances for real success are greatly increased.

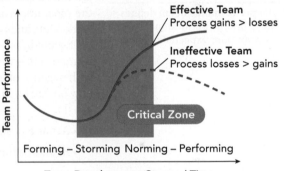

Team Development Challenges

The *forming stage of team development* is one of initial task orientation and interpersonal testing. New members are likely to ask: What can or does the team offer me? What will they ask me to contribute? Can my efforts serve team needs while also meeting my needs? Members begin to identify with one another and the team itself. They focus on getting acquainted, establishing interpersonal relationships, and discovering what is considered acceptable behavior. Difficulties in the forming stage tend to be greater in more culturally and demographically diverse teams.

The *storming stage of team development* is a period of high emotionality. Tension often emerges between members over tasks and interpersonal concerns. There may be periods of conflict, outright hostility, and even infighting as some individuals try to impose their preferences on others. But this is also the stage where members start to clarify task agendas and understand one another. Attention begins to shift toward mastering obstacles, and members start looking for ways to meet team goals while also satisfying individual needs. The storming stage is part of the critical zone where process failures cause lasting problems but process successes set the foundations for future effectiveness.

Cooperation is an important issue in the *norming stage of team development*. Members begin to better coordinate their efforts and share rules of conduct. The team feels a sense of leadership, with each member starting to play a useful role. Most interpersonal hostilities give way to a balancing of forces as norming builds initial integration. Norming is also part of the critical zone of team development. When it is well managed, team members are likely to develop initial feelings of closeness and a sense of shared expectations. This helps protect the team from disintegration while members continue their efforts to work well together.

Teams in the *performing stage of team development* are mature, organized, and well functioning. This is a stage of total integration in which team members are able to creatively deal with complex tasks and interpersonal conflicts. The team has a clear and stable structure, members are motivated by team goals, and the process scores high on the criteria of team maturity shown in **Figure 13.3**.[36]

The *adjourning stage of team development* is the final stage for temporary committees, task forces, and project teams. Here, team members prepare to achieve closure and disband, ideally with a sense that they have accomplished important goals.

TEAM PERFORMANCE IS INFLUENCED BY NORMS.

A **norm** is a behavior, rule, or standard expected to be followed by team members.

Have you ever felt pressure from other group members when you do something wrong—come late to a meeting, fail to complete an assigned task, or act out of character? What you are experiencing is related to group **norms**, the behaviors expected of team members.[37] A norm is a rule or standard that guides behavior. And when a norm is violated, team members are usually pressured to conform. In the extreme, violating a norm can result in expulsion from the group or social ostracism.

Any number of norms can be operating in a group at any given time. During the forming and storming stages of development, norms often focus on expected attendance and levels of commitment. By the time the team reaches the performing stage, norms have formed around adaptability, change, and desired levels of achievement. And without a doubt, one of the most important norms for any team is the **performance norm**. It defines the level of work effort and performance that team members are expected to contribute.

The **performance norm** defines the effort and performance contributions expected of team members.

It shouldn't surprise you that teams with positive performance norms, such as "Reciprocity is important—we all help one another to get things done," are more successful than those with negative ones, such as "Take care of yourself and don't expect someone to help you." But how do you build teams with the right norms? Actually, there are a number of things leaders can do.[38]

- Act as a positive role model.

- Reinforce the desired behaviors with rewards.

		Very poor		Very good	
1. Trust among members	1	2	3	4	5
2. Feedback mechanisms	1	2	3	4	5
3. Open communications	1	2	3	4	5
4. Approach to decisions	1	2	3	4	5
5. Leadership sharing	1	2	3	4	5
6. Acceptance of goals	1	2	3	4	5
7. Valuing diversity	1	2	3	4	5
8. Member cohesiveness	1	2	3	4	5
9. Support for each other	1	2	3	4	5
10. Performance norms	1	2	3	4	5

FIGURE 13.3 What Are the Criteria for Assessing the Process Maturity of a Team?
Teams vary greatly in the degree of maturity they achieve and demonstrate in day-to-day behavior. These criteria are helpful for assessing the development and maturity of a team as it moves through various phases—from forming to storming to norming to performing. We would expect that teams would start to show strong positives on these criteria as members gain experience with one another in the norming stage of team development. We would expect teams to have consistently strong positive scores in the performing stage.

- Control results by performance reviews and regular feedback.
- Train and orient new members to adopt desired behaviors.
- Recruit and select new members who exhibit the desired behaviors.
- Hold regular meetings to discuss progress and ways of improving.
- Use team decision-making methods to reach agreement.

One norm of special interest is the extent to which team members display virtuousness and share a commitment to moral behavior. Scholar Kim Cameron, for example, discusses **team virtuousness** in respect to these five norms or standards of moral behavior.[39] *Optimism*—Team members are expected to strive for success even when experiencing setbacks. *Forgiveness*—Team members are expected to forgive one another's mistakes and avoid assigning blame. *Trust*—Team members are expected to be courteous with one another and interact in respectful, trusting ways. *Compassion*—Team members are expected to help and support one another, and to show kindness in difficult times. *Integrity*—Team members are expected to be honest in what they do and say while working together.

> **Team virtuousness** indicates the extent to which members adopt norms that encourage shared commitments to moral behavior.

TEAM PERFORMANCE IS INFLUENCED BY COHESIVENESS.

Whether the team members will accept and conform to norms is largely determined by **cohesiveness**, the degree to which members are attracted to and motivated to remain part of a team.[40] Members of a highly cohesive team value their membership. They try to conform to norms and behave in ways that meet the expectations of other members, and they get satisfaction from doing so. In this way, at least, a highly cohesive team is good for its members. But does the same hold true for team performance?

> **Cohesiveness** is the degree to which members are attracted to and motivated to remain part of a team.

Figure 13.4 shows that teams perform best when the performance norm is positive and cohesiveness is high. In this best-case scenario, cohesion results in conformity to the positive norm which, in turn, ultimately benefits team performance. When the performance norm is negative in a cohesive team, however, high conformity to the norm creates a worst-case scenario. In this situation, members join together in restricting their efforts and performance contributions.

What are the implications of this relationship between norms and cohesiveness? Basically it boils down to this: Each of us should be aware of what can be done to build both positive norms and high cohesiveness in our teams. In respect to cohesiveness, this means such things as keeping team size as small as possible, working to gain agreements on team goals, increasing interaction among members, rewarding team outcomes rather than individual performance, introducing competition with other teams, and putting together team members who are very similar to one another.

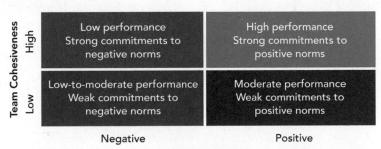

FIGURE 13.4 How Do Norms and Cohesiveness Influence Team Performance?
Group norms are expected behaviors for team members; cohesiveness is the strength of attraction members feel toward the team. When cohesiveness is high, conformity to norms is high. Positive performance norms in a highly cohesive group create a desirable situation, with high-performance outcomes likely. However, negative performance norms in a highly cohesive group can be troublesome; conformity by members to the negative norms creates low-performance outcomes.

TEAM PERFORMANCE IS INFLUENCED BY TASK AND MAINTENANCE ACTIVITIES.

A **task activity** is an action taken by a team member that directly contributes to the group's performance purpose.

A **maintenance activity** is an action taken by a team member that supports the emotional life of the group.

Distributed leadership is when any and all members contribute helpful task and maintenance activities to the team.

Disruptive behaviors are self-serving and cause problems for team effectiveness.

Research on the group process identifies two types of activities that are essential if team members are to work well together over time.[41] **Task activities** contribute directly to the team's performance purpose; **maintenance activities** support the emotional life of the team as an ongoing social system. Although you might expect that these are things that team leaders or managers should be doing, this is only partially correct. In fact, all team members should share the responsibilities for task and maintenance leadership.

The concept of **distributed leadership** in teams makes every member continually responsible for both recognizing when task or maintenance activities are needed and taking actions to provide them. Leading through task activities involves making an effort to define and solve problems and advance work toward performance results. Without task activities, such as initiating agendas and sharing information, teams have difficulty accomplishing their objectives. Leading through maintenance activities, such as encouraging others and reducing tensions, helps strengthen and perpetuate the team as a social system.

Figure 13.5 shows that task and maintenance activities stand in distinct contrast to dysfunctional or **disruptive behaviors**. These include obvious self-serving behaviors that you often see and perhaps even engage in yourself—things such as aggressiveness, excessive joking, and nonparticipation. Think about this the next time one of your groups is drifting toward ineffectiveness. Think also what you and other members can do to correct things by fulfilling distributed leadership responsibilities.

TEAM PERFORMANCE IS INFLUENCED BY COMMUNICATION NETWORKS.

A **decentralized communication network** allows all members to communicate directly with one another.

Teams use the different communication networks shown in **Figure 13.6** as they work and interact together.[42] In a **decentralized communication network**, all members communicate directly with one another. Sometimes called the *all-channel* or *star* structure, this arrangement works well for tasks that require lots of creativity, information processing, and problem solving. Use of a decentralized communication network creates an *interacting team* in which all members actively work together and share information. Member satisfaction on successful interacting teams is usually high.

Distributed leadership roles in teams

Team leaders provide task activities		**Team leaders provide maintenance activities**	
• Initiating	• Elaborating	• Gatekeeping	• Following
• Information sharing	• Opinion giving	• Encouraging	• Harmonizing
• Summarizing			• Reducing tension

Team leaders avoid and discourage disruptive activities	
• Being aggressive	• Competing
• Blocking	• Withdrawal
• Self-confessing	• Horsing around
• Seeking sympathy	• Seeking recognition

FIGURE 13.5 What are the distributed leadership roles in teams?
Teams function with a combination of task and maintenance activities that both appointed leaders and all members are responsible for providing. Task activities directly move the task forward while maintenance activities support the emotional health and social cohesion of the team as a whole. An additional and important distributed leadership responsibility in teams is the avoidance of personal displays of disruptive behaviors and also the discouragement of disruptive behaviors by others.

PATTERN	DIAGRAM	CHARACTERISTICS
Decentralized communication network Interacting Team		High interdependency around a common task Best at complex tasks
Centralized communication network Coaching Team	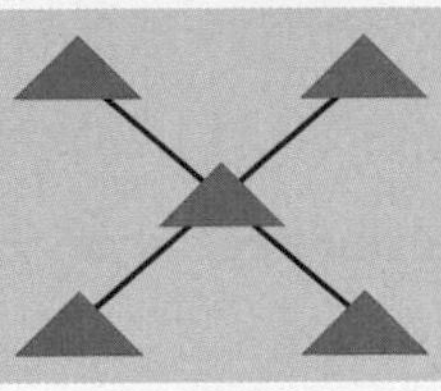	Independent individual efforts on behalf of common task Best at simple tasks
Restricted communication network Counteracting Team	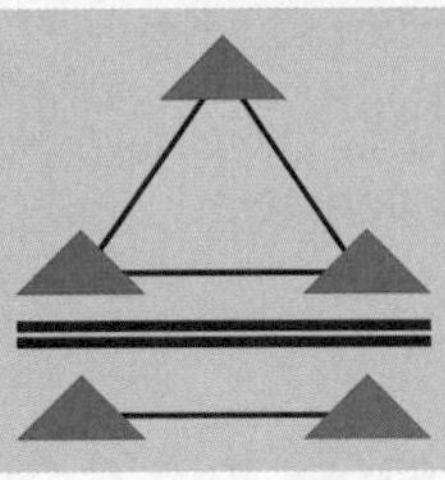	Subgroups in disagreement with one another Slow task accomplishment

FIGURE 13.6 What Communication Networks Are Used in Teams?

Members of teams communicate and interact together in different ways. A decentralized structure is where all members communicate with one another. It works best when tasks are complex and the need for information sharing is high. When tasks are simple and easily broken down into small parts, a centralized structure works well. It coordinates members' communications through one central point. A restricted communication network sometimes forms when subgroups break off to do separate work or due to member alienation. Any lack of communication between the subgroups can create performance problems.

When tasks are more routine and less demanding, team members can often divide up the work and then simply coordinate the final results. This is best done with a **centralized communication network**, sometimes called the *wheel* or *chain* structure. It has a central "hub" through which one member, often the team leader, collects information from and distributes information to all others. This creates a *coaching team* whose members work independently and pass completed tasks to the hub. There, they are put together into a finished product. The hub member often experiences the most satisfaction on successful coaching teams.

When teams break into subgroups, either on purpose or because members are experiencing issue-specific disagreements, this may create a **restricted communication network**. Left unmanaged, this *counteracting team* environment can deteriorate to the point where subgroups fail to adequately communicate with one another and even engage in outwardly antagonistic relations. Although these situations create problems, there are times when counteracting teams might be intentionally set up to encourage conflict, increase creativity, and help double-check the quality of specific decisions or chosen courses of action.

The best teams use all three communication networks—decentralized, centralized, and restricted. But they use them in the right ways and at the right times. When the task is simple and routine, you should organize as a coaching team using a centralized network. When things are getting complicated and unclear, go with an interacting team and the decentralized network. And when there isn't enough critical discussion or you're worried that too much harmony is limiting team creativity, it may be time to form a counteracting team where subgroups in a restricted network engage in a bit of conflict.

In a **centralized communication network**, communication flows only between individual members and a hub or center point.

Subgroups in a **restricted communication network** contest one another's positions and restrict interactions with one another.

STUDYGUIDE

Takeaway 13.2
What Are the Building Blocks of Successful Teamwork?

Terms to Define

Centralized communication network

Cohesiveness

Decentralized communication network

Disruptive behaviors

Distributed leadership

Effective team

Heterogeneous teams

Homogeneous teams

Maintenance activity

Norm

Performance norm

Restricted communication network

Task activity

Team diversity

Team effectiveness equation

Team IQ

Team process

Team virtuousness

Rapid Review

- An effective team achieves high levels of task performance, member satisfaction, and team viability.
- Important team input factors include the membership characteristics, nature of the task, organizational setting, and group size.
- A team matures through various stages of development, including forming, storming, norming, performing, and adjourning.
- Norms are the standards or rules of conduct that influence the behavior of team members; cohesion is the attractiveness of the team to its members.
- In highly cohesive teams, members tend to conform to norms; the best situation is a team with positive performance norms and high cohesiveness.
- Distributed leadership occurs when team members step in to provide helpful task and maintenance activities and discourage disruptive activities.
- Effective teams make use of alternative communication networks and interaction patterns to best complete tasks.

Questions for Discussion

1. What happens if a team can't get past the storming stage?
2. What can a manager do to build positive performance norms on a work team?
3. Why would a manager ever want to reduce the cohesion of a work group?

Be Sure You Can

- **list** the outputs of an effective team
- **identify** inputs that influence team effectiveness
- **discuss** how diversity influences team effectiveness
- **list** five stages of group development
- **explain** how norms and cohesion influence team performance
- **list** ways to build positive norms and change team cohesiveness
- **illustrate** task, maintenance, and disruptive activities in teams
- **describe** how groups use decentralized and centralized communication networks

Career Situation: What Would You Do?

For quite some time you've been watching the performance of your work team slowly deteriorate. Although everyone seems to like one another, the "numbers" in terms of measured daily accomplishments have now fallen to an unacceptable level. It's time to act. What will you look at to identify likely problem issues? What steps might you take to get this team back on track and improve its overall effectiveness?

Takeaway 13.3
How Can Managers Create and Lead High-Performance Teams?

ANSWERS TO COME

■ Team building can improve teamwork and performance.

■ Teams benefit when they use the right decision methods.

■ Teams suffer when groupthink leads to bad decisions.

■ Teams benefit when conflicts are well managed.

THERE'S QUITE A BIT OF AGREEMENT ABOUT THE CHARACTERISTICS OF HIGH-performance teams.[43] They have clear and elevating goals. They are results oriented, and their members are hard working. They have high standards of excellence in a collaborative team culture. They get solid external support and recognition for their accomplishments. And they have strong and principled leaders. It's a great list, isn't it? But how do we get and stay there?

Although we know that high-performance teams generally share the characteristics just noted, not all teams reach this level of excellence. Just as in the world of sports, there are many things that can go wrong and cause problems for teams in the workplace.

TEAM BUILDING CAN IMPROVE TEAMWORK AND PERFORMANCE.

One of the ways to grow capacity for long-term team effectiveness is a practice known as **team building**. This is a set of planned activities used to analyze the functioning of a team and then make changes to improve teamwork and performance.[44] Most systematic approaches to team building begin with awareness that a problem may exist or may develop within the team. The next step is for team members to work together to gather data and fully understand the problem. Action plans are then made, implemented, and evaluated by team members. As difficulties or new problems are discovered, the team-building process recycles.

> **Team building** involves gathering and analyzing data, and making changes to improve teamwork and performance.

There are many methods for gathering data on team functioning, including structured and unstructured interviews, questionnaires, team meetings, and reality experiences. Regardless of the method used, the basic principle of team building remains the same—a careful and collaborative assessment of data on team inputs, processes, and results. It works best when all members participate in data gathering and analysis and then collectively decide on actions to be taken.

Team building can be done with or without the help of outside consultants. It can also be done in the workplace or in off-site locations. It is increasingly popular, for example, to engage in outdoor activities—obstacle courses or special events like geocaching—to create enthusiasm for a team building experience. As one outdoor team-building expert points out, these outdoor team activities "focus on building trust, increasing productivity and emphasizing the importance of being a team player, as well as improving communication and listening skills while learning about group dynamics."[45] It's quite a statement, but the power of team building cannot be denied.

TEAMS BENEFIT WHEN THEY USE THE RIGHT DECISION METHODS.

The best teams don't limit themselves to just one **decision-making** method. Edgar Schein, a respected scholar and consultant, describes six ways teams make decisions.[46] He and other scholars note that teams ideally choose and use methods that best fit the problems at hand.[47] But mistakes are often made.

> **Decision making** is the process of making choices among alternative courses of action.

In *decision by lack of response*, one idea after another is suggested without any discussion taking place. When the team finally accepts an idea, all alternatives have been bypassed and

HOT TOPIC

Can Disharmony Build a Better Team?

Jonathan Daniel/Allsport/Getty Images

"There is no 'I' in team!" they say. But basketball superstar Michael Jordan once said: "There is an 'I' in win." What's his point? Jordan is suggesting that someone as expert as him at a task shouldn't always be subordinated to the team. Rather, it's the team's job to support his talents so that they shine to their brightest.

Sports metaphors abound in the workplace. We talk about "heavy hitters" and ask teammates to "step up to the plate." But, the real world of teamwork is dominated by the quest for cooperation, perhaps at the cost of needed friction. And that, according to Cambridge scholar Mark de Rond, is a potential performance problem. "When teams work well," du Rond says, "it is because, not in spite, of individual differences."

Those in favor of du Rond's views are likely to argue that even if superstars bring a bit of conflict to the situation, the result may well be added creativity and a performance boost. Instead of trying to make everyone happy, perhaps it's time for managers and team leaders to accept that disharmony can be functional. A bit of team tension may be a price worth paying for high performance. *Those worried about du Rond's views* might say there's a fine line between a superstar's real performance contribution and collateral damage or negative impact caused by personality and temperament clashes. And, that line is a hard one to spot and to manage.

HOW ABOUT IT?

Given what we know about teams and your personal experiences with them, should we be finding ways to accommodate the superstar on a team . . . or avoid them?

---

discarded by simple lack of response rather than by critical evaluation. In *decision by authority rule*, the leader, manager, committee head, or some other authority figure makes a decision for the team. Although this is time-efficient, the quality of the decision depends on whether the authority figure has the necessary information. Its implementation depends on how well other team members accept the top-down approach. In *decision by minority rule*, two or three people dominate by "railroading" the team into a decision. How often have you heard: "Does anyone object? Okay, let's go ahead with it."

One of the most common ways teams make decisions, especially when early signs of disagreement arise, is *decision by majority rule*. Although consistent with democratic methods, it is often used without awareness of potential downsides. When votes are taken, some people will be "winners" and others will be "losers." In all likelihood, you've been on the losing side at times. How did it feel? If you're like me, it may have made you feel left out, unenthusiastic about supporting the majority decision, and even hoping for a future chance to win.

Teams are often encouraged to try for *decision by consensus*. This is where full discussion leads to most members favoring one alternative, with the other members agreeing to support it. Even those opposed to the decision know that the others listened to their concerns. Consensus doesn't require unanimity, but it does require that team members be able to argue, debate, and engage in reasonable conflict, while still listening to and getting along with one another.[48]

A *decision by unanimity* means all team members agree on the course of action to take. This is the ideal state of affairs, but it is also very difficult to reach. One of the reasons that teams sometimes turn to authority decisions, majority voting, or even minority decisions is the difficulty of managing team processes to achieve consensus or unanimity.

Keys to Succesful Consensus Decisions

- Don't argue blindly; consider others' reactions to your points.
- Don't change your mind just to reach quick agreement.
- Avoid conflict reduction by voting, coin tossing, bargaining.
- Keep everyone involved in the decision process.
- Allow disagreements to surface so that things can be deliberated.
- Don't focus on winning versus losing; seek acceptable alternatives.
- Discuss assumptions, listen carefully, and encourage inputs by all.

Consensus is reached when all parties believe they have had their say and been listened to, and they agree to support the group's final decision.

TEAMS SUFFER WHEN GROUPTHINK LEADS TO BAD DECISIONS.

How often have you held back from stating your views in a meeting, agreed to someone else's position when it really seemed wrong, or gone along with a boss's suggestions even though you disagreed?[49] If and when you do these things, you are likely trapped by **groupthink**, the tendency for members of highly cohesive groups to lose their critical evaluative capabilities.[50] It occurs when teams strive so hard to reach agreement and avoid disagreement that they end up making bad decisions.[51]

Psychologist Irving Janis says that teams suffering groupthink often fit the description shown in **Table 13.1**.[52] They engage in things like rationalizing disconfirming data, stereotyping competitors as weak, and assuming the team is too good for criticism. They do this because members are trying to hold the group together and maintain harmony at all costs. They avoid doing anything that might detract from feelings of goodwill, such as expressing disagreement or pointing out that the team is moving too fast and needs to deliberate more. Each of these tendencies raises the risk of making bad decisions.

When you are leading or are part of team heading toward groupthink, don't assume there's no way out. Janis notes, for example, that leaders can absent themselves from meetings and allow group members to discuss and debate without them. With the leader absent, members may talk more openly and engage in more frank discussions.

Janis has other advice on how to get a team that is moving toward groupthink back on track.[53] You can assign one member to act as a critical evaluator or "devil's advocate" during each meeting. Subgroups can be assigned to work on issues and then share their findings with the team as a whole. Outsiders can be brought in to observe and participate in team meetings and offer their thoughts on both team processes and tentative decisions. And, the team can hold a "second chance" meeting after an initial decision is made to review, change, and even cancel it. Actions like these encourage helpful conflict and reduce pressures toward premature agreement. With good leadership, there's no reason to let groupthink take a team down the wrong pathway.

TEAMS BENEFIT WHEN CONFLICTS ARE WELL MANAGED.

The ability to deal with conflicts in interpersonal relationships and on a team is critical. When constructive, conflict adds to creativity and reduces tendencies toward groupthink. But when destructive, it breaks down team processes and hurts performance.

At its core, **conflict** involves disagreements among people. And in our experiences, it appears in two quite different forms.[54] **Substantive conflict** involves disagreements

> **Groupthink** is a tendency for highly cohesive teams to lose their evaluative capabilities.

> **Conflict** is a disagreement over issues of substance or clashing emotions.

> **Substantive conflict** involves disagreements over things like goals, tasks, and resources.

TABLE 13.1 Symptoms of Groupthink

Illusions of invulnerability—Members assume that the team is too good for criticism or is beyond attack.

Rationalizing unpleasant and disconfirming data—Members refuse to accept contradictory data or to thoroughly consider alternatives.

Belief in inherent group morality—Members act as though the group is inherently right and above reproach.

Stereotyping competitors as weak, evil, and stupid—Members refuse to look realistically at other groups.

Applying direct pressure to deviants to conform to group wishes—Members refuse to tolerate anyone who suggests the team may be wrong.

Self-censorship by members—Members refuse to communicate personal concerns to the whole team.

Illusions of unanimity—Members accept consensus prematurely, without testing its completeness.

Mind guarding—Members protect the team from hearing disturbing ideas or outside viewpoints.

Emotional conflict results from feelings of anger and distrust, as well as personality clashes.

Avoidance pretends that a conflict doesn't really exist.

Accommodation, or smoothing, plays down differences and highlights similarities.

Competition, or authoritative command, uses force and domination to win a conflict.

Compromise occurs when each party gives up something of value to the other.

Collaboration, or problem solving, works through differences so everyone wins.

Conflict resolution is the removal of substantive or emotional causes of a conflict.

over such things as goals and tasks, the allocation of resources, the distribution of rewards, policies and procedures, and job assignments. **Emotional conflict** results from feelings of anger, distrust, dislike, fear, and resentment as well as relationship problems. You know this form of conflict as a clash of personalities or emotions—when you don't want to agree with another person just because you don't like them or are angry about something they have done.

With all this potential for conflict in and around teams, how do you and others deal with it? Most people respond to conflict through different combinations of cooperative and assertive behaviors.[55] Figure 13.7 shows how they display five conflict management styles—avoidance, accommodation, competition, compromise, and collaboration.[56]

In **avoidance**, everyone withdraws and pretends that conflict doesn't really exist, hoping that it will simply go away. In **accommodation**, peaceful coexistence is the goal. Differences are played down and areas of agreement are highlighted. Both avoidance and accommodation are forms of *lose-lose conflict*. No one achieves what they want and the underlying conflict remains unresolved, often to recur in the future.

In **competition**, one party wins through superior skill or outright domination. It occurs as authoritative command by team leaders and as railroading or minority domination by team members. In **compromise**, trade-offs are made, with each party giving up and gaining something of value. Both competition and compromise are forms of *win-lose conflict*. Each party strives to gain at the other's expense. But whenever one party loses something, seeds for future conflict remain in place.

In **collaboration** both parties try to address the problem and resolve their differences. As you would expect, it is often time-consuming and stressful. But it's also the most effective style in terms of real conflict resolution. Collaboration turns a difficult situation into a *win-win conflict* that creates positive conditions for future teamwork. From experience, you should recognize that this approach depends on the willingness of everyone to dig in, confront the issues, and openly and honestly discuss them.

It's important to point out that each of the five conflict management styles can be useful.[57] Most of us probably use each style at least some of the time. But the question is, are we using them at the right times?

Some suggestions for making good choices about when to use various conflict management strategies are shown in the box. It's worth remembering that unresolved or suppressed conflicts often sow the seeds for future conflicts. Only true **conflict resolution**, characteristic of the collaborative style, eliminates the underlying causes of a conflict in ways that are constructive for future relationships and teamwork.

When to Use Alternative Conflict Management Strategies

- *Collaboration* or *problem solving*—use for true conflict resolution when time and cost permit.
- *Avoidance* or *withdrawal*—use when more important issues are pressing or when "cooling off" time is needed.
- *Competition* or *authoritative command*—use for quick decisions or when unpopular actions must be taken.
- *Accommodation* or *smoothing*—use when issues are more important to others or to build "credits" for future use.
- *Compromise*—use to temporarily settle complex issues or gain quick solutions when time is limited.

FIGURE 13.7

What Are the Five Common Styles of Conflict Management?

A combination of cooperative and aggressive behaviors results in five conflict management styles. Competition occurs when aggression dominates and accommodation occurs when cooperation dominates. Avoidance occurs with both low aggression and cooperation and compromise occurs with moderate amounts of both. True collaboration or problem solving is more likely when both cooperation and aggression are high.

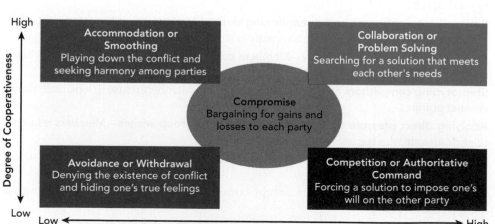

STUDYGUIDE

Takeaway 13.3
How Can Managers Create and Lead High-Performance Teams?

Terms to Define

Accommodation	Compromise	Decision making	Substantive conflict
Avoidance	Conflict	Emotional conflict	
Collaboration	Conflict resolution		Team building
Competition	Consensus	Groupthink	

Rapid Review

- Team building is a collaborative approach to improving group process and performance.
- Teams can make decisions by lack of response, authority rule, minority rule, majority rule, consensus, and unanimity.
- Groupthink is the tendency of members of highly cohesive teams to lose their critical evaluative capabilities and make poor decisions.
- Conflict occurs as disagreements between people over substantive or emotional issues.
- Tendencies toward cooperativeness and assertiveness create the interpersonal conflict management styles of avoidance, accommodation, compromise, competition, and collaboration.

Questions for Discussion

1. How does consensus differ from unanimity in group decision making?
2. Is groupthink found only in highly cohesive teams, or could it exist in precohesive ones?
3. When is it better to avoid conflict rather than directly engage in it?

Be Sure You Can

- **describe** how team building might help one of your groups
- **list** and discuss the different ways groups make decisions
- **define** the term "groupthink" and identify its symptoms
- **list** at least four ways teams can avoid groupthink
- **differentiate** substantive and emotional conflict
- **explain** the conflict management styles of avoidance, accommodation, competition, compromise, and collaboration

Career Situation: What Would You Do?

The members of the executive compensation committee that you are chairing show a high level of cohesiveness. It's obvious that they enjoy being part of the committee and are proud to be on the organization's board of directors. But the committee is about to approve extraordinarily high pay bonuses for the CEO and five other senior executives. This is occurring at a time when executive pay is getting lots of criticism from the press, unions, and the public at large. What can you do to make sure groupthink doesn't cause this committee to make a bad decision?

TEST PREP **13**

Answers to Test Prep questions can be found at the back of the book.

Multiple-Choice Questions

1. _____ occurs when a group of people is able to achieve more than its members could by working individually.
   (a) Distributed leadership
   (b) Consensus
   (c) Team viability
   (d) Synergy

2. One of the recommended strategies for dealing with a group member who engages in social loafing is to _____.
   (a) redefine tasks to make individual contributions more visible
   (b) ask another member to encourage this person to work harder
   (c) give the person extra rewards and hope he or she will feel guilty
   (d) just forget about it

3. An effective team is defined as one that achieves high levels of task performance, high member satisfaction, and _____.
   (a) resource efficiency   (b) team viability
   (c) group consensus   (d) creativity

4. In the open-systems model of teams, the _____ is an important input factor.
   (a) communication network
   (b) decision-making method
   (c) performance norm
   (d) diversity of membership

5. A basic rule of team dynamics might be stated this way: The greater the _____ in a team, the greater the conformity to norms.
   (a) membership diversity
   (b) cohesiveness
   (c) task clarity
   (d) competition among members

6. The team effectiveness equation states the following: Team Effectiveness = Quality of Inputs × (_____ − Process Losses).
   (a) Process Gains   (b) Leadership Impact
   (c) Membership Ability   (d) Problem Complexity

7. Members of a team become more motivated and better able to deal with conflict during the _____ stage of team development.
   (a) forming   (b) norming
   (c) performing   (d) adjourning

8. A team member who does a good job at summarizing discussion, offering new ideas, and clarifying points made by others is providing leadership by contributing _____ activities to the group process.
   (a) required   (b) task
   (c) disruptive   (d) maintenance

9. A team performing very creative and unstructured tasks is most likely to succeed using _____.
   (a) a decentralized communication network
   (b) decisions by majority rule
   (c) decisions by minority rule
   (d) more task than maintenance activities

10. One way for a manager to build positive norms within a team is to _____.
    (a) act as a positive role model
    (b) increase group size
    (c) introduce groupthink
    (d) isolate the team

11. The best way to try to increase the cohesiveness of a team would be to _____.
    (a) start competition with other groups
    (b) add more members
    (c) reduce isolation from other groups
    (d) increase the diversity of members

12. A _____ decision is one in which all members agree on the course of action to be taken.
    (a) consensus   (b) unanimous
    (c) majority   (d) synergy

13. Groupthink is most likely to occur in teams that are _____.
    (a) large in size
    (b) diverse in membership
    (c) high performing
    (d) highly cohesive

14. When people are highly cooperative but not very assertive in a conflict situation, the likelihood is that they will be using which conflict management style?
    (a) Avoidance   (b) Authoritative
    (c) Accommodation   (d) Collaboration

15. The interpersonal conflict management style with the greatest potential for true conflict resolution is _____.
    (a) compromise   (b) competition
    (c) avoidance   (d) collaboration

Short-Response Questions

16. What are the major differences among a task force, an employee involvement group, and a self-managing team?

17. How can a manager influence team performance by modifying group inputs?

18. How do cohesiveness and performance norms together influence team performance?

19. What are two symptoms of groupthink and two possible remedies for them?

Integration and Application Question

20. Valeria Martínez has just been appointed manager of a production team operating the 11 PM to 7 AM shift in a large manufacturing firm. An experienced manager, Valeria is pleased that the team members seem to really like and get along well with one another, but she notices that they also appear to be restricting their task outputs to the minimum acceptable levels.

    Question: How might Valeria improve this situation?

Steps for
Further Learning

BUILD MARKETABLE SKILLS • **DO** A CASE ANALYSIS • **GET** AND STAY INFORMED

BUILD MARKETABLE SKILLS.

EARN BIG CAREER PAYOFFS!

Don't miss these opportunities in the SKILL-BUILDING PORTFOLIO

SELF-ASSESSMENT 13:
Team Leader Skills

Team leadership is coming your way . . . know your strengths and weaknesses.

CLASS EXERCISE 13:
Understanding Team Dynamics

Teams are great . . . understanding how they work can make them better.

TEAM PROJECT 13:
Superstars on the Team

It helps to have a star on the team . . . what happens when the star causes problems?

Many learning resources are found at the end of the book and online within **WileyPLUS Learning Space.**

Practice Critical Thinking—Complete the CHAPTER 13 CASE

CASE SNAPSHOT: Auto Racing—When the Driver Takes a Back Seat[58]

When you think of auto racing, do you first think of drivers . . . or teamwork? Watch any televised race, and the majority of the camera time is dedicated to the drivers and their cars. But, the driver is simply one member of a larger team that works together to achieve maximum performance. When the driver wins, the team wins as well, and the driver is the first to thank them.

DO A CASE ANALYSIS.

STRENGTHEN YOUR CRITICAL THINKING!

MANAGER'S LIBRARY SELECTION
Read for Insights and Wisdom
Crowdsourcing: Why the Power of the Cloud Is Driving the Future of Business (2008, Crown Business) by Jeff Howe

Test: What is a collection of individuals working together to achieve a common purpose? *Digital immigrant's answer*—an organization. *Digital native's answer*—an online community.

So what's next in the world of "crowdsourcing"? In this book Jeff Howe focuses on virtual teamwork that draws on talents of unpaid amateurs to create value comparable to what organizations get from paid experts. There are many variations. Digg.com uses "crowd voting" of 6 million user ratings to promote top news stories. Kiva.org relies on "crowd funding" to gather financing from individuals for small business loans. Wikipedia uses "crowd creation" to create and update an online encyclopedia.

Howe believes crowdsourcing is shifting how organizations approach intellectual capital. It allows large audiences of diverse hobbyists to generate ideas in digital transparency and accelerate innovations quickly in open examination. Past generations largely viewed teamwork as physical actions of paid experts, guided by managers telling them what to do. New generations more likely view teamwork as primarily as a virtual effort of unpaid volunteers, guided by popular opinion that permits them to do what they enjoy. In the past, newspaper editors gathered staffs to determine the news. Today, online bloggers, discussion boards, and "trending now" topics provide much of the news content that is consumed.

GET AND STAY INFORMED.

MAKE YOURSELF VALUABLE!

REFLECT AND REACT How do you use crowdsourcing in everyday life? What work and career applications do you see for it? Should contributors to crowdsourcing be paid? Should members of the crowd remain anonymous or be identified? Should a crowd be led or guided? And, is there any risk of groupthink in crowdsourcing?

Kayak.com's chief technology officer Paul English placed a two-foot-tall toy elephant, Annabelle, in the conference room where it can't be ignored. "So often at work," he says, "people have issues that they can't resolve because they won't talk about it."

Communication 14

Listening Is the Key to Understanding

Management Live
Organizations Push Weekly Happiness Surveys

Dan Dalton/Getty Images

"Does your team leader listen to you?" "Is your manager responsive to questions?" "Did you enjoy your work last week?" "What challenges are you facing today?" Some organizations are asking employees to answer such questions as often as every week. These "quick-fire polls" or "pulse surveys" are online morale surveys. Questions are asked, answered, and analyzed in real time. It's a chance for employers to listen and learn, but some say that "it can get a little bit like homework."

YOUR THOUGHTS?

Pulse surveys can give managers and team leaders early warnings about morale and office problems. How do they sound to you? Is this just another distraction that routinely pops up in a screen window, or is it a real chance to improve communication and employee engagement?

WHAT'S INSIDE

ETHICS CHECK
Blogging is easy, but bloggers beware

FACTS TO CONSIDER
Open Office Designs Have Positive Impact on Behavior

HOT TOPIC
Master the science of persuasion and gain influence

QUICK CASE
"I just got a mediocre performance review"

YOUR CHAPTER 14 TAKEAWAYS

1. Understand the nature of communication and when it is effective.
2. Identify the major barriers to effective communication.
3. Discuss ways to improve communication with people at work.

Takeaway 14.1
What Is Communication, and When Is It Effective?

ANSWERS TO COME

- Communication helps build social capital.
- Communication is a process of sending and receiving messages with meanings attached.
- Communication is effective when the receiver understands the sender's messages.
- Communication is efficient when it is delivered at low cost to the sender.
- Communication is persuasive when the receiver acts as the sender intends.

COMMUNICATION IS AT THE HEART OF THE MANAGEMENT PROCESS. YOU MIGHT think of it as the glue that binds together the four functions of planning, organizing, leading, and controlling.[1] Planning is accomplished and plans are shared through the communication of information. Organizing identifies and structures communication linkages among people and positions. Leading uses communication to achieve positive influence over organization members and stakeholders. And, controlling relies on communication to process information to assess and measure performance results.

COMMUNICATION HELPS BUILD SOCIAL CAPITAL.

Social capital is the capacity to attract support and help from others to get things done.

In many ways communication by managers is all about building something everyone needs—**social capital**. This is the capacity to attract support and help from others in order to get things done. Whereas intellectual capital is basically what you know, social capital comes from who you know and how well you relate to them.

Managers need social capital, and they must be skilled communicators to get and keep it. Communication is a pathway for establishing trust in relationships and becoming valued within interpersonal networks. The best managers and team leaders thrive as communication nerve centers whose social capital grows while they continually gather information, process it, use it for problem solving, and share it with others.[2]

Given all this, does it surprise you that when the American Management Association asked its members to rate the communication skills of their managers, only 22.1% rated them "high"? Does it surprise you that they rated their bosses just slightly above average on putting ideas into words, credibility, listening and asking questions, and written and oral presentations?[3] And even though communication skills regularly top the lists of characteristics looked for by corporate recruiters, why is it that 81% of college professors in one survey rated high school graduates as "fair" or "poor" in writing clearly?[4]

Communication Skills Self-Check

- Convey positive image in communications
- Use e-mail and social media well
- Write clearly and concisely
- Network with peers and mentors
- Run and contribute to meetings
- Give persuasive presentations
- Give and receive constructive feedback

Do a quick self-check. Can you convince a recruiter that you have the communication skills necessary for success in a job? Do you have the baseline communication skills needed to build and maintain social capital for long-term career success?

COMMUNICATION IS A PROCESS OF SENDING AND RECEIVING MESSAGES WITH MEANINGS ATTACHED.

Communication is the process of sending and receiving symbols with meanings attached.

So, just what is this thing called **communication**? It helps to think of it is an interpersonal process of sending and receiving symbols with messages attached to them. Although the definition sounds simple and common sense enough, there is a lot of room for error. All too often things go wrong and our communication attempts end up misunderstood or poorly received.

Figure 14.1 summarizes the key elements in the communication process. A *sender* encodes an intended message into meaningful symbols, both verbal and nonverbal. He or she sends the *message* through a *communication channel* to a *receiver*, who then decodes or interprets its meaning. This *interpretation* may or may not match the sender's original intentions. When present, *feedback* reverses the process and conveys the receiver's response back to the sender.

A useful way to describe the communication process shown in the figure is as a series of questions. "Who?" (sender) "says what?" (message) "in what way?" (channel) "to whom?" (receiver) "with what result?" (interpreted meaning). To check the outcome, it's important to ask yet another important question: Do receiver and sender understand things in the same ways?

COMMUNICATION IS EFFECTIVE WHEN THE RECEIVER UNDERSTANDS THE SENDER'S MESSAGES.

The ability to communicate well both orally and in writing is a critical managerial skill and the foundation of effective leadership. Through communication, people exchange and share information and influence one another's attitudes, behaviors, and understandings. Communication allows managers to establish and maintain interpersonal relationships, listen to others, deal with conflicts, negotiate, and otherwise gain the information needed to make decisions. But all this assumes that the communication goes as intended.

As much as communication is part of our everyday lives, we often fail in using it to our best advantage. One problem is that we take our abilities for granted and end up being disappointed when the process breaks down. Another is that we are too busy, or too lazy, to invest enough time in making sure that the process really works. These problems point to issues of "effectiveness" and "efficiency" in the communication process.

In management, we say that **effective communication** occurs when the receiver fully understands the sender's intended message. In other words, the intended meaning matches the received meaning. As you well know, this outcome doesn't always happen.

> In **effective communication**, the receiver fully understands the intended meaning.

How often have you wondered what an instructor really wants in an assignment or struggled to understand a point during class lecture? How often have you been angry when a friend or loved one just "didn't seem to get" your message and, unfortunately, didn't respond in the desired way? And, how often have you sent a text or e-mail, or left a voice message, only to receive back a confused or even angry reply that wasn't at all appropriate to your intended message? These are all examples of well-intentioned communications that weren't effective. Things don't have to be this way. But it does take effort to achieve effective communication in work and personal affairs.

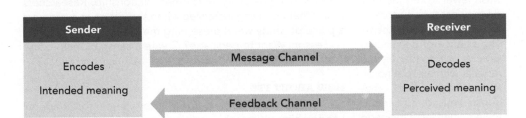

FIGURE 14.1 What Are the Major Elements in the Process of Interpersonal Communication?

The communication process begins when a sender encodes an intended meaning into a message. This message is then transmitted through a channel to a receiver. The receiver next decodes the message into perceived meaning. Finally, the receiver may transmit feedback back to the sender. The communication process is effective when the perceived meaning of the receiver is the same as the intended meaning of the sender.

COMMUNICATION IS EFFICIENT WHEN IT IS DELIVERED AT LOW COST TO THE SENDER.

Efficient communication occurs at minimum cost to the sender.

One reason why communication is not always effective—and the prior examples are good cases in point—is a trade-off between effectiveness and efficiency. **Efficient communication** occurs at minimum cost in terms of resources expended. These costs, time and convenience, in particular, often become very influential in how we choose to communicate.

Picture your instructor speaking individually, face-to-face, with each student about this chapter. Although most likely very effective, it would certainly be inefficient in terms of the cost of his or her time. This is why we often send texts, leave voice-mail, and use e-mail rather than speak directly with other people. These alternatives are more efficient than one-on-one and face-to-face communications. They may also allow us to avoid the discomfort of dealing with a difficult matter face-to-face. But although quick and easy, are these efficient communications always effective?

The next time you have something important to communicate, pause and consider the trade-offs between effectiveness and efficiency. A low-cost approach such as texting may save time, but will it convey to the other party your real intended meaning? By the same token, an effective communication may not always be efficient. If a team leader visits each team member individually to explain a new policy, this may guarantee that everyone truly understands the change. But, it will also take a lot of the leader's time. Holding a team meeting would be more efficient.

COMMUNICATION IS PERSUASIVE WHEN THE RECEIVER ACTS AS THE SENDER INTENDS.

Persuasive communication presents a message in a manner that causes others to accept and support it.

In personal life and at work we often want not just to be heard and understood, but to be followed. We want our communication to "persuade" the other party to believe or behave in a specific way that we intend. **Persuasive communication** gets someone else to accept, support, and act consistent with the sender's message.[5]

If you agree that managers get most things done through other people, you should also agree that managers must be very good at persuasive communication. Yet scholar and consultant Jay Conger believes that many managers "confuse persuasion with bold stands and

---

THE SCIENCE OF PERSUADING SAYS IT'S BEST TO IDENTIFY THE REQUEST WITH A SOCIAL NORM AND CREATE A SENSE OF RECIPROCITY.

HOT TOPIC

Master the Science of Persuasion and Gain Influence

© Rana Faure/Fancy/Corbis

Scene 1. Hoteliers want to wash fewer towels. So how do they get their customers to reuse more of them? The science of persuading says it's best to identify the request with a social norm. Researchers found that guests reused 33% more towels when left a message card that said "75% of customers who stay in this room reuse their towels."

Lesson: Want to persuade? Identify with the social norm.

Scene 2. Restaurant servers want to maximize tips. How can they get more customers to leave bigger ones? The science of persuading says it's best to create a sense of reciprocity in the server–customer relationship. Researchers found that tip giving increased when servers gave customers a piece of candy when presenting the bill.

Lesson: Want to persuade? Create a sense of reciprocity.

HOW ABOUT IT?

Can these lessons be turned into advice for leaders? Leadership ultimately requires success at influencing other people. To what extent is "persuasion" part of your leadership skill portfolio? How about the leaders you work with: Do they pass or fail as masters of the science of persuasion? And if persuasion is so important, should we spend more time learning and practicing to do it really well?

aggressive arguing."[6] This sounds a lot like the so-called debates that we watch on television as advocates of different political viewpoints face off against one another. A lot is said, some of it quite aggressively, but little in the way of influence on the other speaker or the listening audience really takes place.

It's a mistake to believe that an overly confrontational or uncompromising approach is a pathway to persuasion. At its best some compliance will be gained. At its worst, opposing positions will harden and resentment among parties will set the stage for future conflicts.

Persuasion and Credibility

Conger believes that the key to true persuasion is found in credibility. He goes on to define **credible communication** as that which earns trust, respect, and integrity in the eyes of others. He says it is a learned skill, one based on the personal powers of expertise and reference. He points out that those who try to persuade through domination, forcing, and harsh tactics lose credibility. And without credibility, he claims there is little chance for successful persuasion.

Credible communication earns trust, respect, and integrity in the eyes of others.

Persuasion and Charisma

There is renewed interest in the link between leadership charisma and persuasive communication. The latest thinking is that people can gain **charisma**—the ability to inspirationally persuade and motivate others—by mastering and successfully using basic communication skills. Called **charismatic leadership tactics**, these are communication techniques people use to make themselves appear more "leader-like" and be perceived by others as influential and trustworthy.[7]

Charisma is the ability to inspirationally persuade and motivate others.

Do you have what it takes to communicate persuasively? How strong are your charismatic leadership tactics? Why not pause and check your skills at communicating with credibility and charisma? Basic techniques include using words and phrases common to your audience, using clear logic that separates the good from the bad, and displaying emotions through facial gestures, voice intonations, and cadence.

Charismatic leadership tactics are communication techniques people use to make themselves more "leader-like" and be perceived by others as influential and trustworthy.

RECRUITERS GIVE COMMUNICATION AND NETWORKING SKILLS HIGH PRIORITY WHEN SCREENING CANDIDATES FOR COLLEGE INTERNSHIPS AND FIRST JOBS.

EXPLORE YOURSELF

Communication and Networking

Strong **communication and networking** skills are essential in all aspects of our lives. They are the tools for turning ideas into actions, being credible in the eyes of others, listening well and asking relevant questions, and getting your points across in written and oral presentations.

You might think that the attention given to communication and networking as critical management and career skills is overdone. But such attention is warranted. They are key foundations for social capital, the capacity to enlist the help and support of others when needed. They are pathways for getting work done in relationships and with the support of other people. Ultimately, they are the keys to real collaboration.

Recruiters give communication and networking skills high priority when screening candidates for college internships and first jobs. Employers consider it essential that workers be able to communicate well in teams and day-to-day work, and be able to network with others for collaboration and work accomplishment.

Get to know yourself better by taking the self-assessment on **Feedback and Assertiveness** and completing other activities in the *Exploring Management* **Skill-Building Portfolio.**

STUDYGUIDE

Takeaway 14.1
What Is Communication, and When Is It Effective?

Terms to Define

Charisma

Charismatic leadership
  tactics

Communication

Credible
  communication

Effective
  communication

Efficient communication

Persuasive
  communication

Social capital

Rapid Review

- Communication is the interpersonal process of sending and receiving symbols with messages attached to them.
- Effective communication occurs when the sender and the receiver of a message both interpret it in the same way.
- Efficient communication occurs when the sender conveys the message at low cost.
- Persuasive communication results in the recipient acting as the sender intends.
- Credibility earned by expertise and good relationships is essential to persuasive communication.

Questions for Discussion

1. Why do recruiters place so much emphasis on the communications skills of job candidates?
2. Can you describe a work situation where it's okay to accept less communication effectiveness to gain communication efficiency?
3. What can a manager do to gain the credibility needed for truly persuasive communication?

Be Sure You Can

- **describe** the communication process and identify its key components
- **define** and give an example of effective communication
- **define** and give an example of efficient communication
- **explain** why an effective communication is not always efficient
- **explain** the role of credibility in persuasive communication

Career Situation: What Would You Do?

Your boss just sent a text message that he wants you at a meeting starting at 3 PM. Your daughter is performing a music program at her elementary school at 2:45 PM, and she wants you to attend. You're out of the office making sales calls and have scheduled appointments to put you close to the school in the early afternoon. The office is a long way across town. Do you call the boss, text him, or send him an e-mail? What exactly will you say in your response to his message?

Takeaway 14.2
What Are the Major Barriers to Effective Communication?

ANSWERS TO COME

- Poor use of channels makes it hard to communicate effectively.
- Poor written or oral expression makes it hard to communicate effectively.
- Failure to spot nonverbal signals makes it hard to communicate effectively.
- Information filtering makes it hard to communicate effectively.
- Overloads and distractions make it hard to communicate effectively.

JOB INTERVIEW SCENE A COLLEGE SENIOR PAUSES ABOUT 15 MINUTES INTO A JOB interview to answer a call on his smart phone. It lasted a minute and wasn't an emergency. *Salary negotiation scene* A candidate has been offered a job, but doesn't like the salary offer. She has her father call the recruiter to negotiate a higher salary. *Another job interview scene* A college student brings her cat to a job interview and puts the carrier on the interviewer's desk. She played with the cat several times while speaking with the interviewer. *What happened next* None of these candidates were successful.[8] "Life has gotten more casual" for students, says one recruiter. "They don't realize the interview is a sales event."[9]

Whatever the situation—interviewing for a job, giving directions to a team member, asking a boss for help, or even building a personal relationship—everyone must be able to communicate well. So, let's get on with understanding the potential missteps. Look at **Figure 14.2**. It updates our description of the communication process to include **noise**—anything that interferes with the effectiveness of communication. It's important to guard against common sources of noise that find their ways into our conversations and discussions. They include poor choice of communication channels, poor written or oral expression, failures to recognize nonverbal signals, information filtering, and physical distractions.

> **Noise** is anything that interferes with the communication process.

POOR USE OF CHANNELS MAKES IT HARD TO COMMUNICATE EFFECTIVELY.

People communicate with one another using a variety of **communication channels**, the pathways used to carry the message. Good communicators choose the right channel or

> A **communication channel** is the pathway used to carry a message.

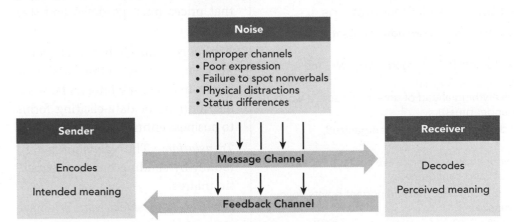

FIGURE 14.2 How Does Noise Interfere with the Communication Process?
Among the types of noise that can interfere with the effectiveness of communication, the following are well worth noting: Semantic problems in the forms of poor written or oral expression, the absence of feedback, improper choice and use of communication channels, physical distractions, status differences between senders and receivers, and cultural differences can all in one way or another complicate the communication process. Unless these factors are given attention, they can reduce communication effectiveness.

Channel richness is the capacity of a communication channel to effectively carry information.

combination of channels to accomplish their intended purpose. They understand differences in **channel richness**, the capacity to carry information in an effective manner.[10]

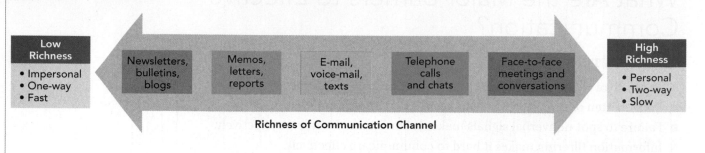

Richness of Communication Channel

The figure shows that face-to-face channels are high in richness. They establish direct personal contacts that can create a supportive, even inspirational, relationship between sender and receiver. Face-to face channels work especially well for complex or difficult messages and when we need immediate feedback. And, with today's technology, don't forget that "face-to-face" can mean being together through online video links.

The richness of communication channels diminishes quickly when you move away from face-to-face interactions. Written channels like memos, e-mails, and texts are efficient for sending basic information and messages. But, they tend to be impersonal and one-way transactions that offer limited, or at best delayed, opportunity for feedback. By the time you receive communications in the form of newsletters and blogs, time and physical distance have removed most channel richness.

POOR WRITTEN OR ORAL EXPRESSION MAKES IT HARD TO COMMUNICATE EFFECTIVELY.

Communication will only be effective when the sender expresses the message in a way that is clearly understood by the receiver. Words must be well chosen and used properly, something we all too often fail to do. Consider the following "bafflegab" found among some executive communications.[11]

A business report said: "Consumer elements are continuing to stress the fundamental necessity of a stabilization of the price structure at a lower level than exists at the present time."

Translation: Consumers keep saying that prices must go down and stay down.

A manager said: "Substantial economies were affected in this division by increasing the time interval between distributions of data-eliciting forms to business entities."

Translation: The division saved money by sending out fewer questionnaires.

A university president said: "We have strived to be as transparent as possible about the strategic alliance plans within the confines of our . . . closed negotiations."

Translation: The negotiations were confidential.

TIPS TO REMEMBER
Essential Ingredients of Successful Presentations

Be prepared—Know what you want to say; know how you want to say it; rehearse saying it.

Do the housekeeping—Attend to details; have room, materials, and arrangements ready to go.

Check technology—Go over everything ahead of time; make sure it works, and be sure you can use it under pressure.

Be professional—Be on time; dress appropriately; act organized, confident, and enthusiastic.

Set the right tone—Focus on your audience; make eye contact; "speak" don't "read"; and act pleasant and confident.

Sequence your points—State your purpose, make important points, follow with details, and then summarize.

Support your points—Give specific reasons for your points; state them in understandable terms.

Accent the presentation—Use good visual aids; provide handouts to add details and a summary overview.

Finish strong—Pull everything together in a concise, clear, and enthusiastic conclusion; invite and welcome questions.

It takes a lot of practice to write a concise letter or report, or deliver a great oral presentation. There's no getting around it—good writing and good speaking are products of plain old hard work.[12] But it's well worth the investment. How many drafts do you write for memos, letters, and reports? Are you getting so used to texting that you can't write a proper sentence? How often do you practice for an oral presentation?

FAILURE TO SPOT NONVERBAL SIGNALS MAKES IT HARD TO COMMUNICATE EFFECTIVELY.

The ways we use **nonverbal communication** can also work for or against our communication effectiveness. It takes place through hand movements, facial expressions, body posture, eye contact, and the use of interpersonal space.[13] And it can be a powerful means of transmitting messages.

> **Nonverbal communication** takes place through gestures, expressions, posture, and even use of interpersonal space.

Research shows that up to 55% of a message's impact comes through nonverbal communication.[14] A good listener, for example, knows how to read the "body language" of a speaker while listening to the words being spoken. In fact, a potential side effect of the growing use of electronic media is that the added value of reading nonverbal signals, such as gestures, voice intonation, or eye movements, gets lost.

Think of how nonverbal signals play out in your own communications. Watch how people behave in meetings, conversations, and even on TV and in videos. A simple hand gesture can show whether someone is positive or negative, excited or bored, or even engaged or disengaged.[15] You might notice, for example, that people tend to lean forward when they like something or someone and lean back when they don't.[16]

Sometimes our body may be "talking" even as we otherwise maintain silence. And when we do speak, our body may be saying different things than our words. This is called a **mixed message**, when a person's words or silence communicate one thing while nonverbal actions communicate something else. Be alert, it's time for caution when you notice someone moving back in their chair or stepping back in a conversation even while voicing agreement with what is being said to them. Chances are that what they are saying and what they believe—including willingness to act—are two different things.

> A **mixed message** results when words communicate one message while actions, body language, or appearance communicate something else.

INFORMATION FILTERING MAKES IT HARD TO COMMUNICATE EFFECTIVELY.

"Criticize my boss? I'd get fired."

"It's her company, not mine."

"I can't tell him that; he'll just get mad at me."

The risk of ineffective communication is high when people are communicating upward to immediate bosses and higher levels in organizations. Status differences in the hierarchy of authority are always potential barriers to effective communication. The fact is that those at higher levels have the power to control rewards and other outcomes affecting lower levels. And, those at lower levels don't always trust the higher-ups to use this power fairly.

Status differences in teams and organizations create a tendency known as **information filtering**—the intentional distortion of information to make it appear favorable to the recipient. You know this as "telling the boss or instructor what he or she wants to hear." And it's more common than many people think. Consultant Tom Peters calls it "Management Enemy Number 1." He also says that "once you become a boss you will never hear the unadulterated truth again."[17]

> **Information filtering** is the intentional distortion of information to make it more favorable to the recipient.

Information filtering involves someone telling the boss only what they think he or she wants to hear. Whether the reason is career protection, fear of retribution for bringing bad news, unwillingness to identify personal mistakes, or just a general desire to please, the end result is the same. The higher level receives biased and inaccurate information from below and ends up making bad decisions.

It's a continuing struggle for managers and team leaders to fight the information filtering problem, and the larger the organization, the bigger the problem seems to get. Leadership consultant Deborah J. Cornwall says: "There's a tendency for people in large, hierarchical organizations to tell the boss what he wants to hear." Former Ford global vice president Martin Zimmerman says: "You get blindsided when things deteriorate. You want to know about mistakes."[18]

OVERLOADS AND DISTRACTIONS MAKE IT HARD TO COMMUNICATE EFFECTIVELY.

Overloads and distractions are common causes of communication problems in our personal and work lives. Just consider the demands placed on us by electronic communications and social media. McKinsey reports that professionals spend up to 28% of their time dealing with e-mail, while the Radicati Group reports that the average business person deals with 108 e-mails per day.[19] Scholar Gloria Mark's research indicates that people check their e-mail inboxes as many as 74 times per day, causing her to say "It's really out of control."[20]

E-mails, messages, and chats pretty much follow us wherever we go 24/7. They all coexist simultaneously, and they compete with one another, social media, and video streams for our attention. The challenge of dealing with an ever-present and shifting mix of overwhelming communication demands spills over into face-to-face environments. Even a scheduled meeting may be compromised by overloads and distractions in the form of telephone interruptions, texts, e-mails, drop-in visitors, and lack of privacy. Consider the following exchange between George and his manager.[21]

> Okay, George, let's hear your problem [phone rings, manager answers it and promises caller to deliver a report "just as soon as I can get it done"]. Uh, now, where were we—oh, you're having a problem with your technician. She's . . . [manager's assistant brings in some papers that need his immediate signature] . . . you say she's overstressed lately, wants to leave. I tell you what, George, why don't you [phone beeps a reminder, boss looks and realizes he has a lunch meeting] . . . uh, take a stab at handling it yourself. I've got to go now [starts texting].

Besides what may have been poor intentions in the first place, this manager did a bad job communicating with George. And it's something that could easily have been prevented. Adequate time should have been set aside for the meeting; steps should have been taken to avoid interruptions; and the visitor's needs to communicate should have gotten more respect. The lesson is: Good communication takes work. When someone needs to communicate with you, respect the request, plan ahead, set aside adequate time, choose the right channel, and then engage—don't waste—the opportunity.

FACTS TO CONSIDER

Open Office Designs Have Positive Impact on Behavior

Dmitriy Shironosov/iStockphoto

A survey by the Ethisphere Institute, a think tank devoted to ethics and social responsibility practices, finds that open offices can have a positive impact on ethical behavior and communication. Respondents in a sample of 200 companies reported the following.

- 60% of companies used mainly open office versus closed office designs.

- 38% changed to open offices in the last 5 years.
- 81% believe staff visibility in open office designs promotes good behavior.
- 21% believe open office designs help reduce ethics violations.

WHAT'S YOUR TAKE?

What is your experience with open versus closed office designs? Would it support Ethisphere's findings? How about the downsides to increased staff visibility? Might a lack of privacy at work contribute to lower morale and even outright dissatisfaction?

STUDYGUIDE

Takeaway 14.2
What Are the Major Barriers to Effective Communication?

Terms to Define

Channel richness	Information filtering	Mixed message	Nonverbal communication
Communication channel		Noise	

Rapid Review

- Noise interferes with the effectiveness of communication.
- Poor choice of channels can reduce communication effectiveness.
- Poor written or oral expression can reduce communication effectiveness.
- Failure to accurately read nonverbal signals can reduce communication effectiveness.
- Filtering caused by status differences can reduce communication effectiveness.

Questions for Discussion

1. When is texting not an appropriate way to convey a message in a work situation?
2. If someone just isn't a good writer or speaker, what can he or she do to improve communication skills?
3. How can a higher-level manager avoid the problem of filtering when lower-level staffers pass information upward to her?

Be Sure You Can

- **list** common sources of noise that can interfere with effective communication
- **discuss** how the choice of channels influences communication effectiveness
- **give** examples of poor language choices in written and oral expression
- **clarify** the notion of mixed messages and how nonverbals affect communication
- **explain** how filtering operates in upward communication

Career Situation: What Would You Do?

As the leader of your work team, some members have come to you and pointed out that there is no way they can complete the current project on time. In fact, they expect to be at least 2 weeks late. This is a "pet" project for your boss, and your understanding is that she has a lot riding on its success for her career advancement. She is aloof and very formal in her dealings with you. Now you're stuck in the middle between her and your team. What actions will you take, and why?

Takeaway 14.3
How Can We Improve Communication with People at Work?

ANSWERS TO COME

- Active listening helps others say what they really mean.
- Constructive feedback is specific, timely, and relevant.
- Office designs can encourage interaction and communication.
- Transparency and openness build trust in communication.
- Appropriate online behavior is a communication essential.
- Sensitivity and etiquette improve cross-cultural communication.

MOST OF US PROBABLY GET IT RIGHT A FAIR AMOUNT OF THE TIME BUT also make too many communication mistakes. That's the story of Richard Herlich. Before participating in workshops held at the Center for Creative Leadership, he said, "I thought I had the perfect style."[22] But in role-playing exercises he learned that wasn't how others saw him. They viewed him as aloof and a poor communicator. Richard went back to his job and made it a point to meet with his team, discuss his style, and become more involved in their projects.

With so much room for error, don't you wonder how we ever communicate effectively? Fortunately, there are a number of things we can do to give things the best possible chance. They include active listening, constructive use of feedback, opening upward communication channels, understanding the use of space, utilizing technology, and valuing diversity.

ACTIVE LISTENING HELPS OTHERS SAY WHAT THEY REALLY MEAN.

When people talk, they are trying to communicate something. That "something" may or may not be what they are saying. This is why managers must be so good at listening. According to the late John Wooden, legendary UCLA men's basketball coach, "Many leaders don't listen. We'd all be a lot wiser if we listened more—not just hearing the words, but listening and not thinking about what you are going to say."[23] Check out these alternative workplace conversations. They contrast a "passive" listener and an "active" listener.

QUESTIONER: "Don't you think employees should be promoted on the basis of seniority?"

Passive Listener's Response: "No, I don't!"

Active Listener's Response: "It seems to you that they should, I take it?"

QUESTIONER: "What does the supervisor expect us to do about these out-of-date computers?"

Passive Listener's Response: "Do the best you can, I guess."

Active listener's response: "You're pretty disgusted with those machines, aren't you?"

Active listening helps the source of a message say what he or she really means.

Active listening is the process of taking action to help others say what they really mean.[24] It requires being sincere while listening to someone and trying to find the full meaning of a message. It also involves being disciplined, controlling one's emotions, and with holding premature evaluations that turn off rather than turn on the other party's willingness to communicate. Look again at the featured questions and answers box. The examples show how active listening can facilitate communication in difficult circumstances, rather than discourage it. But, let's be realistic; it isn't always easy to do. As you think further about active listening skills, keep these rules in mind.[25]

1. *Listen for message content:* Try to hear exactly what content is being conveyed in the message.
2. *Listen for feelings:* Try to identify how the source feels about the content in the message.
3. *Respond to feelings:* Let the source know that her or his feelings are being recognized.
4. *Note all cues:* Be sensitive to nonverbal and verbal messages; be alert for mixed messages.
5. *Paraphrase and restate:* State back to the source what you think you are hearing.

CONSTRUCTIVE FEEDBACK IS SPECIFIC, TIMELY, AND RELEVANT.

Feedback is the process of telling other people how you feel about something they did, said, or about the situation in general. Like active listening, the art of giving feedback is an indispensable skill. Feedback that is poorly given can easily come off as threatening and create more resentment than positive action. But when well delivered, the recipient is more likely to listen and carefully consider the message.[26] See Tips to Remember for advice on making feedback constructive.[27]

Consider someone who comes late to meetings. Feedback from the meeting chair might be *evaluative*— "You are unreliable and always late for everything." It might be *interpretive*— "You're coming late to meetings; you might be spreading yourself too thin and have trouble meeting your obligations." And it might be *descriptive*— "You were 30 minutes late for today's meeting and missed a lot of the context for our discussion."[28] The descriptive

> **Feedback** is the process of telling someone else how you feel about something that person did or said.

TIPS TO REMEMBER
How to Give Constructive Feedback

- *Choose the right time*—Give feedback at a time when the receiver seems most willing or able to accept it.
- *Be genuine*—Give feedback directly and with real feeling, based on trust between you and the receiver.
- *Be specific*—Make feedback specific rather than general; use clear and recent examples to make points.
- *Stick to the essentials*—Make sure the feedback is valid; limit it to things the receiver can be expected to do something about.
- *Keep it manageable*—Give feedback in small doses; never give more than the receiver can handle at any particular time.

"YOU'VE ACTUALLY DONE QUITE WELL, BUT YOU SHOULD KNOW THAT I NEVER GIVE ANYONE HIGH RATINGS TO START WITH."

QUICK CASE

"I Just Got a Mediocre Performance Review"

Andrey Arkusha/Fotalia

A good friend just called and wants to meet for a heart-to-heart chat after work. She was really frantic over a performance review that was a lot lower than what she had been expecting. The review was compounded by the fact that it was her first in a new job and with a new manager. She worried not only that her efforts weren't being appreciated, but also that the mediocre review would hurt her chances for future promotion at the company.

"I just got a mediocre performance review," she said, "and it totally blindsided me. I went into the manager's office with a smile on my face and expecting congratulations for my hard work in this new job. Instead, I got the following message: 'You've actually done quite well, but you should know that I never give anyone high ratings to start with. That doesn't leave any room for improvement.'"

WHAT DO YOU DO?

How do you prepare for this meeting? What should you be ready to say, and not say? She views you as a trusted friend and counselor. How can you play these roles and really help her deal with the situation in the best possible ways?

feedback is more likely to be better received and have a more lasting positive impact on the recipient.

OFFICE DESIGNS CAN ENCOURAGE INTERACTION AND COMMUNICATION.

Look at the margin figure and think about office spaces, yours and those of persons you visit. What messages do the layouts and furnishings send to visitors? Do they help or hinder communication? These are issues of **proxemics**, the study of the ways people use and communicate with space.[29] We know that physical distance between people conveys varying intentions in terms of intimacy, openness, and status as they communicate with one another. But we might not be as sensitive to how the physical layout of work and leisure spaces can do the same things. In fact, they are part of the nonverbal signals we send to others.

Today's organizations are being run with the premise that the better people communicate with one another, the better the organization will perform. We live in an increasingly connected world, and the same levels of connectedness are sought in the workplace. The Facebook brand, for example, is all about sharing and interaction. So, too, is the design for the firm's new headquarters. Designed by Frank Gehry and visualized by founder and CEO Mark Zuckerberg, the building is all on one floor and has no private offices. Zuckerberg and the top management team sit in the center, open and accessible to all. The *Wall Street Journal* describes it a "soaring fishbowl" in which "people can turn or twist their desk clusters to optimize the visual and physical proximity of those with whom they work most closely."[30]

Part of the push toward greater connectedness and more casual conversations is found in what might be called the demise of the office cubicle. It's been popular for awhile to design office spaces with small cubicles for individual workers and larger meeting rooms where they can hold meetings. The new trend is toward smaller teams, less formal meetings, and more frequent casual interaction. Architects and office supply firms are responding with designs that open up or eliminate cubicles—as in the Facebook headquarters—by giving them shorter walls or no walls at all. They are also creating lots of small "focus rooms" where two or just a few people can huddle up while exchanging ideas, working on a project, or just having a chat. Martha Clarkson heads Microsoft's global workplace strategy. She says it's based on a post-cubicle model because "work is really getting done in smaller teams."[31]

TRANSPARENCY AND OPENNESS BUILD TRUST IN COMMUNICATION.

CEO Vineet Nayar believes that one of his most important tasks at the technology outsourcing firm HCL Industries is to create a "culture of trust." And to do that, he says, you have to create transparency. Nayar posts HCL's financial information on the internal Web site, saying "We put all the dirty linen on the table." Results of 360° feedback reviews for HCL's 3,800 managers, including Nayar's, are posted there as well. And when managers present plans to top executives, they also get posted because Nayar wants others to read and comment on them. Why? By the time a plan is approved, it's likely to be a good one, he says, because of the "massive collaborative learning that took place."[32]

Communication transparency involves being honest and openly sharing accurate and complete information about the organization and workplace affairs. Its absence is evident when managers try to hide information and restrict the access of organizational members to it. Whereas lack of transparency creates conditions for distrust and harmful rumor, full transparency can have a positive impact on trust and employee engagement.

Transparency and openness in communication is a characteristic of **open-book management**, where managers provide employees with essential financial information about their companies. This willingness to open the books was evident in the HCL Industries example. At Bailard, Inc., a private investment firm, openness extends to salaries. If you want to know what others are making at the firm, all you need to do is ask the chief financial officer. The firm's co-founder and CEO, Thomas Bailard, believes this approach is a good way to defeat office politics. "As a manager," he says, "if you know that your compensation decisions are essentially going to be public, you have to have pretty strong convictions about any decision you make."[33]

Proxemics is the study of the way we use and communicate with space.

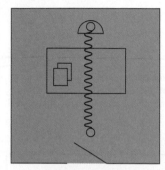

"I am the boss!"

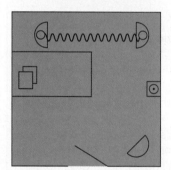

"I am the boss, but let's talk"

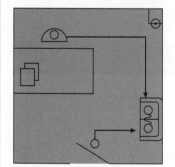

"Forget I'm the boss, let's talk"

Communication transparency involves being honest and openly sharing accurate and complete information.

In **open-book management**, managers provide employees with essential financial information about their employers.

APPROPRIATE ONLINE BEHAVIOR IS A COMMUNICATION ESSENTIAL.

Knowing how and when to use e-mail, texts, and social media is now a top issue in workplace communications. But the goal must always be appropriate—not inappropriate—use. "Thnx for the IView! I Wud Luv to Work 4 U!!;)" may be understandable "textspeak" for some people, but it isn't the follow-up message that most employers like to receive from job candidates.[34]

When Tory Johnson, President of Women for Hire Inc., received a thank-you note by e-mail from an intern candidate, it included "hiya," "thanx," three exclamation points—"!!!," and two emoticons. She says: "That e-mail just ruined it for me." The risk of everyday shorthand in chats and texting is that we become too casual overall in its use, forgetting that how a message is received is in large part determined by the receiver. Even though textspeak and emoticons are the norm in social networks, staffing executives at KPMG, which hires hundreds of new college grads and interns each year, consider them "not professional."

Posting Pitfalls and Strategies

It's not only what a job applicant says or sends directly to a recruiter that counts. Every comment and photo that we post on the Web, or that others post about us, becomes part of our public profile. And, this profile communicates a "personal brand." CareerBuilder points out that close to 40% of recruiters browse social media to check up on job applicants.[35] If what they find fits the impression they are looking for, the personal brand revealed in the online profile works in the applicant's favor. But if it gives the wrong impression, a rejection is likely.

> **Millennial text to baby boomer:**
> Sry abt mtg rdy 4 nxt 1
> **Baby boomer text to Millennial:**
> Missed you at the meeting. Stop by my office. We need to talk about this.

The point is to engage in appropriate online behavior, making technology work for rather than against us. The first step is editing what we put on the Web to minimize negative impressions and maximize positive ones. This might mean something as simple as exercising good judgment on Facebook postings for friends and building another professional profile on LinkedIn. It might also mean crafting a Web presence that backs up your résumé and career goals, such as by posting links to relevant newspaper and magazine articles along with intelligent comments about them. The second step, of course, is to stay vigilant and be Web smart. The founder of reputation.com, Michael Fertik, says: "Assume that every employer is constantly looking at your profile. Just because you don't get negative feedback doesn't mean it's not there."[36]

Privacy at Risk

Even though Facebook's CEO Mark Zuckerberg once said that privacy is "no longer a social norm," we have to take the issue very seriously in personal affairs and at work. Technology makes it easy for employers to monitor what employees do, and when. They get concerned when too much work time gets spent with personal e-mail, chats, Web browsing, and social networking. By the same token, employees are concerned that employers are electronically eavesdropping. But, they can also be casual in time spent on the Web and inappropriate in how they use it. Consider this tweet that became an Internet sensation: "Cisco just offered me a job! Now I have to weigh the utility of a fatty paycheck against the daily commute to San Jose and hating the work."[37] What would you do if you were the recruiter who had just made this job offer?

SENSITIVITY AND ETIQUETTE IMPROVE CROSS-CULTURAL COMMUNICATION.

Nancy McKinstry initiated major changes when taking over as the first American CEO of the Dutch publisher Wolters Kluwer. She cut staff, restructured divisions, and invested in new business areas. She described the new strategy as "aggressive" to her management team.

ETHICS CHECK

Blogging Is Easy, but Bloggers Beware

Photo Edi/Alamy

It is easy and tempting to set up your own blog, write about your experiences and impressions, and then share your thoughts with others online. So, why not do it?

Catherine Sanderson, a British citizen living and working in Paris, might have asked this question before launching her blog, *Le Petite Anglaise*. At one point it was so "successful" that she had 3,000 readers. But, the Internet diary included reports on her experiences at work—and her employer wasn't happy when it became public knowledge.

Even though Sanderson was blogging anonymously, her photo was on the site, and the connection was eventually discovered. Noticed, too, was her running commentary about bosses, colleagues, and life at the office. A Christmas party was described in detail, including an executive's "unforgivable *faux pas*." When her blog came to management attention, Sanderson says that she was "dooced"—a term used to describe being fired for what one writes in a blog. She sued for financial damages and confirmation of her rights, on principle, to have a private blog. The court awarded her a year's salary.

YOUR DECISION?

Just what are the ethics issues here—from the blogger's and the employer's perspectives? What rights do workers have when it comes to communicating in public about their work experiences and impressions? How about employers? Should they be protected from disgruntled employee-bloggers?

When the word wasn't well received by Europeans, she switched to "decisive."[38] "I was coming across as too harsh, too much of a results-driven American to the people I needed to get on board," says McKinstry.

Cultural differences are a ready source of potential problems in communication. But keep in mind that you don't have be doing international business or taking a foreign vacation for this point to be relevant. Think about it—going to work, to class, and out to shop can be a cross-cultural journey for most of us today.

Ethnocentrism is the tendency to consider one's culture superior to any and all others.

You should recall that **ethnocentrism** is a major source of intercultural difficulties. It is the tendency to consider one's culture superior to any and all others. Any such tendencies can hurt cross-cultural communication in at least three ways. First, they may cause someone to not listen well to what others have to say. Second, they may cause someone to address or speak with others in ways that alienate them. And third, they may involve use of inappropriate stereotypes.

Just recognizing tendencies toward ethnocentrism is helpful. You can spot it in conversations as arrogance in tone, manners, gestures, and words. But success in cross-cultural communication also takes sensitivity and a willingness to learn about how different people see, do, and interpret things. This involves **cultural etiquette**, the use of appropriate manners, language, and behaviors when communicating with people from other cultures.

Cultural etiquette is use of appropriate manners and behaviors in cross-cultural situations.

Knowing the etiquette helps us avoid basic cross-cultural mistakes. Messages can easily get lost in translation, as these historical advertising miscues demonstrate. A Pepsi ad in Taiwan that intended to say "the Pepsi generation" came out as "Pepsi will bring your ancestors back from the dead." A KFC ad in China intended to convey "finger lickin' good" came out as "eat your fingers off."[39] Nonverbals are important etiquette issues, too. The American "thumbs-up" sign is an insult in Ghana and Australia. To wave "hello" with an open palm in West Africa is an insult suggesting the other person has five fathers.[40]

STUDYGUIDE

Takeaway 14.3

How Can We Improve Communication with People at Work?

Terms to Define

Active listening

Communication transparency

Cultural etiquette

Ethnocentrism

Feedback

Open-book management

Proxemics

Rapid Review

- Active listening, through reflecting back and paraphrasing, can help overcome barriers and improve communication.
- Organizations can design and use office architecture and physical space toimprove communication.
- Information technology, such as e-mail, instant messaging, and intranets, can improve communication in organizations, but it must be well used.
- Ethnocentrism, a feeling of cultural superiority, can interfere with cross-cultural communication; with sensitivity and cultural etiquette, it can be improved.

Questions for Discussion

1. Which rules for active listening do you think most people break?
2. Is transparency in communications a sure winner, or could a manager have problems with it?
3. How could you redesign your office space, or that of your instructor or boss, to make it more communication-friendly?

Be Sure You Can

- **role**-play the practice of active listening
- **list** the rules for giving constructive feedback
- **explain** how space design influences communication
- **identify** ways technology utilization influences communication
- **explain** the concept of cultural etiquette

Career Situation: What Would You Do?

The restaurant you own and manage is being hit hard by a bad economy. The number of customers is down, as is the amount of the average dinner bill. You employ a staff of 12, but you're going to have to cut back or go to job sharing so that the payroll covers no more than 8. One of the servers just told you that someone is tweeting that the restaurant is going to close its doors after the coming weekend. Loyal customers and staff are "buzzing" about the news, and it's starting to travel more widely. How do you deal with this situation?

TESTPREP 14

Answers to TestPrep questions can be found at the back of the book.

Multiple-Choice Questions

1. Who is responsible for encoding a message in the communication process?
   (a) Sender   (b) Receiver
   (c) Observer   (d) Consultant

2. Issues of "respect" and "integrity" are associated with _____ in communication.
   (a) noise   (b) filtering
   (c) credibility   (d) ethnocentrism

3. Which is the best example of a team leader providing descriptive rather than evaluative feedback to a team member?
   (a) You are a slacker.
   (b) You are not responsible.
   (c) You cause me lots of problems.
   (d) You have been late to meetings three times this month.

4. When interacting with an angry co-worker who is complaining about a work problem, a manager skilled at active listening would most likely try to _____.
   (a) delay the conversation until a better time
   (b) point out that the conversation would be better held at another location
   (c) express displeasure in agreement with the co-worker's complaint
   (d) rephrase the co-worker's complaint to encourage him to say more

5. When the intended meaning of the sender and the interpreted meaning of the receiver are the same, communication is _____.
   (a) effective   (b) persuasive
   (c) passive   (d) efficient

6. What happens when a communication is persuasive?
   (a) The receiver understands the message.
   (b) The sender feels good about the message.
   (c) The receiver acts as the sender intended.
   (d) The sender becomes a passive listener.

7. How can a manager build the credibility needed for persuasive communications?
   (a) Offer rewards for compliance with requests.
   (b) Clarify penalties for noncompliance with requests.
   (c) Remind everyone that she or he is the boss.
   (d) Work hard to establish good relationships with others.

8. One of the rules for giving constructive feedback is to make sure that it is always _____.
   (a) general rather than specific
   (b) indirect rather than direct
   (c) given in small doses
   (d) delivered at a time convenient for the sender

9. When a worker receives an e-mail memo from the boss with information about changes to his job assignment and ends up confused because he doesn't understand it, the boss has erred by making a bad choice of _____ for communicating the message.
   (a) words   (b) channels
   (c) nonverbals   (d) filters

10. The safest conclusion about privacy in electronic communications is _____.
    (a) it's guaranteed by law
    (b) it's not a problem
    (c) it really doesn't exist
    (d) it can be password protected

11. A/An _____ is higher in channel richness than a/an _____.
    (a) memo; voice mail
    (b) letter; video conference
    (c) chat message; e-mail
    (d) voice mail; telephone conversation

12. The negative effects of status differences on communication between lower and higher levels in organizations show up in the form of _____.
    (a) information filtering   (b) proxemics
    (c) ethnocentrism   (d) passive listening

13. A manager who understands the influence of proxemics in communication is likely to _____.
    (a) avoid sending mixed messages
    (b) arrange work spaces to encourage interaction
    (c) be very careful choosing written words
    (d) send frequent e-mail messages to team members

14. When a person's words say one thing but his or her body language suggests something quite different, the person is sending _____.
    (a) a mixed message   (b) noise
    (c) social capital   (d) destructive feedback

15. If a visitor to a foreign culture makes gestures commonly used at home even after learning that they are offensive to locals, the visitor can be described as _____.
    (a) a passive listener   (b) ethnocentric
    (c) more efficient than effective (d) an active listener

Short-Response Questions

16. What is the goal of active listening?

17. Why do managers sometimes make bad decisions based on information received from their subordinates?

18. What are four errors team leaders might make when trying to give constructive feedback to team members?

19. How does ethnocentrism influence cross-cultural communication?

Integration and Application Questions

20. Glenn was recently promoted to be the manager of a new store being opened by a large department store chain. He wants to start out right by making sure that communications are always good between him, the six department heads, and the 50 full-time and part-time sales associates. He knows he'll be making a lot of decisions in the new job, and he wants to be sure that he is always well informed about store operations. He also wants to make sure everyone is always "on the same page" about important priorities. Put yourself in Glenn's shoes.

    Questions: What should Glenn do right from the start to ensure that he and the department managers communicate well with one another? How can he open up and maintain good channels of communication with the sales associates?

Steps for
Further Learning

BUILD MARKETABLE SKILLS • **DO** A CASE ANALYSIS • **GET** AND STAY INFORMED

BUILD MARKETABLE SKILLS.
EARN BIG CAREER PAYOFFS!

Don't miss these opportunities in the SKILL-BUILDING PORTFOLIO

SELF-ASSESSMENT 14:
Feedback and Assertiveness

Stress can take its toll . . . learn how to recognize the symptoms.

CLASS EXERCISE 14:
Difficult Conversations

Not everyone wants the same things . . . it's important to understand individual differences.

TEAM PROJECT 14:
How Words Count

Sometimes it's often others . . . handling difficult personalities is a management challenge.

Many learning resources are found at the end of the book and online within **WileyPLUS Learning Space.**

Practice Critical Thinking—Complete the
CHAPTER 14 CASE

CASE SNAPSHOT: Twitter—Rewriting (or Killing) Communication

Twitter's 140-character text-based messages, or "Twitter-speak," permeate everyday life. But questions about its influence are being asked—by parents, relationship partners, teachers, and employers. Is Twitter reinventing social communication or just abbreviating it? Do tweets create meaningful conversations, or do they dumb down our abilities to write and communicate effectively with one another?

DO A CASE ANALYSIS.
STRENGTHEN YOUR CRITICAL THINKING!

MANAGER'S LIBRARY SELECTION
Read for Insights and Wisdom
Collaboration: How Leaders Avoid the Traps, Build Common Ground, and Reap Big Results **(2009, Harvard Business Press) by Morten Hansen**

Is the sum of the parts greater than the whole? In this book, author Morten Hansen lists four communication problems for team members. First, individuals are hesitant to reach out to others for help because they believe in self-reliance. Second, people are unwilling to help others because they fear it will diminish their power of expertise. Third, members are unable to find experts in large or complex organizations, or they have limited contacts in their networks. And four, they are uncomfortable sharing with people they don't know on a personal level.

GET AND STAY INFORMED.
MAKE YOURSELF VALUABLE!

To resolve these problems, Hansen believes managers must appreciate how difficult collaboration is and limit its use. He thinks improved organizational sharing begins with recruiting and hiring members who can overcome communication barriers. These types of individuals are able to unify with others in common goals because they possess "T-shaped" skills—they work well within their discipline (the vertical bar), but also across other disciplines (the horizontal bar). Managers can also encourage members to build and use personal networks within the organization to alleviate discomfort. Collaborative results should then sum to greater values than individual outcomes.

REFLECT AND REACT Have the four communication barriers identified by Hansen affected teams that you've been on? Would it have been possible to select members that wouldn't have had these problems? Does this concept of "T-shaped skills" make sense as a criterion for selecting team members?

A day at work, a trip to the store, a visit with friends—all bring diversity into our lives. Even a walk across the college campus can be a trip around the world, if you're willing to take it.

Diversity and Global Cultures

15

There Are New Faces in the Neighborhood

Management Live

Cultural Intelligence Opens Doors to Opportunity

Fotosearch RF/Getty Images

Cultural differences can be frustrating and even feel threatening. Our ways of doing things may seem strange or even offensive to others, and vice versa. By nature and upbringing we wear "cultural lenses" that can limit our vision, causing us to see and interpret things with the biases of our own culture. But with cultural intelligence, we can better adapt to new cultures and work well in culturally diverse situations. This includes breaking the habits of our home culture and engaging the ways of others with interest, respect, and learning.

YOUR THOUGHTS?

The cultural diversity of a college campus offers a trip around the world . . . if we're willing to reach out, learn, and embrace it. Are you a cultural joiner or avoider? What are your first tendencies when meeting persons from other cultures?

WHAT'S INSIDE

ETHICS CHECK
Fair-trade fashion

FACTS TO CONSIDER
Employee disengagement varies among world cultures

HOT TOPIC
Explanations vary for motherhood wage gap

QUICK CASE
Silent team members

YOUR CHAPTER 15 TAKEAWAYS

1. Understand what we need to know about diversity in the workplace.
2. Understand what we need to know about diversity among global cultures.

Takeaway 15.1
What Should We Know About Diversity in the Workplace?

ANSWERS TO COME

- Inclusion drives the business case for diversity.
- Multicultural organizations value and support diversity.
- Diversity bias exists in many situations.
- Organizational subcultures create diversity challenges.
- Managing diversity is a leadership priority.

THE U.S. POPULATION IS INCREASINGLY DIVERSE. That we all know. But did you know that by 2044 whites will constitute less than 50% of the U.S. population?[1] Fast forward to 2060 and take another look at the new majority: 38% Hispanic/Latino, 14.7% African American, 9.7% Asian American and Pacific Islander, and 2.7% Native American.[2] Such demographic facts and projections are just windows into our changing social fabric. And, they set the stage for a conversation that should be broad and ongoing.

> **Diversity** describes attributes such as national origin, race, gender, age, sexual orientation, and other individual differences.

Issues of **diversity** are often discussed in respect to national origin, age, race, ethnicity, gender, physical ability, gender identity or expression, and sexual orientation. An even broader definition includes differences in religious beliefs, education, experience, family status, personality, values, and perhaps more. It's common to talk about **surface-level diversity** in respect to the more visible individual attributes such as age, race, gender, and ethnicity. This is the diversity we can often—but not always—recognize on sight. But there is also **deep-level diversity**, which reflects differences in psychological attributes such as personalities and values. This level of diversity is harder to recognize and takes more work to understand in our relationships with others.[3]

> **Surface-level diversity** consists of more visible attributes such as age, race, and ethnicity.

> **Deep-level diversity** consists of psychological attributes like personality and values.

In his book *Beyond Race and Gender*, diversity consultant R. Roosevelt Thomas, Jr., says that "diversity includes everyone . . . white males are as diverse as their colleagues."[4] He also says that diversity is good for organizations, offering a source of competitive advantage. Picture an organization whose diverse employees possess a mix of backgrounds, talents, and perspectives, and that reflect the firm's customers and clients. Wouldn't this be good for the organization and its members?

INCLUSION DRIVES THE BUSINESS CASE FOR DIVERSITY.

Many organizations seem to be good or relatively good at attracting new employees of diverse backgrounds to join. But they aren't always successful in keeping them for the long term. This problem of high employee turnover among minorities and women has been called the **revolving door syndrome**.[5] It can reflect a lack of **inclusion** in the employing organizations—the degree to which they are open to anyone who can perform a job, regardless of race, sexual preference, gender, or any other diversity attribute.[6]

> The **revolving door syndrome** is high turnover among minorities and women.

> **Inclusion** is how open the organization is to anyone who can perform a job.

Research reported in the *Gallup Management Journal* shows that having a diverse and inclusive workplace is good for morale. In a study of 2,014 American workers, those who felt a sense of inclusion were more likely to stay with their employers and recommend them to others. Survey questions asked such things as "Do you always trust your company to be fair to all employees?" "At work, are all employees always treated with respect?" "Does your supervisor always make the best use of employees' skills?"[7] The New York research group Catalyst also reports that companies with a greater percentage of women on their boards outperform those whose boards have the lowest female representation.[8]

Studies like those just cited back what some call a strong "business case for diversity."[9] But, Thomas Kochan and his colleagues at MIT point out that the hoped-for advantages are gained only when managers make diversity a priority by investing in training and supportive human resource practices. They say:[10]

To be successful in working with and gaining value from diversity requires a sustained, systemic approach and long-term commitment. Success is facilitated by a perspective that considers diversity to be an opportunity for everyone in an organization to learn from each other how better to accomplish their work and an occasion that requires a supportive and cooperative organizational culture as well as group leadership and process skills that can facilitate effective group functioning.

MULTICULTURAL ORGANIZATIONS VALUE AND SUPPORT DIVERSITY.

Look around. Think about how people are treating those who differ from themselves. What about your experiences at school and at work? Are you and others always treated with respect and inclusion? Or do you sometimes sense disrespect and exclusion?

The model for inclusivity is a **multicultural organization** that displays commitments to diversity like those in **Table 15.1**—Characteristics of Multicultural Organizations.[11] One such organization is Xerox, the first *Fortune* 500 firm to have an African-American woman, Ursula Burns, as CEO and also the first to have one woman succeed another as CEO. When praising her appointment, Ilene Lang, head of the nonprofit Catalyst, which supports women in business, said: "Most companies have one woman who might be a possibility to become CEO; Xerox has a range of them." The firm has an Executive Diversity Council, runs diversity leadership programs, and evaluates managers on how well they recruit and develop employees from underrepresented groups.[12]

> A **multicultural organization** is based on pluralism and operates with inclusivity and respect for diversity.

DIVERSITY BIAS EXISTS IN MANY SITUATIONS.

We have to be realistic in facing up to the challenges of creating inclusive and multicultural organizations. It isn't always easy to get the members of a workforce to really respect and work well with one another. The word "diversity" basically means the presence of "differences," and differences are potentially challenging in most circumstances. But diversity issues in organizations are especially complicated because such differences are often distributed unequally in the power structure.

Let's be honest. Most senior executives in large businesses are still older, white, and male. There is still more diversity among lower and middle levels of most organizations than at the top. For some women and minority workers, the **glass ceiling** depicted in **Figure 15.1** is a real—albeit hidden—barrier to career advancement. Something called the **leaking pipeline problem** also shows up in male-dominant organizational cultures. It occurs as women drop out of upward career tracks because of glass ceilings and other obstacles, including lack of family-friendly human resource policies and practices.[13]

Minorities and women can face diversity challenges that range from misunderstandings, to lack of sensitivity, to glass-ceiling and leaking-pipeline limitations, to outright harassment

> The **glass ceiling** is a hidden barrier to the career advancement of women and minorities.

> The **leaking pipeline problem** is where glass ceilings and other obstacles cause qualified and high-performing women to drop out of upward career paths.

TABLE 15.1 Characteristics of Multicultural Organizations

Pluralism—Members of minority and majority cultures influence key values and policies.

Structural integration—Minority-culture members are well represented at all levels and in all responsibilities.

Informal network integration—Mentoring and support groups assist career development of minority-culture members.

Absence of prejudice and discrimination—Training and task force activities support the goal of eliminating culture-group biases.

Minimum intergroup conflict—Members of minority and majority cultures avoid destructive conflicts.

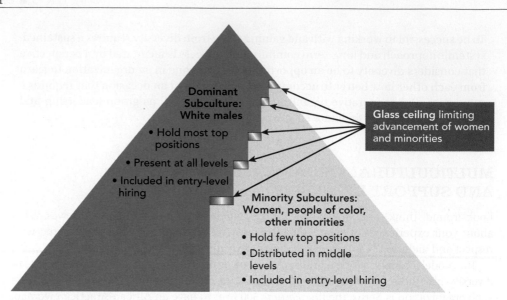

FIGURE 15.1 How Do Glass Ceilings Constrain Career Advancement for Women and Minorities?

Organizations consist of a majority culture (often white males) and minority cultures (including women, people of color, and other minorities). It is likely that members of the majority culture will dominate higher management levels. One of the potential consequences is a "glass ceiling" effect that, although not publicized, acts as a barrier that sometimes makes it hard for women and minorities to advance and gain entry into higher-management ranks.

and job discrimination. One senior executive expressed her surprise on finding that the top performer in her work group, an African-American male, was paid 25% less than anyone else. This wasn't because his pay had been cut to that level; it was because his pay increases had always trailed those given to white co-workers.[14] The U.S. Equal Employment Opportunity Commission (EEOC) reports an increase in both pay and pregnancy discrimination complaints.[15] Sexual harassment in the forms of unwanted sexual advances, requests for

EMPLOYMENT INTERRUPTION TO BEAR CHILDREN CAUSES WOMEN TO SEEK LESS TRAININGANDGO FOR LOWER-WAGE JOBS.

HOT TOPIC

Explanations Vary for Motherhood Wage Gap

Wave break Media Ltd/Alamy

The difference in earnings between mothers and non-mothers is called the "motherhood wage gap." Where and why does it exist? The answer to question one is pretty much everywhere. Some findings from world surveys indicate that it is higher in developing than developed countries, that it increases with size of family, and that it tends to fall with the presence of female versus male children. So, what about question two—why does it exist at all?

Explanations for the motherhood wage gap are several. The *economic explanation* is that employment interruption to bear children causes women to seek less training, go for

lower-wage jobs, and go for flexible jobs versus higher-paying ones. The *sociological explanation* is that women suffer because of role stereotypes, poor access to child care, and employment in lower-paid female-dominant occupations. The *comparative institutionalist* explanation is that women do better in countries with supportive policies on maternity and paternity leaves and where there is less income inequality overall. The *implementation explanation* is that even where protections against discrimination exist, the laws are poorly and unevenly implemented, resulting in unfair treatment of women in the workforce.

HOW ABOUT IT?

Would you agree that the "motherhood wage gap" is a real issue in our society? How about the possible explanations? Do you favor one or more versus others? Do you view this whole issue with a sense of optimism or pessimism, and why?

sexual favors, and sexually laced communications is another problem that sometimes appears in the news and on court agendas, but other times goes unreported.[16]

People respond to bad treatment at work in different ways. Some may challenge the system by filing internal complaints or taking outside legal action. Some may quit to look for better positions elsewhere or to pursue self-employment opportunities. Some may try to "fit in" by adapting through **biculturalism**, attempting to display majority-culture characteristics that seem necessary to succeed in the work environment. For example, lesbian, gay, bisexual, and transgender staff might hide their sexual orientations and gender identities at work—something called staying in the **glass closet**.[17] Similarly, an African-American or Hispanic manager might avoid using words or phrases that white colleagues would consider slang, while a woman might use football or baseball metaphors in conversations with men to gain acceptance into their career networks.

ORGANIZATIONAL SUBCULTURES CREATE DIVERSITY CHALLENGES.

One reason that the truly multicultural organization is hard to find is the complicated dynamics of **organizational subcultures**. These are informal groupings of persons that form around such things as gender, age, race and ethnicity, and even job functions. People can get so caught up in their subcultures that they identify and interact mostly with others who are like themselves. Although perhaps unintentionally, they can develop tendencies toward **ethnocentrism** and act in ways that suggest they believe their subculture is superior to all others.

Job Functions

Occupational subcultures develop as people form shared identities around the work that they do. Some employees may consider themselves "systems people" who are very different from "those marketing people" and even more different still from "those finance people." Even at school, in course project groups, have you noticed how students tend to identify with their majors? Don't some look down on others they consider to be pursuing "easy" majors and view their majors as the superior ones?

Race and Ethnicity

Differences in **racial and ethnic subcultures** exist among people from various races, language groups, regions, and countries. And as we all know, it can be difficult for some to work together across these boundaries. Although one may speak in everyday conversations about "African-American" or "Latino" or "Anglo" cultures, for example, one has to wonder: How well do members of these subcultures really understand one another?[18]

Gender

It's common for **gender subcultures** to form among persons who share the same gender identities. Common ground creates lots of comfort for those inside these subcultures, but fueled by stereotypes it may distance them from outsiders. When men work together, the expected subgroup culture may be one of a competitive behavior set where sports metaphors are common and games and stories often focus on winning and losing.[19] When women work together, the expected subculture may be one of supportive personal relationships and collaboration.[20]

One penalty paid by female leaders caught in subculture expectations is called the **double-bind dilemma**. This occurs when they get criticized as being "too soft" for acting consistent with female subculture stereotypes, but also get criticized as being "too hard" when acting consistent with male subculture stereotypes. In other words, female leaders are "damned if they do, and damned if they don't," often lacking credit for getting leadership just right.[21]

How about transgender and non-binary people? How do they fit in, how do they feel, how do they adapt, and how do they progress in work settings dominated by men and women who identify along traditional gender lines? What subculture dilemmas do trans and non-binary people face in teams and organizations? What penalties do they pay for their gender identities, whether openly expressed or not?

Biculturalism is when minority members adopt characteristics of majority cultures in order to succeed.

The **glass closet** is when lesbians, gays, bisexuals, and transgender workers hide their sexual orientation and gender identities.

Organizational subcultures are groupings of people based on shared demographic and job identities.

Ethnocentrism is the belief that one's membership group or subculture is superior to all others.

Occupational subcultures form among people doing the same kinds of work.

Racial and ethnic subcultures form among people from the same races, language groupings, regions, and nations.

Gender subcultures form among persons who share gender identities and display common patterns of behavior.

In the **double-bind dilemma**, female leaders are criticized when they act consistent with female subculture stereotypes and when they act consistent with male subculture stereotypes.

Discrimination Fears Raised over Social Media Use in Hiring

When at least 6 in 10 recruiters are checking the social media histories of job applicants, there may be more at issue than privacy concerns alone. How do the employment laws on discrimination apply to this new practice? Hearings are being held at the U.S. Equal Employment Opportunity Commission to determine how an employer's peek at a job candidate's postings on Twitter, Instagram, and other social sites may affect discrimination in hiring. If a recruiter can't legally ask an interviewee "Are you married or pregnant?" or "What is your sexual preference?" what are the legalities of finding answers to these questions from the Internet? And if recruiters get social media information on one candidate but not on another, does this amount to discrimination that both aren't being treated equally?

CJG-Technology/Alamy

Age

Generational subcultures form among people in similar age groups.

Age is the basis for **generational subcultures** in organizations. Harris and Conference Board polls report that younger workers tend to be more dissatisfied than older workers.[22] They are also described as more short-term oriented, giving higher priority to work–life balance, and expecting to hold several jobs during their careers.[23] Imagine the conflicts that can occur when members of today's college generation go to work for older managers who grew up with quite different life experiences and even values. Have you had a conflict with a parent, perhaps over a life style or authority issue, that might foreshadow similar ones you might encounter at work someday?

MANAGING DIVERSITY IS A LEADERSHIP PRIORITY.

"Diversity is the mix of talent in your organization," says Anise Wiley-Little, Chief Human Capital and Diversity Officer at Northwestern University's Kellogg School. "Inclusion is how you maximize the talent."[24] Her message is clear and on target. But what can team leaders and managers do so that all persons under their care are treated inclusively?

The pathway to inclusion begins with a willingness to recognize that most workers want the same things, regardless of their backgrounds. They want respect for their talents; they want to be fairly treated; they want to be able to work to the best of their abilities; and they want to achieve their full potential. Meeting these expectations requires the best in diversity leadership.

| Affirmative Action
Create upward mobility
for minorities and
women | Valuing Differences
Build quality
relationships with
respect for diversity | Managing Diversity
Achieve full
utilization of diverse
human resources |

The figure describes what R. Roosevelt Thomas calls a continuum of leadership approaches to diversity.[25] At one end is *affirmative action*. Here, leadership commits the organization to hiring and advancing minorities and women. You might think of this as advancing diversity by increasing the representation of diverse members in the organization's workforce. But this is only a partial solution, and the revolving door syndrome may even negate some of its positive impact.

Thomas says it's a mistake to assume "that once you get representation, people will assimilate." He describes *valuing diversity* as a step beyond affirmative action. Here, a leader commits the organization to educate its workforce so that people better understand and respect differences. The training goal is to help them better deal with "similarities, differences, and tensions" by answering a fundamental question: "Can I work with people who are qualified that are not like me?"[26]

Managing diversity is building an inclusive work environment that allows everyone to reach his or her potential.

The final step in Thomas's continuum is **managing diversity**. A leader who actively manages diversity is always seeking ways to make an organization truly multicultural and inclusive—and keep it that way. Leaders committed to managing diversity build team and organization cultures that are what Thomas calls "diversity mature."[27] They have a diversity mission, one that views inclusion as a true strategic imperative.

STUDYGUIDE

Takeaway 15.1
What Should We Know About Diversity in the Workplace?

Terms to Define

Biculturalism	Ethnocentrism	Inclusion	Organizational
Deep-level diversity	Gender subcultures	Leaking pipeline problem	subcultures
Diversity	Generational	Managing diversity	Revolving door
Double-bind dilemma	subcultures	Multicultural	syndrome
Racial or ethnic	Glass ceiling	organization	Surface-level diversity
subcultures	Glass closet	Occupational	
		subcultures	

Rapid Review

- Workforce diversity can improve business performance by expanding the talent pool of the organization and establishing better understandings of customers and stakeholders.
- Inclusivity is a characteristic of multicultural organizations that values and respects diversity of their members.
- Minorities and women can suffer diversity bias in such forms as job and pay discrimination, sexual harassment, and the glass ceiling effect.
- Organizational subcultures, including those based on occupational, racial, ethnic, age, and gender differences, can create diversity challenges.
- A top leadership priority should be managing diversity to develop an inclusive work environment within which everyone is able to reach their full potential.

Questions for Discussion

1. What subcultures do you see operating at work and/or in school, and how do they affect relationships and daily events?
2. What are some of the things organizations and leaders can do to reduce diversity bias faced by minorities and women in the workplace?
3. What does the existence of an affirmative action policy say about an organization's commitment to diversity?

Be Sure You Can

- **identify** major diversity trends in American society
- **explain** the business case for diversity
- **explain** the concept of inclusivity
- **list** characteristics of multicultural organizations
- **identify** subcultures common to organizations
- **discuss** the types of employment problems faced by minorities and women
- **explain** Thomas's concept of managing diversity

Career Situation: What Would You Do?

One of your co-workers brought along his friend to lunch. When discussing his new female boss, the friend says: "Yeah, she got the job just because she's a Hispanic woman. There's no way that someone like me had a chance given her pedigree. And she now has the gall to act as if we're all one big happy team and the rest of us should accept her leadership. I'm doing my best to make it hard for her to succeed." It was uncomfortable for you just to hear this. Your co-worker looks dismayed but isn't saying anything. What do you do or say? Will you just let the comment go, or do something more?

Takeaway 15.2
What Should We Know About Diversity Among Global Cultures?

ANSWERS TO COME

- Culture shock is discomfort in cross-cultural situations.
- Cultural intelligence is an ability to adapt to different cultures.
- The "silent" languages of cultures include context, time, and space.
- Cultural tightness and looseness varies around the world.
- Hofstede's model identifies value differences among national cultures.
- Intercultural competencies are essential career skills.

A TRIP TO THE GROCERY STORE, A DAY SPENT AT WORK, A VISIT TO OUR CHILDREN'S schools—all are possible opportunities for us to have cross-cultural experiences. And you have to admit, there are a lot of new faces in the neighborhood. At our universities even a walk across campus can be a trip around the world, but we have to be willing to take it. How about you? Do you greet, speak with, and actively engage people of other cultures? Or are you shy, hesitant, and even inclined to avoid them?

CULTURE SHOCK IS DISCOMFORT IN CROSS-CULTURAL SITUATIONS.

Maybe it is a bit awkward to introduce yourself to an international student or foreign visitor to your community. Maybe the appearance of a Muslim woman in a headscarf or a Nigerian man in a long overblouse is unusual to the point of being intimidating. Maybe, too, meeting or working with someone from another culture causes us to experience something known to international travelers as **culture shock**. This is a feeling of confusion and discomfort when in or dealing with an unfamiliar culture.[28]

Global businesses are concerned about culture shock because they need their employees to be successful as they travel and work around the world. Perhaps the same argument might also be applied at home to our everyday cross-cultural experiences on teams at work and in personal activities. Listed here are stages that are often encountered as someone adjusts to the unfamiliar setting of a new culture. The assumption is that knowing about the stages can help us better deal with them.[29]

> **Culture shock** is the confusion and discomfort that a person experiences when in an unfamiliar culture.

- *Confusion*—First contacts with the new culture leave you anxious, uncomfortable, and in need of information and advice.
- *Small victories*—Continued interactions bring some "successes," and your confidence grows in handling daily affairs.
- *Honeymoon*—A time of wonderment, cultural immersion, and even infatuation, with local ways viewed positively.
- *Irritation and anger*—A time when the "negatives" overwhelm the "positives" and the new culture becomes a target of your criticism.
- *Reality*—A time of rebalancing; you are able to enjoy the new culture while accommodating its less-desirable elements.

CULTURAL INTELLIGENCE IS AN ABILITY TO ADAPT TO DIFFERENT CULTURES.

SITUATION: A U.S. businessman meets with a Saudi Arabian official. He sits in the office with crossed legs and the sole of his shoe exposed. He doesn't know this is a sign of disrespect in the local culture. He passes documents to the host using his left hand, which

FACTS TO CONSIDER

Employee Disengagement Varies Among World Cultures

Joshua Hodge Photography/iStockphoto

The Gallup organization regularly measures employee engagement around the world. One recent result showed the following percentages of employees who self-report as "actively disengaged" from their work.

- Australia and New Zealand—16%
- United States and Canada—18%
- Latin America—19%

- Western Europe—20%
- Central and Eastern Europe—26%
- East Asia—26%

WHAT'S YOUR TAKE?

Why do you think disengagement in Australia, New Zealand, the United States, and Canada is lower than that reported in the other regions? Could there be a cultural explanation for the results, or is it more an economic issue? Are you surprised that even the best-scoring countries report active employee disengagement as high as 16% and 18%?

Muslims consider unclean. And, he declines when coffee is offered. This suggests criticism of the Saudi's hospitality. What is the price for these cultural miscues? A $10 million contract is lost to a Korean executive better versed in Saudi ways.[30]

Some might say that this American's behavior was ethnocentric, so self-centered that he ignored and showed no concern for the culture of his Arab host. Others might excuse him as suffering from culture shock. Maybe he was so uncomfortable on arrival in Saudi Arabia that all he could think about was offering his contract and leaving as quickly as possible. Still others might give him the benefit of the doubt. It could have been that he was well intentioned but didn't have time to learn about Saudi culture before making the trip.

Regardless of the possible reasons for the cultural miscues, they still worked to the businessman's disadvantage. There is also no doubt that he failed to show something called "CQ" or **cultural intelligence**—the ability to adapt and adjust to new cultures.[31] People with high CQ have high cultural self-awareness and are flexible in dealing with cultural differences. They are willing to learn from unfamiliar cross-cultural situations and modify their behaviors to act with sensitivity toward another culture's ways. In other words, someone high in cultural intelligence views cultural differences not as threats but as learning opportunities.

> **Cultural intelligence** is the ability to adapt to new cultures and work well in situations of cultural diversity.

Cultural intelligence is probably a good indicator of someone's capacity for success in international assignments, in cross-cultural teamwork, and in everyday relationships with persons of different cultures. How would you rate yourself? Could CQ be one of your important personal assets, or is something that requires attention and more development?

THE "SILENT" LANGUAGES OF CULTURES INCLUDE CONTEXT, TIME, AND SPACE.

HANOI, VIETNAM Visiting former U.S. Secretary of Defense Leon Panetta exchanged war relics with his counterpart, General Phung Quang Thanh. During a short ceremony Thanh presented letters found on a dead U.S. serviceman during the war. The letters were placed on top of a red cloth with yellow fringe. Secretary Panetta presented a diary found on a dead North Vietnamese soldier. He presented the diary in a FedEx envelope.[32]

It is easy to recognize differences in the spoken and written languages used by people around the world. And foreign-language skills can open many doors to cultural understanding. But anthropologist Edward T. Hall points out that there are other "silent" languages of culture that are also very significant. If we look and listen carefully, he believes we should recognize how cultures differ in the ways their members use language in communication.[33] Whether Secretary Panetta realized it or not in the prior example, it wasn't only his words that were communicating to the Vietnamese. The FedEx envelope was, too.

Context

High-context cultures rely on nonverbal and situational cues as well as spoken or written words in communication.

In **high-context cultures** such as Vietnam, what is actually said or written may convey only part, sometimes a very small part, of a message. The rest must be interpreted from nonverbal signals and the situation as a whole—things such as body language, physical setting, and even past relationships among the people involved. Context counts, and cultures and ceremonies are carefully interpreted. Things like dinner parties and social gatherings are also important. They allow potential business partners to get to know one another. It is only after the relationships are established that it becomes possible to discuss and hopefully make business deals.

Low-context cultures emphasize communication via spoken or written words.

In **low-context cultures** most communication takes place via the written or spoken word. This is common in the United States, Canada, and Germany, for example. We rely on words to communicate messages. And as the saying goes: "We say (or write) what we mean, and we mean what we say."

Time

In **monochronic cultures**, people tend to do one thing at a time.

Hall also notes that the way people approach and deal with time varies across cultures.[34] He describes a **monochronic culture** as one in which people tend to do one thing at a time. This is typical of the United States, where most business people schedule a meeting for one person or group to focus on one issue for an allotted time period. And if someone is late for one of those meetings or brings an uninvited guest, we tend not to like it.

In **polychronic cultures**, people accomplish many different things at once.

Members of a **polychronic culture** are more flexible about time and who uses it. They often try to work on many different things at once, perhaps not in any particular order. An American visitor (monochronic culture) to an Egyptian client (polychronic culture) may be frustrated, for example, by interruptions as the client deals with people continually flowing in and out of his office.

Space

Proxemics is the study of how people use and value space.

Space is another important silent language of culture. Hall points out that the ways space communicates varies across cultures. He describes these cultural tendencies in terms of **proxemics**, or how people use and value space.[35] If you visit Japan, you'll notice the difference in proxemics very quickly. Space is precious in Japan; it is respected, and its use is carefully planned. Small and tidy homes, offices, and shops are the norm; gardens are tiny but immaculate; public spaces are carefully organized for most efficient use. Americans, by contrast, tend to like as much space as they can get. We go for big offices, big homes, big yards. We also value personal space and get uncomfortable if others stand too close to us or "talk right in our face."

Cultural Awareness and *The Amazing Race*

Photo by Jeffrey R. Staab/CBS/ Getty Images

The reality series *The Amazing Race* pits teams of players in an around-the-world competition full of cultural and physical challenges. They face grueling travel demands, unfamiliar languages and customs, disrupted sleep and eating schedules, and more. It becomes painfully clear as the race episodes unfold that many of the participants do not know a lot about other countries in the world. They have grown used to the values and patterns of home. But as the teams come face-to-face with one new culture after another, they learn a lot about themselves in the process. When Nat Strand and Kat Chang won the $1 million prize, they were the first female team to do so. Their journey took them to 30 cities across four continents for a total of 32,000 miles. They crossed a lot of national and cultural boundaries along the way, much as today's global organizations do.

> THE JAPANESE AND INDONESIAN TEAM MEMBERS SAID VERY LITTLE, ALTHOUGH THEY HAD EXTENSIVE NOTES OF INFORMATION.

QUICK CASE

Silent Team Members

Stuart Jenner/Shutterstock

The course instructor has assigned teams to complete a case study in two parts spaced 2 weeks apart. Part A requires a preliminary oral presentation; Part B requires a final presentation and written report. Your team has five members, including two internationals from Japan and Indonesia. The team held three face-to-face meetings to finish Part A. The internationals were present and seemed interested, but they didn't directly contribute. The other members and you created the preliminary presentation and assigned short parts for everyone to deliver. The Japanese and Indonesian team members didn't do well. They struggled with their oral presentation and didn't contribute during the question-and-answer session. The instructor said the team's presentation wasn't focused and well integrated. She said things would have to go much better on Part B to earn a high grade. The team is scheduled to meet to night to recap Part A and start work on Part B.

WHAT DO YOU DO?

What can you say and do at this meeting to set the stage for higher performance on Part B? How might team dynamics and cross-cultural diversity have contributed to the Part A results? What insights from cultural models might explain the behavior of your international teammates? How can they be fully engaged so that the team takes best advantage of all of talents going forward? What role can you play during future team meetings to help accomplish this goal?

CULTURAL TIGHTNESS AND LOOSENESS VARIES AROUND THE WORLD.

The nail that sticks up will be hammered down. Asian Proverb

The squeaking wheel gets the grease. American Idiom

Two sayings; two different cultural settings. What are their implications? Picture young children listening to these as words of wisdom passed on by parents and elders. The Asian child grows up being careful to not speak out, stand out, or attract attention. The American grows up trying to speak up and stand out in order to get attention.

This contrast in childhoods introduces the concept of cultural tightness-looseness. Scholars Michele J. Gelfand, Lisa H. Nishii, and Jana L. Raver describe it as "the strength of social norms and degree of sanctioning within societies."[36] Two things are at issue in this definition: (1) the strength of norms that govern social behavior, and (2) the tolerance that exists for any deviations from the norms. Empirical studies have classified 33 societal cultures around the world on their tightness and looseness.[37]

Tight and Loose Cultures

In a **tight culture**, such as ones found in Korea, Japan, or Malaysia, social norms are strong and clear. People know the prevailing norms and let them guide their behavior. They self-govern and try to conform. They also understand that any deviations are likely to be noticed, discouraged, and even sanctioned. The goal in tight cultures, as suggested in the Asian proverb, is to fit in with society's expectations and not stand out.

In a **loose culture**, such as ones found in Australia, Brazil, or Hungary, social norms are mixed and less clear cut. People may be more or less concerned with them, and conformity will vary a good deal. Deviations from norms tend to be tolerated unless they take the form of criminal behavior or reach toward the extremes of morality. It is quite acceptable for individuals in loose cultures, as suggested in the American idiom, to show unique identities and express themselves independent from the masses.

In **tight cultures** social norms are rigid and clear, and members try to conform.

In **loose cultures** social norms are mixed and ambiguous, and conformity varies.

Tight and Loose Culture Tensions

It can be challenging to go from a tight to a loose culture, or vice versa, for travel or work. This calls for lots of cultural awareness to understand differences and a similar amount of self-management to handle the differences well. One of the most common settings where the dynamics of tight and loose cultures play out is a course group or work team whose members come from different cultures. You've probably been there. What did you see and how did it affect team dynamics and accomplishments?

A mix of tightness and looseness on a cross-cultural team may result in soft or unstated conflict, as well as missed performance opportunity. Members from tight cultures may hold back and look toward formal authority for direction, even though on time and prepared. They may be slow to volunteer, criticize, show emotion, or seek praise. Members from loose cultures, by contrast, may act informal toward authority and view punctuality as a hit-or-miss proposition. They may be quick to voice opinions, criticize others, display emotions, and look for recognition.

It takes a lot of cultural awareness for a team leader and team members to spot tight versus loose culture tensions. And, it takes a lot of skill to create a cross cultural team environment where everyone gets their chance to both contribute to team performance and take satisfaction from the experience.

HOFSTEDE'S MODEL IDENTIFIES VALUE DIFFERENCES AMONG NATIONAL CULTURES.

Understanding the ideas just discussed is a good place to start in cultural appreciation, but cultures are still more complex. Scholars offer many models and useful perspectives.[38] One of the most discussed is Geert Hofstede, who explores value differences among national cultures.[39] His work began with a study of employees of a U.S.-based corporation operating in 40 countries. Hofstede identified the four cultural dimensions of power distance, uncertainty avoidance, individualism-collectivism, and masculinity-femininity. Later studies resulted in the addition of a fifth dimension, time orientation.[40] Figure 15.2 shows a sample of how national cultures varied in his research. Can you see why Hofstede's cultural dimensions can be significant in business and management?

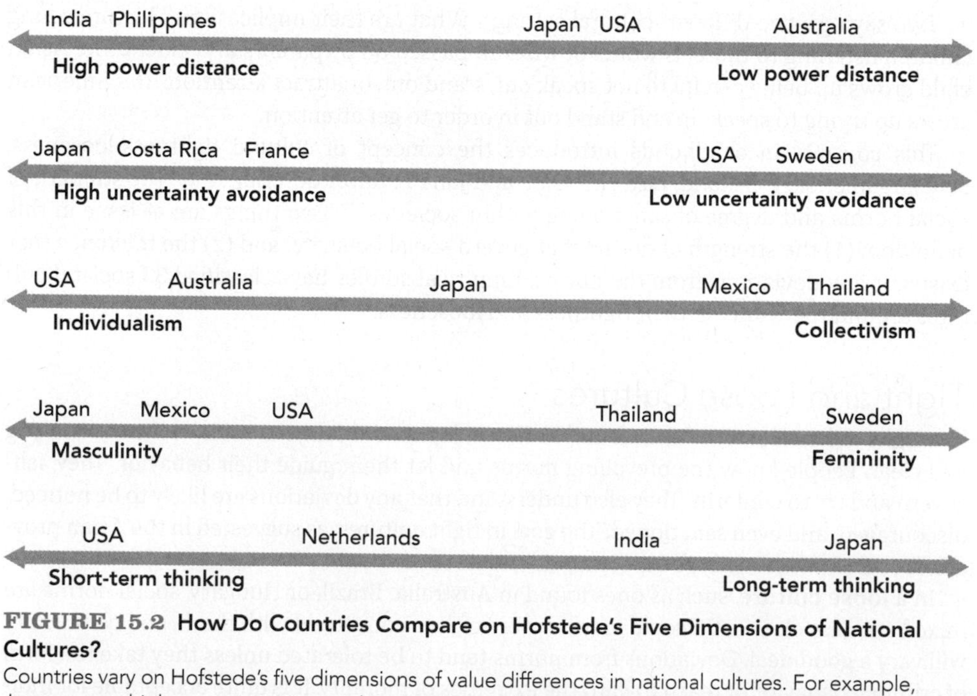

FIGURE 15.2 How Do Countries Compare on Hofstede's Five Dimensions of National Cultures?
Countries vary on Hofstede's five dimensions of value differences in national cultures. For example, Japan scores high on uncertainty avoidance and masculinity; the United States scores high on individualism and short-term thinking. Imagine what this might mean when international business executives try to make deals or when representatives of national governments try to work across these cultural boundaries.

> "WE WILL THEREFORE GUARANTEE THAT EVERY EMPLOYEE WHO MAKES OUR CLOTHING IS PAID A FAIR WAGE, NOT JUST A LEGAL MINIMUM WAGE."

ETHICS CHECK

Fair-Trade Fashion

Andy Manis/The New York Times/Redux Pictures

Are you someone who likes to shop "fair trade"? Do you feel good when buying coffee, for example, that is certified as grown by persons who were paid fairly for their labor?

The clothing retailer Fair Indigo wants to be known for selling fair-trade fashion. It presents itself as "a new clothing company with a different way of doing business" that wants to "create stylish, high-quality clothes while paying a fair and meaningful wage to the people who produce them." Pointing out that there is no certifying body for fair-trade apparel, Fair Indigo offers its own guarantee: "We will therefore guarantee that every employee who makes our clothing is paid a fair wage, not just a legal minimum wage, as is the benchmark in the industry."

Fair Indigo's representatives travel the globe searching for small factories and work cooperatives that meet their standards. CEO Bill Bass says: "The whole evolution of the clothing and manufacturing industry has been to drive prices and wages down, shut factories and move work to countries with lower wages. We said, 'we're going to reverse this and push wages up'."

YOUR DECISION?

Are you willing to pay a bit more for a fair-trade product? And what do you think about Fair Indigo's business model—"fair" wage, not "legal minimum" wage? Is it "fashion" that sells apparel, or fashion plus conditions of origin? Is Fair Indigo at the forefront of a new wave of value creation in retailing—fair-trade fashion?

Dimensions of National Cultures

Power distance is the degree to which a society accepts or rejects the unequal distribution of power in organizations and society. In high power distance cultures such as Japan, we expect to find great respect for age, status, and titles. Could this create problems for an American visitor used to the informalities of a more moderate power distance culture, and perhaps accustomed to first names and casual dress in the office?

Uncertainty avoidance is the degree to which a society tolerates or is uncomfortable with risk, change, and situational uncertainty. In high uncertainty avoidance cultures, such as France, one would expect to find a preference for structure, order, and predictability. Could this be one of the reasons why the French seem to favor employment practices that provide job security?

Individualism-collectivism is the degree to which a society emphasizes individual accomplishments and self-interests, versus collective accomplishments and the interests of groups. In Hofstede's data, the United States had the highest individualism score of any country. Don't you find the "I" and "me" words used a lot in our conversations and meetings? I'm always surprised how often they occur in student team presentations. What are the implications of our cultural tendency toward individualism when we try to work with people from more collectivist national cultures?

Masculinity-femininity is the degree to which a society values assertiveness and materialism, versus feelings, relationships, and quality of life.[41] You might think of it as a tendency to emphasize stereotypical masculine or feminine traits and attitudes toward gender roles. Visitors to Japan, with the highest masculinity score in Hofstede's research, may be surprised at how restricted career opportunities can be for women. The *Wall Street Journal* comments: "In Japan, professional women face a set of socially complex issues—from overt sexism to deep-seated attitudes about the division of labor." One female Japanese manager says: "Men tend to have very fixed ideas about what women are like.[42]

Time orientation is the degree to which a society emphasizes short-term or long-term goals and gratifications.[43] Americans are notorious for being impatient and wanting quick, even instantaneous, gratification. Even our companies are expected to achieve short-term results; those failing to meet quarterly financial targets often suffer immediate stock price declines. Many Asian cultures are quite the opposite, valuing persistence and thrift, and being patient and willing to work for long-term success.

Power distance is the degree to which a society accepts unequal distribution of power.

Uncertainty avoidance is the degree to which a society tolerates risk and uncertainty.

Individualism-collectivism is the degree to which a society emphasizes individuals and their self-interests.

Masculinity-femininity is the degree to which a society values assertiveness and materialism.

Time orientation is the degree to which a society emphasizes short-term or long-term goals.

Ecological Fallacy

The **ecological fallacy** assumes that a generalized cultural value applies equally well to all members of the culture.

Although Hofstede's ideas are insightful, his five value dimensions offer only a ballpark look at national cultures. They're a starting point at best. Hofstede himself even warns that we must avoid the **ecological fallacy**.[44] This is acting with the mistaken assumption that a generalized cultural value, such as individualism in American culture or masculinity in Japanese culture, applies always and equally to all members of the culture.

INTERCULTURAL COMPETENCIES ARE ESSENTIAL CAREER SKILLS.

Intercultural competencies are skills and personal characteristics that help us be successful in cross-cultural situations.

The many complications of cultures place a premium on **intercultural competencies**, skills and personal characteristics that help us function successfully in cross-cultural situations. Think of them as one of the three "must-have goals" for career success today, linking global knowledge on the one hand with management skills on the other.

Foundations for Global Management Success

| *Goal:* Global Knowledge | *Goal:* Intercultral Competency | *Goal:* Management Skills |

Intercultural competencies help us act with confidence when in another culture or participating in culturally mixed teams. Scholars describe these skills as growing from strengths in perception management, relationship management, and self-management.[45]

In terms of *perception management*, a person must be inquisitive and curious about cultural differences and be flexible and nonjudgmental when interpreting and dealing with situations in which differences are at play. In terms of *relationship management*, a person must be genuinely interested in others, sensitive to their emotions and feelings, and able to make personal adjustments while engaging in cross-cultural interactions. In terms of *self-management*, a person must have a strong sense of personal identity, understand their own emotions and values, and be able to stay self-confident even in situations that call for personal adaptations because of cultural differences.

ARE YOU WILLING TO COPE WITH TENSIONS IN ADDRESSING DIVERSITY AND CULTURAL DIFFERENCES?

EXPLORE YOURSELF

Diversity and Cultural Maturity

Today's organizations and the nature of our global workforce demand **diversity and cultural maturity** from anyone who is serious about career success. Being mature about diversity in a global context means being able to answer a confident "yes" to questions such as these:

• Do you understand diversity concepts?

• Do you understand cultural differences?

• Do you make decisions about others based on their abilities, rather than personal characteristics or cultural backgrounds?

• Are you able to cope with tensions when faced with diversity and cultural differences?

Be honest; admit where you still have work left to do. Use your answers to help set future goals to ensure that your actions, not just your words, consistently display positive diversity values.

Get to know yourself better by taking the self-assessment on **Diversity Awareness** and completing other activities in the *Exploring Management* **Skill-Building Portfolio.**

STUDYGUIDE

Takeaway 15.2
What Should We Know About Diversity Among Global Cultures?

Terms to Define

Cultural intelligence

Culture shock

Ecological fallacy

High-context culture

Individualism-collectivism

Intercultural competencies

Loose cultures

Low-context culture

Masculinity-femininity

Monochronic culture

Polychronic culture

Power distance

Proxemics

Tight culture

Time orientation

Uncertainty avoidance

Rapid Review

- People can experience culture shock due to the discomfort experienced in cross-cultural situations.
- Cultural intelligence is an individual capacity to understand, respect, and adapt to cultural differences.
- Hall's silent languages of culture include the role of context in communication, time orientation, and use of interpersonal space.
- Hofstede's five dimensions of value differences in national cultures are power distance, uncertainty avoidance, individualism-collectivism, masculinity-femininity, and time orientation.
- The foundations for intercultural competency are found in perception management, relationship management, and self-management.

Questions for Discussion

1. Should religion be included on Hall's list of the silent languages of culture?
2. Which of Hofstede's cultural dimensions might pose the greatest challenges to U.S. managers working in Asia, the Middle East, or Latin America?
3. Even though cultural differences are readily apparent around the world, is the trend today for cultures to converge and become more like one another?

Be Sure You Can

- **explain** culture shock and how people may respond to it
- **differentiate** low-context and high-context cultures, monochronic and polychronic cultures
- **explain** what makes cultures "tight" and "loose"
- **list** Hofstede's five dimensions of value differences among national cultures
- **contrast** American culture with that of other countries on each of Hofstede's dimensions

Career Situation: What Would You Do?

You've just been asked to join a team being sent to China for 10 days to discuss a new software development project with your firm's Chinese engineers. It's your first trip to China or Asia. In fact, you've only been to Europe as part of a study tour when in college. The trip is scheduled four weeks from today. What can you do to prepare for the trip and for your work with Chinese colleagues? What worries you the most about the trip and how well you'll do in the unfamiliar cultural circumstances?

TEST PREP 15

Answers to TestPrep questions can be found at the back of the book.

Multiple-Choice Questions

1. Which statement is most consistent with arguments that diversity is good for organizations?
   (a) Having a diverse workforce guarantees success.
   (b) Diversity is easy to manage because it is already valued by all people.
   (c) Diverse workforces help organizations deal with diverse customers.
   (d) When workforces are diverse, organizations can spend less on training.

2. When members of minority cultures feel that they have to behave similar to the ways of the majority culture, this tendency is called _____.
   (a) biculturalism   (b) particularism
   (c) the glass ceiling effect   (d) multiculturalism

3. The beliefs that older workers are not creative and prefer routine, low-stress jobs are stereotypes that might create bad feelings among members of different _____ subcultures in organizations.
   (a) gender   (b) generational
   (c) functional   (d) ethnic

4. Among the three leadership approaches to diversity identified by Thomas, which one is primarily directed at making sure that enough minorities and women are hired by the organization?
   (a) Equal employment opportunity   (b) Affirmative action
   (c) Valuing diversity   (d) Managing diversity

5. Pluralism and the absence of discrimination and prejudice in policies and practices are two important hallmarks of _____.
   (a) the glass ceiling effect
   (b) a multicultural organization
   (c) exclusive organizational cultures
   (d) affirmative action

6. The term _____ helps describe an organization that fully integrates members of minority cultures and majority cultures.
   (a) equal employment opportunity   (b) affirmative action
   (c) revolving door syndrome   (d) pluralism

7. When members of the marketing department stick close to one another, as well as share jokes and even a slang language, the likelihood is that a/an _____ subculture is forming.
   (a) occupational   (b) generational
   (c) gender   (d) ethnic

8. When someone experiences culture shock on a study-abroad trip, the first stage is likely to be one of anxiety caused by confusion in the new cultural setting. What is the next stage in culture shock?
   (a) Experiencing a sense of confidence from small victories in dealing with differences.
   (b) Displaying outright irritation and anger at the ways of this new culture.
   (c) Wanting to give up and go home immediately.
   (d) Accepting reality and enjoying the good and bad aspects.

9. When dealing with proxemics as a silent language of culture, what is the issue of most concern?
   (a) How people use the spoken word to communicate
   (b) How people use nonverbal means to communicate
   (c) How people use time to communicate
   (d) How people use space to communicate

10. In _____ cultures, members tend to do one thing at a time; in _____ cultures, members tend to do many things at once.
    (a) monochronic; polychronic   (b) universal; particular
    (c) collectivist; individualist   (d) neutral; affective

11. When a foreign visitor to India attends a dinner and criticizes as "primitive" the local custom of eating with one's fingers, he or she can be described as acting in a/an _____ way.
    (a) culturally intelligent   (b) polychronic
    (c) monochronic   (d) ethnocentric

12. In a high-context culture we would expect to find _____.
    (a) low uncertainty avoidance   (b) high power distance
    (c) monochronic time orientation
    (d) strong emphasis on nonverbal communication

13. It is common in Malaysian culture for people to value teamwork and to display great respect for authority. Hofstede would describe this culture as high in both _____.
    (a) uncertainty avoidance and feminism
    (b) universalism and particularism
    (c) collectivism and power distance
    (d) long-term orientation and masculinity

14. On which dimension of national culture did the United States score highest and Japan score highest in Hofstede's original survey research?
    (a) Masculinity, femininity   (b) Long-term, short-term
    (c) Individualism, masculinity
    (d) High uncertainty avoidance, collectivism

15. If someone commits what Hofstede calls the "ecological fallacy," what are they likely tobe doing?
    (a) Disregarding monochronic behavior
    (b) Assuming all members of a culture fit the popular stereotype
    (c) Emphasizing proxemics over time orientation
    (d) Forgetting that cultural intelligence can be learned

Short-Response Questions

16. What is the difference between valuing diversity and managing diversity?

17. How can subculture differences create diversity challenges in organizations?

18. If you were asked to give a short class presentation on the "silent languages" of culture, what cultural issues would you talk about and what examples would you give?

19. In what ways can the power distance dimension of national culture become an important issue in management?

Integration and Application Questions

20. A friend in West Virginia owns a small manufacturing firm employing about 50 workers. His son spent a semester in Japan as an exchange student. Upon return, he said to his dad: "Boy, the Japanese really do things right; everything is organized in teams; decisions are made by consensus, with everyone participating; no one seems to disagree with anything the bosses say. I think we should immediately start more teamwork and consensus decision making in our factory."

    Questions: The friend asks you for advice. Using insights from Hofstede's framework, what would you say to him? What differences in the Japanese and American cultures should be considered in this situation, and why?

Steps for Further Learning

BUILD MARKETABLE SKILLS • **DO** A CASE ANALYSIS • **GET** AND STAY INFORMED

BUILD MARKETABLE SKILLS.

EARN BIG CAREER PAYOFFS!

Don't miss these opportunities in the SKILL-BUILDING PORTFOLIO

SELF-ASSESSMENT 15:
Diversity Awareness

It's easy to talk about diversity ... where do you stand in day-to-day behavior?

CLASS EXERCISE 15:
Alligator River Story

Ambiguous situations can highlight diversity differences ... compare values with your peers.

TEAM PROJECT 15:
Job Satisfaction Around the World

Discover how the world's workers view job satisfaction ... consider cultural differences in work expectations.

Many learning resources are found at the end of the book and online within **WileyPLUS Learning Space.**

Practice Critical Thinking—Complete the CHAPTER 15 CASE

CASE SNAPSHOT: India, Inc.—How May I Help You?

When you call a toll-free number for customer service assistance, possibly pertaining to finance or banking, an airline reservation, an insurance claim, or technical support for one of your gadgets, there is a good possibility that the person on the other end of the line is half a world away. India and the Philippines are two of the biggest players. Your experience as a caller is part of the quest of multinational companies (think: Dell, American Express, and Verizon) to realize significant cost savings in customer service by outsourcing the work to lower-wage countries. The name for this industry is business process outsourcing, or BPO for short. Its critics worry not just about how customers react. They also worry about its impact on the personalities, lifestyle, careers, and culture of local workers across the world.

DO A CASE ANALYSIS.

STRENGTHEN YOUR CRITICAL THINKING!

MANAGER'S LIBRARY SELECTION
Read for Insights and Wisdom
Half the Sky: Turning Oppression into Opportunity for Women Worldwide (Random House, 2009) by Nicholas Kristof and Sheryl WuDunn

The message is: Women aren't the problem: they're the solution. The book title comes from an ancient Chinese proverb claims that "women hold up half the sky." The harsh reality is that women are oppressed throughout the developing world.

In this book Nicolas Kristof and Sheryl WuDunn outline indignities suffered by poor, uneducated women around the globe. All-too-common gender-specific human rights violations include sex trafficking, rape, and death after childbirth. They equate the modern oppression of women worldwide to that of slavery. In humane treatment of under privileged women continues despite the rule of law. Victimized women are poor, uneducated, and powerless in their societies. Crimes against them are hidden from the developing world and often tolerated in their male-dominated cultures. "Gendercide"—the daily slaughter of girls in the developing world—takes more lives in one decade than any genocide did in the entire 20th century.

The authors say we must first recognize injustices and then speak against them. Ordinary citizens can initiate change by volunteering with global organizations that fight oppression or joining e-mail lists. Educating maltreated women about their moral rights and the economic means to maintain independence is a key. Countries with masculine power structures need female leadership.

REFLECT AND REACT Are our diversity initiatives toward women properly focused on a global scale? Is it more important to increase the ranks of female executives in *Fortune* 500 corporationsor to stop global "gendercide"? Can moral and economic education empower poor, uneducated women to stand against injustice? Does the plight of victimized women get lost because we are too quick to embrace and accept so-called cultural differences?

GET AND STAY INFORMED.

MAKE YOURSELF VALUABLE!

The International Labour Organization reports there are 215 million child laborers worldwide; 115 million of them work in hazardous conditions.

Reuters/Corbis

Globalization and International Business

16

Going Global Isn't Just for Travelers

Management Live
Classic American Company, or Not?

Justin Sullivan/Getty Images

Going to Disney World? Stop by Orlando and visit the headquarters of Tupperware, a classic American company. Or is it? Forty years ago 90% of Tupperware sales were in the U.S. Today 90% are outside of the U.S. Its executive team is transnational. CEO Rick Goings says: "Our number two is English, our head of manufacturing and sourcing is Belgian, our head of human resources is German, our head of tax is Czech, one of our group presidents is a Swede, the other a Colombian. . . . We may be based in America but not a single piece of our DNA today is that of a purely American company."

YOUR THOUGHTS?

What difference does it make whether or not Tupperware is an American company? The product works wherever you are, and the history of the brand is something we can be proud of. So, is this the future of business small and large: Sell anywhere, buy anywhere, staff from everywhere?

YOUR CHAPTER 16 TAKEAWAYS

1. Discuss ways that globalization affects international business.
2. Understand what global corporations are and how they work.

Takeaway 16.1
How Does Globalization Affect International Business?

ANSWERS TO COME

- Globalization increases interdependence of the world's economies.
- Globalization creates international business opportunities.
- Global sourcing is a common international business activity.
- Export/import, licensing, and franchising are market entry forms of international business.
- Joint ventures and wholly owned subsidiaries are direct investment forms of international business.
- International business is complicated by different legal and political systems.
- International businesses deal with regional economic alliances

OUR GLOBAL COMMUNITY IS RICH WITH INFORMATION, OPPORTUNITIES, controversies, and complications. We get on-the-spot news feeds delivered from around the world right to our smart phones. When crises happen, Twitter, Facebook, and other social media get the news out instantaneously. You can board a plane in New York and fly nonstop to Beijing, China; Mumbai, India; or Johannesburg, South Africa. Colleges offer a growing variety of study-abroad programs. And, an international MBA is an increasingly desirable credential.

Here are some conversation starters on the business side of things. Ben & Jerry's Ice Cream is owned by the British-Dutch firm Unilever; Anheuser-Busch is owned by the Belgian firm InBev; India's Tata Group owns Jaguar and Tetley Tea. Honda, Nissan, and Toyota get 80% to 90% of their profits from sales in America; IBM employs more than 40,000 software developers in India. Components for Boeing planes come from 5,400 suppliers in 40 countries, and Nike has manufacturing contracts with more than 120 factories in China alone.[1]

The growing power of global businesses affects all of us as citizens, consumers, and career-seekers. Take a look at what you are wearing. It's hard to find a garment or a shoe that

A World Without Poverty

Nobel Peace Prize Winner Asks Global Firms to Fight Poverty

Micheline Pelletier/Corbis

Should global businesses balance the pursuit of profit with genuine efforts to do public good? A strong and positive "Yes!" is the answer given by Nobel Peace Prize winner Muhammad Yunus. The Bangladeshi economist gained fame for creating the Grameen Bank to offer microcredit loans to help fight poverty in his home country. The bank loans small amounts (as low as $30) to poor applicants (96% women) so that they can start their own small businesses and gain financial independence.

Yunus is now asking global firms to join in a transformational approach that unlocks the power of business to tackle poverty and other enduring social problems. In his book *Creating a World Without Poverty*, Yunus describes a social business model where a company's products or services are targeted to benefit those suffering from social ills. "Now

every time I want to address a problem, I create a business," he says. "These businesses are all focused on problem solving, not on money making."

Danone partnered with Yunus to start Grameen Danone as the world's first multinational social business. The firm manufactures nutritional yogurt and sells it at low cost in an attempt to help Bangladesh's undernourished children. Profits are reinvested to provide even cheaper and better goods and services to customers, rather than being paid out as dividends. "We can create a world where poverty doesn't exist," claims Yunus.

FIND INSPIRATION

When a multinational company enters countries where social problems like poverty, disease, and illiteracy are present, should it find a way to help? Can the social business model really take off in the global business context? Do you agree, or not, that global corporations can become powerful tools for eliminating social problems?

is really "Made in America." What about your favorite T-shirt? Where did you buy it? Where was it made? Where will it end up?

In *The Travels of a T-Shirt in the Global Economy,* economist Pietra Rivoli tracks the origins and disposition of a T-shirt that she bought while on a vacation.[2] It turns out that the common T-shirt lives a complicated global life, as shown in **Figure 16.1**. The life of Rivoli's T-shirt begins with cotton grown in Texas. It moves to China, where the cotton is processed and white T-shirts are manufactured. These are imported by a U.S. firm that silk-screens them and sells them to retail shops for resale to customers like Rivoli. When used T-shirts get donated to charity, many are sold to recyclers. In Rivoli's case the recycler sells them to a vendor in Africa who distributes them to local markets. There they are sold yet again to new customers.

GLOBALIZATION INCREASES INTERDEPENDENCE OF THE WORLD'S ECONOMIES.

We live and work in a **global economy** where labor and resource supplies, capital and product markets, and business competition are worldwide in scope.[3] Pretty much everything we do—from the things we buy to the food we eat to the investments we make—is influenced by the forces of **globalization**. Think of it as the process of growing interconnections among the components of the global economy.[4] Harvard scholar and consultant Rosabeth Moss Kanter describes globalization as "one of the most powerful and pervasive influences on nations, businesses, workplaces, communities, and lives."[5]

Do you have a good idea of how globalization affects your life? It's not just an issue of what you buy and how you invest. What about your work and career plans? In Ohio, for example, you'll find more than 180,000 people working for foreign-owned firms.[6] They hold jobs created by **insourcing,** where a foreign company, say Honda, invests in a business and hires local workers to staff it. Some 5.65 million U.S. jobs are linked to such inward foreign investment. Interestingly, these jobs pay up to 33% more on the average than ones locally created.[7]

Outsourcing is another side of the global economy story. It shifts jobs to foreign locations where businesses save costs by taking advantage of lower-wage skilled labor. John Chambers, CEO of Cisco Systems Inc., pretty much lays it on the line for all of us when he says: "I will put my jobs anywhere in the world where the right infrastructure is, with the right educated workforce, with the right supportive government."[8] Outsourcing has been an important cost-reduction strategy for lots of domestic businesses. But, not everyone is pleased to hear this message. How would you like to be told that your job was being eliminated and outsourced to another country? Should you be planning now for how this possibility might affect future job opportunities in your chosen career?

In the **global economy**, resources, markets, and competition are worldwide in scope.

Globalization is the process of growing interdependence among elements of the global economy.

Insourcing is the creation of domestic jobs by foreign employers.

Outsourcing shifts local jobs to foreign locations to take advantage of lower-wage labor in other countries.

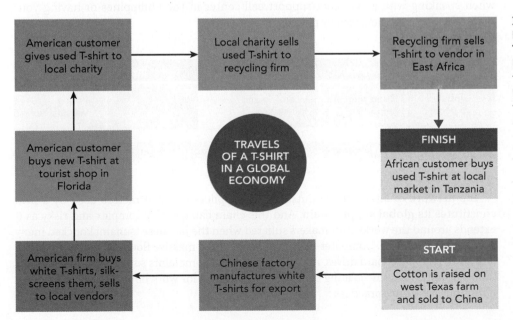

FIGURE 16.1

How Does a T-Shirt Travel Through the World's Global Economy?

This sketch shows the T-shirt beginning as cotton grown in Texas that is shipped to China, where it is processed and white T-shirts are manufactured. The white shirts come back to the United States, where they are silk-screened and sold to retail shops for resale to customers. If customers donate used T-shirts to a charity, they may go to a recycler, who sells them to vendors in other countries, where the used T-shirts get sold again to local customers.

GLOBALIZATION CREATES INTERNATIONAL BUSINESS OPPORTUNITIES.

An **international business** conducts commercial transactions across national boundaries.

Firms like Cisco, Sony, Ford, and IKEA are large **international businesses**. They conduct for-profit transactions of goods and services across national boundaries. Such businesses, from small exporters and importers to the huge multinational corporations, form the foundations of world trade. They move raw materials, finished products, and specialized services from one country to another in the global economy. And, they "go global" for good reasons—profits, customers, suppliers, labor, capital, risk management, and more.[9]

Today you can also add economic development to the list of reasons why some businesses go global. It's a way of helping make the world a better place while supporting sustainability and local business enterprise. An example is found in Rwanda, where coffee giants Green Mountain Coffee Roasters, Peet's Coffee & Tea, and Starbucks work with the nonprofit Techno-Serve. Its goal is to help raise the incomes of African coffee farmers by improving their production and marketing methods. The global firms send advisors to teach coffee growers how to meet international standards. It's a win-win. The global firm gets a quality product at a good price. The growers gain skills and markets, and the local economy improves.[10]

Why Businesses Go Global

- *Profits*—gain profits through expanded operations.
- *Customers*—enter new markets to gain customers.
- *Suppliers*—get access to products, services, and materials.
- *Labor*—hire low-cost, talented workers.
- *Capital*—get access to financial resources.
- *Risk*—spread assets among multiple countries.
- *Economic development*—help make the world a better place.

GLOBAL SOURCING IS A COMMON INTERNATIONAL BUSINESS ACTIVITY.

Just as there is more than one reason for getting into international business, there are several ways of doing it. Nike's swoosh is one of the world's most globally recognized brands. But did you know that Nike, headquartered in Beaverton, Oregon, does no domestic manufacturing? All its products come from sources abroad. New Balance, by contrast, still produces at a few factories in the United States even while making extensive use of global suppliers in China and elsewhere.[11] Although they compete in the same industry, Nike and New Balance are pursuing somewhat different global strategies.

In **global sourcing**, firms purchase materials, manufacturing, or services around the world for local use.

A mainstay of international business is **global sourcing**. This is where a business purchases materials, manufacturing, or services from around the world. It basically takes advantage of international wage gaps by contracting for low-cost goods and services in foreign locations. Nike is a master at this, and you see lots of it in all sorts of manufacturing. Boeing's 787 Dreamliner, for example, has wings and center fuselage from Japan, engines from the U.K. and Canada, and doors from Sweden and France. You also see it in services. Think of this when speaking with a customer-support call center in the Philippines or having your medical x-rays and scans read by physicians in India.

A **global supply chain** is a network of a firm's outsourcing suppliers and contractors.

The network of international outsourcing suppliers and contractors used by a firm constitutes its **global supply chain**. And this chain can get very complex and risky as it extends around the world. Automakers suffered when the Japanese tsunami knocked many parts suppliers offline. Computer makers suffered when massive flooding in Thailand shut down their supply of hard drives. Apple suffered when complaints surfaced that some of its Chinese suppliers were violating company expectations for work hours, worker safety, and hazardous substance practices.[12]

HOT TOPIC

Avoid China and Reshore Our Manufacturing?

Pgiam/iStockphoto

If you were a manufacturer in days past, you went to China, at least as a first stop on your global scouting trip. But things are starting to change. Why so? Light Saver Technologies tried for 2 years to get things done in China. Now its work is back in California. CEO Jerry Anderson says China lost its allure: "It's probably 30 percent cheaper to manufacture in China. But factor in shipping and all the other B.S. that you have to endure."

Transportation costs and time are up for goods moved from China to the U.S. and other world markets. Labor costs are up, rising about 20% a year. Business risks in China, if not up, are at least more visible. Theft of intellectual property is a problem. One small manufacturer says: "They're infamous over there for knocking [products] off." Poor labor standards and work practices are a problem. Just ask Apple CEO Tim Cook about negative publicity over its use of China-based manufacturing.

HOW ABOUT IT?

What's a manufacturing executive to do? *The Economist* says China "is still a manufacturing power." With super-efficient plants and supply chains, it remains a bargain in labor costs. So, are you on the reshoring side or the offshoring side of the issue? What facts are available to support or deny your position? Think of things from a consumer's perspective. If you can buy a child's toy made in China for $8, will you be willing to pay $12 so that it could be labeled "Made in America"? Should more of America's businesses, large and small, say "Not worth the trouble!" when Chinese manufacturers come calling with offers?

Global problems with sketchy suppliers, rising labor and transportation costs, availability of cheaper energy at home, and concerns for good public relations are all reasons why some firms are now modifying their outsourcing strategies. You'll notice an increasing number of news reports about **reshoring** that shifts foreign production—and jobs—back to domestic locations. A survey of large U.S. firms by the Boston Consulting Group found that almost half had plans to return some foreign manufacturing to the United States. The report concluded, "Companies are realizing that the economics of manufacturing are swinging in favor of the U.S."[13]

> **Reshoring** moves foreign production and jobs back to domestic locations.

EXPORT/IMPORT, LICENSING, AND FRANCHISING ARE MARKET ENTRY FORMS OF INTERNATIONAL BUSINESS.

A lot of international business involves **exporting**—selling locally made products in foreign markets, and **importing**—buying foreign-made products and selling them in domestic markets. Exporting in particular is often viewed positively as a driver of economic development. Because the growth of export industries creates local jobs, you'll often read and hear about governments supporting these types of business initiatives.

> In **exporting**, local products are sold abroad.

> **Importing** is the process of acquiring products abroad and selling them in domestic markets.

Another form of international business is the **licensing** agreement, where foreign firms pay a fee for rights to make or sell another company's products in a specified region. The license typically grants access by the foreign firm to a unique manufacturing technology, special patent, or trademark. But, it also carries business risks like stealing and counterfeiting.[14] New Balance, for example, licensed a Chinese supplier to produce one of its brands. Even after New Balance revoked the license, the supplier continued to produce and distribute "New Barlun" shoes around Asia. New Balance ended up facing costly and complex litigation in China's courts.[15]

> In **licensing**, one firm pays a fee for rights to make or sell another company's products.

In **franchising**, a foreign firm buys the rights to use another's name and operating methods in its home country. When companies such as Dunkin' Donuts or Subway franchise internationally, they sell facility designs, equipment, product ingredients, recipes, and management systems to foreign investors. They also typically retain certain product and operating controls to protect their brand's image.

> In **franchising**, a firm pays a fee for rights to use another company's name and operating methods.

JOINT VENTURES AND WHOLLY OWNED SUBSIDIARIES ARE DIRECT INVESTMENT FORMS OF INTERNATIONAL BUSINESS.

A **joint venture** operates in a foreign country through co-ownership with local partners.

Sooner or later, some firms decide to make costly direct investments to set up local operations in foreign countries. One way to do this is by a **joint venture**. This is a co-ownership arrangement in which the foreign and local partners agree to pool resources, share risks, and jointly operate the new business. Sometimes the joint venture is formed when a foreign partner buys part ownership in an existing local firm. In other cases it is formed when the foreign and local partners start an entirely new operation together.

International joint ventures become **global strategic alliances** in which foreign and domestic partners cooperate for mutual gains. Each partner hopes to get from the alliance things they couldn't do or would have a hard time doing alone. For the local partner, an alliance may bring access to technology and opportunities to learn new skills. For the outside partner, an alliance may bring access to new markets and customers and the expert assistance of locals who understand them.[16]

TIPS TO REMEMBER
Checklist for Choosing a Good Joint Venture Partner

- Familiar with your firm's major business
- Employs a strong local workforce
- Values its customers and employees
- Has strong local market for its own products
- Has record of good management
- Has good profit potential
- Has sound financial standing
- Has reputation for ethical decision making
- Has reputation for socially responsible practices

In a **global strategic alliance**, each partner hopes to achieve through cooperation things they couldn't do alone.

A **foreign subsidiary** is a local operation completely owned by a foreign firm.

A **greenfield venture** establishes a foreign subsidiary by building an entirely new operation in a foreign country.

It's important to recognize that joint venture deals pose potential risks, and loss of technology is a big one. Some time ago, for example, GM executives noticed that a new car—the Chery—from a fast-growing local competitor looked very similar to one of their models. This competitor was partially owned by GM's Chinese joint venture partner, and GM claimed its design was copied. Chery Automobile, Ltd., has grown to be China's major automaker and largest car exporter.[17]

In contrast to the international joint venture, which is a cross-border alliance, a **foreign subsidiary** is a local operation completely owned and controlled by a foreign firm. It might be a local firm that was purchased in its entirety or it might be a brand-new operation built from start as a **greenfield venture**. Decisions to set up foreign subsidiaries are most often made only after foreign firms have gained experience in the local environment through earlier joint ventures.

INTERNATIONAL BUSINESS IS COMPLICATED BY DIFFERENT LEGAL AND POLITICAL SYSTEMS.

As you might imagine, the more home-country and host-country laws differ, the more difficult and complex it is for international businesses to operate successfully. And the greater the extent of foreign involvement, the more complex it becomes to understand and adapt to local ways. Common legal problems faced by international businesses involve incorporation practices and business ownership, negotiation and implementation of contracts, handling of foreign exchange, and protection of intellectual property like patents, trademarks, and copyrights.

The issue of intellectual property is particularly sensitive these days. You might know this best in terms of concerns about movie and music downloads, photocopying of books and journals, and sale of fake designer fashions. Many Western businesses know it as lost profits due to their products or designs being copied and sold as imitations by foreign firms. After a lengthy and complex legal battle, for example, Starbucks won a major intellectual property case it had taken to the Chinese courts. A local firm was using Starbucks' Chinese name, "Xingbake" (*Xing* means "star" and *bake* is pronounced "bah kuh"), and was also copying its café designs.[18]

When international businesses believe they are being mistreated in foreign countries, or when local companies believe foreign competitors are disadvantaging them, their respective governments might take the cases to the **World Trade Organization (WTO)**. The 161 members of the WTO give one another **most favored nation status**—the most favorable treatment for imports and exports. Members also agree to work together within its framework to try to resolve some international business problems.

Even though WTO members are supposed to give one another most favored nation status, disputes over trade barriers are still common. Issues relate to **tariffs** or taxes that governments impose on imports. They also include **nontariff barriers** that discourage imports in nontax ways such as quotas and government import restrictions.

A big concern in international business is outright **protectionism**—the attempt by governments to protect local firms from foreign competition and save jobs for local workers. You will see such issues reflected in many political campaigns and debates. And the issues aren't easy. Government leaders face internal political dilemmas involving the often-conflicting goals of seeking freer international trade while still protecting domestic industries. Such dilemmas can make it difficult for countries to reach international agreements on trade matters and hard for the WTO to act as a global arbiter of trade issues.

INTERNATIONAL BUSINESSES DEAL WITH REGIONAL ECONOMIC ALLIANCES.

Globalization has brought with it the growth of regional economic alliances, where nations agree to work together for economic gains. Global firms must understand these alliances in order to do business within and across their borders.

North America

NAFTA, the **North American Free Trade Agreement,** creates a trade zone that frees the flows of goods and services, workers, and investments among the United States, Canada, and Mexico. Many firms have taken advantage of NAFTA by moving production facilities to Mexico and hiring low cost but skilled Mexican workers.

> The **World Trade Organization (WTO)** is a global institution established to promote free trade and open markets around the world.

> **Most favored nation status** gives a trading partner the most favorable treatment for imports and exports.

> **Tariffs** are taxes governments levy on imports from abroad.

> **Nontariff barriers** are nontax policies that governments enact to discourage imports, such as quotas and import restrictions.

> **Protectionism** is a call for tariffs and favorable treatments to protect domestic firms from foreign competition.

> **NAFTA** is the North American Free Trade Agreement linking Canada, the United States, and Mexico in an economic alliance.

BOLIVIA'S PRESIDENT TELLS GLOBAL FIRMS THE COUNTRY'S NATURAL RESOURCES BELONG TO ITS PEOPLE.

ETHICS CHECK

Nationalism and Protectionism

REUTERS/Carlos Hugo Vaca/Landov

The headline read "Bolivia Seizes Control of Oil and Gas Fields." The announcement said: "We are beginning by nationalizing oil and gas; tomorrow we will add mining, forestry, and all natural resources, what our ancestors fought for."

The country's president, Evo Morales, set forth new terms that gave a state-owned firm 82% of all revenues, leaving 18% for the foreign firms. He said: "Only those firms that respect these new terms will be allowed to operate in the country." The implicit threat was that any firms not willing to sign new contracts would be sent home.

Although foreign governments described this nationalization as an "unfriendly move," Morales considered it patriotic. His position was that any existing contracts with the state were in violation of the constitution, and that Bolivia's natural resources belonged to its people.

YOUR DECISION?

If you are the CEO at one of these global firms, do you resist and raise the ethics of honoring your "old" contracts with the Bolivian government? Or do you comply with the new terms being offered? And as an everyday citizen of the world, can you disagree that a country has a right to protect its natural resources from exploitation by foreigners? Just what are the ethics of Morales's decision?

QUICK CASE

16 Hours to J-burg

AMR Image/Getty Images

Just sit back and relax—the flight is underway, and you are sitting in business class on South African Airways flight 204 from JFK to Johannesburg. It's your first overseas assignment as an auditor for Deloitte, and you've been rushing to prepare.

You're flying in alone but will be met by four team members from Deloitte's local office in what they call "J-burg." You expect to be in country about a week.

But, it all happened so fast. One day you're in the office finishing a local audit; that afternoon the boss calls and says he's sending you to Johannesburg; and 3 days later you're on the plane. It's taken all your interim time to finish the last project, pack, and talk with family.

It turns out that your mother isn't very happy—she's not sure a single woman should be sent alone on this job. From your standpoint, though, an international assignment is a real statement that the company believes in your abilities. You even think this might be something you'd like to do more of and that you might make "being good at international" a strong part of your promotion portfolio.

Other than a short "meet-and-greet" video conference with the J-burg team and a description of the project from your boss, you haven't received any other preparation. Now that you're onboard SA204, the question is: Do you have what it takes to succeed with this assignment in a new country and culture?

WHAT DO YOU DO?

The flight is 16 hours long, and you've decided to make some notes on "things I should do and not do." What's on your list and why? As a good auditor, you also decide to self assess on your readiness for cross-cultural teamwork in South Africa. So, you make a balance sheet of "personal assets and liabilities." What goes into each column?

NAFTA has its supporters and critics, and the job shifts just mentioned can be a hot topic in political debates. Arguments on the positive side credit NAFTA with greater cross-border trade and strengthening of the Mexican business environment. Arguments on the negative side blame NAFTA for jobs lost to Mexico and for the willingness of American workers to accept lower wages in order to keep jobs at home.

Europe

> The **EU** or **European Union** is a political and economic alliance of 28 European countries.

The **European Union** or **EU** is a political and economic regional alliance. The EU comprises 28 countries that are integrating politically with a European Parliament and economically by removing barriers to cross-border trade and business development. Nineteen EU members use a common currency—the *euro*—that is a competitor to the U.S. dollar in the global economy.

Asia

It's likely that you will occasionally hear someone say, write, or report that the 21st century will be dominated by developments in Asia—economic, political, and social. As a reflection of that future, **APEC**—short for **Asia-Pacific Economic Cooperation**—links 21 nations to promote free trade and investment in the Pacific region. Its members represent prominent economies such as Australia, Canada, China, the Republic of Korea, Indonesia, Russia, and the United States.

> **APEC** is the **Asia-Pacific Economic Cooperation** that links 21 nations to promote free trade and investment in the Pacific region.

Africa

Africa is fast moving center stage in world business headlines. The region's economies are growing, the middle class is expanding, and regional economic alliances are gaining strength. Among them, the **Southern Africa Development Community, SADC**, links 14 southern African countries in trade and economic development efforts to improve prosperity and living standards for their citizens. Its Web site posts this vision: "a future in a regional community that will ensure economic well-being, improvement of the standards of living and quality of life, freedom and social justice, and peace and security for the peoples of Southern Africa."[19]

> **SADC** is the **Southern Africa Development Community** that links 14 southern African countries in trade and economic development efforts.

STUDYGUIDE

Takeaway 16.1
How Does Globalization Affect International Business?

Terms to Define

APEC (Asia-Pacific Economic Cooperation)	Global sourcing	Joint venture	Protectionism
	Global supply chain	Licensing	Reshoring
EU (European Union)	Global strategic alliance	Most favored nation status	SADC (South Africa Development Community)
Exporting	Globalization	NAFTA (North American Free Trade Agreement)	
Foreign subsidiary	Greenfield venture		Tariffs
Franchising	Importing	Nontariff barriers	World Trade Organization (WTO)
Global economy	Insourcing	Outsourcing	
	International business		

Rapid Review

- The forces of globalization create international business opportunities to pursue profits, customers, capital, and low-cost suppliers and labor in different countries.
- The least costly ways of doing business internationally are to use global sourcing, exporting and importing, and licensing and franchising.
- Direct investment strategies to establish joint ventures or wholly owned subsidiaries in foreign countries represent substantial commitments to international operations.
- Environmental differences, particularly in legal and political systems, can complicate international business activities.
- The World Trade Organization (WTO) is a global institution established to promote free trade and open markets around the world.
- Regional economic alliances link member nations for cooperation in economic and trade development.

Questions for Discussion

1. Why would a government want to prohibit a foreign firm from owning more than 49% of a local joint venture?
2. Are joint ventures worth the risk of being taken advantage of by foreign partners, as with GM's "Chery" case in China?
3. What aspects of the U.S. legal environment might prove complicated for a Russian firm starting new operations in the United States?

Be Sure You Can

- **explain** how globalization affects our lives
- **list** five reasons that companies pursue international business opportunities
- **describe** and give examples of how firms do international business by global sourcing, exporting/importing, franchising/licensing, joint ventures, and foreign subsidiaries
- **discuss** how differences in legal environments can affect businesses operating internationally
- **explain** the purpose of the World Trade Organization

Career Situation: What Would You Do?

Your new design for a revolutionary golf putter has turned out to be a big hit with friends and players on the local golf courses. So, you decide to have some made, start selling them, and see if you can make a business out it. A friend says: "Go to China, someone there will build it cheap and to your quality standard." But you're not sure. Sending your design to China for manufacturing is worrisome, and there's a side of you that would really like to have "Made in America" stamped on the clubs. Make a list of positives and negatives of manufacturing in each place. What factors are likely to drive your final decision on global versus local sourcing?

Takeaway 16.2
What Are Global Corporations, and How Do They Work?

ANSWERS TO COME

- Global corporations have extensive operations in many countries.
- The actions of global corporations can be controversial.
- Managers of global corporations face ethics challenges.
- Planning and controlling are complicated in global corporations.
- Organizing can be difficult in global corporations.
- Leading is challenging in global corporations.

IF YOU TRAVEL ABROAD THESE DAYS, MANY OF YOUR FAVORITE BRANDS AND products will travel with you. You can have a McDonald's sandwich in more than 100 countries, enjoy Häagen-Dazs ice cream in at least 50, and brush up with Procter & Gamble's Crest almost everywhere. The *Economist* magazine even publishes an annual "Big Mac" index to track purchasing power parity among the world's currencies. A recent index listed the dollar cost of a Big Mac as $4.79 in the United States, $2.77 in China, $3.35 in Mexico, and $7.54 in Switzerland.[20]

GLOBAL CORPORATIONS HAVE EXTENSIVE OPERATIONS IN MANY COUNTRIES.

A **global corporation** or **multinational corporation (MNC)** has extensive international operations in many foreign countries and derives a substantial portion of its sales and profits from international sources.[21] The world's largest MNCs are identified in annual listings such as *Fortune*'s Global 500 the *Financial Times*' FT Global 500, and *Forbes*' The World's Largest Public Companies. They include familiar consumer names like Apple, Toyota, Nestlé, BMW, Caterpillar, Sony, and Samsung. But you might be surprised the top four on *Forbes*' list are Chinese banks, while the largest U.S. global firm is Warren Buffet's Berkshire Hathaway followed by JP Morgan Chase and Exxon Mobil.[22]

> A **global corporation** or **multinational corporation (MNC)** has extensive international business dealings in many foreign countries.

Top managers of some global companies are trying to move their firms toward becoming **transnational corporations**. That is, they would like to operate worldwide without being identified with one national home.[23] When you buy Nestlé's products, for example, do you have any idea that it is a registered Swiss company? The firm's executives view the entire world as their domain for acquiring resources, locating production facilities, marketing goods and services, and establishing brand image. They seek total integration of global operations, try to make major decisions from a global perspective, and have top managers from many different countries.

> A **transnational corporation** is an MNC that operates worldwide on a borderless basis.

Even with the goal of becoming transnationals, most MNCs still retain strong national identifications. Is there any doubt in your mind that IBM and Intel are "American" firms, whereas Nissan and Sony are "Japanese"? Most likely not, but that may not be the way their executives would like the firms viewed. And it's certainly not reflected in the sources of earnings. Nissan and Sony thrive on U.S. and European markets. Both IBM and Intel earn more than 75% of their revenues from sales outside of the U.S.

THE ACTIONS OF GLOBAL CORPORATIONS CAN BE CONTROVERSIAL.

What difference does a company's nationality really make? Does it matter to an American whether local jobs come from a domestic giant such as Verizon or a foreign one such as Honda?[24] What about the power global firms wield in the world economy? Is this a problem? The WTO reports that 51 of the 100 largest economies are global firms and that they control

70% of world trade.[25] And how about what some call the **globalization gap**? This is where large multinationals gain disproportionately from the forces of globalization, versus smaller firms and many countries that do not.[26] Should this be on your list of personal concerns about globalization?

Ideally speaking, global corporations and the countries that host them should all benefit. But as **Figure 16.2** shows, things can go both right and wrong in MNC–host country relationships. Although the economic power of global firms is undoubtedly good for business leaders and investors, it can be threatening to small and less-developed countries and their domestic industries.

MNCs may complain that a host country bars it from taking profits out of the country, overprices local resources, and imposes restrictive government rules. Host countries may grumble that an MNC hires the best local talent, fails to respect local customs, makes too much profit, and doesn't transfer really useful technology.[27] Another complaint is that MNCs use unfair practices, such as below-cost pricing, to drive local competitors out of business. This is one of the arguments in favor of *protectionism*, discussed earlier as the use of laws and practices to protect a country's domestic businesses from foreign competitors.

MNCs can also run into difficulties in their home or headquarter countries. If a multinational cuts local jobs and then outsources work to another country, local government and community leaders will quickly criticize the firm for its lack of social responsibility. After all, they will say, shouldn't you be creating local jobs and building the local economy? Perhaps you might agree with this view. But can you see why business executives might disagree?

MANAGERS OF GLOBAL CORPORATIONS FACE ETHICS CHALLENGES.

"Walmart Caught in Huge Bribery Scandal"

"Hewlett-Packard to Pay $108m to Settle Scandal over Bribery of Public Officials"

"UK Banks Launch Reviews over 'Corrupt' FIFA Payments"[28]

Headlines like these are all too common. The ethical aspects of international business are real, complex, and pretty much unavoidable. They put executive decision making to stiff tests.

Corruption

One of the international business ethics issues that is often in the news involves outright **corruption**. This occurs when employees or representatives of MNCs resort to illegal practices such as bribes to further their business interests in foreign countries. The **Foreign Corrupt Practices Act** (FCPA) makes it illegal for U.S. firms and their representatives to engage in corrupt practices overseas. This prohibits them from paying or offering bribes or excessive commissions, including nonmonetary gifts, to foreign officials or employees of state-run companies in return for business favors.[29]

Critics of the FCPA claim that it fails to recognize the realities of business as practiced in many foreign nations. They believe it puts U.S. companies at a competitive disadvantage

The **globalization gap** is where large global firms gain disproportionately from the global economy versus smaller firms.

Corruption involves illegal practices to further one's business interests.

The **Foreign Corrupt Practices Act** makes it illegal for U.S. firms and their representatives to engage in corrupt practices overseas.

FIGURE 16.2
What Can Go Right and Wrong in Relationships Between Global Corporations and Their Host Countries?

When things go right, both the global corporation, or MNC, and its host country gain. The global firm gets profits or resources, and the host country often sees more jobs and employment opportunities, higher tax revenues, and useful technology transfers. But when things go wrong, each finds ways to blame the other.

MNC–HOST COUNTRY RELATIONSHIPS *What should go right*	MNC–HOST COUNTRY RELATIONSHIPS *What can go wrong*	
Mutual benefits	**Host-country complaints about MNCs**	**MNC complaints about host countries**
Shared opportunities with potential for • Growth • Income • Learning • Development	• Excessive profits • Economic domination • Interference with government • Hires best local talent • Limited technology transfer • Disrespect for local customs	• Profit limitations • Overpriced resources • Exploitative rules • Foreign exchange restrictions • Failure to uphold contracts

because they can't offer the same "deals" as businesses from other nations—deals that the locals may regard as standard business practices. And, to some at least, the issues aren't always clear cut. An American executive, for example, says that payoffs are needed to get shipments through customs in Russia even though all legal taxes and tariffs are already paid. "We use customs brokers," he says, "and they build bribes into the invoice."[30]

What do you think? Should the act of paying for what you already deserve to receive be considered a bribe? How do you sort right from wrong when considering how to negotiate local customs and business expectations? Should U.S. legal standards apply to American companies operating abroad? Or should they be allowed to do whatever is locally acceptable?

Sweatshops

Sweatshops employ workers at very low wages, for long hours, and in poor working conditions.

Even the most well-intentioned MNCs can end up in troublesome relationships with their global suppliers. One risk is that the local firms are **sweatshops**, places in which employees work at low wages for long hours and in poor, even unsafe, conditions.

A notorious sweatshop case came to light with the collapse of a building in Bangladesh that housed outsourcing suppliers to major-brand global clothing retailers. The tragedy killed more than 1,100 people and exposed unsafe buildings and sweatshop conditions in factories throughout the country. The local garment industry runs on workers, often female and illiterate, trying to shed lives of poverty. One says her workplace has blocked elevators, filthy tap water, and unclean overflowing toilets.[31] The nonprofit Institute for Global Labour and Human Rights is dedicated to exposing sweatshops as part of its mission "to promote and defend human, women's and workers' rights in the global economy."[32]

Child Labor

Child labor is the full-time employment of children for work otherwise done by adults.

Another global business risk is working with contractors who use **child labor**, the full-time employment of children for work otherwise done by adults.[33] And the facts are startling. The International Labour Organization reports there are some 215 million child laborers worldwide. About 115 million of them work in hazardous conditions.[34] But, the ethics dilemmas of child labor are more complex than these data alone suggest.

Wouldn't you agree that children should go to school and grow up with positive experiences and future prospects? The practice of child labor seems contrary to these aspirations.

TRANSPARENCY INTERNATIONAL SEEKS A WORLD FREE OF CORRUPTION AND BRIBES.

FACTS TO CONSIDER

Corruption and Bribes Haunt Global Business

Daniel Laflor/iStockphoto

If you want a world free of corruption and bribes, you have a lot in common with the nonprofit activist organization Transparency International. Its mission is to "create change for a world free of corruption."

The organization publishes regular surveys and reports on corruption and bribery around the world. Here are some recent data.

Corruption: Best and worst out of 174 countries in perceived public sector corruption.

Best Five—Denmark, New Zealand, Finland, Sweden, Norway

Worst Five—Somalia, Sudan, Afghanistan, Iraq, Turkmenistan

In-Betweens—Canada (#14), United States (#17), South Africa (#67), India (#85), Venezuela (#161)

Bribery: Best and worst of 28 countries in likelihood of home-country firms' willingness to pay bribes abroad.

Best Five—Netherlands, Switzerland, Belgium, Germany, Japan

Worst Five—Russia, China, Mexico, Indonesia, United Arab Emirates

In Betweens—Canada (#6), United States (#10), Brazil (#14), Turkey (#19)

WHAT'S YOUR TAKE?

What patterns do you detect in these data, if any? Does it surprise you that the United States didn't make the "best" lists? How would you differentiate between the terms "corruption" and "bribery" as they apply in international business?

But suppose children and their families live in abject poverty and suffer social harms? Might child labor play a positive role in such settings? A spokesman for UNICEF in Honduras says: "Children need to support their families and themselves, and escape from the gangs."[35]

Where do you stand on this issue? Even if child labor is legal by local standards and the context is one of high poverty, can you justify doing business with one of the employers?

PLANNING AND CONTROLLING ARE COMPLICATED IN GLOBAL CORPORATIONS.

Setting goals, making plans, controlling results—all of these standard management functions can become quite complicated in the international arena. Picture a home office somewhere in the United States, say, Chicago, and foreign operations scattered in Asia, Africa, South America, and Europe. Planning and controlling must somehow span all locations, meeting both home office needs and those of foreign affiliates.

One planning issue in international business is **currency risk**, or profit loss due to fluctuations in foreign exchange rates. Companies such as Starbucks and IBM, for example, make a lot of sales abroad. These sales are in foreign currencies. But as exchange rates vary, the dollar value of sales revenues goes up and down and profits are affected. Companies have to plan for the potential positive and negative impacts of exchange rate fluctuations on their profits.

> **Currency risk** is possible profit loss because of fluctuating exchange rates.

When the dollar is weak against the euro, it takes more dollars to buy 1 euro. This is bad for American consumers, who must pay more to buy European products. But it's good for European consumers, who pay less for American ones. A weak dollar is also good for American companies who make lots of sales in euros and then get more when exchanging them for dollars. But what happens when the dollar strengthens against the euro? Is this good or bad for firms with large sales in euro-zone countries? The boxed example shows that it's bad.

> *Scenario 1:* Weak dollar
> 1 $US = 0.75 euro
> Euro sales = €100,000
> U.S. take-home revenue = $133,000
>
> *Scenario 2:* Strong dollar
> 1 $US = 1.25 euros
> Euro sales = €100,000
> U.S. take-home revenue = $80,000

Global businesses must also deal with **political risk**, potential losses because of instability and political changes in foreign countries. The major threats of political risk today come from terrorism, civil wars, armed conflicts, shifting government systems through elections or forced takeovers, and new laws and economic policies. An example is the surprise nationalization of Bolivia's oil and gas industries that was described earlier in the Ethics Check. Although such things can't be prevented, they can be anticipated to some extent by a planning technique called **political-risk analysis**. It tries to forecast the probability of disruptive events that can threaten the security of a foreign investment. Given the world we now live in, can you see the high stakes of such analysis?

> **Political risk** is possible loss because of instability and political changes in foreign countries.

> **Political-risk analysis** forecasts how political events may have an impact on foreign investments.

ORGANIZING CAN BE DIFFICULT IN GLOBAL CORPORATIONS.

Even after plans are in place, it isn't easy to organize for international operations. In the early stages of international activities, businesses often appoint someone or a specific unit to handle them. But as global business expands, a more complex arrangement is usually necessary.

One possible choice for organizing an MNC is the *global area structure* shown in here. It arranges production and sales functions into separate geographical units and puts top managers in charge—such as Area Manager Africa or Area Manager Europe. This allows business in major areas of the world to be run by executives with special local expertise.

Global area structure

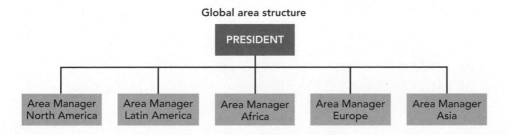

Another organizing option for global corporations is the *global product structure* shown below. It gives worldwide responsibilities to product group managers who are assisted by area specialists on the corporate staff. These specialists provide expert guidance on the cultures, markets, and unique conditions of various countries or regions.

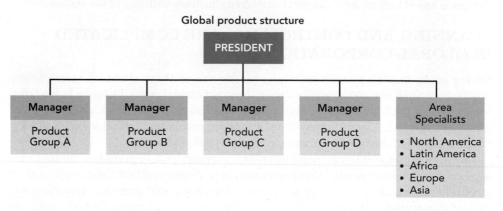

Global product structure

PRESIDENT

Manager	Manager	Manager	Manager	Area Specialists
Product Group A	Product Group B	Product Group C	Product Group D	• North America • Latin America • Africa • Europe • Asia

LEADING IS CHALLENGING IN GLOBAL CORPORATIONS.

As executives in businesses and other types of organizations press forward with global initiatives, the challenges of leading diverse workforces and dealing with customers across national and cultural borders have to be mastered. Globalization and the growth of international businesses are creating needs for more **global managers**, ones aware of international developments and competent in working across cultures.[36]

A **global manager** is culturally aware and informed on international affairs.

The *Wall Street Journal* says that global companies need managers who "understand different countries and cultures" and "intuitively understand the markets they are trying to penetrate."[37] A truly global manager is always inquisitive and informed of international events and complexity in our ever-changing world, such as those featured throughout this book.[38] A truly global manager is also culturally sensitive and aware.

A truly global manager is highly skilled in leadership competencies that travel well across cultural boundaries. Universal facilitators of leadership success are things like being trustworthy, informed, communicative, and inspiring.[39] Regardless of where they live and work, people tend to like leaders who give them confidence and are good with teamwork.

Universal *Facilitators* of Leadership Success

- Acting trustworthy, just, honest
- Being positive, dynamic, motivating
- Inspiring confidence
- Being informed and communicative
- Being a team builder

Universal *Inhibitors* of Leadership Success

- Being a loner
- Acting uncooperative
- Being irritable
- Acting autocratic

Managers who fail in global assignments are likely to display behaviors known as universal inhibitors of leadership success. Things like being a loner and acting irritable, uncooperative, and autocratic are viewed negatively across cultures.

So now we come back to you. Are you willing to admit that the world isn't just for traveling anymore and try to embrace it as a career opportunity? How do you stack up on the nearby lists of leadership facilitators and inhibitors? Is it possible that you might stand out to a potential employer as someone with the leadership skills to excel in international assignments and as a global manager?

STUDYGUIDE

Takeaway 16.2
What Are Global Corporations, and How Do They Work?

Terms to Define

Child labor	Global corporation or multinational corporation (MNC)	Globalization gap	Transnational corporation
Corruption		Political risk	
Currency risk		Political-risk analysis	
Foreign Corrupt Practices Act	Global manager	Sweatshops	

Rapid Review

- A global business or multinational corporation (MNC) has extensive operations in several foreign countries; a transnational corporation attempts to operate without national identity and with a worldwide strategy.

- Global firms benefit host countries by paying taxes, bringing in new technologies, and creating employment opportunities; they can also harm host countries by interfering with local government and politics, extracting excessive profits, and dominating the local economy.

- The Foreign Corrupt Practices Act prohibits representatives of U.S. international businesses from engaging in corrupt practices abroad.

- Planning and controlling global operations must take into account such things as currency risk and political risk in changing environmental conditions.

- Organizing for global operations often involves use of a global product structure or a global area structure.

- Leading global operations requires universal leadership skills and global managers who are capable of working in different cultures and countries.

Questions for Discussion

1. Should becoming a transnational corporation be the goal of all MNCs?

2. Is there anything that global firms and host governments can do to avoid conflicts and bad feelings with one another?

3. Are laws such as the Foreign Corrupt Practices Act unfair to American companies trying to compete around the world?

Be Sure You Can

- **differentiate** a multinational corporation from a transnational corporation

- **list** common host-country complaints and three home-country complaints about MNC operations

- **explain** the international business challenges of corruption, sweatshops, and child labor

- **discuss** the implications of political risk for global businesses

- **differentiate** the global area structure and global product structure

- **list** possible competencies of global managers

Career Situation: What Would You Do?

You've just read in the newspaper that one of your favorite brands of sports shoes is being investigated for being made in sweatshop conditions at factories in Asia. It really disturbs you, but the shoes are great. A student group on campus has a campaign to boycott the brand. Will you join the boycott, or not, and why? How effective are such consumer threats? Is it still too easy for global firms to get away with bad behaviors? If so, what can and should be done about it?

TEST PREP **16**

Answers to Test Prep questions can be found at the back of the book.

Multiple-Choice Questions

1. In addition to gaining new markets, businesses often go international in the search for _____.
   (a) political risk
   (b) protectionism
   (c) lower labor costs
   (d) most favored nation status

2. When boot-maker Rocky Brands bought 70% ownership of a manufacturing company in the Dominican Republic, Rocky was engaging in which form of international business?
   (a) Import/export
   (b) Licensing
   (c) Foreign subsidiary
   (d) Joint venture

3. When Limited Brands buys cotton in Egypt and has tops sewn from it in Sri Lanka according to designs made in Italy and then sells the tops at Victoria's Secret stores in the United States, this is a form of international business known as _____.
   (a) licensing
   (b) importing
   (c) joint venturing
   (d) global sourcing

4. When foreign investment creates new jobs in the U.S., this is a form of _____ that is welcomed by the local economy.
   (a) globalization
   (b) insourcing
   (c) joint venturing
   (d) licensing

5. When a Hong Kong firm makes an agreement with the Walt Disney Company to use the Disney logo and legally make jewelry in the shape of Disney cartoon characters, Disney is engaging in a form of international business known as _____.
   (a) exporting
   (b) licensing
   (c) joint venturing
   (d) franchising

6. One major difference between an international business and a transnational corporation is that the transnational tries to operate _____.
   (a) without a strong national identity
   (b) in at least six foreign countries
   (c) with only domestic managers at the top
   (d) without corruption

7. The Foreign Corrupt Practices Act makes it illegal for _____.
   (a) U.S. businesses to work with subcontractors running foreign sweatshop operations
   (b) foreign businesses to pay bribes to U.S. government officials
   (c) U.S. businesses to make "payoffs" abroad to gain international business contracts
   (d) foreign businesses to steal intellectual property from U.S. firms operating in their countries

8. The World Trade Organization, or WTO, would most likely become involved in disputes between countries over _____.
   (a) exchange rates
   (b) ethnocentrism
   (c) nationalization
   (d) tariffs and protectionism

9. The athletic footwear maker New Balance discovered that exact copies of its running shoe designs were on sale in China under the name "New Barlun." This is an example of a/an _____ problem in international business.
   (a) most favored nation
   (b) global strategic alliance
   (c) joint venture
   (d) intellectual property rights

10. When the profits of large international businesses are disproportionately high relative to those of smaller firms and even the economies of some countries, this is called _____.
    (a) return on risk for business investment
    (b) the globalization gap
    (c) protectionism
    (d) most favored nation status

11. If a government seizes all foreign assets of global firms operating in the country, the loss to foreign firms is considered a _____ risk of international business.
    (a) franchise
    (b) political
    (c) currency
    (d) corruption

12. Who gains most when the dollar weakens versus a foreign currency such as the Brazilian real?
    (a) American consumers of Brazilian products
    (b) Brazilian firms selling products in Europe
    (c) American firms selling products in Brazil
    (d) Brazilian consumers of European products

13. Which of the following is identified by researchers as a universal inhibitor of leadership success across cultures?
    (a) Inspiring confidence
    (b) Acting autocratic
    (c) Being a good planner
    (d) Acting trustworthy

14. If an international business firm has separate vice presidents in charge of its Asian, African, and European divisions, it is most likely using a global _____ structure.
    (a) product
    (b) functional
    (c) area
    (d) matrix

15. Which is the best definition of a truly "global manager?"
    (a) A manager who is competent working across cultures
    (b) A manager who travels internationally on business at least once a year
    (c) A manager who lives and works in a foreign country
    (d) A manager who is employed by a transnational corporation

Short-Response Questions

16. What is the difference between a joint venture and a wholly owned subsidiary?

17. List three reasons why host countries sometimes complain about MNCs.

18. What does it mean in an international business sense if a U.S. senator says she favors "protectionism"?

19. What is the difference between currency risk and political risk in international business?

Integration and Application Question

20. Picture yourself sitting in a discussion group at the local bookstore and proudly signing copies of your newly published book, *Business Transitions in the New Global Economy*. A book buyer invites a comment from you by stating: "I am interested in your point regarding the emergence of transnational corporations. But, try as I might, a company like Ford or Procter & Gamble will always be 'as American as Apple pie' for me."

    Questions: How would you respond in a way that both (a) clarifies the difference between a multinational and a transnational corporation, and (b) explains reasons why Ford or P&G may wish not to operate as or be viewed as "American" companies?

Steps for
Further Learning

BUILD MARKETABLE SKILLS • **DO** A CASE ANALYSIS • **GET** AND STAY INFORMED

BUILD MARKETABLE SKILLS.

EARN BIG CAREER PAYOFFS!

Don't miss these opportunities in the SKILL-BUILDING PORTFOLIO

SELF-ASSESSMENT 16:
Global Intelligence
The world's a complex place . . . are you really up to date?

CLASS EXERCISE 16:
American Football
Cultures are different . . . let sports open your window to the view.

TEAM PROJECT 16:
Globalization Pros and Cons
Coins have two sides . . . getting a handle on globalization may be harder than you think.

Many learning resources are found at the end of the book and online within **WileyPLUS Learning Space.**

Practice Critical Thinking—Complete the CHAPTER 16 CASE

CASE SNAPSHOT: Harley-Davidson— Style and Strategy with a Global Reach

Harley-Davidson is an American success story. It was started in 1903 when two friends since boyhood, William Harley and Arthur Davidson, decided to design a motorized bicycle in a machine shop in Milwaukee, Wisconsin. The Harley-Davidson brand was born when the prototype bike was used to compete in a 1904 motorcycle race. After facing a near-death experience from global competition some years ago, the firm has roared back to reap profits and position itself for strong global growth. Now the Harley Hog is going electric.

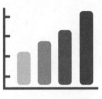

DO A CASE ANALYSIS.

STRENGTHEN YOUR CRITICAL THINKING!

MANAGER'S LIBRARY SELECTION
Read for Insights and Wisdom
The New Digital Age: Reshaping the Future of People, Nations and Business (Knopf, 2013) by Eric Schmidt and Jared Cohen

This book by the executive chairman of Google Eric Schmidt and foreign relations expert Jared Cohen challenges all of us, but especially business and government leaders, to get on top of the "new digital age" of intense global connectivity driven by an ever-developing Internet. Right now, say the authors: "There is a canyon dividing people who understand technology and people charged with addressing the world's toughest geopolitical issues, and no one has built a bridge." In other words, leaders aren't keeping up with what the rest of us are finding out about the utility of changing technology. Schmidt and Cohen believe it's in everyone's best interests to close this divide.

GET AND STAY INFORMED.

MAKE YOURSELF VALUABLE!

War and conflict—physical and in cyberspace—citizen journalists, high-tech gadgets and lifestyle apps, science and health, big data, digital manufacturing, and more are all at issue in a book that claims "technology is natural, people aren't." The authors point toward extreme planning challenges the new digital age poses for executives trying to do business around the world and for those who run or even try to conquer nations. "Authoritarian governments will find their newly connected populations more difficult to control, repress and influence," say Schmidt and Cohen, "while democratic states will be forced to include many more voices (individuals, organizations and companies), in their affairs."

REFLECT AND REACT How is technological change affecting global firms like IBM, Nike, Samsung, and others? What do executives in multinationals have to gain and fear as technology keeps evolving? When the authors say "technology is neutral, but people aren't," what are the implications for you, for your organizations, and for your government? And when it comes to the "new digital age," can politicians afford not to listen to what business executives have to say?

Nick D'Aloisio—17 years old . . . writes Summly app while in high school . . . puts $30 million in the bank. He says: "My parents at first were a bit concerned . . . . You shouldn't be keeping these hours."

Entrepreneurship and Small Business

17

Taking Risks Can Make Dreams Come True

Management Live

Hobby First, New Business Startup Second

Mark Scott/Getty Images

A lot of us dream about it, but not many do it. But, "Yes!" it is possible to turn a hobby into a business. And you don't have to rush it. There's nothing wrong with taking it slow when trying to turn a hobby and leisure-time interest into a profit-making venture. People who do so are "not simply interested in exploiting an opportunity in the market, they're doing something usually for the love of the activity," says Stephen Lipmann of Miami University. His colleague Phillip Kim of Babson College adds: "They're doing something they enjoy, so they're not likely to give up."

YOUR THOUGHTS?

Is there a business opportunity lurking in one of your pastimes and leisure interests? Would you like to be a business owner—part-time or full-time—and enjoy the benefits it might bring? Perhaps now is a good time to start thinking about new venture possibilities in your life.

WHAT'S INSIDE

ETHICS CHECK
Entrepreneurship and social good

FACTS TO CONSIDER
Ups and Downs for Minority Entrepreneurs

HOT TOPIC
Students are crowdfunding their human capital

QUICK CASE
Money's tight. How do we grow further?

YOUR CHAPTER 17 TAKEAWAYS

1. Understand the nature of entrepreneurship and entrepreneurs.
2. Discuss small business and how to start one.

Takeaway 17.1
What Is Entrepreneurship, and Who Are Entrepreneurs?

ANSWERS TO COME

- Entrepreneurs are risk takers who spot and pursue opportunities.
- Entrepreneurs often share similar characteristics and backgrounds.
- Entrepreneurs often share similar personality traits.
- Women and minority entrepreneurs are growing in numbers.
- Social entrepreneurs seek novel solutions to pressing social problems.

JUST OUT OF THE MILITARY AND LOOKING FOR WORK? WHY NOT CREATE YOUR own job? John Raftery did. After a 4-year tour with the Marines—including 2 years on deployment—he earned an accounting degree with help from the G.I. Bill. But after being disappointed with slow advancement at an accounting firm, he answered an e-mail about a free Enterpreneurship Bootcamp for Veterans with Disabilities at Syracuse University. Raftery went and ended up with a business plan to start his own firm.[1]

Struggling with work–life balance as a mother? An interest like child nutrition can become a business proposition. It was for Denise Devine. A former financial executive with Campbell Soup Co., she started Froose Brands to provide nutritional drinks and foods for kids. Called **mompreneurs**, women like Devine are finding opportunity in market niches for healthier products they spot as moms. She says: "As entrepreneurs we're working harder than we did, but we're doing it on our own schedules."

Female, thinking about starting a small business, but don't have the money? Get creative and reach out to organizations like Count-Me-In. Started by co-founders Nell Merlino and Iris Burnett, it provides microcredit loans from $500 to $10,000 to help women start and expand small businesses. Things such as a divorce, time off to raise a family, or age aren't held against applicants. "Women own 38% of all businesses in this country," says Merlino, "but still have far less access to capital than men because of today's process."[2]

The prior examples should be inspiring. Each shows a personal quality that is much valued in society and that offers interesting career possibilities—**entrepreneurship**. Think of it as risk taking to achieve business success.

ENTREPRENEURS ARE RISK TAKERS WHO SPOT AND PURSUE OPPORTUNITIES.

People like John Raftery, Denise Devine, Nell Merlino, and Iris Burnett from our examples acted on their ideas to create value for themselves and for society. They are **entrepreneurs**, sometimes called *classic entrepreneurs*—persons willing to take risks to pursue opportunities that others either fail to recognize or view as problems or threats.

Entrepreneurs aren't only found in the world of business. Nonprofit entrepreneur Scott Beale quit his job with the U.S. State Department to start Atlas Corps, something he calls a "Peace Corps in reverse." The organization brings nonprofit managers from developing countries to the United States to work with local nonprofits while improving their management skills. After a year they return home. "I am just like a business entrepreneur," Beale says, "but instead of making a big paycheck I try to make a big impact."[3]

H. Wayne Huizenga, former owner of AutoNation, Blockbuster Video, and the Miami Dolphins, and a member of the Entrepreneurs' Hall of Fame, describes being an entrepreneur this way: "An important part of being an entrepreneur is a gut instinct that allows you to believe in your heart that something will work even though everyone else says it will not."[4] Huizenga is also a good example of a **serial entrepreneur**. This is someone who starts and runs new ventures—business and nonprofit—over and over again, moving from one interest and opportunity to the next.

Mompreneurs pursue business opportunities they spot as mothers.

Entrepreneurship is risk-taking behavior in pursuit of business success.

An **entrepreneur** is willing to take risks and pursue opportunities in situations that others view as problems or threats.

A **serial entrepreneur** starts and runs businesses and nonprofits over and over again, moving from one interest and opportunity to the next.

A common pattern among successful entrepreneurs—classic and serial—is **first-mover advantage**. They move quickly to spot, exploit, and deliver a product or service to a new market or an unrecognized niche in an existing one. Consider the following brief examples of entrepreneurs who built successful businesses from good ideas and hard work.[5] As you read about these creative and confident individuals, think about how you might apply their experiences to your own life and career. After all, it might be nice to be your own boss someday.

> A **first-mover advantage** comes from being first to exploit a niche or enter a market.

Caterina Fake

From idea to buyout it only took 16 months. That's quite a benchmark for would-be entrepreneurs. Welcome to the world of Caterina Fake. She co-founded Flickr, which turned online photo sharing into a viral Internet phenomenon. Start-up capital came from families, friends, and angel investors. The payoff came when Yahoo! bought them out for $30 million. Fake then started Hunch.com, a Web site

Peter Foley/Bloomberg/GettyImages

designed to help people make decisions (e.g., Should I buy that Porsche?). She sold it to eBay for $80 million. Fake's advice is: "You pick a big, ambitious problem, and look for great people to solve it."

Earl Graves

With a vision and a $175,000 loan, Earl G. Graves Sr. started *Black Enterprise* magazine. That success grew into Earl G. Graves Ltd.—a multimedia company covering television, radio, and digital media including BlackEnterprise.com. Named by *Fortune* magazine as one of the 50 most powerful and influential African Americans in corporate America, he wrote the best-selling book *How to Succeed in Business Without Being White* and is a member of many business and nonprofit boards. Graves says: "I feel that a large part of my role as publisher of *Black Enterprise* is to be a catalyst for black economic development in this country."

Louis Johnny/SIPA/NewsCom

Anita Roddick

Anita Roddick was a 33-year-old housewife looking for a way to support herself and her two children. She spotted a niche for natural-based skin and health care products and started mixing and selling them from a small shop in Brighton, England. The Body Shop PLC has grown to some 1,500 outlets in 47 countries with 24 languages, selling a product every half-second to one of its 86 million customers. Known for her commitment to human rights, the environment, and economic development, the late Roddick believed in business social responsibility, saying: "If you think you're too small to have an impact, try going to bed with a mosquito."

NewsCom

Shawn Corey Carter

Known by most as Jay Z, Carter began rapping on the streets of Brooklyn where he lived with his single mom and three brothers. Hip-hop turned into his ticket to travel. "When I left the block," he told an interviewer, "everyone was saying I was crazy, I was doing well for myself on the streets, and cats around me were like, these rappers . . . just record, tour, and get separated from their families, while some white person takes all their money. I was determined to do it differently." He sure did. Carter used his music millions to found the media firm Roc Nation, co-found the apparel firm Rocawear, and become part owner of the New Jersey Nets.

Andrew Milligan/PA Photos/Landov

TABLE 17.1 Debunking Common Myths about Entrepreneurs

Entrepreneurs are born, not made—Not true! Talent gained and enhanced by experience is a foundation for entrepreneurial success.

Entrepreneurs are gamblers—Not true! Entrepreneurs are risk takers, but the risks are informed and calculated.

Money is the key to entrepreneurial success—Not true! Money is no guarantee of success. There's a lot more to it than that; many entrepreneurs start with very little.

You have to be young to be an entrepreneur—Not true! Age is no barrier to entrepreneurship; with age often come experience, contacts, and other useful resources.

You have to have a degree in business to be an entrepreneur—Not true! But it helps to study and understand business fundamentals.

ENTREPRENEURS OFTEN SHARE SIMILAR CHARACTERISTICS AND BACKGROUNDS.

Is there something in your experience that could be a pathway to business or nonprofit entrepreneurship? There are real people behind all acts of entrepreneurship and you could quite possibly become one of them. But as you think about your potential as an entrepreneur, be sure to set aside the common misconceptions highlighted in **Table 17.1**, Debunking Common Myths About Entrepreneurs.[6]

With the myths out of the way, let's look at some research findings. To begin, we know that most *entrepreneurs often display special personal characteristics*. They tend to be self-confident, determined, self-directing, resilient, adaptable, and driven by excellence.[7] A report in the *Harvard Business Review* suggests that they have strong interests in both "creative production" and "enterprise control." This means that entrepreneurs like to start things—the creative production part. They enjoy working with the unknown and finding unique solutions to problems. It also means that entrepreneurs like to run things—the enterprise control part. They enjoy making progress toward a goal. They like to be in charge, thrive on independence, and value the sense of mastery that comes with earned success.[8]

Evidence shows that many *entrepreneurs tend to have unique backgrounds*.[9] Childhood experiences and family environment seem to make a difference. Evidence links entrepreneurs with parents who were entrepreneurial and self-employed. Similarly, entrepreneurs are often raised in families that encourage responsibility, initiative, and independence. Another pattern is found in career or work history. Entrepreneurs who try one venture often go on to others, and prior work experience in the same business area or industry is helpful.

Entrepreneurs blossom during windows of career opportunity. It seems to make sense that the risk-taking required by entrepreneurship favors the younger set. And indeed, there is lots of entrepreneurship in the college and a bit older age groups. But research by the Kauffman foundation points out that the average age of entrepreneurs starting "high growth" companies is 40, and that the fastest-growing group is actually the 55- to 64-year-olds.[10] A study by the U.S. Small Business Administration has also found that active-duty military veterans are 45% more likely to start their own businesses than those without military experience. The so-called **veteran's advantage** that fosters entrepreneurship includes strong organizational skills and tolerance for risk.[11]

The **veteran's advantage** in entrepreneurship includes strong organizational skills and tolerance for risk.

ENTREPRENEURS OFTEN SHARE SIMILAR PERSONALITY TRAITS.

Although we can't say that there is sure-fit entrepreneurial personality, we can say that certain personality traits are common among entrepreneurs. The following list isn't definitive or limiting, but we can be confident that the more of these traits someone has the more likely it is that they will try entrepreneurship at some point in their careers.[12]

- *Internal locus of control:* Entrepreneurs believe that they are in control of their own destiny; they are self-directing and like autonomy.
- *High energy level:* Entrepreneurs are persistent, hardworking, and willing to exert extraordinary efforts to succeed.
- *High need for achievement:* Entrepreneurs are motivated to accomplish challenging goals; they thrive on performance feedback.
- *Tolerance for ambiguity:* Entrepreneurs are risk takers; they tolerate situations with high degrees of uncertainty.
- *Self-confidence:* Entrepreneurs feel competent, believe in themselves, and are willing to make decisions.
- *Passion and action orientation:* Entrepreneurs try to act ahead of problems; they want to get things done and not waste valuable time.
- *Self-reliance and desire for independence:* Entrepreneurs want independence; they are self-reliant; they want to be their own bosses, not work for others.
- *Flexibility:* Entrepreneurs are willing to admit problems and errors and to change a course of action when plans aren't working.

Take a moment to look at the figure—"Who Are the Entrepreneurs?" How many of the entrepreneurial characteristics can you put a check next to and say with confidence—"Yes, that's me for sure"?[13] Are you surprised at how well you score? Perhaps it's time to further explore the entrepreneur that may reside within you.

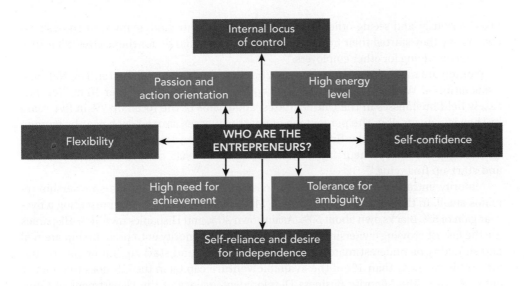

WOMEN AND MINORITY ENTREPRENEURS ARE GROWING IN NUMBERS.

Although background and personality help set the stage, it sometimes takes an outside stimulus or a special set of circumstances to kick-start one's entrepreneurial tendencies. While some entrepreneurs are driven by the desire for new opportunities, others are driven by **necessity-based entrepreneurship**. They start new ventures because they have lost jobs, see no other employment options, or find career doors closed—perhaps due to discrimination. Anita Roddick, featured earlier, once said that she started the first Body Shop store because she needed "to create a livelihood for myself and my two daughters, while my husband, Gordon, was trekking across the Americas."[14]

The fact is that many women and minorities find entrepreneurship a way to strike out on their own and gain both economic and career independence. One survey found that 33% of women leaving private-sector employment to pursue entrepreneurship believed they were not being taken seriously by their prior employer and that 29% experienced what they called "glass ceiling" issues. Another report says that entrepreneurship by women of color is motivated by not being recognized or valued by their prior employers, not being

Necessity-based entrepreneurship occurs when people start new ventures because they have few or no other employment options.

FACTS TO CONSIDER

Ups and Downs for Minority Entrepreneurs

Jacob Wackerhausen/iStockphoto

Minority entrepreneurship is a fast-growing sector of our economy, but challenges to future growth exist.

- There are close to 8 million minority-owned firms in the United States, and they contribute $1+ trillion annually to the economy.

- Minority-owned firms increased 39% in five years by the last census, while nonminority-owned firms decreased by 5%.

- Average annual receipts for minority-owned firms trail those for nonminority-owned, $196,000 to $650,000.

- Loan denials for minority-owners run 31.5% versus 12.3% for non-minority owners.

- Immigrants are twice as likely as native-born Americans to start new businesses.

- Minority entrepreneurs are less successful than majority entrepreneurs when making pitches to angel investors—15% versus 22% success rate.

WHAT'S YOUR TAKE?

Is minority entrepreneurship a way to fight economic disparities in society? What obstacles do minorities in your community face on their pathways toward entrepreneurship? What can be done to improve the start-up and success rates for minority-owned businesses?

---

taken seriously, and seeing others promoted ahead of them. And, many women business owners say they started their firms after realizing they could do for themselves what they were already doing for other employers.[15]

Women are making it as entrepreneurs, but they could do much better. The National Association of Women Business Owners reports that women own over 10 million privately held businesses in the United States, about 36% of the total, up 7% in five years by the last census. But, the percentage of new businesses started each year by women trails that of men, and their firms are generally smaller and more prone to failure. This "gender gap" in entrepreneurship is blamed, in part at least, on lack of access to credit and start-up financing.[16]

Minority entrepreneurs are also on the rise, but their share of business ownership remains small. In the last census they owned 14.6% of small businesses, representing a five-year gain of 5%. Blacks own about 50%, Asians own 30%, and Hispanics own 10%. Hispanics are the fastest growing ownership group.[17] Obstacles to minority entrepreneurship are real and shouldn't be underestimated. Poor access to credit and start-up financing are major problems. Less than 1% of the available venture capital in the U.S. goes to minority entrepreneurs. The Minority Business Development Agency of the Department of Commerce tracks these and related problems. Its goal is to help minority-owned firms grow in "size, scale, and capacity."[18]

SOCIAL ENTREPRENEURS SEEK NOVEL SOLUTIONS TO PRESSING SOCIAL PROBLEMS.

A **social entrepreneur** takes risks to find new ways to solve pressing social problems.

Social entrepreneurs are a growing force in entrepreneurship today. They are persons whose entrepreneurial ventures pursue novel ways to help solve pressing social problems.[19] Think of these problems as the likes of poverty, illiteracy, poor health, and even social oppression. Social entrepreneurs share many characteristics with other entrepreneurs, including backgrounds and personalities. But there is one big difference. Instead of the profit motive, they are driven by a social mission.[20] They want to start and run social enterprises, whose missions are to help make lives better for people who are disadvantaged.[21]

Fast Company magazine says social entrepreneurs run enterprises with "innovative thinking that can transform lives and change the world." It celebrates them with its prestigious Honor Roll of Social Enterprises of the Year. Here are two examples.[22]

- Chip Ransler and Manoj Sinha tackled the lack of electricity for many of India's poor villagers. As University of Virginia business students, they realized that 350 million of the people without reliable power lived in the country's rice-growing regions. And in those regions, tons of rice husks were being discarded with every harvest. Ransler and Sinha found a way to create biogas from the husks and started Husk Power Systems to use the gas to fuel small power plants. But with more than 125,000 villages suffering a lack of power, Ransler says, "There's a lot of work to be done."

- Nissan Bahar and Franky Imbesi want to bring computers to children living in poverty. They created Keepod, whose software puts an Android operating system on a USB drive. It can be used in old and refurbished PCs. This "operating system on a stick" makes each child an "owner" of a PC even when sharing machines with others. Bahar and Imbesi are testing the model in a Nairobi, Kenya, slum and plan to move it around the world. Local workers buy flash drives for about $7, install the Keepod operating system, resell the drives for $9, and use the profit to pay themselves and fuel further expansion.

There's probably quite a bit of social entrepreneurship taking place in your community. Sadly, it may get little notice. Most attention often goes to business entrepreneurs making lots of money—or trying to do so. Yet there are many examples you can find of local people who have made the commitment to social entrepreneurship. Deborah Sardone, for example, owns a housekeeping service in Texas. After noticing that her clients with cancer really struggled with everyday household chores, she started Cleaning for a Reason. It's a nonprofit that networks with cleaning firms around the country that are willing to offer free home cleaning to cancer patients.[23]

How about it? Can you think of ideas that could turn social entrepreneurship by yourself and others into a positive impact on your community?

CAN SMALL BUSINESS SUCCESS WITH CARING CAPITALISM SURVIVE BIG BUSINESS BUYOUTS?

ETHICS CHECK

Entrepreneurship and Social Good

MTC/NewsCom

Would you buy shoes just because their maker is pledged to philanthropy? Blake Mycoskie wants you to. Participation with his sister in the reality TV show *The Amazing Race* whetted his appetite for travel. While visiting Argentina he came face-to-face with lots of young children without shoes and had a revelation: He would return home and start a sustainable business that would help address the problem.

Mycoskie launched TOMS to sell shoes made in a classic Argentinean style, but with a twist—for each pair sold, TOMS donates a pair to needy children. Blake calls this One for One, a "movement" that involves "people making everyday choices that improve the lives of children." After giving away its one-millionth pair of shoes, Mycoskie renamed the company One for One.

Mycoskie's business model can be described as caring capitalism or profits with principles. Two other names associated with this approach are Ben & Jerry's Ice Cream and Tom's of Maine. But each of these firms was sold to a global enterprise—Unilever for Ben & Jerry's and Colgate-Palmolive for Tom's of Maine. The expectation was that the corporate buyers wouldn't compromise on the founders' core values and social goals. Who knows what the future holds if One for One grows to the point where corporate buyers loom?

YOUR DECISION?

What about it? Is Blake's business model one that others should adopt? If an entrepreneurial firm is founded on a caring capitalism model, is it ethical for a future corporate buyer to reduce or limit the emphasis on social benefits?

STUDYGUIDE

Takeaway 17.1
What Is Entrepreneurship, and Who Are Entrepreneurs?

Terms to Define

Classic entrepreneur	First-mover advantage	Necessity-based entrepreneurship	Social entrepreneur
Entrepreneur	Mompreneur	Serial entrepreneur	Veteran's advantage
Entrepreneurship			

Rapid Review

- Entrepreneurship is original thinking that creates value for people, organizations, and society.
- Entrepreneurs take risks to pursue opportunities others may fail to recognize.
- Entrepreneurs tend to be creative people who are self-confident, determined, resilient, adaptable, and driven to excel; they like to be masters of their own destinies.
- Women and minorities are well represented among entrepreneurs, with some of their motivation driven by necessity or the lack of alternative career options.
- Social entrepreneurs apply their energies to create innovations that help to solve important problems in society.

Questions for Discussion

1. Does an entrepreneur always need to have first-mover advantage to succeed?
2. Are there any items on the list of entrepreneurial characteristics that are "must-haves" for someone to succeed in any career, not just entrepreneurship?
3. Could growth of necessity-driven entrepreneurship be an indicator of some deeper problems in our society?

Be Sure You Can

- **explain** the concept of entrepreneurship
- **explain** the concept of first-mover advantage
- **explain** why people such as Caterina Fake and Earl Graves might have become entrepreneurs
- **list** personal characteristics often associated with entrepreneurs
- **explain** trends in entrepreneurship by women and minorities
- **explain** what makes social entrepreneurs unique

Career Situation: What Would You Do?

After reading the examples in this chapter, you're struck by the potential to try entrepreneurship. You're thinking now that it would be very nice to be your own boss, do your own thing, and make a decent living in the process. But how do you get started? One possibility is to start with ideas passed around among your friends and family. Or perhaps there's something that has already been on your mind as a great possible business idea. And then there's the notion of tackling a social problem like poverty or illiteracy. So, tell us about it. What ideas do you have? What would you like to pursue as an entrepreneur and why?

Takeaway 17.2
What Should We Know About Small Businesses and How to Start One?

ANSWERS TO COME

- Small businesses are mainstays of the economy.
- Small businesses must master three life-cycle stages.
- Family-owned businesses face unique challenges.
- Many small businesses fail within 5 years.
- Assistance is available to help small businesses get started.
- A small business should start with a sound business plan.
- There are different forms of small business ownership.
- There are different ways of financing a small business.

THE U.S. SMALL BUSINESS ADMINISTRATION (SBA) DEFINES A SMALL BUSINESS AS one that is independently owned and operated and that does not dominate its industry.[24] It also has 500 or fewer employees, with the number varying a bit by industry. Almost 99% of U.S. businesses meet this definition.

How does owning a **small business** stack up in terms of satisfaction? Pretty well, as it turns out. Data from the Gallup-Healthways Well-Being Index show that business owners rank highest among 10 other occupations in terms of contentment. This includes being happy about things like physical and mental health, job satisfaction, and quality of life overall.[25] Compared to managers who didn't start the businesses they work in, business owners report higher satisfaction with their autonomy and task identity. But also, those starting their businesses out of necessity report lower overall satisfaction than those starting in the pursuit of opportunity.[26]

> A **small business** has fewer than 500 employees, is independently owned and operated, and does not dominate its industry.

SMALL BUSINESSES ARE MAINSTAYS OF THE ECONOMY.

Most nations rely on their small business sector. Why? Among other things, small businesses offer major economic advantages. In the United States, for example, 27.9 million small businesses employ some 49.2% of private-sector workers and provide as many as 2 of every 3 new jobs in the economy.[27] The vast majority employ fewer than 20 persons, and over half are home based. The most common small business areas are restaurants, skilled professions such as craftspeople and doctors, general services such as hairdressers and repair shops, and independent retailers.[28]

Once someone makes a decision to go the small business route, the most common ways to get involved are to start one, buy an existing one, or buy and run a **franchise**—where a business owner sells to another the right to operate the same business in another location. A franchise such as Subway or Domino's Pizza runs under the original owner's business name and guidance. In return, the franchise parent receives a share of income or a flat fee from the franchisee.

> A **franchise** is when one business owner sells to another the right to operate the same business in another location.

Any business—large or small, franchise or start-up—needs a solid underlying **business model**. Think of this as how the business intends to make a profit by generating revenues that are greater than costs. Serial entrepreneur Steven Blank calls business **start-ups** temporary organizations that are trying "to discover a profitable, scalable business model."[29] In other words, a start-up is just that—a "start." It's a new venture that the entrepreneur is hoping will take shape and prove successful as things move forward.

> A **business model** is how the business intends to make a profit by generating revenues that are greater than costs.

> A **start-up** is a new and temporary venture that is trying to discover a profitable business model for future success.

SMALL BUSINESSES MUST MASTER THREE LIFE-CYCLE STAGES.

The typical small business moves through recognizable life-cycle stages.[30] The new firm begins with the *birth stage*, where the entrepreneur struggles to get the new venture

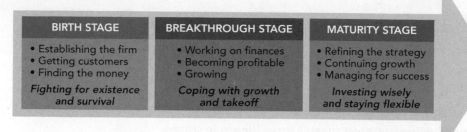

FIGURE 17.1 What Are the Stages in the Life Cycle of an Entrepreneurial Firm?
It is typical for small businesses to move through three life-cycle stages. During the *birth* stage, the entrepreneur focuses on getting things started—bringing a product to market, finding initial customers, and earning enough money to survive. *Breakthrough* is a time of rapid growth when the business model really starts working well. Growth often slows in the *maturity* stage, where financial success is realized but also where the entrepreneur often needs to make adjustments to stay successful in a dynamic marketplace.

established and survive long enough to really test the marketplace. The firm then passes into the *breakthrough stage*, where the business model begins to work well, growth takes place, and the complexity of the business expands significantly. Next is the *maturity stage*, where the entrepreneur experiences market success and financial stability but also has to face competitive challenges in a dynamic environment.

As shown in **Figure 17.1**, small business owners often face somewhat different management dilemmas as their firms move through these life-cycle stages. They start out just fighting for survival. But with growth, they typically face management problems that require a transition from entrepreneurial leadership to strategic leadership. The entrepreneur brings the venture into being and sees it through the early stages of life. The strategist manages and leads the venture into maturity as an ever-evolving enterprise. If the founder can't meet the firm's strategic leadership needs in later life-cycle stages, continued business survival and success may well depend on the business being sold or management control being passed to others with different skill sets.

FAMILY-OWNED BUSINESSES FACE UNIQUE CHALLENGES.

Among the reasons given for getting started in small businesses, you'll find owners saying they were motivated to be their own bosses, be in control of their own futures, fulfill dreams, and become part of a family-owned business.[31] Indeed, **family businesses**, those owned and financially controlled by family members, represent the largest percentage of businesses operating worldwide. The Family Firm Institute reports that family businesses account for 70% to 90% of global domestic product. They create 78% of new jobs in the United States and provide 60% of the nation's employment.[32]

Family businesses must master the same challenges as other small or large businesses, such as devising strategy, achieving competitive advantage, and ensuring operational excellence. When everything goes right, the family firm can be an ideal situation. Everyone works together, sharing values and a common goal—doing well to support the family. But things don't always turn out this way, or stay this way if they do. Changes and complications often test the family bonds, especially as a business changes hands over successive generations.

"Okay, Dad, so he's your brother. But does that mean we have to put up with inferior work and an erratic schedule that we would never tolerate from anyone else in the business?"[33] Welcome to the **family business feud**, a problem that can lead to small business failure. The feud can be about jobs and who does what, business strategy, operating approaches, finances, or other matters. It can be between spouses, among siblings, between parents and children. It really doesn't matter. Unless family business feuds are resolved satisfactorily, the firm may not survive.

Family businesses are owned and financially controlled by family members.

A **family business feud** can lead to small business failure.

A survey of small and midsized family businesses indicated that 66% planned on keeping the business within the family.[34] The management question is: Upon leaving, how will the current head of the company distribute assets and determine who will run the business? This introduces the **succession problem**, how to handle the transfer of leadership from one generation to the next. The data on succession are eye-opening. About 30% of family firms survive to the second generation; 12% survive to the third generation; only 3% are expected to survive beyond that.[35]

> The **succession problem** is the issue of who will run the business when the current head leaves.

If you were the owner of a successful family business, what would you do? Wouldn't you want to have a **succession plan** that clearly spells out how leadership transition and related matters, including financial ones, are to be handled when the time for change-over occurs?

> A **succession plan** describes how the leadership transition and related financial matters will be handled.

MANY SMALL BUSINESSES FAIL WITHIN 5 YEARS.

Does the prospect of starting your own small business sound good? It should, but a word of caution is called for as well. What the last figure on life-cycle stages didn't show is a very common event—small business failure.

Small businesses have a high drop outrate. The SBA reports that as many as 60% to 80% of new businesses fail in their first 5 years of operation.[36] Part of this might be explained as a "counting" issue. The government counts as a "failure" any business that closes, whether it is due to the death or retirement of an owner, the sale to someone else, or the inability to earn a profit.[37] Nevertheless, the fact is that a lot of small business start-ups just don't make it. And, their demise is often due to poor judgment and basic mistakes that could be avoided or overcome with proper planning and good management. Most small business failures are the result of problems like the following.[38]

- *Insufficient financing*—not having enough money available to maintain operations while still building the business and gaining access to customers and markets.
- *Lack of experience*—not having sufficient know-how to run a business in the chosen market or geographical area.
- *Lack of expertise*—not having expertise in the essentials of business operations, including finance, purchasing, selling, and production.
- *Lack of strategy and strategic leadership*—not taking the time to craft a vision and mission, nor to formulate and properly implement a strategy.

SELLING PRESCRIPTION GLASSES FOR $95

Grad School Start-up Takes on Global Competitors

Kathy Willens/AP/Wide World Photos

Did you ever wonder why prescription eyeglasses are so expensive? That's a question four MBA students at Wharton asked. The answer was an oligopoly industry controlled by just a few firms. Their response was to start a company to sell eyeglasses at a reasonable price. Called Warby Parker, their business is described as running with "a rebellious spirit and a lofty objective: to create boutique-quality, classically crafted eyewear at a revolutionary price point."

Founders David Gilboa, Neil Blumenthal, Andrew Hunt, and Jeffrey Raider wrote a Web-driven business plan that many questioned at first. Could eyeglasses be sold over the Internet? Their answer was: "Of course!"

If you're in doubt, check out warbyparker.com. You can buy stylish glasses for as low as $95—frames with prescription lenses and free shipping. They are e-commerce and customer friendly—letting you have free home try-ons of up to five "loaner" pairs. And if you end up buying, you're helping someone who can't afford to buy new glasses for themselves. Warby Parker donates one pair for every pair it sells.

The company's Web site proudly announces: "Let's do good. We're building a company to do good in the world. . . .We think it's good business to do good." They call their business model "eyewear with a purpose." That purpose is anchored in the fact that over a billion people in the world don't have the glasses they need for school, work, and everyday living. It's a problem that Warby Parker's social business model aims to solve.

FIND INSPIRATION

Instead of buying glasses at a boutique for $695, you can buy a stylish pair online from Warby Parker for $95. And your purchase sends a free pair to someone in need. Why aren't there more businesses like this? Why aren't there more entrepreneurs who try to match social problems and business opportunities? How about you—any good ideas here?

- *Poor financial control*—not keeping track of the numbers, and failure to control business finances and use existing monies to best advantage.
- *Growing too fast*—not taking the time to consolidate a position, fine-tune the organization, and systematically meet the challenges of growth.
- *Lack of commitment*—not devoting enough time to the requirements of running a competitive business.
- *Ethical failure*—falling prey to the temptations of fraud, deception, and embezzlement.

Look again at the list and figure. Would you agree that many small business failures may be preventable? If you someday decide to start your own venture—business or nonprofit, you can benefit a lot by learning from, and not repeating, the mistakes of others.

ASSISTANCE IS AVAILABLE TO HELP SMALL BUSINESSES GET STARTED.

Individuals who start small businesses face a variety of challenges. And even though the prospect of being part of a new venture is exciting, the realities of working through complex problems during setup and the early life of the business can be especially daunting. Fortunately, there is often assistance available to help entrepreneurs and owners of small businesses get started.

A **business incubator** is a facility that offers services to help new businesses get established.

One way that start-up difficulties can be managed is through participation in a **business incubator**. These are special facilities that offer space, shared administrative services, and management advice at reduced costs with the goal of helping new businesses get successfully established. Some incubators are focused on specific business areas such as technology, light manufacturing, or professional services; some are located in rural areas, whereas others are urban based; some focus only on socially responsible businesses.

Regardless of their focus or location, business incubators share the common goal of increasing the survival rates for new business start-ups. They want to help build new businesses that will create new jobs and expand economic opportunities in their local communities. In the incubators, small businesses are nurtured and assisted so that they can grow quickly and become healthy enough to survive on their own. An example is the Y Combinator in Mountain View, California. It focuses on nurturing Web start-ups. Members get offices, regular meetings with business experts, access to potential investors, and $15,000 start-up investments. Prominent Y Combinator graduates include Airbnb and Dropbox.[39]

Small Business Development Centers offer guidance to entrepreneurs and small business owners on how to set up and manage business operations.

Another source of assistance for small business development is the U.S. Small Business Administration. The SBA works with state and local agencies as well as the private sector to support a network of more than 1,100 **Small Business Development Centers** nationwide.[40] These SBDCs offer guidance to entrepreneurs and small business owners, actual and prospective, on how to set up and manage business operations. They are often associated with colleges and universities whose students get a chance to work as consultants with small businesses at the same time that they pursue their academic programs. If you are inclined toward entrepreneurship and small business, why not check out your local SBDC—as a client or student consultant?

A SMALL BUSINESS SHOULD START WITH A SOUND BUSINESS PLAN.

A **business plan** describes the direction for a new business and the financing needed to operate it.

When people start new businesses or even start new units within existing ones, they can greatly benefit from another type of plan—a sound **business plan**. This plan describes the goals of the business and the way it intends to operate, ideally in ways that can help obtain any needed start-up financing.[41] Although there is no single template for a

QUICK CASE

Money's Tight. How Do We Grow Further?

Catherine Yeulet/iStockphoto/Getty Images

We're just about a year into full-time work on a high-school tutoring service called BeUrBest. It offers tutoring to underprivileged students at "cost." Tutors work for free, donating their time, while the fees collected pay for operating expenses. It's been popular. We've already branched out into two neighboring communities and are about to host an out-of-state visitor who heard about us from a relative. But, here's the problem. Our bare-bones budget allows no office frills and pays only basic staff wages. We want to grow but need money for expansion and also to attract and support an ever-increasing pool of volunteer tutors. Two ideas are on the table. 1—Offer tutoring also to students who can pay "market" fees, and use the extra income for growth. 2—Connect with community charities and civic organizations to attract financial sponsorships and donations.

WHAT DO YOU DO?

BeUrBest is your baby—you had the idea and you started it. But now the original model is being tested. Which option for obtaining growth financing do you prefer and why? Are there any other options available that could keep you growing while also staying true to your social business model? Or, should you take growth off the table and be content serving one or just a few local communities?

---

successful business plan, most would agree on the general framework presented in Tips to Remember.[42]

Banks and other financiers want to see a business plan before they loan money or invest in a new venture. Senior managers want to see a business plan before they allocate scarce organizational resources to support a new entrepreneurial project. You should also want a small business plan. The detailed and disciplined thinking helps sort out your ideas, map strategies, and pin down your business model. Says Ed Federkeil, who founded a small business called California Custom Sport Trucks: "It gives you direction instead of haphazardly sticking your key in the door every day and saying—'What are we going to do?'"[43]

THERE ARE DIFFERENT FORMS OF SMALL BUSINESS OWNERSHIP.

One of the important choices when starting a new venture is the legal form of ownership. There are a number of alternatives, and each has its own advantages and disadvantages.

A **sole proprietorship** is simply an individual or a married couple that pursues business for a profit. The business often operates under a personal name, such as "Tiana Lopez Designs." Because a sole proprietorship is simple to start, run, and terminate, it is the most common form of U.S. small business ownership. If you choose this form, however, you have to remember—any owner of a sole proprietorship is personally liable for all business debts and claims.

A **partnership** is formed when two or more people contribute resources to start and operate a business together. Most are set up with legal and written agreements that document what each

TIPS TO REMEMBER
What to Include in a Business Plan

- *Executive summary*—business purpose, highlights of plan
- *Industry analysis*—nature of industry, economic trends, legal or regulatory issues, risks
- *Company description*—mission, owners, legal form
- *Products and services*—major goods or services, uniqueness vis-à-vis competition
- *Market description*—size, competitor strengths and weaknesses, 5-year sales goals
- *Marketing strategy*—product characteristics, distribution, promotion, pricing
- *Operations description*—manufacturing or service methods, suppliers, controls
- *Staffing*—management and worker skills needed and available, compensation, human resource systems
- *Financial projection*—cash flow projections 1 to 5 years, breakeven points
- *Capital needs*—amount needed, amount available, amount being requested
- *Milestones*—timetable for completing key stages of new venture

EXPLORE YOURSELF

Risk Taking

Entrepreneurship plays an important role in local economies and the nation as a whole. It can also be a pathway to personal success. There's probably a bit of entrepreneur in each of us. Just how much probably depends on our tendency toward **risk taking**. This is a willingness to take action to achieve a goal even in the face of uncertainty. How would others describe you in this regard? How would you describe yourself?

> Get to know yourself better by taking the self-assessment on **Entrepreneurship Orientation** and completing other activities in the *Exploring Management* **Skill-Building Portfolio**.

In a **general partnership**, owners share management and responsibility for debts and losses.	party contributes as well as how profits and losses are to be shared. You would be ill advised to enter into a serious partnership without such an agreement.

party contributes as well as how profits and losses are to be shared. You would be ill advised to enter into a serious partnership without such an agreement.

In a **general partnership**, owners share management and responsibility for debts and losses.

Once the choice is made to go the partnership route, there are two alternatives. In a **general partnership**, the simplest and most common form, owners share day-to-day management and responsibilities for debts and losses. This differs from a **limited partnership** consisting of a general partner and one or more "limited" partners. The general partner runs the business; the limited partners do not participate in day-to-day management. All partners share in profits, but their losses are limited to the amounts of their investments. This limit to one's liabilities is a major advantage. You'll notice that many professionals, such as accountants and attorneys, work in **limited liability partnerships**—designated as LLP—because they limit the liability of one partner in case of negligence by any others.

In a **limited partnership** owners share profits, but responsibility for losses is limited to original investments.

Limited liability partnerships, LLPs, limit the liability of one partner in case of negligence by any others.

A **corporation**, commonly identified by the "Inc." designation in a name, is a legal entity that exists separately from its owners. Corporations are legally chartered and registered by states. They can be for-profit, such as Microsoft Inc., or not-for-profit, such as Count-Me-In, Inc.—a firm featured early in the chapter as helping women entrepreneurs get started with small loans.

A **corporation** is a legal entity that exists separately from its owners.

There are two major advantages to incorporation. First, the corporate form grants the organization certain legal rights—for example, to engage in contracts. Second, the corporation is responsible for its liabilities. This firm has a life of its own and separates the owners from personal liability. The major disadvantages are the legal costs of setting up the corporation and the complex documentation required to operate as one.

The **benefit corporation**, or B-Corp, is a corporate form for businesses whose stated goals are to combine making a profit with benefiting society and the environment.

The **benefit corporation** is a new corporate form for businesses whose stated goals are to benefit society while making a profit.[45] Businesses that choose this ownership type formally adopt the goals of social entrepreneurship and social enterprises to help solve social and environmental problems. Often called "B-Corps" for short, these goals must be stated in the firm's by laws or rules of corporation. Each B-Corp is then required to file an

Etsy Turns "Handmade" into Entrepreneurship

Brian Ramsay/Modesto Bee/ZumaPress

Etsy's mission is described as empowering people and creating "a world in which very-very small businesses have much-much more sway in shaping the economy." The original idea came from painter and photographer Rob Kalin, who wanted an online market for his works. Along with Chris Maguire and Haim Schoppik, he founded Etsy as an online market place where artisans could showcase their work and link with customers. The business model was as neat as a hand-stitched quilt: take a 3.5% transaction fee and 20¢ listing charge, and sell ads to artists. And it worked. Etsy now has 14 million members.

annual "benefit report" as well as an annual financial report so that both social and financial performance can be properly assessed against stated goals. The adoption of this form by a number of larger and well-recognized businesses, Ben & Jerry's and Patagonia for example, has given it rising public visibility. [46]

The **limited liability corporation (LLC)** has gained popularity as an ownership form. It combines the advantages of sole proprietorship, partnership, and corporation. It functions as a corporation for liability purposes and protects the assets of owners against claims made against the company. For tax purposes, it functions as a partnership in the case of multiple owners and as a sole proprietorship in the case of a single owner.

> A **limited liability corporation (LLC)** combines the advantages of the sole proprietorship, partnership, and corporation.

THERE ARE DIFFERENT WAYS OF FINANCING A SMALL BUSINESS.

Starting a new venture takes money. Unless you possess personal wealth that you are willing to risk, that money has to be raised.

Debt and Equity Financing

Debt financing involves borrowing money from another person, a bank, or a financial institution. This is a loan that must be paid back over time with interest. A loan also requires collateral that pledges business assets or personal assets, such as a home, as security in case of default. You borrow money with a promise to repay both the loan amount and interest. If you can't pay, the security is lost up to the amount of the outstanding loan.

> **Debt financing** involves borrowing money from another person, a bank, or a financial institution.

Equity financing gives ownership shares to outsiders in return for their financial investments. In contrast to debt financing, this money does not need to be paid back. Instead, the investor assumes the risk of potential gains and losses based on the performance of the business. But in return for taking that risk, the equity investor gains something—part of your original ownership. The amount of ownership and control given up is represented in the number and proportion of ownership shares transferred to the equity investors.

> **Equity financing** gives ownership shares to outsiders in return for their financial investments.

Venture Capitalists and Angel Investors

When businesses need equity financing in fairly large amounts, from the tens of thousands to the millions of dollars, they often turn to **venture capitalists**. These are individuals and companies that pool capital to invest in new ventures. They hope that their equity stakes rise in value and can be sold for a profit when the business becomes successful. Venture capitalists can be aggressive in wanting the business to grow in value as soon as possible. This value is often tapped by an **initial public offering (IPO)**. This is when shares in the business are sold to the public at large, most likely by beginning to trade on a major stock exchange.

> **Venture capitalists** make large investments in new ventures in return for an equity stake in the business.

> An **initial public offering (IPO)** is an initial selling of shares of stock to the public at large.

When venture capital isn't available or isn't yet interested, entrepreneurs may try to find an **angel investor**. This is a wealthy individual who invests in return for equity in a new venture. Angel investors are especially helpful in the late birth and early breakthrough stages of a new venture. Once they jump in, it can raise the attractiveness of the investment and make it easier to raise more funds from venture capitalists. When Liz Cobb wanted to start

> An **angel investor** is a wealthy individual willing to invest in return for equity in a new venture.

Would-Be Entrepreneurs Dive for Dollars in the Shark Tank

Michael Ansell/Getty Images

Have you seen the reality TV show, *Shark Tank*? It pits entrepreneurs against potential investors called "sharks." The entrepreneurs present their ideas, and the sharks, people with money to invest, debate the worth whileness of investing in their businesses. Brian Duggan went on the show to pitch his Element Bars, a custom energy bar he developed as an MBA student. He previously tried to get a bank loan, but failed. His presentation impressed the sharks. By show's end they had given him $150,000 to help turn his energy bars into a popular product. But it came at a price. He gave them in return 30% ownership in his business.

her sales compensation firm, Incentive Systems, for example, she contacted 15 to 20 venture capital firms. Only 10 interviewed her, and all of those turned her down. However, after she located $250,000 from two angel investors, the venture capital firms renewed their interest, allowing her to obtain her first $2 million in financing. Her firm grew to employ more than 70 workers.[46]

Crowdfunding

> In **crowdfunding**, new ventures go online to get start-up financing for their businesses from crowds of investors.

The rise of social media has given birth to **crowdfunding**, where those starting new ventures go online to obtain start-up funds from a "crowd" of willing providers. Many options already exist, and more are appearing all the time. Kickstarter, for example, focuses on fund-raising for innovative and imaginative projects from software to literature to films and more. Founder Yancy Strickler describes it as "a place of opportunity for anyone to make things happen."[47] Investors don't get ownership rights, but they do get the satisfaction of sponsorship and in some cases early access to the results. Ownership rights are part of the deal at AngelList, a crowdfunding site that bills itself as the place "Where the world meets startups." AngelList matches entrepreneurs with pools of equity investors—called syndicates—willing to put up as little as $1,000 to back a new venture. All investors are vetted for financial background and legitimacy.[48]

The JOBS Act of 2012—Jumpstart Our Business Startups—made it easier for small U.S. companies to sell equity on the Internet.[49] But the U.S. Securities and Exchange Commission, which oversees the practice, recognizes potential negatives as well as positives. Advocates claim it spurs entrepreneurship by giving small start-ups a better shot at raising investment capital and helps small investors join the venture capital game. Skeptics worry that small investors in a crowd may be easy prey for fraudsters because they won't do enough analysis or have the financial expertise to ensure they are making good investments.[50] As things now stand, crowdfunding is fast expanding both in accessibility and areas of application.

GET MONEY NOW FROM INVESTORS WHO WILL GET A PERCENTAGE OF YOUR FUTURE EARNINGS.

HOT TOPIC

Students Are Crowdfunding Their Human Capital

Kevork DjamsezianJ/Reuters/Corbis

Situation An undergraduate student at an art and design school needs money to pay back student loans and fund ideas for a start-up company. He goes online at Upstart.com and finds investors willing to give him up-front money in return for a portion of what he earns in the future. He signs on and takes in $38,500.

The idea here is to sell equity stakes in your human capital. In other words, get money now from investors hoping for good paybacks from rights to a percentage of your future pre-tax earnings. Terms used to describe this form of crowdfunding are "human-capital contracts" or "social financial agreements."

Those in favor of students' crowdfunding their human capital are likely to say that it helps them get the education or resources they need to succeed. It's also a way of avoiding interest on debt; if the student fails to earn enough or the project fails, the investor loses. And, the investors may turn out to be good mentors and motivators who drive the student to high levels of achievement.

Those against students' crowdfunding their human capital are likely to say that it's a form of servitude. It's not right for one person to indenture themselves to another in this way. Young students, furthermore, may not be mature or insightful enough to make good decisions that commit them to long-term financial contracts. And if the student's "back is to the wall," she or he might make a really bad decision.

HOW ABOUT IT?

Is crowdfunding human capital something that sounds attractive to you? What are the possible risks and returns as you see them? If you were a parent, would you let your child do this? If you were an investor, would you consider this a legitimate way to earn a return on your money?

STUDYGUIDE

Takeaway 17.2
What Should We Know About Small Businesses and How to Start One?

Terms to Define

Angel investor	Debt financing	Limited liability corporation (LLC)	Small Business Development Centers
Benefit corporation	Equity financing	Limited liability partnership (LLP)	Sole proprietorship
Business incubator	Family businesses	Limited partnership	Start-up
Business model	Family business feud	Partnership	Succession plan
Business plan	Franchise	Small business	Succession problem
Corporation	General partnership		Venture capitalists
Crowdfunding	Initial public offering (IPO)		

Rapid Review

- Small businesses constitute the vast majority of businesses in the United States and create 7 of every 10 new jobs in the economy.
- Small businesses have a high failure rate; as many as 60% to 80% of new businesses fail in their first 5 years of operation.
- Small businesses owned by family members can suffer from the succession problem of transferring leadership from one generation to the next.
- A business plan describes the intended nature of a proposed new business, how it will operate, and how it will obtain financing.
- Proprietorships, partnerships, and corporations are different forms of business ownership, with each offering advantages and disadvantages.
- New ventures can be financed through debt financing in the form of loans and through equity financing, which involves the exchange of ownership shares in return for outside investment.
- Venture capitalists and angel investors invest in new ventures in return for an equity stake in the business.

Questions for Discussion

1. Given the economic importance of small businesses, what could local, state, and federal governments do to make it easier for them to prosper?

2. If you were asked to join a small company, what would you look for as potential success indicators in its business plan?

3. Why might the owner of a small but growing business want to be careful when accepting big investments from venture capitalists?

Be Sure You Can

- **state** the SBA definition of small business
- **list** the life-cycle stages of a small business
- **list** several reasons why many small businesses fail
- **discuss** the succession problem in family-owned businesses
- **list** the major elements in a business plan
- **differentiate** the common forms of small business ownership
- **differentiate** debt financing and equity financing
- **explain** the roles of venture capitalists and angel investors in new venture financing

Career Situation: What Would You Do?

Your start-up e-textbook rating Web site is attracting potential investors. One angel is willing to put up $50,000 to help move things to the next level. But you and your two co-founders haven't done anything to legally structure the business. You've operated so far on personal resources and a "handshake" agreement among friends. What's the best choice to legally set up the company? What's your best option for getting the financing needed for future growth while still protecting your ownership?

TEST PREP **17**

Answers to TestPrep questions can be found at the back of the book.

Multiple-Choice Questions

1. An entrepreneur who thrives on uncertainty displays

   _____.
   (a) high tolerance for ambiguity
   (b) internal locus of control
   (c) need for achievement
   (d) action orientation

2. _____ is a personality characteristic common among
   entrepreneurs.
   (a) External locus of control   (b) Inflexibility
   (c) Self-confidence   (d) Low self-reliance

3. When a new business is quick to capture a market niche before
   competitors, this is _____.
   (a) intrapreneurship
   (b) an initial public offering
   (c) succession planning
   (d) first-mover advantage

4. Almost_____% of U.S. businesses meet the definition of
   "small business."
   (a) 40   (b) 99
   (c) 75   (d) 81

5. A small business owner who wants to pass the business to
   other family members after retirement or death should prepare
   a _____ plan.
   (a) retirement   (b) succession
   (c) partnership   (d) liquidation

6. A common reason small business start-ups often fail
   is _____.
   (a) the owner lacks experience and business skills
   (b) there is too much government regulation
   (c) the owner tightly controls money and finances
   (d) the business grows too slowly

7. A pressing problem faced by a small business in the birth or
   start-up stage is _____.
   (a) gaining acceptance in the marketplace
   (b) finding partners for expansion
   (c) preparing the initial public offering
   (d) getting management professional skills

8. A venture capitalist who receives an ownership share in return
   for investing in a new business is providing _____
   financing.
   (a) debt   (b) equity
   (c) limited   (d) corporate

9. In _____ financing, the business owner borrows money as
   a loan that must be repaid.
   (a) debt   (b) equity
   (c) partnership   (d) limited

10. If you start a small business and want to avoid losing any more
    than the original investment, what form of ownership is best?
    (a) Sole proprietorship   (b) General partnership
    (c) Limited partnership   (d) Corporation

11. The first element in a good business plan is _____.
    (a) an industry analysis
    (b) a marketing strategy
    (c) an executive summary
    (d) a set of performance milestones

12. Trends in U.S. small businesses show _____.
    (a) a growing number owned by minorities
    (b) fewer of them using the Internet for business
    (c) more small businesses leaving small communities for the
       big city
    (d) fewer of them being family owned

13. A _____ protects small business owners from personal
    liabilities for losses.
    (a) sole proprietorship
    (b) franchise
    (c) limited partnership
    (d) corporation

14. _____ take ownership shares in a new venture in return
    for start-up funds.
    (a) Business incubators
    (b) Angel investors
    (c) SBDCs
    (d) Intrapreneurs

15. _____ makes social entrepreneurship unique.
    (a) Lack of other career options
    (b) Focus on international markets
    (c) Refusal to finance by loans
    (d) Commitment to solving social problems

Short-Response Questions

16. What is the relationship between diversity and entrepreneur-
    ship?

17. What major challenges are faced at each life-cycle stage of an
    entrepreneurial firm?

18. What are the advantages of a limited partnership form of
    ownership?

19. What is the difference, if any, between a venture capitalist and
    an angel investor?

Integration and Application Question

20. You have a great idea for an Internet-based start-up business. A
    friend advises you to clearly link your business idea to potential
    customers and then describe it well in a business plan. "You
    won't succeed without customers," she says, "and you'll never
    get a chance if you can't attract financial backers with a good
    business plan."

    Questions: What questions will you ask and answer to ensure
    that you are customer focused in this business? What are the
    major areas that you would address in your initial business
    plan?

Steps for
Further Learning

BUILD MARKETABLE SKILLS • **DO** A CASE ANALYSIS • **GET** AND STAY INFORMED

BUILD MARKETABLE SKILLS.

EARN BIG CAREER PAYOFFS!

Don't miss these opportunities in the SKILL-BUILDING PORTFOLIO

SELF-ASSESSMENT 17:
Entrepreneurship Orientation

Lots of people can do it . . . find out if entrepreneurship fits you.

CLASS EXERCISE 17:
Entrepreneur Role Models

Entrepreneurs are all around us . . . find out who are the best role models.

TEAM PROJECT 17:
Community Entrepreneurs

Many of them fly below the radar . . . discover how entrepreneurs help build your community.

Many learning resources are found at the end of the book and online within **WileyPLUS Learning Space.**

Practice Critical Thinking—Complete the CHAPTER 17 CASE

CASE SNAPSHOT: Crowdfunding—The New Mother of Angel Investors

"How do I get financing?" Answering this fundamental question presents one of the greatest challenges to entrepreneurs intent on following their dream of business independence. Never easy, start-up financing has been even harder to get after banks shrank their small business loan portfolios in the recent financial crisis. Many owners of existing small businesses as well as those launching new start-ups are finding it hard to come up with timely and solid business funding options. But, as with so many things, the Web is offering some help. Crowdfunding is an emerging field of financing built around a social media platform. It's still developing, and it's not without controversy; but it's also here to stay.

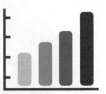

DO A CASE ANALYSIS.

STRENGTHEN YOUR CRITICAL THINKING!

MANAGER'S LIBRARY SELECTION
Read for insights and wisdom
In-N-Out Burger: A Behind-the-Counter Look at the Fast-Food Chain That Breaks all the Rules (2009, HarperCollins), by Stacy Perman

In 1948, Harry and Esther Snyder opened a small hamburger stand beside a busy road in Los Angeles, California. Their restaurant, In-N-Out Burger, is now a successful family-owned chain of drive-through stores. Stacy Perman's book profiles the Snyder's values and the investment they put into every In-N-Out burger, employee, and customer. She claims that dedication to quality, reinvestment in employees, and joy in delighting customers has generated an "uncopyable" competitive advantage. In-N-Out stores match competitors' revenues without advertising, franchising, financing debt, minimum wage labor, or sacrificing quality for volume, speed, and price. They just build a better burger.

GET AND STAY INFORMED.

MAKE YOURSELF VALUABLE!

Part of the In-N-Out difference is a focus on quality—right from the beef to the service. Another part is genuine interest in employee. Called associates, they are paid well above minimum wage and train at In-N-Out University. New stores open only after managers have been carefully trained and tested. The results are unrivaled customer loyalty and a "cult-like" following.

REFLECT AND REACT Do you agree with Perman's assessment of In-N-Out Burger's sources of competitive advantage? How "uncopyable" are these practices in the industry today? Are these practices that could be copied by entrepreneurs seeking successful start-ups in other industries?

Great jobs aren't easy to get. Career success today requires lots of initiative, self-awareness, and continuous personal improvement. The question is: *"Are you ready?"*

Self-Assessments *Class Exercises* **Team Projects**

Self-Assessment 1: Personal Career Readiness

Instructions

Use this scale to rate yourself on the following list of personal characteristics.[1]

S = Strong, I am very confident with this one.
G = Good, but I still have room to grow.
W = Weak, I really need work on this one.
U = Unsure, I just don't know.

_____ 1. *Resistance to stress:* The ability to get work done even under stressful conditions

_____ 2. *Tolerance for uncertainty:* The ability to get work done even under ambiguous and uncertain conditions

_____ 3. *Social objectivity:* The ability to act free of racial, ethnic, gender, and other prejudices or biases

_____ 4. *Inner work standards:* The ability to personally set and work to high performance standards

_____ 5. *Stamina:* The ability to sustain long work hours

_____ 6. *Adaptability:* The ability to be flexible and adapt to changes

_____ 7. *Self-confidence:* The ability to be consistently decisive and display one's personal presence

_____ 8. *Self-objectivity:* The ability to evaluate personal strengths and weaknesses and to understand one's motives and skills relative to a job

_____ 9. *Introspection:* The ability to learn from experience, awareness, and self-study

_____ 10. *Entrepreneurism:* The ability to address problems and take advantage of opportunities for constructive change

Scoring

Give yourself 1 point for each S, and 1/2 point for each G. Do not give yourself points for W or U responses. Total your points and enter the result here: _____ .

Interpretation

This assessment offers a self-described *profile of your management foundations.* Are you a perfect 10 or something less? There shouldn't be too many 10s around. Also ask someone else to assess you on this instrument. You may be surprised at the results, but the insights are well worth thinking about. The items on the list are skills and personal characteristics that should be nurtured now and throughout your career.

Self-Assessment 2: Terminal Values Survey

Instructions

1. Read the following list of things people value.[2] Think about the importance of each value as a guiding principle in your life.

A comfortable life	An exciting life	A sense of accomplishment
A world at peace	A world of beauty	Equality
Family security	Freedom	Happiness
Inner harmony	Mature love	National security
Pleasure	Salvation	Self-respect
Social recognition	True friendship	Wisdom

2. *Circle* six of these 18 values to indicate that they are *most important* to you. If you can, rank-order these most important values by writing a number above them—with "1" the most important value in your life, and so on through "6."

3. *Underline* the six of these 18 values that are *least important* to you.

Interpretation

Terminal values reflect a person's preferences concerning the ends to be achieved. They are the goals individuals would like to achieve in their lifetimes. As you look at the items you have selected as most and least important, what major differences exist among the items in the two sets? Think about this and then answer the following questions.

A) What does your selection of most and least important values say about you as a person?

B) What does your selection of most and least important values suggest about the type of work and career that might be best for you?

C) Which values among your most and least important selections might cause problems for you in the future—at work and/or in your personal life? What problems might they cause, and why? How might you prepare now to best deal with these problems in the future?

D) How might your choices of most and least important values turn out to be major strengths or assets for you—at work and/or in your personal life—and why?

Self-Assessment 3: Maximizer or Satisficer Quick Check

Instructions

Answer the following questions in the way that most often describes your behavior.[3]

Yes   No   1. I am a frequent channel surfer when watching TV.

Yes   No   2. I try on a lot of outfits before purchasing clothes.

Yes   No   3. It's hard for me to choose movies for pleasure viewing.

Yes   No   4. I'm careful about relationships, trying to find the perfect fit.

Yes   No   5. Second best at anything isn't good enough for me.

Yes   No   6. I dream a lot about living a different lifestyle.

Yes   No   7. I write several drafts before being satisfied with a term paper.

Yes   No   8. I often think about changing jobs.

Scoring and Interpretation

The more "Yes" answers, the more you tend toward a "maximizer" decision making approach that tries to find the optimum or absolute best course of action. The more "No" answers, the more you tend toward a "satisficer" approach that seeks a satisfactory course of action that is "good enough" even if not perfect. Researchers link maximizing tendencies with perfectionism and regret, while satisficing is correlated with higher life satisfaction. Psychology Professor Barry Swartz of Swarthmore College says: "Maximizers make good decisions and end up feeling bad about them. Satisficers make good decisions and end up feeling good about them."

Self-Assessment 4: Time Management Profile

Instructions

Indicate Y (yes) or N (no) for each item. Be frank; let your responses describe an accurate picture of how you tend to respond to these kinds of situations.[4]

1. When confronted with several items of similar urgency and importance, I tend to do the easiest one first.
2. I do the most important things during that part of the day when I know I perform best.
3. Most of the time I don't do things someone else can do; I delegate this type of work to others.
4. Even though meetings without a clear and useful purpose upset me, I put up with them.
5. I skim documents before reading them and don't complete any that offer a low return on my time investment.
6. I don't worry much if I don't accomplish at least one significant task each day.
7. I save the most trivial tasks for that time of day when my creative energy is lowest.
8. My workspace is neat and organized.
9. My office door is always "open"; I never work in complete privacy.
10. I schedule my time completely from start to finish every workday.
11. I don't like "to-do" lists, preferring to respond to daily events as they occur.
12. I "block" a certain amount of time each day or week to be dedicated to high-priority activities.

Scoring

Count the number of Y responses to items 2, 3, 5, 7, 8, 12. [Enter that score here _____]. Count the number of N responses to items 1, 4, 6, 9, 10, 11. [Enter that score here _____]. Add together the two scores.

Interpretation

The higher the total score, the more closely your behavior matches recommended time management guidelines. Reread those items where your response did not match the desired one. Why don't they match? Are there reasons for your action tendencies? Think about what you can do to be more consistent with time management guidelines.

Self-Assessment 5: Internal/External Control

Instructions

Circle either a or b to indicate the item you most agree with in each of the following pairs of statements.[5]

1. **(a)** Promotions are earned through hard work and persistence.
   (b) Making a lot of money is largely a matter of breaks.

2. **(a)** Many times the reactions of teachers seem haphazard to me.

    (b) In my experience I have noticed that there is usually a direct connection between how hard I study and the grades I get.

3. **(a)** The number of divorces indicates that more and more people are not trying to make their marriages work.

    (b) Marriage is largely a gamble.

4. **(a)** It is silly to think that one can really change another person's basic attitudes.

    (b) When I am right, I can convince others.

5. **(a)** Getting promoted is really a matter of being a little luckier than the next guy.

    (b) In our society, an individual's future earning power is dependent on his or her ability.

6. **(a)** If one knows how to deal with people, they are really quite easily led.

    (b) I have little influence over the way other people behave.

7. **(a)** In my case, the grades I make are the results of my own efforts; luck has little or nothing to do with it.

    (b) Sometimes I feel that I have little to do with the grades I get.

8. **(a)** People such as I can change the course of world affairs if we make ourselves heard.

    (b) It is only wishful thinking to believe that one can really influence what happens in society at large.

9. **(a)** Much of what happens to me is probably a matter of chance.

    (b) I am the master of my fate.

10. **(a)** Getting along with people is a skill that must be practiced.

    (b) It is almost impossible to figure out how to please some people.

Scoring

Give yourself 1 point for 1b, 2a, 3a, 4b, 5b, 6a, 7a, 8a, 9b, 10a. Total scores of: 8–10 = high *internal* locus of control, 6–7 = moderate *internal* locus of control, 5 = *mixed* locus of control, 3–4 = moderate *external* locus of control, 0–2 = 5 high *external* locus of control.

Interpretation

This instrument offers an impression of your tendency toward an *internal locus of control or external locus of control.* Persons with a high internal locus of control tend to believe they have control over their own destinies. They may be most responsive to opportunities for greater self-control in the workplace. Persons with a high external locus of control tend to believe that what happens to them is largely in the hands of external people or forces. They may be less comfortable with self-control and more responsive to external controls in the workplace.

Self-Assessment 6: Facts and Inferences

Instructions

1. Read the following report.[6]

    A well-liked college instructor had just completed making up the final examination and had turned off the lights in the office. Just then a tall, broad figure with dark glasses appeared and demanded the examination. The professor opened the drawer. Everything in the drawer was picked up, and the individual ran down the corridor. The president was notified immediately.

2. Indicate whether you think the following observations are true (T), false (F), or doubtful in that it may be either true or false (?). Judge each observation in order. Do not reread the observations after you have indicated your judgment, and do not change any of your answers.

    1. The thief was tall, broad, and wore dark glasses.
    2. The professor turned off the lights.
    3. A tall figure demanded the examination.
    4. The examination was picked up by someone.
    5. The examination was picked up by the professor.
    6. A tall, broad figure appeared after the professor turned off the lights in the office.
    7. The man who opened the drawer was the professor.
    8. The professor ran down the corridor.
    9. The drawer was never actually opened.
    10. Three persons are referred to in this report.

Scoring

The correct answers in reverse order (starting with 10) are: ?, F, ?, ?, T, ?, ?, T, T, ?.

Interpretation

To begin, ask yourself if there was a difference between your answers and the correct ones. If so, why? Why do you think people, individually or in groups, may answer these questions incorrectly? Good planning depends on good decision making by the people doing the planning. Being able to distinguish "facts" and understand one's "inferences" are important steps toward improving the planning process. Involving others to help do the same can frequently assist in this process.

Self-Assessment 7: Empowering Others

Instructions

Think of times when you have been in charge of a group—this could be a full-time or part-time work situation, a student work group, or whatever. Complete the following questionnaire by recording how you feel about each statement according to this scale.[7]

> 1 = Strongly disagree   2 = Disagree   3 = Neutral   4 = Agree   5 = Strongly agree

When in charge of a team, I find that

1. Most of the time other people are too inexperienced to do things, so I prefer to do them myself.
2. It often takes more time to explain things to others than to just do them myself.
3. Mistakes made by others are costly, so I don't assign much work to them.
4. Some things simply should not be delegated to others.
5. I often get quicker action by doing a job myself.
6. Many people are good only at very specific tasks, so they can't be assigned additional responsibilities.
7. Many people are too busy to take on additional work.
8. Most people just aren't ready to handle additional responsibilities.
9. In my position, I should be entitled to make my own decisions.

Scoring

Total your responses and enter the score here [_____].

Interpretation

This instrument gives an impression of your willingness to delegate. Possible scores range from 9 to 45. The lower your score, the more willing you appear to be to delegate to others. Willingness to delegate is an important managerial characteristic: It is how you—as a manager—can empower others and give them opportunities to assume responsibility and exercise self-control in their work. With the growing importance of horizontal organizations and empowerment in the new workplace, your willingness to delegate is worth thinking about seriously.

Self-Assessment 8: Tolerance for Ambiguity

Instructions

Rate each of the following items on this seven-point scale.[8]

> Strongly agree   1   2   3   4   5   6   7   Strongly disagree

_____ 1. An expert who doesn't come up with a definite answer probably doesn't know too much.

_____ 2. There is really no such thing as a problem that can't be solved.

_____ 3. I would like to live in a foreign country for a while.

_____ 4. People who fit their lives to a schedule probably miss the joy of living.

_____ 5. A good job is one where what is to be done and how it is to be done are always clear.

_____ 6. In the long run it is possible to get more done by tackling small, simple problems rather than large, complicated ones.

_____ 7. It is more fun to tackle a complicated problem than it is to solve a simple one.

_____ 8. Often the most interesting and stimulating people are those who don't mind being different and original.

_____ 9. What we are used to is always preferable to what is unfamiliar.

_____ 10. A person who leads an even, regular life in which few surprises or unexpected happenings arise really has a lot to be grateful for.

_____ **11.** People who insist upon a yes or no answer just don't know how complicated things really are.

_____ **12.** Many of our most important decisions are based on insufficient information.

_____ **13.** I like parties where I know most of the people more than ones where most of the people are complete strangers.

_____ **14.** The sooner we all acquire ideals, the better.

_____ **15.** Teachers or supervisors who hand out vague assignments give a chance for one to show initiative and originality.

_____ **16.** A good teacher is one who makes you wonder about your way of looking at things.

Scoring and Interpretation

To obtain a score, first *reverse* your scores for items 3, 4, 7, 8, 11, 12, 15, and 16 (i.e., a rating of $1 = 7, 2 = 6, 3 = 5$, etc.). Next add up your scores for all 16 items. The higher your total score, the greater your suggested tolerance for ambiguity.

Self-Assessment 9: Performance Review Assumptions

Instructions

In each of the following pairs of statements, check the alternative that best reflects your assumptions about performance reviews.[9]

1. **(a)** a formal process done annually

   (b) an informal process done continuously

2. **(a)** a process planned for team members

   (b) a process planned with team members

3. **(a)** a process with set procedures

   (b) a process with some flexibility

4. **(a)** a time for managers to evaluate workers' performance

   (b) a time for workers to evaluate their managers

5. **(a)** a time for managers to clarify standards and expectations

   (b) a time for workers to clarify job and career needs

6. **(a)** a time to confront performance problems

   (b) a time to express appreciation for performance accomplishments

7. **(a)** an opportunity to provide direction and control

   (b) an opportunity to increase enthusiasm and commitment

8. **(a)** only as good as the procedure used

   (b) only as good as the team leader's interpersonal and coaching skills

Interpretation

In general, the "a" choices show more emphasis on the *evaluation* function of performance reviews. This largely puts the team leader in the role of documenting a team member's performance for control and administrative purposes. The "b" choices show a stronger emphasis on the *counseling* or *development* function. Here, the team leader is concerned with helping the team member do better in the future and with learning from the team member what he or she needs to achieve this.

Self-Assessment 10: Least Preferred Co-worker Scale

Instructions

Think of all the different people with whom you have ever worked—in jobs, in social clubs, in student projects, or whatever. Next, think of the one person with whom you could work least well—that is, the person with whom you had the most difficulty getting a job done. This is the one person—a peer, boss, or subordinate—with whom you would least want to work. Describe this person by circling numbers at the appropriate points on each of the following pairs of bipolar adjectives. Work rapidly. There is no right or wrong answer.[10]

Pleasant	8 7 6 5 4 3 2 1	Unpleasant
Friendly	8 7 6 5 4 3 2 1	Unfriendly
Rejecting	1 2 3 4 5 6 7 8	Accepting
Tense	1 2 3 4 5 6 7 8	Relaxed
Distant	1 2 3 4 5 6 7 8	Close

Cold	1 2 3 4 5 6 7 8	Warm
Supportive	8 7 6 5 4 3 2 1	Hostile
Boring	1 2 3 4 5 6 7 8	Interesting
Quarrelsome	1 2 3 4 5 6 7 8	Harmonious
Gloomy	1 2 3 4 5 6 7 8	Cheerful
Open	8 7 6 5 4 3 2 1	Guarded
Backbiting	1 2 3 4 5 6 7 8	Loyal
Untrustworthy	1 2 3 4 5 6 7 8	Trustworthy
Considerate	8 7 6 5 4 3 2 1	Inconsiderate
Nasty	1 2 3 4 5 6 7 8	Nice
Agreeable	8 7 6 5 4 3 2 1	Disagreeable
Insincere	1 2 3 4 5 6 7 8	Sincere
Kind	8 7 6 5 4 3 2 1	Unkind

Scoring

This is called the "least-preferred co-worker scale" (LPC). Compute your LPC score by totaling all the numbers you circled; enter that score here [LPC = _____].

Interpretation

If your score is 73 or above on the LPC scale, Fiedler considers you a "relationship-motivated" leader; if it is 64 or below on the scale, he considers you a "task-motivated" leader. If your score is between 65 and 72, Fiedler leaves it up to you to determine which leadership style is most accurate. Remember that Fiedler believes that leadership style is a relatively fixed part of one's personality and is therefore difficult to change.

Self-Assessment 11: Stress Test

Instructions

Complete the following questionnaire. Circle the number that best represents your tendency to behave on each bipolar dimension.[11]

Am casual about appointments	1 2 3 4 5 6 7 8	Am never late for appointments
Am not competitive	1 2 3 4 5 6 7 8	Am very competitive
Never feel rushed	1 2 3 4 5 6 7 8	Always feel rushed
Take things one at a time	1 2 3 4 5 6 7 8	Try to do many things at once
Do things slowly	1 2 3 4 5 6 7 8	Do things fast
Express feelings	1 2 3 4 5 6 7 8	"Sit on" feelings
Have many interests	1 2 3 4 5 6 7 8	Have few interests but work

Scoring and Interpretation

Total the numbers circled for all items, and multiply this by 3; enter the result here [_____]. Scoring as a Type A Personality indicates that you tend to bring stress on to yourself and may have to be more sensitive to stress prevention and stress management strategies.

Points	Personality Type
120+	A+
106–119	A
100–105	A–
90–99	B+
below 90	B

Self-Assessment 12: Two-Factor Profile

Instructions

On each of the following dimensions, distribute a total of 10 points to indicate your preference between the two options. For example:

Summer weather   *(7)*   *(3)*   *Winter weather*

1. Very responsible job   (__)   (__)   Job security
2. Recognition for work accomplishments   (__)   (__)   Good relations with co-workers
3. Advancement opportunities at work   (__)   (__)   A boss who knows his/her job well
4. Opportunities to grow and learn on the job   (__)   (__)   Good working conditions
5. A job that I can do well   (__)   (__)   Supportive rules, policies of employer
6. A prestigious or high-status job   (__)   (__)   A high base wage or salary

Scoring

Summarize your total score for all items in the *left-hand column* and write it here. MF = _____

Summarize your total score for all items in the *right-hand column* and write it here. HF = _____

Interpretation

The *MF score* shows how important *job content* is to you. It indicates the relative importance that you place on the motivating, or satisfier, factors in Herzberg's two-factor theory. The *HF score* shows how important *job context* is to you. It indicates the relative importance that you place on hygiene, or dissatisfier factors in Herzberg's two-factor theory.

Self-Assessment 13: Team Leader Skills

Instructions

Consider your experiences in groups and work teams. Ask: "What skills do I bring to team leadership situations?" Then complete the following inventory by rating yourself on each item using this scale.[12]

1 = Almost never   2 = Seldom   3 = Sometimes   4 = Usually   5 =Almost always

_____ 1. I facilitate communications with and among team members between team meetings.
_____ 2. I provide feedback/coaching to individual team members on their performance.
_____ 3. I encourage creative and out-of-the-box thinking.
_____ 4. I continue to clarify stakeholder needs/expectations.
_____ 5. I keep team members' responsibilities and activities focused within the team's objectives and goals.
_____ 6. I organize and run effective and productive team meetings.
_____ 7. I demonstrate integrity and personal commitment.
_____ 8. I have excellent persuasive and influence skills.
_____ 9. I respect and leverage the team's cross-functional diversity.
_____ 10. I recognize and reward individual contributions to team performance.
_____ 11. I use the appropriate decision-making style for specific issues.
_____ 12. I facilitate and encourage border management with the team's key stakeholders.
_____ 13. I ensure that the team meets its team commitments.
_____ 14. I bring team issues and problems to the team's attention and focus on constructive problem solving.
_____ 15. I provide a clear vision and direction for the team.

Scoring and Interpretation

Add your scores for the items listed next to each dimension below to get an indication of your potential strengths and weaknesses on seven dimensions of team leadership. The higher the score, the more confident you are on the particular skill and leadership capability. When considering the score, ask yourself if others would rate you the same way.

1, 9	Building the team
2, 10	Developing people
3, 11	Team problem solving/decision making
4, 12	Stakeholder relations

5, 13	Team performance
6, 14	Team process
7, 8, 15	Providing personal leadership

Self-Assessment 14: Feedback and Assertiveness

Instructions

For each statement below, decide which of the following answers best fits you.[13]

1 = Never true   2 = Sometimes true   3 = Often true   4 = Always true

_____ **1.** I respond more modestly than I really feel when my work is complimented.

_____ **2.** If people are rude, I will be rude right back.

_____ **3.** Other people find me interesting.

_____ **4.** I find it difficult to speak up in a group of strangers.

_____ **5.** I don't mind using sarcasm if it helps me make a point.

_____ **6.** I ask for a raise when I feel I really deserve it.

_____ **7.** If others interrupt me when I am talking, I suffer in silence.

_____ **8.** If people criticize my work, I find a way to make them back down.

_____ **9.** I can express pride in my accomplishments without being boastful.

_____ **10.** People take advantage of me.

_____ **11.** I tell people what they want to hear if it helps me get what I want.

_____ **12.** I find it easy to ask for help.

_____ **13.** I lend things to others even when I don't really want to.

_____ **14.** I win arguments by dominating the discussion.

_____ **15.** I can express my true feelings to someone I really care for.

_____ **16.** When I feel angry with other people, I bottle it up rather than express it.

_____ **17.** When I criticize someone else's work, they get mad.

_____ **18.** I feel confident in my ability to stand up for my rights.

Scoring and Interpretation

Aggressiveness tendency score—Add items 2, 5, 8, 11, 14, and 17.

Passiveness tendency score—Add items 1, 4, 7, 10, 13, and 16.

Assertiveness tendency score—Add items 3, 6, 9, 12, 15, and 18.

The maximum score in any single area is 24. The minimum score is 6. Try to find someone who knows you well. Have this person complete the instrument also as it relates to you. Compare his or her impression of you with your own score. What is this telling you about your behavior tendencies in social situations?

Self-Assessment 15: Diversity Awareness

Instructions

Write "O" for often, "S" for sometimes, and "N" for never in response to each of the following questions as they pertain to where you work or go to school.

1. How often have you heard jokes or remarks about other people that you consider offensive?

2. How often do you hear men "talk down" to women in an attempt to keep them in an inferior status?

3. How often have you felt personal discomfort as the object of sexual harassment?

4. How often do you work or study with persons of different ethnic or national cultures?

5. How often have you felt disadvantaged because members of ethnic groups other than yours were given special treatment?

6. How often have you seen a woman put in an uncomfortable situation because of unwelcome advances by a man?

7. How often does it seem that members of minority groups seem to "stick together" during work breaks or other leisure situations?

8. How often do you feel uncomfortable about something you did and/or said to someone of the opposite sex or a member of an ethnic or racial group other than yours?

9. How often do you feel efforts are made in this setting to raise the level of cross-cultural understanding among people who work and/or study together?

10. How often do you step in to communicate concerns to others when you feel actions and/or words are used to the disadvantage of minorities?

Interpretation

There are no correct answers for the Diversity Awareness Checklist. The key issue is the extent to which you are sensitive to diversity issues in the workplace or university. Are you comfortable with your responses? How do you think others in your class responded? Why not share your responses with others and examine different viewpoints on this important issue?

Self-Assessment 16: Global Intelligence

Instructions

Use the following scale to rate yourself on these 10 items.[14]

1 = Very poor   2 = Poor   3 = Acceptable   4 = Good   5 = Very good

1. I understand my own culture in terms of its expectations, values, and influence on communication and relationships.

2. When someone presents me with a different point of view, I try to understand it rather than attack it.

3. I am comfortable dealing with situations where the available information is incomplete and the outcomes unpredictable.

4. I am open to new situations and am always looking for new information and learning opportunities.

5. I have a good understanding of the attitudes and perceptions toward my culture as they are held by people from other cultures.

6. I am always gathering information about other countries and cultures and trying to learn from them.

7. I am well informed regarding the major differences in the government, political, and economic systems around the world.

8. I work hard to increase my understanding of people from other cultures.

9. I am able to adjust my communication style to work effectively with people from different cultures.

10. I can recognize when cultural differences are influencing working relationships, and I adjust my attitudes and behavior accordingly.

Scoring

The goal is to score as close to a perfect 5 as possible on each of the three dimensions of global intelligence. Develop your scores as follows:

- Items $(1 + 2 + 3 + 4)/4$ = Global Mindset Score—The extent to which you are receptive to and respectful of cultural differences.
- Items $(5 + 6 + 7)/3$ = Global Knowledge Score—Your openness to know and learn more about other nations and cultures.
- Items $(8 + 9 + 10)/3$ = Global Work Skills Score—Your capacity to work effectively across cultures.

Interpretation

To be successful in the global economy, you must be comfortable with the cultural diversity that it holds. This requires a global mindset that is receptive to and respectful of cultural differences, global knowledge that includes the continuing quest to know and learn more about other nations and cultures, and global work skills that allow you to work effectively across cultures.

Self-Assessment 17: Entrepreneurship Orientation

Instructions

Answer each of the following questions.[15]

1. What portion of your college expenses did you earn (or are you earning)?

(a) 50% or more (b) Less than 50% (c) None

2. In college, your academic performance was/is

(a) above average. (b) average. (c) below average.

3. What is your basic reason for considering opening a business?

(a) I want to make money. (b) I want to control my own destiny. (c) I hate the frustration of working for someone else.

4. Which phrase best describes your attitude toward work?

(a) I can keep going as long as I need to; I don't mind working for something I want. (b) I can work hard for a while, but when I've had enough, I quit. (c) Hard work really doesn't get you anywhere.

5. How would you rate your organizing skills?

   (a) Superorganized (b) Above average (c) Average (d) I do well to find half the things I look for.

6. You are primarily a(n)

   (a) optimist. (b) pessimist. (c) neither.

7. You are faced with a challenging problem. As you work, you realize you are stuck. You will most likely

   (a) give up. (b) ask for help. (c) keep plugging; you'll figure it out.

8. You are playing a game with a group of friends. You are most interested in

   (a) winning. (b) playing well. (c) making sure that everyone has a good time. (d) cheating as much as possible.

9. How would you describe your feelings toward failure?

   (a) Fear of failure paralyzes me. (b) Failure can be a good learning experience. (c) Knowing that I might fail motivates me to work even harder. (d) "Damn the torpedoes! Full speed ahead."

10. Which phrase best describes you?

    (a) I need constant encouragement to get anything done. (b) If someone gets me started, I can keep going. (c) I am energetic and hardworking—a self-starter.

11. Which bet would you most likely accept?

    (a) A wager on a dog race (b) A wager on a racquetball game in which you play an opponent (c) Neither. I never make wagers.

12. At the Kentucky Derby, you would bet on

    (a) the 100-to-1 long shot. (b) the odds-on favorite. (c) the 3-to-1 shot. (d) none of the above.

Scoring

Give yourself 10 points each for answers 1a, 2a, 3c, 4a, 5a, 6a, 7c, 8a, 9c, 10c, 11b, 12c; total the scores and enter the result here [I = _____].

Give yourself 8 points each for answers 3b, 8b, 9b; enter total here [II = _____].

Give yourself 6 points each for answers 2b, 5b; enter total here [III = _____].

Give yourself 5 points for answer 1b; enter result here [IV = _____].

Give yourself 4 points for answer 5c; enter result here [V = _____].

Give yourself 2 points each for answers 2c, 3a, 4b, 6c, 9d, 10b, 11a, 12b; enter total here [VI = _____].

The other answers are worth 0 points.

Total your summary scores for I + II + III + IV + V + VI and enter the result here: My Entrepreneurship Potential Score is _____.

Interpretation

This assessment offers an impression of your *entrepreneurial profile (EP)*. It compares your characteristics with those of typical entrepreneurs, according to this profile: 100+ = Entrepreneur extraordinaire; 80–99 = Entrepreneur; 60–79 = Potential entrepreneur; 0–59 = Entrepreneur in the rough.

Class Exercise 1: My Best Manager

Preparation

Working alone, make a list of the *behavioral attributes* that describe the "best" manager you have ever had.[1] This could be someone you worked for in a full-time or part-time job, summer job, volunteer job, student organization, or elsewhere. If you have trouble identifying an actual manager, make a list of behavioral attributes of the manager you would most like to work for in your next job.

Instructions

Form into teams as assigned by your instructor, or work with a nearby classmate. Share your list of attributes and listen to the lists of others. Be sure to ask questions and make comments on items of special interest. Work together in your team to create a master list that combines the unique attributes of the "best" managers experienced by members of your group. Have a spokesperson share that list with the rest of the class for further discussion.

Class Exercise 2: Confronting Ethical Dilemmas

Preparation

Read and indicate your response to each of the following situations.

1. Ron Jones, vice president of a large construction firm, receives in the mail a large envelope marked "personal." It contains a competitor's cost data for a project that both firms will be bidding on shortly. The data are accompanied by a note from one of Ron's subordinates saying: "This is the real thing!" Ron knows that the data could be a major advantage to his firm in preparing a bid that can win the contract. What should he do?

2. Kay Smith is one of your top-performing team members. She has shared with you her desire to apply for promotion to a new position just announced in a different division of the company. This will be tough on you because recent budget cuts mean you will be unable to replace anyone who leaves, at least for quite some time. Kay knows this and, in all fairness, has asked your permission before she submits an application. It is rumored that the son of a good friend of your boss is going to apply for the job. Although his credentials are less impressive than Kay's, the likelihood is that he will get the job if she doesn't apply. What will you do?

3. Marty José got caught in a bind. She was pleased to represent her firm as head of the local community development committee. In fact, her supervisor's boss once held this position and told her in a hallway conversation, "Do your best and give them every support possible." Going along with this, Marty agreed to pick up the bill (several hundred dollars) for a dinner meeting with local civic and business leaders. Shortly thereafter, her supervisor informed everyone that the entertainment budget was being eliminated in a cost-saving effort. Marty, not wanting to renege on supporting the community development committee, was able to charge the dinner bill to an advertising budget. Eventually, an internal auditor discovered the charge and reported it to you, the personnel director. Marty is scheduled to meet with you in a few minutes. What will you do?

Instructions

Working alone, make the requested decisions in each of these incidents. Think carefully about your justification for the decision. Meet in a group assigned by your instructor. Share your decisions and justifications in each case with other group members. Listen to theirs. Try to reach a group consensus on what to do in each situation and why. Be prepared to share the group decisions, and any dissenting views, in general class discussion.

Class Exercise 3: Lost at Sea

Preparation

Consider This Situation: You are adrift on a private yacht in the South Pacific when a fire of unknown origin destroys the yacht and most of its contents.[2] You and a small group of survivors are now in a large raft with oars. Your location is unclear, but you estimate that you are about 1,000 miles south-southwest of the nearest land. One person has just found in her pockets five $1 bills and a packet of matches. Everyone else's pockets are empty. The following items are available to you on the raft.

	Individual ranking	Team ranking	Expert ranking
Sextant	_____	_____	_____
Shaving mirror	_____	_____	_____
5 gallons water	_____	_____	_____
Mosquito netting	_____	_____	_____

	Individual ranking	Team ranking	Expert ranking
1 survival meal	_____	_____	_____
Maps of Pacific Ocean	_____	_____	_____
Floatable seat cushion	_____	_____	_____
2 gallons oil-gas mix	_____	_____	_____
Small transistor radio	_____	_____	_____
Shark repellent	_____	_____	_____
20 square feet black plastic	_____	_____	_____
1 quart 20-proof rum	_____	_____	_____
15 feet nylon rope	_____	_____	_____
24 chocolate bars	_____	_____	_____
Fishing kit	_____	_____	_____

Instructions

1. *Working alone,* rank the 15 items in order of their importance to your survival (1 is most important and 15 is least important).
2. *Working in an assigned group,* arrive at a "team" ranking of the 15 items. Appoint one person as team spokesperson to report your team ranking to the class.
3. *Do not write in column* 3 until your instructor provides the "expert" ranking.

Class Exercise 4: The Future Workplace

Instructions

Form groups as assigned by the instructor. Brainstorm to develop a master list of the major characteristics you expect to find in the workplace in the year 2025. Use this list as background for completing the following tasks:

1. Write a one-paragraph description of what the typical "Workplace 2020" manager's workday will be like.
2. Draw a "picture" representing what the "Workplace 2025" organization will look like.
3. Summarize in list form what you consider to be the major planning implications of your future workplace scenario for management students today. That is, explain what this means in terms of using academic and extracurricular activities to best prepare for success in this future scenario.
4. Choose a spokesperson to share your results with the class as a whole and explain their implications for the class members.

Class Exercise 5: Stakeholder Maps

Preparation

Review the discussion of organizational stakeholders in the textbook. (1) Make a list of the stakeholders that would apply to all organizations—for example, local communities, employees, and customers. What others would you add to this starter listing? (2) Choose one organization that you are familiar with from each list that follows. (3) Draw a map of key stakeholders for each organization. (4) For each stakeholder, indicate its major interest in the organization. (5) For each organization, make a list of possible conflicts among stakeholders that the top manager should recognize.

Nonprofit	Government	Business
Elementary school	Local mayor's office	Convenience store
Community hospital	State police	Movie theater
Church	U.S. Senator	National retailer
University	Internal Revenue Service	Local pizza shop
United Way	Homeland Security agency	Urgent care medical clinic

Instructions

In groups assigned by your instructor, choose one organization from each list. Create "master" stakeholder maps for each organization, along with statements of stakeholder interests and lists of potential stakeholder conflicts. Assume the position of top manager for each organization. Prepare a "stakeholder management plan" that represents the high-priority issues the manager should be addressing with respect to the stakeholders. Make a presentation to the class for each of your organizations and engage in discussion about the importance and complexity of stakeholder analysis.

Class Exercise 6: Strategic Scenarios

Preparation

In today's turbulent economic climate, it is no longer safe to assume that an organization that was highly successful yesterday will continue to be so tomorrow—or that it will even be in existence.[3] Changing times exact the best from strategic planners. Think about the situations currently facing the following well-known organizations. Think, too, about the futures they may face.

McDonald's	Ford	Sony
Apple Computer	Nordstrom	United Airlines
Yahoo!	National Public Radio	AT&T
Ann Taylor	*The New York Times*	Federal Express

Instructions

Form into groups as assigned by your instructor. Choose one or more organizations from the prior list (or as assigned) and answer the following questions for the organization:

1. What in the future might seriously threaten the success, perhaps the very existence, of this organization? As a group, develop at least three such *future scenarios*.
2. Estimate the probability (0 to 100%) of each future scenario occurring.
3. Develop a strategy for each scenario that will enable the organization to successfully deal with it.
4. Thoroughly discuss these questions within the group and arrive at your best possible consensus answers. Be prepared to share and defend your answers in general class discussion.

Class Exercise 7: Organizational Metaphors

Instructions

Form into groups as assigned by the instructor and do the following:

1. Think about organizations and how they work.
2. Select one of the following sets of organizational metaphors.
   (a) human brain—spiderweb
   (b) rock band—chamber music ensemble
   (c) cup of coffee—beehive
   (d) cement mixer—star galaxy
   (e) about the fifth date in an increasingly serious relationship—a couple celebrating their 25th wedding anniversary
3. Brainstorm how each metaphor in your set can be used to explain how organizations work.
4. Brainstorm how each metaphor in the set is similar to and different from the other in this explanation.
5. Draw pictures or create a short skit to illustrate the contrasts between your two metaphors.
6. Present your metaphorical views of organizations to the class.
7. Explain to the class what managers and team leaders can learn from your metaphors.

Class Exercise 8: Force-Field Analysis

Instructions

1. Form into your class discussion groups and review this model of force-field analysis—the consideration of forces driving in support of a planned change and forces resisting the change.

Driving forces ⋛ Resisting forces

Current state ●●●●●⟩ Desired future state

2. Use force-field analysis and make lists of driving and resisting forces for one of the following situations:

   (a) The dean wants all faculty to put at least some of their courses online—all or in part. This would mean a reduction in the number of required class sessions, but an increase in students' responsibility for completing learning activities and assignments online.

   (b) A new owner has just taken over a small walk-in-and-buy-by-the-slice pizza shop in a college town. There are presently eight employees, three of whom are full-time and five of whom are part-time. The shop is open seven days a week from 10:30 AM to midnight. The new owner believes there is a market niche available for late-night pizza and would like to stay open each night until 4 AM. She wants to make the change as soon as possible.

   (c) A situation assigned by the instructor.

3. Choose the three driving forces that are most significant for the proposed change. For each force, develop ideas on how it could be further increased or mobilized in support of the change.

4. Choose the three resisting forces that are most significant for the proposed change. For each force, develop ideas on how it could be reduced or turned into a driving force.

5. Be prepared to participate in a class discussion led by your instructor.

Class Exercise 9: Upward Appraisal

Instructions

Form into work groups as assigned by the instructor. The instructor will then leave the room. As a group, complete the following tasks:[4]

1. Within each group create a master list of comments, problems, issues, and concerns about the course experience to date that members would like to communicate to the instructor.

2. Select one person from the group to act as a spokesperson who will give your feedback to the instructor when he or she returns to the classroom.

3. Before the instructor returns, the spokespersons from each group should meet to decide how the room should be physically arranged (placement of tables, chairs, etc.) for the feedback session. This arrangement should allow the spokespersons and instructor to communicate while they are being observed by other class members.

4. While the spokespersons are meeting, members remaining in the groups should discuss what they expect to observe during the feedback session.

5. The classroom should be rearranged. The instructor should be invited in.

6. Spokespersons should deliver feedback to the instructor while observers make notes.

7. After the feedback session is complete, the instructor will call on observers for comments, ask the spokespersons for their reactions, and engage the class in general discussion about the exercise and its implications.

Class Exercise 10: Leading by Participation

Procedure

1. For the 10 situations described here, decide which of the three styles you would use for that unique situation. Place the letter A, P, or L on the line before each situation's number.

   A—authority; make the decision alone without additional inputs

   P—consultative; make the decision based on group inputs

   L—group; allow the group to which you belong to make the decision

Decision Situations

_____ 1. You have developed a new work procedure that will increase your team's productivity. Your boss likes the idea and wants you to try it within a few weeks. You view your team members as quite capable and believe that they will be receptive to the change.

_____ 2. Your main product has new competition in the industry. Your organization's revenues have been dropping. You have been told to lay off 3 of 10 employees in 2 weeks. You have been the supervisor for just over 1 year. All employees are very capable.

_____ **3.** Your department has been facing a problem for several months. Many solutions have been tried and have failed. You finally thought of a new possible solution, but you are not sure of its possible consequences or its acceptance by the highly capable employees.

_____ **4.** Flextime has become popular in your organization. Some departments let each employee start and end work whenever they choose. In your department, however, because of the need for cooperative effort, everyone has traditionally worked the same 8 hours. You are not sure of the level of interest in changing to flexible scheduling. Your employees are a very capable group and like to make decisions.

_____ **5.** The technology in your industry is changing faster than the members of your organization can keep up. Top management hired a consultant who has given a recommendation for change. You have 2 weeks to make your decision. Your employees are capable, and they enjoy participating in the decision-making process.

_____ **6.** Your boss called you on the telephone to tell you that someone has requested an order for your department's product with a very short delivery date. She asked that you call her back with the decision about taking the order in 15 minutes. Looking over the work schedule, you realize that it will be very difficult to deliver the order on time. Your employees will have to push hard to make it. They are cooperative, capable, and enjoy being involved in decision making.

_____ **7.** A change has been handed down from top management. How you implement it is your decision. The change takes effect in 1 month. It will personally affect everyone in your department. The acceptance of the department members is critical to the success of the change. In the past they have not shown much interest in being involved in making decisions.

_____ **8.** You believe that performance by your team could be improved. You have some improvement ideas, but you're not sure of them. Your team members are very experienced, and almost all have been in the department longer than you have.

_____ **9.** Top management has decided to make a change that will affect everyone on your team. You know that they will be upset because it will cause them hardship. One or two may even quit. The change goes into effect in 30 days. Your team members are very capable.

_____ **10.** A customer has offered you a profitable contract with a quick delivery date. The offer is open for 2 days. Meeting the contract deadline would require employees to work nights and weekends for 6 weeks. You cannot require them to work overtime. Filling this contract could help get you the raise you want and feel you deserve. However, if you take the contract and don't deliver on time, it will hurt your chances of getting a big raise. Your employees are very capable.

2. Form groups as assigned by your instructor. Share and compare your choices for each decision situation. Reconcile any differences, and be prepared to defend your decision preferences in general class discussion.

Class Exercise 11: Job Satisfaction Preferences

Preparation

Rank the following items from 1 = least important to 9 = most important to your future job satisfaction.[6]

My job will be satisfying when:

1. It is respected by other people.
2. It encourages continued development of knowledge and skills.
3. It provides job security.
4. It provides a feeling of accomplishment.
5. It provides the opportunity to earn a high income.
6. It is intellectually stimulating.
7. It rewards good performance with recognition.
8. It provides comfortable working conditions.
9. It permits advancement to high administrative responsibility.

Instructions

Form into groups as designated by your instructor. Within each group, members of each gender should develop a consensus ranking of the items as they think other genders would rank them. The reasons for the rankings should be shared and discussed so they are clear to everyone. Everyone should discuss possible gender differences in job satisfaction preferences and what their implications are for work teams. A spokesperson for each group should share the group's discussion points with the class.

Class Exercise 12: Why We Work

Preparation

Read this "ancient story."[7]

> In days of old, a wandering youth happened upon a group of men working in a quarry. Stopping by the first man, he said: "What are you doing?" The worker grimaced and groaned as he replied: "I am trying to shape this stone, and it is backbreaking work." Moving to the next man, the youth repeated the question. This man showed little emotion as he answered: "I am shaping a stone for a building." Moving to the third man, our traveler heard him singing as he worked. "What are you doing?" asked the youth. "I am helping to build a cathedral," the man proudly replied.

Instructions

In groups assigned by your instructor, discuss this short story. (1) Ask and answer the question: "What are the motivation and job design lessons of this ancient story?" (2) Have members of the group role-play each of the stonecutters as they are answering this additional question: "Why are you working?" Have someone in the group be prepared to report and share the group's responses with the class as a whole.

Class Exercise 13: Understanding Team Dynamics

Preparation

Think about your course work team, a team you are involved with in another campus activity, or any other team situation suggested by your instructor. Use this scale to indicate how often each of the following statements accurately reflects your experience in the group.[8]

     1 = always   2 = frequently   3 = sometimes   4 = never

1. My ideas get a fair hearing.
2. I am encouraged to offer innovative ideas and take risks.
3. Diverse opinions within the group are encouraged.
4. I have all the responsibility I want.
5. There is a lot of favoritism shown in the group.
6. Members trust one another to do their assigned work.
7. The group sets high standards of performance excellence.
8. People share and change jobs a lot in the group.
9. You can make mistakes and learn from them in this group.
10. This group has good operating rules.

Instructions

Form groups as assigned by your instructor. Ideally, this will be the group you have just rated. Have all group members share their ratings, and then make one master rating for the group as a whole. Circle the items for which there are the biggest differences of opinion. Discuss those items and try to find out why they exist. In general, the better a group scores on this instrument, the higher its creative potential. If everyone has rated the same group, make a list of the five most important things members can do to improve its operations in the future. Nominate a spokesperson to summarize the group discussion for the class as a whole.

Class Exercise 14: Difficult Conversations

Instructions

1. Identify from the list below the three conversations that you find most difficult and uncomfortable when part of a team.[9]
    (a) Telling a friend that she or he must stop coming late to team meetings
    (b) Pointing out to a team member that his or her poor performance is hurting the team

(c) Asking teammates to comment on your criticism of the consensus that seems to be emerging on a particular issue

(d) Telling a teammate who has problems working with others on the team that he or she has to do something about it

(e) Responding to a team member who has just criticized your performance

(f) Responding to a team member who has just criticized your attitude toward the team

(g) Responding to a team member who becomes emotional and defensive when you criticize his or her performance

(h) Having a teammate challenge you to justify your contributions to a discussion

2. Form three-person teams as assigned by your instructor. Identify the three conversations with which each person indicates the most discomfort.

3. Have each team member practice performing these conversations with another member, while the third member acts as an observer. Be direct, but try to hold the conversations in an appropriate way. Listen to feedback from the observer, and try the conversations again, perhaps practicing with different members of the group.

4. When finished, discuss the overall exercise, and be prepared to share highlights of the exercise with the rest of the class.

Class Exercise 15: Alligator River Story

Preparation

Read this story.[10]

> There lived a woman named Abigail who was in love with a man named Gregory. Gregory lived on the shore of a river. Abigail lived on the opposite shore of the same river. The river that separated the two lovers was teeming with dangerous alligators. Abigail wanted to cross the river to be with Gregory. Unfortunately, the bridge had been washed out by a heavy flood the previous week. So she went to ask Sinbad, a riverboat captain, to take her across. He said he would be glad to if she would consent to go to bed with him prior to the voyage. She promptly refused and went to a friend named Ivan to explain her plight. Ivan did not want to get involved at all in the situation. Abigail felt her only alternative was to accept Sinbad's terms. Sinbad fulfilled his promise to Abigail and delivered her into the arms of Gregory. When Abigail told Gregory about her amorous escapade in order to cross the river, Gregory cast her aside with disdain. Heartsick and rejected, Abigail turned to Slug with her tale of woe. Slug, feeling compassion for Abigail, sought out Gregory and beat him brutally. Abigail was overjoyed at the sight of Gregory getting his due. As the sun set on the horizon, people heard Abigail laughing at Gregory.

Instructions

1. After reading the story, rank the five characters in the story beginning with the one you consider the most offensive and ending with the one you consider the least objectionable. That is, the character who seems to be the most reprehensible to you should be entered first in the list, then the second most reprehensible, and so on, with the least reprehensible or objectionable being entered fifth. Of course, you will have your own reasons for why you rank them in the order that you do. Very briefly note these, too.

2. Form groups as assigned by your instructor (at least four persons per group with gender mixed). Each group should

   (a) Elect a spokesperson for the group

   (b) Compare how the group members have ranked the characters

   (c) Examine the reasons used by each of the members for their rankings

   (d) Seek consensus on a final group ranking

3. After completing the prior steps, discuss in the group the outcomes and reasons for agreement or disagreement on the rankings. Pay particular attention to any patterns that emerge.

4. Have a spokesperson be prepared to discuss the results of the exercise and the discussion within your group with the rest of the class.

Class Exercise 16: American Football

Instructions

Form into groups as assigned by the instructor and do the following:

1. Discuss American football—the rules, the way the game is played, the way players and coaches behave, and the roles of owners and fans.[11]

2. Use American football as a metaphor to explain the way U.S. corporations run and how they tend to behave in terms of strategies and goals.

3. Prepare a class presentation for a group of visiting Japanese business executives. In this presentation, use the metaphor of American football to (1) explain American business strategies and practices to the Japanese and (2) critique the potential strengths and weaknesses of the American business approach in terms of success in the global marketplace.

Class Exercise 17: Entrepreneur Role Models

Preparation

Michael Gerber, author and entrepreneur, says: "The entrepreneur in us sees opportunities everywhere we look, but many people see only problems everywhere they look."[12]

Instructions

1. Think about the people you know and deal with. Who among them is the best example of a successful entrepreneur? Write down their name and also a brief justification for your choice.

2. Think about your personal experiences, interests, and ideas that might be sources of personal entrepreneurship. Jot down a few notes that set forth some tentative plans for turning at least one into an actual accomplishment.

3. Form teams as assigned by the instructor. Within the team share both (a) your example of a successful entrepreneur and (b) your personal entrepreneurship plan.

4. Choose one as your team's "exemplar" entrepreneur to share with the class at large. Focus on the entrepreneur as a person, the entrepreneur's business or nonprofit venture, what factors account for success and/or failure in this case, and what the entrepreneur contributes to the local community.

5. Choose one of the entrepreneurship plans from among your teammates, and be prepared to share and explain it as well with the class at large.

Team Project 1: The Multigenerational Workforce

Question

What should Generation Xers, Millennials, and Generation Fs know about one another?

Instructions

1. Gather insights regarding the work and career preferences, values, and expectations of members of different generational subcultures—specifically, Generation Xers, Millennials, and Generation Fs.

2. Analyze the points of potential difference between Generation Xers and Millennials. What advice can you give to a Generation X team leader on how to best deal with a Millennial team member? What advice can you give the Millennial on how to best deal with a Generation Xer boss?

3. Analyze the points of potential difference between Millennials and Generation Fs. What advice can you give to a Millennial team leader on how to best deal with a Generation F team member or intern? What advice can you give the Generation F worker on how to best deal with a Millennial boss?

Team Project 2: Organizational Commitment to Sustainability

Instructions

In your assigned work teams do the following.

1. Reach agreement on a definition of "sustainability" that should fit the operations of any organization.

2. Brainstorm audit criteria that can be used to create a Commitment to Sustainability Scorecard (CSS) that can be used to assess the sustainability practices of an organization.

3. Formalize your list of criteria, and then create a formal CSS worksheet that can be used to conduct an actual audit. Be sure that an organization being audited would not only receive scores on individual dimensions or categories of sustainability performance but also receive a total overall "Sustainability Score" that can be compared with results for other organizations.

4. Present and defend your CSS to the class at large.

5. Use feedback received from the class presentation to revise your CSS to be used in an actual organizational sustainability audit.

6. Use your CSS to conduct a sustainability audit for a local organization.

Team Project 3: Crisis Management Realities

Question

What types of crises do business leaders face, and how do they deal with them?

Instructions

• Identify three crisis events from the recent local, national, and international business news.

• Read at least three different news reports on each crisis, trying to learn as much as possible about its specifics, how it was dealt with, what the results were, and the aftermath of the crisis.

• For each crisis, use a balance sheet approach to list sources or causes of the conflict and management responses to it. Analyze the lists to see if there are any differences based on the nature of the crisis faced in each situation. Also look for any patterns in the responses to them by the business executives.

• Score each crisis (from 1 = low to 5 = high) in terms of how successfully it was handled. Be sure to identify the criteria that you use to describe "success" in handling a crisis situation. Make a master list of "Done Rights" and "Done Wrongs" in crisis management.

• Summarize the results of your study into a report on "Realities of Crisis Management."

Team Project 4: Personal Career Planning

Instructions

1. Complete the following activities and bring the results to class. Your work should be in a written form suitable for grading.[1]

   Activity 1: Strengths and Weaknesses Inventory Different occupations require special talents, abilities, and skills. Each of us, you included, has a repertoire of existing strengths and weaknesses that are "raw materials" we presently offer a potential employer. Actions can (and should!) be taken over time to further develop current strengths and to turn weaknesses into strengths. Make a list identifying your most important strengths and weaknesses in relation to the career direction you are likely to pursue upon graduation. Place a * next to each item you consider most important to focus on for continued personal development.

Activity 2: Five-Year Career Objectives   Make a list of three career objectives that you hope to accomplish within 5 years of graduation. Be sure they are appropriate given your list of personal strengths and weaknesses.

Activity 3: Five-Year Career Action Plans   Write a specific action plan for accomplishing each of the five objectives. State exactly what you will do, and by when, in order to meet each objective. If you will need special support or assistance, identify what it is and state how you will obtain it. An outside observer should be able to read your action plan for each objective and end up feeling confident that he or she knows exactly what you are going to do and why.

2. In class, form into groups as assigned by the instructor. Share your career-planning analysis with the group and listen to those of others. Participate in a discussion that examines any common patterns and major differences among group members. Take advantage of any opportunities to gather feedback and advice from others. Have one group member be prepared to summarize the group discussion for the class as a whole.

Team Project 5: After Meeting/Project Review

Instructions

1. Complete the following assessment after participating in a meeting or a group project.[2]

   1. How satisfied are *you* with the outcome of the meeting project?

      Not at all satisfied   1 2 3 4 5 6 7   Totally satisfied

   2. How do you think *other members of the meeting/project group would rate you* in terms of your *influence* on what took place?

      No influence   1 2 3 4 5 6 7   Very high influence

   3. In your opinion, how *ethical* was any decision that was reached?

      Highly *unethical*   1 2 3 4 5 6 7   Highly ethical

   4. To what extent did you feel *"pushed into"* going along with the decision?

      Not pushed into it at all   1 2 3 4 5 6 7   Very pushed into it

   5. How *committed* are *you* to the agreements reached?

      Not at all committed   1 2 3 4 5 6 7   Highly committed

   6. Did you understand what was expected of you as a member of the meeting or project group?

      Not at all clear   1 2 3 4 5 6 7   Perfectly clear

   7. Were participants in the meeting/project group discussion listening to each other?

      Never   1 2 3 4 5 6 7   Always

   8. Were participants in the meeting/project group discussion honest and open in communicating with one another?

      Never   1 2 3 4 5 6 7   Always

   9. Was the meeting/project completed efficiently?

      Not at all   1 2 3 4 5 6 7   Very much

   10. Was the outcome of the meeting/project something that you felt proud to be a part of?

      Not at all   1 2 3 4 5 6 7   Very much

2. Make sure that everyone in your group completed this assessment for the same team project.

3. Each person in the group should then take the "mirror test." They should ask: (a) What are my thoughts about my team and my contributions to the team, now that the project is finished? (b) What could I do in future situations to end up with a "perfect" score after a meeting or after a project review?

4. Share results of both the assessment and mirror test with one another. Discuss their implications: (a) for the future success of the group on another project and (b) for the members as they go forward to work with other groups on other projects in the future.

5. Be prepared to share your team project results with the class as a whole.

Team Project 6: Contrasting Strategies

Starbucks is the dominant name among coffee kiosks—how does Dunkin' Donuts compete? Google has become the world's search engine of choice—can Bing ever catch up? Does it make a difference to you whether you shop for books at Amazon or Barnes & Noble, or buy gasoline from BP, Shell, or the local convenience store?

Question

How do organizations in the same industry fare when they pursue somewhat or very different strategies?

Instructions

1. Look up recent news reports and analyst summaries for each of the following organizations:
   - Coach and Kate Spade
   - Southwest Airlines and Delta Airlines
   - The *New York Times* and *USA Today*
   - UnderArmour and Lululemon
   - National Public Radio and Sirius Satellite Radio
   - Coca-Cola and PepsiCo

2. Use this information to write a short description of the strategies that each seems to be following in the quest for performance success.

3. Compare the strategies for each organizational pair, with the goal of identifying whether or not one organization has a strategic advantage in the industry.

4. Try to identify other pairs of organizations and do similar strategic comparisons for them.

5. Prepare a summary report highlighting (a) the strategy comparisons and (b) those organizations whose strategies seem best positioned for competitive advantage.

Team Project 7: Network "U"

Question

Is it time to reorganize your college or university as a network organization?

Instructions

Form into groups as assigned by the instructor and do the following:

1. Discuss the concept of the network organization structure as described in the textbook.

2. Create a network organization structure for your college or university. Identify the "core staffing" and what will be outsourced. Identify how outsourcing will be managed.

3. Draw a diagram depicting the various elements in your Network "U."

4. Identify why Network "U" will be able to meet two major goals: (a) create high levels of student learning and (b) operate with cost efficiency.

5. Present and justify your design for Network "U" to the class

Team Project 8: Organizational Culture Walk

Question

What organizational cultures do we encounter and deal with every day, and what are their implications for employees, customers, and organizational performance?

Instructions

1. In your team, make two lists. List A should identify the things that represent the core cultures of organizations. List B should identify the things that represent the observable cultures of organizations. For each item on the two lists, identify one or more indicators that you might use to describe this aspect of the culture for an actual organization.

2. Take an *organizational culture walk* through a major shopping area of your local community. Choose at least three business establishments. Visit each as customers. As you approach, put your "organizational culture senses" to work. Start gathering data on your Lists A and B. Keep gathering it while you are at the business and right through your departure. Take good notes, and gather your thoughts together after leaving. Do this for each of the three organizations you choose.

3. Analyze and compare your data to identify the major cultural attributes of the three organizations and how they influence customers and organizational performance.

4. Use your results to make some general observations and report on the relationship between organizational cultures and performance as well as among organizational cultures, employee motivation, and customer satisfaction.

Team Project 9: Future of Labor Unions

Question

What is the future for labor unions in America?

Instructions

1. Perform library research to identify trends in labor union membership in the United States.
2. Analyze the trends to identify where unions are gaining and losing strength; develop possible explanations.
3. Consider talking with members of labor unions in your community to gather their viewpoints.
4. Consider examining data on labor union trends in other countries.
5. Prepare a report that uses the results of your research to answer the project question.

Team Project 10: Leadership Believe-It-or-Not

Question

What stories do your friends, acquaintances, family members, and you tell about their bosses that are truly hard to believe?

Instructions

1. Listen to others and ask others to talk about the leaders they have had or presently do have. What strange-but-true stories are they telling?
2. Create a journal that can be shared with class members that summarizes, role-plays, or otherwise communicates the real-life experiences of people whose bosses sometimes behave in ways that are hard to believe.
3. For each of the situations in your report, try to explain the boss's behaviors.
4. Also for each of the situations, assume that you observed or heard about it as the boss's supervisor. Describe how you would "coach" or "counsel" the boss to turn the situation into a "learning moment" for positive leadership development.

Team Project 11: Difficult Personalities

Question

What personalities cause the most problems when people work together in teams, and what can be done to best deal with them?

Instructions

1. Do a survey of friends, family, co-workers, and even the public at large to get answers to these questions:
   - When you work in a team, what personalities do you have the most difficulty dealing with?
   - How do these personalities affect you, and how do they affect the team as a whole?
   - In your experience and for each of the "difficult personalities" that you have described, what have you found to be the best way of dealing with them?
   - How would you describe your personality, and are there any circumstances or situations in which you believe others could consider your personality "difficult" to deal with?
   - Do you engage in any self-management when it comes to your personality and how it fits when you are part of a team?
2. Gather the results of your survey, organize them for analysis, and then analyze them to see what patterns and insights your study has uncovered.
3. Prepare a report to share your study with the rest of your class.

Team Project 12: CEO Pay

Question

What is happening in the area of executive compensation, and what do you think about it?

Instructions

1. Check the latest reports on CEO pay. Get the facts and prepare a brief report as if you were writing a short, informative article for *Fortune* magazine. The title of your article should be "Status Report: Where We Stand Today on CEO Pay."

2. Address the equity issue: Are CEOs paid too much, especially relative to the pay of average workers?

3. Address the pay-for-performance issue: Do corporate CEOs get paid for performance or for something else? What do the researchers say? What do the business periodicals say? Find some examples to explain and defend your answers to these questions.

4. Address the social responsibility issue: Should CEOs accept pay that is many times the amounts that workers receive?

5. Take a position: Should a limit be set on CEO pay? If not, why not? If yes, what type of limit should be set? Who, if anyone, should set these limits—the government, company boards of directors, or someone else?

Team Project 13: Superstars on the Team

During a period of reflection following a down cycle for his teams, Sasho Cirovski, head coach of the University of Maryland's men's soccer team, came to a realization. "I was recruiting talent," he said. "I wasn't doing a very good job of recruiting leaders." With a change of strategy, his teams moved back to top-ranked national competition.

Question

What do you do with a "superstar" on your team?

Instructions

1. Everywhere you look—in entertainment, in sports, and in business—a lot of attention these days goes to the superstars. What is the record of teams and groups with superstars? Do they really outperform the rest?

2. What is the real impact of a superstar's presence on a team or in the workplace? What do they add? What do they cost? Consider the potential cost and benefits of having a superstar on a team. What is the bottom line in terms of net value added by having a superstar on the team?

3. Interview athletic coaches and players on your campus. Ask them the previous questions about superstars. Compare and contrast their answers.

4. Develop a set of guidelines for creating team effectiveness in a situation where a superstar is present. Be thorough and practical.

Team Project 14: How Words Count

Question

What words do people use in organizations that carry meanings that create unintended consequences for the speaker?

Instructions

1. Brainstorm with others to make a list of words that you have used or heard used by people and that cause other persons to react or respond negatively and even with anger toward the person speaking them.

2. For each word on the list, write its "positive" meaning and "negative" meaning.

3. Choose two or three of the words that seem especially significant. Write role-plays that display speakers using each word in the positive sense in conversations and in which the words are interpreted positively by the receivers.

4. For these same words, write role-plays that display speakers using each word conversationally with positive intentions but in which they are interpreted negatively by the receiver.

5. Explain the things that make a difference in how the same words are interpreted by receivers.

6. Draft a report that explains how people in organizations can avoid getting trapped unintentionally in problems caused by poor choice and/or use of words in their conversations.

Team Project 15: Job Satisfaction Around the World

Question

Does job satisfaction vary around the world, and does it reflect differences in national cultures?

Instructions

1. Gather together recent reports on job satisfaction among workers in the United States.

2. Gather similar data on workers in other countries—for example, Canada, the United Kingdom, Germany, Brazil, Mexico, Japan, India.

3. Compare the job satisfaction data across countries to answer the project question.

4.   Consider pursuing your results further by researching how the various countries compare on working conditions, labor laws, and related matters. Use this information to add context to your findings.

5.   Prepare a report to share your study with the rest of your class.

Team Project 16: Globalization Pros and Cons

Question

"Globalization" is frequently in the news. You can easily read or listen to both advocates and opponents. What is the bottom line? Is globalization good or bad, and for whom?

Instructions

1.   What does the term "globalization" mean? Review various definitions, and find the common ground.

2.   Read and study the scholarly arguments about globalization. Summarize what the scholars say about the forces and consequences of globalization in the past, present, and future.

3.   Examine current events relating to globalization. Summarize the issues and arguments. What is the positive side of globalization? What are the negatives that some might call its "dark" side?

4.   Consider globalization from the perspective of your local community or one of its major employers. From their perspectives, is globalization a threat or an opportunity, and why?

5.   Take a position on globalization. State what you believe to be the best course for government and business leaders to take. Justify your position.

Team Project 17: Community Entrepreneurs

Entrepreneurs are everywhere. Some might live next door, many own and operate the small businesses of your community, and you might even be one.

Question

Who are the entrepreneurs in your community, and what are they accomplishing?

Instructions

1.   Read the local news, talk to your friends and other locals, and think about where you shop. Make a list of the businesses and other organizations that have an entrepreneurial character. Be as complete as possible—look at both businesses and nonprofits.

2.   For each of the organizations, do further research to identify the persons who are the entrepreneurs responsible for them.

3.   Contact as many of the entrepreneurs as possible and interview them. Try to learn how they got started, why, what they encountered as obstacles or problems, and what they learned about entrepreneurship that could be passed along to others. Add to these questions a list of your own: What do you want to know about entrepreneurship?

4.   Analyze your results for class presentation and discussion. Look for patterns and differences in terms of entrepreneurs as persons, the entrepreneurial experience, and potential insights into business versus social entrepreneurship.

5.   Consider writing short cases that summarize the "founding stories" of the entrepreneurs you find especially interesting.

Skill Building Portfolio Notes

Self-Assessment Notes

[1]Some items included in *Outcome Measurement Project, Phase I and Phase II Reports* (St. Louis: American Assembly of Collegiate Schools of Business, 1986).

[2]Item list from James Weber, "Management Value Orientations: A Typology and Assessment," *International Journal of Value Based Management*, vol. 3, no. 2 (1990), pp. 37–54.

[3]Questions adapted from Barry Swartz, Andrew Ward, John Monterosso, Sonija Lyubomirsky, Katherine White, and Darrin R. Lehman, "Maximizing Versus Satisficing: Happiness Is a Matter of Choice," *Journal of Personality and Social Psychology*, Vol. 83, No. 5 (2006), pp. 1178–1197. Quote from Elizabeth Bernstein, "Decide to Be Happy," *Wall Street Journal* (October 7, 2014), pp. D1, D2.

[4]Suggested by a discussion in Robert Quinn, Sue R. Faerman, Michael P. Thompson, and Michael R. McGrath, *Becoming a Master Manager: A Contemporary Framework* (New York: Wiley, 1990), pp. 75–76.

[5]Julian P. Rotter, "External Control and Internal Control," *Psychology Today* (June, 1971), p. 42. Used by permission.

[6]Joseph A. Devito, *Messages: Building Interpersonal Communication Skills*, 3rd ed. (New York: HarperCollins, 1996), referencing William Haney, *Communicational Behavior: Text and Cases*, 3rd ed. (Homewood, IL: Irwin, 1973). Reprinted by permission.

[7]Questionnaire adapted from L. Steinmetz and R. Todd, *First Line Management*, 4th ed. (Homewood, IL: BPI/Irwin, 1986), pp. 64–67. Used by permission.

[8]Based on S. Budner, "Intolerance of Ambiguity as a Personality Variable," *Journal of Personality*, vol. 30, no. 1 (1962), pp. 29–50.

[9]Suggested by feedback questionnaire in Judith R. Gordon, *A Diagnostic Approach to Organizational Behavior*, 3rd ed. (Boston: Allyn & Bacon, 1991), p. 298.

[10]Fred E. Fiedler and Martin M. Chemers, *Improving Leadership Effectiveness: The Leader Match Concept*, 2nd ed. (New York: Wiley, 1984). Used by permission.

[11]Adapted from R. W. Bortner, "A Short Rating Scale as a Potential Measure of Type A Behavior, "*Journal of Chronic Diseases*, vol. 22 (1966), pp. 87–91. Used by permission.

[12]Developed from Lynda McDermott, Nolan Brawley, and William Waite, *World-Class Teams: Working Across Borders* (New York: Wiley, 1998).

[13]Douglas T. Hall, Donald D. Bowen, Roy J. Lewicki, and Francine S. Hall, *Experiences in Management and Organizational Behavior*, 2nd ed. (New York: Wiley, 1985). Used by permission.

[14]Developed from "Is Your Company Really Global?" *Businessweek* (December 1, 1997).

[15]Instrument adapted from Norman M. Scarborough and Thomas W. Zimmerer, *Effective Small Business Management*, 3rd ed. (Columbus: -Merrill, 1991), pp. 26–27.

Class Exercise Notes

[1]Adapted from John R. Schermerhorn Jr., James G. Hunt, and Richard N. Osborn, *Managing Organizational Behavior*, 3rd ed. (New York: Wiley, 1988), pp. 32–33. Used by permission.

[2]Adapted from "Lost at Sea: A Consensus-Seeking Task," in the 1975 *Handbook for Group Facilitators*.

[3]Suggested by an exercise in John F. Veiga and John N. Yanouzas, *The Dynamics of Organization Theory: Gaining a Macro Perspective* (St. Paul, MN: West, 1979), pp. 69–71.

[4]Developed from Eugene Owens, "Upward Appraisal: An Exercise in Subordinate's Critique of Superior's Performance," *Exchange: The Organizational Behavior Teaching Journal*, vol. 3 (1978), pp. 41–42.

[6]Adapted from Roy J. Lewicki, Donald D. Bowen, Douglas T. Hall, and Francine S. Hall, "What Do You Value in Work?" *Experiences in Management and Organizational Behavior*, 3rd ed. (New York: Wiley, 1988), pp. 23–26. Used by permission.

[7]Developed from Brian Dumaine, "Why Do We Work?" *Fortune* (December 26, 1994), pp. 196–204.

[8]Adapted from William Dyer, *Team Building*, 2nd ed. (Reading, MA: Addison-Wesley, 1987), pp. 123–25.

[9]Suggested by feedback questionnaire in Judith R. Gordon, *A Diagnostic Approach to Organizational Behavior*, 3rd ed. (Boston: Allyn & Bacon, 1991), p. 298.

[10]This exercise was suggested by the discussion in Martin J. Gannon, *Understanding Global Cultures*, 3rd ed. (Thousand Oaks, CA: Sage, 2004).

[11]Quote from woopidoo.com/businessquotes (retrieved September 16, 2006). See also Michael Gerber, *The E-Myth Revisited: Why Most Small Businesses Don't Work and What to Do About It* (New York: HarperCollins, 2001).

Team Project Notes

[1]Developed in part from Roy J. Lewicki, Donald D. Bowen, Douglas T. Hall, and Francine S. Hall, *Experiences in Management and Organizational Behavior*, 3rd ed. (New York: Wiley, 1988), pp. 261–67. Used by permission.

[2]Developed from Roy J. Lewicki, Donald D. Bowen, Douglas T. Hall, and Francine S. Hall, *Experiences in Management and Organizational Behavior*, 4th ed. (New York: Wiley, 1997), pp. 195–97.

Today's problems and opportunities—career and personal—are often complex and unstructured. It takes lots of wisdom and good analytic skills to master them. How about it: are you developing the critical thinking skills needed for future success?

CASES FOR CRITICAL THINKING

Ruaridh Stewart/Zuma Press

CASE 1: Trader Joe's—Managing Less to Gain More

In a space one-fourth the size of its competitors, the average Trader Joe's stocks approximately 4,500 products—a mere 10% of those typically found in a supermarket. Affectionately nicknamed "TJ's" by its loyal customers, the company stands for unique quality items.

Take a walk down any Trader Joe's aisle and you'll see the fundamentals of management at work—planning, organizing, leading, and controlling. It's one reason TJ's has become more than just the "average Joe" of food retailers.

Corner Store to Hundreds More

In 1958, Joe Coulombe, an MBA from Stanford Business School, started a "7-11 style" corner store in the Los Angeles area, which soon grew into a chain. While Coulombe was on vacation in the Caribbean, the Trader Joe South Seas motif resonated with him, particularly when he witnessed firsthand tourists proudly returning home from their travels with hard-to-find food delights. In 1967, he opened the first Trader Joe's store. Twelve years later, he sold the chain to the Albrecht family, billionaires and owners of discount supermarket chain Aldi's, based in Germany.

How did this retail grocer attract an obsessive and diverse cult of followers? Much has to do with its corporate culture, which includes everything from how the company meticulously plans store locations, manages employees, and crafts purchasing and branding strategies . . . and more.

Upside-Down Pyramid

Rather than being given orders, crew members—nonmanagerial employees—are coached. They are supported by "mates" who assist the "captain" or store manager. The store culture is customer-focused, yet laid back. Knowledgeable, friendly, and enthusiastic crew members make placement decisions solely on customer wants and needs. Shoppers are led by cheerful guides to culinary discoveries such as lime and chili cashews, salmon jerky, ginger almond and cashew granola, and baked jalapeño cheese crunchies.

People and Culture

Trader Joe's aggressively courts friendly, customer-oriented employees by highlighting desired soft skills—such as "ambitious and adventurous, enjoy smiling and have a strong sense of values"—as much as actual retail experience. Employees earn more than their counterparts at other chain grocers. Store managers, hired only from within the company, are well compensated. After all, they know the Trader Joe's culture and system inside and out. Future leaders enroll in training programs at Trader Joe's University.

Private-Label House Brands

Most Trader Joe's products are sold under a variant of their house brand—Italian food under the "Trader Giotto's" moniker, Mexican food under the "Trader Jose's" label, vitamins and health supplements under "Trader Darwin's," and Chinese food under the "Trader Ming's" label. The house brand success is no accident. According to now-retired Trader Joe's President Doug Rauch, the company pursued the strategy to "put our destiny in our own hands." You won't find mass-marketed brands at Trader Joe's, but this helps keep costs low and may also increase its appeal to customers as a source of unique products.

TJ's follows a deliciously simple approach to stocking stores. (1) Search out tasty, unusual foods across the globe; (2) contract directly with manufacturers; (3) label each product under one of several catchy house brands or private labels; and (4) maintain a small stock, making each product fight for its place on the shelf. Most of TJ's research and development dollars are spent on travel by its top buyers or "product developers." They go on "product finding missions" to bring back the most unique products at the best value. There's another level of buyers, called category leaders, who manage hordes of vendors and food suppliers eager to land their products on the shelves of Trader Joe's.

Economic Food Democracy

Ten to 15 new products debut each week at Trader Joe's—and the company maintains a strict "one in, one out" policy so as to not increase the total number of unique products it sells. Items that sell poorly or whose costs go up get the heave-ho in favor of new blood, something the company calls the "gangway factor." If the company hears that customers don't like a product, out it goes. Still, discontinued items may be brought back if customers are vocal enough, making Trader Joe's control function the model of an open crowd-sourcing system. "We feel really close to our customers," says Audrey Dumper, vice president of marketing for Trader Joe's East. "When we want to know what's on their minds, we don't need to put them in a sterile room with a swinging bulb. We like to think of Trader Joe's as an economic food democracy."

On to the Future

Shares of Trader Joe's stock are owned by the Albrecht family and not sold to the public. The company stays hyper private and media-shy. It's very guarded about revealing producers of their store brands, and suppliers operate under a Trader Joe's "cloak of secrecy." So, what does the future hold? Will growth threaten Trader Joe's coolness and appeal for employees and customers alike?

Cases for Critical Thinking

CASE ANALYSIS QUESTIONS

1. **DISCUSSION** Review the six "must-have" management skills in Table 1.1. How is each important to the management and culture of Trader Joe's? Are any of these skills more critical than others to implementing an "upside-down-pyramid" management approach?

2. **PROBLEM SOLVING** First-level "mates" and middle-level "captains" are the managers at a Trader Joe's. Suppose you were being hired in as a "mate" right from college. How could you make your efforts with planning, organizing, leading, and controlling fit well with the Trader Joe's culture?

3. **FURTHER RESEARCH** Study recent news reports to find additional information on Trader Joe's management and organization practices. Look for comparisons with its competitors, and try to identify whether Trader Joe's has the right management approach and business model for continued success. Are there any internal weaknesses, external competitors, or industry forces that might create future challenges?

KaiNedden/Iaif/Redux Pictures

CASE 2: Patagonia—Leading a Green Revolution

How has Patagonia managed to stay both green and profitable? Are Patagonia's business practices good for outdoor enthusiasts and good for the environment-sustainable?

Founder's Vision

These questions were on the minds of 1,200 Walmart buyers as they sat in rapt attention in the company's Bentonville, Arkansas, headquarters. They were listening to a small man in a mustard-yellow corduroy sport coat lecture them on the environmental impact of Walmart's purchasing choices. He—Patagonia's founder Yvon Chouinard—wasn't criticizing the company in the abstract, he was criticizing them and how they went about their jobs. But when he finished speaking, the buyers didn't complain and protest. Rather, they leapt to their feet and applauded enthusiastically.

Such is the authenticity of Yvon Chouinard. With his steadfast commitment to environmental sustainability, it's hard to discuss Patagonia without constantly referencing him; for all practical purposes, the two are one. Where Chouinard ends, Patagonia begins. He breathes life into the company while espousing the outdoorsy athleticism of Patagonia's customers. In turn, Patagonia's business practices reflect Chouinard's insistence on minimizing environmental impact, even at the expense of the bottom line.

Hiking the High Road

Patagonia's niche is high-quality, performance-oriented outdoor clothes and gear sold at top price points. Its clothes are designed for fly fishing, rock climbing, surfing, skiing, and more. They are durable, comfortable, and sustainably produced. And they are not cheap. Derided as *Pradagonia* or *Patagucci* by critics, the brand is aligned with top-shelf labels like North Face and Royal Robbins.

It's a good business. "They've become the Rolls-Royce of their product category," says Marshal Cohen, chief industry analyst with market research firm NPD Group. "When people were stepping back, and the industry became copycat, Chouinard didn't sell out, lower prices, and dilute the brand. Sometimes, the less you do, the more provocative and true of a leader you are." Patagonia succeeds by staying true to Chouinard's vision. "Corporations are real weenies," he says. "They are scared to death of everything. My company exists, basically, to take those risks and prove that it's a good business."

Ideal Corporate Behavior

Chouinard is not shy about espousing the environmentalist ideals intertwined with Patagonia's business model. "It's good business to make a great product, and do it with the least amount of damage to the planet," he says. "If Patagonia wasn't profitable or successful, we'd be an environmental organization."

The company publishes online a library of working documents, *The Footprint Chronicles*, that guide employees in making sustainable decisions in even the most mundane office scenarios. Its mission statement reads: "Build the best product, cause no unnecessary harm, use business to inspire and implement solutions to the environmental crisis." Patagonia has long contributed 10% of pre-tax profits or 1% of sales—whichever is greater—to environmental groups each year. Whatever you do, don't call it a handout. "It's not a charity," Chouinard flatly states. "It's a cost of doing business. We use it to support civil democracy." And, employees can leave their jobs for up to two months to volunteer full-time for the environmental cause of their choice, while continuing to receive full pay and benefits from Patagonia.

Green Growing Pains

Patagonia grew from small start-up into a booming manufacturer of outdoor clothing. Along the way they achieved success with products woven with synthetic threads, although the majority of their items were still spun with natural fibers like cotton and wool. So, management commissioned an external audit of the environmental impact of their four major fibers. Bad news about Patagonia's use of petroleum-derived nylon and polyester was expected, but bad news about cotton was not. It turned out that the production of cotton had a more negative impact on the environment than any of their other fibers-destructive soil and water pollution, unproven but apparent health consequences for field workers, and the astounding statistic that 25% of all toxic pesticides used in agriculture are spent in the cultivation of cotton.

To Chouinard and Patagonia, the appropriate response was clear: Source organic fibers for all 66 of their cotton clothing products. Company representatives went directly to organic cotton farmers, ginners, and spinners, seeking pledges from them to increase production, dust off dormant processing equipment, and do whatever it would take to line up enough raw materials to fulfill the company's promise to its customers and the environment. Not surprisingly, Patagonia met its goal, and every cotton garment made since has been spun from organic cotton.

Sustaining Momentum

Chouinard can't lead Patagonia forever. But that's not to say he isn't continuing to find better ways for Patagonia to do business. "I think entrepreneurs are like juvenile delinquents who say, 'This sucks. I'll do it my own way,'" he says. "I'm an innovator because I see things and think I can make it better. So I try it. That's what entrepreneurs do."

"Right now, we're trying to convince zipper companies to make teeth out of polyester or nylon synths, which can be recycled infinitely," he says. "Then we can take a jacket and melt the whole thing down back to its original polymer to make more jackets."

Despite his boundless enthusiasm for all things green, Chouinard admits that no process is truly sustainable. "I avoid using that word as much as I can," he says. He pauses for a moment and adds: "I keep at it, because it's the right thing to do."

CASE ANALYSIS QUESTIONS

1. DISCUSSION Patagonia has a history of putting sustainability ahead of profits. But it also has to face up to everyday business realities and the need for operating capital. How do you think the company decides which products to offer so that the outcomes will be both business practical and environmentally friendly? And, with Chouinard such an important influence on company ideals and values, what can be done now to ensure that his positive impact is still felt long after he leaves the company?

2. PROBLEM SOLVING Let's suppose Yvon Chouinard comes to you, a new employee, and asks for a proposal on a timely and "forward looking" sustainability agenda for the firm. In other words, he wants a program that can drive Patagonia's future and not just celebrate its past. What would you include in this agenda and why?

3. FURTHER RESEARCH Could ethics lose out to greed even in a company with the idealism of Patagonia? See if you can find examples of decisions that forced people in the firm to make difficult choices between ethics and profitability. Look for examples of decisions made at other companies that may have resulted in different ethics versus profitability choices. Try to explain through the examples what makes the difference

between organizations where ethics and social responsibility are part of core values and those where they are more superficial issues.

© J. Emilio Flores/Corbis

CASE 3: Amazon.com—Keeping the Fire Hot

Amazon.com has gained the No. 1 spot as the world's largest Internet retailer. But never content to rest on past laurels, CEO Jeff Bezos keeps introducing and upgrading Amazon products and services.

It's hard to keep pace with new versions of the Amazon Kindle Fire, Prime Instant Video TV, and movie content streamed on demand. There's a variety of cloud computer services. And, Bezos keeps upping investments in new distribution centers staffed increasingly by robots. It's all part of a push to make Amazon the go-to choice for fast—even same-day—deliveries of as many of the products we consume as possible.

Decision Making and Innovation

From its modest beginning in Jeff Bezos's garage in 1995, Amazon.com has grown into the most megalithic online retailer. Bezos continues to diversify Amazon's product offerings and broaden its brand. Beyond simply finding more and more products and services to offer, he knows that he has to innovate in order to prevent his brand from becoming stagnant. No one is ever sure what will come next under Bezos's guidance. His guiding question is: "What kind of innovation can we layer on top of that that will be meaningful for our customers?"

Amazon's Kindle almost single handedly launched the e-book revolution. Amazon Prime was another master stroke. Prime members get free two-day shipping and discounted one-day shipping as well as access to Amazon Instant Video, movie, TV and music streaming, and free content. It's all designed to keep customers plugged into Amazon. And, Bezos calls Amazon Prime "the best bargain in the history of shopping, and it's going to keep getting better."

There's no shortage of competition. Amazon has squared off against Netflix, Apple, and Google in realms of both hardware and digital entertainment. It bought top-shelf audio book vendor Audible.com and later added shoe and clothing merchant Zappos.

com. Then came acquisition of Boston-based Kiva Systems. Kiva's automated guided robots deliver product to workers at pick stations, allowing Amazon increased efficiency (and reduced labor costs) in its worldwide distribution centers.

Bezos as a Decision Maker

Rather than sticking to just the analytical step-by-step process, Bezos isn't afraid of informed intuition. He uses creativity, flexibility, and spontaneity when making key decisions. He seems comfortable with abstraction and lack of structure when making decisions and also isn't afraid to fail.

Seeming not to worry about current earnings per share, Bezos keeps investing to make his company stronger and harder to catch. Its millions of square feet of distribution fulfillment space keep growing domestically and around the globe. The firm's products and services are continuously upgraded and expanded. Drones are ready to fly Amazon deliveries to customers. But will these investments pay off? Is Bezos making the right long-term choices?

Even as Amazon's stock values fluctuate, Bezos still believes that customer service, not the stock ticker, defines the Amazon experience. "I think one of the things people don't understand is we can build more shareholder value by lowering product prices than we can by trying to raise margins," he says. "It's a more patient approach, but we think it leads to a stronger, healthier company. It also serves customers much, much better."

What's Next?

Amazon.com has quickly—not quietly—grown from a home operation into a global e-commerce giant. By forging alliances to ensure that he has what customers want and making astute purchases, Jeff Bezos has made Amazon the go-to brand for online shopping. After its significant investments in new media, services, and distribution, does the company risk losing its original appeal? Will customers continue to flock to Amazon, making it the go-to company for their each and every need?

CASE ANALYSIS QUESTIONS

1. DISCUSSION Bezos once said: "Amazon may break even or even lose money on the sale of its devices." The company expects to recoup the money later through the sale of products, with a further boost from its annual Prime membership fee. In what ways does this strategy show Bezos as a systematic and intuitive thinker?

2. PROBLEM SOLVING It seems like everyone is streaming these days and there are a growing number of providers. Amazon is a player in the digital entertainment market, but as yet they haven't taken a clear lead. Given the strengths of the company, what decisions should be made to ensure that Amazon jumps ahead and becomes the "No. 1" source for digital content streams—with no doubt about it?

3. FURTHER RESEARCH What are the latest initiatives coming out of Amazon? How do they stack up in relation to actual or potential competition? How have the Kiva and Zappos acquisitions worked out? Who are the major competitors of the moment? What about the Chinese e-commerce giant Alibaba? Is it starting to hurt Amazon? Is Bezos making the right decisions as he guides the firm through today's many business and management challenges?

Raymond Boyd/Getty Images

CASE 4: Nordstrom—"High Touch" with "High Tech"

How does Nordstrom stay profitable despite dips in consumer spending, changing fashion trends, and intense competition among retailers? One answer: Acute attention to detail and well-laid plans.

All in the Family

The fourth generation of family members that runs Nordstrom has brought the store's time-honored and successful retail practices into a new era. "Nordstrom, it seems, is that rarity in American business: an enterprise run by a founding family that hasn't wrecked it," says one business writer. The company provides a quality customer experience via personalized service, a compelling merchandise offering, a pleasant shopping environment, and ever better management of its inventory.

Secret of Success

The secret of this company's success lies in its strategic planning efforts and the ability of its management team to set broad, comprehensive, and longer-term action directions, all of which are focused on the customer experience. The current generation of Nordstrom family members was quick to spearhead an ultramodern multi-million-dollar Web-based inventory management system. This upgrade helped the company meet two key goals: (1) correlate purchasing with demand to keep inventory as lean as possible, and (2) give customers and sales associates a comprehensive view of Nordstrom's entire inventory, including every store and warehouse.

Demand Planning

Instead of relying on one-day sales, coupon blitzes, or marking down entire lines of product, Nordstrom discounts only certain items. "Markdown optimization" software assists in planning more profitable sale prices. According to retail analyst, Patricia Edwards, this helps Nordstrom calculate what will sell better at different discounts and forecast which single items should be marked down. If a style is no longer in demand, the company can ship it off to its Nordstrom Rack outlet stores. It's all part of Nordstrom's long-term investment in efficiency. "If we can identify what is not performing and move it out to bring in fresh merchandise," says Pete Nordstrom, "that's a decision we want to make."

Inventory Planning

Although inventory naturally fluctuates, Nordstrom associates can easily locate any item in another store or verify when it will return to stock. Customers on their smart phones and associates behind sales counters see the same thing—the entire inventory of Nordstrom's stores is presented as one selection, which the company refers to as perpetual inventory. "Customer service is not just a friendly, helpful, knowledgeable salesperson helping you buy something," says Robert Spector, retail expert and author of *The Nordstrom Way*. "Part of customer service is having the right item at the right size at the right price at the right time. And that's something perpetual inventory will help with."

The upgraded inventory management system was an immediate hit. As of launch day, Nordstrom found that the percentage of customers who purchased products after searching the Web site for an item doubled. It also learned that multi-channel customers—those who shop from Nordstrom in more than one way—spend on average four times more than one-source customers. This profit more than offsets the cost of hiring additional shipping employees to wrap and mail items from each store. Now Nordstrom doesn't have to turn away the customer who spied a red Marc Jacobs handbag but found it out of stock in her local store. She can buy it online or at the store counter and it will be shipped to her, even from a store located across the country.

Keeping It Lean

By displaying stock both on its Web warehouse and in its stores, Nordstrom has realized some very meaningful sales and customer service results. Items don't stay in stock very long. The chain turns inventory about twice as fast as its competitors, thanks to strong help from Web sales.

Fast-turning inventories are a sign a retailer is well managed, making it more attractive to investors. "The old, classic Nordstrom way is that if you sell more stuff, that compensates for any deficiency you may have in terms of technology," says Robert Spector. "They didn't want to replace the high touch with the high-tech," and they faced striking "that balance between having up-to-date systems and giving that personal service." "Traditional retailers have traditional ways of doing things," echoes Adrianne Shapira, Goldman Sachs retail analyst, "and sometimes those barriers are hard to break down." But Nordstrom's commitments to planning are paying dividends.

CASE ANALYSIS QUESTIONS

1. DISCUSSION What specific planning objectives and measures could Nordstrom use to assess the success of its Web-based inventory integration?

2. PROBLEM SOLVING How might Nordstrom make use of participatory planning for continuous improvements in areas such asproduct purchasing, floor displays, and sales associates' job satisfaction?

3. FURTHER RESEARCH Nordstrom wants to grow in a number of different areas. Research one of its strategies and project it into the future. What changes, revisions, or updates would you plan for the company? What stretch goals come to mind?

TJP/Alamy

CASE 5: Chipotle—Control Keeps Everything Fresh

Since its humble beginnings in Denver, Colorado, Chipotle has implemented the control process with fervor. Whether reviewing sales to cost ratios, same-store sales figures to gauge growth, payment initiatives to speed checkout during peak lunch hours, or tracking stock performance, management control is deeply entrenched in the firm's culture of performance.

The First Burrito

In 1993, Steve Ells, trained in classical French cooking, opened his first Chipotle in Denver, Colorado. He wasn't your average chain-restaurant mogul. After spending time in San Francisco working for famous Chef Jeremiah Tower at the once-famous Stars Restaurant, Ells saw the need for a similar format using high-quality ingredients and classic cooking methods he had learned in culinary school.

With a loan of $85,000 from his father and inspiration from the vast number of taquerias found in San Francisco's Mission district, Ells took over an old Dolly Madison ice cream store near the University of Denver campus. He calculated his first store needed to sell 107 burritos per day to break even. After 1 month, sales of 1,000 burritos a day far exceeded his projections and his wildest dreams. Chipotle was an instant success, and Ells knew he was onto something big.

Culture Clash with McDonald's

After getting 16 stores up and running in Colorado, Ells thought it timely to bring the McDonald's burger empire on board as a minority owner and help fuel his company's growth toward being a national brand. The strategy was for Chipotle to leverage the buying power and supplier networks enjoyed by the burger empire's economies of scale.

During critical growth years, McDonald's invested over $360 million into Chipotle and at one time owned more than 80% of the company. With McDonald's as their partner, Chipotle's store locations skyrocketed. But, the two companies eventually parted ways.

Thinking back on the union, Ells laments that the two cultures could not have been more different. "We just didn't see eye to eye," he said. McDonald's wanted Chipotle to follow its growth model using franchising. Ells wanted to grow the firm through internal expansion and without the use of other people's money as franchise owners. "We wanted to own the economic model. You franchise if you want money and people. We had plenty of money for our growth rate, and we had great people," he said. Chipotle went public in an initial public offering (IPO) to settle the McDonald's breakup.

"Fast-Casual" with a Difference

Chipotle is "fast-casual," a fusion of a fast-food and fine dining restaurant. More and more customers have come to expect higher food quality and service that is more in line with casual dining over that of a fast-food experience. Chipotle is also known for its "less is more" philosophy when it comes to its limited number of menu items, which include burritos, burrito bowls (a burrito without the tortilla), tacos, and salads. Another hallmark is its generous-size burritos and all high-quality, natural, fresh, sustainable ingredients.

At some of its most efficient restaurants, Chipotle averages more than 350 transactions during the lunch hour alone, or on average, one transaction about every 11 seconds. Executives pay close attention to its customers getting through the line quickly, which results in greater sales revenues and a higher-quality customer experience. But discouragingly long lunch and dinner lines still cause problems. "We've come a long way, but there is still a long line, and there are people turning away at the end," says a Chipotle operations executive.

Sustainable Sourcing

Chipotle's vision and mission statement reads: "to change the way people think about and eat fast food." A threefold value philosophy, called "Food with Integrity," includes "finding and sourcing the very best ingredients raised with respect for the animals, the environment and the farmers."

Whenever possible, the company uses meat from animals raised without the use of added hormones or antibiotics and dairy from cows raised without the use of synthetic hormones or recombinant bovine growth hormone (rBGH). As an advocate of animal rights, Steve Ells has tirelessly committed himself to change the way pork is raised in the United States. He learned of the horrific conditions to which pigs were subjected in factory farm settings, and that approximately 99% of the pork consumed in the United States was produced in "confined animal feeding operations."

As a big enough buyer of pork, Ells knew he was in a position to create change, saying: "I knew at that moment I did not want my success to be based on this kind of exploitation, so we started buying all naturally raised meat." His initial curiosity about the meat supply was actually prompted by the fact that he was unimpressed with the quality. By switching sources, he wound up with a product produced by humane animal treatment and tasting better to customers. Despite a price increase, Ells happily reports: "We started selling twice as many carnitas as before."

Fickle Industry

Chipotle is a company that commits itself to constantly seeking new ways to improve performance. But its high stock price and the increasingly competitive nature of the fast casual food industry raise some questions about future growth. Should Chipotle's record of sound management control be enough to quiet the naysayers?

CASE ANALYSIS QUESTIONS

1. DISCUSSION How did CEO Steve Ells use the control process to move Chipotle forward with success? Explain your answer using at least three examples based on the case.

2. PROBLEM SOLVING A balanced scorecard helps top managers exercise strategic control. The scorecard includes customer satisfaction and internal process improvement. What do you recommend that Chipotle do to implement the scorecard approach and consistently score high in each of these categories?

3. FURTHER RESEARCH Go online to find and analyze Chipotle's most recent annual report. Check and critique the company's recent financial performance. Review reports from competitors—e.g., Rubio, Baja Fresh, Qdoba, or Moe's Southwest Grill. How are they doing, and what threats, if any, do they pose to Chipotle? How about product extensions? Could the Chipotle model be copied with Indian or Caribbean food, for example?

JESSICA RINALDI/REUTERS/Newscom

CASE 6: Dunkin' Donuts—Growth Feeds a Sweet Tooth

This java giant is opening hundreds of stores and entering new markets appealing to a new generation of customers. But, can Dunkin' Donuts stay on course with its rapid growth?

Donuts with Passports

Dunkin' Donut's present global travels are a long step from its first coffee shops opened in the Boston, Massachusetts, area in 1950. Now it's an international brand with a reputation for quality that has earned the trust of many loyal customers. Company executives are hoping that careful strategic planning will keep consumers worldwide "Runnin' on Dunkin'."

Part of Dunkin' Donuts' strategic plan of action includes focusing on the sale of its core products—coffee and donuts. With 500 billion cups consumed every year, coffee is the most popular global beverage, and estimates are that Americans drink 400 million cups a day. Dunkin' Donuts serves close to 3 million of them. That equates to about 30 cups per second—and 65% of the company's annual store revenue.

Target on Emerging Markets

Most Americans have had an encounter with the Dunkin' Donuts brand through its almost 11,000 outlets. The Dunkin's brand has managed to carve out an international niche, not only in expected markets such as Canada and Brazil, but also in some unexpected ones like India, Brazil, Qatar, South Korea, Pakistan, and the Philippines.

The company is betting big on emerging economies. "Emerging markets are attractive because they are growing very quickly, they've a fast-growing middle-class [eating out more], and they love American brands," says CEO, Nigel Travis. The company's growth plans include opening between 80 and 100 outlets in India—with 500 stores there within 15 years. "The company plans to locate in Asia a 'disproportionate' number of the 350–450 outlets that it plans to open outside the U.S. this year," Travis said.

New Products

For most of its existence, Dunkin' Donuts' main product focus has been expressed by its name: donuts and coffee in which to dunk them. Since Stan Frankenthaler became executive chef and vice president, Dunkin' has launched about 25 new products annually as a new product innovation initiative. It has stepped up to competition by offering a variety of espresso-based drinks complemented with a broad number of sugar-free flavorings, including caramel, vanilla, and mocha swirl.

Its strategy now includes breakfast sandwich combinations of eggs, cheese, ham, and sausage on Texas toast, as well as English muffins, croissants, bagel sandwiches, and burritos. If plans prove successful, more customers than ever may flock to the shops. However, it may take a while to convince them that Dunkin' Donuts is the place to go to for a big breakfast.

Customer Appeal

Sometimes called the "anti-Starbucks," Dunkin' Donuts has a rich history of offering simple and straightforward morning snacks—earnest and without pretense—to the everyday working class. The company appeals to modest, cost-conscious customers.

Selective Partnerships

Dunkin' Donuts is banking on strategic partnerships to help fuel growth. But "selectivity" rules the partnership decisions. Although it often partners with grocery retailers to create a store-within-a-store concept, the company is very choosy about where it sets up shop.

"We want to be situated in supermarkets that provide a superior overall customer experience," says a Dunkin business developer. "Of course, we also want to ensure that the supermarket is large enough to allow us to provide the full expression of our brand . . . which includes hot and iced coffee, our line of high-quality espresso beverages, donuts, bagels, muffins, and even our breakfast sandwiches." Furthermore, the outlet's location within the supermarket is critical for a successful relationship. "We want to be accessible and visible to customers, because we feel that gives us the best chance to increase incremental traffic and help the supermarket to enhance their overall performance."

Finding the Sweet Spot

If Dunkin' Donuts can find the "sweet spot" by being within most consumers' reach without creating the feel of a mass-retail-like omnipresence, the company's growth strategy may prove fruitful. But this strategy has risks. Offering too many original products in too many locations could dilute the essential brand appeal and alienate longtime customers who respect its history of simplicity. Potential new customers and a younger demographic might view Dunkin' Donuts as an uncool "yesterday's brand." Then too, some older franchises seem long overdue for a makeover, especially when compared to the trendy Italian feel of a nearby Starbucks café. Will Dunkin' Donuts strike the right balance of products and placement needed to outserve its fierce competition?

CASE ANALYSIS QUESTIONS

1. DISCUSSION What does a Porter's Five Forces analysis suggest about the attractiveness of competing in same industry with Starbuck's? What are the strategic implications for Dunkin' Donuts?

2. PROBLEM SOLVING Complete an up-to-date SWOT analysis for Dunkin' Donuts. If you were the CEO of the firm, what would you consider to be the strategic management implications of this SWOT analysis, and why?

3. FURTHER RESEARCH Research the latest moves by Starbucks and other Dunkin' Donuts' competitors. What is each doing that seems similar to and different from the approach of the other? Can you say that Dunkin' is on the right track? Is it carving out new market share? Or, is it going to be more of a copycat player in the industry?

© Richard Clement/Reuters/Corbis

CASE 7: Nike: Spreading Out to Win the Race

Nike is indisputably a giant in the athletics industry. The Portland, Oregon, company is known worldwide for its products, none of which it actually makes. It has thrived by knowing how to stay small, focusing on core competencies, and outsourcing manufacturing.

But if you don't make anything, what do you actually do? If you outsource everything, what's left? A lot of brand recognition, as it turns out.

Behind the Swoosh

Nike continues to outpace the athletic shoe competition while spreading its brand through an ever-widening universe of sports equipment, apparel, and paraphernalia. The ever-present Swoosh graces everything from bumper stickers to sunglasses to high school sports uniforms. Nike products embody a love of sport, discipline, ambition, practice, and all other desirable traits of athleticism.

The company has cleverly kept its advertising agency nestled close to home, but has relied extensively on outsourcing many non-executive and back office responsibilities to reduce overhead. Nike is structured around its core competency in product design—not manufacturing. It has taken outsourcing to a new level, with sub-contractors producing all of its shoes.

Whoops

Although outsourcing production hasn't hurt product quality, it has challenged Nike's reputation for social responsibility, especially regarding work conditions and labor practices at some suppliers. In a move designed to turn critics into converts, Nike posts information on its Web site detailing every one of the hundreds of factories that it uses to make shoes, apparel, and other sporting goods. It released the data in conjunction with a comprehensive corporate responsibility report summarizing the environmental impact and the labor situations of its contract factories.

Nike also encourages designers to develop environmentally sustainable designs like the Nike Free, a lightweight running shoe that boosted sales dramatically. And Nike's Sustainable Business & Innovation Lab funds outside startups focused on alternative energies, more efficient approaches to manufacturing, and the promotion of healthy lifestyles.

Pesky Competition

Pressure is mounting from outside Nike's Beaverton, Oregon, headquarters. German rival Adidas drew a few strides closer to Nike when it purchased Reebok. The new supergroup of shoes isn't far off from Nike's market size. But when faced with such challenges, Nike simply knocks its bat against its cleats and steps up to the plate. Says Nike spokesman Alan Marks: "Of course we're in a competitive business, but we win by staying focused on our strategies and our consumers. And from that perspective nothing has changed."

Putting It Together

Nike has so far balanced size and pressure to remain successful by leveraging a decentralized and networked organization structure. Individual business centers—such as research, production, and marketing—are free to focus on their core competencies without worrying about the effects of corporate bloat.

This company has found continued marketplace success by positioning itself not simply as a sneaker company but as a brand that fulfills the evolving needs of today's athletes and athletes-at-heart. Will Nike continue to profit from its organization structure, or will it spread itself so thin that its competition has a chance to overtake it?

CASE ANALYSIS QUESTIONS

1. DISCUSSION What factors drive Nike's decision to stick with some form of network organizational structure rather than own its manufacturing operations?

2. PROBLEM SOLVING Draw a diagram that shows what you believe Nike's present organizational structure looks like. Be sure to include all possible components. Next look at the diagram as an organization design consultant. Ask: How can this structure be improved? How can Nike gain even more operating efficiency without losing its performance edge in terms of continually coming up with innovative, high-quality, top-design shoes?

3. FURTHER RESEARCH What is the current state of competition in this industry? Is Nike continuing to pull away from rivals, or are they catching up? Are new, sleek, and faster rivals starting to get into the picture? What moves has Nike made in regard to how it handles the vast amount of subcontracting used in its supply chain? Does it still have problems keeping control of this supply chain? Is Nike's organizational structure still a major strength that contributes to its success, or is it creating problems that will call for organizational design changes in the future?

Ann Hermes/The Christian Science Monitor/Getty Images

CASE 8: Gamification—Games Join the Corporate Culture

Would you be surprised if you approached a co-worker only to realize that he was playing a video game, and the boss didn't care? It is getting more common to see people playing games at work and being praised—not criticized—for doing it. Companies are increasingly using "gamification" to increase productivity, creativity, and satisfaction.

Games Hit the Bottom Line

Games are being seen as a way to promote a culture of learning, individualism, and fun, while also focusing attention on the company's bottom-line performance goals. Jesse Schell, CEO of Schell Games, says: "We are shifting into an enjoyment-based economy. And who knows more about making enjoyment than game developers?"

The commercial contexts for gamification range from customer engagement to employee performance to training, to innovation management, to personal development, to sustainability. Game-specific problem solving can enhance critical thinking and analytical abilities, as well as develop desirable personal attributes such as persistence, creativity, and resilience. An IBM executive says the firm's use of gaming for employees that spend lots of time working from home or traveling is a "way to help colleagues connect and stay engaged."

Playing by the Rules

Experts claim that gaming is a great motivator that can increase employees' enthusiasm for their daily activities and the energy they bring to work. But, there's also fear that gaming can breed unhealthy competition and hurt relationships within organizations.

For sure, gamification has to be well integrated with business needs and objectives. "To achieve success for companies starting in gamification," says industry analyst Brian Burke, "the first design point is to motivate players to achieve their goals—and those goals should overlap with the business goals." Kris Duggan, chief executive of game-maker Badgeville, cautions: "Adding gamification to the workplace drives performance but it doesn't make up for bad management."

CASE ANALYSIS QUESTIONS

1. DISCUSSION What arguments can you make that support making gamification part of an organization's culture? What are the arguments against it? What logic or examples can you offer in support of your arguments?

2. PROBLEM SOLVING Consider yourself the go-to "idea person" for friends who head two local organizations—a fire department and a public library. Both complain about morale problems and ask you for advice on creating a positive organizational culture. They want to know how your interest in gaming can be used to improve staff morale and performance. What will you suggest and why?

3. FURTHER RESEARCH Review how organizations, including major corporations, nonprofits, and the military, are using gaming. What role is gaming taking on in these settings, and how does its use affect the organizational cultures? What does the evidence suggest—is gamification merely a passing trend, or is it here to stay and may even grow in use in the future?

Andreas Gebert/DPA/Zuma Press

CASE 9: Two-Tier Wages—Same Job, Different Pay

When domestic auto manufacturers were hit hard by recession and foreign competition, they struggled to control costs and maintain profitability. One response was a two-tier wage system that pays new workers significantly less than existing ones doing the same job. What is the future for such two-tier wage systems?

A New Labor Contract

In Ford, General Motors, and Chrysler manufacturing plants across the United States, newly hired workers are earning an hourly wage that may be half that of their more experienced co-workers who perform identical tasks, roughly $19 versus $28 per hour. Their benefits—health insurance, paid time off, and retirement funding—are also less than those received by experienced workers. These differences are the result of *two-tier contracts* in which labor unions permit corporations to hire new workers with wage and benefit packages below those earned by veteran employees in the same jobs.

At first the two-tier contracts were viewed as stop-gap measures, likely to disappear once the economy picked up again. Now they appear to be here to stay, and it's easy to see why. The auto firms had long paid unionized workers a comfortable salary and a healthy pension. But as labor and pension costs rose, the Big Three needed to restructure labor costs to match wages offered by foreign manufacturers with American plants. The United Auto Workers (UAW) negotiators conceded to two-tier contracts in order to prevent layoffs and protect the union's presence in the auto plants.

Here to Stay?

"This is not going away," said Kristin Dziczek, a labor analyst at Ann Arbor's Center for Automotive Research. "It has allowed the Big Three to reduce labor costs without cutting the pay of incumbent workers. Is it good for the health and competitiveness of the companies? Yes. And is that good for job security? Yes."

"If you know you're going to get to the top wage eventually, the [two-tier] system can work," says Peter Cappelli, a professor at the University of Pennsylvania's Wharton School. "The big problem is when you think you'll never get there." Although lower tier workers can move up to the higher one, there's a lot of uncertainty about how long it takes. The United Auto Workers union wants to shorten and clarify the time to jump tiers and close the pay gap between them.

Mixed Reactions

Labor's reaction to the two-tier wages has been mixed. Although no one relishes the thought of earning 50% as much as the worker across the aisle, "Everybody is appreciative of a job and glad to be working," said Derrick Chatman, a new hire at Chrysler's Jefferson North plant. Before joining Chrysler for $14.65 per hour, he was laid off from Home Depot, worked the odd construction job, and collected unemployment. Gary Wurtz, a line worker at GM's Orion Township, MI, plant, where 40% of his fellow workers receive lower-tier wages, said: "In order to get those guys up, we'll take a signing bonus or profit sharing instead."

That said, two-tier plans still have the potential to divide workers across salary lines. Gary Chaison, a professor of industrial relations at Clark University, points out, "[Lower-tier workers] might even feel sufficiently aggrieved to someday negotiate away the benefits of retired higher-tier workers." A higher-tier autoworker observed: "After we retire, the next generation may ask, 'Why should we defend your pensions? You didn't defend our pay when we were young.'"

Bridging the Gap

For many union members the rallying cry is "No more tiers!" They would like to eliminate the two tiers and move to a higher uniform wage rate for all. The new UAW president Dennis Williams says: "It's time to bridge the gap." But Chrysler CEO Sergio Marchione takes a very different position. He would prefer to eliminate the higher wage tier altogether as senior workers retire.

CASE ANALYSIS QUESTIONS

1. DISCUSSION How do Employee Value Propositions differ for those being paid at different levels in two-tier wage plans? What are the implications of these differences for each phase in the human resource management process—attracting, developing, and maintaining a talented workforce?

2. PROBLEM SOLVING If you were a negotiator for the United Auto Workers Union, what would be your "union" position management proposal to eliminate the highest tier in the existing two-tier pay system as senior workers retire? How would you expect the management negotiators to respond to your position? Do you see any room or way to negotiate a compromise or trade-offs that could protect the union's desire for higher wages and meet management desires to control labor costs? Is there any way to forge a shared agreement in this situation?

3. FURTHER RESEARCH Dig into current events, scholarly research, and even financial analysts' reports for information on two-tier wage systems and their outcomes in various industries. Find the pros and cons from both management and union points of view. Look for interviews with workers who express their real feelings about being on each side of the two-tier system. Create

a report that summarizes for the reader or listener the current status of two-tier plans and what we know about how they work and what direction we can expect from them in the future.

Noah Berger/Bloomberg/Getty Images, Inc.

CASE 10: Zappos—They Do It with Humor

When Zappos CEO Tony Hsieh was the featured guest on The Colbert Report, *host Stephen Colbert grilled him about the company's success and customer loyalty. Hsieh replied that it's Zappos's goal to deliver "WOW" in every shoe or clothing box. The company is consistently ranked highly as one of Fortune's "Best Companies to Work For." Amazon's Jeff Bezos liked Zappos so much he bought the company.*

Customers First

Zappos's relentless pursuit of the ultimate customer experience is the stuff of legend. The company offers fast shipping at no cost and covers return shipping if you are dissatisfied for any reason at any time. The Zappos brand is less about a particular type of product and more about providing good customer service. Hsieh has said, "We could be in any industry that we can differentiate ourselves through better customer service and better customer experience."

Culture to Thrive In

Success at Zappos begins with the company's culture and the unusual amount of openness Hsieh encourages among employees, vendors, and other businesses. "If we get the culture right," he says, "most of the other stuff, like the brand and the customer service will just happen. . . . We want the culture to grow stronger and stronger as we grow."

Named "The Smartest Dude in Town" by business magazine *Vegas Inc.*, Hsieh believes employees have to be free to be themselves. That means no call times or scripts for customer service representatives, regular costume parties, and parades and decorations in each department. Customer service reps are given a lot of leeway to make sure every customer is an enthusiastic customer.

Hsieh shares the Zappos culture with anyone who will listen. In a program called Zappos Insights, "Company Evangelists" lead tour groups of 20 around the Las Vegas headquarters. Office cubicles often overflow with kitschy action figures and brightly colored balloons, giving participants a glimpse of a workplace that prizes individuality and fun as much as satisfied customers. Staffers blow horns and ring cowbells to greet participants in the 16 weekly tours, and each department tries to offer a more outlandish welcome than the last. "The original idea was to add a little fun," Hsieh says, but it grew into a friendly competition "as the next aisle said, 'We can do it better'."

Those who want to learn Zappos's secrets without venturing to Las Vegas can subscribe to a members-only community that grants access to video interviews and chats with Zappos management. Ask nicely and the company will send you a free copy of their *Zappos Family Culture Book*, a compilation of employee's ideas about Zappos's mission and core values. Hsieh has his own tome, too—*Delivering Happiness*.

Enter Holacracy

Hsieh's latest move to shake up the world of organization cultures is to embrace a fashion-forward concept called Holacracy. Trademarked HolacracyOne, it is described as an approach that "replaces today's top-down predict-and-control paradigm with a new way of achieving control by distributing power."

In Zappos's holacracy, employees are partners and managers don't exist. Partners hold power distributed by the Holacracy Constitution. They constitutionally agree to things like creating and acting on projects to fulfill roles, tracking progress, helping one another, and spotting tensions indicating things could be better.

When Zappos adopted Holacracy, Hsieh justified the shift this way: "There's the org chart on paper, and then the one that is exactly how the company operates for real, and then there's the org chart that it would like to have in order to operate more efficiently. . . . [With Holacracy] the idea is to process tensions so that the three org charts are pretty close together."

Wait a Minute

When the switch to Holacracy kicked in, Hsieh faced an unanticipated resistance by some employees, including "ex" managers. About 14% of Zappos "partners" decided that Holacracy wasn't for them and chose to leave the company. One said: "There's a lot of things that haven't been figured out yet . . . people don't know what is going to be in the books for them a year down the line."

Hsieh defends Holacracy and argues that patience is needed. And on the positive side, a partner says that meetings under Holacracy are more efficient and "end with an opportunity for employees to say whatever is on their minds."

Next Laugh?

So, what does the future hold? As Zappos lives within the Amazon umbrella and as Hsieh devotes more time to community service, can the Zappos culture survive growth and a possible leadership transition? Will Zappos continue to be the home of fashion-forward practices like Holacracy? Is Hsieh's unique brand of leadership so built into the firm's practices that Zappos will stay the same even under a new CEO? Will this company continue to remain prosperous and keep its reputation as a great employer far into the future?

CASE ANALYSIS QUESTIONS

1. DISCUSSION What leadership traits and style does Tony Hsieh demonstrate at Zappos? What aspects of his leadership can you criticize, if any? Is his leadership approach transferable to other leaders and other organizations, or is it person and situation specific?

2. PROBLEM SOLVING Tony Hsieh is a big thinker, and Zappos is clearly his baby. But he's also into philanthropy and community development activities that are taking up more of his time. Perhaps he'll come up with other new business ideas as well. As a leadership coach, what steps would you recommend that he take now to ensure that his leadership style and vision live on at Zappos long after his departure? What can a strong and secure leader like Hsieh do to ensure a positive leadership legacy?

3. FURTHER RESEARCH Check the latest on Zappos and Tony Hsieh. How and what are each doing at the present time? Do some research to compare and contrast the leadership style and characteristics of Tony Hsieh with those of his boss at Amazon, Jeff Bezos. How are the leadership styles of the two CEOs alike? In what ways do they differ? For whom would you rather work? Is one style better than the other in its situational context?

© AP/Wide World Photos

CASE 11: Panera Bread— A Company with Personality

Panera Bread is in the business of satisfying customers. With fresh-baked breads, gourmet soups, and efficient service, the franchise has surpassed all expectations for success. How did a start-up food company grow so fast and so successfully? To answer this question, you have to study founder Ron Shaich and appreciate his personality.

Bread and Soup?

What's so exciting about bread and soup? Lots, as it turns out. At Panera Bread, artisan-style bread served with deli sandwiches and soups is a combination proven to please the hungry masses. The company's roots go back to 1981, when Louis Kane and Ron Shaich founded Au Bon Pain Company Inc. In a 1993 expansion move Au Bon Pain purchased the Saint Louis Bread Company, a Missouri-based chain of about 20 bakery-cafés. It renovated the stores and renamed them Panera Bread. Sales skyrocketed. In 1999, Panera Bread was spun off as a separate company that takes great pride that its loaves are handmade and baked fresh daily.

Can Do Personality

According to Ron Shaich, former CEO and now executive chairman of the board of Panera, "Real success never comes by simply responding to the day-to-day pressures; in fact, most of that is simply noise. The key to leading an organization is understanding the long-term trends at play and getting the organization ready to respond."

Growing up in Livingston, New Jersey, Shaich wasn't set on being a bread magnate. He wanted to be a public servant, working in government on public policy. As a high school student he even interned for a congressman from his home state.

Shaich's entrepreneurial spark was ignited during his sophomore year at Clark University when the owner of a local convenience store that didn't cater to students threw him and his friends out. It was at that point when he had the inspiration for the student government at his college—he was the treasurer—to open a store for students, run by students. The store was a huge success at Clark. Shaich went on to become an impassioned advocate of student governments opening their own stores, speaking on the topic across the country.

Belief in People

Shaich's personal transformation from a government–public service focus to a retailing–market focus emerged from the recognition that a store for the people, run by the people, could be a success. Following college, he matriculated to Harvard's business school, where after graduation he went to work for the Original Cookie Company. With a desire to start his own cookie business, he was ultimately able to find a tiny retail location, opening the Cookie Jar in 1980. This first taste of entrepreneurialism ultimately led to a license agreement with Au Bon Pain, and to the story that has become famous with the explosion of Panera Bread Co.

Changing Times

Under Shaich's leadership Panera has demonstrated that sticking to company ideals while staying in the lead on industry trends will please customers time and time again. But can this company continue to navigate the changing dietary trends and concerns about fast food in today's unstable market?

CASE ANALYSIS QUESTIONS

1. DISCUSSION Describe how stereotypes about the fast-food industry might positively and negatively affect Panera. Do you think of Panera as a fast-food restaurant, or has the company managed to distinguish itself from this industry segment?

2. PROBLEM SOLVING You are a leadership succession consultant called in to help hire a new CEO. What personality characteristics of Panera's founder Ron Shaich contributed to his success, and that of the company? How good of a fit are these characteristics with Panera at its post-entrepreneurial stage of operations? What would you identify as the three or four most important of Shaich's personal qualities that should be sought after in the next CEO, and why?

3. FURTHER RESEARCH Find data reporting on Panera's recent sales and product initiatives. Find out more about Shaich and how his values and personality affect the company, its mission, and its strategies. Is Panera on the leading edge of its industry, or are other competitors—especially new entrants—starting to nip away at its traditional customers and markets? Does Panera seem to have what it takes to deal with shifting customer values and perceptions of the fast-food industry?

David Paul Morris/Bloomberg/Getty Images

CASE 12: Salesforce.com: Instant Praise, Instant Criticism

Instead of waiting a year for your annual performance review, how would you like to know where you stand by getting immediate feedback about how you're doing? After all, the once-a-year version might be little more than a boss-administered exercise in unhelpful feedback.

The typical annual review can present information overload for many—including past performance, goal setting, pay, and improvement needs. For goals accomplished today, how valuable and motivating is recognition and feedback 6 months from now? What if you were able to get real-time feedback and coaching by asking colleagues, managers, and peers pointed questions like: "What did you think of my presentation?" or "What can be done better?"

Meaningful Recognition

In today's business environment of rapid speed, employers are beginning to realize the true value of real-time feedback for employee recognition, control, performance, and motivation. When Salesforce bought Rypple, a maker of performance management social software, CEO Mark Benioff, said that "the next generation of HCM [human capital management] is not just about a cloud delivery model; it's about a fundamentally better way to recruit, manage and empower employees in a social world."

Rypple's top management pitched their software this way: "Performance management has become disconnected from real performance. Today, we move faster. We're more connected. This requires a new approach to performance." Rather than waiting a year to learn what managers think of them, employees using Rypple's platform send out a quick (50 words or less) pointed question to folks ranging from managers to peers to customers to suppliers. Some call this just-in-time performance improvement. Benioff called it a winner.

Enter Work.com

Rebranded within Salesforce as Work.com, the Rypple product provides a real-time snapshot of employee performance in a single place, on completion of a goal, project, or quarter. Benefits include the ability to give public thanks and solicit meaningful feedback in a timely manner. A coaching interface allows workers to build coaching networks to spot needed improvements. This helps resolve problems and issues as they arise rather than after the fact. It also means quicker implementation of needed changes.

More or Less Motivation?

Some ask if too much feedback becomes a bad thing. Reliance on so much feedback and what other people say can be a detriment to learning the hard way—by making mistakes. Others believe that people are motivated to work hard when their efforts are recognized in a public way.

Are you willing to wait a year until your next performance review to get some of that much-needed positive feedback? Or would you like to work in an environment where real-time report cards of your progress are common?

CASE ANALYSIS QUESTIONS

1. DISCUSSION Is the annual performance review past its "sell by" date, or just in need of some revisions? If real-time reviews are available using software like Salesforce's Work.com, is there a need for an annual performance review?

2. PROBLEM SOLVING You've just taken a new job in human resource management, and the organization's president gave you this high-priority task: Give us a plan that can make performance reviews motivating to the recipients and their bosses alike. "I'm tired," she says, "of hearing everyone complain that annual reviews are demotivating. We need to review performance. Surely there are ways that we can make ours more valuable." As you sit down to think about this assignment, make a few notes on what you believe the major issues are and the types of things you might recommend. Use insights from motivation theories to justify what's on your list.

3. FURTHER RESEARCH How about the real-time and Web-based approach to performance reviews offered by Salesforce? Do some research and identify the latest developments with it and others like it. Is this online approach to performance assessment the right pathway to a more motivated workforce? What does the evidence say about benefits? What downsides are users reporting? Overall, what's the current verdict on Work.com and similar products—good for bosses, good for employers, good for employees?

CRYSTAL ALISONMACLEOD/CSM /Landov LLC

CASE 13: Auto Racing—When the Driver Takes a Back Seat

When you think of auto racing, do you first think of drivers . . . or teamwork? The majority of camera time, fame, and rewards goes to the drivers. But, they are simply one member of a larger team that works together to achieve maximum performance. When the driver wins, the team wins as well. And the really great drivers are the first to thank them.

Start Your Engines!

In the world of competitive auto racing, the drivers are the sport's rock stars. They're courted by sponsors, adored by fans, and made the subject of interview after interview by the racing press. Although it goes without saying that drivers are absolutely essential to earning a trophy, racing enthusiasts, teammates, and especially drivers will tell you that they can't win the race by themselves—it takes a successful team to win a race.

Although three of the major forms of professional auto racing—NASCAR, Formula One, and rally car racing—each use different vehicles, rules, and team structures, teamwork is the common denominator among them. Ray Evernham, former crew chief and team manager for Hendrick Motorsports' DuPont car, describes teamwork this way: "We're all spark plugs. If one doesn't fire just right, we can't win the race. So no matter whether you are the guy that's doing the fabricating or changing tires on Sundays and that's the only job responsibility you have, if you don't do your job then we're not going to win. And no one is more or less important than you."

What are the qualities of successful racing teams? Let's take a look.

NASCAR Leads the Pack

NASCAR is the most widely known and watched racing sport in the United States, and the popularity and success of Jeff Gordon has more than a little to do with that. Gordon has the most wins in NASCAR's modern era, has the third-most all-time wins, and has become a spokesperson for the importance of teamwork in NASCAR racing. "My job to communicate is probably the most important thing," Gordon has said. "Because I've got to send a message from the race car and the race track back to the team so that they can make the proper adjustments."

Cars running in NASCAR races hit speeds over 200 miles per hour. But winning or losing can be decided by tenths of a second.

Cases for Critical Thinking

Although it's the driver who gets featured in the winner's circle and in all the advertisements, the difference between crossing the finish line first or losing the race often comes down to the pits, where the efforts of teammates with titles like Car Chief, Fueler, Jackman, Tire Carrier, and Changer have to operate together in just the right way. It's in a crowded pit lane that tires get changed, windshields cleaned, fenders bent back into shape, and spring and balance adjustments fine tuned. Any seconds saved by pit crews are a driver's best friends. Little wonder that racing teams give high priority to hiring the right crew chiefs and building high-performance pit crew teams to maximize their winning chances on race days.

In his analysis of successful NASCAR teams, Robert Williamson notes that an essential characteristic is a team's sense of ownership for all actions—"We won the race, we hit the wall, we had a tire problem, we missed the setup for the track, we nailed that pit stop," rather than noting the success or shortcoming of an individual.

It's impossible for a car to complete a NASCAR race without multiple visits to the pit, and these pit stops are often the best example of teamwork in the sport. Aside from the skill and muscle memory of the pit crew members, other teammates contribute by modifying parts and equipment so they can be changed out in less time.

In Sprint Cup racing, NASCAR's highest designation, pit stops can happen in less than 20 seconds. Champion driver Jimmie Johnson cites the importance of cohesive teamwork even before a car is assembled and tested on the track. "If you really know each other then, you know what each other is looking for, you've built that foundation and belief on the teammates [and] the engineers, you can split those hairs and get it right."

Formula One Has the Speed

The Formula One drivers, team members, and fans have one quality that sets them above all other racing participants: the need for speed. Formula One fields the fastest circuit racing cars in the world, screaming down the track at top speeds as high as 225 miles per hour. Unlike in other racing sports, Formula One teams are required to build their own chassis. Although teams procure specialized engines from specific manufacturers, they are primarily responsible for building their cars from the ground up.

Each formula has its own set of rules that eligible cars must meet (*Formula One* being the fastest of these designations). The McLaren team, one of the most successful in Formula One, and engineering director Paddy Lowe understand the importance of teamwork. Speaking on the challenge of incorporating a new component into an existing car, he noted, "You have to factor in the skill of the team to work together in a very short period of time to push in a completely different direction; to understand all the different issues. The reliability, the performance, the skills of the team, all the tools they've created over the years—they all came through to our profit. Everybody moves seamlessly. They know what they've got to do."

Former BMW Motorsport Director Mario Theissen put it simply: "Teamwork is the key to success," he said. "Of course the basis is formed by a competitive technical package, but without a well-integrated, highly motivated team, even the best car will not achieve prolonged success."

Rally Cars Hit the Road

Whereas NASCAR and Formula One racers speed around a paved track, rally car racing frequently heads off the circuit and into territory that would make most any NASCAR driver step on the brakes: Finnish rallies feature long, treacherous stretches of ice and snow. The famed French *Méditerranée-le Cap* ran 10,000 miles from the Mediterranean to South Africa. The reputed Baja 1000 Rally ran the length of the Baja California peninsula, largely over deserts without a road in sight.

In rally car racing, drivers race against the clock instead of each other. Races generally consist of several stages that the driver must compete as quickly as possible, and the winning driver completes all stages in the least amount of time.

You could argue that of all racing sports, rally drivers are the most reliant on teamwork to win. Unlike other forms of circuit racing, the driver is not racing on a fixed track and does not get to see the course before the race begins. Instead, drivers are wholly reliant on a teammate, the navigator, for information on upcoming terrain. Part coach and part copilot, the navigator relies on page notes (detailed information on the sharpness of turns and the steepness of gradients) to keep the driver on course from the passenger seat.

Turkish driver Burcu Çetinkaya had already made a name for herself as a successful snowboarder before deciding to take up rally car racing at the age of 24. She says: "The thing that hooked me about rally driving was working together with a team for a common goal with nature working against you," she said. "I love cars, first of all—I grew up with them and I love every part of them. And I love competition. I have been competing all my life. In a rally, these things come together: nature, competition, teamwork and cars."

Teams Rule on Racedays

Although they may receive the lion's share of the notoriety and adulation, racing drivers are only one member of a larger team, wherein every team member's performance contributes to the team's success. The best drivers don't let the fame go to their heads. As Jeff Gordon—who knows a thing or two about success—put it, "The only way I can do my job correctly is to be totally clear in my mind and have 100% confidence in every person's job that went into this team so that they can have 100% confidence in what I'm doing as a driver."

CASE ANALYSIS QUESTIONS

1. DISCUSSION Racing teams and their leaders make lots of decisions—from the pressures of race day to the routines of everyday team management. When and in what situations are these decisions made by authority rule, minority rule, majority rule, consensus, or unanimity? How do these decision-making approaches fit certain times and situations but not others? Defend your answer.

2. PROBLEM SOLVING Assume you have been retained as a team-building consultant by a famous racing team pit crew whose performance fell badly during the prior season. Design and explain a series of team-building activities you will use to engage team members to strengthen their trust in each other and improve their individual and collective efforts.

3. FURTHER RESEARCH Choose a racing team of interest to you. Research the team, its personnel, and its performance in the most recent racing season. Try to answer this question: What accounts for this team's success or lack of success—driver talent, technology, teamwork, ownership/leadership, or all four? List at least three lessons from your analysis of the racing team that might be valuable and transferable to teams and organizations in any setting.

NICHOLAS KAMM/AFP/Getty Images

CASE 14: Twitter—Rewriting (or Killing?) Communication

Twitter's 140-character text-based messages, or "Twitter-speak," permeate everyday life. But questions about its influence are being asked—by parents, relationship partners, teachers, and employers. Is Twitter reinventing social communication, or is it just abbreviating it? Do tweets create meaningful conversations, or do they dumb down our abilities to write and communicate effectively with one another?

Twitter was conceived on a playground slide during a burrito-fueled brainstorming session by employees of podcasting company Odeo. Co-founder Jack Dorsey suggested the idea of using short, SMS-like messages to connect with a small group. "[W]e came across the word *twitter*, and it was just perfect," he says. "The definition was 'a short burst of inconsequential information' and 'chirps from birds.' And that's exactly what the product was."

Messages With(out) Meanings

Messages have to be terse and to the point given Twitter's 140-character limit. But there's no guarantee they'll be meaningful. When market research firm Pear Analytics analyzed 2,000 U.S. and British tweets sent during daytime hours over 2 weeks, they concluded that 40% of them represented "pointless babble." Social network researcher Danah Boyd has criticized Pear Analytics' results, pointing out that pointless babble could be better characterized as *social grooming*, where tweeters "want to know what the people around them are thinking and doing and feeling."

Tweets Travel Faster

"Twitter lets me hear from a lot of people in a very short period of time," says tech evangelist Robert Scoble. It has also become a de facto emergency broadcast network for breaking news, including natural disaster and dangerous situations—think hostages, civil strife, and armed conflict. Managers are using Twitter to send announcements about upcoming events, post rapid response items, and share links that bear on what's happening within the organization. Twitter is also being used in educational settings as a way to promote student interactions with faculty and administration, and with one another.

Changing Communication

There is no doubt that Twitter's quick and short messages have shortened the stages of communication for users—quick thoughts warrant a tweet. It is also increasing the frequency of communication, as people get attached to the easy and time efficient medium. Yet we also know that well-known tweeters sometimes have to apologize and explain themselves—often at great lengths. The immediacy of tweeting can make it impulsive communication—tweets are oh, so easy to send out—but those 140 characters can create lots of later regrets!

CASE ANALYSIS QUESTIONS

1. DISCUSSION What are the advantages and disadvantages of communicating via Twitter? Can a 140-character tweet really be effective? What guidelines would you recommend for maximizing the effectiveness of a personal tweet?

2. PROBLEM SOLVING You have been given a first assignment as the new summer intern in the office of a corporate CEO. The task is to analyze Twitter and make a presentation to the CEO and her executive team recommending whether or not it should be used for corporate purposes. What points will you make in the presentation to summarize its potential uses, possible downsides, and overall strategic value to the firm?

3. FURTHER RESEARCH Do research to identify current developments with Twitter. What is presently happening with the firm? What are the financial and business analysts saying? Is Twitter still innovating, and if so, what new directions are evident? Is Twitter on a continued path of success, or is its 140-character appeal starting to fade? Who are Twitter's major competitors? Are they real threats, or not? Is the tweet here to stay, or will it soon be displaced by the next best leap forward in communication technology?

© Terry Vine/Blend Images/Corbis

CASE 15: India, Inc. — "How May I Help You?"

When you call a toll-free number for customer service assistance, possibly pertaining to finance or banking, an airline reservation, an insurance

Cases for Critical Thinking

claim, or technical support for one of your gadgets, there is a good possibility that the person on the other end of the line is a half-world away.

Business Process Outsourcing

Your customer service experience is part of an outsourcing arrangement made by multinational companies that realize significant capital and cost savings. This industry has a name—business process outsourcing, or BPO for short. And critics worry not just about customer satisfaction. They also worry about BPO's impact on the personalities, lifestyle, careers, and culture of workers across the world, ones who assist in increasing your credit card limit or getting your cable modem back online. In other words, there's a real person behind the voice on the line or words in the chat box.

"How May I Help You?"

India has a dominant stake in BPO services related to customer management, human resource outsourcing, finance and accounting, banking, financial services, billing, and supply chain management. The serviced industries include retail, insurance, mortgage, banking and finance, healthcare, telecommunications, technology, travel, and hospitality. High transaction volume is found especially in payroll, human resources, accounts payable, and customer data analytics.

The growing BPO industry has had what some believe to be both positive and negative effects on the culture and lifestyle of Indian workers. Americans are quick to share stories of call center experiences and in particular issues understanding the Indian English accent. However, what you might not have considered during your call is its cultural impact. Although India's BPO industry—highlighted by firms like Infosys and Tata—has given tremendous employment opportunities and a reduction in gender disparity, the result for some is a sociocultural shift.

Shehzad Nadeem, author of *Dead Ringers: How Outsourcing Is Changing the Way Indians Understand Themselves*, discusses concerns about "the damaging psychological effects on call-center employees who are expected to ape the Western employees they have replaced in terms of accents, slang, and even names." A popular Indian business magazine says: "Sanjay grew an alter ego as Sam, Nikhil turned into Nick, and Sulekha pretended to be Sally. Hours in training turned a Tamil accent into the Boston twang and the Punjabi gruffness into the Texan drawl."

De-Indianization

Call center training centers operate all over India, and for a fee, they teach Indians who wish to gain employment in a call center how to assimilate when speaking to U.S. callers. The training includes listening to pop music audio and watching videos, CNN and Fox newscasts, and old TV shows like *Friends* and *Frazier*. Students try to learn U.S. accents and acquire a sense of what it's like to live a U.S. lifestyle. Those who aren't able to conform to a Western culture don't make the cut, which many see as a "financial necessity."

Vandana Raj Nath, who works as a call center worker, said: "I have to Americanize my accent so that my client is comfortable speaking with me and does not guess that I'm Indian. Some of them don't like dealing with Indians." In his opinion, the allure of making a wage significantly higher than average has caused the demise of Indian culture. Some of his co-workers, he states, "were way too disillusioned and 'too Westernized' to be happy in India." His conclusion: financial independence for call center employees comes with the risk of an identity crisis.

In a *Mother Jones* magazine article entitled "My Summer at an Indian Call Center," New York native Andrew Marantz recounts his experience as an undercover call center employee and trainee in Gurgaon, a suburb of Delhi in India. Marantz describes what he calls a process of "De-Indianization" by culture trainers, who encourage mostly Indian workers to adapt and "live" the Western culture. This includes eating fast food, taking on a Western name, listening to U.S. pop music, learning to use U.S. idioms, and of course, dealing with irate customers and the job hazard of racial abuse.

Chameleons at Work

Those who disagree with Marantz's claims about culture loss by BPO acknowledge that, to a certain degree, "we are all chameleons at work" and that what Marantz calls "De-Indianization" is overhyped. Has the impact of working in a call center created a sociocultural shift? Although some may think so, others might disagree, claiming that those who work in this environment are already fairly Westernized and that the job doesn't necessarily create the perceived loss of a native culture.

The BPO industry's impact on its Indian call center workers may not be the only factor in what many see as the workers' risk of culture loss. Many young people in countries worldwide, and in particular, students studying abroad, find themselves influenced by cultures other than their own. Does the influence of Western culture for Indian call center workers necessarily mean that the pride and heritage of one's Indian culture is forgotten?

The next time you seek call center support of some kind, what will you think when "Nick" or "Sally" takes your call? Will you worry about their loss of cultural identity, or be pleased about their financial opportunities?

CASE ANALYSIS QUESTIONS

1. DISCUSSION What are the main arguments why the BPO industry contributes to a loss of cultural identity for Indian workers who are asked to "act as Westerners" while serving customers of large multinational firms? Are these arguments on or off point?

2. PROBLEM SOLVING A professor challenged your international business student organization to prepare a position paper on BPO practices. Her main question is: If cultural identity loss is occurring as suggested in this case, do the financial benefits to the workers and employers make its loss worth while? Should loss of cultural identity by BPO workers be a real social concern, or is it just a natural outcome of changes accompanying the global economy? What are the main points you will bring to the meeting where this position paper is to be drafted?

3. FURTHER RESEARCH What is the current status of the business process outsourcing industry in India? Is it still a growth industry, or is it slowing down? What are the pros and cons being discussed on the Indian side . . . on the multinational contractor side? What other countries are big players in BPO? Is BPO in general a good thing for developing countries? How are multinationals responding to customer complaints about BPO? Are they paying any attention to criticisms that the BPO industry causes a loss of cultural identity for its employees? If so, what are they doing about it?

Chuck Burton/AP

CASE 16: Harley-Davidson—Style and Strategy with a Global Reach

Harley-Davidson's American success story began in 1903 when two friends—William Harley and Arthur Davidson—built a motorized bicycle in a machine shop in Milwaukee, Wisconsin. The progeny of that first machine now travel the world—with speed and style. Now the Harley Hog is going electric.

Rebuilding the Hog

When Harley-Davidson was founded it was one of more than 100 firms producing motorcycles in the United States. By the 1950s, it was the only remaining American manufacturer. But in the 1960s, Honda began sales in the United States and Harley had difficulty competing against the Japanese firm's smaller bikes.

The American Machine and Foundry Co. (AMF) bought Harley in 1969 and quickly increased production. However, this rapid expansion led to significant problems with quality, and the better-built Japanese motorcycles began to take over the market. A group of 13 managers bought Harley-Davidson back from AMF in 1981 and began a turnaround with the rallying cry "The Eagle Soars Alone." Richard Teerlink, former CEO of Harley, explained: "The solution was to get back to detail. The key was to know the business, know the customer, and pay attention to detail." The key elements in this turn around were increasing quality and improving service to customers and dealers. Management kept the classic Harley style and focus on heavyweight bikes.

In 1983 Harley-Davidson asked the International Trade Commission (ITC) for tariff protection on the basis that Japanese manufacturers, including Honda, were stockpiling inventory in the United States and providing unfair competition. The request was granted. Harley was confident enough in 1987 to petition the ITC to have the tariff lifted because the company had improved its ability to compete with foreign imports. Once Harley's image had been restored, the company began to increase production and open new facilities.

The average Harley customer in the 1980s was male, late 30s, with an average household income above $40,000. Teerlink said:

"Our customers want the sense of adventure that they get on our bikes.... Harley-Davidson doesn't sell transportation, we sell transformation. We sell excitement, a way of life." The company created a line of Harley accessories available online, by catalog, or through dealers, all adorned with the Harley-Davidson logo. These jackets, caps, T-shirts, and other items became popular with nonbikers as well. In fact, the clothing and parts had a higher profit margin than the motorcycles; nonbike products made up as much as half of sales at some dealerships.

Crossing Borders

Although Harley had been exporting motorcycles ever since it was founded, it was not until the late 1980s that management invested seriously in international markets. Traditionally, the company's ads had been translated word for word into foreign languages. Now, new ads were developed specifically for different markets and Harley rallies were adapted to fit local customs. Harley actively recruited dealers in Europe and Japan, built a large parts warehouse in Germany, and purchased a Japanese distribution company.

Harley's management learned a great deal from these early international activities. Recognizing, for example, that German motorcyclists rode at high speeds—often more than 100 mph—the company began studying ways to give Harleys a smoother ride and emphasizing accessories that would give riders more protection. Its Japanese subsidiary adapted the company's marketing to fit local tastes, even producing shinier and more complete toolkits than those available in the United States. Harley bikes are now symbols of prestige in Japan, and many enthusiasts see themselves as rebels on wheels.

The company has also made inroads into the previously elusive Chinese market. It partnered with China's Zongshen Motorcycle Group, which makes several million small-engine motorcycles each year. Despite China's growing disposable income, the venture has several hurdles ahead of it, including riding restrictions imposed by the government in urban areas.

Growing the Future

The U.S. market still represents a high percentage of Harley's sales. Executives attribute Harley's success to loyal customers and the Harley-Davidson name. "It is a unique brand that is built on personal relationship and deep connections with customers, unmatched riding experiences, and proud history," said Jim Ziemer, Harley's former president and chief executive.

CEO Keith E. Wandell seeks to increase growth by focusing effort and resources on the unique strengths of the Harley-Davidson brand. He also plans to enhance productivity and profitability through continuous improvement. Part of his approach focuses company resources on Harley-Davidson products and experiences, demographic outreach, commitment to core customers, and even more global growth.

The latest innovation is the electric Hog, now in prototype and soon expected to travel the highways of the world. A Harley spokesperson says: "We anticipate it's going to appeal to a younger, more urban demographic" and that it is part of Harley's commitment to "preserving the riding environment."

CASE ANALYSIS QUESTIONS

1. DISCUSSION If you were CEO of Harley-Davidson, how would you compare the advantages and disadvantages of using exports, joint ventures, and foreign subsidiaries as ways of expanding international sales?

2. PROBLEM SOLVING If you were advising Harley's CEO on business expansion in sub-Saharan Africa, what would you recommend in terms of setting up sales centers and manufacturing sites in countries like South Africa, Kenya, and Zimbabwe? When a new location is targeted, what would you suggest as the proper role for locals to play? Should they run everything, or should there be a mix of locals and expatriates? And if the CEO wants to send expatriates from the United States into some locations, what selection criteria would you recommend, and why?

3. FURTHER RESEARCH Is it accurate to say that Harley is still "on top of its game"? How well is the company performing today in both domestic and global markets? Who are its top competitors in other parts of the world, and how well does Harley compete against them? Does the electric Harley have what it takes to fuel the company's next stage of global growth?

Helder Almeida/Shutterstock

CASE 17: Crowdfunding—The New Mother of Angel Investors

Financing is the mother of all constraints on small businesses and new venture start-ups. But for those quick with the Web, social media may turn out to be the mother of all angel investors. A growing number of entrepreneurs are realizing their long-held dreams by using a Web-based tool called crowdfunding. And, it's a force to be reckoned with.

The Game has Changed

Crowdfunding is an online fund-raising platform that acts as an intermediary to help entrepreneurs, artists, writers, filmmakers, and multitudes of others realize their dreams through less-traditional ways of raising seed money. It's already mainstream and available to serve almost any type of project imaginable. You can now go online and find any number of crowdfunding sites, with Kickstarter, AngelList, and Indiegogo prominent among them.

The two basic crowdfunding financing models are All or Nothing (AoN) and Keep it All (KiA). The AoN model allows pledged money to be kept by the entrepreneur only if the initial fundraising goal is met. If it is not met, then no money is collected from the investors—in other words, it's all or nothing. The KiA model allows all collected funds to be kept, regardless of whether the fundraising goal is met.

Kickstarter Says "Support," Not "Own"

Numbers keep growing for the popular crowdfunding platform Kickstarter. Staff must approve projects before they get listed, and they must fit into the world of Art, Comics, Dance, Design, Fashion, Film, Food, Games, Music, Photography, Publishing, Technology, and Theater. Funded projects range from software development to iPhone accessories to graphic novels to indie films shown at the Sundance Film Festival. Its Web site reads: "Kickstarter is full of ambitious, innovative, and imaginative projects that are brought to life through the direct support of others."

Backers, mostly friends and fans, fund each Kickstarter campaign on an altruistic basis—with the desire to help a cause, and/or as a value exchange—in return for something like an early release copy of the completed project. As Kickstarter's Web site says: "Backing a project is more than just giving someone money, it's supporting their dream to create something that they want to see exist in the world."

With Kickstarter there are no equity shares at stake, and investors get no ownership rights. What they do get are updates and the satisfaction of seeing their projects take off. Also common are small tokens of appreciation such as Twitter Shout-outs, autographs, limited editions, tickets to a film's premiere, and, in some cases, a discounted or free product.

Examples of prohibited projects and practices include energy food and drinks, offensive material such as hate speech and encouraging violence, alcohol as a reward, political fundraising, drugs, pornography, and offering financial, money-processing, or credit services.

Crowdfunding Pros and Cons

Those who support the growing crowdfunding phenomenon argue that ideas that don't fit traditional financing can successfully attract funding through the crowd. The initial crowdfunding financing then allows a project to gain traction for future backing from traditional sources.

A disadvantage of crowdfunding is the public disclosure required. Although this isn't a problem for charitable organizations and artists, firms in their early stages of product development can be compromised with well-financed competitors and copycats. Another possible downside is the time associated with managing communication to a broad base of investors and supporters.

President Obama signed into law the Jumpstart Our Business Startups (JOBS) Act, which permits backers who pledge money to projects on crowdfunding sites to earn an equity stake in the project—going beyond the Kickstarter model. If the project becomes a success, the backer cashes in—similar to a venture capital firm. The upside of the act is that many more small businesses will be able to raise capital. But, critics of the act worry that this could be the start of fraudulent crowdfunding sites and those interested solely in profiteering.

CASE ANALYSIS QUESTIONS

1. DISCUSSION What are the pros and cons of crowdfunding? Look at it first from the perspective of the entrepreneur who needs the money. Look at it also from the side of the potential investor. What are the risks that each might face? Is crowdfunding a good option for them, or is it mainly a way for the owners of the crowdfunding sites to make money for themselves?

2. PROBLEM SOLVING (a) As a potential investor, you want to take advantage of crowdfunding to put some excess cash to work. Investigate at least three possible crowdfunding sites that

you might use, with one being Kickstarter. Which would you choose and why? (b) As an entrepreneur who needs money for a new start-up, you want to take advantage of crowdfunding. Investigate at least three possible crowdfunding sites that you might use, with one being Kickstarter. Which would you choose, and why?

3. FURTHER RESEARCH Perform additional research to learn more about the status and implications of Kickstarter, Angel-List, Indiegogo, and other crowdfunding sites. Does one seem to have advantage over the other? Is the "no equity" model of Kickstarter proving more popular than the "with equity" alternatives legitimated by the JOBS Act? Do a quick industry analysis. Who's doing what, why, and with what results? What does the future hold for crowdfunding as a financing alternative for small start-ups and entrepreneurial ventures? After considering the JOBS Act and the crowdfunding industry as a whole, what advice would you offer to small investors attracted to crowdfunding as a way of becoming venture capitalists?

Case References

Case 1 Trader Joe's

Elaine Misonzhink, "Retail Real Estate Pros Laud Trader Joe's Upsized Aspirations," *Retail Traffic Magazine* (November 3, 2011): retailtrafficmag.com. Accessed August 24, 2012.

Amy Groth, "Trader Joe's Is Run by This Ultra-Secretive German Family," *BusinessInsider.com* (August 1, 2011): articles.businessinsider.com. Accessed August 21, 2012.

David Nusbaum, "Two Buck Chuck Price Goes Up," *Los Angeles Business Journal* (January 16, 2013): labusinessjournal.com. Accessed February 7, 2013.

Christopher Palmeri, "Trader Joe's Recipe for Success," *Businessweek* (February 20, 2008): businessweek.com. Accessed August 21, 2012.

Beth Kowitt, "Inside the Secret World of Trader Joe's," *Fortune* (February 23, 2010): money.cnn.com. Accessed August 22, 2012.

Jena McGregor, "Leading Listener: Trader Joe's," (October 1, 2004): fastcompany.com. Accessed February 7, 2013.

Blanca Torres, "Safeway Escalates Food Fight," *San Francisco Business Times* (March 30, 2012): bizjournals.com. Accessed August 22, 2012.

"Trader Joe's Store Manager Salary," *Glassdoor*: glassdoor.com. Accessed July 7, 2013, and May 16, 2014.

"Trader Joe's," *Hoover's Company Records* (February 14, 2012): cobrands.hoovers.com. Accessed March 14, 2014.

Trader Joe's Website, "About," traderjoes.com. Accessed August 22, 2012.

Trader Joe's Website, "Store Management," traderjoes.com. Accessed August 23, 2012.

Matthew Enis, *Supermarket News* (July 19, 2010), Vol. 58 (9).

Kara Zuaro, "The 10 Best Trader Joe's Store-Brand Items," *L Magazine* (February 22, 2012): thelmagazine.com. Accessed August 23, 2012.

"Trader Joe's Private Label World Revealed," *Store Brand Decisions* (August 24, 2010): storebrandsdecisions.com. Accessed August 23, 2012.

Case 2 Patagonia

Monte Burke, "Wal-Mart, Patagonia Team to Green Business," *Forbes* (May 6, 2010): forbes.com. Accessed February 2, 2011.

Kent Garber, "Yvon Chouinard: Patagonia Founder Fights for the Environment," *U.S. News* (October 22, 2009): usnews.com. Accessed February 2, 2011.

Diana Random, "Finding Success by Putting Company Culture First," *Entrepreneur* (April 19, 2011): entrepreneur.com. Accessed March 1, 2012.

Jennifer Wang, "Patagonia, From the Ground Up," *Entrepreneur* (June 10, 2010): entrepreneur.com. Accessed February 2, 2011.

"Environmental Internships," *Patagonia*, patagonia.com. Accessed February 3, 2011.

Case 3 Amazon

SC Digest Editorial Staff, Logistics News: "In Astounding Move, Amazon.com Buys Robotic Material Handling Provider Kiva," *SC Digest.com* (March 21, 2012): scdigest.com. Accessed September 6, 2012.

Mark Brohan, "Amazon plans a 40% expansion in distribution center space, report says," *InternetRetailer* (January 18, 2011): internetretailer.com. Accessed September 6, 2012.

"Retailers Talk Pros and Cons of Selling on Amazon," *Outdoor Industry Association* (March 8, 2012): outdoorindustry.org. Accessed September 7, 2012.

Ron Miller, "Amazon Prime includes Lots of Free Content," *Fierce Content Management* (August 28, 2012).

David Meerman Scott, "The Flip Side of Free," *eContent*, vol. 28, no. 10 October 2005.

"Amazon CEO Takes Long View," *USA Today* (July 6, 2005): usatoday30.usatoday.com. Accessed September 7, 2012.

Thomas Ricker, "Amazon Adds Audible to Its Digital Empire," engadget.com. Accessed September 7, 2012.

Case 4 Nordstrom

Jake Bastell, "Nordstrom Gets in Step with Tracking Its Inventory," *Seattle Times* (February 10, 2002): seattletimes.nwsource.com. Accessed February 14, 2012.

Stephanie Clifford, "Nordstrom Links Online Inventory to Real World," *New York Times* (August 23, 2010): nytimes.com. Accessed September 10, 2012; and, "Nordstrom Uses Web to Locate Items and Increase Sales," *The New York Times* (August 23, 2010): nytimes.com. Accessed February 14, 2012.

Cotton Timberlake, "Nordstrom Beats Macy's and Saks by Moving Inventories," *Bloomberg* (April 8, 2009): bloomberg.com; "Nordstrom Tries an Extreme Makeover with Topshop," *Businessweek* (July 12, 2012); "How Nordstrom Bests Its Retail Rivals," *Businessweek* (August 11, 2011): businessweek.com. All accessed September 10, 2012.

Zacks Equity Search, "Nordstrom's Comps Rise Again," *Zacks Investment Research* (January 6, 2012) zacks.com. Accessed September 10, 2012.

Case 5 Chipotle

Steven Russollilo, "Chipotle Shares Tank on Slowdown Fears," *Wall Street Journal* (July 20, 2012): blogs.wsj.com. Accessed September 17, 2012.

Annie Gasparro, "Restaurant Chains Feel the Need for Speed," *Wall Street Journal* (September 4, 2012): online.wsj.com. Accessed September 17, 2012.

Miriam Jordan, "A CEO's Demand: Fix Immigration," *Wall Street Journal* (December 19, 2011): online.wsj.com. Accessed September 17, 2012.

"Heard on the Street: Overheard: Chipotle's Bean Counters," *Wall Street Journal* (February 27, 2011). online.wsj.com. Accessed September 17, 2012.

Steve Van Tiem, "Superior Management a Key Ingredient to Chipotle's Success," *Motley Fool* (June 20, 2012): beta.fool.com. Accessed September 17, 2012.

Allison Aubrey, "Antibiotic-Free Meat Business Is Booming, Thanks to Chipotle," *NPR Website* (May 31, 2012): npr.org. Accessed September 17, 2012.

"Full of Beans: How a Classically Trained Chef Reinvented Fast Food," *Knowledge at Wharton* (January 20, 2010): knowledge.wharton.upenn.edu. Accessed September 17, 2012.

Case 6 Dunkin' Donuts

R. Jai Krishna and Rumman Ahmed, "Dunkin' Brands Looks at Emerging Markets," *Wall Street Journal* (May 30, 2012): blogs.wsj.com. Accessed September 28, 2012.

Annalyn Censky, "Dunkin' Donuts to Double U.S. Locations," *CNN Money* (January 4, 2012): money.cnn.com. Accessed September 28, 2012.

Vanessa Wong, "Q&A: Dunkin' Donuts' Creative Willy Wonka," *Businessweek* (September 24, 2012): businessweek. Accessed September 28, 2012.

Carolyn Walkup, "Nigel Travel Talks Dunkin's Strategy," *QSR* (September 2010): qsrmagazine.com. Accessed September 28, 2012.

"Menu," dunkindonuts.com. Accessed September 28, 2012.

"Company Snapshot," dunkindonuts.com. Accessed September 28, 2012, and January 18, 2015.

Susan Spielberg, "For Snack Chains, Coffee Drinks the Best Way to Sweeten Profits," *Nation's Restaurant News* (June 27, 2005).

Dunkin' Donuts Press Kit, news. dunkindonuts.com. Accessed September 28, 2012.

"Investor Overview," *Starbucks Web site*: investor.starbucks.com. Accessed September 28, 2012.

Janet Adamy, "Starbucks Takes Plunge into Instant Coffee," *Wall Street Journal* (February 13, 2009), wsj.com. Accessed September 28, 2012

Case 7 Nike

"Sports Industry Overview." *Plunkett Research, Ltd.* plunkettresearch.com/sports-recreation-leisure-market-research/industry-statistics. Accessed February 14, 2012.

nikeresponsibility.com/#workers-factories/active_factories

"Improving Conditions in Our Contract Factories." *Nikebiz*. secure. nikebiz.com/responsibility/workers_and_factories.html. Accessed February 14, 2012.

"Nike Replaces CEO After 13 Months," *USA Today*, January 24, 2006; Olga Kharif and Matt Townsend. "Nike Betting on Venture Capital in Effort to Step Up Innovation." *Bloomberg Businessweek*. Posted September 28, 2011. businessweek.com/technology/nike-betting-on-venture-capital-in-effort-to-step-up-innovation-09282011.html. Accessed February 24, 2012.

Nike 2009 Annual Report. Select Financials.media.corporate-ir.net/media_files/irol/10/100529/AnnualReport/nike-sh09-rev2/index.html#select_financials. Accessed April 6, 2012.

"2011 Letter to the Shareholder." *Nike*. Posted July 13, 2011. investors.nikeinc.com/Theme/Nike/files/doc_financials/AnnualReports/2011/index.html#mark_parker_letter. Accessed February 24, 2012.

Case 8 Gamification

Schell, J. (2010). DICE 2010. *Design Outside the Box Presentation*: g4tv.com/videos.

Douglas MacMillan, "'Gamification': A growing business to invigorate stalewebsites" (January 19, 2011): businessweek.com.

forbes.com/sites/gartnergroup/2013/01/21/the-gamification-of-business.

Debra Weiss, "Management Trend Is Gamification of the Workplace," *ABA Journal* (November 17, 2011): abajournal.com. Accessed October 11, 2012.

Rachel Emma Silverman, "Latest Game Theory: Mixing Work and Play," *Wall Street Journal* (October 10, 2011): professional.wsj.com. Accessed October 11, 2012.

Rachel King, "The Games Companies Play," *Businessweek* (April 4, 2011), businessweek.com. Accessed October 12, 2012.

forbes.com/sites/gartnergroup/2013/01/21/the-gamification-of-business.

Gee, J. P., "Learning and Games," in Katie Salen (Ed.) *The Ecology of Games: Connecting Youth, Games, and Learning (John D. and Catherine T. MacArthur Foundation series on digital media and learning)*. Cambridge, MA: MIT Press, 2008.

McGonigal, J., *Reality Is Broken: Why Games Make Us Better and How They Can Change the World*. New York: Penguin, 2011.

Case 9 Two-Tier Wages

James Martin, "Two-Tier Compensation Structures: Their Impact on Union Employers and Employees." W.E. Upjohn Institute for Employment Research (1990).

Bill Vlasic, "Detroit Sets Its Future on a Foundation of Two-Tier Wages." *New York Times* (September 12, 2011): nytimes.com. Accessed February 13, 2012.

Gary Chaison, "Two-Tier Wage Settlements and the Legitimacy of American Unions," Proceedings of the Fifteenth Congress of the International Industrial Relations Association. Sydney, Australia (December 2008): ilera-directory.org. Accessed February 13, 2012.

Christina Rogers, "UAW's Next Chief Faces a Battle over Wage Disparity," *Wall Street Journal* (June 3, 2014), p. B1.

John D. Stoll, "U.S. Auto Workers Press to Close Pay Gap at Plants," *Wall Street Journal* (March 24, 2015), p. 17.

Case 10 Zappos

"Looking Ahead—Let There Be Anything and Everything." *Zappos*: about.zappos.com. Accessed February 18, 2012.

Andria Cheng. "Zappos, Under Amazon, Keeps its Independent Streak." *MarketWatch*: marketwatch.com. Accessed February 27, 2012.

Jeff Cerny. "10 Questions on Customer Service and 'Delivering Happiness': An Interview with Zappos CEO Tony Hsieh." *TechRepublic*: techrepublic.com. Accessed February 27, 2012.

"Zappos Retails Its Culture." *Businessweek*: businessweek.com. Accessed February 27, 2012.

"Zappos Launches Insights Service." *AdWeek*: Accessed February 27, 2012.

Jeanne Whalen, "This is the Boardroom of the 'Virtual' Biotech," *Wall Street Journal* (June 4, 2014), pp. B1, B2.

Rachel Emma Silverman, "Going Bossless Backfires at Zappos," *Wall Street Journal* (May 21, 2015), pp. A1, A10.

Case 11 Panera

"Panera Company Overview: Company FAQs." panerabread.com. Accessed February 18, 2012.

Ron Shaich, Speech at Annual Meeting 2006, Temple Israel, June 28, 2006.

Beth Kowitt, "A Founder's Bold Gamble on Panera." CNN Money (July 18, 2012): money.cnn.com. Accessed February 16, 2014.

Case 12 Salesforce

Don Tapscott, "Supervising Net Gen," *BusinessWeek* (December 8, 2008): businessweek.com. Accessed November 12, 2012.

"Motivate," *Work.com*, http://work.com. Accessed 11/12/12.

Kate Abbot, "How I Got Here: Salesforce Rypple's Daniel Debow," *Bloomberg Businessweek* (June 27, 2012): businessweek.com. Accessed November 12, 2012.

Rachel Emma Silverman, "Yearly Reviews? Try Weekly," *Wall Street Journal* (September 6, 2011): online.wsj.com. Accessed November 12, 2012.

Samuel Culbert, "Get Rid of the Performance Review," *Wall Street Journal* (June 21, 2012): professional.wsj.com. Accessed November 12, 2012.

Lena Rao, "Salesforce Debuts Rypple Powered Work to Help Companies Manage Talent," *TechCrunch* (September 19, 2012): techcrunch.com. Accessed November 12, 2012.

Case 13 Auto Racing

Robert M. Williamson. "NASCAR Racing: A Model for Equipment Reliability & Teamwork." *Strategic Work Systems*: swspitcrew.com. Accessed February 13, 2012.

"Modern Era Race Winners." *NASCAR.com*. nascar.com. Accessed February 13, 2012; and, Mike Hembree, "CUP: Gordon's Ride Has Been One Of Sport's Grandest," *Speed TV* (posted 11/6/11): nascar.speedtv.com. Accessed February 13, 2012.

Allen St. John, "Racing's Fastest Pit Crew," *Wall Street Journal* (May 9, 2008), p. W4; and, Bonnie Berkowitz, "Pit Crews Keep NASCAR Racers on Track," *Columbus Dispatch* (May 28, 2008), p. D6.

Dave Rodman. "Teamwork More Important with COT Going Full Time." *NASCAR.com* (posted April 14, 2008): nascar.com. Accessed February 13, 2012.

Adam Cooper. "F1: Lowe Credits McLaren Teamwork for Success." *Speed TV* (posted April 27, 2011): formula-one.speedtv.com. Accessed February 13, 2012.

"Teamwork Is the Key to Success—Theissen." *F1 Technical*: f1technical.net. Accessed February 13, 2012.

"Rallying." *Bethelame Indy*: bethelame-indy.org. Accessed February 13, 2012.

Nick Hardy. "The Fastest Woman on Four Wheels?" *Gulf News* (posted November 18, 2011): gulfnews.com. Accessed February 14, 2012.

Case 14 Twitter

Lauren Duggan, "Twitter to Surpass 500 million Registered Users," mediabistro.com (February 21, 2012). Accessed January 15, 2013.

Pew Research, "The Demographics of Twitter Users." mindjumpers.com. Accessed January 15, 2013.

Shea Bennet, "22% of Black Internet Users Are Active on Twitter (Compared to 16% of White)," mediabistro.com: (January 15, 2013). Accessed March 4, 2014.

Ryan Kelly, "Twitter Study Reveals Interesting Results About Usage—40% Is Pointless Babble," pearanalytics.com (August 12, 2009). Accessed February 26, 2014.

Danah Boyd, "Twitter: 'Pointless Babble' or Peripheral Awareness + Social Grooming?" zephoria.org. Accessed February 26, 2014.

Alex Santoso, "10 Quickie Quotes about Twitter," netorama.com. Accessed February 26, 2014.

Jolie O'Dell, "How Egyptians Used Twitter During the January Crisis," mashable.com (January 31, 2011). JochanEmbley, "Twitter Alerts: Service to Help During Emergencies, Natural Disasters Comes to the UK," independent.co.uk (November 18, 2013). Accessed March 4, 2014.

Case 15 India, Inc.

Veenu Sandhu, "For Young BPO Workers, It's a Close Call with Abuse," *Hindustan Times* (January 12, 2008): hindustantimes.com. Accessed November 27, 2012.

R. Sanjeev Kumar, "BPO Culture: Good or Bad for Indian Youth?" *MeriNews* (May 11, 2008): merinews.com. Accessed November 27, 2012.

Andrew Marantz, "My Summer at an Indian Call Center," *Mother Jones* (July/August 2011): motherjones.com. Accessed November 27, 2012.

Kirti Kamboj, "Mother Jones Falls Short: My Summer in an Indian Call Center," *Hyphen* magazine (posted July 18, 2011): hyphenmagazine.com. Accessed November 2, 2012.

Sarah Whitmire, "How Call Centers 'De-Indianize' Workers," *Newser* (Posted July 10, 2011). Accessed November 12, 2012.

Suresh Yannamani, "The Changing Face of Indian BPO Industry," *Silicon-India* (April 8, 2011): siliconindia.com. Accessed November 12, 2012.

Christy Petty, "Gartner Says Worldwide BPO Growth Continues Despite Mixed Fortunes in Developed Countries," *GartnerReport* (August 22, 2011): gartner.com. Accessed November 26, 2012.

Shehzad Nadeem, *Dead Ringers: How Outsourcing Is Changing the Way Indians Understand Themselves* (Princeton, NJ: Princeton University Press, 2011).

Goutam Das and Sunny Sen, "Born Again: India's BPO Industry Losing Voice, Finds Life Elsewhere," *Business Today* (April 1, 2012): businesstoday. intoday. Accessed November 26, 2012.

Case 16 Harley-Davidson

Malia Boyd, "Harley-Davidson Motor Company," *Incentive* (September 1993), pp. 26–27.

Martha H. Peak, "Harley-Davidson: Going Whole Hog to Provide Stakeholder Satisfaction," *Management Review*, vol. 82 (June 1993), p. 53.

Harley-Davidson, 1992 Form 10K, p. 33; and, Harley-Davidson home page.

Susanna Hanner. "Harley, You're Not Getting Any Younger." *New York Times*, nytimes.com (March 3, 2009). Accessed February 17, 2012.

Kevin Kelly and Karen Miller, "The Rumble Heard Round the World: Harley's," *Businessweek* (May 24, 1993), p. 60.

Sandra Dallas and Emily Thornton, "Japan's Bikers: The Tame Ones," *Businessweek* (October 20, 1997), p. 159.

"Introduction of Chongqing Zongshen Automobile Industry Manufacturing Co., Ltd." *Zongshen International*, zongsheninternational.com. Accessed February 18, 2012.

"Global Customer Focus." *Harley-Davidson*. investor.harleydavidson.com. Accessed February 23, 2012.

"Harley-Davidson's CEO Discusses Q1 2014 Results—Earnings Call Transcript," *Seeking Alpha* (April 22, 2014): seekingalpha.com. Accessed: May 22, 2014.

James R. Hagerty and Bob Tita, "Harley Wheels Out an Electric Hog," *Wall Street Journal* (June 20, 2014), p. B2.

Case 17 Crowdfunding

Erik Sofge, "The Good, the Bad and the Crowd Funded," *Wall Street Journal* (August 18, 2012): professional.wsj.com. Accessed November 24, 2012.

Scott Lowe and Ben Popper, "How Much Accountability Should Your Kickstarter Pledge Buy?" *TheVerge.com* (September 14, 2012): theverge.com. Accessed November 24, 2012.

Rachel Arndt, "The World's 50 Most Innovative Entrepreneurs," *Fast Company*, fastcompany.com. Accessed November 24, 2012.

Roger Yu, "Crowd funding fuels businesses, charities, creative ventures," *USA Today* (May 31, 2012): usatoday.com. Accessed November 24, 2012.

Michael Farrell, "Kickstarter Propels Local Entrepreneurs," *Boston Globe* (September 9, 2012): boston.com. Accessed November 24, 2012.

Bethany Clough, "Kickstarter Proves Useful for Entrepreneurs," *Fresno Bee* (September 30, 2012): hispanicbusiness.com. Accessed November 24, 2012.

Ben Hamilton, *PleaseFund.Us website* (September 9, 2011): pleasefund.us. Accessed November 24, 2012.

Rob Walker, "The Trivialities and Transcendence of Kickstarter," *New York Times* (August 5, 2011): nytimes.com. Accessed November 25, 2012.

Test Prep 1

Multiple Choice

1. d. **2.** c. **3.** b. **4.** b. **5.** b. **6.** d. **7.** a. **8.** d.
9. c. **10.** a. **11.** c. **12.** a. **13.** c. **14.** c. **15.** a.

Short Response

16. Prejudice involves holding a negative stereotype or irrational attitude toward a person who is different from one's self. Discrimination occurs when such prejudice leads to decisions that adversely affect the other person in his or her job, in advancement opportunities at work, or in his or her personal life.

17. The "free agent economy" is one in which there is a lot of job-hopping, and people work for several different employers over a career, rather than just one. This relates not only to the preferences of the individuals but also to the nature of organizational employment practices. As more organizations reduce the hiring of full-time workers in favor of more part-timers and independent contractors, this creates fewer long-term job opportunities for potential employees. Thus they become "free agents" who sell their services to different employers on a part-time and contract basis.

18. You will typically find that top managers are more oriented toward the external environment than the first-level or lower-level managers. This means that top managers must be alert to trends, problems, and opportunities that can affect the performance of the organization as a whole. The first-line or lower manager is most concerned with the performance of his or her immediate work unit and managing the people and resources of the unit on an operational day-to-day basis. Top management is likely to be more strategic and long term in orientation.

19. Planning sets the objectives or targets that one hopes to accomplish. Controlling measures actual results against the planning objectives or targets and makes any corrections necessary to better accomplish them. Thus, planning and controlling work together in the management process, with planning setting the stage for controlling.

Integration and Application

20. I consider myself "effective" as a manager if I can help my work unit achieve high performance and the persons in it to achieve job satisfaction. In terms of skills and personal development, the framework of essential management skills offered by Katz is a useful starting point. At the first level of management, technical skills are important, and I would feel capable in this respect. However, I would expect to learn and refine these skills even more through my work experiences. Human skills, the ability to work well with other people, will also be very important. Given the diversity anticipated for this team, I will need good human skills, and I will have to keep improving my capabilities in this area. One area of consideration here is emotional intelligence, or my ability to understand how the emotions of myself and others influence work relationships. I will also have a leadership responsibility to help others on the team develop and utilize these skills so that the team itself can function

effectively. Finally, I would expect opportunities to develop my conceptual or analytical skills in anticipation of higher-level appointments. In terms of personal development, I should recognize that the conceptual skills will increase in importance relative to the technical skills as I move upward in management responsibility, whereas the human skills are consistently important.

Test Prep 2

Multiple Choice

1. a. **2.** c. **3.** d. **4.** a. **5.** c. **6.** b. **7.** c. **8.** b.
9. a. **10.** a. **11.** b. **12.** b. **13.** d. **14.** c. **15.** d.

Short Response

16. Distributive justice means that everyone is treated the same—that there is no discrimination based on things like age, gender, or sexual orientation. An example would be a man and a woman who both apply for the same job. A manager violates distributive justice if he interviews only the man and not the woman as well, or vice versa. Procedural justice means that rules and procedures are fairly followed. For example, a manager violates procedural justice if he or she punishes one person for coming to work late while ignoring late behavior by another person with whom he or she regularly plays golf.

17. The "spotlight questions" for double-checking the ethics of a decision are "How would I feel if my family finds out?" "How would I feel if this were published in the local newspaper or on the Internet?" "What would the person you know or know of who has the strongest character and best ethical judgment do in this situation?"

18. The rationalizations include believing that (1) the behavior is not really illegal, (2) the behavior is really in everyone's best interests, (3) no one will find out, and (4) the organization will protect him or her.

19. The "virtuous circle" concept of social responsibility holds that social responsibility practices do not hurt the bottom line and often help it; when socially responsible actions result in improved financial performance, this encourages more of the same actions in the future—a virtuous circle being created.

Integration and Application

20. If the manager adopts a position of cultural relativism, there will be no perceived problem in working with the Tanzanian firm. The justification would be that as long as it is operating legally in Tanzania, that makes everything okay. The absolutist position would hold that the contract should not be taken because the factory conditions are unacceptable at home and therefore are unacceptable anywhere. The cultural relativism position can be criticized because it makes it easy to do business in places where people are not treated well; the absolutist position can be criticized as trying to impose one's values on people in a different cultural context.

Test Prep 3

Multiple Choice

1. b. **2.** c. **3.** a. **4.** c. **5.** d. **6.** a. **7.** b. **8.** c.
9. c. **10.** a. **11.** a. **12.** b. **13.** c. **14.** d. **15.** b.

Short Response

16. An optimizing decision represents the absolute "best" choice of alternatives. It is selected from a set of all known alternatives. A satisficing decision selects the first alternative that offers a "satisfactory" choice, not necessarily the absolute best choice. It is selected from a limited or incomplete set of alternatives.

17. A risk environment is one in which things are not known for sure—all the possible decision alternatives, all the possible consequences for each alternative—but they can be estimated as probabilities. For example, if I take a new job with a new employer, I can't know for certain that it will turn out as I expect, but I could be 80% sure that I'd like the new responsibilities, or only 60% sure that I might get promoted within a year. In an uncertain environment, things are so speculative that it is hard to even assign such probabilities.

18. A manager using systematic thinking is going to approach problem solving in a logical and rational fashion. The tendency will be to proceed in a linear step-by-step manner, handling one issue at a time. A manager using intuitive thinking will be more spontaneous and open in problem solving. He or she may jump from one stage in the process to the other and deal with many different things at once.

19. Escalating commitment is the tendency of people to keep investing in a previously chosen course of action, continuing to pursue it, even though it is not working. This is a human tendency to try to make things work by trying harder, investing more time, effort, resources, and so on. In other words, I have decided in the past to pursue this major in college; I can't be wrong, can I? The feedback from my grades and course satisfaction suggests it isn't working, but I'm doing it now so I just need to make it work, right? I'll just stick with it and see if things eventually turn out okay. In this example, my decision to continue with the major is most likely an example of escalating commitment.

Integration and Application

20. This is what I would say. On the question of whether a group decision is best or an individual decision is best, the appropriate answer is probably: It all depends on the situation. Sometimes one is preferable to the other; each has its potential advantages and disadvantages. If you are in a situation where the problem being addressed is unclear, the information needed to solve it is uncertain, and you don't have a lot of personal expertise, the group approach to decision making is probably best. Group decisions offer advantages like bringing more information and ideas to bear on a problem; they often allow for more creativity; and they tend to build commitments among participants to work hard to implement any decisions reached. On the other hand, groups can be dominated by one or more members, and they can take a lot of

time making decisions. Thus, when time is short, the individual decision is sometimes a better choice. However, it is important that you, as this individual, be confident that you have the information needed to solve the problem or can get it before making your decision.

Test Prep 4

Multiple Choice

1. d. **2.** a. **3.** b. **4.** b. **5.** d. **6.** c. **7.** a. **8.** d.
9. b. **10.** a. **11.** c. **12.** b. **13.** d. **14.** b. **15.** c.

Short Response

16. The five steps in the formal planning process are (1) define your objectives, (2) determine where you stand relative to objectives, (3) develop premises about future conditions, (4) identify and choose among action alternatives to accomplish objectives, and (5) implement action plans and evaluate results.

17. Planning facilitates controlling because the planning process sets the objectives and standards that become the basis for the control process. If you don't have objectives and standards, you have nothing to compare actual performance with; consequently, control lacks purpose and specificity.

18. Contingency planning essentially makes available optional plans that can be quickly implemented if things go wrong with the original plan. Scenario planning is a longer-term form of contingency planning that tries to project several future scenarios that might develop over time and to associate each scenario with plans for best dealing with it.

19. Participation is good for the planning process, in part because it brings to the process a lot more information, diverse viewpoints, and potential alternatives than would otherwise be available if just one person or a select group of top managers are doing the planning. Furthermore, and very importantly, through participation in the planning process, people develop an understanding of the final plans and the logic used to arrive at them, and they develop personal commitments to trying to follow through and work hard to make implementation of the plans successful.

Integration and Application

20. Benchmarking is the use of external standards to help evaluate one's own situation and develop ideas and directions for improvement. Curt and Rich are both right to a certain extent about its potential value for them. Rich is right in suggesting that there is much to learn by looking at what other bookstores are doing really well. The bookstore owner/manager might visit other bookstores in other towns that are known for their success. By observing and studying the operations of those stores and then comparing his store to them, the owner/manager can develop plans for future action. Curt is also right in suggesting that there is much to be learned potentially from looking outside the bookstore business. They should look at things like inventory management, customer service, and facilities in other settings—not just bookstores; they should also look outside their town as well as within it.

Test Prep 5

Multiple Choice

1. a.   2. a.   3. d.   4. b.   5. b.   6. c.   7. c.   8. d.
9. a.   10. b.   11. c.   12. a.   13. a.   14. b.   15. c.

Short Response

16. The Army's "after-action review" takes place after an action or activity has been completed. This makes it a form of "feedback" control. The primary purpose is to critique the action/activity and try to learn from it so that similar things in the future can be done better and so that the people involved can be best trained.

17. One way to use clan control in a TQM context would be to set up small teams or task forces called "Quality Circles" that bring together persons from various parts of the workplace with a common commitment to quality improvements. You can ask these teams or QCs to meet regularly to discuss quality results and options and to try to maintain a continuous improvement momentum in their work areas. The members should ideally get special quality training. They should also be expected to actively serve as quality champions in their own work areas to implement continuous quality improvements and come up with ideas for new ones.

18. The just-in-time inventory approach reduces the carrying costs of inventories. It does this by trying to have materials arrive at a workstation just in time to be used. When this concept works perfectly, there are no inventory carrying costs. However, even if it is imperfect and some inventory ends up being stockpiled, it should still be less than that which would otherwise be the case. But as the recent tsunami and nuclear disaster in Japan showed, firms that are too reliant on JIT in their supply chains must prepare for the risk of disruptions when crises and natural disasters occur.

19. The four questions to ask when developing a balanced scorecard are (1) *Financial Performance*—To improve financially, how should we appear to our shareholders? (2) *Customer Satisfaction*—To achieve our vision, how should we appear to our customers? (3) *Internal Process Improvement*—To satisfy our customers and shareholders, at what internal business processes should we excel? (4) *Innovation and Learning*—To achieve our vision, how will we sustain our ability to change and improve?

Integration and Application

20. I would begin the speech by describing MBO as an integrated planning and control approach. I would also clarify that the key elements in MBO are objectives and participation. Any objectives should be clear, measurable, and time defined. In addition, these objectives should be set with the full involvement and participation of the employees; they should not be set by the manager and then told to the employees. Given this, I would describe how each business manager should jointly set objectives with each of his or her employees and jointly review progress toward their accomplishment. I would suggest that the employees should work on the required activities while staying in communication with their managers. The managers, in turn, should provide any needed support or assistance to their employees. This whole process could be formally recycled at least twice per year.

Test Prep 6

Multiple Choice

1. a.   2. b.   3. b.   4. c.   5. a.   6. c.   7. d.   8. a.
9. a.   10. b.   11. c.   12. b.   13. d.   14. c.   15. b.

Short Response

16. A corporate strategy sets long-term direction for an enterprise as a whole. Functional strategies set directions so that business functions such as marketing and manufacturing support the overall corporate strategy.

17. If you want to sell at lower prices than competitors and still make a profit, you have to have lower operating costs (profit = revenues − costs). Also, you have to be able to operate at lower costs in ways that are hard for your competitors to copy. This is the point of a cost leadership strategy—always seeking ways to lower costs and operate with greater efficiency than anyone else.

18. A question mark in the BCG matrix has a low market share in a high-growth industry. This means that there is a lot of upside potential, but for now it is uncertain whether or not you will be able to capitalize on it. Thus, hard thinking is required. If you are confident, the recommended strategy is growth; if you aren't, it would be retrenchment, to allow resources to be deployed into more promising opportunities.

19. Strategic leadership is the ability to enthuse people to participate in continuous change, performance enhancement, and the implementation of organizational strategies. The special qualities of the successful strategic leader include the ability to make trade-offs, create a sense of urgency, communicate the strategy, and engage others in continuous learning about the strategy and its performance responsibilities.

Integration and Application

20. A SWOT analysis is useful during strategic planning. It involves the analysis of organizational strengths and weaknesses, and of environmental opportunities and threats. Such a SWOT analysis in this case would help frame Kim's thinking about the current and future positioning of her store, particularly in respect to possible core competencies and competitive opportunities and threats. Then she can use Porter's competitive strategy model for further strategic refinements. This involves the possible use of three alternative strategies: differentiation, cost leadership, and focus. In this situation, the larger department store seems better positioned to follow the cost leadership strategy. This means that Kim may want to consider the other two alternatives. A differentiation strategy would involve trying to distinguish Kim's products from those of the larger store. This might involve a "made in America" theme or an emphasis on leather or canvas or some other type of clothing material. A focus strategy might specifically target college students and try to respond to their tastes and needs rather than those of the larger community population. This might involve special orders and other types of individualized service for the college student market.

Test Prep 7

Multiple Choice

1. b. 2. c. 3. b. 4. a. 5. b. 6. c. 7. b. 8. a.
9. c. 10. b. 11. c. 12. b. 13. c. 14. b. 15. c.

Short Response

16. An organization chart depicts the formal structure of the organization. This is the official picture of the way things are supposed to be. However, the likelihood is that an organization chart quickly becomes out of date in today's dynamic environments. So one issue is whether or not the chart one is viewing actually depicts the current official structure. Second, there is a lot more to the way things work in organizations than what is shown in the organization chart. People are involved in a variety of informal networks that create an informal structure. It operates as a shadow lying above or behind the formal structure and also influences operations. Both the formal structure and informal structure must be understood; at best, an organization chart helps with understanding the formal one.

17. There are two major ways that informal structures can be good for organizations. First, they can help get work done efficiently and well. When people know one another in informal relationships, they can and often do use these relationships as part of their jobs. Sometimes an informal contact makes it a lot easier to get something done or learn how to do something than the formal linkages displayed on an organization chart. Second, being part of informal groups is an important source of potential need satisfaction. Being in an informal network or group can satisfy needs in ways that one's job can't sometimes and can add considerably to the potential satisfactions of the work experience.

18. The matrix structure is organized in a traditional functional fashion in the vertical dimension. For example, a business might have marketing, human resources, finance, and manufacturing functions. On the horizontal dimension, however, it is organized divisionally in a product or project fashion, with a manager heading up each special product or project. Members from the functional departments are assigned to permanent cross-functional teams for each product or project. They report vertically to their functional bosses and horizontally to their product/project bosses. This two-boss system is the heart of the matrix organization.

19. An organic design tends to be quicker and more flexible because it is very strong in lateral communication and empowerment. People at all levels are talking to one another and interacting as they gather and process information and solve problems. They don't wait for the vertical structure and "bosses" to do these things for them. This means that as the environment changes, they are more likely to be on top of things quickly. It also means that when problems are complex and difficult to solve, they will work with multiple people in various parts of the organization to best deal with them.

Integration and Application

20. A network structure often involves one organization "contracting out" aspects of its operations to other organizations that specialize in these aspects. The example used in the text was of a company that contracted out its mailroom services. Through the formation of networks of contracts, the organization is reduced to a core of essential employees whose expertise is concentrated in the primary business areas. The contracts are monitored and maintained in the network to allow the overall operations of the organization to continue even though they are not directly accomplished by full-time employees. There are many possibilities for doing something similar in a university. In one model, the core staff would be the faculty. They would be supported by a few administrators who managed contracts with outsourcing firms for things such as facilities maintenance, mail, technology support, lawn maintenance, food services, housing services, and even things like development, registrar, and student affairs. Another model would have the administrators forming a small core staff who contract out for all this and, in addition, for faculty who would be hired "as needed" and on contracts for specific assignments.

Test Prep 8

Multiple Choice

1. a. 2. c. 3. d. 4. b. 5. b. 6. c. 7. a. 8. c.
9. c. 10. b. 11. d. 12. c. 13. c. 14. b. 15. b.

Short Response

16. The core values that might be found in high-performance organizational cultures include such things as performance excellence, innovation, social responsibility, integrity, worker involvement, customer service, and teamwork.

17. First, process innovations result in better ways of doing things. Second, product innovations result in the creation of new or improved goods and services. Third, business model innovations result in new ways of making money for the firm.

18. Lewin's three phases of planned change are unfreezing, changing, and refreezing. In terms of the change leadership challenges, the major differences in attention would be as follows: unfreezing—preparing a system for change; changing—moving or creating change in a system; and refreezing—stabilizing and reinforcing change once it has occurred.

19. In general, managers can expect that others will be more committed and loyal to changes that are brought about through shared power strategies. Rational persuasion strategies can also create enduring effects if they are accepted. Force-coercion strategies tend to have temporary effects only.

Integration and Application

20. In any change situation, it is important to remember that successful planned change occurs only when all three phases of change—unfreezing, changing, and refreezing—have been taken care of. Thus, I would not rush into the changing phase. Rather, I would work with the people involved to develop a felt need for change based on their ideas and inputs as well as mine. Then I would proceed by supporting the changes and helping to stabilize them into everyday routines. I would also be sensitive to any resistance and respect that resistance as a

signal that something important is being threatened. By listening to resistance, I would be in a position to better modify the change to achieve a better fit with the people and the situation. Finally, I would want to take maximum advantage of the shared power strategy, supported by rational persuasion, and with limited use of force-coercion (if it is used at all). By doing all this, I would like my staff to feel empowered and committed to constructive improvement through planned change. Throughout all this I would strive to perform to the best of my ability and gain trust and credibility with everyone else; in this way I would be a positive role model for change.

Test Prep 9

Multiple Choice

1. a. **2.** b. **3.** c. **4.** b. **5.** b. **6.** d. **7.** a. **8.** b.
9. b. **10.** a. **11.** d. **12.** d. **13.** a. **14.** a. **15.** b.

Short Response

16. Onboarding and orientation activities introduce a new employee to the organization and the work environment. This is a time when the individual may develop key attitudes and when performance expectations will also be established. Good orientation communicates positive attitudes and expectations and reinforces the desired organizational culture. It formally introduces the individual to important policies and procedures that everyone is expected to follow.

17. Mentoring is when a senior and experienced individual adopts a newcomer or more junior person with the goal of helping him or her develop into a successful worker. The mentor may or may not be the individual's immediate supervisor. The mentor meets with the individual and discusses problems, shares advice, and generally supports the individual's attempts to grow and perform. Mentors are considered very useful for persons newly appointed to management positions.

18. Any performance assessment approach should be both valid and reliable. To be valid it must measure accurately what it claims to measure—whether that is some aspect of job performance or personal behavior. To be reliable it must deliver the same results consistently—whether applied by different raters to the same person or when measuring the same person over time. Valid and reliable assessments are free from bias and as objective as possible.

19. The graphic rating scale simply asks a supervisor to rate an employee on an established set of criteria, such as quantity of work or attitude toward work. This leaves much room for subjectivity and debate. The behaviorally anchored rating scale asks the supervisor to rate the employee on specific behaviors that had been identified as positively or negatively affecting performance in a given job. This is a more specific appraisal approach and leaves less room for debate and disagreement.

Integration and Application

20. As Sy's supervisor, you face a difficult but perhaps expected human resource management problem. Not only is Sy influential as an informal leader, but he also has considerable experience on the job and in the company. Even though he is experiencing performance problems using the new computer system, there is no indication that he doesn't want to work hard and continue to perform for the company. Although retirement is an option, Sy may also be transferred, promoted, or simply terminated. The last response seems unjustified and may cause legal problems. Transferring Sy, with his agreement, to another position could be a positive move; promoting Sy to a supervisory position in which his experience and networks would be useful is another possibility. The key in this situation seems to be moving Sy out so that a computer-literate person can take over the job, while continuing to utilize Sy in a job that better fits his talents. Transfer and/or promotion should be actively considered both in his and in the company's best interests.

Test Prep 10

Multiple Choice

1. b. **2.** b. **3.** a. **4.** d. **5.** a. **6.** c. **7.** c. **8.** a.
9. a. **10.** b. **11.** d. **12.** d. **13.** a. **14.** d. **15.** a.

Short Response

16. Position power is based on reward, coercion or punishment, and legitimacy or formal authority. Managers, however, need to have more power than that made available to them by the position alone. Thus, they have to develop personal power through expertise and reference. This personal power is essential in helping managers get things done beyond the scope of their position power alone.

17. Leadership situations are described by Fiedler according to position power—how much power the leader has in terms of rewards, punishments, and legitimacy; leader–member relations—the quality of relationships between the leader and followers; and task structure—the degree to which the task is clear and well defined, or open ended and more ambiguous. Highly favorable situations are high in position power, have good leader–member relations, and have structured tasks; highly unfavorable situations are low in position power, have poor leader–member relations, and have unstructured tasks.

18. According to House's path-goal theory, the following combinations are consistent with successful leadership. Participative leadership works well, for example, when performance incentives are low and people need to find other sources of need satisfaction. Through participation the leader gains knowledge that can help identify important needs and possible ways of satisfying them other than through the available performance incentives. Directive leadership works well, for example, when people aren't clear about their jobs or goals. In these cases the leader can step in and provide direction that channels their efforts toward desired activities and outcomes.

19. Servant leadership is basically other centered and not self-centered. A servant leader is concerned with helping others to perform well so that the organization or group can ultimately do good things for society. The person who accepts the responsibilities of servant leadership is good at empowering others so that they can use their talents while acting independently to do their jobs in the best possible ways.

Integration and Application

20. In his new position, Marcel must understand that the transactional aspects of leadership are not sufficient enough to guarantee him long-term leadership effectiveness. He must move beyond the effective use of task-oriented and people-oriented behaviors—the "transactional" side of leadership—and demonstrate through his behavior and personal qualities the capacity to inspire others and lead with moral integrity—the "transformational" side. A transformational leader develops a unique relationship with followers in which they become enthusiastic, highly loyal, and high achievers. Marcel needs to work very hard to develop positive relationships with the team members. But he must add to this a moral and ethical dimension. He must emphasize in those relationships high aspirations for performance accomplishments, enthusiasm, ethical behavior, integrity and honesty in all dealings, and a clear vision of the future. By working hard with this agenda and by allowing his personality to positively express itself in the team setting, Marcel should make continuous progress as an effective and moral leader.

Test Prep 11

Multiple Choice

1. c.   2. d.   3. b.   4. a.   5. d.   6. a.   7. b.   8. a.
9. b.   10. a.   11. b.   12. d.   13. d.   14. d.   15. c.

Short Response

16. All of the Big Five personality traits are relevant to the workplace. To give some basic examples, consider the following. Extroversion suggests whether or not a person will reach out to relate and work well with others. Agreeableness suggests whether or not a person is open to the ideas of others and willing to go along with group decisions. Conscientiousness suggests whether someone can be depended on to meet commitments and perform agreed-upon tasks. Emotional stability suggests whether or not someone will be relaxed and secure, or uptight and tense, in work situations. Openness suggests whether someone will be open to new ideas or resistant to change.

17. The Type A personality is characteristic of people who bring stress on themselves by virtue of personal characteristics. These tend to be compulsive individuals who are uncomfortable waiting for things to happen, who try to do many things at once, and who generally move fast and have difficulty slowing down. Type A personalities can be stressful for both the individuals and the people around them. Managers must be aware of Type A personality tendencies in their own behavior and among others with whom they work. Ideally, this awareness will help the manager take precautionary steps to best manage the stress caused by this personality type.

18. The halo effect occurs when a single attribute of a person, such as the way he or she dresses, is used to evaluate or form an overall impression of the person. Selective perception occurs when someone focuses in a situation on those aspects that reinforce or are most consistent with his or her existing values, beliefs, or experiences.

19. Job satisfaction is an attitude that reflects how people feel about their jobs, work settings, and the people with whom they work. A typical job satisfaction survey might ask people to respond to questions about their pay, co-worker relationships, quality of supervisor, nature of the work setting, and the type of work they are asked to do. These questions might be framed with a scale ranging from "very satisfied" to "not satisfied at all" for each question or job satisfaction dimension.

Integration and Application

20. Scott needs to be careful. Although there is modest research support for the relationship between job satisfaction and performance, there is no guarantee that simply doing things to make people happier at work will cause them to be higher performers. Scott needs to take a broader perspective on this issue and his responsibilities as a manager. He should be interested in job satisfaction for his therapists and do everything he can to help them to experience it. But he should also be performance oriented and understand that performance is achieved through a combination of skills, support, and motivation. He should be helping the therapists to achieve and maintain high levels of job competency. He should also work with them to find out what obstacles they are facing and what support they need—things that perhaps he can deal with on their behalf. All of this relates as well to research indications that performance can be a source of job satisfaction. And finally, Scott should make sure that the therapists believe they are being properly rewarded for their work, because research shows that rewards have an influence on both job satisfaction and job performance.

Test Prep 12

Multiple Choice

1. b.   2. c.   3. d.   4. d.   5. b.   6. a.   7. b.   8. b.
9. a.   10. d.   11. a.   12. c.   13. c.   14. a.   15. a.

Short Response

16. People high in need for achievement will prefer work settings and jobs in which they have (1) challenging but achievable goals, (2) individual responsibility, and (3) performance feedback.

17. One way for a team leader to use goal-setting principles in working with team members is to engage them in a process of joint goal-setting and performance review. In an earlier chapter on planning and controlling, this type of approach was described as "management by objectives." It is really a good application of goal-setting theory. Participation of both team leader and team member in goal setting offers an opportunity to choose goals to which the member will respond and which also will serve the team and organization as a whole. Furthermore, through goal setting, the team leader and team member can identify performance standards or targets. Progress toward these targets can be positively reinforced by the team leader. This type of approach harnesses the power of goal-setting theory by putting the team leader and team member together in a process where specific, challenging, and measureable goals can be set, and the team member can feel that he or she has helped set them.

18. When perceived negative inequity exists, an individual might (1) quit the job, (2) speak with the boss to try to increase rewards to the point where the inequity no longer exists, or (3) decide to reduce effort to the level that seems consistent with the rewards being received.

19. Shaping encourages the formation of desirable work behaviors by rewarding successive approximations to those behaviors. In this sense, the behavior doesn't have to be perfect to be rewarded—it just has to be moving in the right direction. Over time and with a change of reinforcement scheduling from continuous to intermittent, such rewards can end up drawing forth the desired behavior.

Integration and Application

20. The use of Muzak would be considered improvement in a hygiene factor under Herzberg's two-factor theory. Thus it would not be a source of greater work motivation and performance. Herzberg suggests that job content factors are the satisfiers or motivators. Based in the job itself, they represent such things as responsibility, sense of achievement, and feelings of growth. Job context factors are considered sources of dissatisfaction. They are found in the job environment and include such things as base pay, technical quality of supervision, and working conditions. Whereas improvements in job context such as introduction of Muzak make people less dissatisfied, improvements in job content are considered necessary to motivate them to high performance levels.

Test Prep 13

Multiple Choice

1. d. 2. a. 3. b. 4. d. 5. b. 6. a. 7. c. 8. b.
9. a. 10. a. 11. a. 12. b. 13. d. 14. c. 15. d.

Short Response

16. In a task force, members are brought together to work on a specific assignment. The task force usually disbands when the assignment is finished. In an employee involvement group, perhaps a quality circle, members are brought together to work on an issue or task over time. They meet regularly and always deal with the same issue/task. In a self-managing team, the members of a formal work group provide self-direction. They plan, organize, and evaluate their work, share tasks, and help one another develop skills; they may even make hiring decisions. A true self-managing team does not need the traditional "boss" or supervisor because the team as a whole takes on the supervisory responsibilities.

17. Input factors can have a major impact on group effectiveness. To best prepare a group to perform effectively, a manager should make sure that the right people are put in the group (maximize available talents and abilities), that these people are capable of working well together (membership characteristics should promote good relationships), that the tasks are clear, and that the group has the resources and environment needed to perform up to expectations.

18. A team's performance can be analyzed according to the interaction between cohesiveness and performance norms. In a highly cohesive team, members tend to conform to group norms. Thus, when the performance norm is positive and cohesion is high, we can expect everyone to work hard to support the norm—high performance is likely. By the same token, high cohesion and a low performance norm will act similarly—low performance is likely. With other combinations of norms and cohesion, the performance results will be more mixed.

19. The text lists several symptoms of groupthink along with various strategies for avoiding groupthink. For example, a group whose members censor themselves to refrain from contributing "contrary" or "different" opinions and/or whose members keep talking about outsiders as "weak" or the "enemy" may be suffering from groupthink. This may be avoided or corrected, for example, by asking someone to be the "devil's advocate" for a meeting and by inviting in an outside observer to help gather different viewpoints.

Integration and Application

20. Valeria is faced with a highly cohesive group whose members conform to a negative or low-performance norm. This is a difficult situation that is ideally resolved by changing the performance norm. To gain the group's commitment to a high-performance norm, Valeria should act as a positive role model for the norm. She must communicate the norm clearly and positively to the group. She should not assume that everyone knows what she expects of them. She may also talk to the informal leader and gain his or her commitment to the norm. She might carefully reward high-performance behaviors within the group. She may introduce new members with high-performance records and commitments. And she might hold group meetings in which performance standards and expectations are discussed, with an emphasis on committing to new high-performance directions. If attempts to introduce a high-performance norm fail, Valeria may have to take steps to reduce group cohesiveness so that individual members can pursue higher-performance results without feeling bound by group pressures to restrict their performance.

Test Prep 14

Multiple Choice

1. a. 2. c. 3. d. 4. d. 5. a. 6. c. 7. d. 8. c.
9. b. 10. c. 11. c. 12. a. 13. b. 14. a. 15. b.

Short Response

16. The manager's goal in active listening is to help the subordinate say what he or she really means. To do this, the manager should carefully listen for the content of what someone is saying, paraphrase or reflect back what the person appears to be saying, remain sensitive to nonverbal cues and feelings, and not be evaluative.

17. Well-intentioned managers can make bad decisions when they base decisions on bad information. Because of the manager's position of authority in the organization, those below him or her may be reluctant to communicate upward information that they believe the manager doesn't want to hear. Thus, they may filter the information to make it as agreeable to the manager as possible. As a result of this filtering of upward communication, the manager may end up with poor or incomplete information and subsequently make bad decisions.

18. The four major errors in giving constructive feedback would be (1) being general rather than specific, (2) choosing a poor time, (3) including in the message irrelevant things, and (4) overwhelming the receiver with too much information at once.

19. Ethnocentrism is when a person views his or her own culture as superior to others. It can interfere with cross-cultural communication when the ethnocentrism leads the person to ignore cultural signals that indicate his or her behavior is inappropriate or offensive by local cultural standards. With the ethnocentric attitude of cultural superiority, the individual is inclined not to change personal ways or display the sensitivity to local cultural ways that is necessary to effective communication.

Integration and Application

20. Glenn can do a number of things to establish and maintain a system of communication with his employees and for his department store branch. To begin, he should, as much as possible, try to establish a highly interactive style of management based on credibility and trust. Credibility is earned by building personal power through expertise and reference. With credibility, he might set the tone for the department managers by using MBWA—"managing by wandering around." Once this pattern is established, trust will build between him and other store employees, and he should find that he learns a lot from interacting directly with them. Glenn should also set up a formal communication structure, such as bimonthly store meetings, where he communicates store goals, results, and other issues to the staff, and in which he listens to them in return. An e-mail system whereby Glenn and his staff could send messages to one another from their workstation computers would also be beneficial.

Test Prep 15

Multiple Choice

1. c. **2.** a. **3.** b. **4.** b. **5.** b. **6.** d. **7.** a. **8.** a.
9. d. **10.** a. **11.** d. **12.** d. **13.** c. **14.** c. **15.** b.

Short Response

16. An approach of valuing diversity shows through leadership a commitment to helping people understand their differences, often through education and training programs. An approach of managing diversity, according to Roosevelt Thomas, is a step beyond, in that it is where the leadership commits to changing the culture of the organization to empower everyone and create a fully inclusive environment where human resources are respected and fully utilized.

17. There are numbers of subcultures that form in organizations and can become the source of perceived differences as people work with one another across subculture boundaries. Examples of common organizational subcultures include those based on age, gender, race, ethnicity, and work function. If younger workers stereotype older workers as uncreative and less ambitious, a team consisting of an age mix of members might experience some difficulties. This illustrates an example of problems among generational subcultures.

18. The anthropologist Edward Hall identified communication context, time, and space as silent languages of culture. High-context cultures rely on nonverbal and situational cues as well as the spoken word to convey messages, whereas low-context cultures are more focused on what is being said. An American businessperson might press an Indonesian client to sign a contract immediately, whereas the body language of the client might say she doesn't want to, even though she is offering a reluctant "okay" in their conversation. Monochronic cultures deal with time in a linear fashion, whereas polychronic cultures view it as more nonlinear and dynamic. Whereas the American schedules time, saves time, and tries to meet time deadlines (monochronic behavior), a Mexican might be less concerned about time budgeting like this and more likely to act flexibly in terms of time schedules and engagements. Proxemics involves the use of space in communication. If you observe Americans in conversation, there is likely to be a modest amount of distance maintained between speakers. But in Italy the conversation is likely to take place in much closer face-to-face conditions, and this would likely make the American a bit uncomfortable.

19. Organizations are power structures, and the way people view and respond to power differences in organizations can be very significant in how they operate. In a national culture where power distance is high, there would be a tendency in organizations to respect persons of authority—perhaps defer to them, use job titles and formal greetings, and refrain from challenging their views in public meetings. In a low or moderate power distance culture, by contrast, there might be more informality in using first names without job titles and being more casual in relationships and even in public disagreements with views expressed by senior people.

Integration and Application

20. The friend must recognize that the cultural differences between the United States and Japan may affect the success of group-oriented work practices such as quality circles and work teams. The United States was the most individualistic culture in Hofstede's study of national cultures; Japan is much more collectivist. Group practices such as the quality circle and teams are natural and consistent with the Japanese culture. When introduced into a more individualistic culture, these same practices might cause difficulties or require some time for workers to get used to. At the very least, the friend should proceed with caution, discuss ideas for the new practices with the workers before making any changes, and then monitor the changes closely so that adjustments can be made to improve them as the workers gain familiarity with them and have suggestions of their own.

Test Prep 16

Multiple Choice

1. c. **2.** d. **3.** d. **4.** b. **5.** b. **6.** a. **7.** c. **8.** d.
9. d. **10.** b. **11.** b. **12.** c. **13.** b. **14.** c. **15.** a.

Short Response

16. In a joint venture, the foreign corporation and the local corporation each own a portion of the firm—for example, 75% and 25%. In a wholly owned subsidiary, the foreign firm owns the local subsidiary in its entirety.

17. The relationship between an MNC and a host country should be mutually beneficial. Sometimes, however, host countries complain that MNCs take unfair advantage of them and do not include them in the benefits of their international operations. The complaints against MNCs include taking excessive profits out of the host country, hiring the best local labor, not respecting local laws and customs, and dominating the local economy. Engaging in corrupt practices is another important concern.

18. If a senator says she favors "protectionism" in international trade, it basically means that she wants to make sure that domestic American firms are protected against foreign competitors. In other words, she doesn't want foreign companies coming into America and destroying the local firms through competition. Thus, she wants to protect them in some ways such as imposing import tariffs on the foreign firms' products or imposing legal restrictions on them setting up businesses in America.

19. Currency risk in international business involves the rise and fall of currencies in relationship with one another. For an American company operating in Japan, currency risk involves the value of the dollar vis-à-vis the yen. When the dollar falls relative to the yen (requiring more of them to buy 1 yen), it means that buying products and making investments in Japan will be more costly; the "risk" of this eventuality needs to be planned for when business relationships are entered in foreign countries. Political risk is the potential loss in one's investments in foreign countries due to wars or political changes that might threaten the assets. An example would be a Socialist government coming into power and deciding to "nationalize" or take over ownership of all foreign companies.

Integration and Application

20. This issue of MNC versus transnational is growing in importance. When a large global company such as Ford or IBM is strongly associated with a national identity, the firm might face risk in international business when foreign consumers or governments are angry at the firm's home country; they might stop buying its products or make it hard for them to operate. When the MNC has a strong national identity, its home constituents might express anger and create problems when the firm makes investments in creating jobs in other countries. Also, when the leadership of the MNC views itself as having one national home, it might have a more limited and even ethnocentric approach to international operations. When a firm such as Ford or P&G operates as a transnational, by contrast, it becomes a global citizen and, theoretically at least, is freed from some potential problems identified here. Because a transnational views the world as its home, furthermore, its workforce and leadership are more likely to be globally diverse and have broad international perspectives on the company and its opportunities.

Test Prep 17

Multiple Choice

1. a.   2. c.   3. d.   4. b.   5. b.   6. a.   7. a.   8. b.
9. a.   10. c.   11. c.   12. a.   13. d.   14. b.   15. d.

Short Response

16. Entrepreneurship is rich with diversity. It is an avenue for business entry and career success that is pursued by many women and members of minority groups. Data show almost 40% of U.S. businesses are owned by women. Many report leaving other employment because they had limited opportunities. For them, entrepreneurship made available the opportunities for career success that they lacked. Minority-owned businesses are one of the fastest-growing sectors, with the growth rates highest for Hispanic-owned, Asian-owned, and African-American–owned businesses in that order.

17. The three stages in the life cycle of an entrepreneurial firm are birth, breakthrough, and maturity. In the birth stage, the leader is challenged to get customers, establish a market, and find the money needed to keep the business going. In the breakthrough stage, the challenges shift to becoming and staying profitable and managing growth. In the maturity stage, a leader is more focused on revising/maintaining a good business strategy and more generally managing the firm for continued success and possibly more future growth.

18. The limited partnership form of small business ownership consists of a general partner and one or more "limited partners." The general partner(s) play an active role in managing and operating the business; the limited partners do not. All contribute resources of some value to the partnership for the conduct of the business. The advantage of any partnership form is that the partners may share in profits, but their potential for losses is limited by the size of their original investments.

19. A venture capitalist is an individual or group of individuals that invests money in new start-up companies and gets a portion of ownership in return. The goal is to sell their ownership stakes in the future for a profit. An angel investor is a type of venture capitalist, but on a smaller and individual scale. This is a person who invests in a new venture, taking a share of ownership, and also hoping to gain profit through a future sale of the ownership.

Integration and Application

20. The friend is right—it takes much forethought and planning to prepare the launch of a new business venture. In response to the question of how to ensure that you are really being customer-focused in the new start-up, I would ask and answer the following questions to frame my business model with a strong customer orientation. "Who are my potential customers? What market niche am I shooting for? What do the customers in this market really want? How do these customers make purchase decisions? How much will it cost to produce and distribute my product/service to these customers? How much will it cost to attract and retain customers?" Following an overall executive summary, which includes a commitment to this customer orientation, I would address the following areas in writing up my initial business plan. The plan would address such areas as company description—mission, owners, and legal form—as well as an industry analysis, product and services description, marketing description and strategy, staffing model, financial projections with cash flows, and capital needs.

Glossary

3 Ps of organizational performance The 3 Ps of organizational performance are profit, people, and planet.

360° feedback 360° feedback includes superiors, subordinates, peers, and even customers in the appraisal process.

A

accommodation Accommodation, or smoothing, plays down differences and highlights similarities to reduce conflict.

accountability Accountability is the requirement to show performance results to a supervisor.

active listening Active listening helps the source of a message say what he or she really means.

affirmative action Affirmative action is an effort to give preference in employment to women and minority group members.

after-action review After-action review is a structured review of lessons learned and results accomplished through a completed project, task force assignment, or special operation.

age discrimination Age discrimination penalizes an employee in a job or as a job applicant for being over the age of 40.

agenda setting Agenda setting identifies important action priorities.

agreeableness An agreeable person is trusting, courteous, and helpful, getting along well with others; a disagreeable person is self-serving, skeptical, and tough, creating discomfort for others.

amoral manager An amoral manager fails to consider the ethics of her or his behavior.

analytical competency Analytical competency is the ability to evaluate and analyze information to make actual decisions and solve real problems.

analytics Analytics is the systematic use and analysis of data to solve problems and make informed decisions.

anchoring and adjustment heuristic The anchoring and adjustment heuristic adjusts a previously existing value or starting point to make a decision.

angel investor An angel investor is a wealthy individual willing to invest in return for equity in a new venture.

APEC (Asia-Pacific Economic Cooperation). A regional economic alliance of 21 member nations.

assessment center An assessment center examines how job candidates handle simulated work situations.

attitude An attitude is a predisposition to act in a certain way.

attribution Attribution is the process of creating explanations for events.

authoritarianism Authoritarianism is the degree to which a person defers to authority and accepts status differences.

authority decision An authority decision is made by the leader and then communicated to the group.

autocratic leader An autocratic leader acts in unilateral command-and-control fashion.

availability heuristic The availability heuristic uses readily available information to assess a current situation.

avoidance Avoidance pretends that a conflict doesn't really exist.

B

B2B business strategy A B2B business strategy uses IT and Web portals to link organizations vertically in supply chains.

B2C business strategy A B2C business strategy uses IT and Web portals to link businesses with customers.

balance sheet A balance sheet shows assets and liabilities at one point in time.

balanced scorecard A balanced scorecard measures performance on financial, customer service, internal process, and innovation and learning goals.

BCG Matrix The BCG Matrix analyzes business opportunities according to market growth rate and market share.

behavioral decision model The behavioral decision model describes decision making with limited information and bounded rationality.

behaviorally anchored rating scale (BARS) A behaviorally anchored rating scale (BARS) uses specific descriptions of actual behaviors to rate various levels of performance.

benchmarking Benchmarking uses external comparisons to gain insights for planning.

benefit corporation The benefit corporation, or B-Corp, is a corporate form for businesses whose stated goals are to combine making a profit with benefiting society and the environment.

best practices Best practices are methods that lead to superior performance.

biculturalism Biculturalism is when minority members adopt characteristics of majority cultures to succeed.

big-C creativity Big-C creativity occurs when extraordinary things are done by exceptional people.

board of directors Members of a board of directors are elected by stockholders to represent their ownership interests.

bona fide occupational qualifications Bona fide occupational qualifications are employment criteria justified by capacity to perform a job.

bonus pay Bonus pay plans provide one-time payments based on performance accomplishments.

breakeven analysis Breakeven analysis performs what-if calculations under different revenue and cost conditions.

breakeven point The breakeven point occurs where revenues just equal costs.

budget A budget is a plan that commits resources to projects or activities.

bullying Bullying is antisocial behavior that is intentionally aggressive, intimidating, demeaning, and/or abusive.

bureaucracy A bureaucracy is a rational and efficient form of organization founded on logic, order, and legitimate authority.

bureaucratic control Bureaucratic control influences behavior through authority, policies, procedures, job descriptions, budgets, and day-to-day supervision.

business incubator A business incubator is a facility that offers services to help new businesses get established.

business model A business model is a plan for making a profit by generating revenues that are greater than costs.

business model innovation Business model innovations result in ways for firms to make money.

business plan A business plan describes the direction for a new business and the financing needed to operate it.

business strategy A business strategy identifies how a division or strategic business unit will compete in its product or service domain.

C

C2B business strategy C2B business strategies link customers to businesses that can supply what they need.

C2C business strategy C2C business strategies link customers together to make business transactions.

career development Career development is the process of managing how a person grows and progresses in a career.

career planning Career planning is the process of matching career goals and individual capabilities with opportunities for their fulfillment.

centralization With centralization, top management keeps the power to make most decisions.

centralized communication network In a centralized communication network, communication flows only between individual members and a hub or center point.

certain environment A certain environment offers complete information on possible action alternatives and their consequences.

change leader A change leader tries to change the behavior of another person or social system.

changing Changing is the phase where a planned change actually takes place.

channel richness Channel richness is the capacity of a communication channel to effectively carry information.

Chapter 11 bankruptcy Chapter 11 bankruptcy protects an insolvent firm from creditors during a period of reorganization to restore profitability.

charisma Charisma is the ability to inspirationally persuade and motivate others.

charismatic leader A charismatic leader develops special leader–follower relationships and inspires followers in extraordinary ways.

charismatic leadership tactics Charismatic leadership tactics are communication techniques people use to make themselves more "leaderlike" and be perceived by others as influential and trustworthy.

child labor Child labor is the full-time employment of children for work otherwise done by adults.

clan control Clan control influences behavior through social norms and peer expectations.

classic entrepreneur A classic entrepreneur is someone willing to pursue opportunities in situations others view as problems or threats.

classical decision model The classical decision model describes decision making with complete information.

classical view of CSR The classical view of CSR is that business should focus on the pursuit of profits.

coaching Coaching occurs as an experienced person offers performance advice to a less-experienced person.

code of ethics A code of ethics is a formal statement of values and ethical standards.

coercive power Coercive power achieves influence by punishment.

cognitive dissonance Cognitive dissonance is discomfort felt when attitude and behavior are inconsistent.

cognitive styles Cognitive style is the way an individual deals with information while making decisions.

cohesiveness Cohesiveness is the degree to which members are attracted to and motivated to remain part of a team.

collaboration Collaboration, or problem solving, involves working through conflict differences and solving problems so everyone wins.

collective bargaining Collective bargaining is the process of negotiating, administering, and interpreting a labor contract.

commercializing innovation Commercializing innovation is the process of turning new ideas into salable products.

committee A committee is designated to work on a special task on a continuing basis.

communication Communication is the process of sending and receiving symbols with meanings attached.

communication channel A communication channel is the medium used to carry a message.

communication transparency Communication transparency involves being honest and openly sharing accurate and complete information.

commutative justice Commutative justice focuses on the fairness of exchanges or transactions.

competition Competition, or authoritative command, uses force, superior skill, or domination to win a conflict.

competitive advantage A competitive advantage is an ability to outperform rivals.

complacency trap The complacency trap is being lulled into inaction by current successes or failures.

compressed workweek A compressed workweek allows a worker to complete a full-time job in less than five days.

compromise Compromise occurs when each party to the conflict gives up something of value to the other.

concentration Growth through concentration means expansion within an existing business area.

conceptual skill A conceptual skill is the ability to think analytically and solve complex problems.

concurrent control Concurrent control focuses on what happens during the work process.

confirmation error Confirmation error is when we attend only to information that confirms a decision already made.

conflict Conflict is a disagreement over issues of substance and/or an emotional antagonism.

conflict resolution Conflict resolution is the removal of the substantive and/or emotional reasons for a conflict.

conscientiousness A conscientious person is dependable, organized, and focused on getting things done; a person who lacks conscientiousness is careless, impulsive, and not achievement oriented.

consensus Consensus is reached when all parties believe they have had their say and been listened to, and agree to support the group's final decision.

constructive stress Constructive stress is a positive influence on effort, creativity, and diligence in work.

consultative decision A consultative decision is made by a leader after receiving information, advice, or opinions from group members.

contingency leadership perspective The contingency leadership perspective suggests that what is successful as a leadership style varies according to the situation and the people involved.

contingency planning Contingency planning identifies alternative courses of action to take when things go wrong.

contingency thinking Contingency thinking tries to match management practices with situational demands.

contingency workers Contingency workers or permatemps work part-time hours on a longer-term basis.

continuous improvement Continuous improvement involves always searching for new ways to improve work quality and performance.

control chart Control charts are graphical ways of displaying trends so that exceptions to quality standards can be identified.

controlling Controlling is the process of measuring performance and taking action to ensure desired results.

co-opetition Co-opetition is the strategy of working with rivals on projects of mutual benefit.

core competencies A core competency is a special strength that gives an organization a competitive advantage.

core culture The core culture is found in the underlying values of the organization.

core values Core values are beliefs and values shared by organization members.

corporate governance Corporate governance is oversight of a company's management by a board of directors.

corporate social responsibility Corporate social responsibility is the obligation of an organization to serve its own interests and those of its stakeholders.

corporate strategy A corporate strategy sets long-term direction for the total enterprise.

corporation A corporation is a legal entity that exists separately from its owners.

corruption Corruption involves illegal practices to further one's business interests.

cost-benefit analysis Cost-benefit analysis involves comparing the costs and benefits of each potential course of action.

cost leadership strategy A cost leadership strategy seeks to operate with lower costs than competitors.

CPM/PERT CPM/PERT is a combination of the critical path method and the program evaluation and review technique.

creativity Creativity is the generation of a novel idea or unique approach that solves a problem or crafts an opportunity.

credible communication Credible communication earns trust, respect, and integrity in the eyes of others.

crisis A crisis is an unexpected problem that can lead to disaster if not resolved quickly and appropriately.

critical-incident technique The critical-incident technique keeps a log of someone's effective and ineffective job behaviors.

critical path The critical path is the pathway from project start to conclusion that involves activities with the longest completion times.

cross-functional team A cross-functional team operates with members who come from different functional units of an organization.

crowdfunding In equity crowdfunding, new ventures go online to get startup financing from crowds of investors.

crowdsourcing Crowdsourcing is strategic use of the Internet to engage customers and potential customers in providing opinions and suggestions on products and their designs.

cultural etiquette Cultural etiquette is use of appropriate manners and behaviors in cross-cultural situations.

cultural intelligence Cultural intelligence is the ability to adapt to new cultures.

cultural relativism Cultural relativism suggests there is no one right way to behave; cultural context determines ethical behavior.

culture shock Culture shock is the confusion and discomfort that a person experiences when in an unfamiliar culture.

currency risk Currency risk is possible loss because of fluctuating exchange rates.

customer structure A customer structure groups together people and jobs that serve the same customers or clients.

D

debt financing Debt financing involves borrowing money from another person, a bank, or a financial institution.

decentralization With decentralization, top management allows lower levels to help make many decisions.

decentralized communication network A decentralized communication network allows all members to communicate directly with one another.

decision A decision is a choice among possible alternative courses of action.

decision making Decision making is the process of making choices among alternative courses of action.

decision-making process The decision-making process begins with identification of a problem and ends with evaluation of implemented solutions.

deep-level diversity Deep level diversity consists of psychological attributes like personality and values.

deficit principle Maslow's deficit principle is that people act to satisfy needs for which a satisfaction deficit exists; a satisfied need doesn't motivate behavior.

delegation Delegation is the process of entrusting work to others.

democratic leader A democratic leader encourages participation with an emphasis on task and people.

departmentalization Departmentalization is the process of grouping together people and jobs into work units.

destructive stress Destructive stress is a negative influence on one's performance.

differentiation strategy A differentiation strategy offers products that are unique and different from those of the competition.

discrimination Discrimination actively denies women and minorities the full benefits of organizational membership.

disruptive behaviors Disruptive behaviors are self-serving and cause problems for team effectiveness.

disruptive innovation Disruptive innovation creates products or services that become so widely used that they largely replace prior practices and competitors.

distributed leadership Distributed leadership is when any and all members contribute helpful task and maintenance activities to the team.

distributed team Members of a virtual team or distributed team work together and solve problems through computer-based interactions.

distributive justice Distributive justice focuses on treating people the same regardless of personal characteristics.

diversification Growth through diversification means expansion by entering related or new business areas.

diversity Diversity describes race, gender, age, and other individual differences.

divestiture Divestiture involves selling off parts of the organization to refocus attention on core business areas.

division of labor The division of labor means that people and groups perform different jobs.

divisional structure A divisional structure groups together people working on the same product, in the same area, or with similar customers.

double-bind dilemma In the double-bind dilemma, female leaders are criticized when they act consistent with female subculture stereotypes and when they act consistent with male subculture stereotypes.

downsizing Downsizing decreases the size of operations.

E

e-business strategy An e-business strategy strategically uses the Internet to gain competitive advantage.

ecological fallacy The ecological fallacy assumes that a generalized cultural value applies equally well to all members of the culture.

economic order quantity The economic order quantity method places new orders when inventory levels fall to predetermined points.

effective communication In effective communication the receiver fully understands the intended meaning.

effective manager An effective manager successfully helps others achieve high performance and satisfaction in their work.

effective team An effective team achieves high levels of task performance, membership satisfaction, and future viability.

efficient communication Efficient communication occurs at minimum cost to the sender.

emotion Emotions are strong feelings directed toward someone or something.

emotional conflict Emotional conflict results from feelings of anger, distrust, dislike, fear, and resentment as well as from personality clashes.

emotional intelligence (EI) Emotional intelligence (EI) is the ability to manage our emotions in leadership and social relationships.

emotional intelligence quotient (EQ) Emotional intelligence quotient (EQ) is a measure of a person's ability to manage emotions in leadership and social relationships.

emotional stability A person who is emotionally stable is secure, calm, steady, and self-confident; a person lacking emotional stability is excitable, anxious, nervous, and tense.

employee assistance programs Employee assistance programs help employees cope with personal stresses and problems.

employee engagement Employee engagement is a strong sense of belonging and connection with one's work and employer.

employee involvement team An employee involvement team meets on a regular basis to help achieve continuous improvement.

employee value propositions The employee value proposition, or EVP, is the exchange of value between what the individual and the employer offer each other as part of the employment relationship.

empowerment Empowerment gives people job freedom and power to influence affairs in the organization.

entrepreneur An entrepreneur is willing to pursue opportunities in situations that others view as problems or threats.

entrepreneurship Entrepreneurship is risk-taking behavior in pursuit of business success.

environmental capital or natural capital Environmental capital or natural capital is the storehouse of natural resources—atmosphere, land, water, and minerals—that we use to sustain life and produce goods and services for society.

equal employment opportunity (EEO) Equal employment opportunity (EEO) is the right to employment and advancement without regard to race, sex, religion, color, or national origin.

equity financing Equity financing gives ownership shares to outsiders in return for their financial investments.

escalating commitment Escalating commitment is the continuation of a course of action even though it is not working.

ethical behavior Ethical behavior is "right" or "good" in the context of a governing moral code.

ethical dilemma An ethical dilemma is a situation that, although offering potential benefit or gain, is also unethical.

ethical frameworks Ethical frameworks are well-thought-out personal rules and strategies for ethical decision making.

ethical imperialism Ethical imperialism is an attempt to impose one's ethical standards on other cultures.

ethics Ethics set moral standards of what is "good" and "right" behavior in organizations and in our personal lives.

ethics training Ethics training seeks to help people understand the ethical aspects of decision making and to incorporate high ethical standards into their daily behavior.

ethnic or national subcultures Ethnic or national subcultures form among people from the same races, language groupings, regions, and nations.

ethnocentrism Ethnocentrism is the belief that one's membership group or subculture is superior to all others.

EU (European Union). A regional economic alliance of 28 member nations.

evidence-based management Evidence-based management involves making decisions based on hard facts about what really works.

existence needs Existence needs are desires for physiological and material well-being.

expectancy Expectancy is a person's belief that working hard will result in high task performance.

expert power Expert power achieves influence by special knowledge.

exporting In exporting, local products are sold abroad.

external control External control occurs through direct supervision or administrative systems.

extinction Extinction discourages a behavior by making the removal of a desirable consequence contingent on its occurrence.

extraversion An extravert is talkative, comfortable, and confident in interpersonal relationships; an introvert is more private, withdrawn, and reserved.

F

family business feud A family business feud can lead to small business failure.

family businesses Family businesses are owned and financially controlled by family members.

family-friendly benefits Family-friendly benefits help employees achieve better work-life balance.

feedback Feedback is the process of telling someone else how you feel about something that person did or said.

feedback control Feedback control takes place after completing an action.

feedforward control Feedforward control ensures clear directions and needed resources before the work begins.

first-line managers First-line managers supervise people who perform nonmanagerial duties.

first-mover advantage A first-mover advantage comes from being first to exploit a niche or enter a market.

flameout A flameout occurs when we communicate extreme agitation in interpersonal communication or electronic messages.

flexible benefits Flexible benefits programs allow choice to personalize benefits within a set dollar allowance.

flexible working hours Flexible working hours give employees some choice in daily work hours.

focused cost leadership strategy A focused cost leadership strategy seeks the lowest costs of operations within a special market segment.

focused differentiation strategy A focused differentiation strategy offers a unique product to a special market segment.

force-coercion strategy A force-coercion strategy pursues change through formal authority and/or the use of rewards or punishments.

forecasting Forecasting attempts to predict the future.

Foreign Corrupt Practices Act The Foreign Corrupt Practices Act makes it illegal for U.S. firms and their representatives to engage in corrupt practices overseas.

foreign subsidiary A foreign subsidiary is a local operation completely owned by a foreign firm.

formal structure Formal structure is the official structure of the organization.

formal team A formal team is officially recognized and supported by the organization.

framing error Framing error is solving a problem in the context perceived.

franchise A franchise is when one business owner sells to another the right to operate the same business in another location.

franchising In franchising, a firm pays a fee for rights to use another company's name and operating methods.

free-agent and on-demand economy In a free-agent economy people change jobs more often, and many work on independent contracts with a shifting mix of employers.

fringe benefits Fringe benefits are nonmonetary forms of compensation such as health insurance and retirement plans.

functional chimneys or functional silos problem The functional chimneys, or functional silos, problem is a lack of communication and coordination across functions.

functional plan A functional plan identifies how different parts of an enterprise will contribute to accomplishing strategic plans.

functional strategy A functional strategy guides activities within one specific area of operations.

functional structure A functional structure groups together people with similar skills who perform similar tasks.

fundamental attribution error The fundamental attribution error overestimates internal factors and underestimates external factors as influences on someone's behavior.

G

gain sharing Gain sharing allows employees to share in cost savings or productivity gains realized by their efforts.

Gantt chart A Gantt chart graphically displays the scheduling of tasks required to complete a project.

gender similarities hypothesis The gender similarities hypothesis holds that males and females have similar psychological makeups.

gender subcultures Gender subcultures form among people of the same gender.

general partnership In a general partnership, owners share management responsibilities.

generational subcultures Generational subcultures form among people in similar age groups.

geographic structure A geographical structure brings together people and jobs performed in the same location.

glass ceiling The glass ceiling is a hidden barrier to the advancement of women and minorities.

glass ceiling effect The glass ceiling effect is an invisible barrier limiting career advancement of women and minorities.

glass closet The glass closet is when lesbians, gays, bisexuals, and transgender workers hide their sexual orientation and gender identities.

global corporation or multinational corporation (MNC) A global corporation or multinational corporation (MNC) has extensive international business dealings in many foreign countries.

global economy In the global economy, resources, markets, and competition are worldwide in scope.

global manager A global manager is culturally aware and informed on international affairs.

global sourcing In global sourcing, firms purchase materials or services around the world for local use.

global strategic alliance In a global strategic alliance, each partner hopes to achieve through cooperation things they couldn't do alone.

global supply chain A global supply chain is a network of a firm's outsourcing suppliers and contractors.

globalization Globalization is the worldwide interdependence of resource flows, product markets, and business competition.

globalization gap The globalization gap involves large global firms gaining disproportionately from the global economy versus smaller firms and many countries.

globalization strategy A globalization strategy adopts standardized products and advertising for use worldwide.

governance Governance is oversight of top management by a board of directors or board of trustees.

graphic rating scale A graphic rating scale uses a checklist of traits or characteristics to evaluate performance.

green innovation Green innovation reduces the carbon footprint of an organization or its products.

greenfield venture A greenfield venture establishes a foreign subsidiary by building an entirely new operation in a foreign country.

group decision A group decision is made by group members themselves.

groupthink Groupthink is a tendency for highly cohesive teams to lose their evaluative capabilities.

growth needs Growth needs are desires for continued psychological growth and development.

growth strategy A growth strategy involves expansion of the organization's current operations.

H

halo effect A halo effect uses one attribute to develop an overall impression of a person or situation.

Hawthorne effect The Hawthorne effect is the tendency of persons singled out for special attention to perform as expected.

heterogeneous teams Heterogeneous teams have members with diverse personal characteristics.

hierarchy of objectives In a hierarchy of objectives, lower-level objectives help to accomplish higher-level ones.

high-context culture High-context cultures rely on nonverbal and situational cues as well as spoken or written words in communication.

higher-order needs Higher-order needs are esteem and self-actualization needs in Maslow's hierarchy.

homogeneous teams Homogeneous teams have members with similar personal characteristics.

human capital Human capital is the economic value of people with job-relevant abilities, knowledge, ideas, energies, and commitments.

human relations leader A human relations leader emphasizes people over tasks.

human resource management (HRM) Human resource management (HRM) is the process of attracting, developing, and maintaining a high-quality workforce.

human skill A human skill is the ability to work well in cooperation with other people.

hygiene factors A hygiene factor is found in the job context, such as working conditions, interpersonal relations, organizational policies, and salary.

I

immoral manager An immoral manager chooses to behave unethically.

importing Importing is the process of acquiring products abroad and selling them in domestic markets.

impression management Impression management tries to create desired perceptions in the eyes of others.

improvement objectives Improvement objectives document intentions to improve performance in a specific way.

improvisational change Improvisational change makes continual adjustments as changes are being implemented.

incivility Incivility is antisocial behavior in the forms of disrespectful acts, social exclusion, and use of hurtful language.

inclusion Inclusion is how open the organization is to anyone who can perform a job.

income statement An income statement shows a firm's profits or losses at one point in time.

incremental change Incremental change bends and adjusts existing ways to improve performance.

independent contractors Independent contractors are hired on temporary contracts and are not part of the organization's permanent workforce.

individualism view In the individualism view, ethical behavior advances long-term self-interests.

individualism-collectivism Individualism-collectivism is the degree to which a society emphasizes individuals and their self-interests.

informal group An informal group is unofficial and emerges from relationships and shared interests among members.

informal structure The informal structure is the set of unofficial relationships among an organization's members.

information competency Information competency is the ability to gather and use information to solve problems.

information filtering Information filtering is the intentional distortion of information to make it more favorable to the recipient.

initial public offering (IPO) An initial public offering (IPO) is an initial selling of shares of stock to the public at large.

innovation Innovation is the process of taking a new idea and putting it into practice.

input standards An input standard measures work efforts that go into a performance task.

insourcing Insourcing is the creation of domestic jobs by foreign employers.

instrumental values Instrumental values are preferences regarding the means to desired ends.

instrumentality Instrumentality is a person's belief that various outcomes will occur as a result of task performance.

integrity Integrity in leadership is honesty, credibility, and consistency in putting values into action.

intellectual capital Intellectual capital is the collective brainpower or shared knowledge of a workforce.

intellectual capital equation The intellectual capital equation is: IC = competency $\times$ commitment.

interactional justice Interactional justice is the degree to which others are treated with dignity and respect.

interactive leadership Interactive leadership is strong on communication, participation, and dealing with problems by teamwork.

intercultural competencies Intercultural competencies are skills and personal characteristics that help us be successful in cross-cultural situations.

internal control (self-control) Internal control, or self-control, occurs as people exercise self-discipline in fulfilling job expectations.

international business An international business conducts commercial transactions across national boundaries.

intrapreneurs Intrapreneurs display entrepreneurial behavior as employees of larger firms.

intuitive thinking Intuitive thinking approaches problems in a flexible and spontaneous fashion.

inventory control Inventory control ensures that inventory is only big enough to meet immediate needs.

ISO 14001 ISO 14001 is a global quality standard that certifies organizations that set environmental objectives and targets, account for the environmental impact of their activities, and continuously improve environmental performance.

J

job audition A job audition is a trial hire where the job candidate is given a short-term employment contract to demonstrate performance capabilities.

job burnout Job burnout is physical and mental exhaustion from work stress.

job design Job design is the allocation of specific work tasks to individuals and groups.

job discrimination Job discrimination occurs when someone is denied a job or job assignment for non-job-relevant reasons.

job enrichment Job enrichment increases job content by adding work planning and evaluating duties normally performed by the supervisor.

job migration Job migration occurs when global outsourcing shifts from one country to another.

job satisfaction Job satisfaction is the degree to which an individual feels positive about a job and work experience.

job sharing Job sharing splits one job between two people.

joint venture A joint venture operates in a foreign country through co-ownership with local partners.

just-in-time scheduling (JIT) Just-in-time scheduling (JIT) routes materials to workstations just in time for use.

justice view In the justice view, ethical behavior treats people impartially and fairly.

K

knowledge workers Knowledge workers add value to organizations through their intellectual capabilities.

L

labor contract A labor contract is a formal agreement between a union and an employer about the terms of work for union members.

labor union A labor union is an organization that deals with employers on the workers' collective behalf.

lack-of-participation error Lack-of-participation error is failure to include the right people in the decision-making process.

laissez-faire leader A laissez-faire leader is disengaged, showing low task and people concerns.

law of contingent reinforcement Law of contingent reinforcement—deliver the reward only when desired behavior occurs.

law of effect The law of effect states that behavior followed by pleasant consequences is likely to be repeated; behavior followed by unpleasant consequences is not.

law of immediate reinforcement Law of immediate reinforcement—deliver the reward as soon as possible after the desired behavior occurs.

leadership Leadership is the process of inspiring others to work hard to accomplish important tasks.

leadership style Leadership style is the recurring pattern of behaviors exhibited by a leader.

leading Leading is the process of arousing enthusiasm and inspiring efforts to achieve goals.

leaking pipeline problem The leaking pipeline problem is where glass ceilings and other obstacles cause qualified and high-performing women to drop out of upward career paths.

learning agility Learning agility is the willingness to grow, to learn, to have insatiable curiosity.

learning goals Learning goals set targets to create the knowledge and skills required for performance.

legitimate power Legitimate power achieves influence by formal authority.

licensing In licensing, one firm pays a fee for rights to make or sell another company's products.

lifelong learning Lifelong learning is continuous learning from daily experiences.

limited liability corporation (LLC) A limited liability corporation (LLC) combines the advantages of the sole proprietorship, partnership, and corporation.

limited liability partnership (LLP) Limited liability partnerships, LLPs, limit the liability of one partner in case of negligence by any others.

limited partnership A limited partnership consists of a general partner who manages the business and one or more limited partners.

liquidation Liquidation occurs when a business closes and sells its assets to pay creditors.

little-C creativity Little-C creativity occurs when average people come up with unique ways to deal with daily events and situations.

locus of control Locus of control is the extent to which one believes what happens is within one's control.

long-range plan Long-range plans usually cover three years or more.

loose cultures In loose cultures social norms are mixed and ambiguous, and conformity varies.

low-context culture Low-context cultures emphasize communication via spoken or written words.

lower-order needs Lower-order needs are physiological, safety, and social needs in Maslow's hierarchy.

M

machiavellianism Machiavellianism is the degree to which someone uses power manipulatively.

maintenance activity A maintenance activity is an action taken by a team member that supports the emotional life of the group.

management by exception Management by exception focuses attention on differences between actual and desired performance.

management process The management process is planning, organizing, leading, and controlling the use of resources to accomplish performance goals.

management science and operations research Management science and operational research apply mathematical techniques to solve management problems.

manager A manager is a person who supports and is responsible for the work of others.

managing by objectives Managing by objectives is a process of joint objective setting between a superior and a subordinate.

managing diversity Managing diversity is building an inclusive work environment that allows everyone to reach his or her potential.

market control Market control is essentially the influence of market competition on the behavior of organizations and their members.

masculinity-femininity Masculinity-femininity is the degree to which a society values assertiveness and materialism.

matrix structure A matrix structure combines functional and divisional approaches to emphasize project or program teams.

mechanistic designs Mechanistic designs are bureaucratic, using a centralized and vertical structure.

mentoring Mentoring assigns early-career employees as protégés to more senior ones.

merit pay Merit pay awards pay increases in proportion to performance contributions.

middle managers Middle managers oversee the work of large departments or divisions.

mission The mission is the organization's reason for existence in society.

mixed message A mixed message results when words communicate one message while actions, body language, or appearance communicate something else.

Mompreneur Mompreneurs pursue business opportunities they spot as mothers.

monochronic culture In monochronic cultures people tend to do one thing at a time.

mood Moods are generalized positive and negative feelings or states of mind.

mood contagion Mood contagion is the spillover of one's positive or negative moods onto others.

moral absolutism Moral absolutism suggests ethical standards apply universally across all cultures.

moral leadership Moral leadership has integrity and appears to others as "good" or "right" by ethical standards.

moral manager A moral manager makes ethical behavior a personal goal.

moral overconfidence Moral overconfidence is an overly positive view of one's integrity and strength of character.

moral rights view In the moral rights view, ethical behavior respects and protects fundamental rights.

most favored nation status Most favored nation status gives a trading partner the most favorable treatment for imports and exports.

motion study Motion study is the science of reducing a job or task to its basic physical motions.

motivation Motivation accounts for the level, direction, and persistence of effort expended at work.

multicultural organization A multicultural organization is based on pluralism and operates with inclusivity and respect for diversity.

multidomestic strategy A multidomestic strategy customizes products and advertising to fit local markets.

multiperson comparison A multiperson comparison compares one person's performance with that of others.

N

NAFTA (North American Free Trade Agreement) NAFTA, or the North American Free Trade Agreement, is a regional economic alliance of Canada, Mexico, and the United States.

necessity-based entrepreneurship Necessity-based entrepreneurship occurs when people start new ventures because they have few or no other employment options.

need A need is a physiological or psychological deficiency that a person wants to satisfy.

need for achievement Need for achievement is the desire to do something better, to solve problems, or to master complex tasks.

need for affiliation Need for affiliation is the desire to establish and maintain good relations with people.

need for power Need for power is the desire to control, influence, or be responsible for other people.

negative reinforcement Negative reinforcement strengthens a behavior by making the avoidance of an undesirable consequence contingent on its occurrence.

network structure A network structure uses IT to link with networks of outside suppliers and service contractors.

networking Networking involves building and maintaining positive relationships with other people.

noise Noise is anything that interferes with the communication process.

nonprogrammed decision A nonprogrammed decision applies a specific solution that has been crafted to address a unique problem.

nontariff barriers Nontariff barriers are nontax policies that governments enact to discourage imports, such as quotas and import restrictions.

nonverbal communication Nonverbal communication takes place through gestures, expressions, posture, and even use of interpersonal space.

norm A norm is a behavior, rule, or standard expected to be followed by team members.

O

objectives Objectives are specific results that one wishes to achieve.

observable culture The observable culture is what you see and hear when walking around an organization.

occupational subcultures Occupational subcultures form among people doing the same kinds of work.

onboarding Onboarding is a program of activities that introduce a new hire to the policies, practices, expectations, and culture of the organization and its teams.

open-book management In open-book management, managers provide employees with essential financial information about their employers.

open system An open system transforms resource inputs from the environment into product outputs.

openness to experience A person open to experience is broad-minded, imaginative, and open to new ideas; a person who lacks such openness is narrow-minded, has few interests, and resists change.

operant conditioning Operant conditioning is the control of behavior by manipulating its consequences.

operational (tactical) plan An operational plan or tactical plan sets out ways to implement a strategic plan.

operations management Operations management is the study of how organizations produce goods and services.

optimizing decision An optimizing decision chooses the alternative providing the absolute best solution to a problem.

organic designs Organic designs are adaptive, using a decentralized and horizontal structure.

organization chart An organization chart describes the arrangement of work positions within an organization.

organization structure Organization structure is a system of tasks, reporting relationships, and communication linkages.

organizational citizenship behaviors Organizational citizenship behaviors are things people do to go the extra mile in their work.

organizational culture Organizational culture is a system of shared beliefs and values guiding behavior.

organizational design Organizational design is the process of configuring organizations to meet environmental challenges.

organizational subcultures Organizational subcultures are groupings of people based on shared demographic and job identities.

organizing Organizing is the process of assigning tasks, allocating resources, and coordinating work activities.

orientation Orientation familiarizes new employees with jobs, co-workers, and organizational policies and services.

outcome goals Outcome goals set targets for actual performance results.

output standards An output standard measures performance results in terms of quantity, quality, cost, or time.

outsourcing Outsourcing shifts local jobs to foreign locations to take advantage of lower-wage labor in other countries.

P

P2P business strategies P2P business strategies link persons needing services with those willing to provide them.

participatory planning Participatory planning includes the persons who will be affected by plans and/or who will be asked to implement them.

partnership A partnership is when two or more people agree to contribute resources to start and operate a business together.

pay discrimination Pay discrimination occurs when men and women are paid differently for doing equal work.

perceived negative inequity Perceived negative inequity is discomfort felt over being harmed by unfair treatment.

perceived positive inequity Perceived positive inequity is discomfort felt over benefitting from unfair treatment.

perception Perception is the process through which people receive and interpret information from the environment.

performance appraisal Performance appraisal is the process of formally evaluating performance and providing feedback to a jobholder.

performance norm The performance norm defines the effort and performance contributions expected of team members.

performance opportunity A performance opportunity is a situation that offers the possibility of a better future if the right steps are taken.

performance review Performance review is the process of formally assessing performance and providing feedback to a jobholder.

performance threat A performance threat is a situation where something is wrong or likely to be wrong.

person–culture fit Person–culture fit is the extent to which an individual's values, interests, and behavior are consistent with the culture of the organization.

person–job fit Person–job fit is the match of individual skills, interests, and personal characteristics with the job.

personal brand Your personal brand is your reputation in the eyes of others and your talents as evidenced by unique and timely skills and capabilities of real value to a potential employer.

personal development objectives Personal development objectives document intentions to accomplish personal growth, such as expanded job knowledge or skills.

personal wellness Personal wellness is the pursuit of a personal health-promotion program.

personality Personality is the profile of characteristics making a person unique from others.

persuasive communication Persuasive communication presents a message in a manner that causes others to accept and support it.

plan A plan is a statement of intended means for accomplishing objectives.

planning Planning is the process of setting performance objectives and determining how to accomplish them.

planning fallacy The planning fallacy is underestimating the time required to complete a task.

policy A policy is a standing plan that communicates broad guidelines for decisions and action.

political risk Political risk is possible loss because of instability and political changes in foreign countries.

political-risk analysis Political-risk analysis forecasts how political events may affect foreign investments.

polychronic culture In polychronic cultures people accomplish many different things at once.

positive reinforcement Positive reinforcement strengthens a behavior by making a desirable consequence contingent on its occurrence.

power Power is the ability to get someone else to do something you want done.

power distance Power distance is the degree to which a society accepts unequal distribution of power.

pregnancy discrimination Pregnancy discrimination penalizes a woman in a job or as a job applicant for being pregnant.

prejudice Prejudice is the display of negative, irrational attitudes toward women or minorities.

problem solving Problem solving involves identifying and taking action to resolve problems.

procedural justice Procedural justice focuses on the fair application of policies and rules.

procedure A procedure or rule precisely describes actions to take in specific situations.

process innovations Process innovations result in better ways of doing things.

product innovations Product innovations result in new or improved goods or services.

product structure A product structure groups together people and jobs working on a single product or service.

profit sharing Profit sharing distributes to employees a proportion of net profits earned by the organization.

programmed decision A programmed decision applies a solution from past experience to a routine problem.

progression principle Maslow's progression principle is that a need at any level becomes activated only after the next-lower-level need is satisfied.

project Projects are one-time activities with many component tasks that must be completed in proper order and according to budget.

project management Project management makes sure that activities required to complete a project are planned well and accomplished on time.

project team A project team is convened for a specific purpose and disbands after completing its task.

projection Projection assigns personal attributes to other individuals.

protectionism Protectionism is a call for tariffs and favorable treatments to protect domestic firms from foreign competition.

proxemics Proxemics is the study of the way we use space.

psychological contract The psychological contract is the exchange of value between the individual and the organization in the employment relationship.

punishment Punishment discourages a behavior by making an unpleasant consequence contingent on its occurrence.

Q

quality circle A quality circle is a team of employees who meet periodically to discuss ways of improving work quality.

quality of work life Quality of work life is the overall quality of human experiences in the workplace.

R

rational persuasion strategy A rational persuasion strategy pursues change through empirical data and rational argument.

realistic job previews Realistic job previews provide job candidates with all pertinent information about a job and organization.

recruitment Recruitment is a set of activities designed to attract a qualified pool of job applicants.

referent power Referent power achieves influence by personal identification.

refreezing Refreezing is the phase at which change is stabilized.

relatedness needs Relatedness needs are desires for satisfying interpersonal relationships.

relationship power Relationship power is the ability to get things done through connections and social capital, or who you know.

reliability Reliability means that a selection device gives consistent results over repeated measures.

remote work Remote work, also called **telecommuting** and work-from-home, uses technology to allow workers to do their jobs from outside the office.

representativeness heuristic The representativeness heuristic assesses the likelihood of an occurrence using a stereotyped set of similar events.

reshoring Reshoring moves job back from foreign to domestic locations.

restricted communication network Subgroups in a restricted communication network contest one another's positions and restrict interactions with one another.

restructuring Restructuring reduces the scale or mix of operations.

retrenchment strategy A retrenchment strategy changes operations to correct weaknesses.

reverse innovation Reverse innovation recognizes the potential for valuable innovations to be launched from lower organizational levels and diverse locations, including emerging markets.

reverse mentoring In reverse mentoring, younger and newly hired employees mentor senior executives, often on the latest developments with digital technologies.

revolving door syndrome The revolving door syndrome is high turnover among minorities and women.

reward power Reward power achieves influence by offering something of value.

risk environment A risk environment lacks complete information but offers probabilities of the likely outcomes for possible action alternatives.

S

SADC (South Africa Development Community) SADC, the South Africa Development Community is a regional economic alliance of 15 nations.

satisficing decision A satisficing decision chooses the first satisfactory alternative that presents itself.

satisfier factors A satisfier factor is found in job content, such as a sense of achievement, recognition, responsibility, advancement, or personal growth.

scalar chain principle The scalar chain principle states that organizations should operate with clear and unbroken lines of communication top to bottom.

scenario planning Scenario planning identifies alternative future scenarios and makes plans to deal with each.

scientific management Scientific management emphasizes careful selection and training of workers and supervisory support.

selection Selection is choosing whom to hire from a pool of qualified job applicants.

selective perception Selective perception focuses attention on things consistent with existing beliefs, needs, actions.

self-efficacy Self-efficacy is a person's belief that they are capable of performing a task.

self-fulfilling prophecy A self-fulfilling prophecy occurs when a person acts in ways that confirm another's expectations.

self-management Self-management is the ability to understand oneself, exercise initiative, accept responsibility, and learn from experience.

self-managing team Members of a self-managing team have the authority to make decisions about how they share and complete their work.

self-monitoring Self-monitoring is the degree to which someone is able to adjust behavior in response to external factors.

self-serving bias Self-serving bias underestimates internal factors and overestimates external factors as influences on someone's behavior.

serial entrepreneur A serial entrepreneur starts and runs businesses and nonprofits over and over again, moving from one interest and opportunity to the next.

servant leadership Servant leadership means serving others and helping them use their talents to help organizations best serve society.

shadow organization The shadow organization or informal structure is the network of unofficial relationships among an organization's members.

shamrock organization A shamrock organization operates with a core group of full-time long-term workers supported by others who work on contracts and part time.

shaping Shaping is positive reinforcement of successive approximations to the desired behavior.

shared power strategy A shared power strategy pursues change by participation in assessing change needs, values, and goals.

shared value The shared value view of CSR approaches business decisions with understanding that economic gains and social progress are interconnected.

short-range plan Short-range plans usually cover a year or less.

Six Sigma Six Sigma is a quality standard of 3.4 defects or less per million products or service deliveries.

skunkworks Skunkworks are special creative units set free from the normal structure for the purpose of innovation.

small business A small business has fewer than 500 employees, is independently owned and operated, and does not dominate its industry.

Small Business Development Centers Small Business Development Centers offer guidance to entrepreneurs and small business owners on how to set up and manage business operations.

social business A social business is one in which the underlying business model directly addresses a social problem.

social capital Social capital is the capacity to attract support and help from others to get things done.

social entrepreneurs Social entrepreneurs take business risks to find novel ways to solve pressing social problems.

social innovation Social innovation is business innovation driven by a social conscience.

social loafing Social loafing is the tendency of some people to avoid responsibility by free-riding in groups.

social media strategy A social media strategy uses social media to better engage with an organization's customers, clients, and external audiences in general.

social network analysis Social network analysis identifies the informal structures and their embedded social relationships that are active in an organization.

social responsibility audit A social responsibility audit measures and reports on an organization's performance in various areas of corporate social responsibility.

socialization Socialization is the process through which new members learn the culture of an organization.

socioeconomic view of CSR The socioeconomic view of CSR is that business should focus on contributions to society, not just on making profits.

sole proprietorship A sole proprietorship is an individual pursuing business for a profit.

span of control Span of control is the number of persons directly reporting to a manager.

spotlight questions Spotlight questions highlight the risks of public disclosure of one's actions.

stakeholders Stakeholders are people and institutions most directly affected by an organization's performance.

start-up A start-up is a new and temporary venture that is trying to discover a profitable business model for future success.

stereotype A stereotype assigns attributes commonly associated with a group to an individual.

stock options Stock options give the right to purchase shares at a fixed price in the future.

strategic alliance In a strategic alliance, organizations join together in partnership to pursue an area of mutual interest.

strategic control Strategic control makes sure strategies are well implemented and that poor strategies are scrapped or changed.

strategic human resource management Strategic human resource management mobilizes human capital to implement organizational strategies.

strategic intent Strategic intent focuses organizational energies on achieving a compelling goal.

strategic leadership Strategic leadership inspires people to implement organizational strategies.

strategic management Strategic management is the process of formulating and implementing strategies.

strategic plan A strategic plan identifies long-term directions for the organization.

strategy A strategy is a comprehensive plan guiding resource allocation to achieve long-term organization goals.

strategy formulation Strategy formulation is the process of creating strategies to deliver competitive advantage.

strategy implementation Strategy implementation is the process of putting strategies into action.

stress Stress is a state of tension experienced by individuals facing extraordinary demands, constraints, or opportunities.

stretch goals Stretch goals are performance targets that we have to work extra hard and stretch to reach.

strong cultures Strong cultures are clear, well defined, and widely shared among members.

substantive conflict Substantive conflict involves disagreements over goals, resources, rewards, policies, procedures, and job assignments.

substitutes for leadership Substitutes for leadership are factors in the work setting that direct work efforts without the involvement of a leader.

subsystem A subsystem is a smaller component of a larger system.

succession plan A succession plan describes how the leadership transition and related financial matters will be handled.

succession problem The succession problem is the issue of who will run the business when the current head leaves.

surface-level diversity Surface-level diversity consists of more visible attributes such as age, race, and ethnicity.

sustainability Sustainability is a goal that addresses the rights of present and future generations as co-stakeholders of present-day natural resources.

sustainable business Sustainable business is where firms operate in ways that both meet the needs of customers and protect or advance the well-being of our natural environment.

sustainable competitive advantage A sustainable competitive advantage is achieved in ways that are difficult to imitate.

sustainable development Sustainable development is making use of natural resources to meet today's needs while also preserving and protecting the environment for use by future generations.

sustainable innovation Sustainable innovation or green innovation reduces the carbon footprint of an organization or its products.

sweatshops Sweatshops employ workers at very low wages, for long hours, and in poor working conditions.

SWOT analysis A SWOT analysis examines organizational strengths and weaknesses, as well as environmental opportunities and threats.

synergy Synergy is the creation of a whole greater than the sum of its individual parts.

systematic thinking Systematic thinking approaches problems in a rational and analytical fashion.

T

tariffs Tariffs are taxes governments levy on imports from abroad.

task activity A task activity is an action taken by a team member that directly contributes to the group's performance purpose.

task force A task force or project team is convened for a specific purpose and disbands after completing its task.

team A team is a collection of people who regularly interact to pursue common goals.

team building Team building involves activities to gather and analyze data on a team and make changes to increase its effectiveness.

team diversity Team diversity is the mix of skills, experiences, backgrounds, and personalities of team members.

team effectiveness equation Team Effectiveness = Quality of Inputs + (Process Gains − Process Losses).

team IQ Team IQ is the ability of a team to perform well by using talent and emotional intelligence.

team process Team process is the way team members work together to accomplish tasks.

team structure A team structure uses permanent and temporary cross-functional teams to improve lateral relations.

team virtuousness Team virtuousness indicates the extent to which members adopt norms that encourage shared commitments to moral behavior.

teamwork Teamwork is the process of people actively working together to accomplish common goals.

technical skill A technical skill is the ability to use expertise to perform a task with proficiency.

technological competency Technological competency is the ability to understand new technologies and to use them to their best advantage.

telecommuting Telecommuting involves using IT to work at home or outside the office.

terminal values Terminal values are preferences about desired end states.

theory X Theory X assumes people dislike work, lack ambition, are irresponsible, and prefer to be led.

theory Y Theory Y assumes people are willing to work and accept responsibility, are self-directed, and are creative.

tight culture In tight cultures social norms are rigid and clear, and members try to conform.

time orientation Time orientation is the degree to which a society emphasizes short-term or long-term goals.

top managers Top managers guide the performance of the organization as a whole or of one of its major parts.

total quality management (TQM) Total quality management (TQM) commits to quality objectives, continuous improvement, and doing things right the first time.

transactional leadership Transactional leadership directs the efforts of others through tasks, rewards, and structures.

transformational change Transformational change results in a major and comprehensive redirection of the organization.

transformational leadership Transformational leadership is inspirational and arouses extraordinary effort and performance.

transnational corporation A transnational corporation is an MNC that operates worldwide on a borderless basis.

transnational strategy A transnational strategy integrates global operations without having a strong national identity.

triple bottom line The triple bottom line of organizational performance includes financial, social, and environmental criteria.

two-tier wage systems Two-tier wage systems pay new hires less than workers already doing the same jobs with more seniority.

Type A personality A Type A personality is oriented toward extreme achievement, impatience, and perfectionism.

U

uncertain environment An uncertain environment lacks so much information that it is difficult to assign probabilities to the likely outcomes of alternatives.

uncertainty avoidance Uncertainty avoidance is the degree to which a society tolerates risk and uncertainty.

unfreezing Unfreezing is the phase during which a situation is prepared for change.

unity of command principle The unity of command principle states that a worker should receive orders from only one boss.

upside-down pyramid The upside-down pyramid view puts customers at the top of the organization being served by workers who are supported by managers below them.

utilitarian view In the utilitarian view, ethical behavior delivers the greatest good to the most people.

V

valence Valence is the value a person assigns to work-related outcomes.

validity Validity means that scores on a selection device have demonstrated links with future job performance.

value-based management Value-based management actively develops, communicates, and enacts shared values.

values Values are broad beliefs about what is appropriate behavior.

venture capitalists Venture capitalists make large investments in new ventures in return for an equity stake in the business.

vertical integration Growth through vertical integration occurs by acquiring suppliers or distributors.

veteran's advantage In entrepreneurship, strong organizational skills and tolerance for risk.

virtual organization A virtual organization uses information technologies to operate as a shifting network of alliances.

virtual team Members of a virtual team work together and solve problems through computer-based interactions.

virtuous circle A virtuous circle exists when corporate social responsibility leads to improved financial performance that leads to more social responsibility.

vision A vision clarifies the purpose of the organization and expresses what it hopes to be in the future.

visionary leadership Visionary leadership brings to the situation a clear sense of the future and an understanding of how to get there.

W

whistleblowers Whistleblowers expose misconduct of organizations and their members.

withdrawal behaviors Withdrawal behaviors include absenteeism (not showing up for work) and turnover (quitting one's job).

work sampling Work sampling evaluates applicants as they perform actual work tasks.

workforce diversity Workforce diversity describes differences among workers in gender, race, age, ethnicity, religion, sexual orientation, and able-bodiedness.

work-from-home Work-from-home, also called remote work and telecommuting, uses technology to allow workers to do their jobs from outside the office.

work–life balance Work–life balance involves balancing career demands with personal and family needs.

workplace rage Workplace rage is aggressive behavior toward co-workers or the work setting.

workplace spirituality Workplace spirituality involves practices that create meaning and shared community among organizational members.

World Trade Organization (WTO) The World Trade Organization (WTO) is a global institution established to promote free trade and open markets around the world.

Z

zero-based budget A zero-based budget allocates resources as if each budget were brand new.

Endnotes

Feature Notes 1

Opening Quote—Wayne Niemi, "Zappos Milestone: Q&A with Tony Hsieh," Footwear News (May 4, 2009): about.zappos.com.

Management Live—Information and quotes from Adam Rubenfire, "Can 'Warcraft' Game Skills help Land a Job?" *Wall Street Journal*, Kindle Edition (August 14, 2014).

Ethics Check—Information from Jennifer Valentino-DeVries, "Social Media and Bias in Hiring," *Wall Street Journal* (November 21, 2013), p. B4.

Facts to Consider—Information from Hannah Kuchler, "Silicon Valley's Diversity Reboot," Financial Times, Kindle Edition (August 28, 2014); Barbara Orfutay, "Surveys: Good Karma on Women's Pay Seems Scarce," *Arizona Daily Star* (October 11, 2014), p. A14; and, J. P. Mangalindan, "How Tech Companies compare in Employee Diversity," *Fortune* (August 29, 2014), fortune.com (accessed October 14, 2014).

Hot Topic—Information and quotes from Rachel Feintzeig, "Container Store Bets on $50,000 Retail Worker," *Wall Street Journal* (October 15, 2014), p. B6.

Quick Case—Used by permission from John R. Schermerhorn, Jr. and Daniel G. Bachrach, *Management*, 13th ed. (Hoboken, NJ: Wiley, 2015), p. 26.

Photo Essays—<u>Ursula Burns</u>: Information and quotes from Ellen McGurt, "Fresh Copy," *Fast Company* (December 2011/January 2012), news.xerox.com (accessed August 25, 2012); "Game Changer in Business and Tech: Ursula Burns," *Huffington Post* (November 1, 2011), huffingtonpost.com; and Carol Hymowitz, "Ursula Burns, CEO, Xerox," *Bloomberg BusinessWeek* (August 12–25, 2013), pp. 57–58. <u>Slumdog Millionaire</u>: Information and quotes from Manohla Dargis, "Orphan's Lifeline out of Hell Could Be a Game Show in Mumbai," *New York Times* (November 12, 2008): movies.nytimes.com; and James Christopher, "Slumdog Millionaire," *The Times* (January 8, 2009): entertainment. timesonline.co.uk.

Endnotes 1

[1] Quote from Philip Delves Broughton, "A Compelling Vision of a Dystopian Future for Workers and How to Avoid It," *Financial Times*, Kindle Edition (May 19, 2011). See also Lynda Gratton, *The Shift: The Future of Work Is Already Here* (London: HarperCollins UK, 2011).

[2] See examples in Carol Hymowitz, "As Managers Climb, They Have to Learn How to Act the Parts," *Wall Street Journal* (November 14, 2005), p. B1.

[3] Information from *Wall Street Journal* (September 21, 2005), p. R4.

[4] For a perspective on the first-line manager's job, see Leonard A. Schlesinger and Janice A. Klein, "The First-Line Supervisor: Past, Present and Future," pp. 370–382, in Jay W. Lorsch (ed.), *Handbook of Organizational Behavior* (Englewood Cliffs, NJ: Prentice-Hall, 1987). Research reported in "Remember Us?" *Economist* (February 1, 1992), p. 71.

[5] For a discussion, see Marcus Buckingham, "What Great Managers Do," *Harvard Business Review* (March 2005). Reprint R0503D.

[6] See William H. Starbuck, "Why Corporate Governance Deserves Serious and Creative Thought," *The Academy of Management Perspectives*, Vol. 28 (February, 2014), pp. 15–21.

[7] See Alan M. Webber, "Danger: Toxic Company," *Fast Company* (November 1998), pp. 15–21; and Stewart D. Friedman, Perry Christensen, and Jessica De Groot, "Work and Life: The End of the Zero-Sum Game," *Harvard Business Review* (November/December 1998), pp. 119–129.

[8] Shelly Banjo, "Clutter Bluster's Next Foray," *Wall Street Journal* (March 21, 2013), p. B7.

[9] Henry Mintzberg, *The Nature of Managerial Work* (New York: Harper & Row, 1973, and HarperCollins, 1997), p. 60.

[10] See, for example, John R. Veiga and Kathleen Dechant, "Wired World Woes: www.Help," *Academy of Management Executive*, vol. 11 (August 1997), pp. 73–79.

[11] For a classic study, see Thomas A. Mahoney, Thomas H. Jerdee, and Stephen J. Carroll, "The Job(s) of Management," *Industrial Relations*, vol. 4 (February 1965), pp. 97–110.

[12] This running example is developed from information from "Accountants Have Lives, Too, You Know," *Business Week* (February 23, 1998), pp. 88–90; Silvia Ann Hewlett and Carolyn Buck Luce, "Off-Ramps and On-Ramps: Keeping Talented Women on the Road to Success," *Harvard Business Review* (March 2005), reprint R0503B; and the Ernst & Young Web site: www.Ey.com.

[13] Information on women and men leaving jobs from Hewlett and Luce, op. cit.

[14] See Mintzberg, op. cit. (1973/1997); Henry Mintzberg, "Covert Leadership: The Art of Managing Professionals," *Harvard Business Review* (November/December 1998), pp. 140–147; and Jonathan Gosling and Henry Mintzberg, "The Five Minds of a Manager," *Harvard Business Review* (November 2003), pp. 1–9.

[15] See Mintzberg, op. cit. (1973/1997); Mintzberg, op. cit. (1998); and Gosling and Mintzberg, op. cit. (2003).

[16] From John P. Kotter, "What Effective General Managers Really Do," *Harvard Business Review* (November/December 1982).

[17] See Seok-Woo Kwon and Paul S. Adler, "Social Capital: Maturation of a Field of Research," *Academy of Management Review*, Vol. 39 (4), 2014, pp. 412–422.

[18] Robert L. Katz, "Skills of an Effective Administrator," *Harvard Business Review* (September/October 1974), p. 94.

[19] See Daniel Goleman's books *Emotional Intelligence* (New York: Bantam, 1995) and *Working with Emotional Intelligence* (New York: Bantam, 1998); and his articles "What Makes a Leader," *Harvard Business Review* (November/December 1998), pp. 93–102, and "Leadership That Makes a Difference," *Harvard Business Review* (March/April 2000), pp. 79–90, quote from p. 80.

[20] Quotes from Melissa Korn, "Bosses Seek Critical Thinking, but what is It?" *Wall Street Journal* (October 22, 2014), p. B6.

[21] Ibid.

[22] Information and quote from Lauren Weber, "Here's What Boards Want in Executives," *Wall Street Journal* (December 10, 2014), p. B5.

[23] Henry Mintzberg, "The Manager's Job: Folklore and Fact," *Harvard Business Review*, vol. 53 (July/August 1975), p. 61. See also Mintzberg, op. cit. (1973/1997).

[24] This example is updated from Thomas Friedman, *The World Is Flat: A Brief History of the 21st Century* (New York: Farrar, Straus & Giroux, 2005), pp. 208–209. See www8.hp.com/us/en/hp-information/facts.html (accessed December 7, 2012).

[25] See Joseph E. Stiglitz, *Globalization and Its Discontents* (New York: W.W. Norton, 2003); and Joseph E. Stiglitz, *Making Globalization Work* (New York: W.W. Norton, 2007).

[26] Michael E. Porter, *The Competitive Advantage of Nations: With a New Introduction* (New York: Free Press, 1998).

[27] See for example, John Bussey, "Buck Up America: China Is Getting Too Expensive," *Wall Street Journal* (October 7, 2011), pp. B1, B2.

[28] An Internet search will turn up many news articles reporting the details of the Bernie Madoff scandal.

[29] See William H. Starbuck, "Why Corporate Governance Deserves Serious and Creative Thought," *The Academy of Management Perspectives*, Vol. 28 (No. 1, 2013), pp. 15–21.

[30] Daniel Akst, "Room at the Top for Improvement," *Wall Street Journal* (October 26, 2004), p. D8; and Herb Baum and Tammy King, *The Transparent Leader* (New York: HarperCollins, 2005).

[31] *Workforce 2000: Work and Workers for the 21st Century* (Indianapolis: Towers Perrin/Hudson Institute, 1987); Richard W. Judy and Carol D'Amico (eds.), *Work and Workers for the 21st Century* (Indianapolis: Hudson Institute, 1997). See Richard D. Bucher, *Diversity Consciousness: Opening Our Minds to People, Cultures, and Opportunities* (Upper Saddle River, NJ: Prentice-Hall, 2000); R. Roosevelt Thomas, "From Affirmative Action to Affirming Diversity," *Harvard Business Review* (March/April 1990), pp. 107–17; and *Beyond Race and Gender: Unleashing the Power of Your Total Workforce by Managing Diversity* (New York: AMACOM, 1992).

[32] June Kronholz, "Hispanics Gain in Census," *Wall Street Journal* (May 10, 2006), p. A6; Phillip Toledano, "Demographics: The Population Hourglass,"

Fast Company (March, 2006), p. 56; June Kronholz, "Racial Identity's Gray Area," *Wall Street Journal* (June 12, 2008), p. A10; "We're Getting Old," *Wall Street Journal* (March 26, 2009), p. D2; Les Christie, "Hispanic Population Boom Fuels Rising U.S. Diversity," *CNNMoney:* www.cnn.com; Betsy Towner, "The New Face of 501 America," *AARP Bulletin* (June 2009), p. 31; "Los U.S.A.: Latin Population Grows Faster, Spreads Wider," *Wall Street Journal* (March 25, 2011), p. A1; and, Laura Meckler, "Hispanic Future in the Cards," *Wall Street Journal* (December 13, 2012), p. A3.

[33]Information from "Racism in Hiring Remains, Study Says," *Columbus Dispatch* (January 17, 2003), p. B2.

[34]For discussions of the glass ceiling effect, see Ann M. Morrison, Randall P. White, and Ellen Van Velso, *Breaking the Glass Ceiling* (Reading, MA: Addison-Wesley, 1987); Anne E. Weiss. *The Glass Ceiling: A Look at Women in the Workforce* (New York: Twenty First Century, 1999); and Debra E. Meyerson and Joyce K. Fletcher, "A Modest Manifesto for Shattering the Glass Ceiling," *Harvard Business Review* (January/February 2000).

[35]For background, see Taylor Cox, Jr., "The Multicultural Organization," *Academy of Management Executive,* vol. 5 (1991), pp. 34–47; and *Cultural Diversity in Organizations: Theory, Research and Practice* (San Francisco: Berrett-Koehler, 1993).

[36]See "Women Come on Board," *Business Week* (June 15, 2009), p. 24.

[37]See Tom Peters, "The Brand Called You," *Fast Company* (August/September 1997), p. 83; Reid Hoffman, Ben Casnocha, and Chris Yewh, "Tours of Duty: The New Employer-Employee Compact," *Harvard Business Review,* Vol. 91 (June, 2013), pp 49–58 and, "The Future of Work," *The Economist,* Kindle Edition (December 31, 2014).

[38]Charles Handy, *The Age of Unreason* (Cambridge, MA: Harvard Business School Press, 1990). See also Michael S. Malone, *The Future Arrived Yesterday: The Rise of the Protean Organization and What It Means for You* (New York: Crown Books, 2009).

[39]See Gareille Monaghan, "Don't Get a Job, Get a Portfolio Career," *The Sunday Times* (April 26, 2009), p. 15; Hoffman, op. cit. (2013); and, "The Future of Work," op cit.

[40]Dave Ulrich, "Intellectual Capital = Competency × Commitment," *Harvard Business Review* (Winter, 1998), pp. 15–26.

[41]See Peter F. Drucker, *The Changing World of the Executive* (New York: T.T. Times Books, 1982), and *The Profession of Management* (Cambridge, MA: Harvard Business School Press, 1997); and Francis Horibe, *Managing Knowledge Workers: New Skills and Attitudes to Unlock the Intellectual Capital in Your Organization* (New York: Wiley, 1999).

[42]Daniel Pink, *A Whole New Mind: Moving from the Information Age to the Conceptual Age* (New York: Riverhead Books, 2005).

[43]Peters, op. cit.

[44]Joann S. Lublin, "Your 'Personal Brand' May Need Some Work," *Wall Street Journal* (January 2, 2015), p. B4.

Feature Notes 2

Opening Quote—"Tim Cook Speaks Up," *Bloomberg BusinessWeek* (October 30, 2014), pp. 12–13.

Management Live—Information and quotes from Emma Jacobs, "Strategies for Calling It a Day," *Financial Times,* Kindle edition (August 19, 2014).

Ethics Check—Information and quotes from Eric Spitznagel, "Rise Up, Interns," *Bloomberg BusinessWeek* (June 24–30, 2013), p. 78.

Facts to Consider—Information from Deloitte LLP, "Leadership Counts: 2007 Deloitte & Touche USA Ethics & Workplace Survey Results," *Kiplinger Business Resource Center* (June, 2007): kiplinger.com.

Hot Topic—Information and quotes from Lauren Weber and Rachel Emma Silverman, "On-Demand Workers: 'We are not Robots'," *Wall Street Journal* (January 28, 2015), pp. B1, B7; and, Rachel Emma Silverman, "Judges Skeptical of Uber-Lyft Claims in Labor Cases," *Wall Street Journal* (February 3, 2015), p. B4.

Quick Case—For an example see Sue Shellenbarger, "How Could a Sweet Third-Grader Just Cheat on That School Exam?" *Wall Street Journal* (May 15, 2014), pp. D1, D3.

Photo Essays—Cheating—Pamela Engel, "Students Don't Cheat; They Collaborate?" *The Columbus Dispatch* (September 10, 2012): dispatch.com. Stonyfield Farm—Information and quotes from stonyfieldfarms.com, notablebiographies.com, and "25 Rich Ass Greenies Who Made Their Fortune Saving the Environment," earthfirst.com (August 25, 2008).

Endnotes 2

[1]See the discussion by Terry Thomas, John W. Dienhart, and John R. Schermerhorn, Jr., "Leading Toward Ethical Behavior in Business," *Academy of Management Executive,* vol. 18 (May 2004), pp. 56–66.

[2]See the discussion by Lynn Sharpe Paine, "Managing for Organizational Integrity," *Harvard Business Review* (March/April 1994), pp. 106–117.

[3]Desmond Tutu, "Do More Than Win," *Fortune* (December 30, 1991), p. 59.

[4]Ibid.

[5]For an overview, see Linda K. Trevino and Katherine A. Nelson, *Managing Business Ethics,* 3rd ed. (New York: Wiley, 2003).

[6]Information from Sue Shellenbarger, "How and Why We Lie at the Office: From Pilfered Pens to Padded Accounts," *Wall Street Journal* (March 24, 2005), p. D1.

[7]Case reported in Michelle Conlin, "Cheating—Or Postmodern Learning?" *Business Week* (May 14, 2007), p. 42.

[8]Milton Rokeach, *The Nature of Human Values* (New York: Free Press, 1973). See also W. C. Frederick and J. Weber, "The Values of Corporate Executives and Their Critics: An Empirical Description and Normative Implications," in W. C. Frederick and L. E. Preston (eds.), *Business Ethics: Research Issues and Empirical Studies* (Greenwich, CT: JAI Press, 1990).

[9]See Gerald F. Cavanagh, Dennis J. Moberg, and Manuel Velasquez, "The Ethics of Organizational Politics," *Academy of Management Review,* vol. 6 (1981), pp. 363–74; Justin G. Locknecker, Joseph A. McKinney, and Carlos W. Moore, "Egoism and Independence: Entrepreneurial Ethics," *Organizational Dynamics* (Winter 1988), pp. 64–72; and Justin G. Locknecker, Joseph A. McKinney, and Carlos W. Moore, "The Generation Gap in Business Ethics," *Business Horizons* (September/October 1989), pp. 9–14.

[10]Raymond L. Hilgert, "What Ever Happened to Ethics in Business and in Business Schools?" *The Diary of Alpha Kappa Psi* (April 1989), pp. 4–8.

[11]Jerald Greenburg, "Organizational Justice: Yesterday, Today, and Tomorrow," *Journal of Management,* vol. 16 (1990), pp. 399–432; and Mary A. Konovsky, "Understanding Procedural Justice and Its Impact on Business Organizations," *Journal of Management,* vol. 26 (2000), pp. 489–511.

[12]Interactional justice is described by Robert J. Bies, "The Predicament of Injustice: The Management of Moral Outrage," in L. L. Cummings & B. M. Staw (eds.), *Research in Organizational Behavior,* vol. 9 (Greenwich, CT: JAI Press, 1987), pp. 289–319. The example is from Carol T. Kulik and Robert L. Holbrook, "Demographics in Service Encounters: Effects of Racial and Gender Congruence on Perceived Fairness," *Social Justice Research,* vol. 13 (2000), pp. 375–402.

[13]See, for example, M. Fortin and M. R. Fellenz, "Hypocrisies of Fairness: Towards a More Reflexive Ethical Base in Organizational Justice Research and Practice," *Journal of Business Ethics,* vol. 78 (2008), pp. 415–33.

[14]The United Nations Universal Declaration of Human Rights is available online at: http://www.un.org/Overview/rights.html.

[15]Robert D. Haas, "Ethics—A Global Business Challenge," *Vital Speeches of the Day* (June 1, 1996), pp. 506–09.

[16]This discussion is based on Thomas Donaldson, "Values in Tension: Ethics Away from Home," *Harvard Business Review,* vol. 74 (September/October 1996), pp. 48–62.

[17]Ibid; Thomas Donaldson and Thomas W. Dunfee, "Towards a Unified Conception of Business Ethics: Integrative Social Contracts Theory," *Academy of Management Review,* vol. 19 (1994), pp. 252–85.

[18]Developed from Donaldson, op. cit.

[19]Reported in Barbara Ley Toffler, "Tough Choices: Managers Talk Ethics," *New Management,* vol. 4 (1987), pp. 34–39. See also Barbara Ley Toffler, *Tough Choices: Managers Talk Ethics* (New York: Wiley, 1986).

[20]See discussion by Trevino and Nelson, op. cit., pp. 47–62.

[21]Information from Steven N. Brenner and Earl A. Mollander, "Is the Ethics of Business Changing?" *Harvard Business Review,* vol. 55 (January/February 1977).

[22]Deloitte LLP, "Leadership Counts: 2007 Deloitte & Touche USA Ethics & Workplace Survey Results," *Kiplinger Business Resource Center* (June, 2007): www.kiplinger.com.

[23]"Who's to Blame: Washington or Wall Street?" *Newsweek* (March 30, 2009): www.newsweek.com.

[24]This research is summarized by Archie Carroll, "Pressure May Force Ethical Hand," *BGS International Exchange* (Fall 2004), p. 5.

[25]Ibid.

[26]Ibid.

[27]Saul W. Gellerman, "Why 'Good' Managers Make Bad Ethical Choices," *Harvard Business Review*, vol. 64 (July/August, 1986), pp. 85–90.

[28]Survey results from Del Jones, "48% of Workers Admit to Unethical or Illegal Acts," *USA Today* (April 4, 1997), p. A1.

[29]Lawrence Kohlberg, *The Psychology of Moral Development: The Nature and Validity of Moral Stages* (*Essays in Moral Development*, Volume 2) (New York: HarperCollins, 1984). See also the discussion by Linda K. Trevino, "Moral Reasoning and Business Ethics: Implications for Research, Education, and Management," *Journal of Business Ethics*, vol. 11 (1992), pp. 445–59.

[30]See D. Ordóñez, Maurice E. Schweitzer, Adam D. Galinsky, and Max H. Bazerman, "Goals Gone Wild: How Goals Systematically Harm Individuals and Organizations," *Academy of Management Perspectives*, Vol. 23 (2009), pp. 6–16; and, Edwin A. Locke and Gary P. Latham, "Has Goal Setting Gone Wild, or Have Its Attackers Abandoned Good Scholarship?" *Academy of Management Perspectives*, Vol. 23 (2009), pp. 17–23.

[31]Developed from recommendations of the Government Accountability Project reported in "Blowing the Whistle Without Paying the Piper," *Business Week* (June 3, 1991): businessweek.com/archives.

[32]Archie B. Carroll, "In Search of the Moral Manager," *Business Horizons* (March/April, 2001), pp. 7–15.

[33]Kohlberg, op. cit.

[34]See, for example, David Bielo, "MBA Programs for Social and Environmental Stewardship," *Business Ethics* (Fall 2005), pp. 22–28.

[35]See the Josephson model for ethical decision making: www.josephsoninstitute.org.

[36]Ibid.

[37]Examples from "Whistle-Blowers on Trial," *Business Week* (March 24, 1997), pp. 172–78; and "NLRB Judge Rules for Massachusetts Nurses in Whistle-Blowing Case," *American Nurse* (January/February 1998), p. 7. For a review of whistleblowing, see Marcia P. Micelli and Janet P. Near, *Blowing the Whistle* (Lexington, MA: Lexington Books, 1992); Micelli and Near, "Whistleblowing: Reaping the Benefits," *Academy of Management Executive*, vol. 8 (August 1994), pp. 65–72; and Cynthia Cooper, *Extraordinary Circumstances* (Hoboken, NJ: Wiley, 2009).

[38]Information from James A. Waters, "Catch 20.5: Mortality as an Organizational Phenomenon," *Organizational Dynamics*, vol. 6 (Spring 1978), pp. 3–15.

[39]Information from corporate Web site: www.gapinc.com/community sourcing/vendor_conduct.htm.

[40]See David Vogel, *The Market for Virtue: The Potential and Limits of Corporate Social Responsibility* (Washington, DC: Brookings Institution Press, 2006); and Thomas et al., op. cit.

[41]For more on this notion, see Alfred A. Marcus and Adam R. Fremeth, "Green Management Matters Regardless," *Academy of Management Perspectives*, vol. 23 (August, 2009), pp. 17–26; and Jeffrey Pfeffer, "Building Sustainable Organizations: The Human Factor," *Academy of Management Perspectives*, vol. 24 (February, 2010), pp. 34–45.

[42]Joe Biesecker, "What Today's College Graduates Want: It's Not All About Paychecks," *Central Penn Business Journal* (August 10, 2007).

[43]Sarah E. Needleman, "The Latest Office Perk: Getting Paid to Volunteer," *Wall Street Journal* (April 29, 2008), p. D1.

[44]The historical framework of this discussion is developed from Keith Davis, "The Case For and Against Business Assumption of Social Responsibility," *Academy of Management Journal* (June 1973), pp. 312–22; Keith Davis and William Frederick, *Business and Society: Management: Public Policy, Ethics*, 5th ed. (New York: McGraw-Hill, 1984). This debate is discussed by Joel Makower in *Putting Social Responsibility to Work for Your Business and the World* (New York: Simon & Schuster, 1994), pp. 28–33. See also Aneel Karnani, "The Case Against Social Responsibility," *Wall Street Journal* (August 23, 2010); www.wsj.com.

[45]Quotation is from Milton Friedman, *Capitalism and Freedom* (Chicago: University of Chicago Press, 1962) as cited in Davis, op. cit.

[46]Quotation from Paul A. Samuelson, "Love That Corporation," *Mountain Bell Magazine* (Spring 1971) as cited in Davis, op. cit.

[47]See James K. Glassman, "When Ethics Meet Earnings," *International Herald Tribune* (May 24–25, 2003), p. 15; Simon Zaydek, "The Path to Corporate Social Responsibility," *Harvard Business Review* (December 2004), pp. 125–32.

[48]See Makower, op. cit. (1994), pp. 71–75; Sandra A. Waddock and Samuel B. Graves, "The Corporate Social Performance—Financial Performance Link," *Strategic Management Journal* (1997), pp. 303–19: and Vogel, op. cit. (2006).

[49]Michael E. Porter and Mark R. Kramer, "Shared Value: How to Reinvent Capitalism and Unleash a Wave of Innovation and Growth," *Harvard Business Review* (January–February, 2011), pp. 62–77.

[50]Ibid, p. 64.

[51]Information and quotes from Mara Lemos-Stein, "Talking About Waste with P&G," *Wall Street Journal* (September 13, 2011), p. R8; and "Benefits Flow as Top People Join the Battle," *Financial Times*, Kindle edition (June 23, 2011); www.nestle.com/csv/ruraldevelopment/responsiblesourcing (retrieved February 18, 2012); "How to Create a Green Supply Chain," *Financial Times*, Kindle Edition (November 11, 2010); and Information from Steve Lohr, "First, Make Money. Also, Do Good." *New York Times* (August 13, 2011): nytimes.com.

[52]Abuses of microcredit lending have been publicized in the press, and both the microfinance industry as a whole and the Grameen Bank in particular have been criticized by the Bangladesh government. Muhammad Yunus published his own criticism of the industry and defense of the Grameen Bank model in "Sacrificing Microcredit for Megaprofits," *The New York Times* (January 14, 2011): nytimes.com. A Norwegian documentary that aired criticisms of how Yunus and Grameen Bank handled funds has largely been refuted, but Yunus continues to be criticized by the Bangladesh government.

[53]David Bornstein, *How to Change the World—Social Entrepreneurs and the Power of New Ideas* (Oxford, UK: Oxford University Press, 2004).

[54]See Laura D'Andrea Tyson, "Good Works—With a Business Plan," *Business Week* (May 3, 2004), retrieved from Business Week Online (November 14, 2005) at www.Businessweek.com.

[55]Chip Fleiss, "Social Enterprise—the Fiegling Fourth Sector Soapbox," *Financial Times* (June 15, 2009).

[56]Drucker quote referenced and discussed at www.druckersociety.at/repository/newsletter/09/newsletter.html.

[57]Archie B. Carroll, "A Three-Dimensional Model of Corporate Performance," *Academy of Management Review*, vol. 4 (1979), pp. 497–505. Carroll's continuing work in this area is reported in Mark S. Schwartz and Archie B. Carroll, "Corporate Social Responsibility: A Three Domain Approach," *Business Ethics Quarterly*, vol. 13 (2003), pp. 503–30.

[58]See the discussion by Porter and Kramer, op. cit.

[59]Information and quotes from Angel Gonzales, "1,800 Starbucks Staffers Enrolled in ASU Program," *Arizona Daily Star* (October 8, 2014), p. A8; and, starbucks.com/careers/college-plan and starbucks.com/college-plan/first-starbucks-partner-admitted-to-ASU (accessed October 12, 2014).

[60]Information from Helen Jones, "CEOs Now Find that Principles and Profits Can Mix Well," *Wall Street Journal* (November 22, 2010), p. R5.

[61]Ibid.

[62]Ibid.

[63]Definition from www.sustainablebusiness.com.

[64]www.wbcsd.org.

[65]"Eco-nomics—Creating Environmental Capital," *Wall Street Journal* (March 8, 2010), p. R1.

[66]From www.iso.org.

[67]"Indra Nooyi of Pepsico, View from the Top," *Financial Times*: www.ft.com (February 1, 2010), retrieved March 11, 2010.

[68]Pfeffer, op cit. See also, Jeffrey Pfeffer, "Shareholders First? Not So Fast. . . ." *Harvard Business Review* (July–August, 2009), pp. 89–91.

Feature Notes 3

Opening Quote—"Last Miner Out Hailed as a Shift Boss Who Kept Group Alive," news.blog.cnn.com (October 14, 2010).

Management Live—Information from Lauren Weber, "At Work," *Wall Street Journal* (December 12, 2013), p. B6.

Ethics Check—Story reported in and quotes from *The Economist* (June 17, 2006), vol. 379, issue 8482, pp. 65–66, 2p, 1c.

Facts to Consider—Information and quotes from John Bussey, "Gender Wage Gap Reflects an 'Ask Gap'," *Wall Street Journal* (October 11–12, 2014), p. B4; and, Barbara Orfutay, "Surveys: 'Good Karma on Women's Pay Seems Scarce'," *Arizona Daily Star* (October 11, 2014), p. A14.

Hot Topic—Information and quotes from Claire Suddath, "Work-from-Home Truths, Half-Truths, and Myths," *Bloomberg BusinessWeek* (March 4–10, 2013), p. 75; and, Rick Hampson, "Boss vs. You: The Work-from-Home Tug of War," *USA Today* (March 13, 2013), pp. 2, 2A.

Quick Case—See "Asking for a Raise? Avoid Round Numbers," *Wall Street Journal* (May 29, 2013), p. B10.

Endnotes 3

[1] Information and quotes from "Last Miner Out Hailed as a Shift Boss Who Kept Group Alive," news.blog.cnn.com (October 14, 2010); and Eva Bergara, "Chilean Miners Honored in Ceremony, Football Game," news.yahoo.com (October 25, 2010).

[2] Peter F. Drucker, "Looking Ahead: Implications of the Present," *Harvard Business Review* (September/October 1997), pp. 18–32. See also Shaker A. Zahra, "An Interview with Peter Drucker," *Academy of Management Executive*, vol. 17 (August 2003), pp. 9–12.

[3] For a good discussion, see Michael S. Hopkins, Steve LaValle, Fred Balboni, Nina Kruschwitz, and Rebecca Shokley, "10 Insights: First Look at the New Intelligent Enterprise Survey on Winning with Data," *Sloan Management Review*, Vol. 52 (Fall, 2010), pp. 22–27.

[4] For a good discussion, see Watson H. Agor, *Intuition in Organizations: Leading and Managing Productively* (Newbury Park, CA: Sage, 1989); Herbert A. Simon, "Making Management Decisions: The Role of Intuition and Emotion," *Academy of Management Executive*, vol. 1 (1987), pp. 57–64; Orlando Behling and Norman L. Eckel, "Making Sense Out of Intuition," *Academy of Management Executive*, vol. 1 (1987), pp. 57–64; Orlando Behling and Norman L. Eckel, "Making Sense Out of Intuition," *Academy of Management Executive*, vol. 5 (1991), pp. 46–54.

[5] Alan Deutschman, "Inside the Mind of Jeff Bezos," *Fast Company*, Issue 85 (August, 2004); www.fastcompany.com.

[6] Quote from Susan Carey, "Pilot 'in Shock' as He Landed Jet in River," *Wall Street Journal* (February 9, 2009), p. A6.

[7] Based on Carl Jung's typology, as described in Donald Bowen, "Learning and Problem-Solving: You're Never Too Jung," in Donald D. Bowen, Roy J. Lewicki, Donald T. Hall, and Francine S. Hall, eds., *Experiences in Management and Organizational Behavior*, 4th ed. (New York: Wiley, 1997), pp. 7–13; and John W. Slocum Jr., "Cognitive Style in Learning and Problem Solving," in ibid., pp. 349–53.

[8] See Hugh Courtney, Jane Kirkland, and Patrick Viguerie, "Strategy Under Uncertainty," *Harvard Business Review* (November/December 1997), pp. 67–79.

[9] See George P. Huber, *Managerial Decision Making* (Glenview, IL: Scott, Foresman, 1975). For a comparison, see the steps in Xerox's problem-solving process, as described in David A. Garvin, "Building a Learning Organization," *Harvard Business Review* (July/August 1993), pp. 78–91; and the Josephson model for ethical decision making described at www.josephsoninstitute.org.

[10] Joseph B. White and Lee Hawkins, Jr., "GM Cuts Deeper in North America," *Wall Street Journal* (November 22, 2005), p. A3. See also Rick Wagoner, "A Portrait of My Industry," *Wall Street Journal* (December 6, 2005), p. A20.

[11] See Herbert A. Simon, *Administrative Behavior* (New York: Free Press, 1947); James G. March and Herbert A. Simon, *Organizations* (New York: Wiley, 1958); and Herbert A. Simon, *The New Science of Management Decision* (New York: Harper, 1960).

[12] This figure and the related discussion is developed from conversations with Dr. Alma Acevedo of the University of Puerto Rico at Rio Piedras and her articles "Of Fallacies and Curricula: A Case of Business Ethics," *Teaching Business Ethics*, vol. 5 (2001), pp. 157–70; and "Business Ethics: An Introduction," working paper (2009).

[13] Based on Gerald F. Cavanagh, *American Business Values*, 4th ed. (Upper Saddle River, NJ: Prentice-Hall, 1998).

[14] The third spotlight question is based on the Josephson model for ethical decision making: www.josephsoninstitute.org.

[15] Example from Dayton Fandray, "Assumed Innocent: Hidden and Unexamined Assumptions Can Ruin Your Day," *Continental.com/Magazine* (December 2007), p. 100.

[16] See, for example, Roger von Oech, *A Whack on the Side of the Head* (New York: Warner Books, 1983) and *A Kick in the Seat of the Pants* (New York: Harper & Row, 1986).

[17] For discussions of Big-C creativity and Little-C creativity, see James C. Kaufman and Ronald A. Beghetto, "Beyond Big and Little: The Four C Model of Creativity," *Review of General Psychology*, vol. 13 (2009), pp. 1–12. My thanks go to Dr. Erin Fluge of Southeastern Missouri State University for bringing this useful distinction to my attention.

[18] Teresa M. Amabile, "Motivating Creativity in Organizations," *California Management Review*, vol. 40 (Fall, 1997), pp. 39–58.

[19] Developed from discussions by Edward DeBono, *Lateral Thinking: Creativity Step-by-Step* (New York: HarperCollins, 1970); John S. Dacey and Kathleen H. Lennon, *Understanding Creativity* (San Francisco: Jossey-Bass, 1998); and Bettina von Stamm, *Managing Innovation, Design & Creativity* (Chichester, England: Wiley, 2003).

[20] The classic work is Norman R. Maier, "Assets and Liabilities in Group Problem Solving," *Psychological Review*, vol. 74 (1967), pp. 239–49.

[21] This presentation is based on the work of R. H. Hogarth, D. Kahneman, A. Tversky, and others, as discussed in Max H. Bazerman, *Judgment in Managerial Decision Making*, 3rd ed. (New York: Wiley, 1994).

[22] Barry M. Staw, "The Escalation of Commitment to a Course of Action," *Academy of Management Review*, vol. 6 (1981), pp. 577–87; and Barry M. Staw and Jerry Ross, "Knowing When to Pull the Plug," *Harvard Business Review*, vol. 65 (March/April 1987), pp. 68–74.

[23] For a thorough literature review see Dustin J. Sleesman, Donald E. Conlon, Gerry McNamara, and Jonathan E. Miles," *Academy of Management Journal*, vol. 55, no. 3 (2012), pp. 541–62.

[24] For scholarly reviews, see Dean Tjosvold, "Effects of Crisis Orientation on Managers' Approach to Controversy in Decision Making," *Academy of Management Journal*, vol. 27 (1984), pp. 130–38; and Ian I. Mitroff, Paul Shrivastava, and Firdaus E. Udwadia, "Effective Crisis Management," *Academy of Management Executive*, vol. 1 (1987), pp. 283–92.

[25] Anna Muoio, "Where There's Smoke It Helps to Have a Smoke Jumper," *Fast Company*, vol. 33, p. 290.

Feature Notes 4

Opening Quote—"Japan Widens Evacuation Zone Around Fukushima Nuclear Plant," www.dailytelegraph.com (May 15, 2011).

Management Live—Information from Douglas Belkin, "Should a College Student Pick a Major Based on Possible Future Salaries?" *Wall Street Journal* (March 17, 2014), p. R7.

Ethics Check—See "Electronic Hazardous Waste (E-Waste)," California Department of Toxic Substances Control, www.dtsc.ca.gov (Accessed September 12, 2012); and "E-Cycling," United States Environmental Protection Agency Web site, www.epa.gov (Accessed September 12, 2012).

Facts to Consider—Information from Phred Dvorak, Bob Davis, and Louise Radnofsky, "Firms Confront Boss-Subordinate Love Affairs," *Wall Street Journal* (October 27, 2008), p. B5. Survey data from Society for Human Resource Management.

Hot Topic—These viewpoints were found in the *Advanced Management Journal* (Summer, 1975), and reported in John R. Schermerhorn Jr., James G. Hunt, and Richard N. Osborn, *Managing Organizational Behavior* (New York: John Wiley & Sons, 1982, pp. 550–51.

Quick Case—See Lauren Weber, "Why Dads Don't Take Paternity Leave," *Wall Street Journal* (June 13, 2013), pp. B1, B7; and, Susan Wojcicki, "Paid Maternity Leave Is Good for Business," *Wall Street Journal* (December 17, 2014), p. A17.

Photo Essay—**Apple:** Information from Kathrin Hille and Sarah Mishkin, "Foxconn Admits Employing 14-year Old Interns," *Financial Times*, Kindle Edition (October 18, 2012); and Jessica E. Lessin and James R. Hagerty, "A Mac That's 'Made in U.S.A.'," *Wall Street Journal* (December 7, 2012), pp. B1, B2.

Endnotes 4

[1]*Eaton Corporation Annual Report*, 1985.

[2]Henry Mintzberg, "The Manager's Job: Folklore and Fact," *Harvard Business Review*, vol. 53 (July/August 1975), pp. 54–67; and Henry Mintzberg, "Planning on the Left Side and Managing on the Right," *Harvard Business Review*, vol. 54 (July/August 1976), pp. 46–55.

[3]For a classic study, see Stanley Thune and Robert House, "Where Long-Range Planning Pays Off," *Business Horizons*, vol. 13 (1970), pp. 81–87. For a critical review of the literature, see Milton Leontiades and Ahmet Teel, "Planning Perceptions and Planning Results," *Strategic Management Journal*, vol. 1 (1980), pp. 65–75; and J. Scott Armstrong, "The Value of Formal Planning for Strategic Decisions," *Strategic Management Journal*, vol. 3 (1982), pp. 197–211.

For special attention to the small business setting, see Richard B. Robinson Jr., John A. Pearce II, George S. Vozikis, and Timothy S. Mescon, "The Relationship Between Stage of Development and Small Firm Planning and Performance," *Journal of Small Business Management*, vol. 22 (1984), pp. 45–52; and Christopher Orphen, "The Effects of Long-Range Planning on Small Business Performance: A Further Examination," *Journal of Small Business Management*, vol. 23 (1985), pp. 16–23. For an empirical study of large corporations, see Vasudevan Ramanujam and N. Venkatraman, "Planning and Performance: A New Look at an Old Question," *Business Horizons*, vol. 30 (1987), pp. 19–25.

[4]Quote from Stephen Covey and Roger Merrill, "New Ways to Get Organized at Work," *USA Weekend* (February 6/8, 1998), p. 18. Books by Stephen R. Covey include: *The 7 Habits of Highly Effective People: Powerful Lessons in Personal Change* (New York: Fireside, 1990), and Stephen R. Covey and Sandra Merril Covey, *The 7 Habits of Highly Effective Families: Building a Beautiful Family Culture in a Turbulent World* (New York: Golden Books, 1996).

[5]Information from Carol Hymowitz, "Packed Calendars Rule over Executives," *Wall Street Journal* (June 16, 2008), p. B1.

[6]Quotes from *Businessweek* (August 8, 1994), pp. 78–86.

[7]See William Oncken Jr. and Donald L. Wass, "Management Time: Who's Got the Monkey?" *Harvard Business Review*, vol. 52 (September/October 1974), pp. 75–80, and featured as an HBR classic, *Harvard Business Review* (November/December 1999).

[8]Sumath Reddy, "Why Are You Always Late? It Could Be the Planning Fallacy," *Wall Street Journal* (February 3, 2015), pp. D1, D4.

[9]For more on the long term, see Danny Miller and Isabelle Le Breton-Miller, *Managing for the Long Run* (Cambridge, MA: Harvard Business School Press, 2005).

[10]See Elliot Jaques, *The Form of Time* (New York: Russak & Co., 1982). For an executive commentary on his research, see Walter Kiechel III, "How Executives Think," *Fortune* (December 21, 1987), pp. 139–44.

[11]See Henry Mintzberg, "Rounding Out the Manager's Job," *Sloan Management Review* (Fall 1994), pp. 1–25.

[12]Excerpts in sample sexual harassment policy from American Express's advice to small businesses at www.americanexpress.com (retrieved November 21, 2005).

[13]Forecasts in Stay Informed from "Long-Term Forecasts on EIU Country Data and Market Indicators & Forecasts," *The Economist* Intelligence Unit, www.eiu.com (retrieved November 21, 2005).

[14]Information and quotes from Guy Chazan and Neil King, "BP's Preparedness for Major Crisis Is Questioned," *Wall Street Journal* (May 10, 2010), p. A6; and Ben Casselman and Guy Chazan, "Disaster Plans Lacing at Deep Rigs," *Wall Street Journal* (May 18, 2010), p. A1.

[15]The scenario-planning approach is described in Peter Schwartz, *The Art of the Long View* (New York: Doubleday/Currency, 1991); and Arie de Geus, *The Living Company: Habits for Survival in a Turbulent Business Environment* (Boston: Harvard Business School Press, 1997).

[16]Ibid.

[17]See, for example, Robert C. Camp, *Business Process Benchmarking* (Milwaukee: ASQ Quality Press 1994); Michael J. Spendolini, *The Benchmarking Book* (New York: AMACOM, 1992); and Christopher E. Bogan and Michael J. English, *Benchmarking for Best Practices: Winning Through Innovative Adaptation* (New York: McGraw-Hill, 1994).

[18]David Kiley, "One Ford for the Whole World," *Businessweek* (June 15, 2009), pp. 58–59.

[19]See, for example, Cecile Rohwedder and Keith Johnson, "Pace-setting Zara Seeks More Speed to Fight Its Rising Cheap-Chic Rivals," *Wall Street Journal* (February 20, 2008), pp. B1, B6.

[20]T. J. Rodgers, with William Taylor and Rick Foreman, "No Excuses Management," *World Executive's Digest* (May 1994), pp. 26–30.

[21]See Paul Ingrassia, "The Right Stuff," *Wall Street Journal* (April 8, 2005), p. D5.

[22]Stephanie Banchero, "Columbus, Ohio, School District Hit by Cheating Allegations," *Wall Street Journal* (January 28, 2014); wsj.com (accessed June 10, 2014).

[23]Tom Cohen, "Audit: More Than 120,000 Veterans Waiting or Never Got Care," *CNN* (June 9, 2014), cnn.com (accessed June 10, 2014).

[24]Lisa D. Ordóñez, Maurice E. Schweitzer, Adam D. Galinsky, and Max H. Bazerman, "Goals Gone Wild: How Goals Systematically Harm Individuals and Organizations," *Academy of Management Perspectives*, Vol. 23 (2009), pp. 6–16; and, Edwin A. Locke and Gary P. Latham, "Has Goal Setting Gone Wild, or Have Its Attackers Abandoned Good Scholarship?" *Academy of Management Perspectives*, Vol. 23 (2009), pp. 17–23.

[25]Quotes from Cohen, op cit.

[26]See David T. Welsh and Lisa D. Ordóñez, "The Dark Side of Consecutive High Performance Goals: Linking Goal Setting, Depletion, and Unethical Behavior," Organizational Behavior and Human Decision Processes, Vol. 123 (2014), pp. 79–89; and, Gary P. Latham and Gerard Seijts, "Learning Goals or Performance Goals: Is It the Journey or the Destination?" *Ivey Business Journal* (May/June, 2006): iveybusinessjournal.com (accessed June 10, 2014).

[27]See "Management by Goal-Setting Is Making a Comeback, Its Flaws Supposedly Fixed," *The Economist*, Kindle Edition (March 16, 2015).

[28]Latham and Seijts, op cit.

[29]"How Classy Can 7-Eleven Get?" *Businessweek* (September 1, 1997), pp. 74–75; and Kellie B. Gormly, "7-Eleven Moving Up a Grade," *Columbus Dispatch* (August 3, 2000), pp. C1–C2.

Feature Notes 5

Opening Quote—Daniel R. Ames and Abbie S. Wazlawek, "How to Tell If You're a Jerk in the Office," *Wall Street Journal* (February 23, 2015), p. R2.

Management Live—Information and quote from Michael Shermer, "Book Review: 'The Marshmallow Test' by Walter Mischel," *Wall Street Journal*, Kindle Edition (September 20, 2014).

Ethics Check—See Lauren Weber and Rachel Emma Silverman, "Memo to Staff: Time to Lose a Few Pounds," *Wall Street Journal* (December 17, 2014), pp. B1, B7.

Facts to Consider—Information and quotes from Rachel Emma Silverman, "Here's Why You Won't Finish This Article," *Wall Street Journal* (December 12, 2012), pp. B1, B6.

Hot Topic—See for example, Neil Parmar, "The Best Ways to Bribe Children," *Wall Street Journal* (September 22, 2014), p. R7.

Manager's Library—For views on Sandberg's book see Colleen Taylor, "Sheryl Sandberg Launches 'Lean In' Organization as a Global Community for Workplace Equality," *TechCrunch* (March 6, 2013): techcrunch.com (accessed March 18, 2013); Ann Doyle, "It's Sheryl Sandberg's Courage to Raise Her Voice That's Hot News. Not Leaning In," *Forbes* (March 15, 2013): forbes.com (accessed March 18, 2013); Sheryl Sandberg, "Why I Want Women to Lean In," *Time* (March 7, 2013): ideas.time.com/2013/03/07 (accessed March 18, 2013); Belinda Luscombe, "Confidence Woman," *Time* (March 7, 2013): http://ideas.time.com/2013/03/07 (accessed March 18, 2013); Todd Leopold, "Facebook's Sheryl Sandberg Suddenly in Crossfire," *CNN.com* (March 11, 2013): cnn.com/2013/03/11 (accessed March 18, 2013); and "Feminist Mystique: What Must Change for Women to Make It to the Top," *Economist*, Kindle Edition (March 19, 2013).

Find Inspiration—Whole Foods: Lesley Patton and Bryan Gruley, "Whole Foods' Recession Lessons," *Businessweek* (August 9, 2012): businessweek.com (accessed September 12, 2012); "Quality Standards," wholefoodsmarket.com (accessed September 12, 2012); and "Our Mission and Culture," wholefoodsmarket.com (accessed September 12, 2012).

Endnotes 5

[1] For an interesting commentary, see Gates, op. cit.

[2] Information and quote on Toyota from Sharon Terlep and Josh Mitchell, "U.S. Widens Toyota Probe to Electronics," *Wall Street Journal* (February 4, 2010), pp. B1, B12; and "An Open Letter to Toyota Customers," *Columbus Dispatch* (February 4, 2010), p. A12. Information and quote on Lululemon from Claire Suddath, "Lululemon, Exposed," *Bloomberg Businessweek* (April 1–April 7, 2013), p. 81.

[3] "The Renewal Factor: Friendly Fact, Congenial Controls," *Businessweek* (September 14, 1987), p. 105.

[4] Rob Cross and Lloyd Baird, "Technology Is Not Enough: Improving Performance by Building Institutional Memory," *Sloan Management Review* (Spring 2000), p. 73.

[5] Information from Pep Sappal, "Integrated Inclusion Initiative," *Wall Street Journal* (October 3, 2006), p. A2.

[6] Example from George Anders, "Management Guru Turns Focus to Orchestras, Hospitals," *Wall Street Journal* (November 21, 2005), pp. B1, B5.

[7] Information from Leon E. Wynter, "Allstate Rates Managers on Handling Diversity," *Wall Street Journal* (October 1, 1997), p. B1.

[8] Information from Kathryn Kranhold, "U.S. Firms Raise Ethics Focus," *Wall Street Journal* (November 28, 2005), p. B4.

[9] Based on discussion by Harold Koontz and Cyril O'Donnell, *Essentials of Management* (New York: McGraw-Hill, 1974), pp. 362–65; see also Cross and Baird, op. cit.

[10] Information from Louis Lee, "I'm Proud of What I've Made Myself Into—What I've Created," *Wall Street Journal* (August 27, 1997), pp. B1, B5; and Jim Collins, "Bigger, Better, Faster," *Fast Company*, vol. 71 (June 2003), p. 74.

[11] See Sue Shellenbarger, "If You Need to Work Better, Maybe Try Working Less," *Wall Street Journal* (September 23, 2009), p. D1.

[12] Douglas McGregor, *The Human Side of Enterprise* (New York: McGraw-Hill, 1960).

[13] This distinction is made in William G. Ouchi, "Markets, Bureaucracies and Clans," *Administrative Science Quarterly*, vol. 25 (1980), pp. 129–41.

[14] Martin LaMonica, "Wal-Mart Readies Long-Term Move into Solar Power," *CNET News.com* (January 3, 2007).

[15] See Dale D. McConkey, *How to Manage by Results*, 3rd ed. (New York: AMACOM, 1976); Stephen J. Carroll Jr. and Henry J. Tosi Jr., *Management by Objectives: Applications and Research* (New York: Macmillan, 1973); and Anthony P. Raia, *Managing by Objectives* (Glenview, IL: Scott, Foresman, 1974).

[16] For a discussion of research on MBO, see Carroll and Tosi, op. cit.; Raia, op. cit.: and Steven Kerr, "Overcoming the Dysfunctions of MBO," *Management by Objectives*, vol. 5, no. 1 (1976). Information in part from Dylan Loeb McClain, "Job Forecast: Internet's Still Hot," *New York Times* (January 30, 2001), p. 9.

[17] The work on goal setting and motivation is summarized in Edwin A. Locke and Gary P. Latham, *Goal Setting: A Motivational Technique That Works!* (Englewood Cliffs, NJ: Prentice-Hall, 1984).

[18] McGregor, op. cit.

[19] The "hot stove rules" are developed from R. Bruce McAfee and William Poffenberger, *Productivity Strategies: Enhancing Employee Job Performance* (Englewood Cliffs, NJ: Prentice-Hall, 1982), pp. 54–55. They are originally attributed to Douglas McGregor, "Hot Stove Rules of Discipline," in G. Strauss and L. Sayles (eds.), *Personnel: The Human Problems of Management* (Englewood Cliffs, NJ: Prentice-Hall, 1967).

[20] For basic readings on quality control, see Joseph M. Juran, *Quality Control Handbook*, 3rd ed. (New York: McGraw-Hill, 1979); and "The Quality Trilogy: A Universal Approach to Managing for Quality," in H. Costin (ed.), *Total Quality Management* (New York: Dryden, 1994); W. Edwards Deming, *Out of Crisis* (Cambridge, MA: MIT Press, 1986) and "Deming's Quality Manifesto," *Best of Business Quarterly*, vol. 12 (Winter 1990–1991), pp. 6–101; Howard S. Gitlow and Shelly J. Gitlow, *The Deming Guide to Quality and Competitive Position* (Englewood Cliffs, NJ: Prentice-Hall, 1987); and Rafael Aguay, *Dr. Deming: The American Who Taught the Japanese About Quality* (New York: Free Press, 1997).

[21] Aguay, op. cit.; W. Edwards Deming, op. cit. (1986).

[22] Ibid.

[23] See "Downsides of Just-In-Time Inventory," *Bloomberg Businessweek* (March 28–April 3, 2011), pp. 17–18.

[24] Information from Karen Carney, "Successful Performance Measurement: A Checklist," *Harvard Management Update* (No. U9911B), 1999.

[25] Robert S. Kaplan and David P. Norton, *The Balanced Scorecard* (Cambridge, MA: Harvard Business School Press, 1996); and, "The Balanced Scorecard: Measures That Drive Performance," *Harvard Business Review* (July/August, 2005).

Feature Notes 6

Opening Quote—Information and quote from Walter Mossberg, "Changing the Economics of Education," *Wall Street Journal* (June 4, 2012), p. R8.

Management Live—Information and quotes from "Financial Gains Linked to Diverse Leadership," *Wall Street Journal* (January 21, 2015), p. B7.

Ethics Check— Information and quotes from "Life and Death at the iPad Factory," *Bloomberg Businessweek* (June 7–13, 2010), pp. 35–36; and Paul Mozur and Lorraine Luk, "Apple Contractor's Robots Hit a Glitch," *Wall Street Journal* (December 13, 2012), p. B4.

Facts to Consider—Information from Daniel Costello, "The Drought Is Over (at Least for CEOs)," *New York Times* (April 9, 2011); nytimes.com (accessed May 3, 2011); Joann S. Lublin, "CEO Pay in 2010 Jumped 11%," *Wall Street Journal* (May 9, 2011), p. 81; and, AFL-CIO, "2011 CEO Paywatch," aflcio.org.

Hot Topic—Information and quotes from Rachel Botsman and Andrew Keen, "Can the Sharing Economy Create Good Jobs?" *Wall Street Journal* (May 11, 2015), p. R6.

Quick Case—Used by permission from John R. Schermerhorn, Jr., and Daniel G. Bachrach, *Management*, 13th ed. (Hoboken, NJ: John Wiley & Sons, Inc., 2015), pp. 238, 239.

Manager's Library—See "Rebooting Work: Transform How You Work in the Age of Entrepreneurship," amazon.com (accessed March 25, 2013); "Rebooting Work," maynardwebb.com (accessed March 25, 2013); Maynard Webb, "The Future of Mentorship in the Age of Entrepreneurs," *Fast Company* (December 13, 2012), fastcompany.com (accessed March 25, 2013); and, Dan Schwabel, "Maynard Webb: Rethink Your Workplace Habits to Become Successful," *Forbes* (January 28, 2013): forbes.com (accessed March 25, 2013).

Endnotes 6

[1] Information and quote from Walter Mossberg, "Changing the Economics of Education," *Wall Street Journal* (June 4, 2012), p. R8.

[2] Information and quotes from Marcia Stepanek, "How Fast Is Net Fast?" *Businessweek E-Biz* (November 1, 1999), pp. EB52–54.

[3] Keith H. Hammonds, "Michael Porter's Big Ideas," *Fast Company* (March 2001), pp. 150–56.

[4] See khanacademy.org.

[5] Gary Hamel and C. K. Prahalad, "Strategic Intent," *Harvard Business Review* (May/June 1989), pp. 63–76; and, Donald C. Hambrick and James W. Fredrickson, "Are You Sure You have a Strategy?" *Academy of Management Executive*, Vol. 15, No. 4 (2001), pp. 48–59.

[6] Geoffrey A. Fowler and Nick Wingfield, "Apple's Showman Takes the Stage," *Wall Street Journal* (March 3, 2011), p. B1.

[7] khanacademy.org, op cit.

[8] Michael A. Hitt, R. Duane Ireland, and Robert E. Hoskisson, *Strategic Management: Competitiveness and Globalization* (Minneapolis: West, 1997), p. 197.

[9] See William McKinley, Carol M. Sanchez, and A. G. Schick, "Organizational Downsizing: Constraining, Cloning, Learning," *Academy of Management Executive*, vol. 9 (August 1995), pp. 32–44.

[10] Kim S. Cameron, Sara J. Freeman, and A. K. Mishra, "Best Practices in White-Collar Downsizing: Managing Contradictions," *Academy of Management Executive*, vol. 4 (August 1991), pp. 57–73.

[11] "Overheard," *Wall Street Journal* (April 16, 2009), p. C10; and Geoffrey A. Fowler and Evan Ramstad, "eBay Looks Abroad for Growth," *Wall Street Journal* (April 16, 2009), p. B2.

[12]This strategy classification is found in Hitt et al., op. cit.; the attitudes are from a discussion by Howard V. Perlmutter, "The Tortuous Evolution of the Multinational Corporation," *Columbia Journal of World Business,* vol. 4 (January/February 1969).

[13]Fowler and Ramstad, op. cit., 2009.

[14]Adam M. Brandenburger and Barry J. Nalebuff, *Co-Opetition: A Revolution Mindset That Combines Competition and Cooperation* (New York: Bantam, 1996).

[15]Jonathan Spiva, "BMW ActiveHybrid 7 Review," the dieseldriver.com (July 1, 2010).

[16]See Michael E. Porter, "Strategy and the Internet," *Harvard Business Review* (March 2001), pp. 63–78; and Michael Rappa, *Business Models on the Web* (www.ecommerce.ncsu.edu/business_models.html. February 6, 2001).

[17]See threadless.com.

[18]Peter F. Drucker, *Management: Tasks, Responsibilities, Practices* (New York: Harper & Row, 1973), p. 122.

[19]See Laura Nash, "Mission Statements—Mirrors and Windows," *Harvard Business Review* (March/April 1988), pp. 155–56; James C. Collins and Jerry I. Porras, "Building Your Company's Vision," *Harvard Business Review* (September/October 1996), pp. 65–77; and James C. Collins and Jerry I. Porras, *Built to Last: Successful Habits of Visionary Companies* (New York: Harper Business, 1997). See also Peter F. Drucker's views on organizational objectives in his classic books *The Practice of Management* (New York: Harper & Row, 1954) and *Management: Tasks, Responsibilities, Practices* (New York: Harper & Row, 1973). For a more recent commentary, see his article "Management: The Problems of Success," *Academy of Management Executive,* vol. 1 (1987), pp. 13–19.

[20]C. K. Prahalad and Gary Hamel, "The Core Competencies of the Corporation," *Harvard Business Review* (May/June 1990), pp. 79–91; see also Hitt et al., op. cit., pp. 99–103.

[21]For a discussion of Michael Porter's approach to strategic planning, see his books *Competitive Strategy: Techniques for Analyzing Industries and Competitors* (New York: Free Press, 1980) and *Competitive Advantage: Creating and Sustaining Superior Performance* (New York: Free Press, 1986) and his article "What Is Strategy?" *Harvard Business Review* (November/December 1996), pp. 61–78; and Richard M. Hodgetts's interview "A Conversation with Michael E. Porter: A Significant Extension Toward Operational Improvement and Positioning," *Organizational Dynamics* (Summer 1999), pp. 24–33.

[22]See Porter, op. cit. (1980 and 1986).

[23]Information from www.polo.com.

[24]Richard G. Hammermesh, "Making Planning Strategic," *Harvard Business Review,* vol. 64 (July/August 1986), pp. 115–20; and Richard G. Hammermesh, *Making Strategy Work* (New York: Wiley, 1986).

[25]See Gerald B. Allan, "A Note on the Boston Consulting Group Concept of Competitive Analysis and Corporate Strategy," Harvard Business School, Intercollegiate Case Clearing House, ICCH9-175-175 (Boston: Harvard Business School, June 1976).

[26]R. Duane Ireland and Michael A. Hitt, "Achieving and Maintaining Strategic Competitiveness in the 21st Century," *Academy of Management Executive,* vol. 13 (1999), pp. 43–57.

[27]Hammond, op. cit.

[28]For a discussion see Paul J. H. Shoemaker, Steve Krupp, and Samantha Howland, "Strategic Leadership: The Essential Skills," *Harvard Business Review,* vol. 91 (January–February 2013), pp. 131–34.

[29]patagonia.com/web/us/patagonia.go?assetid = 3351.

Feature Notes 7

Management Live—Information and quotes from Douglas Belkin, "Skills Gap Found in College Students," *Wall Street Journal* (January 17–18, 2015), p. A5.

Facts to Consider—Information and quote from "Bosses Overestimate Their Managing Skills," *Wall Street Journal* (November 1, 2010), p. B10.

Hot Topic— Information from Rachel Feintzeig, "The New Science of Who Sits Where at Work," *Wall Street Journal* (October 8, 2013): online.wsj.com (accessed October 9, 2013).

Quick Case—Information from Rachel Emma Silverman and Leslie Kwoh, "Peer Performance Reviews Take Off," *Wall Street Journal* (August 1, 2012), p. B6.

Photo Essays—*Holacracy*: Jeanne Whalen, "This is the Boardroom of the 'Virtual' Biotech," *Wall Street Journal* (June 4, 2014), pp. B1, B2. *Virtual Biotech*: Jeanne Whalen, "This Is the Boardroom of the 'Virtual' Biotech," *Wall Street Journal* (June 4, 2014), pp. B1, B2.

Endnotes 7

[1]Henry Mintzberg and Ludo Van der Heyden, "Organigraphs: Drawing How Companies Really Work," *Harvard Business Review* (September/October 1999), pp. 87–94.

[2]Ibid.

[3]See for example "Employee Engagement: A Leading Indicator of Financial Performance," gallup.com/consulting (accessed June 24, 2012).

[4]The classic work is Alfred D. Chandler, *Strategy and Structure* (Cambridge, MA: MIT Press, 1962).

[5]See Alfred D. Chandler Jr., "Origins of the Organization Chart," *Harvard Business Review* (March/April 1988), pp. 156–57.

[6]Ibid.

[7]See David Krackhardt and Jeffrey R. Hanson, "Informal Networks: The Company Behind the Chart," *Harvard Business Review* (July/August 1993), pp. 104–11.

[8]Information from Jena McGregor, "The Office Chart That Really Counts," *Businessweek* (February 27, 2006), pp. 48–49.

[9]See Phred Dvorak, "Engineering Firm Charts Ties," *Wall Street Journal* (January 26, 2009): www.wsj.com.

[10]Information from Ellen Byron, "A New Odd Couple: Google, P&G Swap Workers to Spur Innovation," *Wall Street Journal* (November 19, 2008), pp. A1, A18.

[11]For a discussion of departmentalization, see H. I. Ansoff and R. G. Bradenburg, "A Language for Organization Design," *Management Science,* vol. 17 (August 1971), pp. B705–31; Mariann Jelinek, "Organization Structure: The Basic Conformations," in Mariann Jelinek, Joseph A. Litterer, and Raymond E. Miles (eds.), *Organizations by Design: Theory and Practice* (Plano, TX: Business Publications, 1981), pp. 293–302; Henry Mintzberg, "The Structuring of Organizations," in James Brian Quinn, Henry Mintzberg, and Robert M. James (eds.), *The Strategy Process: Concepts, Contexts, and Cases* (Englewood Cliffs, NJ: Prentice-Hall, 1988), pp. 276–304.

[12]"A Question of Management," op. cit.

[13]Example reported in "Top Business Teams: A Lesson Straight from Mars," *Time* (February 9, 2009), p. 40; and Howard M. Guttman, *Great Business Teams* (Hoboken, NJ: Wiley, 2009).

[14]These alternatives are well described by Mintzberg, op. cit.

[15]Norihiko Shirouzu, "Toyota Plans a Major Overhaul in U.S.," *Wall Street Journal* (April 10, 2009), p. B3.

[16]Information and quotes from "Management Shake-Up to Create 'Leaner Structure'," *Financial Times* (June 11, 2009).

[17]Information and quote from "Revamped GM Updates Image of Core Brands," *Financial Times* (June 18, 2009).

[18]Excellent reviews of matrix concepts are found in Stanley M. Davis and Paul R. Lawrence, *Matrix* (Reading, MA: Addison-Wesley, 1977); Paul R. Lawrence, Harvey F. Kolodny, and Stanley M. Davis, "The Human Side of the Matrix," *Organizational Dynamics,* vol. 6 (1977), pp. 43–61; and Harvey F. Kolodny, "Evolution to a Matrix Organization," *Academy of Management Review,* vol. 4 (1979), pp. 543–53.

[19]Davis and Lawrence, op. cit.

[20]Susan Albers Mohrman, Susan G. Cohen, and Allan M. Mohrman Jr., *Designing Team-Based Organizations* (San Francisco: Jossey-Bass, 1996).

[21]See Glenn M. Parker, *Cross-Functional Teams* (San Francisco: Jossey-Bass, 1995).

[22]Andrew Hill, "Is Radical Innovation a Thing of the Past?" *Financial Times,* Kindle Edition (September 27, 2011).

[23]See the discussion by Jay R. Galbraith, "Designing the Networked Organization: Leveraging Size and Competencies," in Susan Albers Mohrman, Jay R. Galbraith, Edward E. Lawler III, and associates, *Tomorrow's Organizations: Crafting Winning Strategies in a Dynamic World* (San Francisco: Jossey-Bass,

1998), pp. 76–102. See also Rupert F. Chisholm, *Developing Network Organizations: Learning from Practice and Theory* (Reading, MA: Addison-Wesley, 1998); and Michael S. Malone, *The Future Arrived Yesterday: The Rise of the Protean Corporation and What It Means for You* (New York: Crown Books, 2009).

[24]See Jerome Barthelemy, "The Seven Deadly Sins of Outsourcing," *Academy of Management Executive,* vol. 17 (2003), pp. 87–98; and Paulo Prada and Jiraj Sheth, "Delta Air Ends Use of India Call Centers," *Wall Street Journal* (April 18–19, 2009), pp. B1, B5.

[25]See the collection of articles by Cary L. Cooper and Denise M. Rousseau (eds.), *The Virtual Organization: Vol. 6, Trends in Organizational Behavior* (New York: Wiley, 2000).

[26]For a discussion of organization theory, see W. Richard Scott, *Organizations: Rational, Natural, and Open Systems,* 4th ed. (Upper Saddle River, NJ: Prentice-Hall, 1998).

[27]For a classic work, see Jay R. Galbraith, *Organizational Design* (Reading, MA: Addison-Wesley, 1977).

[28]David Van Fleet, "Span of Management Research and Issues," *Academy of Management Journal,* vol. 26 (1983), pp. 546–52.

[29]Information from "The Troubling Dean-to-Professor Ratio," *Bloomberg BusinessWeek* (November 26–December 2, 2012), p. 40.

[30]Information from Tim Stevens, "Winning the World Over," *Industry Week* (November 15, 1999).

[31]See George P. Huber, "A Theory of Effects of Advanced Information Technologies on Organizational Design, Intelligence, and Decision Making," *Academy of Management Review,* vol. 15 (1990), pp. 67–71.

[32]Developed from Roger Fritz, *Rate Your Executive Potential* (New York: Wiley, 1988), pp. 185–86; Roy J. Lewicki, Donald D. Bowen, Douglas T. Hall, and Francine S. Hall, *Experiences in Management and Organizational Behavior,* 3rd ed. (New York: Wiley, 1988), p. 144.

[33]Max Weber, *The Theory of Social and Economic Organization,* A. M. Henderson (trans.) and H. T. Parsons (ed.) (New York: Free Press, 1974). For classic treatments of bureaucracy, see also Alvin Gouldner, *Patterns of Industrial Bureaucracy* (New York: Free Press, 1954); and Robert K. Merton, *Social Theory and Social Structure* (New York: Free Press, 1957).

[34]Tom Burns and George M. Stalker, *The Management of Innovation* (London: Tavistock, 1961), republished (London: Oxford University Press, 1994). See also Wesley D. Sine, Hitoshi Mitsuhashi, and David A. Kirsch, "Revisiting Burns and Stalker: Formal Structure and New Venture Performance in Emerging Economic Sectors," *Academy of Management Journal,* vol. 49 (2006), pp. 121–32. The Burns and Stalker study was later extended by Paul R. Lawrence and Jay W. Lorsch, *Organizations and Environment* (Boston: Division of Research, Graduate School of Business Administration, Harvard University, 1967).

[35]See Henry Mintzberg, *Structure in Fives: Designing Effective Organizations* (Englewood Cliffs, NJ: Prentice-Hall, 1983).

[36]"What Ails Microsoft?" *Businessweek* (September 26, 2005), p. 101.

[37]"Should Microsoft Break Up, on Its Own?" *Wall Street Journal* (November 26–27, 2005), p. B16.

[38]See, for example, Jay R. Galbraith, Edward E. Lawler III, and Associates, *Organizing for the Future* (San Francisco: Jossey-Bass, 1993); and Mohrman et al., op. cit.

[39]Peter Senge, *The Fifth Discipline: The Art and Practice of the Learning Organization* (New York: Doubleday, 1994).

[40]Barney Olmsted and Suzanne Smith, *Creating a Flexible Workplace: How to Select and Manage Alternative Work Options* (New York: American Management Association, 1989).

[41]See Allen R. Cohen and Herman Gadon, *Alternative Work Schedules: Integrating Individual and Organizational Needs* (Reading, MA: Addison-Wesley, 1978), p. 125; Simcha Ronen and Sophia B. Primps, "The Compressed Work Week as Organizational Change: Behavioral and Attitudinal Outcomes," *Academy of Management Review,* vol. 6 (1981), pp. 61–74.

[42]Information from Lesli Hicks, "Workers, Employers Praise Their Four-Day Workweek," *Columbus Dispatch* (August 22, 1994), p. 6.

[43]Business for Social Responsibility Resource Center: www.bsr.org/resourcecenter (January 24, 2001); Anusha Shrivastava, "Flextime Is Now Key Benefit for Mom-Friendly Employers," *Columbus Dispatch* (September 23, 2003), p. C2; Sue Shellenbarger, "Number of Women Managers Rises," *Wall Street Journal* (September 30, 2003), p. D2.

[44]"Networked Workers," *Businessweek* (October 6, 1997), p. 8; and Diane E. Lewis, "Flexible Work Arrangements as Important as Salary to Some," *Columbus Dispatch* (May 25, 1998), p. 8.

[45]Christopher Rhoads and Sara Silver, "Working at Home Gets Easier," *Wall Street Journal* (December 29, 2005), p. B4.

[46]Information and quotes from Claire Suddath, "Work-from-Home Truths, Half-Truths, and Myths," *Bloomberg BusinessWeek* (March 4–10, 2013), p. 75; and Rick Hampson, "Boss vs. You: The Work-from-Home Tug of War," *USA Today* (March 13, 2013), pp. 2, 2A.

[47]For a review, see Wayne F. Cascio, "Managing a Virtual Workplace," *Academy of Management Executive,* vol. 14 (2000), pp. 81–90.

[48]Suddath, op cit.; Hampson, op cit.

[49]Information and quotes from Emily Glazer, "Can't Afford an Office? Rent a Desk for $275," *Wall Street Journal* (October 4, 2011), p. B4.

Feature Notes 8

Opening Quote—Quote from Shelly Banjo, "Clutter Buster's Next Foray," *Wall Street Journal* (March 21, 2013), p. B7.

Management Live—Information and quotes from Adam Auriemma, "Chiefs at Big Firms Often Last to Know," *Wall Street Journal* (April 3, 2014), pp. B1, B2; and, Jeff Bennett and Mike Ramsey, "GM Takes Blame, Vows Culture Shift," *Wall Street Journal* (June 6, 2014), pp. A1, A2.

Facts to Consider—Information data reported in "A Saner Workplace," *Businessweek* (June 1, 2009), pp. 66–69, and based on excerpt from Claire Shipman and Katty Kay, *Womenomics: Write Your Own Rules for Success* (New York: Harper Business, 2009); and "A to Z of Generation Y Attitudes," *Financial Times* (June 18, 2009).

Hot Topic—Information from Sue Shellenbarger, "Believers in the 'Project Beard' and Other Office Rituals," *Wall Street Journal* (June 26, 2013), pp. D1, D2.

Quick Case—Information and quotes from Leslie Kwoh, "More Firms Bow to Generation Y's Demands," *Wall Street Journal* (August 22, 2012), Kindle Edition.

Find Inspiration—Clif Bar: Information from Marnie Hanel, "Clif Bar's Offices Keep Employees Limber," *Bloomberg Businessweek* (November 21–27, 2011), pp. 104–05; and clifbar.com.

Photo Essay—Social Entrepreneur: Information and quotes from Aubrey Henvetty, "Seeds of Change," *Kellogg* (Summer, 2006), p. 13; "Amid Turmoil, Social Entrepreneur Sows Hope in Africa," *Kellogg* (Spring, 2008), p. 7; and Updates: Andrew Youn (KSM06), *Kellogg* (Winter, 2012), p. 57.

Endnotes 8

[1]See the discussion of Anthropologie in William C. Taylor and Polly LaBarre, *Mavericks at Work: Why the Most Original Minds in Business Win* (New York: William Morrow, 2006).

[2]Edgar H. Schein, "Organizational Culture," *American Psychologist,* vol. 45 (1990), pp. 109–19. See also Schein's *Organizational Culture and Leadership,* 2nd ed. (San Francisco: Jossey-Bass, 1997); and *The Corporate Culture Survival Guide* (San Francisco: Jossey-Bass, 1999).

[3]Information and quotes from Christopher Palmeri, "Now for Sale, the Zappos Culture," *Businessweek* (January 11, 2010), p. 57.

[4]Jena McGregor, "Zappos' Secret: It's an Open Book," *Businessweek* (March 23 and 30, 2009), p. 62; and, Jena McGregor, "Zappos Gives Employees Exit Prize If Culture Change Is Turnoff," *Columbus Dispatch* (April 6, 2015), p. C3.

[5]James Collins and Jerry Porras, *Built to Last* (New York: Harper Business, 1994).

[6]For the positive side of strong cultures see Schein, op. cit. (1997); Terrence E. Deal and Alan A. Kennedy, *Corporate Cultures: The Rites and Rituals of Corporate Life* (Reading, MA: Addison-Wesley, 1982); and Ralph Kilmann, *Beyond the Quick Fix* (San Francisco: Jossey-Bass, 1984). For the negative side of strong cultures see Adam Auriemma, "Chiefs at Big Firms Often Last to Know," *Wall Street Journal* (April 3, 2014), pp. B1, B2; and, Jeff Bennett and Mike Ramsey, "GM Takes Blame, Vows Culture Shift," *Wall Street Journal* (June 6, 2014), pp. A1, A2.

[7]Schein, op. cit. (1997).

[8]John P. Wanous, *Organizational Entry,* 2nd ed. (New York: Addison-Wesley, 1992).

[9]Scott Madison Patton, "Service Quality, Disney Style" (Lake Buena Vista, FL: Disney Institute, 1997).

[10]See Schein, op cit., 1990, 1997, 1999; Collins and Porras, op cit.; Deal and Kennedy, op cit.

[11]This framework is described by Kim S. Cameron and Robert E. Quinn, *Diagnosing and Changing Organizational Culture: Based on the Competing Values Framework* (Reading, MA: Addison-Wesley, 1999).

[12]"Workplace Cultures Come in Four Kinds," *Wall Street Journal* (February 7, 2012), p. B6.

[13]This is a simplified model developed from Schein, op. cit. (1997).

[14]James C. Collins and Jerry I. Porras, "Building Your Company's Vision," *Harvard Business Review* (September/October 1996), pp. 65–77.

[15]See corporate Web sites.

[16]Tom's of Maine example is from Jenny C. McCune, "Making Lemonade," *Management Review* (June 1997), pp. 49–53.

[17]See Robert A. Giacalone and Carol L. Jurkiewicz (Eds.), *Handbook of Workplace Spirituality and Organizational Performance* (Armonk, NY: M. E. Sharpe, 2003).

[18]See Peter F. Drucker, "The Discipline of Innovation," *Harvard Business Review* (November/December 1998), pp. 3–8.

[19]Peter F. Drucker, *Management: Tasks, Responsibilities, and Practices* (New York: Harper & Row, 1973), p. 797.

[20]See Cortis R. Carlson and William W. Wilmont, *Getting to "Aha"* (New York: Crown Business, 2006).

[21]See "Green Business Innovations" and "New Life for Old Threads," both in *Businessweek* (April 28, 2008), special advertising section.

[22]David Bornstein, *How to Change the World: Social Entrepreneurs and the Power of New Ideas* (Oxford, UK: Oxford University Press, 2004).

[23]Peter F. Drucker, *Management: Tasks, Responsibilities, and Practices* (New York: Harper-Row, 1973), p. 797.

[24]Quote from "How to Measure Up," *Kellogg* (Summer, 2009), p. 17.

[25]See Gary Hamel, *Leading the Revolution* (Boston: Harvard Business School Press, 2000).

[26]Based on Edward B. Roberts, "Managing Invention and Innovation," *Research Technology Management* (January/February 1988), pp. 1–19.

[27]"The Joys and Perils of 'Reverse Innovation'." *Businessweek* (October 5, 2009), p. 12.

[28]Ibid. Also, example and quotes from "How to Compete in a World Turned Upside Down," *Financial Times*, Kindle edition (October 6, 2009).

[29]Clay Christensen, *The Innovator's Dilemma: When New Technologies Cause Great Firms to Fail*, Reprint Edition (New York: Harper Paperbacks, 2011); and Clay Christensen, Jeff Dyer, and Hal Gregersen, *The Innovator's DNA: Mastering the Five Skills of Disruptive Innovators* (Cambridge, MA: Harvard Business Press, 2011).

[30]Walter Mossberg, "Changing the Economics of Education," *Wall Street Journal* (June 4, 2012), p. R8.

[31]Information and quotes from Nancy Gohring, "Microsoft: Stodgy or Innovative? It's All About Perception," *PC World* (July 25, 2008).

[32]This discussion is stimulated by James Brian Quinn, "Managing Innovation: Controlled Chaos," *Harvard Business Review*, vol. 63 (May/June 1985), 73–84.

[33]Quote from www.ideo.com (retrieved March 11, 2009).

[34]"'Mosh Pits' of Creativity," *Businessweek* (November 7, 2005), p. 99.

[35]Quote from Brad Stone, "Amid the Gloom, an E-Commerce War," *New York Times* (October 12, 2008): www.nytimes.com.

[36]For a review of scholarly work on organizational change, see W. Warner Burke, *Organizational Change: Theory and Practice*, 2nd ed. (Thousand Oaks, CA: Sage, 2008).

[37]Quote from Pilita Clark, "Delayed, Not Cancelled," *Financial Times* (December 19, 2009).

[38]For an overview, see W. Warner Burke, *Organization Change: Theory and Practice* (Thousand Oaks, CA: Sage, 2002).

[39]For a discussion of alternative types of change, see David A. Nadler and Michael L. Tushman, *Strategic Organizational Design* (Glenview, II: Scott, Foresman, 1988); John P. Kotter, "Leading Change: Why Transformation Efforts Fail," *Harvard Business Review* (March/April 1995), pp. 59–67; and Burke, op. cit.

[40]Michael Beer and Nitin Nohria, "Cracking the Code of Change," *Harvard Business Review* (May–June 2000), pp. 138–41; "Change Management, An Inside Job," *Economist* (July 15, 2000), p. 61; and Mark Hughes, "Do 70 Per Cent of All Organizational Change Initiatives Really Fail?" *Journal of Change Management*, Vol. 11, No. 4 (2011), pp. 451–64.

[41]Ibid; Beer and Nohria, op. cit.; and "Change Management, An Inside Job," *Economist* (July 15, 2000), p. 61.

[42]Based on Kotter, op. cit.

[43]This is based on Rosabeth Moss Kanter's "Innovation Pyramid," *BusinessWeek* (March 2007), p. IN 3.

[44]Kurt Lewin, "Group Decision and Social Change," in G. E. Swanson, T. M. Newcomb, and E. L. Hartley (eds.), *Readings in Social Psychology* (New York: Holt, Rinehart, 1952), pp. 459–73.

[45]See Wanda J. Orlikowski and J. Debra Hofman, "An Improvisational Model for Change Management: The Case of Groupware Technologies," *Sloan Management Review* (Winter 1997), pp. 11–21.

[46]This discussion is based on Robert Chin and Kenneth D. Benne, "General Strategies for Effecting Changes in Human Systems," in Warren G. Bennis, Kenneth D. Benne, Robert Chin, and Kenneth E. Corey (eds.), *The Planning of Change*, 3rd ed. (New York: Holt, Rinehart, 1969), pp. 22–45.

[47]The change agent descriptions here and following are developed from an exercise reported in J. William Pfeiffer and John E. Jones, *A Handbook of Structured Experiences for Human Relations Training*, vol. 2 (La Jolla, CA: University Associates, 1973).

[48]Information from Mike Schneider, "Disney Teaching Execs Magic of Customer Service," *Columbus Dispatch* (December 17, 2000), p. G9.

[49]Teresa M. Amabile, "How to Kill Creativity," *Harvard Business Review* (September/October 1998), pp. 77–87.

[50]See Jeffrey D. Ford and Laurie W. Ford, "Decoding Resistance to Change," *Harvard Business Review* (April, 2009), pp. 99–103.

[51]John P. Kotter and Leonard A. Schlesinger, "Choosing Strategies for Change," *Harvard Business Review*, vol. 57 (March/April 1979), pp. 109–12.

Feature Notes 9

Opening Quote: Information from "Men Are People Too," *Bloomberg Businessweek* (June 3–June 6, 2013), pp. 59–63.

Management Live—Information and quotes from Melissa Korn, "The Amazon Interview," *Wall Street Journal* (May 2, 2013), p. B7.

Ethics Check—Information from "What Prospective Employers Hope to See in Your Facebook Account," forbes.com (October 3, 2011): accessed November 26, 2011; Manuel Valdes and Shannon McFarland, "Drug Test? Now It's Facebook Password," *The Columbus Dispatch* (March 21, 2012), pp. A1, A4; and, Lauren Weber and Elizabeth Dwoskin, "As Personality Tests Multiply, Employers Are Split," *Wall Street Journal* (September 30, 2014), pp. A1, A12.

Facts to Consider—Information from Joe Light, "Human Resource Executives Say Reviews Are Off the Mark," *Wall Street Journal* (November 8, 2010), p. B8.

Hot Topic—Information from Jenny Marlar, "Underemployed Report Spending 36% Less Than Employed," *Gallup.com*, February 23, 2010 (retrieved December 8, 2011); gallup.com/poll/125639/gallup-daily-workforce.aspx; Jordan Weissman, "44% of Young College Grads Are Underemployed (and That's Good News)," *The Atlantic*, theatlantic.com (June 28, 2013).

Quick Case—See, for example, "NU Players Cast Secret Ballots," *ESPN.com news services* (April 26, 2014): espn.go.com (accessed May 14, 2015).

Photo Essay—Employees that Quit: Information from George Anders, "When the Best Employees Quit, Can You Handle the Truth?" *Forbes* (March 18, 2014): forbes.com (accessed April 2, 2104).

Endnotes 9

[1]Jeffrey Pfeffer, *The Human Equation: Building Profits by Putting People First* (Boston: Harvard University Press, 1998).

[2]Jeffrey Pfeffer and John F. Veiga, "Putting People First for Organizational Success," *Academy of Management Executive*, vol. 13 (May 1999), pp. 37–48.

[3]Ibid. and Pfeffer, op. cit.

[4]Quote from William Bridges, "The End of the Job," *Fortune* (September 19, 1994), p. 68.

[5]See James N. Baron and David M. Kreps, *Strategic Human Resources: Frameworks for General Managers* (New York: Wiley, 1999).

[6]Quotes from Andrew Hill, "Wanted: Flexible Strategies for Fast Changing Times," *Financial Times* (March 25, 2015), p. 8.

[7]Information from Adam Lashinsky, "Zappos: Life After Acquisition," tech.fortune.cnn.com (November 24, 2010); Nicholas Boothman, "Will You be my Friend?" *Bloomberg Businessweek* (January 7–January 13, 2013), pp. 63–65; and, Jena McGregor, "Zappos Gives Employees Exit Prize If Culture Change Is Turnoff," *Columbus Dispatch* (April 6, 2015), p. C3.

[8]Julie Jargon and Douglas Belkin, "Starbucks to Subsidize Online Degrees," *Wall Street Journal* (June 16, 2013), p. B3.

[9]See also R. Roosevelt Thomas Jr.'s books, *Beyond Race and Gender* (New York: Amacom, 1999) and (with Marjorie I. Woodruff) *Building a House for Diversity* (New York: Amacom, 1999); and Richard D. Bucher, *Diversity Consciousness* (Englewood Cliffs, NJ: Prentice-Hall, 2000).

[10]For a discussion of affirmative action, see R. Roosevelt Thomas, Jr., "From 'Affirmative Action' to 'Affirming Diversity,'" *Harvard Business Review* (November/December 1990), pp. 107–17.

[11]See the discussion by David A. DeCenzo and Stephen P. Robbins, *Human Resource Management*, 6th ed. (New York: Wiley, 1999), pp. 66–68 and 81–83.

[12]Ibid., pp. 77–79.

[13]Case reported in Sue Shellenbarger, "Work & Family Mailbox," *Wall Street Journal* (March 11, 2009), p. D6.

[14]Information from Sheryl Gay Stolberg, "Obama Signs Equal-Pay Legislation," *New York Times* (January 30, 2009): www.nytimes.com.

[15]"What to Expect When You're Expecting," *Businessweek* (May 26, 2008), p. 17.

[16]Ibid; and Madeline Heilman and Tyhler G. Okimoto, "Motherhood: A Potential Source of Bias in Employment Decisions," *Journal of Applied Psychology*, vol. 93, no. 1 (2008), pp. 189–98.

[17]Information and quotes from Jennifer Levitz and Philip Shiskin, "More Workers Cite Age Bias After Layoffs," *Wall Street Journal* (March 11, 2009), pp. D1, D2.

[18]See Frederick S. Lane, *The Naked Employee: How Technology Is Compromising Workplace Privacy* (New York: Amacom, 2003).

[19]This and other cases are described in Debra Cassens Weiss, "Companies Face 'Legal Potholes' as They Crack Down on Workers' Social Media Posts," ABAJournal.com (posted January 24, 2011).

[20]John P. Kotter, "The Psychological Contract: Managing the Joining Up Process," *California Management Review*, vol. 15 (Spring 1973), pp. 91–99; Denise Rousseau, ed., *Psychological Contracts in Organizations* (San Francisco: Jossey-Bass, 1995); Denise Rousseau, "Changing the Deal While Keeping the People," *Academy of Management Executive*, vol. 10 (1996), pp. 50–59; and Denise Rousseau and Rene Schalk, eds., *Psychological Contracts in Employment: Cross-Cultural Perspectives* (San Francisco: Jossey-Bass, 2000).

[21]"Finding Job Candidates Who Aren't Looking," *Bloomberg Businessweek* (December 17–23, 2012), pp. 41–42; and, Rachel Emma Silverman and Lauren Weber, "The New Résumé: It's 140 Characters," *Wall Street Journal* (April 10, 2013), p. B8.

[22]Information and quote from Sarah E. Needleman, "The New Trouble on the Line," *Wall Street Journal* (June 2, 2009): www.wsj.com.

[23]See Sarah E. Needleman, "Initial Phone Interviews Do Count," *Wall Street Journal* (February 7, 2006), p. 29.

[24]Data reported in "At Work," *Wall Street Journal* (December 12, 2012), p. B6.

[25]See John P. Wanous, *Organizational Entry: Recruitment, Selection, and Socialization of Newcomers* (Reading, MA: Addison-Wesley, 1980), pp. 34–44.

[26]Josey Puliyenthuruthel, "How Google Searches for Talent," *Businessweek* (April 11, 2005), p. 52.

[27]Quote from Ronald Henkoff, "Finding, Training, and Keeping the Best Service Workers," *Fortune* (October 3, 1994), pp. 110–22.

[28]See Harry J. Martin, "Lessons Learned," *Wall Street Journal* (December 15, 2008), p. R11.

[29]"A to Z of Generation Y Attitudes," *Financial Times* (June 18, 2009); and "When Three Generations Can Work Better Than One," *Financial Times* (September 16, 2009).

[30]Dick Grote, "Performance Appraisal Reappraised," *Harvard Business Review Best Practice* (1999), Reprint F00105.

[31]See Larry L. Cummings and Donald P. Schwab, *Performance in Organizations: Determinants and Appraisal* (Glenview, IL: Scott, Foresman, 1973).

[32]For a good review, see Gary P. Latham, Joan Almost, Sara Mann, and Celia Moore, "New Developments in Performance Management," *Organizational Dynamics*, vol. 34, no. 1 (2005), pp. 77–87.

[33]See Mark R. Edwards and Ann J. Ewen, *360-Degree Feedback: The Powerful New Tool for Employee Feedback and Performance Improvement* (New York: Amacom, 1996).

[34]Examples are from Jena McGregor, "Job Review in 140 Keystrokes," *Businessweek* (March 23 & 30, 2009), p. 58.

[35]Timothy Butler and James Waldroop, "Job Sculpting: The Art of Retaining Your Best People," *Harvard Business Review* (September/October 1999), pp. 144–52.

[36]Information from "What Are the Most Effective Retention Tools?" *Fortune* (October 9, 2000), p. S7.

[37]Quote from "Men Are People Too," *Bloomberg Businessweek* (June 3–June 6, 2013), pp. 59–63.

[38]See Betty Friedan, *Beyond Gender: The New Politics of Work and the Family* (Washington, DC: Woodrow Wilson Center Press, 1997); and James A. Levine, *Working Fathers: New Strategies for Balancing Work and Family* (Reading, MA: Addison-Wesley, 1997).

[39]See Ravi S. Gajendran and David A. Harrison, "The Good, the Bad, and the Unknown About Telecommuting: Meta-Analysis of Psychological Mediators and Individual Consequences," *Journal of Applied Psychology*, vol. 92 (2007), pp. 1524–41.

[40]Claire Suddath, "Work-from-Home Truths, Half-Truths, and Myths," *Bloomberg Businessweek* (March 4–March 10, 2013), p. 75.

[41]Ibid.

[42]Ibid.

[43]Examples from Amy Saunders, "A Creative Approach to Work," *Columbus Dispatch* (May 2, 2008), pp. C1, C9; Shellenbarger, op. cit. (2007); and Michelle Conlin and Jay Greene, "How to Make a Microserf Smile," *Businessweek* (September 10, 2007), pp. 57–59.

[44]Reid Hoffman, Ben Casnocha, and Chris Yewh, "Tours of Duty: The New Employer-Employee Compact," *Harvard Business Review*, Vol. 91 (June, 2013), pp. 49–58.

[45]Erin Hatton, "The Rise of the Permanent Temp Economy," *New York Times* (January 26, 2013), nytimes.com (accessed April 16, 2013).

[46]Michael Orey, "They're Employees, No, They're Not," *Businessweek* (November 16, 2009), pp. 73–74.

[47]Information and quotes from Peter Coy, Michelle Conlin, and Moira Herbst, "The Disposable Worker," *Businessweek* (January 18, 2010), pp. 33–39.

[48]See Kaja Whitehouse, "More Companies Offer Packages Linking Pay Plans to Performance," *Wall Street Journal* (December 13, 2005), p. B6.

[49]Ibid.

[50]Erin White, "How to Reduce Turnover," *Wall Street Journal* (November 21, 2005), p. B5.

[51]Information from Susan Pulliam, "New Dot-Com Mantra: 'Just Pay Me in Cash, Please,'" *Wall Street Journal* (November 28, 2000), p. C1.

[52]Nanette Byrnes, "Pain, but No Layoffs at Nucor," *Businessweek* (March 26, 2009), www.businessweek.com.

[53]Information from www.intel.com; and "Stock Ownership for Everyone," *Hewitt Associates* (November 27, 2000): www.hewitt.com.

[54]"Benefits: For Companies, the Runaway Train Is Slowing Down," *Businessweek* (February 16, 2009), p. 15.

[55]Quote from Jeffrey Sparshott, "Workplace Benefits Get Focus," *Wall Street Journal* (June 24, 2014), p. A6.

[56]Angus Loten and Sarah E. Needleman, "Laws on Paid Sick Leave Divide Businesses," *Wall Street Journal* (February 6, 2014), p. B5.

[57]For reviews, see Richard B. Freeman and James L. Medoff, *What Do Unions Do?* (New York: Basic Books, 1984); Charles C. Heckscher, *The New Unionism* (New York: Basic Books, 1988); and Barry T. Hirsch, *Labor Unions and the Economic Performance of Firms* (Kalamazoo, MI: W. E. Upjohn Institute for Employment Research, 1991).

[58]Melanie Trottman, "Union Membership Stagnates Around 11%," *Wall Street Journal* (January 24–25, 2015), p. A3.

[59]Example from Timothy Aeppel, "Pay Scales Divide Factory Floors," *Wall Street Journal* (April 9, 2008), p. B4.

[60]Matthew Dolan, "Ford to Begin Hiring at Much Lower Wages," *Wall Street Journal* (January 26, 2010), p. B1.

[61]Leslie Kwoh, "More Firms Bow to Generation Y's Demands." *Wall Street Journal* (August 22, 2012): online.wsj.com (accessed March 21, 2013); David Burstein, "TEDxNYU—David Burstein—Fast Future: The Rise of The

Millennial Generation." Speech, May 11, 2012: YouTube.com; David Burstein Website, "About" and "Fast Future," davidburstein.com (accessed March 21, 2013).

Feature Notes 10

Opening Quote—Full texts of the "I Have a Dream" speech are available online; see, for example, usconstitution.net/dream.html.

Management Live—Information from John Antonakis, Marika Fenley, and Sue Liechti, "Learning Charisma," *Harvard Business Review*, Vol. 90 (June 2012), pp. 127–130; and, Alicia Clegg, "The Subtle Secrets of Charisma," *Financial Times*, Kindle Edition (January 3, 2013).

Facts to Consider—Information from "Many U.S. Employees Have Negative Attitudes to Their Jobs, Employers and Top Managers," Harris Poll #38 (May 6, 2005), retrieved from www.harrisinteractive.com.

Find Inspiration—Information and quotes from Lorraine Monroe, "Leadership Is about Making Vision Happen—What I Call 'Vision Acts,'" *Fast Company* (March 2001), p. 98; Lorraine Monroe Leadership Institute website: lorrainemonroe.com. See also, Lorraine Monroe, *Nothing's Impossible: Leadership Lessons from Inside and Outside the Classroom* (New York: PublicAffairs Books, 1999), and *The Monroe Doctrine: An ABC Guide to What Great Bosses Do* (New York: PublicAffairs Books, 2003).

Hot Topic—Information and incident from Julian Sancton, "Milgram at McDonald's," *Bloomberg Businessweek* (August 27–September 2, 2012), pp. 74–75.

Endnotes 10

[1]Abraham Zaleznick, "Leaders and Managers: Are They Different?" *Harvard Business Review* (May/June 1977), pp. 67–78.

[2]Tom Peters, "Rule #3: Leadership Is Confusing as Hell," *Fast Company* (March 2001), pp. 124–40.

[3]Quotations from Marshall Loeb, "Where Leaders Come From," *Fortune* (September 19, 1994), pp. 241–42; Genevieve Capowski, "Anatomy of a Leader: Where Are the Leaders of Tomorrow?" *Management Review* (March 1994), pp. 10–17. For additional thoughts, see Warren Bennis, *Why Leaders Can't Lead* (San Francisco: Jossey-Bass, 1996).

[4]See Jean Lipman-Blumen, *Connective Leadership: Managing in a Changing World* (New York: Oxford University Press, 1996), pp. 3–11.

[5]Rosabeth Moss Kanter, "Power Failure in Management Circuits," *Harvard Business Review* (July/August 1979), pp. 65–75.

[6]The classic treatment of these power bases is John R. P. French, Jr., and Bertram Raven, "The Bases of Social Power," in Darwin Cartwright (ed.), *Group Dynamics: Research and Theory* (Evanson, IL: Row, Peterson, 1962), pp. 607–13.

[7]For managerial applications of this basic framework, see Gary Yukl and Tom Taber, "The Effective Use of Managerial Power," *Personnel*, vol. 60 (1983), pp. 37–49; and Robert C. Benfari, Harry E. Wilkinson, and Charles D. Orth, "The Effective Use of Power," *Business Horizons*, vol. 29 (1986), pp. 12–16. Gary A. Yukl, *Leadership in Organizations*, 4th ed. (Englewood Cliffs, NJ: Prentice-Hall, 1998), includes "information" as a separate, but related, power source.

[8]James M. Kouzes and Barry Z. Posner, "The Leadership Challenge," *Success* (April 1988), p. 68. See also their books *Credibility: How Leaders Gain and Lose It: Why People Demand It* (San Francisco: Jossey-Bass, 1996); *Encouraging the Heart: A Leader's Guide to Rewarding and Recognizing Others* (San Francisco: Jossey-Bass, 1999); and *The Leadership Challenge: How to Get Extraordinary Things Done in Organizations*, 3rd ed. (San Francisco: Jossey-Bass, 2002).

[9]Quote from Andy Serwer, "Game Changers: Legendary Basketball Coach John Wooden and Starbucks' Howard Schultz Talk About a Common Interest—Leadership," *Fortune* (August 11, 2008): www.cnnmoney.com.

[10]Burt Nanus, *Visionary Leadership: Creating a Compelling Sense of Vision for Your Organization* (San Francisco: Jossey-Bass, 1992).

[11]The early work on leader traits is well represented in Ralph M. Stogdill, "Personal Factors Associated with Leadership: A Survey of the Literature," *Journal of Psychology*, vol. 25 (1948), pp. 35–71. See also Edwin E. Ghiselli, *Explorations in Management Talent* (Santa Monica, CA: Goodyear, 1971); and Shirley A. Kirkpatrick and Edwin A. Locke, "Leadership: Do Traits Really Matter?" *Academy of Management Executive* (1991), pp. 48–60.

[12]See also John W. Gardner's article, "The Context and Attributes of Leadership," *New Management*, vol. 5 (1988), pp. 18–22; John P. Kotter, *The Leadership Factor* (New York: Free Press, 1988); and Bernard M. Bass, *Stogdill's Handbook of Leadership* (New York: Free Press, 1990).

[13]Kirkpatrick and Locke, op. cit. (1991).

[14]This terminology comes from Robert R. Blake and Jane Strygley Mouton, *The New Managerial Grid III* (Houston: Gulf Publishing, 1985) and the classic studies by Kurt Lewin and his associates at the University of Iowa. See, for example, K. Lewin and R. Lippitt, "An Experimental Approach to the Study of Autocracy and Democracy: A Preliminary Note," *Sociometry*, vol. 1 (1938), pp. 292–300; K. Lewin, "Field Theory and Experiment in Social Psychology: Concepts and Methods," *American Journal of Sociology*, vol. 44 (1939); and K. Lewin, R. Lippitt, and R. K. White, "Patterns of Aggressive Behavior in Experimentally Created Social Climates," *Journal of Social Psychology*, vol. 10 (1939), pp. 271–301.

[15]See Blake and Mouton, op. cit.

[16]For a good discussion of this theory, see Fred E. Fiedler, Martin M. Chemers, and Linda Mahar, *The Leadership Match Concept* (New York: Wiley, 1978); Fiedler's current contingency research with the cognitive resource theory is summarized in Fred E. Fiedler and Joseph E. Garcia, *New Approaches to Effective Leadership* (New York: Wiley, 1987).

[17]Paul Hersey and Kenneth H. Blanchard, *Management and Organizational Behavior* (Englewood Cliffs, NJ: Prentice-Hall, 1988). For an interview with Paul Hersey on the origins of the model, see John R. Schermerhorn Jr., "Situational Leadership: Conversations with Paul Hersey," *Mid-American Journal of Business* (Fall 1997), pp. 5–12.

[18]See Claude L. Graeff, "The Situational Leadership Theory: A Critical View," *Academy of Management Review*, vol. 8 (1983), pp. 285–91; and Carmen F. Fernandez and Robert P. Vecchio, "Situational Leadership Theory Revisited: A Test of an Across-Jobs Perspective," *Leadership Quarterly*, vol. 8 (summer 1997), pp. 67–84.

[19]See, for example, Robert J. House, "A Path-Goal Theory of Leader Effectiveness," *Administrative Sciences Quarterly*, vol. 16 (1971), pp. 321–38; and Robert J. House and Terrence R. Mitchell, "Path-Goal Theory of Leadership," *Journal of Contemporary Business* (Autumn 1974), pp. 81–97. The path-goal theory is reviewed by Bass, op. cit., and Yukl, op. cit. A supportive review of research is offered in Julie Indvik, "Path-Goal Theory of Leadership. A Meta-Analysis," in John A. Pearce II and Richard B. Robinson, Jr. (eds.), *Academy of Management Best Paper Proceedings* (1986), pp. 189–92.

[20]See the discussions of path-goal theory in Yukl, op. cit.; and Bernard M. Bass, "Leadership: Good, Better, Best," *Organizational Dynamics* (Winter 1985), pp. 26–40.

[21]See Steven Kerr and John Jermier, "Substitutes for Leadership: Their Meaning and Measurement," *Organizational Behavior and Human Performance*, vol. 22 (1978), pp. 375–403; Jon P. Howell and Peter W. Dorfman, "Leadership and Substitutes for Leadership Among Professional and Nonprofessional Workers," *Journal of Applied Behavioral Science*, vol. 22 (1986), pp. 29–46.

[22]An early presentation of the theory is F. Dansereau Jr., G. Graen, and W. J. Haga, "A Vertical Dyad Linkage Approach to Leadership Within Formal Organizations: A Longitudinal Investigation of the Role Making Process," *Organizational Behavior and Human Performance*, vol. 13, pp. 46–78.

[23]This discussion is based on Yukl, op. cit., pp. 117–22.

[24]Ibid.

[25]Victor H. Vroom and Arthur G. Jago, *The New Leadership: Managing Participation in Organizations* (Englewood Cliffs, NJ: Prentice-Hall, 1988). This is based on earlier work by Victor H. Vroom, "A New Look in Managerial Decision-Making," *Organizational Dynamics* (Spring 1973), pp. 66–80; and Victor H. Vroom and Phillip Yetton, *Leadership and Decision-Making* (Pittsburgh: University of Pittsburgh Press, 1973).

[26]Vroom and Jago, op. cit.

[27]For a related discussion, see Edgar H. Schein, *Process Consultation Revisited: Building the Helping Relationship* (Reading, MA: Addison-Wesley, 1999).

[28]For a review, see Yukl, op. cit.

[29]See the discussion by Victor H. Vroom, "Leadership and the Decision Making Process," *Organizational Dynamics*, vol. 28 (2000), pp. 82–94.

[30]Survey data from Gallup Leadership Institute, *Briefings Report 2005-01* (Lincoln: University of Nebraska–Lincoln); "The Stat," *Businessweek*

(September 12, 2005), p. 16; and "U.S. Job Satisfaction Keeps Falling, the Conference Board Reports Today," The Conference Board (February 28, 2005), retrieved from www.conference-board.org.

[31]Among the popular books addressing this point of view are Warren Bennis and Burt Nanus, *Leaders: The Strategies for Taking Charge* (New York: Harper Business 1997); Max DePree, *Leadership Is an Art* (New York: Doubleday, 1989); Kouzes and Posner, op. cit. (2002).

[32]The distinction was originally made by James McGregor Burns, *Leadership* (New York: Harper & Row, 1978) and was further developed by Bernard Bass, *Leadership and Performance Beyond Expectations* (New York: Free Press, 1985), and Bernard M. Bass. "Leadership: Good, Better, Best," *Organizational Dynamics* (Winter 1985), pp. 26–40. See also Bernard M. Bass, "Does the Transactional-Transformational Leadership Paradigm Transcend Organizational and National Boundaries?" *American Psychologist*, vol. 52 (February 1997), pp. 130–39.

[33]See the discussion in Bass, op. cit., 1997.

[34]This list is based on Kouzes and Posner, op. cit.; Gardner, op. cit.

[35]Daniel Goleman, "Leadership That Gets Results," *Harvard Business Review* (March/April 2000), pp. 78–90. See also his books *Emotional Intelligence* (New York: Bantam Books, 1995) and *Working with Emotional Intelligence* (New York: Bantam Books, 1998).

[36]Daniel Goleman, Annie McKee, and Richard E. Boyatzis, *Primal Leadership: Realizing the Power of Emotional Intelligence* (Boston: Harvard Business School Press, 2002), p. 3.

[37]Daniel Goleman, "What Makes a Leader?" *Harvard Business Review* (November/December 1998), pp. 93–102.

[38]Goleman, Working with Emotional Intelligence, op. cit. (1998).

[39]Information from "Women and Men, Work and Power," *Fast Company*, issue 13 (1998), p. 71.

[40]Jane Shibley Hyde, "The Gender Similarities Hypothesis," *American Psychologist*, vol. 60, no. 6 (2005), pp. 581–92.

[41]A. H. Eagley, S. J. Daran, and M. G. Makhijani, "Gender and the Effectiveness of Leaders: A Meta-Analysis," *Psychological Bulletin*, vol. 117 (1995), pp. 125–45.

[42]Research on gender issues in leadership is reported in Sally Helgesen, *The Female Advantage: Women's Ways of Leadership* (New York: Doubleday, 1990); Judith B. Rosener, "Ways Women Lead," *Harvard Business Review* (November/December 1990), pp. 119–25; Alice H. Eagley, Steven J. Karau, and Blair T. Johnson, "Gender and Leadership Style Among School Principals: A Meta Analysis," *Administrative Science Quarterly*, vol. 27 (1992), pp. 76–102; Lipman-Blumen, op. cit.; Alice H. Eagley, Mary C. Johannesen-Smith, and Marloes L. van Engen, "Transformational, Transactional and Laissez-Faire Leadership: A Meta-Analysis of Women and Men," *Psychological Bulletin*, vol. 124, no. 4 (2003), pp. 569–91; and Carol Hymowitz, "Too Many Women Fall for Stereotypes of Selves, Study Says," *Wall Street Journal* (October 24, 2005), p. B1.

[43]Data reported by Rochelle Sharpe, "As Women Rule," *Businessweek* (November 20, 2000), p. 75.

[44]Eagley et al., op. cit. (2003); Hymowitz, op. cit.; Rosener, op. cit.; Vroom, op. cit.,1973 and 2000; and, Ibarra and Obodaru, op. cit.

[45]Herminia Ibarra and Otilia Obodaru, "Women and the Vision Thing," *Harvard Business Review* (January, 2009): Reprint R0901E.

[46]Rosener, op. cit. (1990).

[47]See research summarized by Stephanie Armour, "Do Women Compete in Unhealthy Ways at Work?" *USA Today* (December 30, 2005), pp. B1–B2.

[48]Quote from "As Leaders, Women Rule," *Businessweek* (November 20, 2000), pp. 75–84. Rosabeth Moss Kanter is the author of *Men and Women of the Corporation*, 2nd ed. (New York: Basic Books, 1993).

[49]See Del Jones, "Women CEOs Slowly Gain on Corporate America," *USA Today* (January 1, 2009): www.usatoday.com; Morice Mendoza, "Davos 2009: Where Are the Women?" *Businessweek* (January 26, 2009): www.businessweek.com; and Susan Bulkeley Butler, *Women Count: A Guide to Changing the World* (South Bend, IN: Purdue University Press, 2010).

[50]Hyde, op. cit.; Hymowitz, op. cit.

[51]For debate on whether some transformational leadership qualities tend to be associated more with female than male leaders, see "Debate: Ways Women and Men Lead," *Harvard Business Review* (January/February 1991), pp. 150–60.

[52]See Terry Thomas, John R. Schermerhorn Jr., and John W. Dienhart, "Strategic Leadership of Ethical Behavior in Business," *Academy of Management Executive*, vol. 18 (May 2004), pp. 56–66.

[53]"Many U.S. Employees Have Negative Attitudes to Their Jobs, Employers and Top Managers," Harris Poll #38 (May 6, 2005), retrieved from www.harrisinteractive.com.

[54]Information from "The Stat," *Businessweek* (September 12, 2005), p. 16.

[55]See Thomas et al., op. cit.

[56]Doug May, Adrian Chan, Timothy Hodges, and Bruce Avolio, "Developing the Moral Component of Authentic Leadership," *Organizational Dynamics,* vol. 32 (2003), pp. 247–60.

[57]Peter F. Drucker, "Leadership: More Doing than Dash," *Wall Street Journal* (January 6, 1988), p. 16.

[58]"Information from Southwest CEO Puts Emphasis on Character," *USA Today* (September 26, 2004), retrieved from www.usatoday/money/companies/management on December 12, 2005.

[59]Nitin Nohria, "The Big Question: What Should We Teach Our Business Leaders?" *Bloomberg Businessweek* (November 14–20, 2011), p. 68.

[60]Ibid.

[61]See Drucker, op cit., 1988.

[62]Robert K. Greenleaf and Larry C. Spears, *The Power of Servant Leadership: Essays* (San Francisco: Berrett-Koehler, 1996).

[63]Jay A. Conger, "Leadership: The Art of Empowering Others," *Academy of Management Executive*, vol. 3 (1989), pp. 17–24.

[64]Max DePree, "An Old Pro's Wisdom: It Begins with a Belief in People," *New York Times* (September 10, 1989), p. F2; DePree, op. cit.; David Woodruff, "Herman Miller: How Green Is My Factory," *Businessweek* (September 16, 1991), pp. 54–56; and Max DePree, *Leadership Jazz* (New York: Doubleday, 1992).

[65]Lorraine Monroe, "Leadership Is About Making Vision Happen—What I Call 'Vision Acts,'" *Fast Company* (March 2001), p. 98; School Leadership Academy Web site: www.lorrainemonroe.com.

[66]Greenleaf and Spears, op. cit., p. 78.

Feature Notes 11

Management Live—Information and quotes from Ron Friedman, "Work–Life Balance is Dead," *CNN Opinion*: cnn.com (December 9, 2014).

Facts to Consider—Information from Christine Porath and Christine Pearson, "The Price of Incivility: Lack of Respect Hurts Morale and the Bottom Line," *Harvard Business Review*, Vol. 91 (January–February, 2013), pp. 114–21.

Hot Topic—Information and quotes from Sumathi Reddy, "Study Finds Some Teens Can Excel at Multitasking," *Wall Street Journal* (October 14, 2014), pp. D1, D5.

Quick Case—See Sue Shellenbarger, "Companies Deal with Employees Who Refuse to Take Time Off by Requiring Vacations, Paying Them to Go," *Wall Street Journal*, Kindle Edition (August 14, 2014).

Photo Essays—Bias Against Black Leaders: from Andrew M. Carton and Ashleigh Shelby Rosette, "Explaining Bias Against Black Leaders: Integrating Theory on Information Processing and Goal-Based Stereotyping," *Academy of Management Journal*, vol. 54, No. 6 (2011), pp. 1141–58.

Find Inspiration—Life Is Good: Information from Leigh Buchanan, "Life Lessons," *Inc.* inc.com/magazine (accessed June 6, 2006); "A Fortune Coined from Cheerfulness Entrepreneurship," *Financial Times* (May 20, 2009); and, lifeisgood.com/about.

Endnotes 11

[1]This example is reported in *Esquire* (December 1986), p. 243. Emphasis is added to the quotation. Note: Nussbaum became director of the Labor Department's Women's Bureau during the Clinton administration and subsequently moved to the AFL–CIO as head of the Women's Bureau.

[2]See H. R. Schiffman, *Sensation and Perception: An Integrated Approach,* 3rd ed. (New York: Wiley, 1990).

[3]Information from "Misconceptions About Women in the Global Arena Keep Their Numbers Low," Catalyst study: www.catalystwomen.org; Yochanan Altman and Susan Shortland, "Women and International Assignments: Taking Stock," *Human Resource Management*, vol. 47 (2008), pp. 196–216; and Sebastian Reiche, "Expatriatus," *IESE Business School Blog* (March 29, 2011): blog.iese.edu (accessed April 28, 2013).

4The classic work is Dewitt C. Dearborn and Herbert A. Simon, "Selective Perception: A Note on the Departmental Identification of Executives," *Sociometry*, vol. 21 (1958), pp. 140–44. See also J. P. Walsh, "Selectivity and Selective Perception: Belief Structures and Information Processing," *Academy of Management Journal*, vol. 24 (1988), pp. 453–70.

5Quote from Sheila O'Flanagan, "Underestimate Casual Dressers at Your Peril," *The Irish Times* (July 22, 2005).

6See William L. Gardner and Mark J. Martinko, "Impression Management in Organizations," Journal of Management (June 1988), pp. 332–43.

7Sandy Wayne and Robert Liden, "Effects of Impression Management on Performance Ratings," *Academy of Management Journal* (February 2005), pp. 232–52.

8See M. R. Barrick and M. K. Mount, "The Big Five Personality Dimensions and Job Performance: A Meta-Analysis," *Personnel Psychology*, vol. 44 (1991), pp. 1–26.

9For a sample of research, see G. M. Hurtz and J. J. Donovan, "Personality and Job Performance: The Big Five Revisited," *Journal of Applied Psychology*, vol. 85 (2000), pp. 869–79; and T. A. Judge and R. Ilies, "Relationship of Personality to Performance Motivation: A Meta-Analytic Review," *Journal of Applied Psychology*, vol. 87 (2002), pp. 797–807.

10Carl G. Jung, *Psychological Types*, H. G. Baynes trans. (Princeton, NJ: Princeton University Press, 1971).

11I. Briggs-Myers, *Introduction to Type* (Palo Alto, CA: Consulting Psychologists Press, 1980).

12See, for example, William L. Gardner and Mark J. Martinko, "Using the Myers-Briggs Type Indicator to Study Managers: A Literature Review and Research Agenda," *Journal of Management*, vol. 22 (1996), pp. 45–83; Naomi L. Quenk, *Essentials of Myers-Briggs Type Indicator Assessment* (New York: Wiley, 2000).

13This discussion based in part on John R. Schermerhorn, Jr., James G. Hunt, and Richard N. Osborn, *Organizational Behavior*, 9th ed. (New York: Wiley, 2005), pp. 54–60.

14Douglas Belkin, "Colleges Put the Emphasis on Personality," *Wall Street Journal* (January 9, 2015), p. A3.

15J. B. Rotter, "Generalized Expectancies for Internal Versus External Control of Reinforcement," *Psychological Monographs*, vol. 80 (1966), pp. 1–28.

16T. W. Adorno, E. Frenkel-Brunswick, D. J. Levinson, and R. N. Sanford, *The Authoritarian Personality* (New York: Harper & Row, 1950).

17Niccolo Machiavelli, *The Prince*, trans. George Bull (Middlesex, UK: Penguin, 1961).

18See M. Snyder, *Public Appearances/Private Realities: The Psychology of Self-Monitoring* (New York: Freeman, 1987).

19See Arthur P. Brief, Randall S. Schuler, and Mary Van Sell, *Managing Job Stress* (Boston: Little, Brown, 1981), pp. 7, 8.

20The classic work is Meyer Friedman and Ray Roseman, *Type A Behavior and Your Heart* (New York: Knopf, 1974).

21Sue Shellenbarger, "Do We Work More or Not? Either Way, We Feel Frazzled," *Wall Street Journal* (July 30, 1997), p. B1; and "Arggh! American Workers Are at the Breaking Point," *The Pony Blog*, cnbc.com (April 9, 2013), accessed April 11, 2013.

22Ibid.

23Carol Hymowitz, "Can Workplace Stress Get *Worse?*" *Wall Street Journal* (January 16, 2001), pp. B1, B3.

24Hans Selye, *Stress in Health and Disease* (Boston: Butterworth, 1976); and, Steve M. Jex, *Stress and Job Performance* (San Francisco: Jossey-Bass, 1998).

25The extreme case of "workplace violence" is discussed by Richard V. Denenberg and Mark Braverman, *The Violence-Prone Workplace* (Ithaca, NY: Cornell University Press, 1999).

26David Gauthier-Villars and Leila Abboud, "In France, CEOs Can Become Hostages," *Wall Street Journal* (April 3, 2009), pp. B1, B4.

27See Daniel C. Ganster and Larry Murphy, "Workplace Interventions to Prevent Stress-Related Illness: Lessons from Research and Practice," Chapter 2 in Cary L. Cooper and Edwin A. Locke (eds.), *Industrial and Organizational Psychology: Linking Theory with Practice* (Malden, MA: Blackwell Business, 2000); Jonathan D. Quick, Amy B. Henley, and James Campbell Quick, "The Balancing Act—At Work and at Home," *Organizational Dynamics*, vol. 33 (2004), pp. 426–37.

28See Melinda Beck, "Stress So Bad It Hurts—Really," *Wall Street Journal* (March 17, 2009), pp. D1, D6.

29Information and quote from Joann S. Lublin, "How One Black Woman Lands Her Top Jobs: Risks and Networking," *Wall Street Journal* (March 4, 2003), p. B1.

30Martin Fishbein and Icek Ajzen, *Belief, Attitude, Intention and Behavior: An Introduction to Theory and Research* (Reading, MA: Addison-Wesley, 1973).

31See Leon Festinger, *A Theory of Cognitive Dissonance* (Palo Alto, CA: Stanford University Press, 1957).

32For an overview, see Paul E. Spector, *Job Satisfaction* (Thousand Oaks, CA: Sage, 1997); Timothy A. Judge and Allan H. Church, "Job Satisfaction: Research and Practice," Chapter 7 in Cooper and Locke (eds.), op. cit. (2000); Timothy A. Judge, "Promote Job Satisfaction Through Mental Challenge," Chapter 6 in Edwin A. Locke (ed.), *The Blackwell Handbook of Principles of Organizational Behavior* (Malden, MA: Blackwell, 2004).

33Information in Stay Informed from Linda Grant, "Happy Workers, High Returns," *Fortune* (January 12, 1998), p. 81; Judge and Church, op. cit. (2004); "U.S. Employees More Dissatisfied with Their Jobs," Associated Press (February 28, 2005), retrieved from www.msnbc.com; "U.S. Job Satisfaction Keeps Falling, the Conference Board Reports Today," *The Conference Board* (February 28, 2005), retrieved from www.conference-board.org; and Salary.com, "Survey Shows Impact of Downturn on Job Satisfaction," *OH&S: Occupational Health and Safety* (February 7, 2009): www.ohsonline.com.

34*What Workers Want: A Worldwide Study of Attitudes to Work and Work-Life Balance* (London: FDS International, 2007).

35Data reported in "When Loyalty Erodes, So Do Profits," *Businessweek* (August 13, 2001), p. 8.

36Dennis W. Organ, *Organizational Citizenship Behavior: The Good Soldier Syndrome* (Lexington, MA: Lexington Books, 1988).

37See Mark C. Bolino and William H. Turnley, "Going the Extra Mile: Cultivating and Managing Employee Citizenship Behavior," *Academy of Management Executive*, vol. 17 (August 2003), pp. 60–67.

38Christine Porath and Christine Pearson, "The Price of Incivility: Lack of Respect Hurts Morale and the Bottom Line," *Harvard Business Review*, Vol. 91 (January–February 2013), pp. 114–21.

39See Sandra L. Robinson and Rebecca J. Bennett, "A Typology of Deviant Workplace Behaviors: A Multidimensional Scaling Study," *Academy of Management Journal* 38 (1995), pp. 555–72; Reeshad S. Dalal, "A Meta-Analysis of the Relationship Among Organizational Citizenship Behavior and Counterproductive Work Behavior," *Journal of Applied Psychology* 90 (2005), pp. 1241–55; and, HealthForceOntario, *Bullying in the Workplace: A Handbook for the Workplace* (Toronto: Ontario Safety Association for Community and Health Care, 2009).

40Tony DiRomualdo, "The High Cost of Employee Disengagement" (July 7, 2004): www.wistechnology.com.

41These relationships are discussed in Charles N. Greene, "The Satisfaction-Performance Controversy," *Business Horizons*, vol. 15 (1982), pp. 31; Michelle T. Iaffaldano and Paul M. Muchinsky, "Job Satisfaction and Job Performance: A Meta Analysis," *Psychological Bulletin*, vol. 97 (1985), pp. 251–73.

42This discussion follows conclusions in Judge, op. cit. (2004). For a summary of the early research, see Iaffaldano and Muchinsky, op. cit.

43Incident reported in Jon Ostrower, "Pressure Mounts on Boeing's Top Salesman," *Wall Street Journal* (October 9, 2013), p. B10.

44Daniel Goleman, "Leadership That Gets Results," *Harvard Business Review* (March–April 2000), pp. 78–90. See also his books *Emotional Intelligence* (New York: Bantam Books, 1995) and *Working with Emotional Intelligence* (New York: Bantam Books, 1998).

45"Charm Offensive: Why America's CEOs Are So Eager to Be Loved," *Businessweek* (June 26, 2006): businessweek.com (retrieved September 20, 2008).

46See Robert G. Lord, Richard J. Klimoski, and Ruth Knafer (eds.), *Emotions in the Workplace; Understanding the Structure and Role of Emotions in Organizational Behavior* (San Francisco: Jossey-Bass, 2002); Roy L. Payne and Cary L. Cooper (eds.), *Emotions at Work: Theory Research and Applications for Management* (Chichester, UK: Wiley, 2004); and Daniel Goleman and Richard Boyatzis, "Social Intelligence and the Biology of Leadership," *Harvard Business Review* (September 2008), Reprint R0809E.

47J. E. Bono and R. Ilies, "Charisma, Positive Emotions and Mood Contagion," *Leadership Quarterly*, vol. 17 (2006), pp. 317–34; and Goleman and Boyatzis, op. cit.

Feature Notes 12

Opening Quote—J. K. Rowling, *Harry Potter and the Half-Blood Prince.*

Management Live—Information and quotes from Juloia La Roche, "A Wells Fargo Employee Emailed the CEO asking for a $10,000 raise and he CC'd 200,000 other Employees," businessinsider.com (October 10, 2014). Accessed October 12, 2014.

Ethics Check—Information on this situation from Jared Sandberg, "Why You May Regret Looking at Papers Left on the Office Copier," *Wall Street Journal* (June 20, 2006), p. B1.

Facts to Consider—Information from "UK Headhunters Pledge New Focus on Gender," *Financial Times*, Kindle Edition (May 11, 2011); Joseph Schumpeter, "The Mommy Track," *The Economist*, Kindle Edition (August 25, 2012); Jill Parkin, "Women at Director Level Help to Make a Marque," *Financial Times*, Kindle Edition (May 22, 2012); "Gender Politics," *The Economist*, Kindle Edition (September 7, 2012); Joann S. Lublin, "Europe's Boards Recruit U.S. Women," *Wall Street Journal* (September 12, 2012), p. B8; James Fontanella-Khan, "EU Scraps Board Quotas for Women," *Financial Times*, Kindle Edition (October 24, 2012); and Jeff Green, "The Boardroom's Still the Boys' Room," *Bloomberg Businessweek* (October 29–November 4, 2012), pp. 25–26.

Find Inspiration—Information from "HopeLab Video Games for Health," *Fast Company* (December, 2008/ January, 2009), p. 116; "Zamzee Works! Research, Iteration and Positive New Results" (September 24, 2012): blog. hopelab.org; and hopelab.org.

Hot Topic—Information and quotes from Ron Alsop, *The Trophy Kids Grow Up* (San Francisco: Jossey-Bass, 2008); Mark H. Daniel, *World of Risk: Next Generation Strategy for a Volatile Era* (New York: Wiley, 2000) "Bobcats Don't Deserve Post-Season Adulation," *Athens Messenger* (March 21, 2014), p. A4; and, Jon Gold, "Romar: No Regrets, even with Challenges," *Arizona Daily Star* (January 21, 2013), pp. B1, B2.

Quick Case—Information and quotes from Katie Little, "Noodles CEO Dishes on No-Tip Policy, Minimum Wage," *CNBC* (March 19, 2014): cnbc. com (accessed March 20, 2014); and, Al Lewis, "Skip the Tip at Noodles & Company," *Dow Jones Newswires* (May 25, 2014): denverpost.com (accessed January 5, 2015).

Endnotes 12

[1]Melinda Beck, "If at First You Don't Succeed, You're in Excellent Company," *Wall Street Journal* (April 29, 2008), p. D1.

[2]Jerry Krueger and Emily Killham, "At Work, Feeling Good Matters," *Gallup Management Journal* (December 8, 2005): gmj.gallup.com; and, Ellen Wulfhorst, "Morale Is Low, Say Quarter of Employers in Poll," *Reuters Bulletin* (November 17, 2009): reuters.com; and, Julie Ray, "Gallup's Top 10 World News Findings of 2013," *Gallup World* (December 27, 2013): gallup.com (accessed June 19, 2014).

[3]See Abraham H. Maslow, *Eupsychian Management* (Homewood, IL: Richard D. Irwin, 1965); and Abraham H. Maslow, *Motivation and Personality*, 2nd ed. (New York: Harper & Row, 1970). For a research perspective, see Mahmoud A. Wahba and Lawrence G. Bridwell, "Maslow Reconsidered: A Review of Research on the Need Hierarchy," *Organizational Behavior and Human Performance*, vol. 16 (1976), pp. 212–40.

[4]Clayton P. Alderfer, *Existence, Relatedness, and Growth* (New York: Free Press, 1972).

[5]Examples and quotes from Jane Hodges, "A Virtual Matchmaker for Volunteers," *Wall Street Journal* (February 12, 2009), p. D3; Dana Mattioli, "The Laid-Off Can Do Well Doing Good," *Wall Street Journal* (March 17, 2009), p. D1; Elizabeth Garone, "Paying It Forward Is a Full-Time Job," *Wall Street Journal* (March 17, 2009), p. D4.

[6]Developed originally from a discussion in Edward E. Lawler III, *Motivation in Work Organizations* (Monterey, CA: Brooks/Cole Publishing, 1973), pp. 30–36.

[7]For a collection of McClelland's work, see David C. McClelland, *The Achieving Society* (New York: Van Nostrand, 1961); "Business Drive and National Achievement," *Harvard Business Review*, vol. 40 (July/August 1962), pp. 99–112; David C. McClelland, *Human Motivation* (Glenview, IL: Scott, Foresman, 1985); David C. McClelland and Richard E. Boyatsis, "The Leadership Motive Pattern and Long-Term Success in Management," *Journal of Applied Psychology*, vol. 67 (1982), pp. 737–43.

[8]David C. McClelland and David H. Burnham, "Power Is the Great Motivator," *Harvard Business Review* (March/April 1976), pp. 100–10.

[9]The complete two-factor theory is in Frederick Herzberg, Bernard Mausner, and Barbara Block Synderman, *The Motivation to Work*, 2nd ed. (New York: Wiley, 1967); Frederick Herzberg, "One More Time: How Do You Motivate Employees?" *Harvard Business Review* (January/February 1968), pp. 53–62, and reprinted as an *HBR classic* (September/October 1987), pp. 109–20.

[10]Critical reviews are provided by Robert J. House and Lawrence A. Wigdor, "Herzberg's Dual-Factor Theory of Job Satisfaction and Motivation: A Review of the Evidence and a Criticism," *Personnel Psychology*, vol. 20 (Winter 1967), pp. 369–89; and Steven Kerr, Anne Harlan, and Ralph Stogdill, "Preference for Motivator and Hygiene Factors in a Hypothetical Interview Situation," *Personnel Psychology*, vol. 27 (Winter 1974), pp. 109–24. See also Frederick Herzberg, "Workers' Needs: The Same Around the World," *Industry Week* (September 21, 1987), pp. 29–32.

[11]See, for example, Greg R. Oldham and J. Richard Hackman, "Not What It Was and Not What It Will Be: The Future of Job Design Research," *Journal of Organizational Behavior*, vol. 31 (2010), pp. 463–479.

[12]See Herzberg et al., op. cit. (1967). The quotation is from Herzberg, op. cit. (1968).

[13]For a complete description of the core characteristics model, see J. Richard Hackman and Greg R. Oldham, *Work Redesign* (Reading, MA: Addison-Wesley, 1980).

[14]See, for example, J. Stacy Adams, "Toward an Understanding of Inequity," *Journal of Abnormal and Social Psychology*, vol. 67 (1963), pp. 422–36; and J. Stacy Adams, "Inequity in Social Exchange," in vol. 2, L. Berkowitz (ed.), *Advances in Experimental Social Psychology* (New York: Academic Press, 1965), pp. 267–300.

[15]See, for example, J. W. Harder, "Play for Pay: Effects of Inequity in a Pay-for-Performance Context," *Administrative Science Quarterly*, vol. 37 (1992), pp. 321–35.

[16]Information and quotes from Alistair Barr, "A Look at Some of the Most Luxurious Executive Perks," *Columbus Dispatch* (May 24, 2009), p. D1.

[17]Victor H. Vroom, *Work and Motivation* (New York: Wiley, 1964; republished by Jossey-Bass, 1994).

[18]"The Boss: Goal by Goal," *New York Times* (August 31, 2008), p. 10.

[19]The work on goal-setting theory is well summarized in Edwin A. Locke and Gary P. Latham, *Goal Setting: A Motivational Technique That Works!* (Englewood Cliffs, NJ: Prentice Hall, 1984). See also Edwin A. Locke, Kenneth N. Shaw, Lisa A. Saari, and Gary P. Latham, "Goal Setting and Task Performance 1969–1980," *Psychological Bulletin*, vol. 90 (1981), pp. 125–52; Mark E. Tubbs, "Goal Setting: A Meta-Analytic Examination of the Empirical Evidence," *Journal of Applied Psychology*, vol. 71 (1986), pp. 474–83; and Terence R. Mitchell, Kenneth R. Thompson, and Jane George-Falvy, "Goal Setting: Theory and Practice," Chapter 9 in Cary L. Cooper and Edwin A. Locke (eds.), *Industrial and Organizational Psychology: Linking Theory with Practice* (Malden, MA: Blackwell Business, 2000), pp. 211–49.

[20]For a recent critical discussion of goal-setting theory, see Lisa D. Ordóñez, Maurice E. Schweitzer, Adam D. Galinsky, and Max H. Bazerman, "Goals Gone Wild: The Systematic Side Effects of Overprescribing Goal Setting," *Academy of Management Perspectives*, vol. 23 (February 2009), pp. 6–16; and Edwin A. Locke and Gary P. Latham, "Has Goal Setting Gone Wild, or Have Its Attackers Abandoned Good Scholarship?" *Academy of Management Perspectives*, vol. 23 (February 2009), pp. 17–23.

[21]Gary P. Latham and Edwin A. Locke, "Self-Regulation Through Goal Setting," *Organizational Behavior and Human Decision Processes*, vol. 50 (1991), pp. 212–47.

[22]Edwin A. Locke, "Guest Editor's Introduction: Goal-Setting Theory and Its Applications to the World of Business," *Academy of Management Executive*, vol. 18, no. 4 (2004), pp. 124–25.

[23]Ordóñez et al., op. cit.; Locke and Latham, op. cit.

[24]"Pressured Schedulers Masked Wait Times, According to VA Audit," *Arizona Daily Star* (May 31, 2014, p. A3; and, Tom Cohen, "Audit: More Than 120,000 Veterans Waiting or Never Got Care," *CNN* (June 9, 2014), cnn.com: accessed June 10, 2014.

[25]Quotes from Cohen, op. cit.

[26]Richard Simon, "Lawmakers Attack VA's 'Culture' of Bonuses," *Columbus Dispatch* (June 21, 2014), p. A6.

27See David T. Welsh and Lisa D. Ordóñez, "The Dark Side of Consecutive High Performance Goals: Linking Goal Setting, Depletion, and Unethical Behavior," *Organizational Behavior and Human Decision Processes*, vol. 123 (2014), pp. 79–89; and, Gary P. Latham and Gerard Seijts, "Learning Goals or Performance Goals: Is It the Journey or the Destination?" *Ivey Business Journal* (May/June, 2006): iveybusinessjournal.com (accessed June 10, 2014).

28Latham and Seijts, op cit.

29E. L. Thorndike, *Animal Intelligence* (New York: Macmillan, 1911), p. 244.

30B. F. Skinner, *Walden Two* (New York: Macmillan, 1948); *Science and Human Behavior* (New York: Macmillan, 1953); *Contingencies of Reinforcement* (New York: Appleton-Century-Crofts, 1969).

31For a good review, see Lee W. Frederickson (ed.), *Handbook of Organizational Behavior Management* (New York: Wiley-Interscience, 1982); Fred Luthans and Robert Kreitner, *Organizational Behavior Modification* (Glenview, IL: Scott-Foresman, 1985); and Andrew D. Stajkovic and Fred Luthans, "A Meta-Analysis of the Effects of Organizational Behavior Modification on Task Performance 1975–95," *Academy of Management Journal*, vol. 40 (1997), pp. 1122–49.

32Knowledge@Wharton, "The Importance of Being Richard Branson," *Wharton School Publishing* (June 3, 2005): www.whartonsp.com.

33Richard Gibson, "Pitchman in the Corner Office," *Wall Street Journal* (October 24, 2007), p. D10. See also David Novak, *The Education of an Accidental CEO: Lessons Learned from the Trailer Park to the Corner Office* (New York: Crown Business, 2007).

34Michael Mankins, Alan Bird, and James Root, "Making Star Teams Out of Star Players," *Harvard Business Review*, vol. 91 (January–February 2013), pp. 74–78.

35Edwin A. Locke, "The Myths of Behavior Mod in Organizations," *Academy of Management Review*, vol. 2 (October 1977), pp. 543–53.

Feature Notes 13

Management Live—Information and quote from Rachael Emma Silverman, "No More Angling for the Best Seat: More Meetings Are Stand-Up Jobs," *Wall Street Journal* (February 2, 2012), pp. A9, A10.

Ethics Check—Some information from Bib Latané, Kipling Williams, and Stephen Harkins, "Many Hands Make Light the Work: The Causes and Consequences of Social Loafing," *Journal of Personality and Social Psychology*, Vol. 37 (1978), pp. 822–32; and W. Jack Duncan, "Why Some People Loaf in Groups and Others Loaf Alone," *Academy of Management Executive*, Vol. 8 (1994), pp. 79–80.

Facts to Consider—Information from "Two Wasted Days at Work," *CNNMoney.com* (March 16, 2005): www.cnnmoney.com.

Hot Topic—Information from Ravi Mattu, "Be a Good Sport and You Might Be a Better Manager," *Financial Times*, Kindle Edition (October 11, 2012); and Andrew Hill, "The Right Number of Stars for a Team," *Financial Times*, Kindle Edition (August 12, 2012). See also Mark de Rond, *There Is an I in Team: What Elite Athletes and Coaches Really Know about High Performance* (Cambridge, MA: Harvard Business Review Press, 2012).

Quick Case—Information from "Do Headphones in the Office Suggest I Lack Team Spirit," *Financial Times*, Kindle Edition (January 16, 2013).

Endnotes 13

1See, for example, Edward E. Lawler III, Susan Albers Mohrman, and Gerald E. Ledford, Jr., *Employee Involvement and Total Quality Management: Practices and Results in Fortune 1000 Companies* (San Francisco: Jossey-Bass, 1992); Susan A. Mohrman, Susan A. Cohen, and Monty A. Mohrman, *Designing Team-Based Organizations: New Forms for Knowledge Work* (San Francisco: Jossey-Bass, 1995).

2Jon R. Katzenbach and Douglas K. Smith, *The Wisdom of Teams: Creating the High Performance Organization* (Boston: Harvard Business School Press, 1993).

3See Edward E. Lawler III, *From the Ground Up: Six Principles for Building the New Logic Corporation* (San Francisco: Jossey-Bass, 1996), p. 131.

4Data from Lynda C. McDermott, Nolan Brawley, and William A. Waite, *World-Class Teams: Working Across Borders* (New York: Wiley, 1998), p. 5; survey reported in "Meetings Among Top Ten Time Wasters," *San Francisco Business Times* (April 7, 2003); www.bizjournals.com.

5Information from Scott Thurm, "Teamwork Raises Everyone's Game," *Wall Street Journal* (November 7, 2005), p. B7.

6Harold J. Leavitt, "Suppose We Took Groups More Seriously," in Eugene L. Cass and Frederick G. Zimmer (eds.), *Man and Work in Society* (New York: Van Nostrand Reinhold, 1975), pp. 67–77.

7See Marvin E. Shaw, *Group Dynamics: The Psychology of Small Group Behavior*, 2nd ed. (New York: McGraw-Hill, 1976); Leavitt, op. cit.

8A classic work is Bib Latané, Kipling Williams, and Stephen Harkins, "Many Hands Make Light the Work: The Causes and Consequences of Social Loafing," *Journal of Personality and Social Psychology*, vol. 37 (1978), pp. 822–32. See also John M. George, "Extrinsic and Intrinsic Origins of Perceived Social Loafing in Organizations," *Academy of Management Journal* (March 1992), pp. 191–202; and W. Jack Duncan, "Why Some People Loaf in Groups While Others Loaf Alone," *Academy of Management Executive*, vol. 8 (1994), pp. 79–80.

9The "linking pin" concept is introduced in Rensis Likert, *New Patterns of Management* (New York: McGraw-Hill, 1962).

10See discussion by Susan G. Cohen and Don Mankin, "The Changing Nature of Work," in Susan Albers Mohrman, Jay R. Galbraith, Edward E. Lawler III, and associates, *Tomorrow's Organization: Crafting Winning Capabilities in a Dynamic World* (San Francisco: Jossey-Bass, 1998), pp. 154–78.

11Information from "Diversity: America's Strength," special advertising section, *Fortune* (June 23, 1997); and American Express corporate communication (1998).

12See Susan D. Van Raalte, "Preparing the Task Force to Get Good Results," *S.A.M. Advanced Management Journal*, vol. 47 (Winter 1982), pp. 11–16; Walter Kiechel III, "The Art of the Corporate Task Force," *Fortune* (January 28, 1991), pp. 104–06.

13Developed from Eric Matson, "The Seven Sins of Deadly Meetings," *Fast Company* (April/May 1996), p. 122.

14Mohrman et al., op. cit. (1998).

15For a good discussion of quality circles, see Edward E. Lawler III and Susan A. Mohrman, "Quality Circles After the Fad," *Harvard Business Review*, vol. 63 (January/February 1985), pp. 65–71; Edward E. Lawler III and Susan Albers Mohrman, "Employee Involvement, Reengineering, and TQM: Focusing on Capability Development," in Mohrman et al. (1998), pp. 179–208.

16See Wayne F. Cascio, "Managing a Virtual Workplace," *Academy of Management Executive*, vol. 14 (2000), pp. 81–90.

17See Sheila Simsarian Webber, "Virtual Teams: A Meta-Analysis," http://www.shrm.org.

18See Stacie A. Furst, Martha Reeves, Benson Rosen, and Richard S. Blackburn, "Managing the Life Cycle of Virtual Teams," *Academy of Management Executive*, vol. 18, no. 2 (2004), pp. 6–11.

19R. Brent Gallupe and William H. Cooper, "Brainstorming Electronically," *Sloan Management Review* (Winter 1997), pp. 11–21; Cascio, op. cit.

20Quote from Chris Tosic, "Tactics for Remote Teamwork," *Financial Times*, Kindle Edition (February 14, 2010).

21Cascio, op. cit.; Furst et al., op. cit.

22See, for example, Paul S. Goodman, Rukmini Devadas, and Terri L. Griffith Hughson, "Groups and Productivity: Analyzing the Effectiveness of Self-Managing Teams," in John R. Campbell and Richard J. Campbell, *Productivity in Organizations* (San Francisco: Jossey-Bass, 1988); Jack Orsbrun, Linda Moran, Ed Musslewhite, and John H. Zenger, with Craig Perrin, *Self-Directed Work Teams: The New American Challenge* (Homewood, IL: Business One Irwin, 1990); Dale E. Yeatts and Cloyd Hyten, *High Performing Self-Managed Work Teams* (Thousand Oaks, CA: Sage, 1997).

23See, for example, J. Richard Hackman and Nancy Katz, "Group Behavior and Performance," in Susan T. Fiske, Daniel T. Gilbert, and Gardner Lindzey (eds.), *Handbook of Social Psychology*, 5th ed. (Hoboken, NJ: Wiley, 2010), pp. 1208–51.

24Goodman et al., op. cit.; Orsbrun et al., op. cit.; Yeatts and Hyten, op. cit.; and Lawler et al., op. cit., 1992.

25For a review of research on group effectiveness, see J. Richard Hackman, "The Design of Work Teams," in Jay W. Lorsch (ed.), *Handbook of Organizational Behavior* (Englewood Cliffs, NJ: Prentice-Hall, 1987), pp. 315–42; and J. Richard Hackman, Ruth Wageman, Thomas M. Ruddy, and Charles L. Ray, "Team Effectiveness in Theory and Practice," in Cary L. Cooper and Edwin A. Locke, *Industrial and Organizational Psychology: Linking Theory with Practice* (Malden, MA: Blackwell, 2000).

[26]For a discussion of effectiveness in the context of top management teams, see Edward E. Lawler III, David Finegold, and Jay A. Conger, "Corporate Boards: Developing Effectiveness at the Top," in Mohrman, op. cit. (1998), pp. 23–50.

[27]Quote from Alex Markels, "Money & Business," *U.S. News online* (October 22, 2006).

[28]See for example, Michael Mankins, Alan Bird, and James Root, "Making Star Teams Out of Star Players," *Harvard Business Review*, vol. 91 (January–February, 2013), pp. 74–78.

[29]"Dream Teams," *Northwestern* (Winter 2005), p. 10; Matt Golosinski, "Teamwork Takes Center Stage," *Northwestern* (Winter 2005), p. 39.

[30]Golosinski, op. cit., p. 39.

[31]See for example, Warren Watson, "Cultural Diversity's Impact on Interaction Process and Performance" *Academy of Management Journal*, vol. 16 (1993); Christopher Earley and Elaine Mosakowski, "Creating Hybrid Team Structures: An Empirical Test of Transnational Team Functioning," *Academy of Management Journal*, vol. 5 (February 2000), pp. 26–49; Eric Kearney, Diether Gebert, and Sven C. Voilpel, "When and How Diversity Benefits Teams: The Importance of Team Members' Need for Cognition," *Academy of Management Journal*, vol. 52 (2009), pp. 582–98; and Aparna Joshi and Hyuntak Roh, "The Role of Context in Work Team Diversity Research: A Meta-Analytic Approach," *Academy of Management Journal*, vol. 52 (2009), pp. 599–628.

[32]Information from Susan Carey, "Racing to Improve," *Wall Street Journal* (March 24, 2006), pp. B1, B6.

[33]Daniel Goleman, "Emotional Intelligence Teams," danielgoleman.info (January 27, 2007): accessed October 6, 2012.

[34]J. Steven Heinen and Eugene Jacobson, "A Model of Task Group Development in Complex Organizations and a Strategy of Implementation," *Academy of Management Review*, vol. 1 (1976), pp. 98–111; Bruce W. Tuckman, "Developmental Sequence in Small Groups," *Psychological Bulletin*, vol. 63 (1965), pp. 384–99; Bruce W. Tuckman and Mary Ann C. Jensen, "Stages of Small-Group Development Revisited," *Group & Organization Studies*, vol. 2 (1977), pp. 419–27.

[35]See Warren Watson, "Cultural Diversity's Impact on Interaction Process and Performance," *Academy of Management Journal*, vol. 16 (1993); Christopher Earley and Elaine Mosakowski, "Creating Hybrid Team Structures: An Empirical Test of Transnational Team Functioning," *Academy of Management Journal*, vol. 5 (February 2000), pp. 26–49; Eric Kearney, Diether Gebert, and Sven C. Voilpel, "When and How Diversity Benefits Teams: The Importance of Team Members' Need for Cognition," *Academy of Management Journal*, vol. 52 (2009), pp. 582–598; and Aparna Joshi and Hyuntak Roh, "The Role of Context in Work Team Diversity Research: A Meta-Analytic Approach," *Academy of Management Journal*, vol. 52 (2009), pp. 599–628.

[36]See, for example, Edgar Schein, *Process Consultation* (Reading, MA: Addison-Wesley, 1988); and Linda C. McDermott, Nolan Brawley, and William A. Waite, *World-Class Teams: Working Across Borders* (New York: Wiley, 1998).

[37]For a good discussion, see Robert F. Allen and Saul Pilnick, "Confronting the Shadow Organization: How to Detect and Defeat Negative Norms," *Organizational Dynamics* (Spring 1973), pp. 13–16.

[38]See Schein, op. cit., pp. 76–79; Rachel Feintzeig, "What Not to Expect at the Office? Help." *Wall Street Journal* (March 1, 2015), p. B7.

[39]See Kim S. Cameron & Bradley Winn, "Virtuousness in Organizations," pp. 231–245 in Kim S. Cameron and Gretchen M. Spreitzer (eds.), *The Oxford Handbook of Positive Organizational Scholarship* (Oxford: Oxford University Press, 2012).

[40]Marvin E. Shaw, *Group Dynamics: The Psychology of Small Group Behavior* (New York: McGraw-Hill, 1976).

[41]A classic work in this area is K. Benne and P. Sheets, "Functional Roles of Group Members," *Journal of Social Issues*, vol. 2 (1948), pp. 42–47; see also Likert, op. cit., pp. 166–69; Schein, op. cit., pp. 49–56.

[42]Based on John R. Schermerhorn Jr., James G. Hunt, and Richard N. Osborn, *Organizational Behavior*, 7th ed. (New York: Wiley, 2000), pp. 345–46.

[43]Schein, op. cit., pp. 69–75.

[44]A good overview is William D. Dyer, *Team-Building* (Reading, MA: Addison-Wesley, 1977).

[45]Quote from Terah Shelton Harris, "True Grit: How a Little Mud & Muscle Can Inspire Leaders and Build Teams," *Convention South*, vol. 29 (February, 2013), p. 10–11.

[46]Schein, op. cit., pp. 69–75.

[47]Victor H. Vroom and Arthur G. Jago, *The New Leadership: Managing Participation in Organizations* (Englewood Cliffs, NJ: Prentice Hall, 1988); Victor H. Vroom, "A New Look in Managerial Decision-Making," *Organizational Dynamics* (Spring 1973), pp. 66–80; Victor H. Vroom and Phillip Yetton, *Leadership and Decision-Making* (Pittsburgh: University of Pittsburgh Press, 1973).

[48]See Kathleen M. Eisenhardt, Jean L. Kahwajy, and L. J. Bourgeois III, "How Management Teams Can Have a Good Fight," *Harvard Business Review* (July/August 1997), pp. 77–85.

[49]Michael A. Roberto, "Why Making the Decisions the Right Way Is More Important Than Making the Right Decisions," *Ivey Business Journal* (September/October 2005), pp. 1–7.

[50]See Irving L. Janis, "Groupthink," *Psychology Today* (November 1971), pp. 43–46; and *Victims of Groupthink*, 2nd ed. (Boston: Houghton Mifflin, 1982).

[51]See also Michael Harvey, M. Ronald Buckley, Milorad M. Novicevic, and Jonathon R. B. Halbesleben, "The Abilene Paradox After Thirty Years: A Global Perspective," *Organizational Dynamics*, vol. 33 (2004), pp. 215–26.

[52]Janis, op. cit.

[53]Ibid.

[54]Richard E. Walton, *Interpersonal Peacemaking: Confrontations and Third-Party Consultation* (Reading, MA: Addison-Wesley, 1969), p. 2.

[55]See Kenneth W. Thomas, "Conflict and Conflict Management," in M. D. Dunnett (ed.), *Handbook of Industrial and Organizational Behavior* (Chicago: Rand McNally, 1976), pp. 889–935.

[56]See Robert R. Blake and Jane Strygley Mouton, "The Fifth Achievement," *Journal of Applied Behavioral Science*, vol. 6 (1970), pp. 413–27; Alan C. Filley, *Interpersonal Conflict Resolution* (Glenview, IL: Scott, Foresman, 1975); and L. David Brown, *Managing Conflict at Organizational Interfaces* (Reading, MA: Addison-Wesley, 1983).

[57]Filley, op. cit.

[58]Used by permission from John R. Schermerhorn, Jr. and Daniel G. Bachrach, *Management*, 13th ed. (Hoboken, NJ: John Wiley & Sons, 2015), pp. 459–61.

Feature Notes 14

Opening Quote—Quote from Claire Suddath, "Inside the Elephant in the Room," *Bloomberg BusinessWeek* (December 10–December 16, 2012), pp. 83–85.

Management Live—Information and quotes from Rachel Emma Silverman, "Are you happy in Your Job? Bosses Push Weekly Surveys," *Wall Street Journal* (December 3, 2014), pp. B1, B4.

Ethics Check—Information from Bridget Jones, "Blogger Fire Fury," CNN.com (July 19, 2006); and Bobbie Johnson, "Briton Sacked for Writing Paris Blog Wins Tribunal Case," *The Guardian* (March 29, 2007): guardian.co.uk.

Facts to Consider—Information from *Survey on the Influence of Workplace Design & Practices on the Ethical Environment* (New York: Ethisphere, 2010): ethisphere.com (accessed May 29, 2015).

Hot Topic—Information and quotes from Parminder Bahra, "The Science Behind Persuading People," *Wall Street Journal* (December 27, 2012), p. D5.

Endnotes 14

[1]See Henry Mintzberg, *The Nature of Managerial Work* (New York: Harper & Row, 1973 and Harper-Collins, 1997; John P. Kotter, "What Effective General Managers Really Do," *Harvard Business Review*, vol. 60 (November/December 1982), pp. 156–157; and *The General Managers* (New York: Macmillan, 1986).

[2]Mintzberg, op cit.

[3]Information from American Management Association (AMA), "The Passionate Organization Fast-Response Survey" (September 25–29, 2000), and organization Web site: http://www.amanet.org.

[4]Survey information from "What Do Recruiters Want?" *BizEd* (November/December 2002), p. 9; "Much to Learn, Professors Say," *USA Today* (July 5, 2001), p. 8D; and AMA, op. cit.

[5] Jay A. Conger, *Winning 'Em Over: A New Model for Managing in the Age of Persuasion* (New York: Simon & Schuster, 1998), pp. 24–79.

[6] Ibid.

[7] John Antonakis, Marika Fenley, and Sue Liechti, "Learning Charisma," *Harvard Business Review*, vol. 90 (June 2012), pp. 127–30; and Alicia Clegg, "The Subtle Secrets of Charisma," *Financial Times*, Kindle Edition (January 3, 2013).

[8] Information from Paul Davidson, "Managers to Millennials: Job Interview No Time to Text," *USA Today* (April 29, 2013), cnbc.com: accessed April 29, 2013.

[9] Ibid.

[10] See Robert H. Lengel and Richard L. Daft, "The Selection of Communication Media as an Executive Skill," *Academy of Management Executive*, vol. 2 (August 1988), pp. 225–32.

[11] Information from Sam Dillon, "What Corporate America Can't Build: A Sentence," *New York Times* (December 7, 2004); and, Melissa Korn, "Business School Copes with Deal Backlash," *Wall Street Journal* (January 29, 2014), p. B5.

[12] See Eric Matson, "Now That We Have Your Complete Attention," *Fast Company* (February/March 1997), pp. 124–32.

[13] David McNeill, *Hand and Mind: What Gestures Reveal About Thought* (Chicago: University of Chicago Press, 1992).

[14] Martin J. Gannon, *Paradoxes of Culture and Globalization* (Los Angeles: Sage, 2008), p. 76.

[15] McNeill, op. cit.

[16] Janelle Harris, "The Body Language of Business," *Black MBA* (Winter/Spring, 2012), pp. 34–37.

[17] Tom Peters and Nancy Austin, *A Passion for Excellence* (New York: Random House, 1985). "Epigrams and Insights from the Original Modern Guru," *Financial Times*, Kindle edition (March 4, 2010). See also Tom Peters, *The Little Big Things: 163 Ways to Pursue Excellence* (New York: Harper Studio, 2010).

[18] Quotes from Adam Auriemma, "Chiefs at Big Firms Often Last to Know," *Wall Street Journal* (April 3, 2014), pp. B1, B2.

[19] Information from "How to Cope with Email Overload," *Financial Times*, Kindle Edition (February 10, 2014).

[20] Rachel Feintzeig, "A Company Without Email? Not So Fast," *Wall Street Journal* (June 18, 2014), p. B7.

[21] Suggested by an incident from Richard V. Farace, Peter R. Monge, and Hamish M. Russell, *Communicating and Organizing* (Reading, MA: Addison-Wesley, 1977), pp. 97–98.

[22] Quote from Andy Serwer, "Game Changers: Legendary Basketball Coach John Wooden and Starbucks' Howard Schultz Talk about a Common Interest—Leadership," *Fortune* (August 11, 2008): www.cnnmoney.com.

[24] This discussion is based on Carl R. Rogers and Richard E. Farson, "Active Listening" (Chicago: Industrial Relations Center of the University of Chicago, n.d.); see also Carl R. Rogers and Fritz J. Roethlisberger, "Barriers and Gateways to Communication," *Harvard Business Review* (November/December, 2001), Reprint 91610.

[25] Ibid.

[26] A useful source of guidelines is John J. Gabarro and Linda A. Hill, "Managing Performance," Note 9-96-022 (Boston, MA: Harvard Business School Publishing, n.d.).

[27] Developed from John Anderson, "Giving and Receiving Feedback," in Paul R. Lawrence, Louis B. Barnes, and Jay W. Lorsch (eds.), *Organizational Behavior and Administration*, 3rd ed. (Homewood, IL: Richard D. Irwin, 1976), p. 109.

[28] Sue DeWine, *The Consultant's Craft* (Boston: Bedford/St. Martin's Press, 2001), pp. 307–14.

[29] A classic work on proxemics is Edward T. Hall's book *The Hidden Dimension* (Garden City, NY: Doubleday, 1986).

[30] Information and quote from James S. Russell, "Architecture Review: An Exclusive Look at Facebook's New Building," *Wall Street Journal* (May 7, 2015): wsj.com (accessed May 29, 2015).

[31] Information and quotes from Ben Kesling and James R. Hagerty, "Say Goodbye to the Office Cubicle," *Wall Street Journal* (April 3, 2013), pp. B1, 2.

[32] Information and quotes from Adam Bryant, "Creating Trust by Destroying Hierarchy," *Global Edition of the New York Times* (February 15, 2010), p. 19.

[33] Information and quote from Kelly K. Spors, "Top Small Workplaces 2009," *Wall Street Journal* (September 28, 2009), pp. R1–R4.

[34] Information and quotes from Sarah E. Needleman, "Thnx for the IView! I Wud Luv to Work 4 U!!;)," *Wall Street Journal Online* (July 31, 2008).

[35] Kevin Joy, "Online Introduction," *Columbus Dispatch* (April 19, 2013), pp. D1, D2.

[36] Information and quotes from Rhymer Rigby, "Assume that Every Employer Is Looking at Your Profiles," *Financial Times*, Kindle Edition (April 22, 2013).

[37] Information and quotes from Michelle Conlin and Douglas MacMillan, "Managing the Tweets," *Businessweek* (June 1, 2009), pp. 20–21. For P. Smith and Filiz Tabak, "Monitoring Employee E-Mails: Is There Any Room for Privacy?" *Academy of Management Perspectives*, vol. 23 (November, 2009), pp. 33–48.

[38] Information from Carol Hymowitz, "More American Chiefs Are Taking Top Posts at Overseas Concerns," *Wall Street Journal* (October 17, 2005), p. B1.

[39] Examples reported in Martin J. Gannon, *Paradoxes of Culture and Globalization* (Los Angeles: Sage Publications, 2008), p. 80.

[40] Information from Ben Brown, "Atlanta Out to Mind Its Manners," *USA Today* (March 14, 1996), p. 7.

Feature Notes 15

Management Live—On "cultural lenses," see Richard D. Lewis, *The Cultural Imperative: Global Trends in the 21st Century* (Yarmouth, ME: Intercultural Press, 2002). On "cultural intelligence," see P. Christopher Earley and Elaine Mosakowski, "Toward Cultural Intelligence: Turning Cultural Differences into Workplace Advantage," *Academy of Management Executive*, vol. 18 (2004), pp. 151–57.

Ethics Check—Information and quotes from Susan Chandler, "'Fair Trade' Label Enters Retail Market," *Columbus Dispatch* (October 16, 2006), p. G6; and www.fairindigo.com.

Facts to Consider—Information from "Worldwide, 13% of Employees Are Engaged at Work," Gallup World, *gallup.org* (October 8, 2013). Accessed February 9, 2015.

Hot Topic—Information and quotes from *Global Wage Report 2014/2015: Wages and Inequality* (Geneva: International Labour Office, 2015).

Photo Essay—The Amazing Race—E. R. Goldstein, "What If 'English Only' Isn't Wrong?" *Wall Street Journal* (August 2010). Retrieved December 8, 2010, from online.wsj.com.

Endnotes 15

[1] Laura B. Shrestha and Elayne J. Heisler, *The Changing Demographic Profile of the United States* (Washington: Congressional Research Service, 2011); Conor Dougherty and Miriam Jordan, "Minority Births Are New Majority," *Wall Street Journal* (May 17, 2012), p. A4; and Laura Meckler, "Hispanic Future in the Cards," *Wall Street Journal* (December 13, 2012), p. A3.

[2] Data from "Facts and Figures," Diversity Inc., diversityinc.com (accessed February 10, 2015).

[3] On diversity in general, see Lee Gardenswartz and Anita Rowe, *Managing Diversity: A Complete Desk Reference and Planning Guide* (Chicago: Irwin, 1993). For insights on surface-level versus deep-level diversity, see Alice H. Eagley and Jean Lau Chin, "Are Memberships in Race, Ethnicity, and Gender Categories Merely Surface Characteristics?" *American Psychologist*, Vol. 9 (2010), p. 934.

[4] R. Roosevelt Thomas, Jr., *Beyond Race and Gender* (New York: AMACOM, 1992), p. 10; see also R. Roosevelt Thomas, Jr., "'From Affirmative Action' to 'Affirming Diversity,'" *Harvard Business Review* (November/December 1990), pp. 107–17; R. Roosevelt Thomas, Jr., with Marjorie I. Woodruff, *Building a House for Diversity* (New York: AMACOM, 1999).

[5] Oliver, op. cit.

[6] Gardenswartz and Rowe, op. cit., p. 220.

[7] Survey reported in "The Most Inclusive Workplaces Generate the Most Loyal Employees," *Gallup Management Journal* (December 2001), retrieved from http://gmj.gallup.com.

[8] Carol Stephenson, "Leveraging Diversity to Maximum Advantage: The Business Case for Appointing More Women to Boards," *Ivey Business Journal* (September/October 2004), Reprint #9B04TE03, pp. 1–8.

[9]Donald H. Oliver, "Achieving Results Through Diversity: A Strategy for Success," *Ivey Business Journal* (March/April, 2005), Reprint #9B05TB09, pp. 1–6.

[10]Thomas Kochan, Katerina Bezrukova, Robin Ely, Susan Jackson, Aparna Joshi, Karen Jehn, Jonathan Leonard, David Levine, and David Thomas, "The Effects of Diversity on Business Performance: Report of the Diversity Research Network," reported in *SHRM Foundation Research Findings* (retrieved from www.shrm.org/foundation/findings.asp). Full article published in *Human Resource Management*, vol. 42 (2003), pp. 3–21.

[11]Taylor Cox Jr., *Cultural Diversity in Organizations* (San Francisco: Berrett Koehler, 1994).

[12]Nanette Byrnes and Roger O. Crockett, "An Historic Succession at Xerox," *Businessweek* (June 9, 2008), pp. 18–21; and, PaxEllevate Women's Global Index Fund, "Leading Companies," *paxellevate.com* (April 30, 2015): accessed May 30, 2015.

[13]Sue Shellenbarger, "The XX Factor: What's Holding Women Back?" *Wall Street Journal* (May 7, 2012), pp. B7–B12.

[14]Rob Walker, "Sex vs. Ethics," *Fast Company* (June, 2008), pp. 72–78.

[15]Sue Shellenbarger, "More Women Pursue Claims of Pregnancy Discrimination," *Wall Street Journal* (March 27, 2008), p. D1.

[16]"Bias Cases by Workers Increase by 9%," *Wall Street Journal* (March 6, 2008), p. D6.

[17] John Browne, *The Glass Closet: Why Coming Out Is Good Business* (New York: HarperBusiness, 2014).

[18]See Anthony Robbins and Joseph McClendon III, *Unlimited Power: A Black Choice* (New York: Free Press, 1997); and Augusto Failde and William Doyle, *Latino Success: Insights from America's Most Powerful Latino Executives* (New York: Free Press, 1996).

[19]Barbara Benedict Bunker, "Appreciating Diversity and Modifying Organizational Cultures: Men and Women at Work," in Suresh Srivastava and David L. Cooperrider, *Appreciative Management and Leadership* (San-Francisco: Jossey-Bass, 1990), Chapter 5.

[20]See Gary N. Powell, *Women-Men in Management* (Thousand Oaks, CA: Sage, 1993); and Cliff Cheng (ed.), *Masculinities in Organizations* (Thousand Oaks, CA: Sage, 1996). For added background, see also Sally Helgesen, *Everyday Revolutionaries: Working Women and the Transformation of American Life* (New York: Doubleday, 1998).

[21]See Kathleen Hall Jamieson, *Beyond the Double Bind: Women and Leadership* (New York: Oxford University Press, 1997).

[22]"Demographics: The Young and the Restful," *Harvard Business Review* (November 2004), p. 25. "Many U.S. Employees Have Negative Attitudes to Their Jobs, Employers and Top Managers," *The Harris Poll #38* (May 6, 2005), available from www.harrisinteractive.com; and "U.S. Job Satisfaction Keeps Falling," *The Conference Board Reports Today* (February 25, 2005; retrieved from www.conference-board.org).

[23]Mayo Clinic, "Workplace Generation Gap: Understand Differences Among Colleagues" (July 6, 2005), retrieved from http://www.cnn.com.

[24]"Transformation through Diversity," *Kellogg* (Spring/Summer, 2015), p. 6.

[25]Thomas, op. cit. (1990, 1992).

[26]Quotes from Thomas, op. cit. (1992), p. 17.

[27]Thomas, op. cit. (1992), p. 17.

[28]Bunker, op. cit.

[29]Ibid., pp. 127–49.

[30]Examples reported in Neil Chesanow, *The World-Class Executive* (New York: Rawson Associates, 1985).

[31]P. Christopher Earley and Elaine Mosakowski, "Toward Cultural Intelligence: Turning Cultural Differences into Workplace Advantage," *Academy of Management Executive*, vol. 18 (2004), pp. 151–57.

[32]Example from Julian E. Barnes, "U.S., Vietnam Exchange War Relics," *Wall Street Journal* (June 5, 2012), p. A15.

[33]Edward T. Hall, *Beyond Culture* (New York: Doubleday, 1976).

[34]Edward T. Hall, *Hidden Differences* (New York: Doubleday, 1990).

[35] Hall, op cit., 1990.

[36]Michele J. Gelfand, Lisa H. Nishii, and Jana L. Raver, "On the Nature and Importance of Cultural Tightness-Looseness," *Journal of Applied Psychology*, vol. 91 (2006), pp. 1225–44.

[37]Michele J. Gelfand and 42 co-authors, "Differences Between Tight and Loose Cultures: A 33-Nation Study," *Science*, vol. 332 (May 2011), pp. 1100–04.

[38]See, for example, Fons Trompenaars, *Riding the Waves of Culture: Understanding Cultural Diversity in Business* (London: Nicholas Brealey Publishing, 1993); Harry C. Triandis, *Culture and Social Behavior* (New York: McGraw-Hill, 1994); Steven H. Schwartz, "A Theory of Cultural Values and Some Implications for Work," *Applied Psychology: An International Review*, vol. 48 (1999), pp. 23–49; Martin J. Gannon, *Understanding Global Cultures*, 3rd ed. (Thousand Oaks, CA: Sage, 2004); and Robert J. House, Paul J. Hanges, Mansour Javidan, Peter W. Dorfman, and Vipin Gupta (eds.), *Culture, Leadership and Organizations: The GLOBE Study of 62 Societies* (Thousand Oaks, CA: Sage, 2004).

[39]Geert Hofstede, *Culture's Consequences* (Beverly Hills, CA: Sage, 1984), and *Culture's Consequences: Comparing Values, Behaviors, Institutions and Organizations Across Nations*, 2nd ed. (Thousand Oaks, CA: Sage, 2001). See also Michael H. Hoppe, "An Interview with Geert Hofstede," *Academy of Management Executive*, vol. 18 (2004), pp. 75–79.

[40]Geert Hofstede and Michael H. Bond, "The Confucius Connection: From Cultural Roots to Economic Growth," *Organizational Dynamics*, vol. 16 (1988), pp. 4–21.

[41]This dimension is explained more thoroughly by Geert Hofstede et al., *Masculinity and Femininity: The Taboo Dimension of National Cultures* (Thousand Oaks, CA.: Sage, 1998).

[42]Information from "The Conundrum of the Glass Ceiling," op cit.; and "Japan's Diversity Problem," *Wall Street Journal* (October 24, 2005), pp. B1, B5.

[43]See Hofstede and Bond, op. cit.

[44]See Geert Hofstede, *Culture and Organizations: Software of the Mind* (London: McGraw-Hill, 1991).

[45]Discussion based on Allan Bird, Mark Mendenhall, Michael J. Stevens, and Gary Oddou, "Defining the Content Domain of Intercultural Competence for Global Leaders," *Journal of Managerial Psychology*, vol. 25 (2010), pp. 810–28.

Feature Notes 16

Opening Quote—International Labour Organization, *Facts on Child Labor 2010* (Geneva, Switzerland: April 1, 2010).

Management Live—Information and quotes from Gillian Tett, "Global Shift in US Business is a Headache for Washington," *Financial Times*, Kindle Edition (August 13, 2012).

Ethics Check—Information and quotes Raul Burgoa, "Bolivia Seizes Control of Oil and Gas Fields," *Bangkok Post* (May 3, 2006), p. B5.

Facts to Consider—Information from Transparency International, "Corruption Perceptions Index 2014," and "Bribe Payers Index (2011)" www.transparency.org (accessed June 1, 2015).

Hot Topic—Information and quotes from David Rocks and Nick Leiber, "Made in China? Not Worth the Trouble," *Bloomberg BusinessWeek* (June 25–July 1, 2012), pp. 49–50; and "The End of Cheap China," *The Economist* (March 10, 2012): www.economist.com (accessed January 9, 2013).

Find Inspiration—Information and quotes from Muhammad Yunus, *Creating a World Without Poverty: Social Business and the Future of Capitalism* (New York: Public Affairs, 2009); "Fighting Poverty with $30 Loans," *USA Today* (April 25, 2013), p. 11A; and, David Bornstein, "Beyond Profit: A Talk with Muhammad Yunus," *New York Times*, opinionator.blogs.nytimes.com (April 17, 2013), accessed May 5, 2013.

Endnotes 16

[1]Sample articles include "Globalization Bites Boeing," *Businessweek* (March 24, 2008), p. 32; "One World, One Car, One Name," *Businessweek* (March 24, 2008), p. 32; Eric Bellman and Jackie Range, "Indian-Style Mergers: Buy a Brand, Leave it Alone," *Wall Street Journal* (March 22–23, 2008), pp. A9, A14; David Kiley, "One Ford for the Whole Wide World," *Businessweek* (June 15, 2009), pp. 58–59; and, "Boeing: Faster, Faster, Faster," *The Economist*, Kindle Edition (January 29, 2012).

[2]Pietra Rivoli, *The Travels of a T-Shirt in the Global Economy*, 2nd ed. (Hoboken, NJ: Wiley, 2009).

[3]See for example Kenichi Ohmae's books *The Borderless World: Power and Strategy in the Interlinked Economy* (New York: Harper, 1989); *The End of the Nation State* (New York: Free Press, 1996); *The Invisible Continent: Four Strategic Imperatives of the New Economy* (New York: Harper, 1999); and *The Next Global Stage: Challenges and Opportunities in Our Borderless World* (Philadelphia: Wharton School Publishing, 2006).

[4]For a discussion of globalization, see Thomas L. Friedman, *The Lexus and the Olive Tree: Understanding Globalization* (New York: Bantam Doubleday Dell, 2000); John Micklethwait and Adrian Woodridge, *A Future Perfect: The Challenges and Hidden Promise of Globalization* (New York: Crown, 2000); and Thomas L. Friedman, *The World Is Flat: A Brief History of the Twenty-First Century* (New York: Farrar, Straus and Giroux, 2005).

[5]Rosabeth Moss Kanter, *World Class: Thinking Locally in the Global Economy* (New York: Simon & Schuster, 1995), preface.

[6]Paul Wilson, "Foreign Companies Big Employers in Ohio," *Columbus Dispatch* (December 26, 2005), p. F6.

[7]Jose W. Fernandez, "Foreign Direct Investment Supports U.S. Jobs," *DipNote: U.S. Department of State Official Blog* (October 07, 2011), accessed March 3, 2012.

[8]Quote from John A. Byrne, "Visionary vs. Visionary," *Businessweek* (August 28, 2000), p. 210.

[9]See Mauro F. Guillén and Esteban García-Canal, "The American Model of the Multinational Firm and the 'New' Multinationals from Emerging Economies," *Academy of Management Perspectives,* vol. 23 (2009), pp. 23–35.

[10]Information and quote from Steve Hamm, "Into Africa: Capitalism from the Ground Up," *Businessweek* (May, 4 2009), pp. 60–61.

[11]Information from newbalance.com/corporate.

[12]David Murphy, "A Foxconn Breakdown: Its Strengths, Strangeness, and Scrutiny," *PC Magazine* (January 22, 2012): pcmag.com.

[13]Information and quote from "More than a Third of Large Manufacturers Are Considering Reshoring from China to the U.S.," Boston Consulting Group press release, bcg.com (April 20, 2012): accessed May 5, 2013; and, "A Revolution in the Making," *Wall Street Journal* (June 11, 2013), pp. R1, R2.

[14]"Survey: Intellectual Property Theft Now Accounts for 31% of Global Counterfeiting," *Gieschen Consultancy,* February 25, 2005.

[15]Information from "Not Exactly Counterfeit," *Fortune* (April 26, 2006): oney.cnn.com.

[16]Criteria for choosing joint venture partners developed from Anthony J. F. O'Reilly, "Establishing Successful Joint Ventures in Developing Nations: A CEO's Perspective," *Columbia Journal of World Business* (Spring 1988), pp. 65–71; and "Best Practices for Global Competitiveness," *Fortune* (March 30, 1998), pp. S1–S3, special advertising section.

[17]Karby Leggett, "U.S. Auto Makers Find Promise—and Peril—in China," *Wall Street Journal* (June 19, 2003), p. B1; "Did Spark Spark a Copycat?" *Businessweek* (February 7, 2005), p. 64; and "Overview: Chery Automobile Co., Ltd.," Cheryinternational.com (accessed May 5, 2013).

[18]"Starbucks Wins Trademark Case," *Economic Times,* Bangalore (January 3, 2006), p. 8.

[19]sadc.int/about_sadc/vision.php.

[20]This index is reported annually in *The Economist.* These data were published January 22, 2015.

[21]Many newspapers and magazines publish annual lists of the world's largest multinational corporations. *Fortune's* annual listing is available from www.fortune.com.

[22]These examples are from "The World's Biggest Public Companies," *Forbes*: forbes.com (accessed May 31, 2015).

[23]See Peter F. Drucker, "The Global Economy and the Nation-State," *Foreign Affairs,* vol. 76 (September/October 1997), pp. 159–71.

[24]Michael Mandel, "Multinationals: Are They Good for America?" *Businessweek* (February 28, 2008): businessweek.com.

[25]"Trade Liberalisation Statistics, World Trade Organization: gatt.org (accessed June 1, 2015).

[26]Mandel, op. cit.

[27]Adapted from R. Hall Mason, "Conflicts Between Host Countries and Multinational Enterprise," *California Management Review,* vol. 17 (1974), pp. 6, 7.

[28]Headlines from Henry Blodget, "Busted: Walmart Caught in Huge Bribery Scandal," Business Insider: businessinsider.com (April 22, 2012); Juliet Garside, "Hewlett-Packard to Pay $108m to Settle Scandal over Bribery of Public Officials," *The Guardian* (April 9, 2014): theguardian.com (accessed June 1, 2015); and, "UK Banks Launch Reviews over 'Corrupt' FIFA Payments," *The Telegraph* (May 31, 2015): reported by Institute for Business Ethics (accessed June 1, 2015).

[29]See Dionne Searcey, "U.S. Cracks Down on Corporate Bribes," *Wall Street Journal* (May 26, 2009), pp. A1–A4.

[30]Quote from Carol Matlack, "The Peril and Promise of Investing in Russia," *Businessweek* (October 5, 2009), pp. 48–51.

[31]"The Paradox of Bangladesh," *Bloomberg Businessweek* (May 13–May 19, 2013), pp. 14–15.

[32]Information and quote from Andrew Morse and Nick Wingfield, "Microsoft Will Investigate Conditions at Chinese Plant," *Wall Street Journal* (April 16, 2010), p. B7; and "About Us: Institute for Global Labour and Human Rights," globallabourrights.org (accessed May 5, 2013).

[33]"An Industry Monitors Child Labour," *New York Times* (October 16, 1997), pp. B1, B9; and Rugmark International Web site: www.rugmark.de.

[34]International Labour Organization, *Facts on Child Labor 2010* (Geneva, Switzerland: April 1, 2010).

[35]Alberto Arce, "Young Laborers," *The Columbus Dispatch* (December 24, 2014), pp. A1, A11.

[36]See Robert B. Reich, "Who Is Them?" *Harvard Business Review* (March/April 1991), pp. 77–88.

[37]Carol Hymowitz, "The New Diversity," *Wall Street Journal* (November 14, 2005), p. R1.

[38]See for example, Melissa Korn, "Yale Redefines Global," *Wall Street Journal* (June 7, 2012), p. B9.

[39]This summary is based on Mansour Javidan, P. Dorfman, Mary Sully de Luque, and Robert J. House, "In the Eye of the Beholder: Cross Cultural Lessons in Leadership from Project GLOBE," *Academy of Management Perspectives* (February 2006), pp. 67–90; and Martin J. Gannon, *Paradoxes of Culture and Globalization* (Thousand Oaks, CA: Sage, 2008), p. 52.

Feature Notes 17

Opening Quote—"Charlie Rose Talks to Nick D'Aloisio," *Bloomberg Businessweek* (April 1–April 7, 2013), p. 40.

Ethics Check—Information from Jessica Shambora, "The Story Behind the World's Hottest Shoemaker," *Financial Times,* Kindle edition (March 21, 2010); www.toms.com, and John Tozzi, "The Ben & Jerry's Law: Principles Before Profit," *Bloomberg Businessweek* (April 26–May 2, 2010), pp. 69, 70.

Facts to Consider—Information from Jules Lichtenstein, "Demographic Characteristics of Business Owners," *SBA Office of Advocacy, Issue Brief Number 2* (January 16, 2014); "Minority-Owned Business Growth & Global Reach," U.S. Department of Commerce MBDA: www.mbda.org (accessed February 11, 2015); "Minority-Owned Businesses," *Jobenomics* (January 10, 2014), jobeconomicsblog.com (accessed June 5, 2015); and, Ruth Simon, "Keys to '14 Business Creation," *Wall Street Journal* (May 28, 2015), p. B6; and, "U.S. Minority-Owned Firms Continue to Outpace Growth of Nonminority-owned Firms," *PRNewswire* (August 19, 2015): prnewswire.com (accessed August 26, 2015).

Hot Topic—Information and quotes from "Crowdfunding Students: Start Me Up," *The Economist* (June 15, 2013), economist.com (accessed June 20, 2013).

Management Live—Information and quotes from Caitlin Huston, "First Comes the Hobby. Then the Startup. And, Eventually, Profits," *Wall Street Journal* (January 26, 2015), p. R2.

Photo Essay—Shark Tank—Information from Carolyn T. Geer, "Innovation 101," *Wall Street Journal* (October 17, 2011), p. R5.

Find Inspiration—Information and quotes from "A Startup's New Prescription for Eyewear," *Bloomberg Businessweek* (July 4–10, 2011), pp. 49–551; (January 12, 2013); and warbyparker.com. Etsy—Information from Etsy.com; and "Space Oddities," *Bloomberg Businessweek* (February 13–1, 2012), pp. 78–79.

Endnotes 17

[1]Information from Gwen Moran, "How Military Veterans Are Finding Success in Small Business," *Entrepreneur* (February 20, 2012), entrepreneur.com (accessed January 11, 2013). See also, Ian Mount, "Open for Business," *USAA Magazine* (Summer 2012), pp. 20–24.

[2]Information from "Women Business Owners Receive First-Ever Micro Loans Via the Internet," *Business Wire* (August 9, 2000); Jim Hopkins, "Non-Profit Loan Group Takes Risks on Women in Business," *USA Today* (August 9, 2000), p. 2B; and "Women's Group Grants First Loans to Entrepreneurs," *Columbus Dispatch* (August 10, 2000), p. B2.

[3]Information from Thomas Heath, "Value Added: The Nonprofit Entrepreneur," voices.washingtonpost.com.

[4]Speech at the Lloyd Greif Center for Entrepreneurial Studies, Marshall School of Business, University of Southern California, 1996.

[5]Information and quotes from the corporate Websites; "Disruptor of the Day: Caterina Fake—Because She Had a Flickr of a Hunch About an Etsy," *Daily Disruption* (January 31, 2012), dailydisruption.com; Entrepreneur's Hall of Fame at www.1tbn.com; Anita Roddick, *Business as Unusual: My Entrepreneurial Journey, Profits with Principles* (West Sussex, England: Anita Roddick Books, 2005); Zack O'Malley Greenburg, "Jay-Z's Business Commandments" (March 16, 2011): forbes.com; and "Shawn 'Jay Z' Carter," BlackEntrepreneurProfile.com (accessed March 8, 2012): www.hunch.com.

[6]This list is developed from Jeffry A. Timmons, *New Venture Creation: Entrepreneurship for the 21st Century* (New York: Irwin/McGraw-Hill, 1999), pp. 47–48; and Robert D. Hisrich and Michael P. Peters, *Entrepreneurship*, 4th ed. (New York: Irwin/McGraw-Hill, 1998), pp. 67–70.

[7]For a review and discussion of the entrepreneurial mind, see Timmons, op. cit., pp. 219–25.

[8]Timothy Butler and James Waldroop, "Job Sculpting: The Art of Retaining Your Best People," *Harvard Business Review* (September/October 1999), pp. 144–52.

[9]Based on research summarized by Hisrich and Peters, op. cit., pp. 70–74.

[10]Data in Arnaud Bertrand, "Age Versus the Cult of Youth Entrepreneurship," *Financial Times*, Kindle Edition (December 13, 2012).

[11]Gwen Moran, "How Military Veterans Are Finding Success in Small Business," *Entrepreneur* (February 20, 2012): entrepreneur.com (accessed January 11, 2013).

[12]See the review by Hisrich and Peters, op. cit.; and Paulette Thomas, "Entrepreneurs' Biggest Problems and How They Solve Them," *Wall Street Journal Reports* (March 17, 2003), pp. R1, R2.

[13]Ibid.

[14]Quote from www.anitaroddick.com/aboutanita.php (accessed April 24, 2010).

[15]*Paths to Entrepreneurship: New Directions for Women in Business* (New York: Catalyst, 1998) as summarized on the National Foundation for Women Business Owners Web site: www.nfwbo.org.; and *Women Business Owners of Color: Challenges and Accomplishments* (Washington, DC: National Foundation for Women Business Owners, 1998).

[16]National Association of Women Business Owners, "Open State of Women-Owned Businesses 2014," nawbo.org (accessed June 5, 2015); Ruth Simon, "Gender Gap Widens for Entrepreneurs," *Wall Street Journal* (May 14, 2015), p. B7; Christine Kymn, "Access to Capital for Women- and Minority-owned Businesses: Revisiting Key Variables," *SBA Office of Advocacy, Issue Brief Number 3* (January 29, 2014); Ruth Simon, "Keys to '14 Business Creation," *Wall Street Journal* (May 28, 2015), p. B6; and, Ruth Simon, "Women Make Strides in Business Ownership," *Wall Street Journal* (August 19, 2015): wsj.com (accessed August 24, 2015).

[17]Jules Lichtenstein, "Demographic Characteristics of Business Owners," *SBA Office of Advocacy, Issue Brief Number 2* (January 16, 2014); and, Tanzina Vega, "U.S. Sees Big Spike in Black and Hispanic Women Entrepreneurs," *CNNMoney*, (August 20, 2015): money.cnn.com (accessed August 25, 2015). Note also that new data from the U.S. Census Bureau are scheduled for release in late 2015.

[18]Information from www.mbda.gov; and Leah Yomtovian, "The Funding Landscape for Minority Entrepreneurs," *ideacrossing.org* (February 16, 2011); and, Kymn, op cit., 2014.

[19]David Bornstein, *How to Change the World: Social Entrepreneurs and the Power of New Ideas* (Oxford, UK: Oxford University Press, 2004).

[20]See Laura D'Andrea Tyson, "Good Works—With a Business Plan," *Businessweek* (May 3, 2004), retrieved from *Businessweek Online* (November 14, 2005) at www.businessweek.com.

[21]David Bornstein, *How to Change the World: Social Entrepreneurs and the Power of New Ideas* (Oxford, UK: Oxford University Press, 2004).

[22]"The 10 Best Social Enterprises of 2009," *Fast Company* (December 1, 2009), www.fastcompany.com/magazine (accessed April 24, 2010); and Dan Simmons, "Keepod: Can a $7 Stick Provide Billions Computer Access?" *BBC* (May 9, 2014): bbccom (accessed May 9, 2014).

[23]Examples are from "Growing Green Business," *Northwestern* (Winter 2007), p. 19; and Regina McEnery, "Cancer Patients Getting the White-Glove Treatment," *Columbus Dispatch* (March 1, 2008).

[24]*The Facts About Small Business 1999* (Washington, DC: U.S. Small Business Administration, Office of Advocacy).

[25]Reported by Sue Shellenbarger, "Plumbing for Joy? Be Your Own Boss," *Wall Street Journal* (September 16, 2009), pp. D1, D2.

[26]Data reported in Charlie Wells, "Why Some Entrepreneurs Feel Fulfilled—But Others Don't," *Wall Street Journal* (May 26, 2015), pp. R1, R2.

[27]Jared Hecht, "Are Small Businesses Really the Backbone of the U.S. Economy?" *Inc.* (December 17, 2014): inc.com (accessed June 5, 2015). For updated data, seeperiodic reports from the U.S. Small Business Administration Web site: www.sba.gov.

[28]Charles Kenny, "Small Isn't Beautiful," *Bloomberg Businessweek* (October 3–9, 2011), pp. 10–11.

[29]Information and quotes from Steve Lohr, "The Rise of the Fleet-Footed Start-Up," *New York Times* (April 23, 2010): www.nytimes.com.

[30]Discussion based on "The Life Cycle of Entrepreneurial Firms," in Ricky Griffin (ed.), *Management*, 6th ed. (New York: Houghton Mifflin, 1999), pp. 309–10; and Neil C. Churchill and Virginia L. Lewis, "The Five Stages of Small Business Growth," *Harvard Business Review* (May/June 1993), pp. 30–50.

[31]Information reported in "The Rewards," *Inc. State of Small Business* (May 20–21, 2001), pp. 50–51.

[32]"The Business of Education," *Financial Times*, Kindle Edition (January 14, 2013); and The Family Firm Institute: www.ffi.org (accessed May 16, 2013).

[33]Conversation from the case "Am I My Uncle's Keeper?" by Paul I. Karofsky (Northeastern University Center for Family Business) and published at www.fambiz.com/contprov.cfm? ContProvCode=NECFB&ID=140.

[34]*Survey of Small and Mid-Sized Businesses: Trends for 2000*, conducted by Arthur Andersen and National Small Business United.

[35]Ibid.

[36]See U.S. Small Business Administration Web site: www.sba.gov.

[37]See Deborah Gage, "Venture Capital's Secret—3 out of 4 Start-Ups Fail," *Wall Street Journal* (September 20, 2012), pp. B1, B2.

[38]Based on Norman M. Scarborough and Thomas W. Zimmerer, *Effective Small Business Management* (Englewood Cliffs, NJ: Prentice-Hall, 2000), pp. 25–30; and Scott Clark, "Most Small-Business Failures Tied to Poor Management," *Business Journal* (April 10, 2000).

[39]Anne Field, "Business Incubators Are Growing Up," *Businessweek* (November 16, 2009), p. 76.

[40]See www.sba.gov/aboutsba.

[41]Developed from William S. Sahlman, "How to Write a Great Business Plan," *Harvard Business Review* (July/August 1997), pp. 98–108.

[42]Marcia H. Pounds, "Business Plan Sets Course for Growth," *Columbus Dispatch* (March 16, 1998), p. 9; see also firm Web site: www.calcustoms.com.

[43]Standard components of business plans are described in many books, such as Linda Pinson, *Anatomy of a Business Plan: The Step-by-Step Guide to Building the Business and Securing Your Company's Future* (Tustin, CA: Out of Your Mind . . . and Into the Marketplace, 2008). Scarborough and Zimmerer, op. cit.; and on Web sites such as American Express Small Business Services, Business Town.com, and BizplanIt.com.

[44]Angus Loten. "With New Law, Profits Take a Back Seat," *Wall Street Journal* (January 19, 2012): wsj.com (accessed November 24, 2012); Mark Underberg, "Benefit Corporations vs. 'Regular' Corporations: A Harmful Dichotomy"(June 18, 2012): *Businessethics.com* (accessed November 24, 2012); and Angus Loten, "Can Firms Aim to Do Good If It Hurts Profits?" *Wall Street Journal* (April 11, 2013), p. B6.

[45]As of this writing the B-Corp is legal in 12 states and is being considered in 20 others. For an update see Certified B Corporation: www.bcorporation.net.

[46]"You've Come a Long Way Baby," *Businessweek Frontier* (July 10, 2000).

[47]"Charlie Rose Talks to Yancy Strickler," *Bloomberg Businessweek* (March 20, 2014), p. 46.

[48]See kickstarter.com and angel.co.

[49]See Jean Eaglesham, "Crowdfunding Efforts Draw Suspicion," *Wall Street Journal* (January 18, 2013), p. C1.

[50]Information from "Should Equity-Based Crowd Funding Be Legal?" *Wall Street Journal* (March 19, 2012), p. R3; and Angus Loten, "Avoiding the Equity Crowd Funding," *Wall Street Journal* (March 29, 2012); wsj.com.

Name Index

Organization Index

Subject Index